ROBERT EVANS NYE

School of Music
University of Oregon

VERNICE TROUSDALE NYE

College of Education
University of Oregon

Music in the Elementary School

third edition

PRENTICE-HALL, INC., ENGLEWOOD CLIFFS, NEW JERSEY

PRENTICE-HALL INTERNATIONAL, INC., London
PRENTICE-HALL OF AUSTRALIA, PTY. LTD., Sydney
PRENTICE-HALL OF CANADA, LTD., Toronto
PRENTICE-HALL OF INDIA PRIVATE LTD., New Delhi
PRENTICE-HALL OF JAPAN INC., Tokyo

preface

This third edition of *Music in the Elementary School* is designed as a text and resource book for the elementary education major, the music major, the student teacher, and the teacher-in-service. It is a comprehensive book from which the college teacher and his students can select problems and activities that are pertinent to their needs, leaving other problems and activities for later use. For example, the elementary education major can be assigned selected activities in his music methods class, then continue to use this book as a resource in his student teaching and, still later, in his professional teaching. Graduate students will find much from which they can profit.

A major purpose is to establish music as part of the core of the curriculum, to bring music into the mainstream of educational thought, so that it is no longer a peripheral subject standing in semi-isolation. To do this, it is necessary that the teacher of music be able to communicate clearly with teachers in other areas of education; this book aims to make this communication possible. The various thought processes, individualization of instruction, levels of accomplishment, discovery, inquiry, the conceptual approach, and other aspects of educational thought and theory become a part of music teaching. The learning sequence—from data to concepts to generalizations—is explained and exemplified. The music classroom becomes a laboratory for learning.

The college course in elementary music methods has undergone considerable change from the remote past, when it was organized in a prescriptive way. In this third edition the authors have recognized that the essence of conceptual learning and the inquiry method is that the learner has access to a large amount of data. They have attempted to provide the learner with an opportunity to select from these data that which contributes most effectively to his formulation of musical concepts, generalizations, and strategies for teaching music. Thus, music learning, selection of data, and the choosing of strategies come into focus, rather than an easy prescribed routine which research shows to be ineffective in the development of understandings, wholesome attitudes, values, and interests for most students.

The *grade level* approach has become less tenable because of the stress on the importance of teaching each child at his level of understanding and the growing trend to organize children in non-graded groups. Therefore, this edition emphasizes levels of learning for each child. However, those who maintain the grade level organization will find that the book provides for it also.

The reader will find new chapters: Dominant Trends in Teaching Music, Music and the Learning Process, Planning to Teach Music, Instructional Media and the Differentiated Staff, Music in Early Childhood, and Music for the Disadvantaged and the Handicapped. Other chapters are organized differently from before, being based more clearly on the elements of music. Aspects of music fundamentals are reviewed and certain concepts are expanded, because fundamentals provide a basis for the data from which concepts and generalizations grow. The "Conceptual Structure of Music" chart is a new feature upon which the book is in large part organized. It is a condensed, abbreviated outline of the generalizations on which the learning and teaching of music are based, together with the concepts that support them. Inquiry and Suggested Activities sections at the end of each chapter provide a listing of pertinent activities from which the college teacher and students can select. The sections titled "Some Activities and Suggestions for Lesson Plans" provide a large number of activities that encourage students to analyze, adapt, or create strategies for teaching. The "Scope and Sequence Chart of Conceptual Learnings," reproduced by permission of the Los Angeles Schools, is included for further assistance in planning lessons. Several types of lesson plans are suggested. Another new feature is the "Source Index of Songs Mentioned in the Book."

Music has the potential for being one of the most valuable subjects for enhancing the human personality through complete involvement in inquiry techniques and creative approaches to learning. Yet, it has often been taught in as rigid or prescribed a manner as any subject in the curriculum. There has been little research undertaken specifically with musical conceptualization. It is known, however, that the conceptual approach to learning should be integrated with learning by doing. A balance of teaching strategies is recommended by the authors, and it should be kept in mind that music should be taught as an experience to be lived, rather than as a subject to be learned.

The education and teaching experience of one of the authors has been primarily within the field of music; that of the other has been primarily within the field of education. They hope that their collaboration will reinforce the concept of music as an essential part of elementary education.

The authors acknowledge their debts of gratitude to the many persons who have provided assistance, encouragement, and inspiration in the compiling of this volume.

R.E.N.
V.T.N.

contents

4

music and the learning process, 51

5

developing a responsive environment for learning, 85

6

planning to teach music, 105

7

instructional media and the differentiated staff, 153

8

tempo, dynamics, and rhythm, 182

9

pitch, melody, and singing, 262

10

polyphony, harmony, and texture, 371

II
tone quality, 441

I2
form, 466

I3
styles and listening, 481

I4
creativity; more about notation, 516

15
music in early childhood, 536

16
music for the disadvantaged and the handicapped, 558

17
relating with other areas, 584

18
performance, 604

19

THE ARTS AND
THE FULL MEANING OF LIFE

by Charles E. Brown

There are many things that I want my children —and yours—to gain from education:

I want them to know something of beauty—the forms it takes, the many ways in which it is revealed, the sometimes unexpected places in which we find it, the art of expressing it.

I want them to be sensitive to the world around them—to feel the wind, to see —to really see—the stars, and the moon, and the trees, to hear the sounds of nature, to live as one with their environment.

I want them to develop a sense of aesthetic taste—to have a feeling for and about the things in their lives, to be something other than a passive recipient of someone else's sense of what is aesthetically appealing.

I want them to be discriminating —not only in their intellectual tastes but in their artistic and cultural tastes as well.

I want them to know, in full measure, the wonder of being human—I want them to be sensitive to the human condition, to know themselves and to see themselves clearly in relation to others, to know that man has struggled since the beginning of his existence to express his thoughts, his convictions, his fears, his dreams—and that he has done this in a variety of ways.

I want them to realize that history is the story of man—to sense that in this story are found many examples of man's attempts to liberate himself from the limitations and restrictions imposed upon him by the society of which he was a part—to know that some men have never made this attempt—that they have in Thomas Wolfe's words remained in the "unspeakable and incommunicable prison of this earth."

I want them to realize fully that every man, as long as he lives, must make some kind of response to certain fundamental experiences of human life, ranging from birth to death and all that lies in-between; man, in his own fashion, must respond also to such aspects of his search for meaning as trust, compassion, authority, discipline, freedom, hope, beauty, truth, love.

The question, "How shall I find the full meaning of life?" has reference to every individual, and the answer, or more accurately, the parts of the answer, come from many sources.

My strong conviction is that the schools must provide part of the answer, and that in the arts we have one of our richest resources for working toward this end.

This statement concluded a paper presented by the author, Superintendent of Schools, Newton, Massachusetts, at the Music Educators National Conference, Eastern Division, Tanglewood Symposium Project Session, February 9, 1967, Boston, Massachusetts.

Reprinted by permission of the author and the Music Educators Journal.

1

an introduction to music education

THE IMPORTANCE OF MUSIC INSTRUCTION

When children respond to music, they respond with their feelings and emotions, manipulative skills, through intellectual means, and by combinations of these. Contemporary education names these three ways as "domains," the affective, the psycho-motor, and the cognitive. James L. Mursell summed this up by stating that "the purpose of all music teaching must be to bring about the evolution of musical responsiveness or musicality."[1]

There is an interesting history of such statements which reveals some past uncertainty with regard to the specific purposes and functions of music in the school curriculum. Not many years ago music education was apt to be justified by various non-musical goals such as worthy citizenship and personality development. Following this was a reaction which not only attempted to justify music with strictly musical goals such as "musicality," but tended to belittle music's contribution to the attainment of non-musical goals. Today we believe we possess a more balanced view of music's place in education. The primary purposes of music instruction are, of course, musical. However, music is acknowledged to be of valued assistance in the realization of non-musical objectives. The teacher is responsible for knowing specifically what he is doing with music; is he *teaching* it? or

---

[1] The 57th Yearbook of the National Society for the Study of Education, *Basic Concepts in Music Education* (Chicago: The University of Chicago Press, 1958), p. 146.

3

is he *using* it for some other purpose? Music teachers in the past have done well in helping children enjoy and perform music. Today's teachers must add to these accomplishments by helping children *understand* music.

Music fills a basic human desire in that it satisfies the need to comprehend tonal beauty that man *hears*. Only music does this; therefore music education has a unique function in serving this need. School music qualifies as an educational subject whenever it provides with clarity more of what the learner needs than he is able to absorb informally from his environment. It is a serious matter that modern man, unlike his primitive ancestors who lived in a world surrounded by silence, is almost overwhelmed by sound—most of this outright noise. Therefore, many children learn at an early age to shut out this din by learning *not* to listen, an attempt at self-protection. However, today's listener, by means of recordings, radio, and television is hearing more varied, interesting, and exciting music than at any time in our history. He is hearing the results of invention and experimentation in forms and instruments, as well as subject matter created by poets, musicians, arrangers, performers, and technicians. The teacher has the responsibility of helping the contemporary child to learn to listen and to hear the fascinating musical sounds which he could not fully comprehend without assistance and to continue to develop his understanding of music throughout his school life. Schwadron says, "Man's relationship to music becomes educational when succeeding generations are assisted in becoming critically intelligent about musical styles and forms, about the organization and design of sound, and about the social, emotional, and physical phenomena which characterize music as an art form."[2] Leonhard and House add, "Music is *not* a specialty reserved for the talented; it is universally important to every human being and his culture. It can be taught frankly on that basis."[3]

Foster McMurray's view of the aim of music instruction and the justification for music in the curriculum is as follows:

By translation from the universal aim of general education, the aim of music education may be explained in this way. It is: to help everyone to further awareness of patterns of sound as an aesthetic component in the world of experience; to increase each person's capacity to control the availability of aesthetic richness through music; and to transform the public musical culture into a recognized part of each person's environment. . . . Music

---

[2] Abraham A. Schwadron, *Aesthetics: Dimensions for Music Education* (Washington, D.C.: Music Educators National Conference, 1967), p. 5.

[3] Charles Leonhard and Robert W. House, *Foundations and Principles of Music Education* (New York: McGraw-Hill Book Company, 1959), p. 66.

education is justified because, when the more refined portions of our musical culture are communicated, the person to whom they are communicated will find in music what he would not have been able to find otherwise, thereby expanding his environment and increasing his power to find a good life through deliberate guidance of his behavior and its outcomes.[4]

The aims of music education and its justification rest on firm ground educationally, culturally, and historically. However, the need for improvement of its quality is voiced from many sources. Alexander Ringer, a musicologist speaking at the International Seminar on Teacher Education in Music (University of Michigan, 1966), said, "Nearly thirty years ago, the American composer and poet, Paul Bowles, remarked that the American people tended to regard music as a 'form of decoration' rather than 'a system of thought.' If amazingly little has changed in this respect it is largely because our music teachers have been similarly conditioned." Grant Beglarian is another friendly critic who differentiates education and entertainment:

The arts educate, instruct, civilize; they glorify our human potential for imagination and discipline. Let the tired businessman sleep or watch television at night. Let vacationing families take pleasure cruises or go to the zoo. But let us not confuse them with those who seek insights and experiences in the arts that educate, instruct, and civilize. We, as educators, are responsible to these persons in this generation, and the next, and the next. . . .[5]

According to the above statements, music is an important form of entertainment but its primary function in the elementary schools is in the realm of aesthetic education. The 1959 Resolutions of the American Association of School Administrators supports this in a frequently-quoted excerpt:

We believe in a well-balanced school curriculum in which music, drama, painting, poetry, sculpture, architecture, and the like are included side by side with other important subjects such as mathematics, history, and science. It is important that pupils, as a part of general education, learn to appreciate, to understand, to create, and to criticize with discrimination those products of the mind, the voice, the hand, and the body which give dignity to the person and exalt the spirit of man.

[4] The 57th Yearbook of the National Society for the Study of Education, *Basic Concepts in Music Education* (Chicago: The University of Chicago Press, 1958), p. 146.

[5] Grant Beglarian, "Focus on the Arts," *National Elementary Principal*, XLVII, No. 1 (September, 1967), 9–13.

Charles Leonhard complains that some elementary schools provide no more than a casual contact with music:

> In many elementary schools, for example, children dance, play games, and paint to music; they sometimes listen to recordings but with no purpose beyond that of immediate satisfaction and pleasure.

> Teachers often use music for recreational purposes and for a kind of emotional catharsis. When children are tired from concentration on reading and arithmetic, bored, overwrought, or obstreperous, it's time for music. This use of music is appropriate, healthy, and consistent with music's great powers, but it does not represent a valid music education program because it leads nowhere and results in no significant musical learning.[6]

TEACHING MUSIC

Knowledge of music comes primarily from the study of *the music itself*. The learning of facts about music, such as those concerned with music theory and composers, is best derived from this study. Children need to discover what music communicates and by what technical means this communication takes place. Such communication is based upon the feelings and responses of the listener or performer. It may be a mood, a description, a story, or it may have nonprogrammatic meaning such as beauty for its own sake, contrast, tension and release, form or other intellectual design. The vehicles of this communication include such elements and concepts as rhythm, melody, tempo, dynamics, harmony, repetition, contrast, variation, and tone quality.

The ability to use musical skills and knowledge in the solution of musical problems indicates the degree of *understanding* possessed by the learner. Problems are confronted and solved that concern listening, composing, performing, reading notation, improvising, and interpreting music. Music has as much intellectual content as any other area of education; thus it can serve intellectual development well. A balance should be maintained between emotional responses and the intellectual factors of knowledge and understanding.

Hoffer writes that when one guides students to comprehend and manipulate sounds, he is teaching music.[7] He asks, "What is a good teacher? He is one who feels music fully. He comprehends the place of

---

[6] Charles Leonhard, "The Place of Music in our Elementary and Secondary Schools," NEA *Journal* (April, 1963), p. 40.

[7] Charles R. Hoffer, *Teaching Music in the Secondary School* (Belmont, California: Wadsworth Publishing Company, 1964), p. 2.

music in the educational program. He understands the students he is to teach; he finds out what motivates them, and what their hopes and fears are. Then, knowing music and understanding his students, he organizes the music program to reach each student. He selects music that provides for maximum learning."[8] He plans classroom strategies that enable the students to form concepts and generalizations important in understanding music.

As standards for teaching music rise, the question of the place of the classroom teacher in the music program deserves closer scrutiny. It is widely accepted that the classroom teacher is a valuable partner in the music education effort. While the amount and kind of contribution will vary from teacher to teacher, he is in a superior position to know the children, to relate music to the total school curriculum, and to work with the specialist in helping children master concepts and form generalizations. It is possible that both music specialists and classroom teachers may leave their college preparatory courses in music with a faulty understanding of the functions of music fundamentals and performance skills in music education. It is essential to keep in mind that the expressive, emotional, communicative, and aesthetic elements are central, and that music fundamentals and skills are *contributory* to these. They are the avenues by which children can be guided to discover what music communicates and the structure of music as a discipline.

The teacher of today is called upon to break away from some of the concepts of the elementary school classroom he may have learned through his experience.

School classrooms in the future must more often be laboratory workshops and studios rather than neat rows of desks in which obedient children sit and do as they are told according to a prescribed text. The surest way to retard learning and stultify thinking is to place children in the old-fashioned conventional classroom with its excessive emphasis on the conservative and its tremendous restriction of the creative. If we want children to think for themselves, we must allow them to express their ideas in a variety of media.[9]

The elementary school child of today is to be a composer, critic, and researcher as well as a performer of music.

---

[8] *Ibid.* p. 6.

[9] Excerpt from an address by Dr. N.V. Scarfe, Dean, School of Education, University of British Columbia, at the Conference to Improve the Effectiveness of Music Education in Oregon Elementary Schools, Gearhart, Oregon, April 27–28, 1967. State Department of Education, Salem, Oregon.

INQUIRY AND SUGGESTED ACTIVITIES

1. From statements in this chapter and elsewhere concerning the purpose and/or justification of music in the schools, prepare a defensible rationale of why music should be in the curriculum.

2. Discuss this statement: "In a world which compels men's minds to invent the machines of destruction, the arts must remind it of the beneficence of beauty and the worth of an individual." (Oleta Benn, in the 57th Yearbook of the National Society for the Study of Education: *Basic Concepts in Music Education,* 1958, p. 355.)

3. Role-play a situation in which a local school board is confronted by some disturbed taxpayers who want art and music eliminated from the educational offerings in order to reduce the local tax burden. Include among the players a music teacher and a parent who want a good music program. The other class members can be the audience at the regular meeting of the board. Later, exchange the roles. Afterwards, identify the ideas that became evident in the performance.

4. It has been said that certain school subjects have to do with *making* a living while others have to do with the *quality* of living. Discuss whether there is a reasonable priority of importance implied or whether these two aspects of education are equal in importance.

5. It seems agreed that it does not matter who teaches music as long as children are the beneficiaries of a good music program. Discuss possible deficiencies of both music specialists and classroom teachers, and advance propositions concerning how both can do better in the future.

REFERENCES

ANDREWS, FRANCIS, "Guideposts for Beginning Teachers," *Music Educators Journal* (October, 1967), pp. 37–38. Every beginning teacher should study this short article.

BLOOM, BENJAMIN S., ED., *Taxonomy of Educational Objectives,* Handbook I, Cognitive Domain. New York: David McKay Company, 1956.

BIRGE, EDWARD B., *History of Public School Music in the United States.* Philadelphia: Oliver Ditson Company, 1937. Reprinted by the Music Educators National Conference, Washington, D.C., 1967.

BRITTON, ALLEN P., "Music Education: An American Specialty," *Music Educators Journal* (June-July, 1962), pp. 27–29, 55–60. A short history and discussion of American music education. Reprinted from *One Hundred Years of Music in America,* ed. Paul Henry Lang. New York: G. Schirmer, Inc., 1961.

BROUDY, HARRY S., "Educational Theory and the Music Curriculum," *Perspectives in Music Education: Source Book III.* Washington, D.C.: Music Educators National Conference, 1966, pp. 173–184. Justification of music education.

EDUCATIONAL POLICIES COMMISSION, *The Role of the Fine Arts in Education*. Washington, D.C.: National Education Association, 1968.

GEHRKENS, KARL WILSON, "Five Decades of Music Education," *Education* (March, 1956).

KRATHWOHL, DAVID R., et. al., *Taxonomy of Educational Objectives*: Handbook II, Affective Domain. New York: David McKay Company, 1964.

SCHUMAN, DANIEL, "Music Education Is Coming of Age," *College Music Symposium* (Fall, 1966), pp. 33–48. A good summary of indications pointing to increasing maturity of music education in the United States.

TANGLEWOOD SYMPOSIUM REPORT, "Music in American Society," *Music Educators Journal*, LIV, No. 3 (November, 1967), 49–80 The Tanglewood Declaration, p. 51, places music in the core of the curriculum. Implications and recommendations are stated for the curriculum, educational processes, evaluation, music in higher education and in the community.

Film

Bringing Music into the Classroom, American Music Conference, 332 South Michigan Blvd., Chicago 60604. A film for classroom teachers that illustrates the importance of some familiar teaching tools; it orients teachers-to-be to their need for music teaching skills. 25 minutes. Postage only.

Posters

National Leaders Speak for Music, Music Educators National Conference, Washington, D.C., 1967. A portfolio of separate sheets for each of fifteen testimonials, suitable for bulletin board posting.

2

dominant trends in the teaching of music

The function of this chapter is to introduce major trends which will be discussed in later chapters.

Teachers of school music have always been interested in improving the quality of music instruction, and action toward this goal has been accelerating in the past few years. Through the concern of the Music Educators National Conference and its state affiliates, consultants in music in state departments of education, and groups of inservice teachers, a unified effort is being exerted to carefully analyze the status of present music curricula and to devise ways of improving them and their implementation. Special curriculum projects are in progress, and centers for studying and developing new materials have been organized. Innovative ideas, programs, and materials are being tested and evaluated. The current high point of enthusiasm, work, and support for an improved music program is believed to be giving new direction, depth, quality, and significance to music as a worthy area of the curriculum for boys and girls. Knowledge of current trends and developments is necessary in order to be able to analyze, evaluate, and improve programs and the teaching-learning process.

AN EMPHASIS ON THE STRUCTURE OF MUSIC

One of the emphases in the teaching of music today is on the structure of music as a discipline. It is both necessary and logical that the study of music be centered upon the fundamental ideas which are the concepts and generalizations concerned with the elements comprising music: tempo, dynamics, rhythm, melody, harmony, form, texture, tone quality, and style. The content of music as an area of the curriculum and method of inquiry are derived from these ideas, as are also units of study, guides for teachers, and the materials of instruction. In order to approach this structure of music effectively, the teacher utilizes two other bases: society and the learner. In considering society, he studies its evaluation of music, its musical goals, and the changing conditions of music in society. In considering the learner, he knows the developmental characteristics of children, the ways children learn, and the stages of cognitive development. Music programs are devised to meet the needs of children and the needs of society, with the structure of music as the focus of study. The trend is toward giving adequate attention to each of the three bases.

The following example shows the relation between some related concepts and a generalization that can be drawn from them, expressed in adult terms.

Concepts: beat, accent, meter, bar line, measure, meter signature, duple meter, triple meter

Generalization: metrical metered rhythm is characterized by a fixed unit of time called a beat and an accent recurring at regular intervals which comprise measures.

As children explore and create music, they are guided in experiences in which data are examined, organized, and summarized into concepts and into generalizations. It is not easy for the teacher-in-preparation to work with the idea that *the same musical term may be an identifying word, a concept, imply a cluster of concepts, or be expanded into a generalization, depending upon how the teacher uses it in his plans.* For example, the term "music" can be used to identify a type of sound, the *concept* of a combination of sounds, the *cluster of concepts* consisting of rhythm, melody, harmony, form, and tone quality, and can lead to a *generalization* which might be something like: Music is concerned with the combination of sounds and silences to the end that beauty of form and the expression of thought and feeling result.

DISCOVERY AND INQUIRY

Charles B. Fowler states that, "The discovery method is an exciting, stimulating, and rewarding way to learn, because the student is not provided with all the answers, but is invited to come into his own proud possession of them. . . . Adoption of discovery method would have a marked effect throughout the music education program. It could result in the development of an intrinsic, self-motivated musical interest, in the achievement of deeper aesthetic understandings, and in the growth of independence in taste and judgment."[1]

Learning takes place best when children are actively involved in the teaching-learning process. For the young learner, music should be the discovery of musical sound—what it is like, what produces it, how he might respond to it, how it is organized, and how he might manipulate it. On his level he is a researcher (young musicologist), writer of music (composer), a listener (analyst and critic), and a performer of music. Musical instruments, music notation, books, body responses, films, and musical performance should be considered as sources of information that can be used to answer questions, try out theories, verify conclusions, and alter generalizations. The child's quest for musical knowledge should be in answer to questions, not only those he has asked, but some that are prompted, as well as those discovered through his experiences with music.

To attempt a music curriculum in which the children discover *everything* for themselves is not possible, nor is it even logical.

There is not enough time in the school day to permit the discovery of every aspect of musical learning. What is needed is a *balance of types of learning* which includes discovery and inquiry. This yields for the learner the excitement of discovery and a genuine insight into how musical problems are met and solved. Thus, in good music programs both teacher-directed and student-discovery learning have a place; the problem is that each be given its necessary amount of attention and emphasis. The teacher plans and guides learning experience so that concepts are developed which children can use to solve musical problems. Certain music skills are taught in a systematic way for children to use them in their own pursuits. The teacher should strive, however, to organize learning experiences in such a way that the children are actively seeking

---

[1] Charles B. Fowler, "Discovery Method; Its Relevance for Music Education," *Journal of Research in Music Education,* XIV (Summer, 1966), 133–134.

new ideas and finding ways to attack musical problems, whether the study is teacher-directed or learner-discovered. There should be times when the learning is more teacher-directed, times when it is a co-operative endeavor on the part of both teacher and children, and times when the children define their own problems, seek solutions, discover relationships, and investigate and analyze music in their own ways.

In summary, today's effective teacher does more specific planning, guiding, and explaining of musical concepts and understandings than ever before. This is not done, however, at the expense of depriving children of the opportunity to use the inductive method of learning which includes time necessary to explore, discover, analyze, inquire, relate, summarize, and formulate generalizations.

INTERCULTURAL UNDERSTANDING

A major trend emphasized in social studies and shared by music is intercultural understanding, of which international understanding is a sub-head. Although music educators have been slow in recognizing the sophistication of music of other cultures, the interest and concern about it today has outdistanced the resources presently available for these studies in elementary schools. However, it is possible for teachers to do independent research in scholarly books concerned with music of India, China, Indonesia, Arabian countries, and Central Africa. But in many cases new methods of approach must be developed. Currently, the Seattle Schools have projects underway which will result in strategies to approach music of Africa and Asia, and the reports of these projects may be available now. Recorded music of cultures other than Western have assisted the study of intercultural music in the classroom. Depth studies dealing with comparative treatment of musical elements (rhythm, texture, melody) in both our culture and a non-Western culture are possible with children possessing a mental age of from nine years upward.

THOUGHT PROCESSES

Teachers in all areas of education are more aware today of the importance of helping children to develop the ability to think effectively in relation to living in a democracy and in a rapidly changing world. This ability can be gained in the study of music in the same general ways as in any other subject—by means of defining problems; hypothesizing;

locating, analyzing and evaluating information; drawing conclusions and testing them; classifying, summarizing; and formulating and stating generalizations. Teachers have become acquainted with and are utilizing various thought processes, such as cognitive-memory, divergent thinking, convergent thinking, and evaluative thinking.

INDIVIDUALIZATION OF INSTRUCTION

The following excerpts from the September, 1967, Supplementary Edition of the Association for Supervision and Curriculum Development *New Exchange* explains this trend. "There is decreasing emphasis on the teaching of a class and more on the teaching of small groups and the individual child. Much of school work is on an individualized basis, and the teachers want and need materials available for individual children whether presented by the teachers themselves or in a tutorial situation over a listening center or over an audio- or video-retrieval system. Increasingly, there is a trend toward having the student take more responsibility for his own learning and toward the student instructing himself. No longer do we consider the teacher the mediator of all learning. Teaching is . . . an endeavor in which *students* are provided an opportunity through use of materials to discover, make generalizations on their own, and to think critically. The growing emphasis today is on self-directed, informal *learning* activities, as well as systematic, instructional *teaching* activities."

RE-EVALUATION OF EUROPEAN MUSIC TEACHING

In the effort to improve music teaching, American music educators are giving renewed consideration to how teachers in other nations organize and teach music. Those methods receiving marked attention are those of the Hungarian composer-educator Zoltan Kodaly and those of the German composer Carl Orff. Involved in these are reconsiderations of techniques like Latin syllables and hand signals in which there had been declining interest.

LEVELS OF ACCOMPLISHMENT RATHER THAN GRADE LEVELS

"Level" no longer means exclusively grade level; the term now refers to a level of pupil accomplishment. These levels are organized differently in different situations. For example, one large city system has eight levels of pupil accomplishment from kindergarten through grade six. A method of classroom music instruction distributed by one publisher is organized in four levels from grades one through six. Ideally, the learner is placed in the proper level for his best learning experience without regard to the old grade level placement.

In situations where the "levels" idea is used, children are grouped, then helped as individuals to master the level at which they can profit before advancing to a more sophisticated one. In order for the level idea to function effectively, teachers must analyze each student in terms of his understanding and performance, his personal interests, and his attitude toward music in general. Then each student is placed at the level where he can succeed. When he masters that level he is promoted to the next level. Obviously, the lengths of time spent at each level will vary for each child, depending on the difficulty and sophistication found in a level as well as on the child's level of achievement, experience, and background.

This type of organization is highly appropriate in our migratory society in which many families move from place to place, from school to school, city to city, and from one school system to another.

EARLIER STUDY OF CONCEPTS—MUSIC FOR EARLY CHILDHOOD

In music as in other areas of education, appropriately selected concepts and understandings, skills, and attitudes about music are fostered at a much earlier age today. This is done partly because of research findings that support providing children with meaningful, purposeful, and challenging learning experiences on their maturity level. And it is also done as a means to challenge the capacities and interests of the child regardless of his level—slow, average, or fast developing. Formerly we spoke of children's readiness or lack of readiness for certain musical experiences. Today we do not wait for them to "get ready"; *we simplify concepts and generalizations and teach them at their level of understanding.* According to research it is often difficult to develop certain basic understandings and appreciations in later years.

MUSIC FOR THE DISADVANTAGED

Today effort is being exerted to aid children who are considered to be disadvantaged. The goal is to assist these students in restructuring their mental and emotional operations and to formulate processes of learning how to learn. These students often lack self-confidence, purpose, ambition, and mastery of basic academic and interpersonal skills. Many are apt to consider traditional school activities as drudgery without meaning or value. Music teachers are advised to seek out the music these children accept as real, and to begin work from this point. Their tasks include devising ways to stimulate interest in learning music, guiding them, freeing them to experiment and to find meaning in music as it relates to their life experiences. The aim is to assist each individual to develop the skills necessary to achieve measures of satisfaction and success, thereby enabling him to grow in self-esteem.

Since attention to and emphasis on improving the musical experiences of the disadvantaged are relatively new, the program remains in a state of experimentation. Naturally the approach which has achieved relatively satisfactory success with both middle and upper cultural level groups does not answer the needs of these disadvantaged children. Thus, the content of the curriculum may be selected from both conventional and unconventional sources in order for school music to communicate sucessfully with the disadvantaged. See Chapter 16, "Music for the Disadvantaged and the Handicapped," for a detailed discussion of this trend.

MUSIC FOR THE PHYSICALLY HANDICAPPED

Society is concerned more today than in any period of history with the education of the handicapped child. Attempts are being made to encourage this child to develop to the limits of his potential, thus preparing him for life, aiding him to become a more independent and secure individual, and providing him with the opportunity for developing his creative talents that will contribute to his adjustment to society and to his acceptance of self and others.

There is a consensus that music delights these children and is good for them. Juliette Alvin writes that if this is so, we must ask ourselves certain pertinent questions and seek the best possible solutions.

> If this is so, could we not use music at a deeper and more effective level in order to help specifically towards the mental, emotional, and social maturation of handicapped children in need of integrating and enriching experiences at their level? Could we not find out why music is good for them—why they respond so well to music—what their responses are due to, and what are their responses on which we can build? Furthermore, can we not find a relationship between their response to certain musical experiences and their mental, physical, and emotional state? And if so, in which way could music contribute to their intellectual, social, or emotional

development? We may also ask how musical experiences can be adapted to any kind or degree of handicap, so that the child can benefit from them.[2]

Answers to these questions remain incomplete, although many teachers have found great pleasure in working with this group of children in music. As a rule, musicians are not trained in strategies for teaching the handicapped, and those who specialize in education for the handicapped seldom have the skills and knowledges in music which are needed. Both the musician and the specialist who deals with the handicapped agree that music has a great unused potential with which to help these children. See Chapter 16.

STUDY OF CONTEMPORARY MUSIC

Much of the music of our time is experimental in nature. The teacher whose musical background included little attention to contemporary music could not understand this kind of music. Thus, when experienced in the elementary classroom, it was usually treated apart from the regular study of music. Today aspects of contemporary music are incorporated into the normal study of musical elements: rhythm, melody, harmony, tone quality, texture, form, and style. It is treated in this manner in this book. Children should be able to analyze and compare its major characteristics, compose music illustrative of some of its techniques, and find interest in its experimental nature.

RELATION TO OTHER AREAS

Music is recognized as a school subject in its own right. There were times in the past when school music was regarded by some as 1) entertainment rather than a field of study, and 2) an activity with which to enhance other subjects or to promote non-musical goals. Today, with attention centered upon the structure of music, its concepts and generalizations, music is seen as a basic school subject which is useful and valuable in other areas as well.

INSTRUCTIONAL MEDIA

The emphasis upon the process of learning and the learning of concepts and generalizations has brought about demand for a greater variety

[2] Juliette Alvin, *Music for the Handicapped Child* (New York: Oxford University Press, 1965), p. 2.

of materials of instruction and learning resources that assist in specific aspects of this learning. The former emphasis on singing and playing or the memorization of musical facts as final goals no longer holds. Music skills are viewed as important activities which are part of a process by means of which children can explore, discover, and learn concepts and form generalizations related to the study of music as a discipline, and to demonstrate desirable musical values, attitudes, and appreciations. This has meant a rather sudden out-dating of many existing publications and a need for new or revised publications and other types of instructional media to accommodate the newer educational trends. Needless to say, all existing materials and resources are currently under critical reappraisal by teachers. The question, "Does this (film, music series, book, song, activity, recording) aid children in the realization of specific behavioral objectives and do they in turn contribute to the learning of musical concepts and generalizations?" is a crucial one.

EVALUATION

There is increased emphasis on evaluating the success of learning experiences in terms of children's behavior. The trend is toward the use of many devices that measure and evaluate all aspects of learning—what the child is capable of doing as a result of teaching; what concepts and generalizations he understands and uses; what skills he can utilize; how and how well he thinks, and what he feels and values. One of the most realistic and effective ways to find what the student has learned is to ask him to behave in ways that demonstrate what he has learned. This is reflected in the recent method of explaining instructional objectives in behavioral terms, using them as the basis for the evaluation of all aspects of accomplishment and learning.

DIFFERENTIATION OF STAFF

Another trend is a new type of staff organization, currently thought of in terms of "the teacher and his staff." Such a differentiated staff would have approximately four levels of teacher assignments with specific responsibilities for each level. One level would include teacher aides, part-time and supplementary staff. This type of organization presents a concept of staff which could include two or three adults working cooperatively with the same group of children. The implications of this are more types of team teaching and more detailed and exacting staff planning. The differentiated staff is necessary in order to utilize and organize the achievement level concept discussed earlier.

INQUIRY AND SUGGESTED ACTIVITIES

1. Describe the elementary music program you experienced in your childhood. What were its strengths? What were its weaknesses? What improvements can you suggest for it?
2. Analyze each trend as to its possibilities for improving the teaching of music in the elementary school. Suggest ways of incorporating these trends into the music curriculum.
3. Gather data and formulate a generalization as to the meaning of "structure" as applied to the study of music. Illustrate with your own example how data, concepts, and generalizations are related. Select a music series book and try to utilize the given data to formulate concepts and generalizations useful in learning music. See pp. 113–127.
4. Determine the rationale supporting the inquiry approach to learning music.
5. Select a nation or a culture and do a preliminary investigation of its music.
6. Explore the different types of thinking and suggest possible ways to develop these in music learning.
7. Interview a classroom teacher or a music specialist to see how he identifies individual differences and how he handles them in music teaching.
8. Investigate one or more of the European methods of music teaching listed in the references at the end of Chapter 7. Try to identify elements which appear to be innovative, to be strengths, and to be weaknesses. Could these methods be incorporated in a conceptual approach to music learning?
9. Examine music guides and courses of study to determine whether their scope and sequence is built on grade levels or performance levels.
10. Visit a nursery school or kindergarten to observe the musical environment. What music concepts are being developed at this age?
11. Listen to aspects of contemporary music recorded on the following discs: *Sounds of New Music* FX 6160, and *Electronic Music* FM 3436, both by Folkways Records, 906 Sylvan Ave., Englewood Cliffs, N.J. 07632. Study the descriptive notes; be able to explain the origins of the different sounds. Identify current television programs employing such music.
12. Survey the types of instructional materials and media available in school music teaching in your local schools. Determine to what degree these are being used or could be used effectively in the classroom.

13. Investigate to what extent the differentiated staff organization is utilized in the immediate school community and throughout the nation in the teaching of music. Interview school administrators to learn how such a program is organized and implemented.

REFERENCES

CONTEMPORARY MUSIC PROJECT, *Experiments in Musical Creativity*. Washington, D.C.: Music Educators National Conference, 1966.

FOWLER, CHARLES B., "Discovery Method; Its Relevance for Music Education," *Journal of Research in Music Education,* XIV (Summer, 1966).

GRAY, CHARLES L., ED., *The Study of Music in the Elementary School: A Conceptual Approach.* Washington, D.C.: Music Educators National Conference, 1967.

KAPLAN, ABRAHAM, *The Conduct of Inquiry.* San Francisco: Chandler Publishing Company, 1964.

LEEPER, ROBERT R., *Strategy for Curriculum Change.* Washington, D.C.: Association for Supervision and Curriculum Development, 1965.

LEEPER, SARAH HAMMOND, ET. AL., *Good Schools for Young Children* (2nd ed.). New York: The Macmillan Company, 1968. Chap. 17, "The Creative Arts."

NYE, ROBERT E., "Music in Changing Times," *Perspectives in Music Education: Source Book III.* Washington, D.C.: Music Educators National Conference, 1966, pp. 74–78. The condition and trends of music in the United States in the 1960's.

NYE, VERNICE T., ROBERT E. NYE, AND H. VIRGINIA NYE, *Toward World Understanding With Song.* Belmont, California: Wadsworth Publishing Company, 1967. One way to introduce and study music of different cultures.

REIMER, BENNETT, "New Curriculum Developments in Music Education," *Influences in Curriculum Change,* eds. Glenys G. Unruh, and Robert R. Leeper. Washington, D.C.: Association for Supervision and Curriculum Development.

SIEGEL, LAURENCE, ED., *Instruction: Some Contemporary Viewpoints.* San Francisco: Chandler Publishing Company, 1967.

TABA, HILDA, AND DEBORAH ELKINS, *Teaching Strategies for the Culturally Disadvantaged.* Chicago: Rand McNally & Co., 1967.

THOMAS, RONALD B., "Innovative Music Education Programs," *Music Educators Journal* (May, 1967), pp. 50–52.

WILHELMS, FRED T., ED., *Evaluation as Feedback and Guide.* Washington, D.C.: Association for Supervision and Curriculum Development, 1967.

BILL OF RIGHTS

Let me grow as I be
And try to understand why I want to grow like me;
Not like my Mom wants me to be,
Nor like my Dad hopes I'll be
Or my teacher thinks I should be.
Please try to understand and help me grow
Just like me!

3

music and the child

MUSIC CONTRIBUTES TO INDIVIDUAL DEVELOPMENT

A child needs the opportunity to participate spontaneously, enthusiastically, and completely, in the various aspects of music. No other life experience can bring more thrills and enjoyment, a feeling of individual worth and self-completeness, than experiences in some or all areas of music. With the many opportunities music provides the child for self-involvement and personally initiated activities, it is an effective way for the individual to become acquainted with his unique musical abilities, his ways of solving musical problems and expressing himself creatively. Self-respect, acceptance, and respect by his peers may result from satisfying musical accomplishments.

TEACHERS MUST KNOW THE LEARNERS

When teachers do not know and understand children, they fail to find ways to bridge the gap between the child and the subject content. The problem of the teacher's knowing the subject matter but failing to know and understand the learner is a very old one. It has affected all levels of learning.

Rath writes:

> It is obvious to most teachers that concerns for the child and for the subject matter are met only as the characteristics of both are known, prized, and preserved. The problem that has plagued teachers and curriculum formulators for ages is how to do just that—plan a course of study based on knowledge of children *and* subject matter.[1]

NEW CONCEPTS OF CHILD DEVELOPMENT

Changes in our view of the world bring with them changes in our view of the child and of man. Today's psychologists are emphasizing the fact that all aspects of development are neither fixed nor necessarily orderly. The concept that development is modifiable is extremely important. Educators once believed that the child at age six would behave in a "six" way, and the child at seven in a "seven" way. They knew that there were individual differences in rate of development, that a particular youngster might reach the six year old "stage" at five or at seven. However, there was an order commonly believed that every child would go through, and one simply waited it out.

Research indicates that this is not necessarily so. It is not so in a variety of ways. For example, not long ago it was a "fact" that children could not ride a two-wheeled bicycle until they were twelve years old. Today many children do this at age five. The concepts of both grade levels and age levels in terms of what children are able to accomplish have been undergoing revision. It is now recognized that individual differences among children are far greater than had once been thought, and it is known that some young children can accomplish certain feats believed possible only of older children some years ago. There have been changes on the intellectual level. Under certain conditions young children can intellectualize on a plane thought impossible until recently.[2] Children are maturing earlier and educators are learning that even the physical characteristics of the age groups have undergone change.

What, then, is the value of child development charts where a norm is "established" for various groups of children? Despite the exceptions, it is still necessary for teachers to know the common characteristics of

---

[1] James Rath, "Mutuality of Effective Functioning and School Experience," *Learning and Mental Health:* 1966 Yearbook of the Association for Supervision and Curriculum Development, Washington, D.C., p. 9.

[2] For Piaget's description of children's thought processes at different stages, see Chapter 4, pp. 52–54.

50% or more of a particular group. By knowing this norm, he can judge whether or not his class of a certain age is performing on that level, or if its *mental* age is higher or lower than this age would indicate. Child development consists of mental, social, emotional, and physical growth. Any child can be above or below the norm for any one of these characteristics. Knowing this, the teacher will plan for the child's musical education on the level where he is, and this implies extensive individualization of instruction.

The developmental characteristics stated below are descriptions of development; they are not limitations or prescriptions. They describe similarities in patterns of physical, mental, social, and emotional growth at certain stages or ages of development. Effective teachers utilize this knowledge. The following chart serves as a basis for analyzing a child's developmental level and as a guide for organizing music curricula and daily lesson plans.

Developmental Characteristics	Suggested Implications for the Teacher of Music
NURSERY SCHOOL AND KINDERGARTEN: AGES FOUR AND FIVE	
Large muscles better developed than small muscles; constantly physically active; right or left handedness is established.	Physical activities involving large muscles are stressed; fundamental movements such as walking, running, and hopping are related to music; can skip rope; can play simple percussion instruments; movements of animals are imitated; activities include free rhythmic responses to recordings and piano selections that "tell what to do"; *the teacher's accompaniment follows the movement at first,* then later the child learns to follow the music; *simple* directed singing games and dances; creative and spontaneous movement; space is needed for physical movement because these children are apt to fall.
Language development is limited; speech skills are little developed but both language and speech are improving rapidly.	Chants and calls, singing games and songs with words that are colorful, rhythmic, repetitious and sometimes nonsensical; provision for much spontaneous and creative response to the

sound of words and to music; singing and chanting of Mother Goose rhymes and neutral syllables; Latin syllables so-mi, then so-mi-la-so-mi, and finally so-la-so-mi-do can be *slowly* introduced with accompanying pitch levels and arm movements or hand signals.

Attention span is relatively short, depending on the interest and the activity; most children are very active, affectionate, and aggressive.

Plan music through the day for short periods of time; utilize music in other areas of instruction and to change the tempo of the day by creating activity and rest; use a variety of types of songs to relieve tension and fatigue and stimulate relaxation; include songs involving names, touching objects and repeating phrases; provide opportunity for each child to learn perseverance on his own level.

Some children are shy and are limited in ways of expressing ideas and feelings.

Help children to listen to music in creative ways; encourage dramatizations and imitations of people, animals and things.

Very self-centered; wants to be involved and motivated; cares little what his peers think; is very individualistic; emotions are intense, with brief extremes of happiness, anger, hate.

Give individual help, the opportunity to sing alone and in small groups before singing in larger groups; he will sing co-operatively in large groups when he is socially and intellectually mature enough to co-operate in a group; provision is made for his enjoyment of music plus help in gradually and sequentially increasing his understanding of it; the teacher must establish limits in group response activities; the child needs help in learning to co-operate in singing, taking turns, listening to others; songs in which the child is clearly identified are utilized; the teacher substitutes the child's name for the name in the song; the teacher leads in creating calls, chants, and conversational singing which include the child's name; short, repetitious songs for fun, acting out and singing are used.

They have little understanding of ownership.

Create chants such as "This belongs to Mary," (55365–3–) and "The new shoes are Johnny's" (35–365–3–).

Sex roles are not clearly identified.

Songs and singing games in which each sex has its logical role.

The harmonic sense is rudimentary.

The teacher emphasizes the melodic line and the rhythm, not harmony; songs that require no chord changes in their accompaniment are preferable; complex harmonic accompaniments are avoided or kept to a minimum.

Enjoys the security of repetitious activity.

Repetitive songs, motions or ideas, and repetitive manipulative experiences with percussion instruments and bells are employed.

Desires to be accepted by adults; needs warmth and security from them; enjoys individual attention.

The teacher and parent sing to the child often, and provide a simple, pleasant and secure environment; they give security and respect, avoiding unpleasant experiences and situations; they get the child involved by planning activities in which he can succeed; children will feel success with music that is interesting and appealing; provision should be made for spontaneous and creative responses to music; the teacher and parent should give encouragement and recognition for children's efforts in music; music should be provided to suit the moods of the children.

Beginning to develop independence; tries to help himself; gradually depends less upon adults.

The teacher should be certain that each child is helped in singing, interpreting or playing music as increased music skills develop self-confidence and independence; song content can aid children in adjusting to new or frightening experiences; encourage children to make up new words, chants, motions or rhythms, to play different percussion instruments, and to experiment with sound; discussions and evaluations assist social development; opportunities are provided for children to help plan music activities, to select songs, recordings, appropriate percussion instruments, and to decide how to interpret music.

Teeth and bony structures are growing and changing; vigorous action results in fatigue.

A variety of music activities from very active to restful is employed; a *minimum* of twenty minutes of music is distributed throughout the day; action songs and finger plays are used; children listen to many kinds of music, including types that encourage rest and relaxation; creative body movements and use of percussion instruments are encouraged.

The beginning of co-operative play in relatively small groups. Most learning is non-verbal.

Music activities should help children grow in understanding and appreciation of others, as well as the quality of work done; brief periods of discussion and evaluation aid children in developing their powers of communication and in their ability to relate to and respect others; social consciousness should be nurtured.

Very inquisitive about his surroundings; he is eager to learn and to respond; is very alert; learns through manipulating concrete objects and re-enacting real situations.

Provide opportunity to use and experiment with a variety of musical materials; plan music experiences that build sensitivity to beauty of melody, rhythm, and form, and recognition of happy, sad, slow, fast, high, and low; experiment with types of sounds obtainable from wood, metal, glass, stone and various percussion instruments, introducing them one at a time; simple imitations and dramatizations are employed; high-low can be equated with right-left in playing keyboard instruments.

Interested in the "here and now," "what and what for," and in realizing immediate goals.

Songs about everyday experiences such as mother and family, playthings, people they know, pets and animals; children need simple directions, demonstrated clearly and explicitly, and musical activities that can be completed in short periods of time;

the teacher gives each child opportunities to succeed; music is used as a "core" for learning content in other areas.

Lives in a world of make-believe and imagination; the child is imitative.

Provide the chance for creative responses in singing, listening, and rhythm; children should imitate the movement of animals and dramatize songs in a simple manner; songs about inanimate objects and talking animals and the creative activities related to them should aid in children's enjoyment, encourage initiative, develop self-confidence, help children recognize their own possibilities, limitations, and capabilities in learning co-operation with the group, stimulating imagination, overcoming shyness, relieving aggressive feelings, and expressing their ideas and personal feelings; songs are taught by rote; the teacher's voice and recordings should be good models; the teacher's attitudes, skills, appreciations and enthusiasm are imitated by the children; musical models in the home are very important too; the child learns to appreciate the type of music he is exposed to most.

Voices are small; the pitch is often underdeveloped.

Many children need help in finding their singing voices; the teacher uses tone-matching games, calls, chants, and singing conversations to build up, down, or same pitch concepts; the teacher establishes the pitch of songs by means of the piano, pitch pipe, or bells; he gives individual and small-group assistance in finding the singing voice and its range; children are helped with learning to listen to pitches and to recorded music; the teacher has the children imitate vocally sounds of their environment—train and factory whistles, church bells, chimes,

the sounds of animals and machines;
oral, aural, and visual aids are necessary in building pitch concepts; the
teacher makes certain that children
enjoy music and want to take part in
singing; children have opportunities
to play very simple songs or parts of
songs on the bells; the teacher emphasizes listening to singing, then having
children imitate the example.

Creative, spontaneous, and uninhibited.

The teacher encourages creating chants,
interesting word-rhythms, rhythmic
movement, and dramatizations; spontaneous singing is encouraged as
children play; children dramatize
roles of people and animals well
known to them; space is provided for
the children to move freely; percussion instruments, scarves, and balloons
can assist creative responses to rhythm.

They work alone or in very small groups.

Create the opportunity for individual
musical experimentation and for small
group activities.

Early Elementary: Ages Six and Seven

Extend and refine the experiences indicated for five-year-olds. Children in many
school systems do not have kindergarten experience and many six-year-olds
perform on the level of five-year-olds.

*Many children are still unable to sing in
tune; most voices are light and high in
quality, but some are low, and there are
usually many different ranges present. The
overlapping of the different ranges at beginning of the school year will permit about five
or six consecutive pitches to be sung by the
large majority of the class, usually from
middle C to the G or A above.*

The teacher assists each child in
learning to sing in tune; children are
guided to do much individual singing,
singing in pairs, and in small groups
within the large group; the teacher
helps children to experiment with their
voices to determine the difference
between speaking and singing;
children need good models to imitate
both in school and at home; the
teacher begins the school year with
songs of limited range to assure the
largest degree of success; this range
is gradually extended; individual

singing independent of the teacher's voice or the recording is encouraged; the children use body movements and hand levels to reveal their comprehension of high and low pitch.

Slow growth; children want warm, personal attention.

The teacher employs a small repertory of simple songs well learned and frequently repeated; music repetition is necessary in learning to hear pitch differences and to match tones; nursery rhymes are reviewed; children are seated near the teacher when they sing; children's names are often substituted for those in songs and are used in question-answer games and in singing conversations; most children learn to sing simple melodies accurately; they comprehend melodic movement.

Large muscles are more developed than small muscles; children tend to move with the entire body as a unit; a lengthening of the limbs.

Free rhythmic movements and fundamental movements such as walking, running, skipping, hopping, and galloping are stressed; finger plays develop small muscles; emphasis is given to impersonation of animals, people, and things; keeping perfect time in various tempos is not expected of most children because they need to experiment in their own ways to develop muscular control; all children are encouraged to improvise rhythmic responses of their own and to take part in activities that lead to improvement in poise, balance, and bodily control in response to rhythmical stimuli; at first the accompaniment follows the response, then later the children become able to respond to accompaniments of various tempos; suitable furniture and seating arrangements are provided; they grow in ability to sing with rhythmic accuracy; they can repeat rhythmic patterns in body movements and on percussion instruments; they become aware of the beat and can demonstrate it in body movements and on percussion instruments; they can improvise melodic fragments on simple instruments and play them by numeral notation; they become more aware of meter.

At age six eye-hand co-ordination is poorly developed.

Rote singing and rote playing are emphasized; use is made of large-sized notation written on chart paper.

At age seven the heart grows rapidly; muscular development is uneven; motor skills are steadily developing; eye-hand co-ordination improves; attention span increases.

Time allotted to strenuous physical activity should be brief; active musical activities should be interspersed with quiet responses; singing games and dances can be more complex; there can be greater variety and skill in fundamental movements; percussion instruments are played with more ability and control; some children will play piano, bells, and Autoharp; more songs and longer songs with more verses can be learned.

Eyes of the six-year-olds not ready for close work; eyes of seven-year-olds better developed but still not ready for sustained close work.

Emphasize a "by-ear" approach to music; contour lines are associated with melodic direction; line notation can help in expanding the concept of duration in rhythm patterns; the teacher uses simple notation on large charts, flannel board and chalk board—easy chants, phrases, parts for singing and playing; children observe the teacher as he notates songs they have created; rote songs are sung from large charts; music textbooks with large clear print are usually introduced in the second grade; the teacher sings short songs already familiar to the children while the class does guided observation of aspects of notation in the books; children read rhythm notation (from large charts) and write some of it in simple form on the chalkboard; seven-year-olds can identify similar and different notated patterns, step-wise and skip-wise melodic notation.

Missing front teeth of seven-year-olds make perfect pronunciation and diction difficult.

The teacher emphasizes vowel sounds rather than consonant sounds in simple chants and singing activities; Latin syllables and neutral syllables such as *loo* and *la* can be sung; pronunciation and enunciation should not be overstressed.

Six-year-olds are extremely active and constantly on the move; they have a relatively short attention span; they are easily fatigued; at age seven children alternate between very active and quiet behavior.

Use music to permit necessary activity and rest and to relieve tensions and fatigue; children need short, frequent, and varied periods of music; listening experiences should be of brief duration; purposes for listening should not only be minimal but explicitly stated; listening skills should be developed gradually as the nervous system becomes more mature.

Eager and anxious to learn.

Involve the child in planning and evaluating a variety of musical experiences; gradually and consistently introduce music vocabulary; expand the types and number of musical experiences.

The harmonic sense is largely undeveloped.

The teacher includes songs and chants that need no chord changes in accompaniments; complex harmonic accompaniments are avoided, chants and two-part rounds are sung.

Children are highly competitive; they fight with words rather than with fists; six-year-olds are aggressive, egotistical, and often unco-operative.

The teacher gives children chance to perform and to succeed individually; he develops social consciousness and social skills by guiding the children to appreciate each other's accomplishments, to help each other, and to appreciate the rewards of co-operative effort.

Children are highly imaginative and enjoy imitating; they are interested in and are curious about their surrounding environment; they enjoy sounds and sound effects.

Children reveal knowledge of similar and contrasting phrases by selecting same or different accompanying instruments; they become aware of introductions and codas by playing them on instruments and inventing them; they create their own short songs; numerals and/or syllables can be used in singing melodic fragments; they become aware of the need for chord changes in harmonic accompaniments; common musical instruments can be identified by sight and sound; opportunity is provided for creative reproduction of rhythms from the environment; the teacher should stimulate interest in aesthetic aspects of the environment through the use of the senses—hearing, seeing, feeling, and smelling; in spontaneous and guided dramatizations children imitate sounds and movements of airplanes, missiles, jets, trains, and other machines, the sound of wind and evidence of its action, water, thunder, people's speech, sounds and movements of animals, and the movements and moods of people; to implement the above, the teacher employs a variety of materials that may include recordings, piano, percussion instruments, bells, pictures, music charts, bulletin boards, chalk board, recorder, opaque and overhead projectors, slides, film strips and movies; there is experimenting with various materials to discover different sounds resulting from them and the way they are struck; children help decide suitable sound effects to enhance their songs; they create accompaniments to songs and recorded music with percussion instruments; sounds heard in the environment are reproduced or imitated; they can be sensitive to the suitability of volume (loud-soft) in their musical activities.

Rudimentary understanding of time, space, and money values.

The teacher uses line notation to show relative length of note values that have been felt through physical responses; this is later compared with music notation; the teacher begins to teach the understanding of simple music design such as the phrase, contrasting sections, tonal and rhythm patterns, expanded concepts of fast and slow, high and low, and related moods; children learn to comprehend simple note values through identification with simple rhythmic responses involving the entire body.

Learn through use of concrete materials, in terms of experience background, and through participation under wise supervision; limited utilization of the abstract.

Plan time to experiment, to listen, and to participate in learning tone production on wood, metal, skin and other media; relate scale tones to hand signals and the keyboard; step bells are useful in developing the scale concept; explore uses of simple instruments, introducing them gradually, one at a time, and teach the use of each thoroughly after stimulating interest in what each can do; listen to and watch various types of musical performance; create and explore uses of voice, instruments, words, tunes, and accompaniments; guide listening with a few *specific* purposes; do creative development of music through interpretation, dramatization, body movement, and the addition of codas, introductions, and instrumental parts; teach songs and music of quality that deal with the here and now, including those that reflect the expanding technological age in which these children live, but on their maturity level (remember that some of today's six-year-olds have been all over the world by means of direct and simple physical responses, feelings and moods; they are able to do only very simple analysis of music).

Children need encouragement, acceptance, and praise from adults.

See that each child develops his special talents and interests in music to the maximum degree; have each child perform acceptably alone and in groups in order to feel success and acceptance from the teacher, and to grow in assuming responsibility, co-operation, and in social competency; provide a warm, interesting, challenging environment that includes a teacher who knows when and how to give encouragement and praise; because of the children's great need for acceptance by adults, they try to imitate, and thus are susceptible to the teacher's example of enthusiasm, interest, skill, and love for music; teachers should not underestimate this age, but should offer a music program of quality that sets the stage for greater ability in performance, listening, and appreciation of music; it is here that the teacher can utilize this characteristic of seeking the approval of adults, not to dictate learning, but to develop the skills that will progressively be used as a basis for children's future growth in musical competencies, and in their self-reliance and their independence from adults.

At age seven group activities are increasing in popularity; there is some evidence that interests of boys and girls are diverging.

Prepare group singing games, action songs, and percussion instrument experiences; boys and girls should be given some opportunity to select songs and activities in accordance with possible different interests.

At age seven the concept of the right and wrong ways of doing things is beginning to emerge.

Now the children are ready to evaluate the quality of singing and playing; work with children on ways to improve the sound of their singing and playing, and on the proper care of instruments and other materials.

MIDDLE ELEMENTARY: AGES EIGHT AND NINE

The attention span is expanded.

The music period is extended to as long as thirty minutes, depending on the nature and variety of the activities; children can do guided listening to music for a longer period of time; longer songs with greater variety of content and skills can be taught; two- and three-part song forms and rondo forms can be discovered and identified; obvious cultural characteristics of national or ethnic music can be recognized; there is interest in comparing major and minor tonalities; 2 to 1 and 3 to 1 note value relationships can be recognized.

Slow steady growth; girls are more mature than boys; this age group has better co-ordination, is conscious of detail, and is able to devote attention to activities that require control of small muscles of body, hands, feet, and eyes; children are more interested in detailed and intricate work.

The teacher provides opportunities to make substantial use of music notation, in singing, playing, and creating music; more detailed work is planned in the reading of music; use of music text books is expanded; more complex folk dances can be learned; children can conduct all common meters, with some able to direct music activities of the class; syncopated patterns can be introduced; the Autoharp can be played from chord designations with increased skill; children reveal their expanding concepts of repetition and contrast in body movement, in creating music, and in exploring musical forms; sequential tonal patterns can be identified in melodic lines; the teacher guides the consistent progress in standards of musical performance; percussion instruments are played more effectively; recorder-type instruments can be played by the nine-year-olds; the teacher gives each child time to develop his musical and dramatic skills; individual and group lessons in band and orchestra instruments often begin in fourth grade for the physically mature; lessons on half-sized string instruments are sometimes begun in third grade, and for the less physically mature nine-year-olds; there is increasing utilization of the piano and other keyboard instruments by children in the music class and at home; songs of wider range can be sung.

Posture needs attention.

Moving to music and proper singing can aid posture; a variety of music activities can relieve tension and fatigue that cause poor posture.

Vocal cords and lungs are developing rapidly; more control of voice and of breathing; the singing voice of the nine-year-old is better in quality, range, and dependability.

More complex song material of wider ranges can be used; part singing is a goal; the children can study the problem of finding the best places in songs to take breaths.

The harmonic sense is not well developed for the eight-year-olds, but a growing number of nine-year-olds possess it.

The teacher selects special added parts for children who possess ability to sing harmony; rounds and easy descants are used in working for the harmonic readiness of the group; the Autoharp is employed in listening activities to help children become aware of the necessity of chord changes; simple two-part singing is achieved during the fourth grade year; I, IV and V_7 chords can be identified by ear; intervals of thirds and sixths can be identified by sound and sight; playing Autoharp by ear reveals harmonic comprehension; some can chord piano accompaniments.

Communication skills are more highly developed, including reading skills and a larger vocabulary.

Music reading can be emphasized with the eight-year-old; a useful vocabulary of musical symbols and terms increases; numbers and/or syllables are useful in solving problems in singing and creating music; the functions of meter and key signatures are discovered and applied in creative work; notation of two-part songs is interpreted by nine-year-olds; music textbooks are used more analytically; music is read from books, charts, flannel boards, magnetic boards, and from projections on a screen; the repertoire of songs increases.

Need for encouragement, acceptance, and praise from adults; sensitive to criticism.

Provide opportunity and encouragement for each child to develop his special talents and interests in music to a maximum degree; provide opportunity to perform acceptably both individually and in groups in order to feel success and acceptance from the teacher and to grow in responsibility, co-operation, and social competence; create a warm, interesting, challenging environment with an understanding teacher who knows when and how to give encouragement and praise; because of children's great need for acceptance from adults they try to imitate the teacher's example in enthusiasm, interest, and skill in music; this sets the stage for greater skill in performance and appreciation of music; there is pride in creating one's own songs and instrumental pieces.

Peers become important; children are better able to co-operate and work in groups; interest in gangs of the same sex and secret codes is strong, particularly at age nine; this is a time of joining groups; eight-year-olds are usually interested in cowboys, rough and ready play, and they are prone to accidents.

Plan group exploration, discussion, experimentation, sharing, creating and evaluating; music clubs and choruses can be organized; use "mystery tunes," notation treated as a code, and songs about Scouts and other groups; permit time for singing, dancing, creating, dramatizing, and playing instruments in and for groups. These activities are planned by the teacher to improve mutual acceptance of children and the individual child's relationship to, as well as status with, his peers; songs that involve group endeavor and songs of action are emphasized; easy folk dances, play-party games, fun and stunt songs, call and response songs are enjoyed; dialogue songs are used in which boys sing one part and girls another; there is improved group activity in music.

The age of hero worship begins to emerge at about age nine; children need good adult models; children are interested in patriotism.

Provision is made for reading books written for this age level about composers, musicians, instruments, and the history of music; song material and recordings can relate to musical or historical heroes; dramatizations of the lives of composers, musicians, or heroes are employed in musical ways; patriotic songs and songs concerned with great men are stressed.

Interest in other cultures and in the expanding world environment.

The teacher utilizes songs about the problems of the peoples of the world community, with words that mention mechanical progress in production, travel, and communication throughout history; cultural characteristics are identified in terms of specific instruments, rhythm patterns, and dances.

Children enjoy ridiculous humor and the humor in everyday situations; a growing appreciation of imaginary adventure.

The teacher uses songs of humor and nonsense, and plans listening experiences involving adventure and humor; dramatizations and interpretations include comedy.

They are rather indiscriminately interested in anything new to them, particularly the eight-year-olds; they are eager to expand their knowledge.

The teacher introduces new and more complex aspects of music notation and vocabulary; a system of note reading can be employed; information about band and orchestra instruments is emphasized; the structure of major and pentatonic scales is explored.

An increasing number of individual differences and abilities appear; a wide range of reading abilities is evident.

The teacher uses a variety of techniques to learn the background and level of musical performance of each child: parent-teacher conferences, teacher-pupil conferences, observations, anecdotal records of children's performance and attitude, the study of cumulative records and reports, interviews with former teachers, simple and appropriate tests—both standard and teacher-prepared; the teacher plans for the development of each child's musical abilities and needs; attention is given to special individual problems as well as to developing group skills; a music program possessing a variety of activities for the advanced, slow, and average child is a necessity; emphasize reading and pronouncing the words of songs.

Rapid development in independence and in work-study habits.

The teacher strives for the development of creative ideas; special class instruction in piano and strings may begin in third grade, in woodwinds and brasses in fourth grade; the teacher uses pupil leaders in singing and directing; guidance is necessary to establish progressive and consistently high standards of work and performance; provision for independent work is made, such as individual reading of books, playing instruments, composing, bringing from home selected favorite recordings with the stipulation that the child is able to explain to the class the reason for the recording's special worth.

These children need guidance and experience in evaluation of their individual performances and of the performances of others; greater ability in self-evaluation.

The teacher plans successful music activities to build self-confidence; there should be freedom for musical experimentation and invention; guidance is provided in choices and evaluation of related motion pictures, radio and television programs, and of recordings; emphasis is given to improving tone quality in singing, more critical listening, and in developing musical discrimination and taste; good standards of musical quality should be provided by the teacher, some of the children, and recordings.

Nine-year-olds are very conscious of what is right and what is wrong; they desire to do things correctly; they seek help on specific skills and on mastering information.

The teacher gives guidance in evaluating and using music skills and materials; help is given to the uncertain singer; special individual and group work is planned for those who need them and for the specially talented; teachers should not "sell this age short"—they should plan a music program of high quality and stimulate appeal for it.

Continue to learn best through use of varied and concrete materials and through active participation under wise supervision.

Provide varied music activities and materials, and opportunity to explore the potentialities of voices and instruments; create words, tunes, instrumental accompaniments, introductions, codas, and interludes; plan guided listening with specific purposes; allow for creative interpretations of music, including dramatization and body movement; use music that deals with the present and the known.

Understand concepts of simple fractions, time, and money.

Meter signatures are learned.

LATER ELEMENTARY: AGES TEN AND ELEVEN

A pause in physical growth to be followed by a period of rapid growth; girls mature more rapidly than boys; rapid growth implies an awkward stage.

Rhythmic activities that develop muscular co-ordination, grace, and poise are employed; some Dalcroze eurythmics exercises are appropriate; plan activities that reduce awkwardness and self-consciousness; more complex folk dances and formal period dances are good choices; in work dependent upon physical maturity, the teacher does not expect as much from boys as he does from girls; the teacher discusses the effects of physical change on the voice and the ability to play certain band and orchestra instruments; children can play the more complex instruments.

The harmonic sense develops rapidly; the voice range extends; the diaphragm is developing and expanding; some sixth-grade boys will develop the initial stage of the changing voice.

I, IV and V_7 chords in minor can be recognized; polyphonic and harmonic textures can be identified and compared; two-and eventually three-part songs are sung; accompanying chords can be determined by ear and by analysis of melody lines; part singing is stressed; more complex songs are attempted; the first stage of the changing voice retains the unchanged voice quality but lowers the range about a fourth; part singing becomes a necessity for boys whose voices have started to change; the tape recorder can assist the evaluation of voice qualities and general vocal performance; activities are planned to expand the vocal range; a chorus is organized.

Seeks the approval of the peer group; needs to "belong"; is inclined to be overcritical of self and others; is often prejudiced.

The teacher provides opportunity to work and play together and to learn and share music experiences in group situations; he plans for the success of each child in some aspect of music; band, orchestra, and chorus groups are offered; the teacher guides the children in development of appreciation of each child's contributions and skills; he emphasizes the unique contributions of all peoples of the world through study of music; performers from various racial and socio-economic groups are invited to demonstrate their characteristic music and abilities to the class.

The ability to work both independently and with others is more highly developed; the ability to follow the leadership of others is present.

The teacher helps children formulate standards that encourage the best efforts of individuals and groups; he aids the child in consistent, sequential, and thoroughly learned activities and gives children the opportunity to analyze, evaluate and improve their musical learning; the children have the chance to suggest, organize, plan, create, initiate and evaluate many types of music activities for individuals and groups; time and assistance help the children to improve and perfect needed musical skills, attitudes, and appreciations by working alone with books, instruments, recordings, tape recorders, and learning packages.

Pre-adolescents often become extremely critical, unpredictable, and defiant.

To avoid or eliminate this implied problem, a music lesson should include activities that are made meaningful and purposeful through co-operative selecting, planning, developing, and team evaluation by the teacher and the children; ask children to assume leadership roles; offer encouragement and praise as it is deserved and needed; the music activities should be selected in terms of interests, needs, and abilities of each child.

Children have increased energy; they are interested in activity.

Teach various dance steps related to music, social studies, or physical education.

A wide range of individual ability.

The teacher analyzes every child in terms of his abilities, capabilities, level of performance, and needs; the teacher must possess the knowledge of the various levels of musical accomplishment present in kindergarten through grade seven in singing, playing, rhythmic responses, listening, creating, comprehension of notation, and must apply this knowledge in organizing a music program that meets these individual differences; provide opportunity for every child, including the specially talented, to progress at his own rate; when necessary the teacher seeks assistance from guidance personnel, parents, other school music teachers, and private music teachers, in the community; the school must have a wide variety of types and levels of instructional materials.

Interests of boys and girls are usually divergent.

The teacher includes activities in which boys and girls sing in turn or have separate parts, and in which dance partners change frequently; he selects songs and rhythmic responses that appeal to both boys and girls; he encourages children to create according to their own musical interests.

Teasing and hostility between boys and girls.

The teacher attempts to offset this through carefully planned coeducational activities that involve both sexes in participation and evaluation; feelings and relationships are discussed.

Listless at times, but highly active generally.

The teacher plans both quiet and active types of music including listening to recordings, listening to performances of others, quiet songs, action songs, singing games, rhythmic responses, dramatizations, and playing instruments; music is interspersed throughout the day as it is needed to relieve emotional tensions or fatigue and to supply variety.

Resentment of any kind of attention or activity that appears to cause an individual to lose status with his group; seeks to conform to standards exemplified by child leaders in the group and by the majority of his peers.

The teacher refrains from types of criticism and overpraise that would cause an individual to lose status with the group; encouragement and praise is often given privately; the teacher utilizes the child "leaders" to establish standards of performance and behavior.

There is desire for the approval and understanding of adults even though the effort is to become more independent of them.

Provide increased opportunities for children to assume responsibility for their actions and ideas, to pursue their own interests, to explore, to experiment, and to create.

They are often silly; they giggle unnecessarily; they are loud, rough, and like to joke.

Provide songs, rhythmic responses, and instrumental activities that help self-understanding and provide opportunities for release of energy and relief from emotional tension.

Attracted to adults who possess humor, understanding and warmth, and who are constructive, mature, and positive in their approach.

The teacher shows interest, confidence, and enthusiasm; he reveals appreciation of appropriate humor; he is considerate and appreciative of each child's musical efforts; he respects each child's personality and utilizes constructive, positive criticism.

Interested in music concerned with adventure, mystery, humor, work, transportation, inventions, outer space; girls are also interested in music concerned with home and family life.

The teacher includes the content mentioned in the music selected for study; a balance and variety of music content should be sought; music of Asia and Africa can be explored.

Wants to know why as well as how; is inquisitive about scientific reasons that support facts, situations, and theories.

The study of acoustics is introduced; the scientific foundations of vocal and instrumental tone production, including their characteristic types and qualities, are explored; harmonic principles as related to chord structure are studied; the causes of the future voice change, particularly in the boys, are defined; the music structure in songs and in larger forms is analyzed.

Interest in and increased understanding of an expanding environment including time and number concepts. More complete understanding of the contributions of past achievements to present-day culture.

Emphasis is given to understanding various cultures of the world through music that reflects history, customs, religious and social problems; the children create, notate, and invent appropriate music as an outgrowth of their knowledge of history, customs, and cultures, and of time and number concepts related to notation; include the opportunity to understand and appreciate the history of music and the musical contributions of all peoples; there should be some familiarity with the large vocal and instrumental forms; the learner can recognize scales, modes, tone rows, all common intervals, and unusual meters.

Possess the background for understanding and enjoying fantasy.

The teacher provides opportunity for creative composition and dramatization inspired by fantasy; music that has fantasy content is utilized in listening activities; the ways in which musical tones communicate stories are explored and analyzed.

Sustained and intense interest in activities that hold meaning and purpose.

The music period can be lengthened; opportunity is provided to participate in band, orchestra, chorus, musical composition, reading books about music and musicians, the planning of special programs; the teacher involves the children in activities in which time is provided for them to attempt to perfect the activity; creative activities are highly important and can include dance interpretations of recorded music, adding chants and ostinatos to songs, experimenting with pentatonic, modal, tone row, and invented scale tonal organizations; constructing "new" chords, employing rondo and variation forms; experimenting with tape loops and aspects of contemporary music.

In summary, we have attempted to point out the importance of knowing, understanding, and analyzing the capabilities as well as the needs of children in addition to the importance of preparing a music curriculum in terms of the uniqueness of each child. This obviously implies the planning and implementation of a very exacting and effectively organized music curriculum. The emphasis on the individual learner is a revolutionary concept in education when one compares it to what has been common practice. Engleman comments on this:

> The idea of sending a man to the moon and bringing him back safe and sound is a puny concept and a simple undertaking compared to the belief that every man is unique and important and that education can be designed and executed so that every man can achieve his full potential.[3]

INQUIRY AND SUGGESTED ACTIVITIES

1. Present an example, true story or contrived, in which a teacher of music understands his subject but fails to understand the learner. What do you recommend to make this problem less likely in the future?
2. What instances do you know of young children being able to learn something which had been thought impossible for a child in this age group? How do you account for this? In what ways might precocious learners be helped by this early learning? Harmed by it?
3. In what respects are child development musical growth charts inaccurate? If they are not accurate, what good are they?
4. Try to draw relationships between individualization of instruction, flexible scheduling, the ungraded school, levels of instruction, and the elimination of traditional grading? What are possible implications for music teaching?
5. What is the relationship of the selection and use of instructional resources and media to the guidance of individual inquiry and learning?
6. How might effectively organized team teaching and the use of teacher aides be used to improve the individual's learning of music? Design a plan; specify the role and responsibility of each.
7. Education in the United States has been characterized by ideals of a lofty character. What does the ideal of believing "every man to be unique and important and that education can be designed to bring forth his full potential" do to 1) the learner, 2) the teacher, and 3) the public's attitude toward education?

[3] Finis E. Engleman et. al., *Vignettes on the Theory and Practice of School Administration.* (New York: The Macmillan Company, 1963), p. 200.

8. How might an enriched musical environment affect child growth and development in music? Apply this to your own elementary school music experience; how much more might you have known about music today had your school music environment been better?

9. Discuss the growth characteristics and implications suggested for different age levels. Visit a music class; identify and list ideas that might be added to those in this chapter.

REFERENCES

BERGETHON, BJORNAR, AND EUNICE BOARDMAN, *Musical Growth in the Elementary School*. New York: Holt, Rinehart & Winston, Inc., 1963. Musical Growth Charts, pp. 16–27.

COMBS, ARTHUR, ED., *Perceiving, Behaving, Becoming,* 1962 Yearbook. Washington, D.C.: Association for Supervision and Curriculum Development, 1962. Chaps. 3, 4, 5.

FLAVELL, J. H., *The Developmental Psychology of Jean Piaget*. Princeton, New Jersey: D. Van Nostrand, Inc., 1963. A detailed review of Piaget's philosophy.

GAGNE, ROBERT, ED., *Learning and Individual Differences*. Columbus, Ohio: Charles E. Merrill Books, Inc., 1966. Innovations and studies.

HERMANN, EDWARD J., *Supervising Music in the Elementary School*. Englewood Cliffs, New Jersey: Prentice-Hall, Inc., 1965. Developmental characteristics, pp. 27–35.

JENKINS, GLADYS G., ET. AL., *These Are Your Children*. Chicago, Ill.: Scott, Foresman & Company, 1966.

JOINT PROJECT, *A Climate for Individuality*. Washington, D.C.: Association for Supervision and Curriculum Development, 1965.

PASSOW, HARRY, ED., *Nurturing Individual Potential,* Papers and Reports from the ASCD Seventh Curriculum Research Institute. Washington, D.C.: Association for Supervision and Curriculum Development, 1964.

RASMUSSEN, MARGARET, ED., *Children's Views of Themselves*. Washington, D.C.: Association for Childhood Education International, 1959.

————, *Individualizing Instruction*. Washington, D.C.: Association for Childhood Education International, 1964.

TORRANCE, E. PAUL, *Constructive Behavior: Stress, Personality, and Mental Health*. Belmont, California: Wadsworth Publishing Company, Inc., 1965.

In our teaching of men we hardly do more than the housemaid's humble chore of raising the blinds to let the sunlight stream into the house. The teacher's work is to remove impediments to a man's own seeing, to remove the things that would block the light. He cannot reach into another man's mind to insert knowledge; neither can he furnish the light to that mind by which it will see the truth. He merely sets nature free to work, as a doctor's medicine helps nature to throw off a disease; his is the humble work of helping nature, imitating its procedures, but never supplanting it. . . . He cannot offer the comfort of a superior intellect, as an angel can, for in fact his intellect is not superior; it is of exactly the same kind as that of the student.

St. Thomas Aquinas

4

music and the learning process

In Chapter 3 consideration was given to child development. Because child development and learning cannot be separated, this chapter is in essence an extension of the previous chapter. It deals with the learning process as it relates to music.

Any discussion of the teaching of music requires attention to the new concepts concerning acceptable theories of learning that contemporary research has introduced. What conditions aid learning and stimulate its persistence? How much do we know about a child's ability to think? Do children learn particular aspects of music better at certain ages than at others? Are there optimal ages, for example, for learning concrete facts? Are there optimal ages for generalizing? Today's teacher must develop some directional criteria for improving the child's intellectual development. These should not attempt to project learning upon him for which he has insufficient background of understanding, nor should they delay learning past the time when he can satisfactorily master it in terms of his present needs and interests. Such knowledge and issues as these are almost constantly undergoing revision. However, the teacher has little choice but to seek out the most recent pertinent data and research findings that can aid in revising and updating the principles of learning used to guide more effective and efficient mastering of music.

INTELLIGENCE

Research has shown that the amount and quality of learning is in direct proportion to experiences. Another way of saying this is if children lack certain experiences they cannot learn. One of the most encouraging and optimistic beliefs of our time is that intelligence is *something that can be changed* to an important degree by improving the quality and amount of experiencing. This belief serves as the foundation for the processes of inquiry and discovery in today's education.

The findings of a number of distinguished researchers have resulted in the definition of intelligence as the variety of ways an individual has available for processing or organizing incoming information.

Piaget believes that there are rather definite stages of the development of intelligence, each carrying with it the embryonic elements of behavior or intelligence required in the succeeding stage. Unless these embryonic elements are encouraged to grow they can contribute little or nothing to the next stage. The various stages or levels of development have a fixed order, but their time of appearance varies with the individual and with the society or culture of which the individual is a product.

Piaget's first stage is the *sensory-motor* or pre-verbal stage. It is prior to language development. Information is acquired through hearing, sight, smell, taste, and touch (texture).

The second stage is called *pre-operational* representation. The child begins to use language; he can utilize symbols or representations of objects, and can acquire labels and names for experiences, a type of concept formation. He reconstructs all that was developed on the previous level.

A third stage is called *concrete-operational;* the child acts with objects but does not express verbal hypotheses about them. He classifies, orders, numbers, utilizes concepts of space and time, and learns to discriminate in increasing degrees of exactness. He can soon deal with two related aspects of an object.

The fourth and last stage, is the *hypothetic-deductive operational* stage. The child can now reason on the basis of hypotheses and the abstract, not just on the basis of objects or the concrete. He constructs new operations, attains new structures and grouping of structures, and develops relationships between and among ideas. Level four is the highest level of intellectual thought.

It is clear that the child must acquire mental processes and systems in order to be able to assimilate, to act, to think, and to reorganize and reclassify information. For instance, until a small child has learned to control pitch (at least to some degree) with his singing voice, he cannot sing a recognizable tune or learn a new one. The spiral concept of the curriculum is acceptable to Piaget, who calls this concept a series of encounters with ideas or situations in which the child successively accomodates himself. There are two kinds of experiences, physical experience with objects or situations and logical-mathematical, in which there is an ordering. Neither physical maturation nor experiences fully account for the growth of intelligence; a third factor is the social or linguistic or educational transmission. Small children cannot be taught complexities dependent upon verbal transmission because they do not have the experience background from which to formulate structures to assist them in processing such ideas. A fourth factor is what Piaget calls the factor of equilibration or autoregulation, where development progresses as limited understandings are revised, expanded, and related to each other.

This process of equilibration takes the form of a succession of levels of equilibrium, and the levels have a sequence. It is not possible to reach the second level unless equilibrium has been reached on the first level. That is, each level is determined by the preceding level and learning will not progress until equilibration has occurred on the first level.

The importance of the fourth factor lies in the fact that the other three are situations in which the environment does something to the rather passive learner; the fourth factor is a situation in which the learner is active and he acts intellectually upon his environment in order to change it.

In order to develop children's intelligence, it is important that they become involved in their own learning process. The teacher's task is to employ situations in which children are free to experiment and to manipulate. The children pose questions and search for answers. They compare their findings with those of other children.

Piaget states that, "The principal goal of education is to create men who are capable of doing new things, not simply of repeating what other generations have done—men who are creative, inventive, and discoverers. The second goal of education is to form minds which can be critical, can verify, and not accept everything they are offered. The great danger today is of slogans, collective opinions, ready-made trends of thought. We have to be able to resist individually, to criticize, to distinguish between what is proved and what is not. So we need pupils who are active, who learn early to find out by themselves, partly by their own spontaneous activity and partly through material we set up for them;

who learn early to tell what is verifiable and what is simply the first idea to come to them."[1]

It should be remembered that musical and intellectual growth are influenced by both hereditary and environmental factors. Intelligence is not a fixed entity, but will expand if heredity and the experiential environment are conducive to such growth.

Developing Thinking Processes

One of the basic goals of education has become the cultivation of the ability to think. In explaining the definition of thinking Russell states that, "Thinking is a process rather than a fixed state. It involves a sequence of ideas moving from some beginning through some sort of relationships to some goal or conclusion."[2]

In order for teachers to be able to assist children in thinking it is necessary for them to understand clearly what is entailed in the process. Thinking as a process may be employed when an individual has to act in a particular situation or has to decide upon a specific choice.

Crabtree and Shaftel say that in general, thinking consists of a sequence of ideas; how directed the sequence is, however, depends upon the purposes the children hold. Thinking procedures vary from fantasy and pure enjoyment to critical and creative problem solving.[3] Consideration will now be given to some of the different processes of thinking.

PERCEPTION AND ASSOCIATIVE THINKING

There are two levels of associative thinking. The first level may be called cognitive-memory. This type of thinking involves the simple reproduction of facts through recognition, rote memory, or recall. The learner associates a present experience with past encounters and meanings in an automatic, routine, uncritical manner, making a one-to-one match of incidents, situations or occurrences without questioning or analyzing the reasons why. This is the simplest form of thinking.

[1] Richard Ripple and Verne Rockcastle, eds., *Piaget Rediscovered* (Ithaca: School of Education, Cornell University, 1964), p. 5.

[2] David Russell, *Children's Thinking* (Boston: Ginn and Company, 1956), p. 27.

[3] Charlotte Crabtree and Fannie Shaftel, "Fostering Thinking," *Curriculum for Today's Boys and Girls,* ed. Robert S. Fleming (Columbus, Ohio: Charles E. Merrill Books, Inc., 1963), p. 250.

The second type of associative thinking which is more complex than the cognitive-memory type is deductive or convergent thinking in which the learner analyzes and organizes various types of data and information. A question involving convergent thinking might be as follows: "In what ways are all types of drums alike?"

In guiding children in the use of deductive-convergent thinking the teacher needs to assist them in:

identifying what is to be studied
exploring relationships
formulating implications
making inferences by contrasting and comparing

Children can deduce from available or remembered data the logical and acceptable answers, conclusions, and/or generalizations.

Both types of associative thinking indicated above have value but should not be used to the neglect of other types of thinking.

PROGRESSING TO CONCEPT FORMATION AND ABILITY TO GENERALIZE

To think conceptually one progresses from the level of perception of objects, events, and situations to making associations, to formulating concepts, to grouping two or more concepts to form his own generalization, to applying the generalization in solving related problems. In thinking inductively the learner begins with a problem, collects and analyzes his data, and then formulates concepts which in turn are combined and summarized as generalizations.

When a young child examines a bell set, he feels it, may attempt to taste it, looks at its shiny, smooth surfaces, eventually discovers that it can produce a sound and experiments with this characteristic; he may form a mental image (*percept*) of a bell set which becomes stored in his mind, then retrieved when he needs it. Later, when he relates this percept to other types of keyboard instruments, he has made an *association* based on the common elements of the appearance of the keyboard and the fact that it can produce pitches on the different instruments. Through this series of experiences he gains the *concept* of keyboard instruments. This concept continues to expand as he acquires progressively more experiences with it, and it becomes a part of his thinking process. For example, when he first sees a celesta, he will want to find out what new manner of keyboard instrument it is, what it is used for in the orchestra, how the sound is produced, and why it sounds different from other keyboard instruments he knows. He will be able to do this because he has acquired a concept he can utilize when confronted with a problem concerning keyboard instruments. The more he knows about the construction of these instruments, what produces the sound, and what makes the tone qualities differ, the more he will be able to think and act in terms of keyboard instruments.

The lesson for the teacher implied from the above is this: he should assist children to have accurate and clear perception of any aspect of music under study because children cannot develop precise associations and meanings unless they can differentiate between the characteristics of what is being studied—in this instance, the bell set. The teacher is needed to help the children make the associations they cannot make well enough by themselves. He seeks ways to set up purposes in the minds of the children and assists them in their observations, discussions, and in summarizing or evaluating the outcomes of their experiences. Children's findings should be listed, grouped, labeled, analyzed, and related whenever possible. This entire process may be initiated with questions such as "What is it?" "How do people use it?" "Is it like any other instrument?" "How is it different from other instruments?" Vocabulary is introduced and utilized in order for pupil discussion to take place.

Some musical concepts are not *concrete* like the bell set; they are *intangible* like the interdependence of the various elements of music. In its earlier stages this concept is introduced when children find that recognizable melody cannot take place without some form of rhythm. This concept is gradually acquired through experiences with a number of melodies and rhythms. For instance, "Happy Birthday to You" and "The Star-Spangled Banner" are completely different melodies, but there is a rhythm pattern common to both. The child should discover that the first parts of these two songs have identical rhythm and that "Joy to the World" utilizes the major scale in its beginning measure, but it is the rhythm that clearly distinguishes it from the way the major scale is commonly played. The children can try to invent a melody without rhythm to find that rhythmic feeling may be reduced but cannot be eliminated. Out of all of these experiences grows the generalization that the interdependence of pitch and rhythm produces melody. Later on, harmony and other musical elements will expand the generalization of the interdependence of these elements in producing various types of music, and the children will use this principle in creating their own music.

Unless the teacher plans the lesson in such a way that the children know what they are listening for in melody and rhythm, a child might conclude that he is simply singing a song or clapping a rhythm because the teacher told him to do it. The teacher must bring the focus of the lesson clearly to the attention of the children. This is done by planning some type of activity that reveals to the teacher what the children already know about the content of the lesson, or one which connects with the children's past experiences. Then the focusing of the lesson may be brought about through questioning or class discussion of the problem before it, and writing important points on the chalkboard. In class discussions there should be references to past experience, to possible future activities, and the problem should be defined and clarified. Unless the purpose for what the class is doing is made clear in the thinking of the students, little learning will take place.

"Musical understanding results from learning, and may be approached fundamentally by grasping combinations of sounds and the succession patterns by which these sounds become interrelated. Isolated tones become meaningful when associated with other tones. Problems in the perception of rhythm, harmonic progression, texture, and formal design require similar modes of studied relationships. Habits of concentrated attention to stimulate memory and frequent comparisons to motivate critical attitudes are then essential to the task of coordinating the intellect with sense perception."[4]

HIGHER LEVELS OF THINKING: DISCOVERY, INFERENTIAL AND CREATIVE-PROBLEM SOLVING

These ways of thinking include features of perceptual, associative, and conceptual processes; thus there is interrelatedness in practice.

In order to teach for the development of higher and more sophisticated levels of thinking, teachers must involve the learner in identifying problems, planning for their solution and in the evaluation of their endeavors. Teachers can lead children to search by asking "open-ended" questions that cause them to imagine, to speculate, to analyze, and to experiment. The teacher should plan and formulate questions which stimulate the children to use all the different types of thought processes and responses.

[4] Abraham A. Schwadron, *Aesthetics: Dimensions for Music Education.* (Washington, D.C.: Music Educators National Conference, 1967), p. 95.

Gallagher suggests that teachers employ the use of a variety of types of questions carefully selected and ordered to develop the logical solutions of problems and to guide the children into higher levels of thinking and problem-solving skills. Under each type of thinking stated below he indicates key terms to use as guides in formulating questions:[5]

KEY TERMS FOR VARIOUS THINKING OPERATIONS

CIA Project—Gallagher

Divergent Thinking
What would happen if . . . ?
How many ways can you . . . ?
Give me all of the reasons you can think of . . .
Present as many possible solutions to our problem as you can . . .
Give all the synonyms you can think of for . . .

Convergent Thinking
Explain how this could happen . . .
Tell us why you think so.
Give your reasons for such a judgment.
How did you reach that conclusion?
Why is it called . . . ?
What conclusion have you reached . . . ?

Cognitive-Memory
What is the name for . . . ?
Who is . . . ?
Where is the . . . ?
What is the meaning of . . . ?
Describe . . .
What is a . . . ?

Evaluative Thinking
What is the most important . . . ?
Name the two most influential causes . . .
What are the chances that . . . ?
Give an estimate of . . .
In your judgment, what is the best course of action . . . ?
What do you think of my choice?

As children become involved through the use of various types of questions and in the process of inquiry, they become more able to direct and control their own learning.

[5] James J. Gallagher, "Key Terms for Various Thinking Operations," presented in mimeograph form from CIA Project.

CREATIVE PROBLEM-SOLVING

For many years creative problem solving has been recognized as a very effective way of learning. One of the major roles of the teacher is to assist children in suspending judgment until all the data has been assembled, then have them draw conclusions from relevant data to either prove or disprove a hypothesis. The sequential steps in the problem solving process are listed below but seldom can or will these steps be employed sequentially in approaching the solution to problems; they are often used by skipping about:

1. Recognizing and defining a problem
2. Gathering data
3. Forming tentative solutions or hypotheses
4. Testing these by organizing and interpreting data
5. Drawing and testing conclusions
6. Applying the accepted conclusion to related situations

An example of this might be the case of Johnnie, who in fifth grade is learning to play the trumpet. He notices that in music of the eighteenth century the trumpet plays only chord-line melodies or repeated note parts, and this is a problem worth investigating because he likes to play diatonic tunes as well as bugle-type music. His problem is "Why do the trumpets play only chord-line parts in this music?" Johnnie and his classmates collect data by listening to more music. They find that later on in the nineteenth century the trumpets are assigned scale-line melodies by the composers. Their theories about this include:

> The composers of the eighteenth and early nineteenth centuries did not want the trumpet to play melodies that were step-wise in construction.
>
> The trumpet players did not like to play anything that did not have bugle-call or repeated-note characteristics.
>
> Nobody had thought of the trumpet as an instrument that should play scale-line parts.
>
> The players did not know the fingering, so could not play scale-line parts.

At this point they decide that they have insufficient data to test any of these theories, so it is necessary to collect more data. They go to the library to seek help. The librarian guides them to books on instruments. What they find leads them to agree that none of their theories is correct, because the reason the trumpet did not play scale-line melodies was that it was mechanically unable to do so; the valve had not yet been invented.

The problem had been solved, but led to more questions about other instruments and their history. The concepts the children worked with led them to the generalization, "Present-day musical instruments have evolved from earlier forms; a series of inventions which expanded the capabilities of instruments gradually gave the composers more pitches and tone qualities with which to work." In this process their concept of music through the ages and into the future was expanded, and the class had gained another way to think about instrumental music and its human relationships. Their new generalization about the evolution of instruments and expansion of tone qualities was guided by the teacher to include consideration of the electronic music of today and the strong possibilities of new tonal resources being added to music as far into the future as the children could imagine. It is vital to the learning process that validated concepts and generalizations are applied to new and related situations in this way in order that learnings be extended.

CREATIVE INQUIRY THINKING   Alice S. Beer implies that the creative-inquiry approach is synonymous with the conceptual approach. In an article in *Baltimore Public Schools Bulletin of Education,* XLII, No. 4, she wrote:

> Children are learning more about music by creating music themselves. In effect, children are acting as composers and by composing are acquiring a first-hand understanding of the process of composing. In trying to create music, children find a need to learn a great deal about the nature of music, its composition, structure, balance, unity, variety, beauty, tone color, expression, dynamics, tension and release, scales, harmony, rhythm, melody, and of course, its notation.
> As the children evaluate their own compositions, they feel a need to refine, rework, and improve. This is essentially the conceptual approach to learning rather than the imposition of a pre-established set of ideas. In the process of creativity, students learn through discovery—discovery of their own need for knowledge that can be immediately put to use.

She describes children's dramatizations of "The Three Billy Goats Gruff," in which they experimented with telling the story by selecting a rhythm instrument for each character. They added a cymbal to provide tension and heighten the dramatic effect of the fight between the Troll and Billy Goat Gruff. This experience helped children discover how sound and music can tell a story. An intermediate grade utilized a tone row as a backdrop for sounds of instruments and other classroom resources in working out a musical description of a busy city street. This led to a better understanding of how Gershwin accomplished this in *An American in Paris*. Other classes explored composition approached through words—using children's names to create a rondo, using old sayings, original poetry, television commercials, names of birds, etc. Some children developed compositions based upon exploring terms such as *theme* and *variation* which they had found applied to a number of compositions. In writing their variations they learned much about how a composer works. Others learned how composers add descants, ostinatos, and counter-melodies, and still others learned more about using chords and tone clusters, adding and subtracting instruments, and how composers end compositions. She concluded:

> The conceptual approach promises an effective way of presenting music to children, more effective perhaps than memorizing a certain number of songs and rote-learning certain musical facts. Like the *New Math* and other educational innovations, creative approaches to music education place the student in the center of a learning process. Thus, his music education emanates from his capacity and skill in musical expression and response and leads to understanding and maturity in performance and musical literacy.

The creative process is necessary for self-fulfillment. It seems that children respond to learning whenever they can become personally involved in this process, regardless of aptitude or socio-economic background. To be creative is to think in new and different ways. Creative people work with problems. Every person has creative potential. What we know about creativity leads us to believe that childhood is a very significant period during which creativity can be encouraged or be stifled. Leonhard says:

> Psychologists have recognized that in connection with many abilities, there is a critical stage in the development of the child. If education is delayed past this critical stage, the child can never fulfill his potential. It is likely that there is a critical stage in the development of musicianship and aesthetic sensitivity, and present evidence indicates that it occurs early —probably before the age of nine.[6]

[6] Excerpt from address by Dr. Charles Leonhard at the Conference to Improve the Effectiveness of Music Education in Oregon Elementary Schools, Gearhart, Oregon, April 27–28, 1967. State Department of Education, Salem, Oregon.

There are four suggested phases of the creative process for adults:

1. Preparation. Exploring ideas to identify a problem.

2. Incubation period. This phase may last a few moments or even years. During this period there is little conscious work on the problem but it seems to be mulling about in the back of a person's mind.

3. Illumination, or Insight. Ideas begin to flow; new relationships are discovered; novel combinations of the elements of the problem occur. Excitement comes with illumination.

4. Verification. During this phase the new idea is tested and the details refined and revised. The experiment may be repeated again and again, and finally the relevant phases are selected for application.

The creative problem solving steps and the four phases of the creative process are highly similar. Children proceed through these same steps in a less sophisticated manner.

It is commonly said that children need to be "free" in order to create, and this has led to much misunderstanding. Some have mistakenly believed that children must not be restricted. In the first place, there must be certain restrictions to make it possible to have a classroom situation in which creativity can flourish. At the beginning of the process, to give children the confidence that they can produce their own music, many music teachers restrict these children to using only a few tones of the pentatonic scale on metalophones and xylophones. This restriction frees them to create because they are protected from the complexities of the complete major scale with its leading tones. Conformity to basic rules, such as how and when to play instruments, the care and storage of equipment, the distribution of various music materials and their collection, and taking turns in class discussion, are necessary routine matters. Such things get in the way only when they become ends in themselves instead of being truly functional.

The creative imagination can be energized and guided from birth. If it is stifled early, it will only become imitative if it survives at all. It is true that a vigorous creative imagination can survive early stifling and opposition, but if it learns only to act vigorously without direction, it becomes dangerous.

According to Dr. Paul Torrance we can now do a better job of individualizing instruction. Although curiosity and creativity, as well as creative thinking ability, are apparently universal enough to make creative ways of learning valuable for all children, such ways of learning must not be regarded as an exclusive way of learning for all children—nor for any child. No one method of instruction seems to be the best method for all children. Even some of the most successful experiments in (music) education show that some children fail to profit by the experimental procedure.[7]

Dr. Torrance further argues that as creative processes give us a better understanding of the human mind and its functioning and a new vision of what man may become, it will lead us towards a more humane kind of education—a kind of education which will give every child a better chance to realize his potentialities. If this dream is to come true, however, a number of steps must be taken.

1. Creative development must no longer be left to chance.

2. Children must be given more opportunities for using their creative thinking abilities in acquiring knowledge and in using what they acquire.

3. We must do a better job of individualizing instruction, making it possible for many children who do not now profit very much from education to succeed.

4. We must somehow reduce the discontinuities in education and begin developing early the motivations and skills for continued learning.

5. We must shift our emphasis from covering an ever-increasing curriculum content to inquiry, discovery, and the creative application of knowledge.

6. We must move from a preoccupation with personality adjustment to a concern about mental health and self-actualization.

7. We must place a greater emphasis upon courage and honesty, without which there can be no true creativity.

These are the directions in which I believe creativity research is leading us.[8]

CRITICAL-EVALUATIVE THINKING

This type of thinking is a matter of using judgment. Critical thinking makes evaluations in accordance with standards or criteria. Children will

[7] From a paper prepared for presentation at George Peabody College, Nashville, Tennessee, July 16, 1963, "Where is Research in Creativity Leading Us?" Bureau of Educational Research, University of Minnesota.

[8] *Ibid.*

examine music, symbols, or processes in order to deduce the extent to which the criteria are met. In order to do this, the underlying concepts must be well understood, what is being evaluated must be clearly perceived, and feelings must be restrained to avoid interference with the appraisal.

In music there is much critical examination of performance and recordings in terms of pitch, tone qualities, tempo, dynamics, articulation, tension and release, form, and the balance of musical elements. When evaluating a song, the relation of the words and the melody is also under scrutiny. Questions involved could be: "Listen to the song we just sang as I play it back to you on the tape recorder. Have we utilized all appropriate ways for singing it expressively?" "Is the form of this recorded composition logical in terms of what the composer has named it? He called it "Theme and Variations." "Which percussion instruments are most suitable to accompany this music? Why?" "Does this melody make good sense in terms of what the words are communicating? Why or why not?" Such questions cannot be answered by a simple *yes* or *no:* they always imply a logical defense of a *yes* or *no* in terms of standards derived from past experience or from current class determination of them—standards which are recorded in writing or are understood. The teacher will see to it that opinions and facts are not confused.

When concerts are presented in elementary schools, it is necessary to set up standards for how to act when one is at a concert. When children and teachers plan together for such events, their criteria would be appropriate standards of behavior they would expect both as members of the visiting performance group and as members of an audience. Against these criteria they would plan their behavior critically. After the concert the students would evaluate the behavior of the performers and themselves in terms of their stated criteria.

This type of thinking involves value judgments and beliefs. As the learner reflects, refines, and tests his beliefs he should become more able to defend them on factual grounds rather than on an emotional basis. In this way values and beliefs acquire additional meaning and significance. The child develops the ability to make value judgments, to act on the basis of hypothetical propositions, to test, prove, and seek new data if needed, and to prize values.

The following chart assists teachers in guiding children in critical and evaluative listening.

Listening Critically to Recordings

Listen for musical elements or ideas
related to questions and problems
under consideration.

The criteria to assist
judgment are either listed or
commonly understood.

Listen for musical ideas which act
as cues to guide the listener to
answer the question or solve the
problem.

If the music is program music,
listen for the musical means
the composer utilizes to
communicate the story or
description, and evaluate their effectiveness.

If the music is pure music,
listen for the interrelation
of the musical elements under
consideration, and evaluate its effectiveness.

If tone color is under appraisal,
instrument identification is of
importance when considered in
light of the choice of the composer
in the type of tone qualities
necessary for his communication,
either of program music or of
pure music. Evaluate its suitability.

Application of Steps in Concept
Formation Using Various Types of Thinking

In developing cognitive processes in this section, all of the types
of thinking discussed in the preceding pages are utilized and exemplified
in the steps of concept formation, moving from simple perception to the
higher levels of thinking.

DEVELOPING COGNITIVE PROCESSES

In developing thinking processes, the teacher begins by providing
learners with data-collecting experiences by means of which concepts can

be built. Degrees of mastery of these concepts yield an increasing mental ability to interpret and to make generalizations. From there the process moves on to a higher level in which the learner has practice in analyzing and synthesizing data, evaluating and judging as required by the experience or problem, and then he has an opportunity to make application of this knowledge in solving new problems. It is highly important that in music learning, these thinking abilities which call for the utilization of music skills as well as music knowledge be activated.

CONCEPT FORMATION

COLLECTING AND ORGANIZING DATA   Concept formation is basic to other cognitive processes and is the necessary foundation for formulating generalizations. In general, the sequence by which this development takes place in the mind of the learner is as follows:

1. Identifying and enumerating through use of the ear, eye, and body various musical characteristics, elements, objects, and events such as pitch, rhythm, instruments, and concerts. What did you hear? See? Feel? (Identify. List. Examine. Compare.)

2. Grouping in accordance with common qualities, uses, or other characteristics. For example, types of chords, even and uneven meters, types of phrases, and classifications of instruments. How can we group these most logically? If we don't know, what can we do or where can we go to find out?

3. Discriminating between the features of these and abstracting common characteristics or elements, like the instances of 4/4, 5/4, 6/8, and 7/8 meters being different, yet containing the same note values or possibly using the same tempos. How are they alike? What names should we give to these categories?

Related concepts can be linked together to form a *concept group*. An example would be the various meter signatures; when each is viewed as a concept, they then can form a concept group. Similarly, major, minor, and other less common tonalities form a concept group because each has a tonal center. The *label* "tonality" can be applied to each of them, thus to the group.

INTERPRETING DATA AND GENERALIZING   After data have been assembled and ordered, and after an understanding of the relevant concepts has been achieved, it is possible to relate concepts and use them to form generalizations. Some important points to consider are as follows:

1. Examining the same aspect of music in several different compositions. Example: What are the outstanding rhythm patterns in each of these songs?

2. Comparing the same aspect of music in several different compositions. Example: Contrast these rhythm patterns; how are they the same; how are they different?

3. Generalizing. Example: This type of song tends to have a characteristic rhythm pattern.

4. Explaining. Example: The characteristic rhythm pattern is the result of each song's relationship to the same national dance.

APPLICATION OF CONCEPTS AND GENERALIZATIONS   Concepts, concept groups, and generalizations can be used to:

1. Compare objects, performances, activities, or phenomena.
    Example: How can we use the concept of a stage work in comparing a stage play with an opera? A ballet with a musical comedy?

2. Predict possibilities.
    Example: What do you think would happen if there were no woodwinds in symphony orchestras? If there were no percussion section? What would happen if there were no symbols to depict accidentals in music?

3. Supporting predictions.
    Example: Why do you believe the woodwinds are needed in symphony orchestras? What evidence can you give to prove that the percussion section is important? How do you know that it would not sound *better* if all accidentals were abandoned?

4. Verifying.
    Example: How can we find out if orchestras in Asia have woodwinds? Are drums in African orchestras more or less important than drums in our orchestras? Where can we find evidence to prove this?

ANALYZING   Analysis is used to dissect music and requires the mastery of data and concepts. One must have knowledge and understanding about music in order to deal with analysis of average complexity. The process may be developed by the following types of activities:

1. Analyzing specific details or elements in music.
    Example: What is the form of this music? What is there about the structure of the melody that gives us this feeling?

2. Analyzing musical relationships.
   Example: How are rhythm and melody related? What have the note values to do with tension and release in this song?

SYNTHESIZING   Synthesis is used to bring the elements of music together to form a unified whole. It requires thinking of a high order and ordinarily can be encountered at about the sixth-grade level.

1. Discovering relationships.
   Example: How are harmony and the melody line related in this song? Why did Saint-Saëns choose the tone quality of the cello for the melody in *The Swan*? What other instruments might be as appropriate?

2. Solving problems creatively.
   Example: Write a composition describing an afternoon at the beach, including original sound effects: notation will probably have to be specially invented.

3. Organizing.
   Example: Plan a program for room parents that relates and explains the musical learnings of the term.

4. Relating elements.
   Example: Create an appropriate background of musical sounds by which to heighten the effect of this poem.

EVALUATING   This is thinking which is involved with value, choice, and judging. It is the highest level of thinking.

Example: According to our criteria, how well did the performer play? Who is the most important symphony orchestra conductor in the United States?

Theories of Teaching and Learning

Teachers in the past have been more concerned with *what* the child did than *why* or *how* he did it. There was more concern with what the child did in terms of what the teacher wanted him to do than concern about what motivated him, how he learned, or his thought processes. There is still too little understanding of the differences between a musical problem in which children advance their theories concerning data they collected and one in which they attempt to find the correct inference from facts the teacher has told them.

What children already know greatly influences what they perceive. A very young child will be able to identify something as music by hearing it, but an intellectually mature child who has had many more experiences will hear the same music and be able to hear different elements which constitute music and to describe what these elements are doing in this music. The more intellectually mature child will be able to hear both the music as a whole and as a sum of a number of parts which he can, to some extent, analyze. Let us imagine that this music gives this child a new experience; it is 5/4 meter. The fact that the learner has had experiences with 2/4, 3/4, and 4/4 meters serves him as an *organizer*[9] because through this prior experience he can organize the selection, grouping, and ordering of experiences involving his concept of meter. The organizer, which is a condition of the mind, permits *meaning* to be produced in response to the experience. This learner tries to feel the accents which help to determine meter. He may find either a $3 + 2$ or a $2 + 3$ pattern of beats. He may also find every fifth beat the stronger one. From this he may theorize the new meter, 5/4. Thus, past experience makes an organizer possible. The teacher can be sure that:

1. The more experiences the learner has had, the greater the possibility is that he can acquire new meanings.
2. The more organizers the learner has to draw upon, the more meaning he can extract from his experiences.

The availability of organizers, therefore, is a key to children's learning. *The order of events is from experience to organizer to meaning.*

It is not surprising that in today's computerized world, the mind is considered by some to be similar to a computer, with intake (perception), control, and storage facilities. For instance, stored experiences are a form of organizer, but they also serve the learner by helping him to abstract, categorize, and analyze the raw experiences by constructing and utilizing *systems* or ways for processing these experiences. A child, for example, hears something he identifies as music. His concepts of various tone qualities serve as an organizer to enable him to identify the music as band music, not orchestra music nor dance band music. The learner has also stored *systems* he has learned. These organize similarities and

[9] J. Richard Suchman, "A Model for the Language of Education," *The Instructor* (September, 1966).

differences and may consist of aspects of music—loud and soft, fast and slow, sharps and flats, duple and triple, major and minor, woodwinds and brass. A great deal of teaching is of the type that constructs systems the learner uses to make sense out of his world of experiences. The learner is also given a great deal of *data* that come from applying systems to experiences; such data are selected by the teacher, as a rule. Examples might be that Middle C is a note on a leger line between the bass and treble clefs, and that F is the name of the first space of the treble clef.

Eventually the learner begins to abstract or construct beliefs, theories, generalizations, and principles describing the characteristics of the type of data he has met. This is called *inference* or *induction*. For example, Steve has experienced the different common meters. As a result of examining these, he generalizes that: meter is a type of mathematical measurement applied to beats and to rhythm patterns. Such inferences can be stored, then drawn upon to be used as organizers for some future experience with meter and note values. In storage are four kinds of organizers: experiences, systems, data, and inferences. Let us try to use these in anaylzing a teaching-learning example.

Miss Ferrens brings a two-tone (two drums of different pitch) bongo drum into her classroom. The drum remains on the music table for a week while the children respond with curiosity to Miss Ferrens' invitation that they examine the drum to find out how much they can learn about it. She suggests from time to time that they perform simple experiments with it to see what types of sounds come from it, under what conditions the most resonant sounds can be made, why there is a difference in pitch, and how the drum might be struck to produce what the children believe are the best results. After a few days she asks: "In what different ways do people play drums?" The children theorize that they can be played by hitting with some kind of stick and with the hands. One boy who had observed a dance band drummer said that some drums can be struck by using the foot on a mechanical striker. The children are then urged to observe drumming whenever they can on television and in rehearsals of the school band and orchestra in order to test their theories resulting from the re-stated question: "How are drums best played, and in how many different ways?" Later Miss Ferrens brings in other drums, the snare drum, hand drum, and conga drum. The children play them and compare their characteristics and study them to find out how each was made. Eventually the tambourine is added to be compared with the drums, and the children try to find more drums of different kinds.

Analysis: Miss Ferrens first planned for a common set of experiences for all the children with the one drum. As the children experimented with it, they produced additional experiences for themselves. They were freed for *action* through which their experiences took place and which made those experiences more meaningful because they were self-involving. The children drew on organizers such as prior experiences with pitch, with tone qualities, and with ways of striking objects. After experiences with the other drums they were able to discover common characteristics as well as differences (such as the snare). The bringing in of the tambourine was an interesting *discrepant event* whereby the children discovered that its sound was different and its construction varied in one respect from the concept of the membrane drum: it had metal jingles on it, and this made its tone quality different in a special way. To gather more data a field trip was made to a music store which had many drums on display; later the class visited the band rehearsal room where the drummers played the different drums and answered questions. Inferences were made about the functions of drums in the world of man as well as the world of music.

Compare all of this with a lecture given by a teacher during which pictures of drums are displayed, then a recording of the sound of a number of drums is heard. Contrast this with Miss Ferrens' approach in terms of experiences, systems, data, inferences and action. How much decision-making by the children took place?

MOTIVATION

The problem with motivation in the past has been that too often the child became active in the learning process to please the teacher or to conform to his peer group (extrinsic motivation) instead of becoming active in learning because he wanted to find out something for himself (intrinsic motivation—also inquiry). The learner has choices he can make. He may gather information in order to solve a problem or try to do it in a disorganized pattern. He can select from storage ideas or facts to apply as organizers in a different situation. He may act upon the problem, turn to something else, or decide to ignore the entire process for a while. Teachers need to know more about these possible choices and why the learner makes them.

Suchman claims there are three levels of motivation.[10] One is the

---

[10] J. Richard Suchman, "Motivation," *The Instructor* (December, 1966).

visceral in which the learner is motivated by body needs and the urge to survive. Another is the *social-ego* level in which the learner seeks to be accepted by peers and adults. Teachers frequently employ this level to bring pressures to bear on students; grades are usually included among the status symbols. The third is the *cognitive* level. Suchman emphasizes at least three basic kinds of cognitive motivations; CLOSURE, when the learner is faced with a situation in which his knowledge is not adequate to cope with it and he then desires a solution, answer or explanation; CURIOSITY, when the learner actively enjoys the process of finding answers to questions, (This type of learner may not accept the five-line staff without wondering why it has five lines and not three or seven); and POWER, when the learner realizes that knowledge gives him control over his environment and he wants the security and confidence this can give him.

The type of motivation affects the way the learner is apt to behave. Visceral motivation, which implies physical danger or discomfort, is not a type that permits much of any sifting of ideas or theorizing; the child thinks only of what will work to get him out of a very uncomfortable situation. Since productive reflection demands security, visceral motivation denies such reflection at the outset, and the child who is afraid, overtired, or hungry is regularly not a good learner. The school should avoid this type of motivation. The pressures of social-ego motivation can generate worry about failure or non-acceptance. Children under these pressures are apt to think about themselves rather than about the world outside of them. In both of these types of motivation the vital process of inquiry is defeated. The mind is hemmed in by external pressures that prevent its being occupied with creative matching and ordering of organizers and experiences, which is necessary for inquiry to take place.

Example: Mr. Sperry asks his class a divergent question on a piece of music the class knows well: "Why has Bach's 'Air for the G String' become a universal favorite?" All are free to contribute their thoughts. One student says she believes it is because of the calm and flowing style of the composition. Another believes that the interesting combination of a leading melody with polyphonic texture has made the piece appealing. Another says that if Bach's name had not appeared as the composer, the music would probably be unknown today. The class listens to each theory, discusses and examines it. New evidence is given to assist evaluating the theories. No final answers result, and there are no right or wrong answers. The class is motivated by the thrill of thinking, gathering data, and then of more thinking.

Compare this with another class in which "Air for the G String" has been studied. The teacher's motive is to try to find out how much the class knows about the music. He has a list of questions and goes around the class, asking one question of each student in turn. If a student fails to answer a question, the teacher goes on to the next student. After the class has been questioned in this way, the teacher gives a short lecture in which he states specifically why this music has become a universal favorite. The class takes notes part of the time. Some of the students do not take notes; they furtively draw pictures or look out of the window. How has social-ego pressure been used? How much creativity can there be in this class? In which class will there be more anxiety?

The first of the above two examples is an example of inquiry learning, which is learning that may be teacher planned but is learner directed and controlled as it unfolds. The teacher promotes learner growth by knowing how and when *to get out of the way* of the developing learner and how to encourage continued development.

Play and *discussion* are important. Genuine play is satisfying in itself; one is not necessarily concerned about its consequences because play *seems* not to have significance. This frees the learner to experiment and explore without fear. Music teachers often utilize play and games in connection with ear training drills. Young children are assumed not to identify the activity as anything but a game, which frees them to do relatively uninhibited play for which the teacher may have one purpose and they another. Discussion is of vital importance, for it can give direction and structure to thinking. The teacher should keep discussion free and open, participate at times, and introduce specifically-related facts and organizers which stimulate discussion and raise its intellectual level. Children must be able to verbalize their experiences. This permits them to profit from ideas of other learners and increase their number of organizers. The teacher's role requires planning play and discussion activities that children will enjoy, not fearing the consequences of mental actions they may make. Later, it is hoped that the learner will be so attracted by these types of learning that he will risk consequences in unprotected situations. Suchman says that such risk taking will form the core of a creative person and a creative society.

DIDACTICS[11]

Didactic teaching is that in which the teacher controls the situation by means of rapid-fire questioning, making comparisons, using pictures and charts as organizers, lecturing, and reading. It is perhaps the most common method in situations where the teacher's primary goal is acquisition of knowledge and comprehension. For example, the music teacher provides a chart of a certain kind of scale, asks questions about it, shows its use in a song, compares it with charts of other scales, shows the scales on a chart of the keyboard, plays scales and has the children identify them aurally; he illustrates these in songs, lectures briefly about different scale systems and in general manipulates the matching of new experiences with existing organizers. In contrast, a teacher stressing inquiry might have made chromatic bell sets available to small groups of children, given the children a week in which to find out how many different scales there might be within a specific octave, and in effect have the learner develop the quest for information from there.

The didactic teaching method attracts many teachers because they are "in control," feel that they are truly "teaching," and it seems to be to the point, thus efficient. Also, children do not grope for information nor do they theorize misconceptions. The disadvantages can be that the easy and accurate handling of data and experiences by the teacher is less attractive to most learners than understanding something because of their own efforts. In addition, the motivation is largely external.

OTHER ASPECTS OF LEARNING

Drill,[12] while bearing the burden of some negative concepts today, is not necessarily dull and uninteresting. *If children have their own reasons for memorizing,* they not only will want some helpful drill, but will enjoy the feeling of power as they master the skill or information in question. *Recitation* is learning in which the children respond to questions put to them by the teacher that show whether they have or have not accumulated knowledge. This serves to restrict the learners to specifics, permitting little opportunity for expansion of comprehension and knowledge. Open, free inquiry is not a part of this type of teaching. Fortunately, there is less recitation in today's schools than formerly. *Projects* can be valuable

---

[11] J. Richard Suchman, "Didactics," *The Instructor* (March, 1967).
[12] J. Richard Suchman, "Three Old Standbys," *The Instructor* (May, 1967).

or not, depending upon many factors. The project, like other aspects of teaching, has to be judged in terms of what is happening to the learner, as well as what the teacher wants accomplished. If the motivation for the project is social-ego based rather than cognitive, then the learner is not likely to strike out in new paths in his quest for knowledge. He will conform instead to a pattern best designed to give him teacher or group approval.

A BALANCE OF STRATEGIES

All strategies of learning have a place in a balanced learning program, and the teacher should know his reasons for the selection and employment of any one of them. Because music, as taught years ago, was unbalanced with overemphasis on drill, performance, rote learning, and recitations, it behooves today's teachers to plan to bring inquiry learning into balance with other teaching strategies. The learner should have more autonomy; his musical education should be planned with and for him as an individual; he should be permitted to search for meaning rather than to seek "success" as determined by extrinsic standards; he should be permitted to learn for himself. To encourage inquiry learning the teacher provides the environment for it, and facilitates it by helping children with self-directed investigation of the wonders of music. He helps children to become aware of the learning process, how to structure it, and how to discuss it. The teacher gives the children direction by providing motivation to inquire; he gives them the freedom to pursue their quest for knowledge and for answers; he makes available to the child resources by means of which he can answer his questions, improve his skills, test his theories, and locate data.

Acquiring Attitudes and Values

Knowledge alone is insufficient as a goal of education. Unless constructive attitudes and values accompany it, knowledge is at least neutralized, and is even dangerous on occasion.

An attitude may be defined as a predisposition to react in a certain way to objects, persons, ideas, or subjects. It may be conscious and willful, or subconscious; it may be rational or irrational.[13] Attitudes and

[13] John Jarolimek, *Social Studies in the Elementary School* (3rd ed.) (New York: The Macmillan Company, 1967), p. 59.

values result from an individual's total experience. They are flexible, and change as the learner's experiences in living are expanded. They are therefore extremely personal.

Attitudes deal primarily with feelings and emotions—with the *affective* processes. Because both attitudes and values are more affective than cognitive there is general belief that they cannot be taught in a direct manner. For example, the importance or beauty of a musical selection is not taught alone by the teacher informing the children how important and beautiful it is, or by the children merely verbalizing on its importance and beauty. The children must *internalize* such importance and beauty to the extent that their conduct toward music, and their response to and understanding of other music, are affected. Children's valuing is far more, therefore, than a class presentation on how valuable something is to humanity.

Jarolimek points out that because attitudes and feelings are related, the emotional climate of the classroom must be one that furthers emotional growth.[14] When the environment frustrates children by failing to meet social and emotional needs, there is little in it to contribute to the development of wholesome attitudes. A learning environment that permits destructive, negative opinions of music or of people tends to destroy values rather than to discover them. Hostility and aggression are products of such practices. Attitudes and emotions, whether good or bad, will be developed in the classroom; it is the teacher's responsibility that they be healthy and constructive. Therefore, teachers must plan for this important type of learning. Raths, Harmin, and Simon[15] suggest that teachers:

Encourage children to make choices and to make them freely.

Help them discover and examine available alternatives when faced with choices.

Help children weigh alternatives thoughtfully, reflecting on the consequences of each.

Encourage children to consider what it is they prize and cherish.

Give them opportunities to make public affirmation of their choices.

[14] *Ibid.*, p. 60.
[15] Louis E. Raths, Merrill Harmin, and Sidney B. Simon, *Values and Teaching: Working with Values in the Classroom* (Columbus, Ohio: Charles E. Merrill Books, Inc., 1966), pp. 38–39.

Encourage them to act, behave, live in accordance with their choices.

Help them to examine repeated behaviors or patterns in their own lives.

Research indicates that children's attitudes and values regarding music may reflect the attitudes of both the peer group and those of high-status adults. It also indicates a relationship between attitudes and the emotional make-up of the individual. Thus it is possible that a child's musical attitudes and values can be weakened by contradictory musical influences emanating from adults and peers (radio, television, recordings). As children experience conflicting musical values, attention is sometimes necessary on an individual basis. At the same time, music teachers should not strive nor expect to have all children acquire the same set of musical values.

The attitudes and values of teachers are highly important in the instructional process. The chance remark of a teacher might have a lasting influence on a child. The teacher's attitude toward music, with its great variety of values and uses in human life, will usually affect children's valuing more than formal class presentations on learning to value.

Different types of music affect people differently. Therefore, the teacher should work toward an "open-type" classroom environment in which the varied opinions of children toward works of music are listened to with interest, valued, defended with musical knowledge when necessary. (Why did you like or dislike this music?) Such environment permits disagreements that can be expressed in ways that permit personal differences while arguing intellectual points in support of positions taken. Musical values and attitudes toward music cannot be separated entirely from respect, concern for the feelings of others, and the acknowledgment that people can hold differing values—especially in a classroom situation in which there is neither hostility nor aggression. An intellectually sound position for a music teacher to take is one that attempts to judge "good" music in accordance with how well it performs its function, and to operate in a climate of openness that admits the exploration of every type of music to attempt to find out what it is used for, how it is constructed, and how good it is in its category. In this atmosphere every facet of music from Renaissance to jazz and electronic has a place, and their values are to be discovered by children in their personal learning of music.

Suggested Principles for Learning Music

The following suggestions are reflections of educational research. Understanding them stimulates teachers to seek better ways in which to help children grow and develop in their musical responsiveness. Children learn best when:

1. There is a planned, sequential but flexible program of music instruction from level to level.

2. Teachers know the purposes of their music instruction and when they make these purposes understood by the children.

3. The teacher is an active guide for learning who utilizes all types of questions in relation to the various thought processes.

4. They are in a rich and stimulating musical environment.

5. There is a free, responsive, and democratic social environment.

6. Teachers and parents work together to provide children with opportunity to develop worthwhile interest in and sensitivity to various types of music.

7. They experience wholesome social and emotional relationships with peers and with their teachers.

8. They have good models with which to identify (peers, teachers, parents).

9. They have satisfying experiences with music.

10. They have an opportunity to develop favorable self-concepts.

11. Their music activities are on their own physical, intellectual, and social maturity level.

12. Individual differences and levels of musical proficiency are recognized, studied, and accommodated.

13. There is a problem to be solved.

14. They see meaning and purpose in what they are doing, can make functional application of what they are doing, and have a part in establishing their purposes.

15. They employ a variety of activities and materials.

16. The conceptual approach to music teaching involves the children in intrinsic learning.

17. There is consistent evaluation of student progress in which children participate.

18. The teacher has obvious confidence in the child's ability to learn.

LEARNING IN INNOVATIVE MUSIC PROGRAMS

It is significant that experimental or innovative music programs yield relationships to the content of this chapter. When Thomas[16] examined these attempts to explore new ways to improve the teaching of music, he reported certain common characteristics. Some are:

Each program had clearly defined objectives in music learning.

There was concern for the student's frame of reference, for the way he perceived music, and for the direction of his inquiry.

Few of the programs were designed on the premise that cognitive results would stem directly from an emphasis on skill training.

Teachers were resource persons who shared in class activities; they guided and provided leadership rather than authoritarian control.

Learning strategies were planned that encouraged the youngster to use his intuitive and inductive powers; the student had opportunity to experiment, gain experience, and develop judgments through his own discovery.

INQUIRY AND SUGGESTED ACTIVITIES

1. Discuss ways you believe the teaching of music to be similar and dissimilar to the teaching of other subjects.
2. Formulate a definition of thinking. How do perception and associative thinking affect the learning of music? Give examples and explain.
3. Explore possible functional and creative ways to use the steps in creative problem solving explained in this chapter.
4. Contrast the Socratic and the inquiry methods of teaching.
5. Prepare cognitive-memory, convergent, divergent (inductive), and evaluative types of questions to use in teaching a musical concept, skill, or appreciation. Refer to the examples stated in this chapter.
6. Identify a concept and a generalization. Discuss the rationale of conceptual learning. Why is such learning considered to be essential?
7. Discuss the relationship of concept formation to other cognitive processes and to the formulation of generalizations.
8. Explore ways of teaching children to formulate concepts and generalizations. Take note of the sequential steps suggested in this chapter.

[16] Ronald B. Thomas, "Innovative Music Education Programs," *Music Educators Journal* (May, 1967), pp. 50–52.

9. Select a concept and apply the sequential steps in guiding children in the formulation of a concept.
10. Identify and list important musical concepts to be developed in the teaching of rhythm for a level of your choice.
11. Read the section of this chapter dealing with "Theories of Thinking and Learning" and apply what you have read to the teaching of music.
12. Investigate and discuss the importance of using more than one strategy (a "balance" of strategies) in teaching music.
13. Explore and indicate ways that music contributes to the affective (values, appreciations, and feelings) aspect of learning.
14. Investigate ways to use in a music class Raths' sequence of steps suggested for guiding children in learning how to value.
15. Explore and discuss each of the suggested Principles for Learning Music as to their implications for improving music teaching and learning.
16. Examine one or two children's music textbooks and take note of the content, notation, and accompaniments of songs, questions, suggested teaching strategies in the teacher's book and other aspects that could possibly be used in developing problem-solving, cognitive-memory, convergent, divergent (inductive), and evaluative thinking. What other resources are needed? Why is a variety of instructional resources and media necessary to develop these thinking processes?

REFERENCES

ALMY, MILLIE YOUNG, *Children's Thinking*. Columbia University, New York: Teachers College Press, 1966. A presentation and interpretation of Piaget's work.

BRUNER, JEROME S., *The Process of Education*. Cambridge, Mass.: Harvard University Press, 1960.

————, ET. AL., *A Study of Thinking*. New York: Science Editions, 1962.

BUSWELL, G. T., *Learning and the Teacher*. Washington, D.C.: Association for Supervision and Curriculum Development, 1959. Chaps. 2, 5, 6, 8.

COMBS, ARTHUR, ED., *Perceiving, Behaving, Becoming*. Washington, D.C.: Association for Supervision and Curriculum Development, 1962.

FLAVELL, J. H., *The Developmental Psychology of Jean Piaget*. Princeton, New Jersey: D. Van Nostrand Company, Inc., 1963. An analytical summary of Piaget's philosophy.

FLEMING, ROBERT S., *Curriculum for Today's Boys and Girls*. Columbus, Ohio: Charles E. Merrill Books, Inc., 1963. Chap. 4.

FRAZIER, ALEXANDER, ED., *Freeing Capacity to Learn*. Washington D.C.: Association for Supervision and Curriculum Development, 1960.

GAGNE, ROBERT, *The Conditions of Learning*. New York: Holt, Rinehart & Winston, Inc., 1965. Several types of learning are discussed.

GRAISSER, PHILIP, *How to Use the Fine Art of Questioning.* Englewood Cliffs, New Jersey: Prentice-Hall, Inc., 1964.

KAPLAN, ABRAHAM, *The Conduct of Inquiry.* San Francisco: Chandler Publishing Company, 1964.

KLAUSMEIER, H. J., AND CHESTER W. HARRIS, EDS., *Analyses of Concept Learning.* New York: Academic Press, 1966. Describes the learning and teaching of concepts.

LEEPER, ROBERT R., ED., *Humanizing Education: The Person in the Process.* Washington, D.C.: Association for Supervision and Curriculum Development, 1967.

MACDONALD, JAMES, ED., *Theories of Instruction.* Washington, D.C.: Association for Supervision and Curriculum Development, 1965.

MANHATTANVILLE PROJECT, "A Study of New Concepts, Procedures, and Achievements in Music Learning as Developed in Selected Music Education Programs," Manhattanville College, Purchase, New York, Ronald B. Thomas, Director. U.S. Office of Education.

MURSELL, JAMES L., "Growth Processes in Music Education," *Basic Concepts in Music Education,* ed. Nelson B. Henry. Chicago, Ill.: University of Chicago Press, 1958, pp. 140–162.

OLSON, REES G., "Teaching Music Concepts by the Discovery Method," *Music Educators Journal* (September, 1967), pp. 51–53.

PARKER, J. CECIL, ET. AL., *Process As Content: Curriculum Design and the Application of Knowledge.* Chicago: Rand McNally & Co., 1966.

PFLEDERER, MARILYN, "The Responses of Children to Musical Tasks Embodying Piaget's Principle of Conservation" (Unpublished doctoral dissertation, University of Illinois, 1963), *Dissertation Abstracts,* XXXIV/11/4730.

———, "How Children Conceptually Organize Musical Sounds," *Bulletin,* No. 7, Council for Research in Music Education (Spring, 1966).

RATHS, LOUIS E. ET. AL., *Values and Teaching: Working With Values in the Classroom.* Columbus, Ohio: Charles E. Merrill Books, Inc., 1966.

RUSSELL, DAVID, *Children's Thinking.* Boston: Ginn and Company, 1956.

SANDERS, NORRIS M., *Classroom Questions, What Kinds?* New York: Harper & Row, Publishers, 1966.

SHULMAN, LEE S., AND EVANS R. KEISLAR, EDS., *Learning by Discovery.* Chicago: Rand McNally & Co., 1966. A treatment and appraisal of discovery learning.

SMITH, JAMES A., *Creative Teaching of the Creative Arts in the Elementary School.* Boston: Allyn and Bacon, Inc., 1967.

SUCHMAN, J. R., *The Elementary School Training Program in Scientific Inquiry,* Title 7, Project N. 216. Urbana: Publications Office, University of Illinois, 1962. A project of the Illinois Studies in Inquiry Training.

———, "Inquiry Training: Building Skills for Autonomous Discovery," *Merrill-Palmer Quarterly* (1961), pp. 7, 147–69.

THORPE, LOUIS P., "Learning Theory and Music Teaching," *Basic Concepts in Music Education.* Chicago: University of Chicago Press, 1958, pp. 163–94.

TORRANCE, E. PAUL, *Guiding Creative Talent*. Englewood Cliffs, New Jersey: Prentice-Hall, Inc., 1962. Includes ways to foster creativity.

WAETJEN, WALTER B., ED., *Human Variability and Learning*. Washington, D.C.: Association for Supervision and Curriculum Development, 1961.

————, ED., *Learning and Mental Health in the Schools*. Washington, D.C.: Association for Supervision and Curriculum Development, 1966.

WALLACH, MICHAEL A., AND NATHAN KOGAN, *Modes of Thinking in Young Children*. New York: Holt, Rinehart & Winston, Inc., 1965. Suggestions, examples of, and implications for teaching.

WOODRUFF, ASAHEL D., "The Use of Concepts in Teaching and Learning," *Journal of Teacher Education*, XV (1964), 81–99.

A WORLD TO KNOW

by James S. Tippett

Beautiful, wonderful sights to see
And wonderful sounds to hear;
The world is a place for a seeing eye
And a place for a listening ear.

Puppies and lambs and kittens to touch!
Satins and silks to feel!
Sugar and salt and honey to taste!
Fragrant fruits to peel!

Beautiful, wonderful, pleasant world!
And a child who would know it well
Has everything to see and hear,
To touch and taste and smell.

5

developing a responsive environment for learning

A Responsive Environment

The child needs the type of learning environment that furthers the understanding of "self" and his relations with others. In addition, the environment should assist him in inquiring into the various related elements of music in some depth—exploring, experimenting, analyzing, evaluating, concluding, and generalizing. Inquiry, not rote learning, typifies this kind of environment. The emphasis is on the formulation of musical hypotheses. "You decided that this melodic line sounds incomplete. Why do you think it sounds that way? What can you do about it?"

Teachers who cultivate this type of environment exert great effort to teach students to consider their knowledge and standards as tentative and emerging, to make them responsible for their decisions, and to help them relate to others in cooperative inquiry. The child is, therefore, encouraged to form freer and more satisfactory relationships with others, to accept uncertainty about knowledge, to seek and weigh evidence, and to treat others, as well as himself, with respect. Failure is considered a source of information rather than a threat to his self concept and dignity. "We know the song sounds bad again in the same place. What do you think we can do to improve it?" The child also shares in the development of standards of musical performance. "In what ways have we made real progress with this music? Are there places where we can make it sound even better?"

The effective environment is one of security, precision, calmness, and purpose that requires great understanding and persistence on the part of the teacher. It takes time for students to develop their own standards; they will stumble many times. Students need freedom, with the necessary restraints, to develop open minds plus an attitude favorable to change; both are essential for developing conceptual learning.

THE INDIVIDUAL AND THE GROUP

While the music teacher must think in terms of each learner, the relation of the individual learner to the group is of enormous importance, whether this is applied toward living in a democratic society or toward growth as an individual in a music class. One can learn cooperation and leadership only in a group. Also, the nature of the group has great effect upon the individual. For example, in a large group such as in a community where adults participate in music activities to a marked degree, children are apt to be strongly inclined toward music. The same is true in the family group, and it can be true in the elementary classroom also, with the cultural standard being established not only by the teacher but by the peer group. The values which prevail in a culture will be reflected in the children of that culture, and if music is an esteemed value, it is highly likely to be esteemed by the young people. Thus, both the social and artistic climate can influence the attitude of the learner toward music. Dorothy Lee writes that when a value is present and strong in a culture, no obstacle can stop its expression, and if an obstacle does act as an interference, it is because the value is either weak or not truly present. "The secret lies in the supporting values of the home and the community as well as in the encouragement of a questioning mind, of a mind that demands the right to come to its own conclusions."[1] The implication is that the teacher of music should strive to build a group acceptance for, and love of, music in the home, the community, and the school.

THE INDIVIDUAL

Group valuing of music is necessary, but it is not enough. Added to this cultural stamp of approval for music, there should be certain personal attitudes and intellectual characteristics teachers will help the

[1] Lee, Dorothy, "Developing the Drive to Learn," *Freeing the Capacity to Learn* (Washington, D.C.: Association for Supervision and Curriculum Development, 1960), pp. 12, 20.

individual learner to acquire. These include an inquiring and challenging mind, the capacity to analyze on his level, making original interpretations, and a tendency to try out things and to experiment. He should ultimately be able to manipulate the components of music in creative ways. Thus, individuality must be reflected in the music curriculum. To individualize instruction means that the teacher must plan learning experiences appropriate for the learner at the proper time. It does not demand a one-to-one teacher-pupil relationship. Although there needs to be a given framework within which the group operates, within this framework there should be no set curriculum for everyone. Each learner should be permitted to begin to operate on his level of thinking and performing, and to move at his own pace, setting his own temporary limits. His study should begin with primary musical sources—music he hears and in which he participates in the home and community. Out of these everyday experiences could come his own musical composition, much of which he may do at home, treating environmental sources as data to examine, question, analyze, compare, interpret, and to infer from, but not as unquestioned authority.

Similarly, within the music class the major effort should be to establish a favorable climate for the growth of each child in musical knowledge, understanding, and responsiveness. There follow some general conditions essential to attain this goal.

DISCUSSION IN A RESPONSIVE ENVIRONMENT

If the environment is a responsive one, children are "freely" engaged in attempting to solve musical problems by exploring, questioning, discussing, performing, analyzing, generalizing and hypothesizing. In a musical environment which is conducive to the development of the above inquiry skills, children are guided in focusing their attention upon problems which have no single solution.

The comments of both the students and the teacher are accepted because of their pertinence to the solution of the problem being investigated. All students, as well as the teacher, are given equal freedom to discuss, question, suggest, analyze, generalize, and hypothesize. Each statement is carefully and critically evaluated as to its relevance to a hypothesis.

The teacher functions in this environment by asking questions which challenge the learners and questions which he cannot answer himself but is perplexed about. He demonstrates by example to the students that there are many more important things he also would like to learn about music. The teacher's attitude challenges the students to seek more significant and penetrating answers and solutions as well as to stimulate more research and discussion among the pupils and between the teacher and the pupils. Students should question each other and freely discuss alternate solutions as they pertain to musical problems and to a hypothesis which gives the discussion focus. The problem outlines the general direction of pursuit. The teacher uses all types of thinking and questioning—cognitive-memory, convergent (deductive), divergent (creative, inductive) and evaluative. These types are used as they are needed to develop a musical attitude, value, concept, generalization, or skill.

It should be remembered that in music classes some types of musical learning may not take place if talking and discussion predominate, since the skills of musical performance and many understandings about it are gained by actively performing music. Proper questions in music class are based upon music activities, directed toward musical learnings, and follow the activity as well as precede it. They stimulate better listening, better singing, better rhythmic responses, better playing of instruments, more creativity, more use of notation, and better understanding of all of the components of music.

AROUSING INTEREST

The teacher surrounds the learners with a variety of stimuli—recordings, films, charts, songs, instruments, sound-producing objects, pictures, speakers, and demonstrators. There may be field trips to concerts, to rehearsals of high school music groups, and to music stores. These experiences are at first exploratory; later they serve as sources of data upon which the teacher bases specific learning experiences. He selects exact data from which chosen concepts of the structure of music will be built, and utilizes these in ways which will lead to the discovery of these concepts by the learners. Later the children will form their own generalizations from these concepts. The children's environment grows richer in stimuli as they develop competence in the various areas of musical expression: performance, composing, critical evaluation and analysis. The teacher knows that significant musical subject matter serves as the primary stimulus for arousing interest, when it is utilized in ways that promote intrinsic learning.

FREEDOM TO TAKE RISKS

Freedom from fear and from unnecessary restraints, freedom to discover the world of music for oneself, serves as a powerful generator of interest, meaning, and creativity. It leads to exploring, to daring, to attempting, and to growth—those things which are more difficult than previous achievements. Of course, because music classes are generally taught in groups, freedom must be within the context of teacher-pupil established standards of order. An essential element of freedom is responsibility; without it, freedom is meaningless and chaotic. Responsibility is the basis for self-respect and confidence; it is essential to self-testing and to a developing sense of achievement. The learner needs to have a greater responsibility for identifying learning problems and for decisions as to how to solve them. Such involvement stimulates strong personal motivation to learn music.

ACCEPTANCE AND ENCOURAGEMENT

The highest form of encouragement is unconditional personal respect. There is unquestioned scientific evidence that respect and love are prime conditions for growth. It is obvious that the school cannot supply love in the same sense that the home can or should. Nevertheless, the teacher can accept the worth of each child, showing faith and trust in him. If a child is to grow to his fullest potential, he must live in an environment where he knows he *belongs,* is *wanted,* and *respected.*

SUCCESS

Regardless of how difficult the task might be, the teacher must guide each child into successful accomplishment of some aspect of music each day. Success builds upon success; each success releases energy for the next try, and it must be genuine. The need for success does not imply that failure is not present—or even necessary at times. When failures lead to eventual solution of musical problems, they form a necessary part of the learning process. Properly handled, failure can be good for a child because it serves to give him a realistic image of life. Failure can be bad for a child when the greater percentage of his efforts result in it. Furthermore, it must be impressed upon the child that success need not mean being the "best"; it means doing well whatever one needs to do—seeing clearly what the job is and knowing that one has done it to the best of his ability. Thus the child becomes aware of his strengths and limitations. Music teachers need to provide a great diversity of ways in which children can succeed. Fortunately, music's many facets make this rather easy. When music teaching is being planned, the teacher should be alert to build many roads to success into the lesson, and plan for the many ways individual children can contribute to the whole activity. The good teacher recognizes that the music class has within its organization the means to approach a musical composition in different ways, to arrive at somewhat different conclusions, and to contain different levels of achievement.

INTRINSIC MOTIVATION

When the classroom environment promotes intrinsic motivation, it has set free one of the most powerful stimuli for learning. The learner is working toward a goal that *he* wants to achieve. This goal has become a personal matter, not an extrinsic item such as what the teacher told him to do. Learning usually takes place best when the learner's purposes are his own, and when he values them personally.

SELF-CONCEPT

Of all the school subjects that offer possibilities for the development of wholesome and positive self-concepts, music is probably the most pertinent. The many opportunities offered in types of performance, including body responses to music, and in composing, evaluating, and analyzing music, provide a great number of outlets for self-expression which can result in personal satisfaction and in the gaining of status within the peer group. Since one of the greatest blocks to learning is a faulty or negative self-concept, music can be an important means for promoting learning by making possible the improvement of children's self-images. The good teacher will make full use of this by planning and encouraging successful experiences in music which enhance children's opinions of themselves and self-respect for their ability to achieve in satisfying ways.

Organizing the Classroom

A teacher's knowledge and skill in music are of value in the classroom only in terms of his ability to organize and manage the music activities in that classroom so that they strike a balance between the routine and the creative, between stability and change. Efficient routine is necessary to avoid overlooking detail; the main reason for taking care of detail is to provide more pupil-teacher time and energy for creative and problem-solving types of learning and teaching. A teacher needs to know procedures that should be routinized and those that should not. The most effective and efficient routine procedures should be selected, then they should be used consistently so that they become habitual. They should be such that they have value in similar situations elsewhere in life. The children should have a part in planning classroom routines and in using them to facilitate learning; they should understand the value of these procedures, exactly how they are to be done, and then they should evaluate the degree of efficiency resulting from them. It is important that a new teacher at the beginning not change routines already established unless there is good and sufficient reason for change. When change is made the children must be guided into the new and more efficient routines in a gradual way.

PHYSICAL CONDITIONS OF THE ROOM ENVIRONMENT

It is obvious that learning is difficult when attempted in impure air, uncomfortable temperatures, and improper lighting. The busy teacher who is in the same classroom all day will sometimes fail to notice insufficient ventilation, unhealthy temperatures, and faulty lighting because of the gradual changes in the room as the day progresses. While teachers should be alert to these factors, children should assume part of this responsibility. Classroom committees can be established to give children experience in assuming responsibility and to relieve the teacher of part of this routine task.

A LEARNING LABORATORY

A room that is conducive to effective learning has a child-centered appearance. It is organized in the form of a learning laboratory with specific centers of interest and a variety of instructional materials and equipment that challenge students of varying interests and abilities. The music center has been called the "music corner." It is located out of the traffic lines, in a place in the room which is both relatively secluded, yet accessible. It may consist of one large table or several smaller ones upon which may be placed interesting materials such as books, bells and other small instruments, music to play on the instruments, recordings, record player with ear phones, a viewer, film strips and film strip machine, a tape recorder and various sound-producing materials and machines for experimentation. The center could include bulletin boards which assist musical learning, and on them can be mounted information about community musical events, composers, recommended radio and television programs, musical achievements of students, charts, musical symbols, cartoons, jackets from books about music and from recordings, newspaper and magazine clippings, notation of unnamed familiar songs which are to be identified by studying this notation, favorite songs, rhythm patterns, and pictures relating to musical subjects. However, the bulletin board must be arranged attractively and changed frequently, if it is to accomplish its mission of attracting maximum interest.

Children should be free to experiment and explore with materials and equipment in gathering data from which to develop musical concepts, understandings, skills, generalizations, attitudes, and values. Soft mallets for the bells and earphones with the record player can eliminate interference with other activities in the room. By teacher-pupil planning, standards for the use of the music materials and equipment are established. These standards should also indicate when and how children are to work in the music center.

The music program requires extensive instructional materials and equipment, all of which should be properly stored. Series books should have their definite place on shelves or in cabinets if they are not in the children's desks. Recordings, tapes, Autoharp, bells, song flutes, record player, tape recorder, percussion instruments, and charts have their special places, too. Children share in the storing of these items, and are taught to take responsibility for keeping their equipment in order and in good condition. It is assumed that by involving students in deciding why and how to take care of and use the room, instructional materials, and equipment, they will continue to explore ways of using their environment for learning after they have left the music class and the school. The learning environment should be ordered by the children and the teacher. Its appearance should reflect the types of learning experiences occurring in it.

The Manhattanville Music Curriculum Program (USOE 6–1999) deals more with ways of learning than with specific strategies. Its principles are assumed to be appropriate for children at all levels of learning. Its concept of the music class is that of a laboratory for discovery, dealing with sounds and skills. It is a place in which pupils can explore music on their level of understanding—a place where children perform, compose, and evaluate music. The teacher is assumed to be a guide, a creator of problems to be solved by children, a resource person for children, and a good musician. He stimulates rather than dominates; he encourages rather than controls; he questions more than he answers; and he remains sensitive both to children and to the art of music. In this laboratory the children act as musicians who have a world of sound to explore.

FLEXIBLE USE OF ROOMS

The arrangement of the furniture influences the type of learning that takes place. Seating for the entire class should be appropriately arranged to make it possible for students to participate in discussion as well as in individual and small group work, and to provide opportunity for listening effectively and courteously to any class member who is speaking, singing, or playing an instrument.

The varied activities in music make movable furniture a necessity. Seating (or temporary standing) will be changed at times for singing in large and small groups, playing instruments, creative interpretations, rhythmic responses, and dance. Special seating may be needed if some of the children have difficulty hearing or seeing. The manner in which the children will move from one activity to another is established by clear instructions from the teacher and by teacher-pupil planning. This needs well-planned questions from the teacher that stimulate the children to plan and take responsibility for this part of classroom routine. Leaving and entering a music room, going to and from a music room or assembly room, and moving books, instruments, and other materials are additional aspects of school routine that need planning, reminders, and repetition so that good habits are formed that may prevent problems from arising.

The placement of the teacher's desk in an inconspicuous place makes it easier for him to circulate freely among the students to observe and assist them.

Another use of the room is in connection with listening to recordings, when, to reflect the mood of compositions, shades might be drawn, lights turned on, color employed, or objects placed in a way to heighten the aural effect.

EXPANDING CLASSROOM WALLS Music teachers of today are utilizing work space other than the classroom. They also use cultural resources in the community to enrich learning in music. The expansion of the learning environment makes it necessary for the teacher to become familiar with all areas and facilities of the school plant and community which can be useful for music instruction. When students explore the musical resources of the community, and when parents and other community resource people contribute to the school music program, the musical learning laboratory is thereby expanded.

SELECTION AND HANDLING OF MATERIALS

When series books are selected, the teacher considers such things as print, size, clarity of notation, a good grade of paper that is free from eye-straining high gloss, ease of handling by children, color, illustrations, absence of clutter, general attractiveness, well organized and comprehensive indices, content that appeals to the age group, quality of content, general durability, quality of the cover, simplicity and musicality of accompaniments, helpfulness of the teachers' manuals, quality and usefulness of the recordings.

When instruments and equipment are selected, the teacher chooses those that produce excellent tone quality, that are durable, attractive, and easy to store, that are suitable for the age group; instruments meeting these qualifications are often those designed and sold for school use. Chairs and desks should be selected to fit the varying sizes of children found in a class.

When songs are selected, the teacher looks for simplicity and variety in the melody, repeated parts that assist rapid learning, content interesting to the age group, proper range for the voices, appropriate length for the age level, rhythmic appeal, and a suitable, attractive accompaniment. He examines the song to find what teaching purpose it can serve. It must pass these tests: "Is this song worth learning?" "Is it a worthy art song or a folk song that is authentic?" and "Does it contribute to the realization of the stated objectives?"

Teachers should have the required materials assembled, should know how to use them, and should plan the necessary routine with the children. A system of distributing materials and collecting them should be planned with and executed by the children, who should know where and how to store them. For example, if Tonettes are used, each should be labeled with the child's name; they should be placed in the plastic bags that are made for them in order to keep them clean; they should not be taken home until the child can play reasonably well; a place should be selected to store them, such as a box on a shelf, and they should be played and treated as musical instruments, not as noisemakers. For sanitary reasons children should not exchange instruments, but if this is necessary, a disinfectant for plastic must be used; the instruments must be cleaned periodically with disinfectant applied with a small brush or cotton swab.

Standards must be established, preferably with the children, for proper use of the room in viewing television and films, listening to radio programs, and using the music center. Provision should be made for displays of music materials other than at the music center, and for the filing or storing of music charts when they are not on display. A classified card file of recordings, a card file of available books about music, and a vertical file of pictures should be part of the teacher's equipment, placed for his convenience.

ROUTINE AND SYSTEMATIC PROCEDURES

While over-routinization can stifle creativity, a proper amount saves time and assists the orderly procedure of events in the music period. Experienced teachers have found certain ideas helpful.

A chord played on piano or Autoharp, or a tone played on the bells can be a signal for a change of activity. Such musical means for giving directions are more conducive to pleasant feelings than the teacher's voice directing children to do something.

Part of preparation for the music class is the removal of any objects or materials from the desks that could take attention from the lesson. Proper posture for singing should become habitual (see Chapter 9) for reasons known and understood by the children. Books should be held in a manner that encourages good singing posture and makes it easy to see the teacher.

Definite purposes and directions should be established with the children. The teacher can occasionally make certain of this by asking a child to state in order the things that were decided upon.

Special music teachers who teach in a music room should assign seats to pupils so the roll can be taken in the shortest possible time. When this is done, children are given a reasonable choice of seats and a part in the planning of this seating arrangement so that they understand the necessity for it. Children in intermediate grades can take the roll, with the roll-takers alternating each week or so. Other children can be class monitors to distribute and collect books and other materials. Still others can be delegated responsibility for room temperature, ventilation, and lighting. These responsibilities develop needed social skills, self-esteem, and a feeling of contributing to the welfare of others. Teacher and pupils should evaluate the effectiveness from time to time.

All materials used in a lesson should be assembled in advance. Special music teachers often have some of these on carts that they wheel from room to room. When a teacher makes advance preparations for a lesson by doing such routine things as assembling materials, writing on the chalkboard the titles and page numbers of the songs, words of rote songs, notation for class study, the order of music activities, and other directions, he promotes general efficiency. Through pupil discussion, evaluation and modification of the order and directions of activities indicated, children have a part in the planning, and see meaning and purpose in the sequences of activities included in the lesson. Valuable time is saved. When verbal directions are given they are stated clearly and concisely, thus lessening the need for repeating them. The teacher should make certain that every child can see and hear what is spoken, sung, played, danced, or dramatized.

Testing devices in singing, rhythmic responses, playing, observation of performance and attitudes, and checklists or other evaluative techniques can be planned to determine readiness for music activities. The teacher needs to know how much the class knows in order to plan teaching strategies wisely. Finding out how much a group knows about symbols of notation or what its vocal range is will reveal to the teacher what some of his purposes will be—purposes based upon "where the children are" musically at this particular time. Later, the teacher must know "where every child is" in musical understanding and responsiveness in order to plan and guide learning skillfully.

Children who are in advance of the class musically are given the opportunity to continue to grow at their own rate. Such a child might prepare a song to teach to the class, practice an instrumental part to add to a song, create an accompaniment on the piano, play a song on the bells, prepare a descant to add to a song, or present a short listening lesson based upon a teacher-approved recording of his choice.

All teachers should know the *names* of the children. Even before they see the children, names can be learned from photographs in the school records. Special music teachers sometimes have the children wear name tags until they can remember the names. Knowledge and use of names places a teacher in closer relation to children at once, has profound influence on discipline, and is a vital aspect of good classroom management. Special effort must be made by every teacher to learn children's names as rapidly as possible.

Interruptions are to be expected. These can include visits by the principal, another teacher or pupil, parent, or supervisor. A child should be appointed to be the host or hostess to care for visitors' needs; this responsibility changes each week to another child. When a visitor comes into the room to observe, the child will see that there is a chair and a music book for him so that he can follow the lesson and perhaps join in the singing. This procedure eliminates the stopping of the lesson by the teacher. With children prepared for the possibility of such visits, the class will continue without interruptions, not only saving time and confusion, but contributing to the children's learning of courtesy, social abilities, and proper human relations. Unscheduled announcements over intercom systems are another type of interruption for which children should be prepared and for which teacher-pupil planning should result in an agreed-upon response.

In teaching rote singing there is a simple technique that relates to good classroom management: The teacher points to himself when he wants the class to listen to his voice, then points toward the class when it is their turn. By such simple signals, the teacher is able to convey ideas without having to give spoken directions. This saves his voice and increases efficiency.

COLLECTING DATA FOR EFFECTIVE MUSIC TEACHING   Planning for effective music teaching is based upon the knowledge of children and how they learn, on knowledge of available music materials and supplies, knowledge of appropriate teaching strategies, and knowledge of the curriculum. Some of this information can come from observing and noting children's musical performance and attitudes in music classes, while some can come from cumulative school records. Still more of it comes from knowledge of the home environment and general community environment. Obviously, some of this can be accumulated and recorded rather quickly, while other aspects may take considerably more time to assemble. It is also obvious that until a teacher "knows" each child's musical status, it is not possible to plan music lessons that will foster each child's musical growth. Knowledge of available music materials and supplies comes from school inventories. Knowledge of children and how they learn, as well as knowledge of the curriculum, comes from individual study, experimentation, observation, research, and participation in professional group study.

In the classroom the teacher observes vocal ranges, attitudes, social aptitudes, rhythmic ability, evidence of special talents, special interests, evidences of musical understanding, and special problems. After each music class, he should record such information, perhaps in a card file or on a special form that he uses for each child. At times he will work with individuals and small groups to determine such things as exact voice ranges.

From school records and from questioning teachers who taught the children in prior years, relevant information can be gleaned. This information may include health records, past musical experiences and achievements, data assembled from parent conferences over the years, family histories, and information regarding social and emotional adjustments. Any pertinent facts should be recorded in the teacher's files and made readily accessible for use in planning music lessons that contain activities that help each child. Parent conferences and questionnaires given to the children can reveal needed information about the home and community musical environment (parents' musical abilities and interests, musical activities of brothers and sisters, radio and television program preferences, and record collections).

The teacher should consult school and classroom accession and inventory records to familiarize himself with available music materials and supplies; he should also know what materials and resource people are available in the school system administration building. Teachers in the entire school should work cooperatively to inventory and make available to each other the materials centered in the general supply room of the school as well as in each classroom. Such inventories should always be kept up-to-date, revealing the latest acquisitions.

Encouraging Self-Control and Democratic Behavior

Class control is a complicated process, involving many different personalities, each unique. There are no specific solutions that will apply in all situations. Every teacher is different, and each must determine what techniques function best for him in terms of both his personality and those of the children. In order for learning to take place, there must be appropriate order and control. The nature of the activity determines to an extent the type of order and control. The learning climate is improved when each child accepts his responsibilities and carries them out without disturbing others. Democratic behavior is furthered through teacher-pupil planning in which the children have a major part in defining the conditions necessary to learn most effectively, and deciding how to achieve them. The feeling is developed that the classroom is the *children's* class-room and that each child has a definite responsibility in helping establish and maintain the standards by which it functions. In such a classroom the teacher helps develop the importance of the individual, a sense of respect for others, ability to work with others, and a maximum of self-control. Since the teacher realizes that self-control develops slowly, and that children regress from time to time, he and the children evaluate the established standards for each specific activity, their success in maintaining these standards, and what they need to do next time to improve. Standards for a listening activity will obviously be different from those for a singing activity. After the standards are well established and incorporated into the behavior of most of the pupils, the teacher works with the individual who is having difficulty, analyzing his behavior and planning ways of modifying it.

FACTORS AFFECTING CLASS CONTROL

There are many factors that influence children's behavior. Most classroom misbehavior is the direct result of conditions in the learning environment. The misbehavior could have been prevented had the teacher given proper consideration to the following:

PHYSICAL COMFORT   Children who are too cold, too warm, too crowded, who must breathe stale air, who cannot see or hear what is going on, who are not comfortably seated, or have been seated too long, or have been physically active for too long, often misbehave. Children should be seated so as to facilitate their participation in, and concentration on, the activity at hand.

ORGANIZATION AND PROPER ROUTINE   Teachers who are well prepared, and who have made provision for proper directions and routine, usually exemplify a feeling of confidence and security that is reflected in the behavior of the child. Children sense insecurity in teachers, and they are disturbed by it. Therefore, the teacher must make careful plans for the learning activities and assemble all materials needed in developing them. He must also give attention to such details as how to begin and conclude the lesson, how to keep it progressing steadily and thoroughly toward realization of the intended purposes, how to seat or group the children for specific activities, how to distribute and collect materials, when to change or alternate activities, and how to evaluate and summarize with the children the accomplishments of the day.

CHALLENGING EVERY CHILD   Children who are engaged in activities that are interesting and worthwhile to them are normally well-behaved. Those who fail to find interest and purpose in what they are asked to do become bored and often disturb others. If children have a part in the planning of activities, and an opportunity to identify, analyze, and explore problems on their own level of performance, they are ordinarily interested in them.

THE TEACHER   The teacher will find ways to recognize and encourage those who show improvements in behavior and in work habits. He shows respect for the personality of each child. The teacher knows that children reflect his enthusiasm, interest, and confidence. This confidence is fundamentally based upon the knowledge that what he is teaching is significant to the physical, social, emotional, aesthetic, and intellectual development of children. A teacher should be happy, well-adjusted, and should truly want to teach. He assists children in solving their own behavior problems, but when unable to do this in specific cases, he seeks assistance. He knows that he loses prestige if he repeatedly sends pupils to the principal, and does this only as a last resort. His own behavior is consistent, understanding, and firm, and he has a sincere interest in every child. He has a good sense of humor, sees humor in many situations, and knows that humor can help in the solution of problems. He refrains from using ridicule and sarcasm, and is mature in his behavior. As an adult, he is objective—not overly friendly or emotionally attached to the children. If he is in error, or does not know the answer to a problem, he admits it. He retains his self-control, and is a dependable adult in whom children can have confidence and faith. As much as possible he deals with individuals who have behavior problems privately, since this is usually more effective and is less disturbing to both the troublemaker and the class. The class is not made to suffer for what one or two children may do. The teacher is generous with his praise whenever it is needed, with appropriate reinforcement. His speaking voice is pleasant and varies in pitch and intensity. He knows that a tense voice disturbs children. His singing voice is natural, sincere, and pleasing. He approaches difficult situations calmly, and seeks the reasons for behavior problems. In order to accomplish these things, he tends to his own physical and mental health by getting sufficient rest and wholesome recreation. His personal appearance is such that it increases the children's respect and serves to remind them to be neat and orderly in their appearance.

The teacher knows the children's names and uses class leaders. Books and materials are distributed after directions for an activity have been determined, or after the standards established for the activity have been reviewed. He anticipates possible problems, and plans ways to offset them; intersperses appropriate music throughout the day to relieve tensions and to unify the group. Through thoughtful selection of music, a teacher can calm or stimulate the class as he desires. Small difficulties can be avoided by simple actions. For example, if a teacher sees a child about to trip another in rhythmic movement, or about to throw an eraser, he can ask the child a direct question that brings him back into the group activity at once. The teacher keeps eye contact with the various members of the class at all times. He cannot focus his attention on notation in a music book or on piano accompaniments so exclusively that he cannot see the class. This necessitates complete familiarity with the song being taught and its accompaniment. The division of the class at times into several groups, one singing, one accompanying, and the third evaluating the musical performance of the others, is conducive to class control because it gives every child something specific to do. Other purposeful ways to involve children include tending the record player, pressing the buttons on an Autoharp, playing the bells, conducting, or interpreting music creatively through body movement or dramatization. The teacher usually refuses to talk when children are talking, and when he begins to speak, does so in a low-pitched, calm, positive, soft but easily heard voice.

All behavior is goal-centered and has specific causes. Teachers must continually collect information about pupils in order to understand the motives for their behavior and to attempt to deal with the causes of it. They should endeavor to treat the causes, and not confuse them with the symptoms, which may be the overt actions of the child. When a child must be corrected in behavior, this should be done with due consideration for his background and motives. Because every child is different, the manner of rebuke appropriate for one may not be appropriate for another.

The ultimate goal of the teacher is to assist the child in developing the ability and desire to assume responsibility for his own behavior. Such competence is necessary in a democratic society.

INQUIRY AND SUGGESTED ACTIVITIES

In preparation for formulating your own plans for teaching music in Chapter 6, do the following:

1. Ask a music teacher to discuss his lesson plan with you. Note to what extent he organizes the lesson for the children to work part of the time as individuals and part of the time as members of both small and large class groups. Discuss the behavioral objectives stated in the plan and the teaching strategies, questions and activities planned to realize these objectives. Follow the plan as the teacher guides the children and observe how the lesson is developed. Observe how he moves the children from one type of class organization to another; estimate the degree of success achieved in the functioning of each type of class organization—individual learning, small group, and class; discuss with the teacher the strategies used in each type of organization; note to what extent the behavioral objectives stated in the lesson plan were realized; try to determine the quality of the emotional and social climate in the classroom, what the effects of this climate are on the children and why.

2. Next, try to identify ways you think the lesson could be improved in the organization of the class and the development of the lesson.

3. Observe a music class to study the physical conditions of the room; how learning centers are used; how space is utilized; types of grouping; ways individual needs are met; types of materials and media available and how they are used; the specific routines—who establishes them and how and when they are employed.

REFERENCES

ADDICOTT, IRWIN O., *Constructive Classroom Control*. San Francisco: Chandler Publishing Company, 1958.

BROWN, EDWIN JOHN, and ARTHUR THOMAS PHELPS, *Managing the Classroom: the Teacher's Part in School Administration*. New York: The Ronald Press Company, 1961.

FOX, ROBERT, et. al., *Diagnosing Classroom Learning Environments*. Chicago: Science Associates, 1966.

GARY, CHARLES L., ed., *Music Buildings, Rooms and Equipment*. Washington, D.C.: Music Educators National Conference, 1966.

WRIGHTSTONE, WAYNE J., *Class Organization for Instruction,* What Research Says to the Teacher Series. Washington, D.C.: National Education Association, Department of Classroom Teachers, 1957.

THE CHILD'S BILL OF RIGHTS IN MUSIC

I

Every child has the right to full and free opportunity to explore and develop his capacities in the field of music in such ways as may bring him happiness and a sense of well-being; stimulate his imagination and stir his creative activities; and make him so responsive that he will cherish and seek to renew the fine feelings induced by music.

II

As his right, every child shall have the opportunity to experience music with other people so that his own enjoyment shall be heightened and he shall be led into greater appreciation of the feelings and aspirations of others.

III

As his right, every child shall have the opportunity to make music through being guided and instructed in singing, in playing at least one instrument both alone and with others, and, so far as his powers and interests permit, in composing music.

IV

As his right, every child shall have opportunity to grow in musical appreciation, knowledge, and skill, through instruction equal to that given in any other subject in all the free public educational programs that may be offered to children and youths.

V

As his right, every child shall be given the opportunity to have his interest and power in music explored and developed to the end that unusual talent may be utilized for the enrichment of the individual and society.

6

planning to teach music

Classroom teachers are concerned primarily with the grade level or grade levels, performance level or performance levels, they are assigned to teach. Music specialists are concerned with a span of grade and performance levels varying from several to all of them. However, since music learning is developmental, every teacher needs to have a more comprehensive knowledge of musical learning than that limited to one or two grade levels. He needs to understand the total developmental process in music from its beginnings if he is to assist every child. He needs to know the reasons why music is a part of general education, the goals of music education, its organizational plan, and its sequence of content. The teacher is best able to organize music in his classroom when he understands its relation to the total framework of the music curriculum. Only then can wise decisions be made which involve the continuity and sequential learning of music. Children need a planned program which includes both normal developmental patterns and provision for individual differences, of which there are many.

Planning at National, State, and Community Levels

The Constitution of the United States designates the control of education to the individual states. However, the United States Office of Education has a music specialist to assist state officials in the improvement of music education. A notable effort of the Office of Education in recent years to influence music education was the government-financed Yale Seminar on Music Education held in 1963.[1] This had as its purpose the improvement of elementary and secondary music education. Federal funds have stimulated the recent addition of music consultants in some state departments of education. Many states now have this type of personnel. Federal funds have been made available for the purchase of music textbooks and other materials; curriculum improvement is being speeded with funds made available by the Elementary and Secondary Education Act of 1965 (Public Law 89–10). The Music Educators National Conference[2] is a large and important national organization of public school music teachers who work together with college teachers and the music industry for better music programs in the schools. It is common practice for the different state departments of education to publish general curriculum guides or bulletins which outline objectives of music instruction, what is deemed appropriate for levels of instruction, and offer teaching suggestions. Every teacher should be familiar with the music guide published by the department of education in the state in which he teaches, or plans to teach. The local schools are expected to establish the music curricula suited to the particular community within the framework of the guide. The state department ordinarily offers assistance in organizing, planning, and evaluating such music programs.

PLANNING AT THE COMMUNITY LEVEL

In the United States there is a strong feeling that the schools belong to the local people and these people should have major control of what takes place in them. Therefore, the great diversity in wealth, population density, socio-economic condition, and occupations of the people comprising these communities indicates that there are many reasons for the varying emphases among general educational needs, and even

[1] Palisca, Claude V., ed. *Music in Our Schools:* Report of the Yale Seminar on Music Education (Washington, D.C.: U.S. Department of Health, Education, and Welfare, Office of Education, OE–33033, Bulletin 1964, No. 28.)

[2] Music Educators National Conference, 1201 Sixteenth St. N.W., Washington, D.C. 20036.

some educational needs unique to certain situations. The cultural roots of the local population may influence the organization of the music program and the selection of materials of instruction. Thus, local curriculum studies, guides, and courses of study are prepared, building upon the general guides provided by the state department of education. Teachers participate in such planning in many ways:

Serving on committees to select textbooks, purchase materials, develop teaching guides, prepare special teaching units, determine goals for each grade or level, develop sequential approaches to phases of music learning

Taking part in workshops to develop audio-visual aids, to learn to use teaching guides, to plan ways of improving music instruction

Participating in grade or level meetings involved in the above

Attending institutes, conventions, and other professional meetings which involve the most recent practices and procedures in music teaching

Becoming involved with research activities such as testing materials or procedures in the classroom, evaluating instructional materials, and developing new teaching strategies

PLANNING AT THE SCHOOL LEVEL

When teachers plan in terms of the child's past experiences and in terms of what his future experiences in music are to be, music learnings should form a natural, logical pattern for the child's progress through the elementary and secondary school. A plan of music instruction from kindergarten through high school is essential to ensure the sequential development necessary for maximum learning. To provide for continuity in children's music learning it is necessary for the teacher to provide information for the next teacher of the children that includes the repertoire learned, specific musical topics studied, books and materials used, films and film strips utilized, concerts attended, field trips taken, and any other pertinent information concerning individual children or the group.

Most teachers are curriculum builders. They serve on curriculum committees and plan learning experiences for children. They need, therefore, to be familiar with the construction and use of curriculum guides. The best guides possess the following characteristics:

They are flexible—to be used as a guide, not as an edict.
They recommend instructional procedures.
They list instructional materials and resources.
They suggest ways of evaluating both learning and programs.
They are based on sound principles of child growth and development.
They recognize that guides are tentative rather than final—they are under continuous study for possible changes, deletions, and additions.

PLANNING AT THE ROOM LEVEL

As has been indicated above, the teacher plans his music program for the year in terms of assistance available at the state, community, and school levels. He studies state and local music guides; ask questions of his principal and fellow teachers; studies appropriate school files and permanent records of each child; finds out what the children accomplished the previous year; and knows the music program the children will have after they leave his room. Then he formulates the major objectives to work toward in the year immediately ahead. He will consider local, state, and national events and seasons, holidays and special days to determine whether they have any relation to his plans. He will locate all available music materials at the school, see which of these he will utilize and decide whether his personal music books, record collection, or other musical possessions can or should be used. He will incorporate flexibility into the details of his planning so that the children can make some decisions and choices, and he will realize that there will be continuous planning, day by day, guided by his master plan for the year.

A properly designed music curriculum will be concerned with knowledges, understandings, attitudes, and skills. These are usually suggested in a general way at the state level and affect the curriculum at all levels. However, in the classroom more detailed and specific planning is necessary because of the special needs of the particular school, class, or child. Good planning is flexible, not rigid or over-prescriptive. Children can and should have a part in the planning of selected experiences. However, it is unsound to believe that a music curriculum should be planned *entirely* by the children; the responsibility for planning instructional programs is an adult task.

When children have a part in formulating some of the objectives that are meaningful to them, they can be highly motivated to work to realize them. Often an objective of one music lesson will grow naturally and directly from the previous one. For example, the children may feel, after learning an American Indian song, that a ceremonial dance is needed to convey its meaning; this becomes their objective. The creative teacher will plan to utilize this interest, guiding the class to discover the form of the music through its relation to the new dance, and leading the children to notate, study, and compare the basic rhythm patterns employed both in the song and in the dance. In the same manner objectives emerge for the next day's lesson. *Notice that the teacher's objectives and the children's objectives are not always the same*. In this example the children aim to create a dance; the teacher may have several objectives—musical form, rhythm, and notation as well as furthering creative efforts. The teacher sometimes assists the children in finding a need for objectives that are initially obscure to them but challenging when identified and clarified.

Some teachers have difficulty in realizing what children's objectives are. They need to ask themselves why the children need or want to do a certain activity, then try to think of it from their point of view. For example, a teacher may be concerned with growth in comprehending the meter signature. He should consider why the child should want or need to know this. After some creative thinking, this could emerge: "To be able to use the understanding of meter in order to direct songs." Notice that the purpose and the activity are united in a child's mind. The good teacher always considers the child's point of view as well as his purpose for learning.

Organization of Content

Teaching music has to do with concepts and generalizations of importance concerning rhythm, melody, harmony, texture, tone quality, dynamics, tempo, and form. These represent conceptual approaches to selection and organization of the content of the music curriculum.

In curriculum development the term *concept* has a precise and limited meaning, commonly expressed in the form of a word or phrase. Man's ability to conceptualize provides a way for him to organize and classify knowledge systematically. An example would be *rondo,* which is the conceptualizing of a type of composition having the characteristic of a recurrent section. High, low, fast, slow are more simple concepts. Musical concepts, then, are those learned from working with the elements of music. Needless to say, children learn these best when they engage in active musical explorations, experiments, performances, and problem-solving activities.

Generalizations are commonly expressed in the form of complete sentences which show the relationship between two on more concepts. A sub-generalization differs from a generalization in that it has limited rather than general application. In contrast, concepts are personal and subjective and vary from individual to individual in accordance with their experience, point of view, or cultural background. Generalizations will contain two or more concepts, whereas concepts (stated as words or phrases) cannot include a generalization.

When concepts are taught, the teacher introduces them in musical context rather than in isolation. If possible, concepts should be presented in more than one context in order to reveal their different degrees of meaning. Children should have the opportunity to formulate their own understanding of concepts before the teacher offers his guidance and direction. As students discover the various meanings and features of concepts, they will increase their understanding, use, and retention of them. Immediately following the introduction of a concept, the students should explore it by moving, singing, playing, reading, listening, and notating, when these are applicable. The teacher determines which concepts are important, then plans learning activities for the children that will help them acquire these concepts. Many examples of this that are related to the structure of music are found in *The Study of Music in the Elementary School: A Conceptual Approach,* published by the Music Educators National Conference in 1967. This book reflects the thinking of a committee of teachers in Southern California. The Committee states most of the "concepts" in the form of generalizations.

Concepts can be classified as dealing with 1) the tangible: concrete objects, signs, and symbols, and 2) abstract terms such as: feeling, thinking, and behaving. Examples of the first type are clarinet, clef sign, and crescendo; examples of the second type are patriotic music, impressionism, and how to act at a concert. Young children understand concepts which relate to tangible things more easily than those which are abstract in nature.

Children learn concepts and generalizations through many planned experiences and through contact with facts in relation to those experiences. From problem solving and inquiry they learn the meaning of concepts. Ultimately they grow in their understanding of these to the point where they are able to combine two or more into conclusions. When they do this, they are forming their own generalizations, and because they are their own, they have special meaning for them. For this reason, problem solving and inquiry approaches are encouraged whenever possible. Ideally, we begin with problems and conclude with generalizations. Concepts and generalizations are taught at various levels. One of the most frequently-quoted beliefs of our time is one from Jerome Bruner, "The foundations of any subject may be taught to anybody at any age in some form. . . . The role of structure in learning . . . lies in giving students an understanding of the fundamental structure of whatever subjects we choose to teach."[3] As important as this is, let us not forget that it must be combined with an understanding of how an individual learns. And added to these must be a teacher's faith in the child's ability to learn.

USING CONCEPTS AND GENERALIZATIONS IN PLANNING

Curriculum planners follow logical steps:

1. Identify the important concepts and generalizations to be developed.
2. Scale these down into levels of difficulty which enable them to be worked with at appropriate grade or performance levels.
3. Base planning on children's prior experience—on what they already know. Then gradually widen their horizons.

The second step should be emphasized because the basic elements of any subject may be profound and complex. The teacher is called upon to utilize imagination when examining these elements with their supporting generalizations, concepts, and data, and *then re-write or otherwise change them* to suit his own purposes at the level of instruction for which he is planning.

SELECTION OF CONTENT

Every teacher needs to justify in his own mind the importance of what he teaches. In the selection of music content and skills he can ask himself:

Does this help the child to live better in today's world?
Does this assist the child to formulate important generalizations and to realize objectives?
How has this helped me or how can it help me in my own life?

The teacher's problem is to select from the vast world of music that small but highly important portion he will be able to work with in one school year. However, teachers are not entirely free to select these topics. They can exercise choice within certain limits.

...in order to co-ordinate the efforts of individual teachers, school districts often empower groups of teachers and administrators to impose constraints in the form of curricular designs or suggested sequences for instructional units of work. Teachers are not often free, nor should they

[3] Jerome S. Bruner, *The Process of Education* (Cambridge, Mass.: Harvard University Press, 1962), pp. 11–12.

be, to consider any topic whatever in the classroom. Instructional choices are limited so as to fall within a predetermined pattern that promises to tie together the efforts of an entire staff. A variety of other restrictions are also necessary and prudent in the conduct of schools, in order to provide for the safety of the children and a balanced school program. The restrictions encountered in teaching are of several kinds; they may vary in number or in their power to constrain, but they exist. It is within the context of restraint that teachers exercise choice.[4]

The transfer student constitutes an additional problem when choice of subject matter is considered. In our increasingly mobile society, there are students constantly leaving and entering schools. Thus, the normal amount of individual differences in music classes, staggering enough in itself, is aggravated further. The task of the teacher is to find out how much each student knows, then plan a program of instruction psychologically sequential for individual learners. This is possible in music because of the variety of activities to further learning and because most musical experiences can be made as complex or as simple as need be. Consequently, if a child is familiar with what is to be learned in music, the teacher can plan for him to extend his knowledge of it. While there should be a course of study that is logically sequential, it is also important that the learnings are sequential for each child.

From Children's Learning Toward Teacher Planning

Thus far, the ways children learn have been emphasized; now we shall turn our attention to the bases from which teachers plan. When children learn, they begin with facts (data), but when teachers plan, they begin with generalizations. This is illustrated at the top of page 113.
The teacher seldom tells children generalizations; the children form them and state them in their own words after doing pertinent and necessary collecting, analyzing, and organizing of data.

Despite the reverse appearance of the two columns, it should be obvious by now that the teacher's planning will reflect the learning process of children. To review the three steps above, the first is *perceptual*. The child learns facts by means of his senses, and the good music teacher plans to encourage the child's use of every appropriate sense, ear, eye,

---

[4] Clements, H. Millard, William R. Fielder, and B. Robert Tabachnick, *Social Study: Inquiry in Elementary Classrooms* (The Bobbs-Merrill Company, Inc., New York, 1966), pp. 115–16.

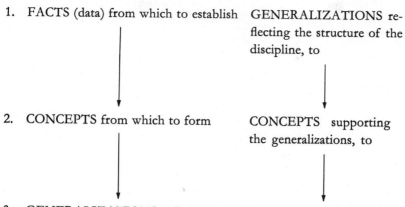

CHILDREN'S LEARNING

1. FACTS (data) from which to establish

2. CONCEPTS from which to form

3. GENERALIZATIONS reflecting the structure of the discipline

TEACHER PLANNING

GENERALIZATIONS reflecting the structure of the discipline, to

CONCEPTS supporting the generalizations, to

FACTS (data) necessary to build concepts

and feeling, in order that he can receive all the meaning necessary for him to produce a mental image. The second step requires associative *thinking* in that the images are retrieved from mental storage, re-examined, explored, and organized so that concepts may be formed from them. The third step has to do with forming generalizations based on experience with concepts, and applying these generalizations in new situations to test them and to change and refine them.

A major task of the teacher is to engage in a type of questioning that guides discussion, assists children in their comprehension of pertinent aspects of the matter at hand, helps them relate the parts to the whole, encourages them to explore, theorize, experiment, and so on. It is important that children verbalize their experiences. They work with musical facts, concepts, and generalizations in two ways: 1) listening to music, and 2) producing music by performing it and composing it. Habits, attitudes, and values are influenced by this process, the type of classroom environment (both physical and social), and the example set either consciously or unconsciously by the teacher in his attitude toward music.

The selection of materials of instruction that most clearly reveal the essentials of the lesson is vital and poses another important task for the teacher. All of this is necessary to relate the learning process to the teaching process.

A balance of questions involving the various types of thinking are used by teacher and pupils as they assemble data and seek solutions to problems. In the exploration of problems they usually begin at the data level, move to the concept level, and then to the generalization level. Examples of different types of questions are indicated in the following illustration:

STEPS IN DEVELOPING CONCEPTS AND GENERALIZATIONS

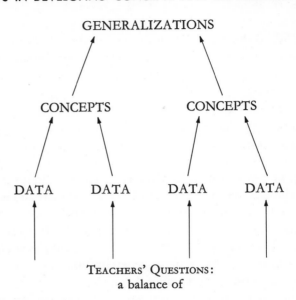

TEACHERS' QUESTIONS:
a balance of

Cognitive-memory Questions

"What is meant by this term or symbol?"

Convergent Questions

"Under what conditions are musical terms and symbols used?"

Divergent Questions

"What would happen if there were no terms or symbols?"

Evaluative Questions

"Are these the most appropriate terms and symbols needed for the best communication of this song's message?"

Jerome Bruner writes, "Grasping the structure of a subject is understanding it in a way that permits many other things to be related to it meaningfully. To learn structure, in short, is to learn how things are related."[5] " . . . the curriculum of a subject should be determined by

[5] Jerome Bruner, *The Process of Education* (Cambridge, Mass.: Harvard University Press, 1960), p. 7.

the most fundamental understanding that can be achieved of the underlying principles that give structure to a subject."[6] Understanding the structure of music means being able to comprehend the relationships of the elements which comprise music and to use this understanding in dealing with music. This structure will guide the selection of course content. It is further assumed that such subject matter will lead the learner to act in a manner of identifying and solving problems on his level, which is very similar to that of the expert performer, composer, and critic on their adult level. When we seek course content in light of music's structure, we find that the teacher's task becomes one to help children learn and expand their concepts of aspects of rhythm, dynamics, tempo, pitch, melody, polyphony, harmony, texture, tone quality, form, and style.

The terms *scope* and *sequence* are used in curriculum building. Scope pertains to what is learned and its comprehensiveness; sequence refers to the order of learnings in a program designed to further logical continuity. Presently the emphasis in scope is more on what children are to learn about music than on the topics or skills they are to study. Topics and skills are regarded as vehicles by means of which learning can take place. Many schools define the scope of their music programs in terms of the elements that comprise music as a discipline. These "big ideas" are expressed in terms of concepts and generalizations and form a conceptual approach to subject content. When knowledge is organized around the comparatively few basic ideas which underlie the study of music, it is believed that this provides the learner with more possibilities of associative relationships than does a large amount of scattered or less related facts about music.

Possible Steps in the Development of the Concept *Melody*

1. The learner first experiences a melody by hearing it.

2. He responds to it with body movement.

3. He experiences other melodies and begins to form a notion of what a melody is.

4. He experiments with performing melodies by singing, playing instruments, and body movement.

5. He compares his performance with melodies performed by others.

6. By further effort he is better able to comprehend the rhythm which unites with pitch to form melody.

[6] Ibid. p. 31.

7. He sees a familiar melody in an understandable form of notation.

8. He revises and expands his concept of melody; he then uses his newly revised concept in exploring other aspects of melody.

The following structure of music outline is one drawn by the authors only as an example; it does not represent any final word. Anyone can organize his own outline of music's basic structure, and the authors encourage both students and teachers in service to do so. This example is highly condensed and can be expanded easily. There are *many* more generalizations than are stated in it. Some time and effort are necessary to learn to use such an outline flexibly.

The generalizations stated in formal, adult language are of use to the teacher in *setting his intellectual compass in the right direction*. He does not recite them to the children nor does he expect to hear the children form them in these words; in most cases they are to *discover* generalizations for themselves and express them in their own ways. Notice some examples of ways children might state them which appear in the Suggested Conceptual Structure of Music.

When children explore music within the framework of the following Structure or one similar to it, they should be able to *think* musically. The good teacher remembers that children do not learn concepts by memorizing definitions. Instead, the learner develops the meanings of concepts through many and varied experiences and by selecting and using pertinent facts. This has an inductive nature about it. The learner is assisted to develop his own generalizations. *Most generalizations are tentative;* they will be tested, refined, and explored further. The same "big idea" is often studied at the various levels of instruction. Bruner writes, "A curriculum, as it develops, should revisit these basic ideas repeatedly, building upon them. . . . "[7] Young children can learn that "Sound and silence have duration," but such a generalization will be expanded, refined, and made more specific as these children study it again and again as they proceed through the elementary school years. The good teacher does not "teach" concepts; he plans experiences through which the children develop them.

To introduce the following Structure of Music, it may be helpful to decide what music is in its barest essentials. It is sound which is intended to be music taking place in time. It may be very simple or

[7] Jerome Bruner, *The Process of Education* (Cambridge, Mass.: Harvard University Press, 1963), p. 53.

very complex. In its more simple forms it will contain only some type of sound in some type of pattern. In its more complex forms it may involve all of the elements of music. This Structure of Music is expressed in adult terms; children will state generalizations *in their own vocabulary*.

A SUGGESTED CONCEPTUAL STRUCTURE OF MUSIC

Tempo

Generalization[8]: Tempo pertains to degrees of fast and slow.

Sub-generalization: There are commonly employed words and abbreviations for degrees of fast and slow.

Concepts:		
	lento	slow
	largo	broad and slow
	andante	moderately slow
	allegretto	moderately fast
	allegro	lively
	vivace	spirited
	presto	very fast
	a tempo	in original tempo
	accelerando (accel.)	gradually faster
	rallentando (rall.)	gradually slower
	ritardando (rit.)	gradually slower

Dynamics

Generalization: Dynamics pertains to degrees of loud and soft which supply variety and meaning to music.

Sub-generalization: There are commonly employed words, abbreviations, and signs for degrees of loud and soft.

Concepts:			
	accent	∧—>	more than usual stress
	pianissimo	pp	very soft
	piano	p	soft
	mezzo piano	mp	medium soft
	mezzo forte	mf	medium loud
	forte	f	loud

---

[8] All generalizations should lead to the goal of the learner's musical responsiveness based on understanding the interdependence of the components of music.

fortissimo	ff	very loud
sforzato or sforzando	sf	heavy accent
crescendo	cresc.	gradually increasing loudness
decrescendo	decresc.	gradually decreasing loudness
diminuendo	dim.	gradually decreasing loudness

sign for crescendo:

sign for decrescendo:

Sub-generalization: There are relationships between changes of dynamics and tempo, and melody, harmony, and texture.

Rhythm

Generalization: Rhythm in music is a grouping of sounds and silences of varying duration, usually controlled by a regular beat.

Sub-generalization: Sound and silence have duration.

Concepts: beat
equal divisions of the beat
unequal divisions of the beat
one-to-two relation of note values
one-to-three relation of note values
one-to-four relation of note values
notated rhythm
dotted notes
rests
speech-rhythm
notated speech-rhythm
articulation such as staccato and legatto
fermata (⌒)

Sub-generalization: Musical sound has duration and pitch.

Concepts: word-rhythms related to duration
word-rhythms related to duration and pitch
notation of word-rhythms
notation of melody

Sub-generalization: Accent or lack of accent governs types of rhythm.

Concepts: metrical rhythm
meter, bar line, measure, upbeat (anacrusis),

downbeat, meter signature, duple meter, triple meter, primary accent, secondary accent, rhythm pattern
asymmetrical rhythm (5/4, 7/8, etc.)
"measured" rhythm (no regular recurring beat, such as in Gregorian chant)
free rhythm
rallentando (rall.)
accelerando (accel.)
rubato
no common metrical beat (such as some Oriental, Indian, and Hungarian music which cannot be expressed in traditional notation)
syncopation as a disturbance of the normal pulse of meter, accent, and rhythm

Sub-generalization: Devices related to rhythm are used by composers to add interest to their compositions.

Concepts: rhythm patterns
rhythmic ostinati
augmentation
diminution
canonic imitation
polyrhythm
free rhythm (rit., rall., accel., rubato, syncopation)
syncopation

Sub-generalization: There are rhythms which are characteristic of peoples and nations.

Concepts: distinctive rhythms in national songs
distinctive rhythms in national dances
(minuet, waltz, polka, schottische, square dance, etc.)
distinctive rhythms associated with ethnic groups

Generalization: Rhythm is universal and has meanings beyond music.

Concepts: Rhythm in—
the seasons
waves of the ocean
the grain of wood
architecture
painting
the heartbeat
day and night
life cycles of plants and animals
the speech and movement of man

Melody

Generalization: A melody is a linear succession of tones which are rhythmically controlled and are perceived by the human ear as a meaningful grouping of tones. (Children might say, "A melody is a line of tones in rhythm that sounds right.")

Sub-generalization—Direction: The tones of melodies may go up, down, or remain the same in pitch.

Concepts: pitch and vibration
high and low
contour
relation to tension, climax, and release
notation of pitch
staff, note, clef, numerals and syllables to identify pitches

Sub-generalization—Duration: Melodies are formed by a union of pitch and rhythm.

Concepts: relation of song melodies to word rhythms
note values (see RHYTHM)
rhythm patterns in, or related to, melodies

Sub-generalization: The tones of melodies may have adjacent (scale-line) pitches or skips (chord-line pitches).

Concepts: scale (major, minor, diatonic, modal, pentatonic, chromatic, the tone row derived from the chromatic, whole-tone, ethnic, invented)
passive and active scale tones (tension and release)
tonal centers
home tone
key
key signature
accidental
intervals
relation to chords (see HARMONY)

Sub-generalization: Form: Melodies are usually formed of distinct parts or sections.

Concepts: phrase
phrase arrangement (repetition and contrast; unary, binary, and ternary song forms)
sequence
tonal patterns and their alterations

Sub-generalization: Devices: Melodies can be manipulated. (Children might say, "Melodies can be changed in different ways.")

Concepts: transposition
            diminution
            augmentation
            inversion
            retrograde
            melodic variation
            rhythmic variation

Sub-generalization: Melodies may reflect national or cultural styles.

Sub-generalization: Some melodies are functional in that they tend to communicate ideas and moods.

Harmony, Polyphony, and Texture

Generalization: Harmony pertains to the vertical aspect of music, the successions of chords and the relationships among them. (Children might say, "Harmony means chords and their changes.")

Generalization: Texture, a term derived from weaving, pertains to vertical and horizontal elements ("threads") in music which produce such effects as light, heavy, thick, and thin, and which include styles of composition such as homophonic and polyphonic.

Sub-generalization: Homophonic music consists primarily of one melody with an accompaniment.

Concepts: accompanied song
            accompanied instrumental solo
            music of the nineteenth century
            harmony suggested by chord tones in melodies

Sub-generalization: Polyphonic music has two or more melodic lines sounding at the same time; these melodic lines are connected in tonal music by harmonic relationships.

Concepts: round, canon
            counterpoint
            contrary motion
            fugue
            fugal entry

music of Palestrina and J. S. Bach
harmony suggested by chord tones in melodies
descriptive terms: contrapuntal, imitative, canonic, fugal,
atonal polyphony.

Sub-generalization: A chord is any simultaneous combination of three or
more pitches; some may be more agreeable to the ear
than others. (Children might say, "A chord is three or
more notes sounded together.")

Concepts: chord construction—3rds, 4ths, 5ths, clusters, contrived
chords
inversions
relation to key centers
triad
scale
major
minor
question and answer (V_7—I)
cadence: full, half, plagal
relation to melody
harmonizing a tune
chord tones
passing tones
consonance
dissonance
primary and secondary chords
chording
chords relating to no tonal center
atonality
chords as conjunctions of melodic lines
parallel chords

Sub-generalization: Identical harmonies can be sounded at different pitch
levels.

Concepts: transposition
key signatures

Sub-generalization: Harmonies can be combined.

Concepts: bitonality
polytonality

Form

Generalization: Musical forms are similar to plans of construction made
by architects.

Form in Music
Sub-generalization: Melodies may be divided into parts.

Concepts: phrase
period
sequence

Sub-generalization: Melodies can be extended and altered.

Concepts: introduction   diminution
coda   inversion
interlude   retrograde
sequence
repetition
section
thematic development
augmentation

Forms of Music
Sub-generalization: Most musical form is based on the principle of repetition-contrast (same-different, unity-variety)

Concepts: a a
a b
a b a
A B A sections
rondo (A B A C A; A B A C A B A)
rondeau (A B A C A D . . . A)
variation

Sub-generalization: Some forms can be classified as contrapuntal.

Concepts: round
canon
fugue

Sub-generalization: A compound form comes into being when several movements are combined to form a complete musical composition.

Concepts: movement
instrumental compound forms
  sonata-allegro
  concerto
  suite
    classic dance
    ballet
    other
  symphony
  overture

     vocal compound forms
      opera
      oratorio
      cantata

Sub-generalization: Some forms are dictated by poems or stories.

  Concepts: art song
       symphonic poem (tone poem)
       vocal compound forms

Generalization: Principles of form such as repetition, contrast, balance, and unity have meanings beyond music.

  Concepts: art
       architecture
       poetry and stories
       clothing and textiles
       nature

Tone Quality

Generalization: Tone quality (timbre, tone color) is the difference heard between tones of the same pitch produced by different voices and instruments; it distinguishes the sound of one instrument or voice from another.

Sub-generalization: Voices and instruments can be classified according to tone quality and range.

  Concepts: classification of voices
      soprano
      alto
      tenor } and their subdivisions
      bass
     classification of instruments
      strings
       bowed
       plucked
       keyboard
     woodwinds
      flue
      reed
     percussion
     brass
     organ
     electronic
     folk

Sub-generalization: Instruments can be played in ways that produce different sounds.

    Concepts: legato
                  staccato
                  spiccato, as concerns bowing
                  mute, as concerns strings, trumpets, French horn
                  vibrato
                  use of extreme ranges of high or low
                  stop, as concerns the organ
                  glissando, as concerns the harp and other instruments
                  experimental ways

Sub-generalization: Voices and instruments may be combined to produce infinite variety of tone colors.

Sub-generalization: Composers and arrangers select different voices, instruments, and tone colors for specific reasons.

Sub-generalization: The difference in tone qualities can be explained scientifically.

    Concepts: resonance
                  harmonics
                  overtone series
                  partials
                  vibrato

Style

A Synthesis of Musical Elements

Generalization: Musical style is the result of the particular combination of qualities of melody, rhythm, harmony, texture, form, tone color, tempo, dynamics, national origin, time in history, and the unique characteristics of individual composers; to analyze and identify style indicates knowledge and understanding of the musical elements and the ability to relate and synthesize them, together with historical, social, and psychological influences.

Sub-generalization: Composers utilize devices and methods of composition which contribute to their individual style.

    Concepts: canon, sequence, augmentation, diminution, inversion, retrograde, retrograde inversion, open harmony (texture), closed harmony (texture), repetition, counterpoint, homophony, tone color, etc.

Sub-generalization: Composers have written types of music such as mood music, descriptive music, music based on stories, and non-programatic music; these can be identified and analyzed to examine style.

Sub-generalization: The music of any composer can be examined to determine its style; there will be distinctive musical elements and nonmusical influences of his life and times.

Sub-generalization: There are stylistic elements of melody, rhythm, harmony, texture, etc., which are of national or ethnic origin.

Sub-generalization: There are style periods in music related to historical times; the outstanding characteristics of any style period can be discovered and identified.

Concepts: renaissance
baroque
classic
romantic
impressionist
contemporary

Sub-generalization: Style is influenced by the type of composition.

Concepts: operatic
symphonic
motet
church
popular
etc.

Sub-generalization: Style is influenced by the performance medium.

Concepts: instrumental
vocal
keyboard
etc.

An example of using this Structure of Music in the intermediate grades follows. The teacher has abstracted his own generalization from the outline, "The family of reed instruments includes the oboe, bassoon, clarinet, and saxophone." In developing this generalization, concepts of each of these instruments must be formed. When considering the bassoon, data such as these will be learned by the children:

Data   a long tube which doubles back on itself
         a double reed made of cane
         a conical bore
         a tone of cavernous quality
         a bass instrument
         a very wide range of pitches

Concept   the standard bassoon

Generalization   (assuming concepts of the four instruments have developed)
The family of reed instruments includes the oboe, bassoon, clarinet, and saxophone.[9]

This generalization may later be refined and expanded if the teacher chooses to work with it further. For example, he could plan the discovery of the *metal* reed as a *discrepant event* which would bring the attention of the children to the function of reeds in the accordion, harmonica, and reed organ. Then the concept of the "family of reed instruments" will expand and the concept of "reed" will grow. Children can discover that each metal reed is constructed to produce a definite pitch, while each cane reed must in some way accommodate difference in pitch. Thus discovery grows out of discovery as the teacher guides the process in a helpful but unobtrusive way. The children are guided to discuss their findings and problems as they work with the tone qualities, range, appearance, and mechanical features of reed instruments. Such study as this is ordinarily *only a part* of a lesson plan which includes a variety of musical activities such as singing, playing instruments, body responses, and listening, all selected to assist progress toward specific objectives.

In developing concepts, children may listen to music, perform music, compose it, write it, analyze it, and discuss it. The aim is to clarify the mental image of the aspect of music under study. This is done best by genuine student involvement with musical problems, not by the teacher's presentation of pre-digested facts. The children should be guided to develop concepts and generalizations concerned with tone qualities, arrangements of pitches melodically, harmonically, rhythmically, and contrapuntally, and of the relations between these and other elements of music such as form, tempo, and dynamics.

[9] Notice where this teacher found his generalization in the Suggested Structure of Music. He selected what might be termed a sub-concept in the Tone Quality section and re-stated it as a generalization to use for his own purposes. Find his source.

To close this part of the chapter, a concept is said to be a clear and complete thought about something. Musical knowledge is made up of data from which concepts and generalizations will ultimately be formed. Musical understanding is the ability to use concepts and generalizations to solve musical problems.

Teaching Music

When the teacher begins his work in planning the teaching of music, it is wise for him to ponder the warning of Charles Leonhard not to overemphasize the intellectual aspects:

> We should exercise caution in abandoning the goals we have worked toward under the often vague term appreciation. One danger that I see in the current emphasis on concepts and structured learning is that we may become so involved in the specifics and minutiae of music that we forget that the musical experience is basically an affective experience. Whatever else it may achieve, music loses its value when it fails to touch the hearts and stir the feelings of people.[10]

The above words urge the teacher to consider children's appreciative responses to music and to realize that they are often of non-verbal character. This is part of affective learning—the feelings and emotions aspect. Music is always a reflection of humanity; the technical aspects of music are only a means of communication. It is necessary to be reminded of this in a day when stress is being placed on concept development and the structure of disciplines. *Music is an aesthetic experience and a social language before it is an intellectual experience,* and the good music teacher never forgets this when he plans the music lesson.

OBJECTIVES

The Pictorial Description of Music Content indicates the four major categories of music teaching: the components of music as a discipline; musical skills; attitudes, values, and behaviors; and musical thinking. These form the framework from which the teacher selects justifiable objectives, then plans learning experiences which serve to promote them.

[10] Excerpt from an address by Dr. Charles Leonhard at the Conference to Improve the Effectiveness of Music Education in Oregon Elementary Schools, Gearhart, Oregon, April 27–28, 1967. State Department of Education, Salem, Oregon.

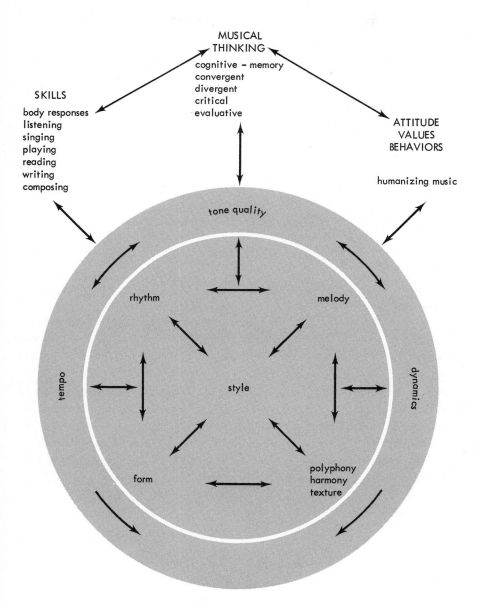

A Pictorial Description of Music Content

Such learning experiences should provide for multiple learnings contributing to two or more objectives. For example, an experience which furthers basic knowledge of music should also further development of some music skill, as well as advancing the ability to think musically.

After many years of confusing activities with musical objectives, teachers are now more clear in their concepts of what they are teaching. In the past, objectives tended to center around performance skills. The development of basic skills is a part of teaching any elementary school subject, which means that skills in singing, rhythmic response, playing instruments, listening to music, reading music, writing music notation, and composing music are defensible objectives. Most objectives today are directed toward learning the structure of music, and *skills are generally viewed as activities through which one learns about music* instead of being viewed as ends in themselves. Consequently, skills are often vehicles by means of which objectives are attained. Objectives may be selected for a day, a week, a month, a term, or a year.

Behavioral Objectives A recent trend is to state pupil objectives in behavioral terms. Teachers who state objectives behaviorally think of them in terms of the child's performance, thus one might consider a behavioral objective as a performance objective. An example might be: "The children will be able to identify all common reed instruments both by their tone qualities and by sight." This is much more precise than an objective written as: "The reed instruments will be studied at the fifth-grade level," because it is stated in language which enables the teacher to tell whether or not, or to what extent, the objective has been achieved. The behavioral objective incorporates a means of evaluation by indicating what the child will be able to do as a result of his learning experience. A practical way to identify a behavioral objective is to ask, "Specifically, what will the children be able to do?"

Examples of behavioral objectives:

The children will be able to clap these rhythm patterns from the chalkboard and from the chart.

The children will be able to *classify* the names of these instruments into brass and woodwind families.

Given a four-measure phrase of notation which consists of these note patterns, the children will be able to sight-sing the phrase with ease.

The class will be able to *identify* the forms as either ABA or rondo when they hear them in unfamiliar recorded compositions.

As a result of the lesson, the learner will behave or perform in a variety of ways, some of which are:[11]

> *Identifying* a musical instrument, term, symbol, or aspect of notation by picking it up, pointing to it, touching it, or communicating it verbally.
>
> *Naming* an instrument, form, term, symbol, or relationship.
>
> *Arranging* three or more phrases, terms, symbols, measures, or events in order based on a stated plan.
>
> *Describing* properties sufficient to identify a type of song, phrase, term, symbol, or relationship.
>
> *Selecting* an object, term, symbol, or phrase from two or more which might be confused.
>
> *Composing* or *constructing* music, accompaniments, musical instruments, a drawing, and written or verbal statements which indicate ability to infer, hypothesize, and evaluate.
>
> *Demonstrating* the sequence of operations necessary to carry out a musical procedure.
>
> *Deriving* an answer to a musical problem by employing the behaviors stated above, and organizing these into various types of data derived from such behaviors into a musical concept or generalization to be applied in the solution of other musical problems.

ADVANCE PLANNING

When a teacher plans a year's program, he works from knowledge of the competencies of children at the beginning of the year toward the long-range objectives to be reached at the year's end. When he plans a daily lesson, he utilizes activities the children can manage at their current level of musical development, activities which will lead them toward achieving the long-range objectives. When the teacher formulates objectives, he does this to give direction and depth to the music program as well as to guide each child's learning of music in the most effective way he can devise. He makes daily plans which will be likely to *involve* the learners in exploratory and inquiry activities and techniques of the learning process. It is assumed that the teacher knows the developmental characteristics of each child as outlined in Chapter Three.

To know the children and their musical ability at the beginning of the year, the teacher can utilize information which should be available in school records. He can study these before school begins and from them

[11] Nye, Robert E., Vernice T. Nye, Neva Aubin, and George Kyme, *Singing With Children,* 2nd ed. (Belmont, Calif., Wadsworth Publishing Company, Inc., 1970, Introduction.)

he can learn many things about the children's musical background. Ordinarily information he can obtain prior to the opening of school may be from:

1. Health records — that may reveal any deviation from the norm affecting music learning, including eyesight, hearing, and muscular coordination.

2. Cumulative records — that begin when a child first enters school; they may indicate the scope and sequence of his musical learning.

3. Checklists — that indicate types of musical experiences and levels of competency.

4. Tape recordings — of musical performances of the previous year.

5. Interviews with previous teachers — that may reveal musical problems and experiences which relate to the present.

6. Interviews with private music teachers — that reveal abilities, interests, and attitudes.

7. Anecdotal records — that are dated records of significant observed behavior of the child by previous teachers.

In the first weeks of school the teacher may obtain information by:

1. Pupil-teacher conferences — to learn about children's interests, musical experiences, and family musical background.

2. Observations — of attitudes, facial expression revealing degrees of enjoyment, emotional involvement, ease of voice production, ability to stay on pitch, facility with instruments, ability in part singing, muscular coordination, rhythmic skill, and creative responses.

3. Class discussions — that reveal likes, dislikes, prejudices, problems, interests, appreciations, knowledge, and understanding.

4. Parent-teacher conferences — that reveal family musical interests and cultural and economic conditions affecting present musical responsiveness.

Fortified with this information, the teacher can plan the first music experience with more confidence. In the nursery school, kindergarten, and first grade, the first encounter with music may begin with listening to the teacher sing attractive and appealing songs with subject content meaningful to the age group, combined with opportunities for physical responses. The teacher will be alert to the degrees of response indicated by the children's behavior, and will begin to plan from there. In subsequent days she will provide opportunities for many individual and small group responses to judge abilities to respond to the beat, comprehend ptich, match tones, and coordinate muscle responses with music. With eight-year-olds and older, abilities and attitudes can be assessed by asking children to recall favorite songs and musical activities from last year, or from summer camps. Again, observation will provide clues as to what to plan for the experiences to follow.

To be able to hear and observe children, the teacher must ordinarily move about the room. This requires limiting the use of the piano, not only to be able to see the children and move around among them, but in order to hear each voice without the hindrance of the sounds of the piano. While this large instrument can be utilized constructively for other purposes, it cannot be used in group situations when the teacher needs to hear each child's voice in order to assess pitch accuracy or vocal tone quality. Therefore, many unaccompanied songs will be sung, or "sing along" recordings may be used; a child may accompany on the Autoharp, the teacher may accompany on the guitar—and because the guitar is portable, it frees the teacher to move among the children, listen to them, and be in contact with each child. Of course, in this assessment of musical responses the teacher's manner is casual and interested, not inspectorial. He observes each child, how he responds to rhythm, sings or plays, and reacts to various types of games or tests the teacher devises to help measure "where the class is" in music at the beginning of the year.

EVALUATION

Evaluation is a two-edged device; it appraises both children's musical growth and the teacher's success. Skills and concept building can be tested, but evaluation is a term that relates to *all* aspects of musical growth—knowledge of facts, concepts, generalizations, skills, thinking, habits, attitudes and values. Some of these can be evaluated subjectively by teachers' observations. A common definition of evaluation is *that which determines to what extent objectives have been realized.*

Musical understanding can be revealed behaviorally by students' ability to manipulate the components of music in creative work: making up songs, instrumental pieces, codas, introductions, interludes, descants, harmony parts, and variations. Ability to improvise can be a means of assessing musical sensitivity and taste. Musical knowledge is frequently demonstrated through written tests on factual items such as terms, forms, dynamic marks, notation, and information about composers. Tests of more complex types measure both knowledge and understanding. In such tests, children prove their understanding by using facts and concepts to solve musical problems. The level of attainment in performance abilities can be observed, as can skill in moving to music. Note reading talents are observed when children sight sing or sight read music, and when they write notation in response to pitch dictation, which is also a listening skill. Students' ability to analyze music aurally is a measure of their skill in listening, while their ability to analyze music from the printed page is a measure of their musical understanding in an intellectual sense. Attitudes and habits are reflected by degrees (tastes and amounts) of liking music, participating in it, reading about it, and in musical activities outside of school. Habits are revealed through singing, playing instruments, writing music creatively as a hobby, improvising music, listening to recordings and worthwhile radio programs, viewing worthwhile television programs, and attending concerts.

By stating objectives behaviorally and by evaluating the child's ability to behave and perform in certain ways, there is immediate "feed back" to the teacher and the learner of his accomplishments in skills, concepts, understandings, attitudes, and appreciations. Obviously the child's goals are in a state of constant adjustment as he matures and advances in musical growth.

The Daily Lesson Plan

The inexperienced teacher may feel that a great many things must be packed into a lesson in order that the year's objectives can be realized; thus he may err by striving to "cover" too much in his teaching plan. The fear of leaving out something of importance can cause the acquisition of information to become the objective rather than nurturing the capacity to pursue fruitful learnings. Such an approach negates the idea of conceptual learning because in order for concepts to be learned and for generalizations to be formed, there must be studies *in depth* in which the main idea(s) is approached from every angle and by all appropriate senses. This is different from a random acquisition-of-information approach.

LESSON PLAN ORGANIZATIONS

There are many different types of lesson plan organizations. However, most effective plans should be designed to free the teacher to establish a learning situation in which the children can become involved in the exploration of music and in autonomous learning. Teachers sometimes become slaves of rigid lesson plans which emphasize musical content and musical skills as ends within themselves. Today it is important that the process of learning be emphasized. Overly rigid lesson plans can be a major cause of a pupil's lack of interest in music and consequently in his limited learning of musical concepts.

Even though there is no specific model of a lesson plan to be used in all music classes, there are important essential components of any effective lesson. They are as follows:

1.	Objective(s)	What the pupils are to learn.
2.	Materials and Equipment	The materials and equipment needed for developing the lesson.
3.	Interest and Initiation	Ways of preparing the pupils for the lesson; ways of launching the lesson.
4.	Work Study and Teaching Strategies	What activities the children will engage in in order to realize their identified objective(s), as well as other related learnings.
5.	Summary and Evaluation	What the teacher and pupils will do to conclude and evaluate the lesson.

Any lesson plan must be designed in terms of the pupils' past musical experiences, competencies, and interests in music. It must also reflect the individuality and creativity of the teacher and be kept flexible to allow for pupil involvement in the exploration and solution of musical problems.

The first lessons of the year are usually centered around pleasurable singing and getting acquainted experiences. From the standpoint of music activities they might include something like the following:

First Day   Sing familiar songs.

                What did you learn to sing at camp last summer?

                What are your favorite songs from past years?

                Common repertoire songs.

Second Day   Review familiar songs; try to add something new to them.

                Discover or invent a rhythm pattern to be used with percussion instruments with a song.

                Learn a new song.

                Begin to utilize songs or parts of songs for individual and group tone matching.

Third Day   Sing familiar songs.

                Make up a tune for a short poem.

                Introduce a new recording for listening purposes; create some appropriate physical responses.

The following *Suggested Form for a Daily Lesson Plan* is one designed to emphasize concept development. It accommodates the planning of those teachers who wish to stress relating to the structure of music as a discipline, the learning of data, the forming of concepts and generalizations by children, children's behavioral objectives, and teaching strategies including carefully formed questions of different types.

SUGGESTED FORM FOR A DAILY LESSON PLAN

Date_____

Generalization or Main Idea_____   Name_____

pacing	musical content	behavioral objectives	teaching strategies (learning experiences and teacher's questions)	materials

	Sub-generalization (focus of the lesson) concepts supporting data (There can be more than one sub-generalization, each with its supporting concepts and data.)		A. Introduction
			  1. Question(s)
			  2. Activities
			B. Development or work-study activities and pertinent questions
			C. Questions and activities for concluding and evaluating the lesson.	

EXPLANATION OF DAILY LESSON PLAN

PACING   This is an estimate of the time the teacher will spend on any one part of the lesson.

MUSICAL CONTENT   This has to do with the focus of the lesson— the important understanding(s) or sub-generalization(s) the teacher is to help the children learn.

BEHAVIORAL OBJECTIVES   Writing objectives for children in behavioral terms helps the teacher to project what he expects the learners *to be able to do* at the end of the lesson.

TEACHING STRATEGIES   This is the "how to do it" part of the plan. What the teacher does and what the students are doing in each activity is included here, as are the teacher's questions. The teacher tries to use as many different types of questions as are logically appropriate in exploring an idea or concept—convergent, cognitive, evaluative, and divergent types of questions. This section can be divided into three distinct parts: 1) Introduction, which may include a review of a previous lesson, building readiness for the lesson of the day, and establishing purposes, 2) Developmental strategies, the work-study-game activities the children will engage in, and 3) Concluding and evaluative strategies, specific techniques to be used to determine if the behavioral objectives and the focus of the lesson have been realized. Teacher and children generalize and summarize what has been accomplished or learned, what they planned to do but did not complete, how well they did what they did, where they could improve, and what they need to continue to work on in the next lesson.

MATERIALS   List all media and/or materials needed for the lesson— projectors, films, slides, transparencies, tapes, recordings, charts, maps, books, poems, songs, paper, instruments, objects, etc. Pre-service teachers should be specific when listing sources; state the title of a book, with publisher and page numbers; state the manufacturer of a recording and the record number.

The above plan is useful for the beginning teacher because it assists in learning how to organize a lesson. Less detailed plans are used by the experienced teacher because he knows many of the details and procedures and does not need to write them out. The experienced classroom teacher and the music specialist who must go quickly from room to room can write very brief plans. One example is the following:

Concepts (or objectives) (or subject matter)	Activities and Strategies	Materials

The extremely busy music specialist sometimes makes only a list of the materials to be used for each classroom, knowing the other parts of the lesson plan from memory.

Some teachers may prefer the standard traditional lesson plan:

Purposes: Establish teacher's and children's specific purposes.[12]

Materials: Prepare and assemble all necessary books, instruments, and audio-visual aids.

Procedure: Plan the steps and activities needed to realize the purposes, beginning with motivation and review those stemming from the previous lesson, if any; establish the purposes of today's plan with the children.

Evaluation: At the end of the lesson, summarize and evaluate with the children what was accomplished and what needs further emphasis in the next lesson. After the lesson the teacher analyzes the strengths and weaknesses of the plan and gleans implications from these for the next time.

The following lesson plan for second or third grade follows the design of the one which emphasizes concept development. For illustrative purposes it includes some of the possible teacher-pupil interaction which obviously would not be written in a teacher's daily lesson plan.

[12] Another possible plan has seven parts: materials, concepts to be learned, strategies (describe procedures to learn each concept or generalization), items to review, related learnings, observable outcomes.

Lesson Plan for Second or Third Grade

(30 minutes)

GENERALIZATION: The tones of melodies may have adjacent (scale-line) pitches or skips (chord-line pitches).

SUB-GENERALIZATION: (focus of the lesson) Some melodies move in skips or steps.

Concepts	*Data*
high	line
low	space
skip	measure
step	etc.
scale	
melodic line	
chord	

BEHAVIORAL OBJECTIVE: The children will be able to identify parts of melodies which move along chord-lines and parts which move along scale-lines.

Pacing TEACHING STRATEGIES (expanded here for illustrative purposes):

five A. Introduction:
min.

    Teacher: What do we remember about the last song we sang yesterday? (Teacher writes major points on chalkboard as children state them.)

    Child: We sang "Taps" last.

    Teacher: Why did we sing it last?

    Child: Because it is a song to end with; it begins, "Day is done."

    Teacher: Today we are going to do more with this song. Let's sing it again. Each of you think of a way to show the high and low pitches. Try to remember how the tune goes. Can you hear it in your head without singing it?

Children demonstrate with hands, bodies, etc.

    Teacher: Where did you begin?

    Children: Low.

Teacher establishes the pitch and the class sings the song.

twenty B. Development:
min.

Teacher directs students to sing "Planting Cabbages," and says, Sing it as you did last week, with part of the class singing measures one and two, five and six, and the rest singing measures three and four, seven and eight. (The teacher has assigned the more difficult chord-line measures to good singers, and the less difficult scale-line measures to the less certain singers.)

PLANTING CABBAGES

Can you plant the cab-bage so, Just as we do, just as we do?

Can you plant the cab-bage so, Just the same as we can do?

2. You can plant it with your feet. . . . .

3. You can plant it with your hands. . . .

TAPS

Day is done, gone the sun from the lake from the hills,

from the sky. Safe-ly rest all is well God is nigh.

Class sings the song as directed.

> *Teacher:* Now comes the puzzle: In what way are these songs alike? (pause)

> *Child:* Could we sing the songs again?

Class sings the songs again.

> *Sally:* The tunes are different.

> *Fred:* The rhythm is not the same.

> *Marie:* The way we sing "Can you plant the cabbages so" is a little like "Day is done, gone the sun."

> *Teacher:* Why do you think they are alike, Marie?

> *Marie:* The tune in both places skips instead of going in steps.

Teacher produces charts of the notation of each song and asks Marie to explain what she means by pointing to the measures.

> *Teacher:* Does anyone have another theory? Let's sing these songs again, watch the notes, and think how it sounds when the melody skips lines and spaces.

Class sings the songs again.

Teacher: Was there any part of these two songs that didn't skip lines and spaces?

Bob: The part I sing in "Planting Cabbages" doesn't skip.

Teacher: I see that you have examined this song carefully, Bob. Look at the chart and show us the part that you think doesn't skip.

Bob points to measures three and four.

Teacher: Play those measures on the bells, Pete. (He does) What did you discover?

Pete: The notes were all next to each other; there were no skips.

Teacher: Play measures seven and eight. (He does) What do you find there?

Pete: There is a skip in measure seven.

Teacher: Can you change the song so there isn't a skip there, Pete?

Pete experiments and adds an E between notes D and F to eliminate the skip. Teacher writes the E into the chart by making D and E eighth notes which are slurred on the word "same." Pete plays measures seven and eight as revised.

Teacher: Let's all sing measures seven and eight to see if we like them this way.

The class sings the measures and likes the change. Pete volunteers that it is easier to play on the bells this way.

Teacher: Can we analyze the melody of "Taps?" He holds up the chart of "Taps."

Child: It's all skips; it has some repeated notes.

Child: There are dotted notes.

Teacher: Let's examine "Planting Cabbages." Can you use the chart to explain what you find?

Children: It's half skips and half steps; measures 1–2, 5–6 are skips, and measures 3–4 and 7–8 are steps; it's in 6/8 meter.

Teacher: Everyone sing the measures that skip along chord lines and let Pete play the measures that step along scale lines.

The class does as directed.

The teacher next tests the class on its comprehension of chord lines and scale lines by the following process:

1. A familiar song is sung as the children move to show skips and steps as they hear them in the melody.
2. The class decides if skips or steps are present and states where they are found in the song.
3. The teacher shows a transparency of the notation on the screen to enable the class to verify its decision.

The children will find:

"A Hunting We Will Go"	to be	all steps
"Merrily We Roll Along"	to be	all steps except one skip at the end of the first phrase
"Little Tom Tinker"	to be	all skips and repeated notes until steps in the last measure
"Bow Belinda"	to be	a skip pattern one step lower, then one step higher, with steps in the last measure.

five
min.

C. Concluding the Lesson:

Teacher: Let's see if we can state in one sentence all the important things we learned about melodies today.

Class: Some melodies move in steps, some move in skips, and some move in steps and skips. (Notice how the children summarized the day's lesson by stating their findings in the form of a generalization.)

The concluding activity is the singing of "Bow, Belinda" and clapping the beat while volunteer pairs of children improvise dances in turn.

MATERIALS

Chalkboard

Songs the children know. Source: *Basic Music,* 3rd ed., Nye and Bergethon, Prentice-Hall, Inc., 1968.

Charts of the notation of "Taps," p. 63, and "Planting Cabbages," p. 63.

Bell set

Transparencies of "Merrily We Roll Along," p. 78, "A Hunting We Will Go," p. 85, "Little Tom Tinker," p. 98, and "Bow, Belinda," p. 69.

COMMENTS Notice that the teacher plans to work toward *many more goals* than stated in the focus of the lesson. Besides working toward the generalization and behavioral objective stated, this teacher will give attention to:

Tonal memory (can you hear it in your head without singing it?)

High and low pitch

Body movement in relation to high and low in pitch

Grouping children in accordance with their degree of ability to sing accurately on pitch

Using notation to solve musical problems

Playing an instrument (why do you think the teacher chose Pete to play the bells?)

Manipulating a melody by changing it

Comparing measures seven and eight with the changed version to judge if the new version is acceptable

Emphasizing listening skills

A concluding activity which involves body movement in dance improvisation (creative), clapping the beat (rhythm), and which may involve "pure enjoyment" as well as possible application of melodic skips and steps and repeated notes to dance movements.

For reasons of his own, the teacher does not plan to relate chord line melodies with chords; he is probably reserving this for a later lesson. There may be questions as to whether he should have planned to use the words "chord line" and "scale line" when he did. Either his class has sufficient background so that no student would question his use of them or the teacher is using them in the hope that someone might ask about them; then he will be able to propose study of these on another day as a suggestion that came from the class. He did not plan to develop the references by children to repeated notes or repeated note groups; he will lead the class in activities that emphasize skips and steps—his stated purpose.

The concluding activity can be questioned if it leaves the children in an emotional state that would make their learning in a following subject difficult. It would be assumed that it will not, or if it did, this teacher would follow it with another concluding activity to quiet the children, or that the class is followed by dismissal for the day or for recess or physical education.

To guide his effectiveness in planning for teaching, the teacher may use the following questions:

1. What objectives am I seeking? What pupil behaviors am I seeking to change?

2. What musical activities are appropriate for the achievement of the objectives? How will the learner react to the musical environment planned for him?

3. How shall I organize my teaching strategies? What takes place first? What is appropriate for whom? What important skills and values will be worked with over the years? How will I assure continuity of learning?

4. How will I measure progress?

After teaching a lesson, the teacher might ask himself:

1. Did I encourage student inquiry and discovery of concepts rather than tell them in lecture style?

2. Did I encourage student creativity?

3. Did I keep the learner active?

4. Were the activities pertinent to the realization of the objectives?

5. Did both teacher and learner evaluate the lesson in terms of their objectives?

At this point it may be well to think about a broad but briefly-stated view of musical learning from the cradle through the sixth grade:

1. The learner observes music in his life and in society about him. He begins to comprehend that man expresses himself, his activities, and his feelings by means of music.

2. As the learner continues to examine music, he gradually finds the same musical elements that the adult musician knows—rhythm, melody, harmony, form, and other elements.

3. The learner begins to manipulate the musical elements through his performance and composition of music. He arrives at a number of generalizations concerning music. He analyzes and evaluates music.

4. The learner is able to make hypotheses and important generalizations as he learns more about music through his many experiences with it. His increased grasp of data assists him in revising, expanding, and restating his concepts and generalizations. He learns through this process that musical knowledge is not static, but is tentative and changing. Because he has learned to revise his concepts and to work with musical problems he will be better able to understand the music of the future, which will not be the same as the music of today.

In conclusion, the following principles of organization and planning will prove to be helpful to the beginning teacher.

Some Principles of Organization and Planning

1. Children do not have minds alike; they do not all learn in the same ways. Therefore, the teacher of music needs to know a variety of approaches in order to be able to help every child advance in musical learning.

Assesses the needs of the children in terms of their growth and development	Analyzes and evaluates all aspects of his teaching
Examines the values, goals, and changing conditions in the community with regard to music	Utilizes a variety of teaching strategies and/or procedures, employing all appropriate senses

The Effective Music Teacher

Selects and organizes generalizations, concepts, and data to be studied	Involves the children as individuals, members of small groups, and members of the large group, always considering individual needs and capabilities
Identifies objectives appropriate for the development of necessary skills, attitudes, and appreciations	Organizes the class (large group, small group, individual child) for the execution of his plans, including a responsive environment
Selects appropriate instructional materials and activities by means of which to approach the study	Designs both long-term and immediate plans for the children, including specific daily lesson plans

2. The choice of teaching techniques is dictated by the nature of the learner—his background of musical knowledge and experience, his age, his physical qualities, and all the influences which have brought him to his present state of being. The teacher, therefore, is a constant student of children, observing and analyzing each of them for clues he uses in order to select or create appropriate strategies of teaching.

3. Plan for children to approach music by using all of the appropriate senses—ear, eye, and tactile.

4. The range of musical interests, aptitudes, skills, and knowledge is so great at any given grade level or age that non-graded plans of school organization present few new problems to the teacher who has been aware of students' individual differences and who has been providing for them in his grade level planning.

5. An effective concept of team teaching is one in which the classroom teacher and the music specialist plan and work together for the good of the children.

INQUIRY AND SUGGESTED ACTIVITIES

1. How might a predetermined scope and sequence in music be a disadvantage to a teacher? How might it be an advantage?
2. Explain by example the difference between a fact, a concept, and a generalization in music. How are they related?
3. What is meant by the structure of a subject?
4. Evaluate this statement: "We have a wonderful music teaching guide in our school; it tells the teacher exactly what to do each day."
5. How might a sequence of music study that is well-organized in terms of subject matter fail to be sequential for a learner?
6. What are the advantages and disadvantages of a national curriculum in music?
7. It was pointed out that when a teacher follows a lesson plan, he will teach toward many goals other than those stated in the generalizations and behavioral objectives. Re-read the Lesson Plan for Second or Third Grade to find the place where the teacher works to *extend* the singing skill of the "less certain" singers. What other unwritten goals might a teacher work toward in a lesson?
8. Analyze the types of questions the teacher asks in the Lesson Plan for Second or Third Grade.
9. Read *Preparing Instructional Objectives* by Robert F. Mager; then formulate behavioral objectives for the teaching of a musical concept.
10. Select three or four concepts or a concept cluster from the Suggested Structure of Music Outline. Show how you would develop these in a teaching plan. Follow the procedure suggested in this chapter. Do the same with a selected generalization.
11. Plan what you believe to be an effective and desirable music program for ages 5–12. Consider all the elements of music. Discuss your formulated program with others.
12. Examine the music curriculum guides used in the school system nearest you and appraise the suggested music learnings for each age and perfor-

mance level. Compare these suggested learnings with those in a guide from another school system. How might these be improved to meet the musical needs and conditions in your area?

13. Examine a music course of study used in a nearby school system to answer the following questions:

> What musical content, facts, concepts and generalizations are stated or suggested?
>
> Do you find serious omissions?
>
> What suggestions are made for the spiral development of key ideas and concepts?
>
> Are objectives stated in behavioral or general terms?
>
> What teaching strategies, types of questions and methods of inquiry are listed?
>
> What musical skills and abilities are indicated?
>
> What musical attitudes, appreciations, habits, and values are encouraged?

14. Role play planning for music learning at the national, state, local community, school and classroom level. A class committee can represent each level and explore aspects of curriculum and planning. The types of planning at each level are to be identified, and the interrelation of all of the levels is to be explored and demonstrated.

15. Relate the approach presented in *The Study of Music in the Elementary School: A Conceptual Approach* (MENC, 1967), with the Structure of Music Outline of this chapter.

16. Analyze the Structure of Music Outline and revise it to suit your purposes. Add or delete generalizations, sub-generalizations, and concepts, or reword them. Determine how you will use this suggested structure in teaching the elements of music.

17. In the history of United States music education, whenever teachers have concentrated exclusively on facts about music rather than on the beauty and the satisfactions of music, children's appreciation of this subject has declined. How can teachers prevent this negative development and still utilize the conceptual approach?

18. After learning the types of lesson plans presented in this chapter, study those in *New Approaches to Music in the Elementary School,* by Lois Raebeck and Lawrence Wheeler, Wm. C. Brown Publishers, Dubuque, Iowa, 1964, *Musical Growth in the Elementary School,* by Bjornar Bergethon and Eunice Boardman, Holt, Rinehart and Winston, Inc., 1963, and the implications for lesson plans in *The Study of Music in the Elementary School: A Conceptual Approach,* Music Educators National Conference, 1967. Explore the following features of these plans:

> Objectives
>
> Relation to the structure of music
>
> Learning music skills
>
> Relations to attitudes, feelings, and values (humanizing music)

Keeping the learner active
Intrinsic motivation
Extrinsic motivation
Facts, concepts, and generalizations
Teacher's questions
Provision for individual differences
Grouping
Evaluation

These books can be useful as sources of ideas for your lesson plans. *Be sure* to refer to listed activities near the end of chapters 8–13 in this book which help the learner in skill and concept development.

19. If possible, prepare a three-minute lesson in which one music concept is introduced and taught. Video-tape it and present it to the class for an impersonal analysis.

REFERENCES

BRUNER, JEROME, *The Process of Education.* Cambridge, Mass., Harvard University Press, 1961.

———, *Toward a Theory of Instruction.* Cambridge, Mass., Harvard University Press, 1966.

GAINES, JOAN, *Approaches to Public Relations for the Music Educator,* Music Educators National Conference, Washington, D.C., 1968.

GARY, CHARLES L., ED., *The Study of Music in the Elementary School: A Conceptual Approach.* Music Educators National Conference, Washington, D.C., 1967.

GROISSER, PHILIP, *How to Use the Fine Art of Questioning.* Englewood Cliffs, New Jersey, Prentice-Hall Education Series, Teachers' Practical Press, 1964.

HABERMEN, MARTIN, "Behavioral Objectives: Bandwagon or Breakthrough?" *The Journal of Teacher Education,* XIX, No. 1 (1968), 91.

HILGARD, ERNEST R., ED., *Theories of Learning and Instruction.* Chicago, University of Chicago Press, 1964. The 63rd Yearbook of the National Society for the Study of Education.

HITCHCOCK, CURTICE, *The Way Teaching Is.* Washington, D.C., Association for Supervision and Curriculum Development, 1966.

JOYCE, BRUCE R., *Strategies for Elementary Social Science Education.* Chicago, Science Research Associates, Inc., 1965.

———, *The Structure of Teaching.* Chicago, Science Research Associates, 1967.

LOS ANGELES SCHOOLS, "A Scope and Sequence Chart of Conceptual Learnings Related to the Elements of Music." See Appendix A.

MACDONALD, JAMES, ED., *Theories of Instruction,* Association for Supervision and Curriculum Development, Washington, D.C., 1965.

MAGER, ROBERT F., *Preparing Instructional Objectives*. Palo Alto, Calif., Fearon Publishers, 1962.

SANDERS, NORRIS, *Classroom Questions: What Kinds?* New York, Harper & Row, 1966.

SHUMSKY, ABRAHAM, *Creative Teaching in the Elementary School*. New York, Appleton-Century-Crofts, 1965. Chapters 2, 3, 4, and 9.

SMITH, JAMES A., *Creative Teaching of the Creative Arts in the Elementary School*. Boston, Mass., Allyn and Bacon, Inc., 1967.

TABA, HILDA, *Teacher's Handbook for Elementary Social Studies*. Palo Alto, Calif., Addison-Wesley Publishing Company, 1969.

*The possibilities of using new and different technology
in teaching music creatively are limited only by the teachers'
imagination and willingness to keep up to date.*

From Music in American Society, *an interpretive report of the Tanglewood
Symposium. Music Educators National Conference, 1968, p. 53.*

7

instructional media and the differentiated staff

The provision and selection of instructional materials are of greater importance in the new music education than in music education of previous years because music teaching today is organized around concepts and main ideas, rather than around music activities and skills. When music is concerned with these concepts or main ideas, instructional materials are selected and provided that support this type of course content. Thus, such materials become a part of the learning process.

It is necessary that the teacher understand the use of the many types of instructional materials available. Some are old and familiar; others may be new and strange. An important responsibility of the music teacher is his continuous search for more appropriate, better organized, and more authentic instructional materials.

The school environment should provide rich sources of musical data which the children will be helped to analyze. While some aspects of performance and composition can be studied from real life examples, many aspects of music must be studied from indirect means provided by materials—books, recordings, pictures, video tapes and films. Some of these should lead directly into the music used by all socio-economic groups living within the community. Some should provide information about music of the past and the music of distant cultures. It is important that children know music as it exists in the world about them; it is also important that they know about man's relation to music in the past and man's uses of music in distant places.

The first requirement of instructional media is that the material provide authentic information about the most significant aspects of the subject of music. In addition, the material must supply data that is organized in a way that promotes the building of concepts that explain or solve musical problems. The order in which teachers make materials available to children is important. The folk music of Japan may be followed by folk music of Hungary because the contrast is likely to stimulate the building of useful concepts regarding scale, rhythm, meter, and dynamics. Children's books about music should be examined for their conceptual content. Materials that are useful and interesting to children are then combined with teaching strategies which assist children to interpret data, construct concepts, and further their inquiry into music. This requires a rich supply of materials of instruction in order to accommodate the learning of each individual. Much of this can be collected, created, and written by teachers.

Teachers can ask themselves questions such as:

What specific purposes can be served by the use of this item or equipment?
What facts, concepts, or generalizations can the children gain from it?
How does it affect values, attitudes, interests, and appreciations?
How does it assist in developing the children's ability to do research, discuss music intelligently, and solve their musical problems?

Joyce emphasizes two important purposes to consider in the selection and use of all instructional materials:

Instructional materials have two purposes. One is to give children access to data. The other is to draw meaning from data. These two operations cannot, in practice, be separated effectively. It is clearly insufficient to present children with data (teach them the "facts") and conclude teaching at that point. [At the same time] it is clearly impossible for children to develop organizing concepts and methods of inquiry without dealing with data.[1]

---

[1] Bruce R. Joyce, *Strategies for Elementary Social Science Education* (Chicago: Science Research Associates, Inc., 1965), p. 192.

The new view of the classroom is that it is a laboratory where children use equipment and materials which stimulate their learning. The teacher selects various media to focus upon facts, problems, or explorations taking place. Depending upon what is under consideration at the time, he chooses pictures, maps, musical instruments, notated examples, charts, tapes, recordings, exhibits, films, filmstrips, and materials on bulletin, magnetic, and chalk boards to assist children's thinking. Books, field trips, and other resources and activities could follow. For example, if a sixth grade decided to expand its generalization, "Many individuals and groups have contributed to the development of music in the United States," the following order of activities may take place:

1. Identify and list the major types of music found in the United States; list types of musical contributions and the people and country making contributions to the music of the United States; then group these types from the list and label them. Classifications, lists, and groupings will vary in direct relation to the points of emphasis chosen as well as the frame of reference, or point of view, of both teacher and students.

2. A large retrieval chart could accommodate major contributions to American music and these could be listed as the students find them. Information from this chart is used as a basis for formulating concepts and generalizations.

3. Notebooks could be kept by each child. It is much better for the students to decide that a notebook is an effective and convenient means of organizing data than to make it a requirement.

4. Direct the students to library resources concerned with the generalization. Some music books written for junior high school may be helpful.

5. Provide films and filmstrips dealing with the problem.

6. The class could contribute to files of pertinent newspaper and magazine articles and of pictures concerning important men and women in American music.

7. Consider uses of radio and television.

8. Utilize recordings of American music. Students could select examples they consider important, and explain why.

9. A dramatized musical event or events important in the history of American music can be considered; American music of significance can be performed.

10. Individualized reading can be done by members of the class concerned with the contributions of various nations and races to American music.

11. Invite parents or other adults from the community or older students to perform American folk music; the students may try to trace its origins.

12. Students summarize their findings and formulate the generalization again, basing it on their new data.

COMMUNITY RESOURCES

The school and the children in it are extensions of the community; thus the community is a laboratory for the examination of and inquiry into music in the lives of the local people. What adults and young people are doing with music in the community can be logically incorporated into music instruction in the classroom. Field trips can be made to museums, concerts, and rehearsals of community music groups; observations can be made of youth and adult music classes, and study groups which are now part of the expanding area of education sponsored by colleges, school systems, and park boards. When field trips are made, the particular aspect of music under study is usually well advanced. By that time the children should have found questions to be answered and information to seek which can be supplied by the field trip. An exception, of course, is when the purpose of a field trip is to stimulate curiosity and raise questions to be studied and solved later. Surveys can be made in the community to answer problems uncovered by the children.

Parents who are musicians, adults and young people of various cultural origins, and other musicians in the community, as well as older students, can answer students' questions, speak to and perform for the school class. Children should plan questions to ask in advance of their appearance; they should help plan any out-of-school trip in terms of its capacity to supply them with data and its assistance in the solution of their musical problems; they should know what questions the trip is likely to answer. Following the trip the data should be assembled, organized, and applied to whatever problem is under study.

Community performing groups can present programs for combined classes of children. There must be careful preparation for such events. (See Chapter 18, *Performances.*)

AUDIO-VISUAL RESOURCES

Among the instructional materials are tangible items—musical instruments, models of bands and orchestras, and art objects which concern music. Children should be allowed to handle such objects. However, if they are fragile, they should be demonstrated by someone who knows how to manipulate them with proper care. They should be used in relation to specific problems that arise in the study of music, not as entertaining objects. They could be used, for example, in relation to a visit to a concert or rehearsal of an instrumental group. The bell set is a very useful audio-visual aid; it sounds pitches and the learner can observe relationships between the bars, their arrangement, as well as concepts of pitch, high and low, scales, sharps and flats, and intervals.

This type of instructional material should be used to advance inquiry in music. The above objects, and those similar to them, should be accompanied by related books, pictures, films, and resource people. Teachers and children look for additional materials whenever an unexpected need arises. Observations and comparisons are vital to inquiry.

Teachers sometimes find it difficult to conceive of simple objects— water bottles, water glasses, small tunable drums, other types of drums, the piano keys and mechanism—as audio-visual equipment. Children need to examine sound-producing objects in order to learn about music in a personal and direct way. While instruments and equipment should not be abused, neither should they be so protected from possible abuse that children cannot utilize them in musical learning. Even though risk of damage is always present, to fail to let children handle instruments and to experiment with them is to fail to provide a challenging and responsive learning environment. There are some commercial items for experimenting with sound, among them being the Musikits and Soundkits made by Peripole, Inc., 51–17 Rockaway Beach Boulevard, Far Rockaway, New York 11691.

FILM AND FILMSTRIPS

To use motion pictures effectively, teachers preview them carefully, selecting them in accordance with the needs and problems of the class. A good film is authentic, up-to-date, and on the child's level of comprehension. The best current source for music educators is the 1968 edition of the *Film Guide for Music Educators,* by Donald J. Shetler, published by the Music Educators National Conference, 1201 Sixteenth Street, Washington, D. C. It is a selective and classified annotated listing of value.

Films are selected to contribute to the concepts, generalizations and objectives toward which the children are working. Teachers should be aware of any places in a film where there are difficult ideas which will require additional explanation, and provide for these. Prior to the showing of a film, a teacher might ask, "What do you think a film of this title might tell us?" and list the ideas the children present. This assists them to search actively for ideas they hope to find expressed or explained in the film. After the showing, the teacher will ask if the film showed them what they hoped for, and if it did not, what it did reveal to them. In all of this, teachers' questions are to guide the children's thinking toward the ideas, concepts, and generalizations of most significance. Some specific suggestions for how to use films follow:

A. Purpose: to acquire information to be generalized.
    1. "What did you learn from this film that interested you?"
        Technique: An open question followed by listing of information.
    2. "What do we have listed about melody and form?" "How do these items relate to each other?" "How is this information related to what we know about rhythm?"
        Technique: Relate points of information to each other and to what the learners know about other elements of music.
    3. "Can we state this in a way that makes clear what the relationship is?"
        Technique: Try to draw a generalization from the class.
    4. "Can we combine all that we know about melody, rhythm, and form into a statement that relates to all the other elements of music?"
        Technique: Try to combine sub-generalizations into one broad generalization.

B. Purpose: to verify generalizations developed earlier.
    1. What did we find in the film that would indicate to us that our sentence relating melody and form is true or not true?
    2. Continue this process of verification and clarification with other earlier developed generalizations.

C. Purpose: to test generalizations developed earlier.
    1. Show a film of a new, but related musical experience.
    2. "If we were to visit this country and listen to its music, what would we expect to hear?"

D. Purpose: To acquire specific data.
    1. "As we watch this film, let's find as many new ideas as we can about melody and form."
    2. List data and incorporate it into charts for later study.

An important newer use of films for individual instruction is the three-to-ten minute 8 mm cartridge which the learner injects into a specially-designed projector. Children of all school ages can operate these machines. In the viewing and listening center a student or a small group of students may view 8 mm single concept films or 35 mm filmstrips. Filmstrips accompanied with recorded sound may be viewed while listening to the recorded commentary or music related to the film. Teachers should carefully select and guide children in selecting filmstrips that are pertinent.

Filmstrips are made by many companies; the Jam Handy Organization, Bowmar Records, and the Society for Visual Education produce sound filmstrips concerned with music stories, music fundamentals, composers, and instruments of the orchestra. Filmstrips can also be made by teachers with a 35 mm camera and the assistance of either a school audio-visual expert or advice from a photography supply house. They are rather inexpensive, are easy to store, and convenient to use. Some purposes will require only a few frames, while others will use the entire filmstrip.

Schools having closed circuit television with taping facilities can video-tape important musical events and replay them in the classroom for further analysis and discussion.

PICTURES, SLIDES, AND TRANSPARENCIES

As in the instance of recordings, the concept of "picture" has grown to include pictures in books, magazines, and newspapers; pictures are projected on a screen in order to enlarge them and make group study of them possible. Posters and charts, pictures of instruments are obtained from a fairly large number of commercial sources—one free source being the attractive catalogs of musical instrument manufacturers. Opaque projections of pages in a book, pictures, drawings, single copies of songs, scores, can be used in a darkened room. The opaque projector is the one device that will make it possible for a class to examine their notated compositions without the teacher having to make transparencies of them.

With the aid of an overhead projector and a sheet of transparent plastic, music teachers or students can face the class while drawing music notation to illustrate a problem at hand. To project a creative production or to present parts of the entire song, they can point to notation or pictures on transparencies as they are shown on the screen. By making overlays, they can add notation to a musical score or sections of the orcherstra one by one until the full orcherstra is shown. Because rooms need not be darkened, and the student or teacher can face the class while referring to the transparency, overhead projectors are easy to use and they serve to "focus" the attention of the class. Care should be taken to place the screen high so that no "machinery" blocks the view of any child, and to slant the screen so that the bottom is farther from the projector than the top.

Among the uses of overhead transparencies are showing illustrations of conducting patterns, themes of symphonic works, drawings or pictures of instruments, building triads and their inversions, comparing different scales, notes, beats and rests. A teacher can plan a review of music fundamentals with the use of overlays; he first shows the staff, then adds leger lines, then names of lines and spaces, clef signs, and the grand staff. It is much easier to show this with overlay transparencies than by means of a chalkboard. The musical themes for Bowmar Orchestral Library Series 3 are now presented compactly on one cell to be flashed on a screen. Teaching is becoming more and more screen-centered.

Spirit-transparency masters are available which are both masters for duplicating machines and transparencies for overhead projection. Teachers can make transparencies from pictures which are on clay-coated paper with clear sheets of acetate and a waterproof adhesive. A thermal copying machine can produce a transparency in four seconds. Many packets of transparencies are now available commercially (Tecnifax Corporation, Holyoke, Massachusetts, and Educom, Box 388, Mount Kisco, New York 10549 being among the sources for music education).

Slides are convenient to use and to store. Many are produced commercially or teachers may produce their own. The 35 mm single-lens reflex camera is well suited for school use. A 35 mm slide-copying device is available which can duplicate slides or filmstrips, make filmstrips from slides, add titles and textures, correct color balance and compensate for errors in exposure. Recent improvements in equipment can add motion to specially prepared slides, and two projectors coupled with dissolve control can eliminate the dark interval between slide changes. Companies such as Multiplex (Warne and Carter Avenues, St. Louis, Missouri 63107) make special cabinets in which to organize and store slides. Modern equipment makes it possible to produce on a slide anything produced for filmstrips. Collections of slides can easily be organized for the use of both classroom teaching and individual research.

Bulletin boards, which can be considered an extension of the picture idea, are highly interesting to children if they are attractively arranged, changed frequently, and are pertinent to either the study at hand or to continuing concerns. They should create interest in aspects of music, contain an element of challenge which stimulates students to question, hypothesize, analyze and infer. Teachers do not arrange all bulletin boards; the children should be involved in planning and arranging some of them.

Music teachers use flannel and magnetic boards largely to make it easy for children to see notation clearly, to "write" notation with ease, and to experience notation kinesthetically. It is easier and much quicker to place a felt note or a metal magnet on a staff than to draw a good-looking note. Furthermore, if the note is placed in the wrong position, no one need erase it.

The ever-present chalkboard is almost too commonplace to mention. However, it is one of the most accessible and effective visual aids when properly used. It is very useful as a place to list instructions, such as the page numbers of the textbook the class will use, which saves the teacher much repetition and serves to increase efficiency. It is useful when the teacher finds it necessary to present something in notation which is spontaneous to the situation and for which no chart or other illustration could have been prepared. Students illustrate, write words and notation on the chalkboard as they create, analyze, demonstrate and explain music. Room lighting should be adjusted so that there is no glare; the teacher should write legibly, and high enough on the board so that every child can read what is written.

RADIO AND TELEVISION

A marked advantage of these media is that they can place real events in the classroom as they occur. Also, programs can be recorded on tape, video tape, or film for future use. Outstanding musicians can be brought into the classroom with these media. Schools which have closed circuit television equipment can show commercial programs recorded on video tape when these are suitable. The teacher's responsibility includes identifying the programs suited for classroom use and those suited for individual viewing at home. School systems often supply program guides; other sources of programs include newspapers, magazines, TV guides, and special music publications such as *Young Keyboard Junior* (1346 Chapel Street, New Haven, Connecticut 06511), which relates some of its content to forthcoming television programs. Fellow teachers and audio-visual directors can assist the new teacher in identifying programs that have been used with success. Many of the better programs are scheduled for weekends and evenings. This implies some form of organization in which children are encouraged to listen to them, either alone or in small groups of neighboring children in the home, and to report back to the class what they found interesting and valuable. This class discussion stimulates other children to plan to listen to future presentations. In preparation for these programs, certain skills in listening and viewing should be reviewed. First, there should be a clear purpose for listening. Second, during the listening, the learner demonstrates critical attentiveness. Eyes should be on the television or radio set; pencil and paper should be ready for note-taking; questions should be stated for the class discussion to follow; the listener should be prepared to question and to comment on the points brought up in class; and to seek data to substantiate his agreement or disagreement with them; ideas and concepts that are discovered or changed by the experience should be noted.

The most successful televised music programs have dealt with rhythm in the primary grades and music appreciation in the intermediate grades. Because children learn from good models, television obviously possesses great potential for certain types of music instruction. Some schools have weekly television programs as a part of the general music program. In this way a skilled music specialist can be seen and heard in many classrooms simultaneously. The room teachers are expected to prepare for each telecast in advance—usually following the directions given in a teacher's guide—and to continue teaching each day what is initiated in the lesson presented by the specialist. It should be remembered that these television programs are *not* meant to be substitutes for the regular music program. The room teacher bears the primary responsibility because he is the only teacher who can plan a music program for each student and the only teacher who can assist each student. The best type of television lesson is one which presents those aspects of music which cannot normally be a part of daily classroom lessons. Elaine Shakely, a music specialist who produced a television series for grades four, five and six describes such lessons:

> We were told that we should bring lessons into the classroom which the teacher would not have available. I accepted the challenge and planned lessons using a lute, viola da gamba, a natural trumpet, an interview with Henry Mancini, a lesson on the history of the guitar, the history of ballet, the bell choir, the harpsichord, the organ, and many others. I called on many fine friends who are professional musicians to help me present these

programs and the response was overwhelming. I, in my heart, knew that these programs would stretch the children in their music horizons yet I never felt the material was beyond their grasp.

Mrs. Shakely lists other television lessons based on subjects such as a child prodigy, a concert flutist, a university professor and some of his talented students, a four year old violinist who is learning by means of the Suzuki method, children performing on instruments designed by Carl Orff, an operetta written by elementary school children, original songs written by children, and a sixth-grade folk singer who writes her own music. She adds: "When the teacher has sufficient interest to prepare the children, the results are positive. When she . . . lets the children plunge into the lesson without a word of explanation, the results are negative."[2]

Examples of part of a television series teacher's guide follow. The need to be met is one the teachers could not manage for themselves—how to initiate the composition of electronic music in sixth grade. The video tapes of programs like these are the most widely used by music teachers in the school systems which produce them because television is supplying information and assistance of types that cannot normally be expected of the room teacher.

LESSON 28[3]

Focus

Creating electronic music by altering the sound of the human voice.

Objective

At the end of this lesson the students should be able to:

Work with the voice through song, poetry, and chant as a source for creating electronic sounds.

Before the Telecast

Chant a simple poem such as MARY HAD A LITTLE LAMB.

Have the students clap the rhythm of the poem.

Discuss what happens to the sound when a 78 speed recording is played on 33 1/3 speed on the phonograph.

[2] Elaine M. Shakely, "Television Teaching," *Phi Delta Gamma Journal* (June, 1966), p. 50.

[3] By permission of the Eugene Public Schools, Eugene, Oregon.

Telecast

We will sing a familiar song and manipulate it electronically to create new sounds.

Song: familiar folk song such as MICHAEL, ROW THE BOAT ASHORE

Follow-up

1. Listen to examples of electronic music on recordings:
   a. The Lane County IMC has available for teachers in the Cooperative districts the recording and tape of the Bell Telephone: COMPUTER SPEECH: HE SAW THE CAT. It includes examples of synthesized speech and one computer singing BICYCLE BUILT FOR TWO accompanied by another computer with a brief explanation of how this is done.
   b. RUSTY IN ORCHESTRAVILLE, Capitol Records, is another recording that can be used to show an example of an electronic voice imitating the characteristics of the instruments of the orchestra. The talking and singing is by Sonovox.
   c. Have the children identify television commercials, science-fiction movies and other telecasts that use electronic sounds.
   d. As other examples of electronic music, try to secure the records:
      THE SCIENCE OF SOUND—Folkways FX6007
      MUSIC FROM MATHEMATICS—Decca DL9103
      SCIENCE FICTION SOUND EFFECTS—Folkways FX6250

2. Try making electronic music in your classroom.
   a. Make a tape loop by following these simple steps:
      Record the human voice. Nursery rhymes, chants, and simple songs could be the sound source.
      Cut a segment approximately 12″ to 20″ in length of this recorded sound and splice the segment together. (Be sure to use splicing tape on the shiny side so that no pop will occur in the sound.)
   b. Thread the recorder as usual except for going around the reels, and play the tape loop. It may be necessary to hold the tape taut by letting it pass around your finger. The same sound will repeat over and over creating an ostinato (repeated pattern.). Try playing the loop at different speeds.
   c. Create another tape loop and using two recorders play the two loops simultaneously while recording this sound on a third tape recorder. This is called "mixing the sounds."
   d. After having taped and manipulated many sounds such as human voice, instruments, natural sounds (door slamming, etc.), splice these products together in any sequence to create an original complete electronic composition.

3. Electronic experimentation is probably most successful when done individually or in a small group. After introducing the above techniques to the students, allow them to work independently to develop their own compositions.

LESSON 29

Focus

Electronic music altering sounds of instruments and sounds of nature.

Objective

At the end of this lesson the students should be able to:

Work with instruments and other sound sources to create an original electronic music composition.

Before the Telecast

Review the results of the preceding lesson: Altering the sound of the human voice.

Discuss how the same techniques could be used to alter other sounds.

Telecast

We will continue our study into altering sounds electronically using materials other than the human voice. We hope to investigate how to *complete* an electronic music composition.

Follow-up

1. Listen to Electronic Compositions: one source, series book recordings:

   a. LEILYA AND THE POET, Halim El-Dabh

   Note that the composer used the three sound sources described in the follow-up activity #2-d of lesson 28.

   b. STEREO ELECTRONIC MUSIC NO. 1, Bulent Arel

   Note that the sound source for this composition is completely electronic.

   c. COMPOSITION FOR SYNTHESIZER, Milton Babbitt

   Note that this composition was created using the RCA Electronic Sound Synthesizer. Using a machine such as this, the composer had to continually keep in mind the aural limitations of the listener.

2. Try making electronic music in your classroom:

   a. Make a tape loop like that described in the follow-up activity #2-a of lesson 28. Woodblocks and cymbals can be used to produce the sound. Try running the recorder at different speeds.

Turn the tape over and listen to the sounds backwards. This activity will require a full-track tape recorder—or record the same sounds on both half-tracks, then play it backwards.

b. Semi-conductors can be used by shading them from light with the hand to change the pitch level. This is an example of transistors and tubes producing the tone as contrasted with microphone-recorded actual sounds such as: laughter, clapping, musical instruments, sounds of nature. The semi-conductors will be available through the Lane County IMC for teachers in the Cooperative ITV Project.

c. If one of your students plays the electric guitar, it would be of interest to your students to listen to the sound produced by using the echo chamber of the amplifier when strumming the guitar.

3. A point of interest: When you listen to a record, the sounds are being communicated by vibrations of the cone in the speaker of the record player, consequently this sound is being produced by electronic means.

4. For further study, refer to series book p. 186–190.

RECORDINGS

The concept of recordings has broadened considerably in recent years. Whereas it once meant a disc record placed on a record player, today it may mean a tape recording, either commercial or teacher-made. While the disc record is certainly useful, many teachers find that taping the parts of long musical selections they wish to use in class is far easier and more efficient than hunting for the right spot to place the needle on a micro-groove record. Furthermore, micro-groove records can be damaged by such needle placement unless the player is equipped with a special counter-balanced tone arm which can be operated manually to lower very gently. Also, the tape recorder and video tapes can be used as an immediate play-back of classroom performance; this is a very important study tool and motivator to improve the quality of performance. Another use is for accompaniments that can be taped for classroom or rehearsal purposes. Programs for radio or television broadcasts can be taped, as can programs for exchange between classrooms in the same school— or even with classrooms abroad. A child can tape record his own performance, listen to it, analyze what he hears, record the performance again, compare it with the first one, and find ways to improve his performing ability. Tapes can be used in listening centers having earphones in the same ways disc recordings are commonly used. Children in upper grades are composing electronic music by using two stereophonic tape recorders, sometimes with a tone generator. Such taped music can be played for classes, the music explained by the young composers, and the compositions analyzed critically by the students.

Tape cartridges can be played by children of any school age on the appropriate machine.

The disc recording should not be underestimated, however. Recent improvements in recording, such as exemplified in the Bowmar Orchestral Library Series III, include groove spreads which enable the teacher or student to pin-point the location of certain important sections or themes without interrupting the music. Recordings are a part of every music series, and commonly provide many different types of accompaniments for songs, music for analysis, and music for rhythmic responses. An advantage of some of the series is that the voices on the recordings are of every type and age, from young child to adult, providing both variety and a study of the human voice at all stages of development. Besides the recordings which are part of the textbook series, RCA Victor offers two popular basic collections, The Basic Record Library for Elementary Schools and Adventures in Music. Bowmar offers three sets of orchestral recordings. There are sets of recordings for use in rhythmic development. These and other collections and individual discs are listed elsewhere in this book. Records for the study of music of other cultures are found from sources such as Folkways Records and the Columbia World Library of Folk and Primitive Music.

PROGRAMED INSTRUCTION

In the elementary school the trend in programed instruction is toward short programs to be used by any student who needs its content. While little is available currently in music, it can be predicted with confidence that types of "learning packages" will soon be on the market. Centers for the development and distribution of teacher-made programs of this short type are being formed on a cooperative basis. They are also being encouraged by a number of state departments of education. In the experimental-development stage in music today, they may be commonplace within a few years. The goal is for the teacher to have access to a large number of these programs, and when any child has need for an appropriate one, the teacher will make it available to him to use. Some of these are short versions of workbooks, containing all their advantages and disadvantages. One of the problems is how to build elements into these programs that will further the development of inductive and creative thinking, making them interesting and challenging to children. If they aid in providing for individual differences in a creative way, they can become a very powerful force in the betterment of music education.

Packages which include recordings, a teacher's manual, and a student's book are appearing in increasing numbers. One publisher has this equipment for grades two through six, with only grade one lacking a "workbook" for each child. Teachers must decide if such programed instruction is only the old lock-step workbook in new garb, whether it is suitable for the individual learner, and whether it provides for individual differences or only for differences in the rate of learning. One can assume that the best of the learning packages will assist greatly in the acquisition of data. Some commercial booklets for students are written to assist in learning to listen to great works of music. Obviously with the virtual flood of materials, both old and new, college classes and workshops dealing with the evaluation of instructional media become more necessary each year.

Laurence Siegel explains the position of the teacher in relation to television and automated instruction:

> Contrary to the view held in some quarters, that televised teaching and automated instruction are techniques for coping with education's quantitative problems, such devices and techniques will probably find their most significant applications in helping effect qualitative improvements.

> Now that teachers' fears about 'technological unemployment' are largely dispelled, the teacher can be envisioned as a learning-resources specialist. In this role he will identify each student's level of attainment and cognitive development, establishing legitimate goals for that student, and select from the full armamentarium of instructional aids (including books, seminars, televised lectures, programed courses, and the like) those that are best calculated to help *that* learner reach his goals.[4]

CHARTS

Charts have been an important item of equipment since the beginning of music education in the schools of the United States. Lowell Mason (1792–1872) designed, used, and sold a large number of charts for use

---

[4] Laurence Siegel, ed., "Integration and Reactions," *Instruction: Some Contemporary Viewpoints* (Chandler Publishing Co., San Francisco, 1967), pp. 332–33.

by adult singing schools and by school classes. Today we find them in the materials of Mary Helen Richards, Howard Doolin, Bowmar Records, and the music series. In wider use than any of these are charts teachers make for their own specific purposes to assist children's learning. The following examples are self-explanatory.

Where is the half-step?
G   A   B – C
So   La   Ti – Do
5   6   7 – 8

NOTES CAN MOVE

UP

DOWN

or
STAY THE SAME

G	do	C	F
F♯	ti	B	E
E	la	A	D
D	so	G	C
C	fa	F	B♭
B	mi	E	A
A	re	D	G
G	do	C	F

Find these scales on the bells and play them.
How do they relate to the syllables?
Find the I-chord in each scale (do mi so).
Where is the V-chord (so ti re)?

When teachers make charts consisting of notation, they should take care to write the notation so that the viewer sees clearly where the beats fall. The following examples illustrate the wrong and right ways to do this. Each measure should occupy the same space regardless of the number of notes, and each beat should be lined up vertically.

MUSIC SERIES BOOKS

The elementary school music textbooks have been standard equipment for many years; they are commonly called "music series" books. In order for children and teachers to have sufficient materials for selection, each classroom in grades two through six should have a minimum of two different series books from which to seek appropriate songs and other information. Because there are now eight or nine publishers with competing music textbooks, there is more opportunity today to select books that are well suited to the particular school district. At the same time, the content of the books and their sequence of materials should be reasonably consistent with the guides and handbooks of the state department of education in the state in which the school system is located. The content should be meaningful in terms of pupil needs, experience, interests, and understandings, and the sequence of materials should be consistent with the findings of recent research in child growth and development, accepted instructional techniques, and validity of content. Organization of content based on conceptual design will be a favorable factor. Another favorable factor is a multi-ethnic treatment which adequately reflects intercultural music and the achievements and contributions of the minority groups which have contributed to the development and evolution of the United States and its music.

The textbooks should make provision for the many individual differences to be found in children's musical interests and capacities. The music should possess intrinsic value; it should provide many clear examples of and relationships to the facts, concepts, and generalizations of the study of music. The words of songs should portray literary merit, be of interest to and understood by the children of the level for which they are used; the text and the musical phrase should coincide. The range should be varied in order to provide for both high and low voices, with many songs in medium range.

Because music series books are multi-purpose books, they are expected to include songs for rote singing, for reading notation, which contain tonal and rhythmic patterns, employ instruments to teach musical concepts, develop ability to hear and sing parts, provide special helps for uncertain singers, provide chants and ostinatos, have lower-range parts for some of the older boys, employ instrumental accompaniments, contain songs for the general repertory, folk songs of many countries, songs and thematic material by recognized composers (both past and contemporary), songs with foreign language words, and songs that are seasonal. There should also be rounds and canons, and adequate number of harmonic part songs, and some songs related to other areas of the curriculum. Songs with irregular phrase structure, modal tonalities, unmeasured or unusual meters, and with contemporary characteristics should also be present.

On pages of the children's books should be found informative material relative to songs, instruments, and musical concepts, questions and suggestions directed to the child to stimulate his thinking about music. Both cyclical and sequential plans of learning should be clearly revealed through the series.

The teacher's book should incorporate clear helpful suggestions for teaching each song; simple piano accompaniments should be provided. Recordings of many of the songs should be included. These should employ many types of voices, both child and adult, and many different examples of instrumental accompaniments. The accompaniments should reflect the character of the songs, and be accurate in tone quality, pitch, tempo, diction, and phrasing.

The illustrations should serve the understanding of the song or the development of musical concepts; they should not interfere with the comprehension of the notation either by their content or their color.

There may be as many as three indexes: alphabetical, classified, and music learning. Music should be well spaced on the page without crowding, usually with the length of the staff corresponding to the length of the phrase. Staff, piano keyboard, and Autoharp charts should be printed in the pupil's text. The books should contain suggestions for listening to recordings; these will include themes from some of the great works of music.

The books should contain suggestions for children's compositions, for making up descants, chants, and ostinatos, for rhythmic body movements, for dramatizing songs, for playing simple instruments, for writing simple instrumental orchestrations, and for ear training games.

State departments of education often provide helpful criteria to school personnel involved with textbook selection. Children can assist by reading comparable sections of textbooks, then giving the teacher their reactions and the reasons for them.

SCHOOL RESOURCE PERSONNEL: THE DIFFERENTIATED STAFF

The concept of the differentiated staff includes not only the assignment of teachers to various levels of responsibility but the inclusion of modifications of team teaching to include teacher aides—the paraprofessional staff member who works alongside the professional teacher and under his direction. For example, the instructional staff in a given situation could include a music consultant, a classroom teacher, two interns or student teachers, and two teacher aides. The interns are elementary or music education majors who are learning to teach, and the aides may be qualified parents or other adults from the community who are interested in assisting in music instruction. High school students who plan to be music teachers may also be involved as another type of aide. These interns and aides work under the supervision of the professional instructional team in types of teaching responsibilities or in an instructional center providing music materials.

While certain kinds of teaching are done only by the professionals, all these resource persons cooperate in certain teaching roles. The paraprofessionals also assist in making the general educational environment attractive and efficient, in setting up the necessary equipment, and in moving students. The personnel of various instructional centers or laboratories can be considered as extended members of the team of school resource persons.

Resource Laboratories

THE COMPUTER CENTER

At the present time such centers serve approximately twenty instructional teams. They are staffed by experts in computer-assisted instruction with assisting paraprofessionals. Objective tests can be scored with extreme speed, thus saving enormous amounts of teacher time, thereby encouraging teachers to test more freely. Other activities include automating programed materials and adapting them for local purposes. The use of the computer in organizing modular (flexible) scheduling is well known.

> The computer has a vast array of usages: computer-assisted instruction (an extension of programed instruction), information storage and retrieval, and sound synthesis. Computer-assisted instruction involves the use of a computer with some other type of mechanical teaching procedure. The huge information-processing capacity of computers allows them to adapt mechanical teaching routines to the needs and past performance of the individual student, who may then study, learn, and progress at his own rate of speed. Such a teaching method is especially valuable for handling such routine tasks as memorizing facts.[5]

THE INDIVIDUAL INSTRUCTION CENTER

This center contains programed materials and learning packages for self-instruction, some from commercial sources and some that are teacher made. It may have carrels to which children can go; these are booths equipped with record players, tape recorders, musical instruments, and other types of machinery. Special materials can be adapted or developed here which serve the needs of instructional teams.

THE INQUIRY CENTER

This is the modern school library, fully equipped with printed sources, slides, records, record machines, tape recordings, and machines for viewing. The staff assists children in their individual inquiry. Library specialists gather materials for the instructional team, develop units of study, and work with in-service training programs for teachers.

[5] Judith Murphy and George Sullivan, *Music in American Society,* an interpretive report of the Tanglewood Symposium, Music Educators National Conference, Washington, D.C., 1968, p. 54.

THE MATERIALS DEVELOPMENT CENTER

In large school systems such centers are staffed by audio-visual experts, writers, and artists. Materials which commercial publishers do not produce can be created here—from books to video taping. These centers can produce materials for special needs of the children of the particular school or class.

Implications

Modern technology can produce nearly any teaching device anyone can imagine, and education is only at the threshold of the "teaching machine" age. If a school desires portable equipment on wheels that can play both records and tapes in stereophonic sound, provide a microphone to enable the teacher to superimpose his comments when appropriate, tape record all that is going on during the class, play back tapes of performing groups at full volume, and have multiple headphones for small group listening, it is on the market and can be purchased. If a teacher would like a chalkboard-type staff which shows the relation of the lines and spaces to the keyboard and which *sounds* the note electronically as a pointer touches it, he may order one, providing the budget permits it.

Properly selected, teaching machines of many types become part of an educational laboratory. These may soon become as important as books, musical instruments, radio, and television in the music learning process. They can provide a feedback, often at once, so the learner can tell whether or not he is correct, and what to do about it if he is not. Machines are being developed to assist children's sense of pitch; the individual can go to a machine and learn by himself. Types of programed instruction in music fundamentals exist and more are being prepared. Young children learn to deal with computers; some of the computers can carry on conversations with the children. Some of the drill aspects of music may be taught in an interesting and challenging way to individuals, each at his machine. At present most of this instruction is factual, but more will be thought-provoking in the future. The machine has a type of democratic aura—it responds equally to everyone regardless of wealth, race, or creed. A possible handicap may be its failure to do enough for creativity and the affective domain. If the teacher will utilize the time the machines save him to encourage creativity and the affective aspect of learning, marked progress in music learning should result.

Instructional Materials Checklist[6]

Purpose

_____Does the manual suggest practical and worthwhile purposes?
_____What main ideas can be developed?
_____What questions can be answered?
_____How does it fit into individual or group inquiry with other resources?
_____What skills, attitudes, and appreciations can be improved?

Readiness

_____What concepts need development?
_____What experiences should be recalled and discussed?
_____How can it be related to problems in the unit?
_____What difficulties or understandings need explanation in advance?
_____Is a new point of view presented?
_____Does the manual suggest techniques for introducing it?

During Use

_____Should children observe? _____Take notes? _____Raise questions?
_____Should supplementary comments be made? _____Should a break be allowed during use for rest, questions, and comments?
_____Should the resource be used in its entirety without interruption?
_____Should the resource be used a second time to emphasize points, clarify questions, and make explanations?
_____Should supplementary materials be used with it?
_____Does the manual suggest activities for children?

Follow-Through

_____Is group discussion sufficient?
_____Is group planning needed to explore new questions and problems?
_____Can stated questions be answered?
_____What conclusions can be made? _____Should a summary be made?
_____Should a short test be given on key ideas?
_____Should other resources be consulted to check points at issue?
_____Are related activities suggested, such as map making, chart making, reading, committee work, construction, dramatization, processing of materials, other activities?
_____Does the manual suggest follow-through activities?

[6] Michaelis, John, *Social Studies for Children in a Democracy,* 4th ed., © 1968. (Reprinted by permission of Prentice-Hall, Inc., Englewood Cliffs, New Jersey.)

Teacher Evaluation

_____Was the resource satisfactory for the group involved?
_____How can its use be improved?
_____Should supplementary resources be available before or after its use?
_____Any special difficulties that should be noted for future reference?
_____Does the manual suggest points for evaluation?
_____How well does the resource serve to realize the stated objectives?

INQUIRY AND SUGGESTED ACTIVITIES

1. Explore the many ways a teacher of music can use a tape recorder. Select one you believe to be of distinct value and demonstrate it before the class.
2. Investigate the use of the tape recorder in creative music composition. For a starter, try to communicate a scary Halloween atmosphere by having one classmate stroke the strings of a piano (inside the piano) while one group moans when you so direct, another group makes a hissing sound upon your signal, one student plays the woodblock when directed, and another plays a twelve tone row on a melody instrument of appropriate tone quality. (A muted trumpet would be fine.) Try these sounds in various combinations. When ready, record this music, then play it back for evaluation. Then try other experiments in composing with the tape recorder.
3. Select an important musical idea to be visualized in a class you may someday teach. Then select the type of graphic material needed to communicate this. Why did you choose it? What other audio-visual materials will you need to build a readiness for understanding this graphic material?
4. Investigate the use of IBM cards in taking an objective test in music, and the use of a computer to correct the test.
5. Explore possible field trips and identify possible qualified people available in your community to assist in realizing your objectives in teaching elementary school music.
6. What purposes of your music teaching can be reached through the use of observation of and experimentation with real objects? Why did you decide that observation would be necessary to realize the purpose? Indicate where you can locate and obtain the real objects.
7. Select one field trip which is desirable for realizing a musical objective. Prior to taking the children on the trip, investigate the learning possibilities inherent in the situation. Then make your preliminary plans.
8. Invite a resource person to appear before your class. Prior to his appearance, formulate questions with the children which will give direction to the person in what he is to do. What type of follow-up activities might be appropriate?

9. Assume that you are going to borrow an unusual musical instrument from someone in the community to use in your class. Describe how you would involve your class in the study of this instrument by gathering data and forming concepts. What kinds of concepts might result from this exploration? (Some might not be musical.)

10. You are going to have a display of musical instruments and the music they play. How much do you do, and what do the children do, in setting this up? What are some of the possible groups or categories of instruments that might be shown in this display?

11. Assume that the college class is going on a field trip to seek answers to musical problems and questions. Make plans; assign duties and responsibilities; plan ways of organizing, analyzing, and using data obtained from the trip.

12. Invite self-taught musicians from the school and community to an inquiry session. Collect data concerning the interests, talents, and musical pleasures of these people.

13. Have the class establish criteria for the selection and use of pictures to assist music learning. Have each class member select such a picture and have him explain how the picture can contribute to the realization of a particular objective.

14. Have the class establish creative ways to use the opaque projector. Prepare materials to be used on this projector.

15. Identify different ways transparencies might be used on the overhead projector; establish criteria for their use. Prepare a transparency to be used in the music lesson and demonstrate its use in class.

16. Students who own tape recorders can demonstrate examples of radio and television programs they record at home for later classroom use.

17. Assign different radio stations to small groups in the class. Each group will investigate the programing of music on a station for a day or for a week. What categories of music are broadcast, and how much time is spent with each type?

18. Observe the use of an educational radio or television broadcast in a school music class. Analyze the situation in regard to the objectives that were being realized, the extent to which they were realized, preparation for the presentation, the kind of data being gathered, and the types of concepts and generalizations to which the experience contributed. Was there an indicated follow-up?

19. Explore the different types of programed learning and evaluate them.

20. Write your own program for a small part of a music learning experience.

21. Compare the flannel board, magnetic board, and chalk board in their use and efficiency in music learning experiences.

22. Visit an instructional materials center and examine the types of musical resources available. Select one instructional resource and make plans for using it in teaching a music concept and in the realization of behavioral objectives identified in a music lesson.

23. Establish criteria to be used in selecting musical resources for a specific situation.

REFERENCES

BACON, DENISE, "Kodaly and Orff: Report from Europe," *Music Educators Journal,* April, 1969, pp. 53–56.

BROWN, JAMES W., ET. AL., *A-V Instruction: Materials and Methods.* New York: McGraw-Hill Book Company, 1964. A comprehensive treatment of principles and procedures for using all types of instructional materials, resources, and media; lists sources of materials.

DALE, EDGAR, *Audio-Visual Methods of Teaching,* rev. ed., New York: The Dryden Press, Inc., 1954. A comprehensive coverage of instructional materials.

DOOLIN, HOWARD, *A New Introduction to Music,* General Words and Music Company, 525 Busse Highway, Park Ridge, Ill., 60068, 1967. Four levels of instruction; one class chart sequence on an easel; three sets of students' books on individual easels; Teacher's Score and Manual for Levels Two, Three, and Four.

ERICKSON, CARLTON W. H., *Fundamentals of Teaching With Audio-Visual Technology.* New York: The Macmillan Company, 1965. Instructional technology as applied professionally to the achievement of educational objectives.

FISH, ARNOLD, ED., "An Enlarged Music Repertory for Kindergarten Through Grade Six," Juilliard School of Music, New York. U. S. Office of Education, Washington, D.C.

FOWLER, CHARLES B., "The Misrepresentation of Music: A View of Elementary and Junior High School Music Materials," *Perspectives in Music Education: Source Book III,* Charles L. Gary, ed., Music Educators National Conference, 1966, pp. 289–95. A critical and controversial view of music series books.

FRY, E., *Teaching Machines and Programmed Instruction.* New York: McGraw Hill, 1963.

JOYCE, BRUCE R., *Strategies for Elementary Social Science Education,* Chicago: Science Research Associates, 1965. Suggestions for using various types of instructional media.

————, *The Teacher and His Staff: Man, Media and Machines.* Washington, D.C.: National Education Association, 1967.

KODALY, ZOLTAN, *Choral Method,* adapted by Percy M. Young, New York: Boosey & Hawkes Music Publishers, Ltd., 1964. Fifteen volumes including *333 Exercises, Bicinia Hungarica I, II, III, IV, Pentatonic Music I, II, III, IV, Tricinia,* and others.

McKENNA, BERNARD H., *School Staffing Patterns and Pupil Interpersonal Behavior.* Burlingame, Calif.: California Teachers Association, 1967.

MIESSNER, W. Otto, "How to Master Rhythms," *Music Educators Journal,* Nov., 1966, pp. 48–9. The story of an invention to meet the rhythmic needs of students.

MURPHY, JUDITH, AND GEORGE SULLIVAN, *Music in American Society,* an interpretive report of the Tanglewood Symposium, Music Educators National Conference, Washington, D.C., 1968, pp. 53–4.

NASH, GRACE, *Music With Children,* Swartwout Enterprises, P.O. Box 476, Scottsdale, Arizona 95252. Films, records, and books in an adaptation of Orff methods.

NATIONAL EDUCATION ASSOCIATION, DEPARTMENT OF AUDIO-VISUAL INSTRUCTION, "Mediated Self-Instruction," *Audiovisual Instruction* 12: 421–542; May, 1967.

NOAR, GERTRUDE, *Teacher Aides at Work.* Washington, D.C.: National Education Association, 1967.

OFIESH, GABRIEL D., ET. AL., *Trends in Programmed Instruction.* Washington D.C.: National Education Association, Department of Audio-Visual Instruction, 1964.

ORFF, CARL, *Music for Children,* American Edition, prepared by Doreen Hall and Arnold Walter, New York: Associated Music Publishers, Inc., 609 Fifth Ave., 10017. Volume I—Pentatonic; Volume II—Major: Bordun; Volume III—Major: Triads; Volume IV—Minor: Bordun; Volume V—Minor: Triads.

Orff Music Catalog, Magnamusic-Baton, Inc., 6394 Delmar Blvd., St. Louis, Mo., 63130.

RICHARDS, MARY HELEN, *Threshold To Music,* Harper & Row, Publishers, 2500 Crawford Ave., Evanston, Ill. 60201.

SÁNDOR, FRIGYES, *Musical Education in Hungary.* London: Barrie and Rockliff, 1966.

SCHWARTZ, ELWYN, "Sources of Audio-Visual Aids," *Music Education in Action,* Archie Jones, ed., Dubuque, Iowa: Wm. C. Brown Publishers, pp. 473–93.

SKINNER, B. F., "Why We Need Teaching Machines," *Harvard Educational Review,* 1961, 31, 377–398.

WYMAN, RAYMOND, "Audio Media in Music Education," *Music Educators Journal,* Feb.-March, 1966, pp. 105–8.

Films

Children Learn from Filmstrips, 16 mm motion picture, McGraw-Hill (National Film Board of Canada), black and white, 16 minutes. This film evaluates filmstrips.

Choosing a Classroom, 16 mm motion picture, McGraw-Hill, black and white or color, 18 minutes. Identifies valid bases for choices.

Selecting and Using Ready Made Materials, 16 mm, McGraw-Hill, black and white or color, 17 minutes.

Tape Recorder

207 Ways to Use a Tape Recorder, Midwestern Instruments, 41st and Sheridan Road, Tulsa, Oklahoma.

Music is all-of-a-piece; it is not made of separate elements such as rhythm, melody, harmony, as textbook chapter titles seem to indicate. From this viewpoint, the organization of textbooks like this one would appear to be artificial.

There are two reasons why chapter divisions of this kind are commonly used, 1) to concentrate upon and emphasize a particular aspect of music, and 2) because the mind finds it necessary to identify and classify as part of the learning process. When we try to hold a mental microscope to one element of music such as rhythm, it does not mean ignoring the rest of music but placing full attention on a segment of it before putting it back into its rightful position in the union of all elements which comprise music.

It is not intended in this chapter that aspects of music other than rhythm be ignored; it is practically impossible to do this. The reader should feel free to draw upon his knowledge of other aspects of music and relate these to the study of rhythm in every way he is able to do. The same attitude should be taken with the other chapters dealing with specific musical elements.

8

tempo, dynamics and rhythm

It is the aim of the good teacher to help children hear, feel, and see rhythm. They will listen to rhythm, they will feel it and express it in movement with their bodies, and they will see it in the world around them—in the motions of people, in the movement of waves against the shore, in painting and architecture, and in notation which is man's remarkable way of recording sound on paper. A true sense of rhythm comes from the innermost parts of the body and seems to extend beyond the fingers and the toes into space. Teachers of dance have always known this. Teachers of music have not always had this insight. A Swiss musician, Emil Jaques-Dalcroze,[1] found in the early part of this century that unless rhythm is first felt by the whole body, the would-be musician might produce music mechanically, without feeling, thus never developing the responsiveness essential to genuine musicianship.

Expressing rhythm through movement is an activity that music shares to an extent with physical education and creative dramatics. Music assists physical education by helping physical movement be more rhythmic; it assists creative dramatics by

[1] Emil Jaques-Dalcroze, *Eurhythmics, Music,* and *Education* (New York: G. P. Putnam's Sons, 1921.)

182

heightening the dramatic expression. When physical education gives children more control over their bodies, and when creative dramatics helps to free them to interpret what they hear in music, these areas can in turn contribute to understanding music. By moving to music, children can learn to hear music with perception, to respond to it with imagination, and to explore the expressive ideas it contains.

Of primary concern is listening to the rhythm in music and responding to it with physical movement. Singing will be actively engaged in but will not be stressed here. In the authors' opinion there is good reason for this initial emphasis upon physically active listening, particularly in the primary grades. When children aged five, six, and seven begin their school year, many of them will not be able to sing in tune. Therefore there is logic in first listening to music, then responding by physical movement to what is heard, and in the process becoming oriented to rhythm, pitch, and mood. This builds a background of experience for better singing a little later. In college classes students may prefer beginning with the study of rhythm rather than to stress singing at the very outset.

However, there are important values in rhythmic responses other than the building of a background for successful singing. Among these are the development of body control, imagination, willingness to experiment, rhythmic responsiveness, and concepts of fast and slow, heavy and light, loud and soft, and long and short, in terms of body movement. Furthermore, rhythmic activity is a necessity in carrying out a balanced daily program of education for children. As stated earlier, it is *unnatural* for boys and girls to sit quietly for long periods of time. There is evidence to show that teachers who guide their pupils in appropriate rhythmic responses, and who know the proper times to do this, can reduce pupil tension and fatigue to a marked degree, which makes learning much more likely.

FUNDAMENTAL MOVEMENTS AND FREE RHYTHMIC PLAY

"Fundamental movement" is a term used in physical education. It describes simple, basic movements such as walking, running, skipping, and galloping. Series books for kindergarten and first grade contain helpful song and piano material as well as suggestions for teaching such movements. Also, teachers can quickly learn to use percussion instruments or a few notes on the piano keyboard to improvise rhythms for the simple fundamental movements to which children learn to respond. In these grades the teacher should not expect every child to respond in the same way; some children need time to experiment before being able to do what the others do. It is necessary that children learn fundamental movements because command of them is essential to being able to engage in free rhythmic play, some action songs, and singing games and dances. Each child needs time in which to explore *his own* tempo. Thus, at first the teacher observes and uses the child's natural tempo before asking him to conform to one predetermined by the teacher.

As has been indicated, music is not always required to initiate rhythmic response. For example, words for walking can be chanted, then clapped, then walked, before appropriate music is added in the tempo and rhythm of the children's walking. Other fundamental movements can be introduced by the teacher's drum beat or by word rhythms and learned by clapping before the children move to them with their whole bodies. The music can then be brought in after the rhythm is learned. (The words of songs can be learned first in rhythmic speech, and the melody added later.)

Further understanding of fundamental movements can be gained by using songs that suggest impersonation (imitative play). Children who are five and six years of age tend strongly to *be* what they impersonate, such as the horses that gallop and the rabbits that hop. The teaching of fundamental rhythms can continue also from the point of view of free rhythmic play. The teacher may tap a drum, play the piano, or use a recording, and ask the children what it "makes them feel like doing." From their prior experience should come such movements as clapping, walking, running, skipping, galloping, sliding, hopping, and jumping. Through the freedom of children to respond to the rhythms of music they can discover other body movements which may include swinging, pushing, bouncing, pulling, bending, stretching, and striking. During all of this the teacher controls and guides the learning situation by helping the children relate familiar physical responses to the music they are hearing. The teacher should do this in such a manner that each child feels he has made his personal contribution.

WALKING is commonly done to 4/4 and 2/4 meters, depending on the tempo. It is relaxed and swinging, never tense and jerky. Children may develop different types of walking by pretending they are different characters or animals. Marching is an outgrowth of walking.

RUNNING is done to 4/4, 2/4, and 6/8 meters, depending on the tempo. Running on tiptoe is commonly stressed, and the movement should be kept light.

SKIPPING is generally done to fast 6/8 or 2/4 meters. It is a step, hop, first on one foot and then on the other. Children enjoy a large fast skip that gives them the feeling of moving high in the air.

GALLOPING is ordinarily done to fast 6/8 meter. One foot is kept ahead of the other throughout, and the back foot is brought up to meet it. Heels never touch the floor. Children pretend they are ponies or horses.

HOPPING AND JUMPING are done to several meters, depending on the tempo. Hopping is done on one foot while jumping is done with both feet together. Children can imitate jumping rope, kangaroos jumping, and playing hopscotch. Overly heavy movements are avoided.

SWINGING, SWAYING, AND ROWING can relax the children after the stimulation of the more active movements. Swaying trees, branches or flowers are often imitated, as are swings, the pendulum of a clock, rocking a baby to sleep, and rowing a boat.

In kindergarten and first grade the terms "walking note" and "running note" make sense to the child because they represent body movement he knows. Since children in these grades have limited knowledge about fractions, terms like "quarter" and "eighth" are without much meaning. However, learning the adult terminology should follow learning the "movement" terms as soon as this seems practical.

It takes time to develop skill in these activities; the beginning teacher is likely to try too many things at first. He should "make haste slowly," striving for a simple and thorough approach. By the end of the first grade most children will have learned to walk, skip, run, and hop in time to music. During the second grade most children will have learned to slide, jump rope, and bounce a ball in rhythm. In third grade the ability to leap and step-hop is generally acquired.

Occasionally teachers take a rhythm from something a child is doing, or from nature or machines outside the classroom, and repeat this on a percussion instrument or on a piano. For example, they may clap or tap the rhythm of such sounds as those made by a train, hoof beats, the rain, footsteps, sawing, or a clock. The children are then asked to move to the rhythm they have heard. Percussion instruments may be selected to accompany or to represent the rhythm.

Children should not be asked to respond to rhythm until they have had the opportunity to listen carefully. Teachers often ask them to close their eyes while they listen. After this comes the question, "What did the music tell you to do?" There may follow a discussion, then the music will be repeated and the children will begin to contribute ideas to the group. The teacher will often help free rhythmic responses to grow naturally by asking such questions as, "Does the music make you feel like walking or running or skipping?" "Is it happy, sad, fast, slow?" "How many different motions are good to use with this music?"

Free rhythmic responses are so numerous that it is doubtful that any listing of them can ever be complete, particularly since each of them can be varied almost endlessly. Some, in addition to those already mentioned, are:

trotting	tapping	stroking	swaying
dipping	reaching	patting	rolling
tripping	grasping	creeping	hammering
stamping	banging	rocking	whirling
tossing	circling	crawling	tumbling
skating	beating	turning	sliding

Others are rising and falling in terms of crescendo (gradually louder) and decrescendo (gradually softer) and in terms of rising and falling pitch, bouncing a ball and jumping rope. For example, one way in which crescendo and decrescendo can be acted out is by a circle of children coming together at the height of the crescendo, and being at the farthest point apart at the lowest level of the decrescendo. Also, accelerando (gradually faster) and ritard (gradually slower) can be felt and seen when two children throw and catch a large ball as the music changes tempo. In this, they come closer together for a more rapid bouncing of the ball, and farther apart for the slower tempo.

Space is needed for freedom of movement, and it must be admitted that it is at a premium in some classrooms. However, excellent work can be done despite admitted handicaps, by keeping the following suggestions in mind. First, rhythmic activities need never be boisterous or unruly. Second, activities requiring space may be arranged in some larger room. However, this room should seldom be the size of a gymnasium because this can destroy the intimate feeling desirable for this type of music work. Third, many substitute responses can be made. Children seated quietly at their desks can "walk" with their hands in the air above their heads, and they can "march" with their heels while their toes remain on the floor. When clapping is required, it can be done in quiet ways such as striking the tips of the fingers of both hands together rather than using the palms, or striking the fingertips of one hand on the palm of the other hand. Fourth, part of a class often can do the rhythmic activity while others sing, chant, clap, evaluate, or perform a quiet substitute for the activity.

To sustain interest, variety is essential. No child enjoys skipping to the same music over a long period of time. A variety of accompaniments is also recommended. The teacher may use recordings, the piano, various percussion instruments, and the chanting of the voice. Still more variety may be attained by changing the tempo of the music. When song material is used, more effective results are often obtained when part of the group sings while part does the rhythmic responses—a division into performing and accompanying groups. Jumping ropes, bouncing balls, scarves, flags, and balloons may be used to make appropriate activities more colorful and impressive. These often aid the self-conscious child by focusing attention on the object, and assist the development of big, free movements. Scarves for this purpose are made of silk or lightweight nylon, longer than the child. Such length permits many uses, including dramatization.

It is important that teachers know the physical limitations of the various age groups they guide in activities that require some physical exertion. For example, if a student teacher is unaware that to "waddle like a duck" during a song about a duck is a strenuous exercise for children in first grade (or any grade), he might easily continue this activity for too long a time and see children fall down from exhaustion. Any teacher who intends to ask children to do such things should try them himself in advance. The developmental chart in Chapter 3 is helpful in learning about the physical development of children.

There is recorded music designed to use with rhythmic activities. Besides special albums relating directly to rhythm such as "Rhythmic Activities" in the *RCA Basic Record Library for Elementary Schools* and those made by Bowmar Records, recordings for these purposes are produced by some music series publishers and many other companies. Also, recordings of symphonic music which is appropriate to the activity can be used. Another interesting source is found in the ethnic recordings of such firms as Folkways Records and Columbia. Children can listen to these and perform with the rhythmic music of peoples from all over the world.

Music selected for any rhythmic activity should have tempo suited to the activity and to the children's stage of physical development; it should suggest clearly to the children the movement, mood, or dramatization to which the teacher wishes them to respond.

Action Songs, Singing Games, and Dances

Action songs and singing games are emphasized in the primary grades, and dances are emphasized in the intermediate grades because children aged nine to eleven have gained the physical control and coordination that enables them to perform and enjoy this more patterned social activity. However, each of these responses appears to some extent in all the grades. Their major musical purpose is to help children to feel rhythm and to respond to it with physical movements.

Although many action songs can be done without first acquiring a background of fundamental movements, this is not true of most singing games and dances. The title of this section is stated in an order that implies increasing complexity. *Action songs* are those to which children can add appropriate motions. *Singing games* are those that involve elements of game, chance, and sometimes dance. *Dances* are more formalized. Teachers and children who have imagination will find that they can transform some "ordinary" songs into action songs, singing games, and dances of their own invention.

Most folk dances are easily taught in the intermediate grades. Some of them are taught to primary grade children in simplified versions. The easiest "dance" would be the American Indian type in which six-year-olds do a thumping walk or hop. Occasionally a simplified waltz is introduced in those grades also. However, most basic dance steps are taught in grades four and five, and they are embellished in grade six. Children in these grades can easily learn the polka, schottische, minuet, polonaise, and mazurka.

When children sing and at the same time do extensive bodily movement, the result is usually detrimental to either good singing or good rhythmic action or both. Consequently it is best to divide the children into two groups that alternate in singing and in doing the game or dance. The group that does the singing frequently adds hand clapping and percussion instruments to its accompaniment.

Many singing games and dances contribute to organized play on the playground. The song forms the accompaniment. When these activities take place indoors, the piano and recordings provide variety.

One of the values of certain singing games and folk dances is the contribution they can make to social studies, for through them children can come to a better understanding of the peoples of the world and their customs.

While children need rhythm, and lots of it, there is some danger in identifying folk dancing too closely with the music program. Granting that it is a part of a balanced music program, it should be acknowledged that it is essentially a part of physical education. Therefore, any extensive development of this activity removes it in a sense from the objectives of a balanced music program. Because the time available for the education of children is limited, and because there are so many aspects of music to be taught, it is not logical to consider any large amount of time spent in dancing as time spent in music class. However, any teacher of music needs to be able, when necessary, to teach folk dances to serve musical objectives. The teacher of a well-planned music class will know his musical purposes for employing folk dances, and therefore will have no problem of confusing physical education and music.

Tempo and Dynamics

Tempo and dynamics can be clearly associated with rhythm and melody. Fast-slow and loud-soft are among the first music-related concepts young children are asked to learn at the beginning of their school music instruction.

The teacher can help each child discover his own natural tempo by playing a drum or the piano to his step as he walks across the room, perhaps on some errand or as part of a game. After the relation between his step and the sound the teacher makes has been learned, the child will be able to govern his steps in accordance with the tempo the teacher plays, and can walk slower or faster. This can be a challenging game at this stage of his development. The character of slow and fast music can be examined by comparing two songs, one of then slow and the other fast. Children can be guided to discover that much fast music is "light" and much slow music is smooth, calm, or perhaps "heavy." These descriptions of slow and fast music should be discovered through and reinforced by physical responses to music, and these responses may include aspects of impersonation and dramatization, often of animal movements. Body movement, percussion instruments, and hand clapping are used to develop the concepts *accelerando* (gradually faster) and *rallentando* and *ritardando* (gradually slower). These can be easily taught in the primary grades, with the children first imitating the teacher, then identifying them in music. Another way would be to lead the children to discover them in their experiences with selected songs and recordings, then act them out with body movement.

Loud and soft are easily-understood concepts, and from them are gradually learned the gradations of relative degrees of loud and soft. Percussion instruments and hand clapping can assist in learning about

crescendo ＿＿＿＿＿＿ (gradually louder) and *decrescendo* or *diminuendo*

＿＿＿＿＿ (gradually softer). Some teachers have children imitate them as they clap hands or sound an instrument softly when held low, near the floor, then gradually increase the volume as the hands move higher. This becomes *crescendo* and its reverse becomes *decrescendo*. These aspects of musical expression should be related to, or discovered and identified in, songs and recordings at once, and reviewed and identified repeatedly. *Accent* is a quality of dynamics easily taught in relation to loud-soft and to meter. *Adventures in Music* recordings which can help teach this concept include "Petite Ballerina," Shostakovitch; "Can Can," Rossini; "Departure," Prokofieff (all from II), "Dagger Dance," Herbert; and "Tarantella," Rossini (from III).

From the third grade up, recordings such as "Pacific 321," Honegger, (concerning a railway locomotive of World War I vintage), and "Fêtes," Debussy (concerning a festival) can be useful in studying tempo and dynamics on a large scale. Attention should always be given to their function in the music being studied. Songs should be selected which exemplify their use. Indexes of music textbooks will be helpful. The teacher can draw the attention of the children to tempo and dynamics by well-planned questions: "Would this song be better if it were sung (slower, faster, softer, louder)? "Let's try it that way." "Was it better, or not as good?" "Why do you think so?" "Can you think of other ways we might try it (perhaps utilizing accent, crescendo, decrescendo)?" "Let's try to find the very best ways to sing the song expressively."

As for terminology, English terms are ordinarily learned in the primary grades and their Italian counterparts introduced in the intermediate grades. Some of the terms in more common use are listed in the Structure of Music Outline, Chapter Six. Such a vocabulary should be a *useful* one—not one to be learned because a book lists terms. They are terms that need to be employed by teacher and children to describe the tempo and dynamics of any given piece of music, to explain *how* fast or slow, loud or soft the children's own compositions should be performed, and to be able to discuss music intelligently. Memorization of this terminology is usually boring and self-defeating, but practical use of it makes good sense. In the intermediate grades a glossary of musical terms should be made available to the children to help them solve their musical problems and to enable them to answer their own questions. Some music series books have such glossaries. Other terms related to the character of performance are:

cantabile	in a singing style	*maestoso*	majestic
dolce	sweetly	*molto*	very much
grandioso	grand, pompous, majestic	*poco*	a little

Some teachers and children have made imaginative posters illustrating terminology. For example, *adagio* might be illustrated by the turtle, *allegro* by a swift-flying bird, *accelerando* by a rocket taking off, and *grandioso* by a regal king.

As work on tempo and dynamics continues through the years, relationships between these and the other elements of music should be discovered, and appreciation of them should grow. There are relationships between tempo and dynamics, and between them and melody, harmony, form, and texture. These are waiting to be explored through experiences planned by teachers.

The Beat and Its Subdivisions

Adults are apt to overlook or underestimate the need children have for a great deal of experience with the regular and continuous beat that is characteristic of most music. To the adult, this regular beat seems to be too simple for much consideration and some teachers tend to give it too little attention. The result of this becomes obvious when children have difficulty understanding divisions of the beat and meter, and when a large number of adults cannot march, keep in step or walk in a natural, rhythmic manner. All children need extensive rhythmic experience, and they need teachers who realize how important it is to musical growth, as well as physical and personality development.

Beat and pulse are terms for the same concept, and most people use them interchangeably. The authors will use only the term beat in this book, in the sense that in moderate tempo the 4/4 measure has four beats.

The ear, the eye, and the body are employed in building the concept of the beat. The child *listens* to the teacher's playing on a drum, the piano, or as he claps his hands. He also listens to selected recordings which stress the beat. He *sees* the teacher as he plays the drum or claps his hands, and tries to imitate the motions he sees the teacher make, learning little by little to be "in time" with others. He explores and analyzes the beat for himself through his body responses and by experimenting with various percussion instruments. He also sees the beat pictured in simple notation.

(Notice that these simple 4/4 measures are written in a manner corresponding in miniature to the printed page of a reader.)

The body is employed in a number of ways. The child *feels* the beat with his whole body by walking, marching, swaying, hopping, or by clapping, slapping thighs, and making other hand-arm movements. He can also respond with words that reflect the beat and its subdivisions which are repeated over and over, such as:

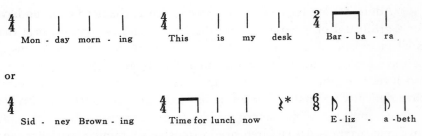

or

* Percussion instruments or hand clapping are often employed when a rest falls on the last beat of the measure.

An aim of the teacher is to have all children feel the beat together. It is a *good* feeling, enjoyed by all the people of the world.

Word Patterns[2]

CHANT	PLAY INSTRUMENTS	
Chant in a deliberate manner, emphasizing the last word in each line of the following:	*Six children, each with a different instrument, play in turn the underlying beat, while the class chants.*	
Bonefish, bluebird, black sheep, CROW	Triangle	
Chickadee, doodlebug, robins in a Row	Tambourine	
Banty rooster, peep squirrel, caterpillar, FLEA	Sticks	
Muley on the mountain and a BIG BUMBLE BEE	Drum	
Fly in the cream jar, frog in the POOL	Finger cymbals	
Clap for all the children here at SCHOOL	Maracas	

From street calls and jingles most children have experienced the beat and many of its divisions. For example:

> One potato, two potato, three potato, four;
> Five potato, six potato, seven potato, more.

Teachers should bring such playground rhymes into the classroom and make use of them.

The quarter rest can be introduced by challenging the children to invent motions to do when the beats are like this:

Mrs. Richards, in her *Threshold to Music* materials tells of Hungarian children throwing their two hands up and away and saying "Sw-sh." Perhaps your children will think of other ways to express or act out the quarter rest. After involving the children this way, and deciding on a motion, the symbol for the rest ⸰ is written in. Another approach is with pictures. Mrs. Richards' Chart 4 of the First Year Charts, with the empty dog houses as rests, has become a favorite.

Music series books for the kindergarten and first grade provide easy piano pieces which encourage responses to the beat, and their publishers provide recordings of marches, march-like songs and dance songs which do the same for all grade levels. Other commonly-used recordings include the RCA Basic Record Library for Elementary Schools, the Adventures in Music albums (also RCA), and the Bowmar Orchestral Library, particularly Album 54. The teacher should seek out these collections, study the suggestions provided for teachers, and select the music most appropriate to the needs of his class.

ECHO-CLAPPING

Echo-clapping is one appropriate introduction to rhythmic instruction because normal children of school age have the physical co-ordination to do it with ease (although a few six-year-olds need to be taught how). If children can imitate the teacher's clapping perfectly, the teacher knows that they are comprehending the rhythms he claps and that they possess the physical co-ordination to respond. Children of all ages are interested when the teacher suddenly says, "Listen to what I clap; then you clap it." First, establish the beat, then:

Soon children will be able to clap improvised rhythms to be echoed by the class.

Beginning with very simple rhythm patterns, the complexity and length can grow with the increasing skill of the children in this rhythmic imitation. The activity can relate to song material and to the teaching of notation by use of a pattern or patterns that are outstanding in a song. Then, after the imitative clapping has helped the children feel the rhythm with their bodies, they can be shown what this looks like in notation, and asked if they can discover, find, or see this rhythm in the song. Perhaps the rhythm or rhythms can be played on percussion instruments to enhance the song and written on the chalkboard for use with the instruments. Thus, beginning with rhythm, the activity unfolds to include notation, singing, and experiments in creating a percussion score that, if properly guided, will increase musical sensitivity and discrimination. Particularly in the upper grades teachers can relate clapping to notation quite directly by first doing the clapping, then showing the class a chart of the rhythms clapped, and finally learning to read a song based on these rhythms. In such an instance, the rhythm patterns used would be found by the teacher by analyzing the song as a part of his preparation for the daily music lesson, and the rhythmic exercise would be a part of learning the song, and of understanding and using music notation as well as to develop good rhythmic responses.

Another interesting type of echo-clapping is the question-and-answer, in which the teacher or a child claps a rhythmic question to be answered creatively, such as:

This activity leads to discovering and creating questions and answers in melody, and to increasing comprehension of the phrase.

Later on, echo-clapping in canon form can develop rhythmic memory. In this activity the class echoes perhaps one measure behind

Body Movements, Rhythm Words, and Notation

Movement	Line Notation	Words	Music Notation	Meter
walking thigh slapping hopping clapping	— — —	ta ta ta ta	𝅘𝅥 𝅘𝅥 𝅘𝅥 𝅘𝅥	$\frac{2}{4}$ or $\frac{4}{4}$
running clapping tapping	– – –	ti-ti ti-ti ti-ti	♫ ♫ ♫	$\frac{2}{4}$ or $\frac{4}{4}$
skipping, galloping	– – –	ta-ti ta-ti ta-ti ti-idi ti-idi ti-idi		$\frac{6}{8}$ $\frac{2}{4}$ or $\frac{4}{4}$
swaying sliding skating rocking swinging	——	ta-a-a	𝅗𝅥.	$\frac{3}{4}$
step-bend jumping	——	ta-a ta-a	𝅗𝅥	$\frac{2}{4}$ or $\frac{4}{4}$

the leader and in so doing must 1) remember what was clapped and repeat it later *while at the same time* 2) hearing and remembering what the leader is doing at the moment. For example:

Children can take the part of the leader, and percussion instruments can be used instead of the clapping or along with it.

Some Possible Responses Relating to Note Values

Note	Clapping	Speaking	Stepping
Whole	clap-flick-flick-flick	ta-a-a-a or who-o-ole-note	step-point-point-point
Dotted Half	clap-flick-flick	ta-a-a or half-note-dot	step-point-point
Half	clap-flick	ta-a or half-note	step-bend
Quarter ♩	clap	ta or quart-er	walk
Eighth ♫	clap-clap	ti-ti or eighth-eighth	run-run
♩ ♪	clap-clap	ta-ti or skip-ty	skip-ping
♫♩	clap-clap-clap	tri-ple-ti	run-run-run

After children have learned to respond to note values in the above ways, they can analyze the notation of simple songs by clapping, speaking, and stepping. Songs such as "Hot Cross Buns" can be studied in this way by young children.

Some teachers make charts such as the following for children to study.

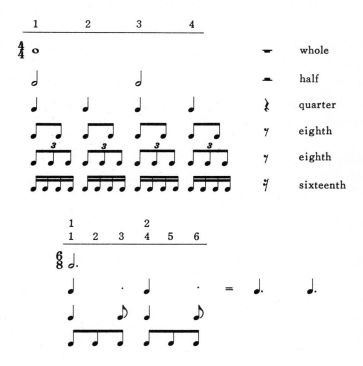

DIVISIONS OF THE BEAT

The necessity for divisions of the beat appears very soon after learning the concept of the steady beat. Although the beat may be fast or slow, the impressive aspect of divisions of the beat comes from relative length. Words such as "Rain, rain, go a-way" demand ⎟ ⎟ ⊓ ⎟ and provide learners with obvious instances where the short-short sound is equal to one long sound. Another way of picturing this is in short and long lines: __ __ __ __ __. The Hungarian methods "speak" the quarter note beat *ta* (tah) and the eight note as *ti* (tee). Thus, the above rhythm pattern would be *ta ta ti-ti ta*. Young children can easily read and write this introductory form of notation. Later on, they can add a slanted line to form the note head ♩ . The triplet ♪♪♪ was once regarded as a complexity to be taught in intermediate grades but today the young child can easily identify it as *tri-ple-ti* and begin to comprehend that in this division of the beat he finds three notes to one beat

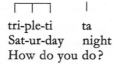

tri-ple-ti   ta
Sat-ur-day   night
How do you do?

and can identify a composer's use of this pattern in the beginning of Beethoven's Fifth Symphony. From this beginning, the seven year old can eventually use and understand the concept of four-to-one or

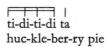

ti-di-ti-di ta
huc-kle-ber-ry pie

and its variants.

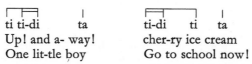

ti ti-di   ta   ti-di   ti   ta
Up! and a- way!   cher-ry ice cream
One lit-tle boy   Go to school now!

Any division of the beat should be studied in relation to words, body movement, songs (melody-rhythms), and children's improvised percussion patterns. For example, let us say that the children are guided to sense and observe the rhythm of the melody of "Hey, Betty Martin," which begins with a fast *long short-short long* or, in this instance, a *ti ti-di ti ti* pattern.

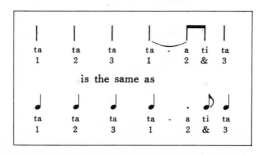

Later they can find that "Ten Little Indians" is constructed from the same rhythm pattern used in a different way, with the first part of it repeated many times.

Dotted Notes. While the rhythm of the dotted quarter note may have been felt for some time and practiced by imitation, emphasis on this concept is usually in third and fourth grades. A familiar song like "America" is useful. By writing it in notation, the fact of the dot being worth half again the value of the note it follows is pictured. Also, the class should be guided to discover where the second beat-point falls (on the dot). A teacher-made chart can then be studied. It could be:

ta	ta	ta	ta	- a	ti	ta
1	2	3	1	2	&	3

is the same as

ta	ta	ta	ta	- a	ti	ta
1	2	3	1	2	&	3

All uses for the dot should be explored in the notation of songs, and the fact that the dot adds half again the original value of the note it follows should be reviewed as frequently as it is needed to understand the music being performed or composed by the children.

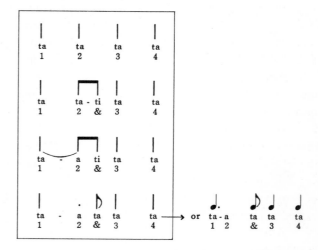

When this relationship of notes and beats has been established, it is not difficult to apply it to the dotted-eighth-and-sixteenth note pattern. This is identical to the dotted-quarter-and-eighth pattern except that it is ordinarily (but not always) twice as fast. "Battle Hymn of the Republic" is a song often used in this study. The children should have numerous experiences with the rhythm of this melody, singing it, clapping it, listening to recorded versions, and listening to performances of it by members of the class. They might conduct experiments with changing the rhythm, such as singing it in even eighth notes, then discussing if this would be preferred to the uneven rhythm of the written song. They should examine the notation carefully. After comparing the even eighth notes with the dotted-eighth-sixteenth notes, the following teacher-made chart could be studied:

By means of the chart the children should be able to analyze the divisions of the beat by dividing it into halves (eighth notes) and then into quarters (sixteenth notes) to understand mathematically and visually the dotted note rhythm they already "know" from previous listening, clapping, and singing. Sixth graders might discover something more—that as notation becomes more complex it sometimes becomes less accurate. It is doubtful that "Battle Hymn of the Republic" is performed with the mathematically exact division of the beat—the 3-to-1 relationship of ♩. ♪ . It is usually only *approximately* this. As any jazz musician can tell us, notation in some instances is highly indicative, but not exactly representative of what is performed.

By means of the types of activities mentioned above, children can be discovering and identifying, as well as feeling, beat units and divisions of the beat. They can find them in words, with clapping, by playing on percussion instruments, and in the melodies of songs. By looking at notation of music they have worked with and know, they will find that beat units can be written in different note values:

$$\text{♩, ♩., ♩, ♪.}$$

They will discover equal division of the beat:

$$\text{♩♩, ♫, ♬, ♬♬,}$$

and unequal divisions:

$$\begin{aligned}
\tfrac{6}{8} \quad &♩. \;=\; ♩ \;♪ \quad (\text{♫♩}) \\
\tfrac{2}{4} \quad &♩ \;=\; ♩. \;♪ \quad (\text{♬♬}) \\
&♩ \;=\; ♬\;♪ \quad (\text{♬♬}) \\
&♩ \;=\; ♫. \quad\;\; (\text{♬♬}) \\
&♩ \;=\; ♬♩ \quad (\text{♬♬})
\end{aligned}$$

They will also find that three notes of equal value can occupy a beat unit normally divided in two's:

Good teachers will remember that it is much more fun for learners to find these for themselves than to be lectured about them.

Staccato and *legato* can be included in the study of the duration of sounds. These are expressive aspects of music having relationships with note values. They are ways of *articulation*, staccato being detached or disconnected sounds and legato being smooth and connected, with no silence between the sounds. The German folk song "My Hat" can be sung in either staccato or legato style; the children can "think over" and evaluate the effect of each of these kinds of articulation in this and other songs and instrumental pieces.

MY HAT

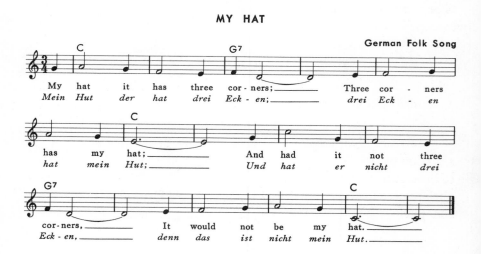

This becomes an action song by touching the chest for "my," the head for "hat," holding three fingers high for "three," and drawing the three corners in the air for "corners." After this, the actions are continued, but one of the four action words, probably "hat," is omitted, leaving only silence in its place. The next time another word is omitted until all four words are indicated only by the action.

Among the many recordings which illustrate articulation are:

legato	Blue Danube Waltz	J. Strauss	Keyboard Junior Recordings
	Berceuse	Stravinsky	Adventures in Music 1
	To a Wild Rose	MacDowell	Keyboard Junior Recordings
	Barcarolle	Offenbach	Adventures in Music 3 v. 1
	Skater's Waltz	Waldteufel	Bowmar 55; RCA WE 74
staccato	Syncopated Clock	Anderson	Keyboard Junior Recordings
	March	Prokofieff	Adventures in Music 1
	March Past of the Kitchen Utensils	Vaughan-Williams	Adventures in Music 3 v. 1
	Danse Infernale	Stravinsky	Keyboard Junior Recordings

Another aspect of duration of sound is the *fermata,* or hold (⌢). This is found in some familiar songs such as "Erie Canal" and "We Three Kings of Orient Are." It can be identified in recorded compositions when the regular beat stops for a time and one tone or chord is sustained before the beat and the melody continue. It should become another tool the children can use in their own compositions.

Rhythm and Pitch

Rhythm is an integral part of melody. As soon as pitch is added to a rhythm pattern some kind of melodic fragment or tune results. Because of the ease in singing the descending minor third interval, this descending pitch pattern has become an important beginning point in relating rhythm and pitch.

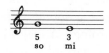

These two notes represent *high* and *low* pitch concepts, thus the beat, divisions of the beat, and high-low pitch concepts can be taught or involved simultaneously. Many simple words can be sung in quarter-and-eighth note patterns:

Young children need musical (singing) conversations like this, and enjoy having teachers sing instructions to them rather than always speaking them. They also enjoy the creative possibilities in singing answers to the teachers' statements; they need not always reply with the same pitches the teacher sings. The experience with 5–5–3 is quickly expanded to include other pitches; the next one is usually scale tone 6 or *la*. In the classroom, working on problems of rhythm and pitch are often integrally related. For example, speak the following words to decide upon their natural rhythm:

> *Star-light, star bright,*
> *First star I see to-night;*
> *Wish I may, wish I might,*
> *Have the wish I wish to-night.*

Then ask a few classmates to sing the words in this rhythm, using only scale tones 5 and 3. When the class agrees that a version so improvised is logical and pleasing, notate it. Next, have some other students improvise tunes using scale tones 5, 3 and 6. Notate a pleasing version of this. Finally, ask others to improvise tunes with scale tones 5, 3, 6, 2, and 1, and notate the best tune. Remember that what the college class can do in a few minutes may take weeks at certain elementary school levels.

Accent, Meter, and Rhythm Patterns

RHYTHMIC EXERCISES

Beginning with very easy movements, teachers help children to feel basic rhythm by having them perform knee-slapping, finger-snapping, desk-tapping, and heel-stamping sounds, first as exercises, then in connection with songs and recordings. A major purpose is to build concepts of metrical rhythm. The long-term objective has three stages, beginning with the concept of symmetrical meters—those divisible by two or three—because they are easiest and therefore the logical starting point. These include the familiar 2/4, 3/4, 4/4, and 6/8. Next the children meet the interesting stage of discovering, exploring, and devising alternations and combinations of these meters. The third stage is learning asymmetrical meters such as 5/4, 7/8 and others not divisible by two or three, which adds irregular accents. Ten and eleven-year olds will discern that these are formed from the familiar two and three beat groups they know from their study of the more conventional meters, but now arranged in a different, less regular order. Spoken words or phrases can be found or invented to help the children learn to feel these meters just as appropriate words helped them with the common ones. Reasons for learning asymmetrical meters include the facts that such meters are commonly used in the musics of Africa and Asia and that they comprise an important element in Western music being written today. Thus, school music has been freed from the metrical straight-jacket of earlier years and is ready to undergo an exciting expansion in the area of rhythm. Some examples of rhythmic exercises follow.

March rhythms such as "This Old Man," "The Caisson Song," and "Pop! Goes the Weasel!"

Waltz rhythms such as "Ach du lieber Augustin" ("The More We Get Together").

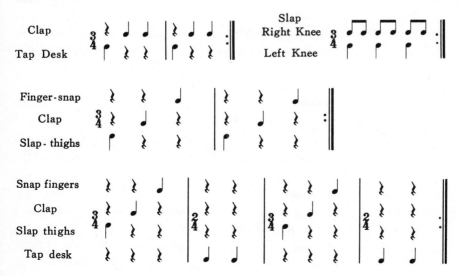

The above pattern could be written as two measures in 5/4 meter.

Other rhythmic exercises:

Percussion instruments can be used instead of body movements to produce the sound in such exercises. Even tone bars or bell sets can be employed. While the class does one pattern softly in unison, one child can improvise rhythmically by clapping or by playing a percussion instrument. If the basic beat is felt and understood, children should be able to place many of their patterns in notation. They should be guided to discover that the natural accent produces the measure by dictating where the bar lines are placed.

Conductors' beat patterns are another rhythmic response to the meter, usually in intermediate grades, and after they have been learned they can be used by the children to identify meters they hear from recordings. The entire class can perform these with songs or recordings. The primary (heavy) accent of each measure is indicated by a downbeat, as illustrated. A drum played on this beat (marked 1) will help the children to hear and feel the accent. A secondary accent occurs in 4/4 and slow 6/8 meters on beats 3 and 4, respectively.

Left-handed children will conduct all left and right motions as right and left—the reverse of the drawings. Such an exercise by children while

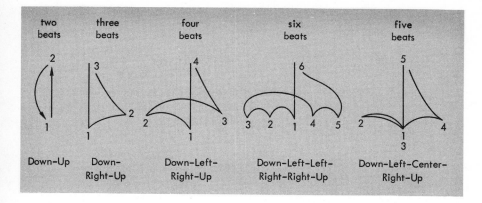

two beats — Down–Up

three beats — Down–Right–Up

four beats — Down–Left–Right–Up

six beats — Down–Left–Left–Right–Right–Up

five beats — Down–Left–Center–Right–Up

singing a song will assist them in giving each measure the correct number of beats. One of the Dalcroze exercises consists of children's conducting different meters while marching. While marching is ordinarily done to duple meter, it can be done to triple meter, as testified by some brilliant Spanish marches in 3/4 time.

WORD-RHYTHMS

The use of word-rhythms is a natural way to introduce rhythmic response. There is rhythm to be discovered in the spoken word, and children use and enjoy this rhythm in their play. The *sound* of words attracts children in the early primary grades, and people of all ages react to them, as testified by the rhythmic cheers at athletic events. Also, the rhythms of both simple and complex note values can be assimilated with ease when teachers relate these to familiar words.

Examples:

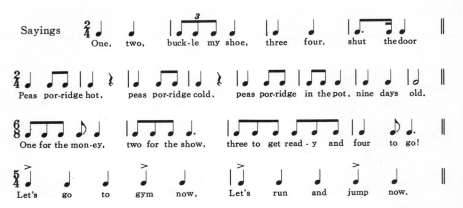

Percussion instruments, clapping, and the use of feet can be added to enhance the rhythm and add to the interest—for names can be "said" with feet and instruments. The teacher should be alert to the fact that most of these word-rhythms can be altered according to different ways of accenting words. For example, "Lemon cream pie" might be:

Several different rhythms can be correct for one word. Rhythms of some radio and television commercials are interesting to work with; they have the advantage of being well-known by the children.

EXPLORING COMMON METERS

When short word rhythms are repeated and when longer groups of rhythmic words are spoken, there is a natural tendency to group the beats by accenting some of them. In their most common usage these accents are spaced regularly, at intervals of two or three beats. If children lower their hands on the accents and raise them on beats between the accents they can find out whether the beats are grouped in two's or three's. This can be done with real music—songs or recordings—but the teacher may find it necessary to introduce the search for meter with a drum. From these groupings, formed by accents, they can theorize on what the meter may be.

Songs and recorded music useful for exploring common meters are very easily found because most of the music for elementary school exemplifies such meters. A few examples are "Marching to Pretoria,"

2 beats, 2/2 meter; "Row, Row, Row Your Boat," 2 beats, 6/8 meter; "When Johnny Comes Marching Home," 2 beats, 6/8 meter; "When Jesus Wept," 3 beats, 3/2 meter (*This Is Music,* Book 6); and "Down in the Valley," 3 beats, 9/8 meter. Examples of recordings for the same purpose are "Gigue" from *Suite Number Three,* Bach, Adventures in Music 1, 2 beats, 6/8 meter; "Ballet of the Sylphs," Berlioz, Adventures in Music 1, 3 beats; "Waltz of the Doll," Delibes, Adventures in Music 1, 3/4 meter; "Minuet" from *Don Giovanni,* Mozart, RCA Rhythm V. 5, 3/4 meter; "Cortège of the Sardar," Ippolitov-Ivanov, Bowmar #54, 4 beats; "Royal March of the Lion," Saint-Saëns, Bowmar #51, 4 beats; "Dagger Dance" from *Natoma,* Herbert, Adventures in Music 3, v. 1, 4/4; "Barcarolle" from *Tales of Hoffman,* Offenbach, Adventures in Music 3, v. 2, 6/8.

EXPLORING LESS COMMON METERS

Music of our day reflects a desire for some contrasts to the more commonplace meters and rhythms. Thus there is new emphasis on exploring less familiar meters once the common ones have been mastered. Some examples of songs and recordings are:

Meter	*Title*	*Source*
5/4 (3+2)	"Rune"	*Music Near and Far,* Silver Burdett
5/4 (3+2)	"Second Movement"	*Sixth Symphony,* Tschaikowsky
7/8 (3+2+2)	"Jingling Bracelets"	*Music Near and Far,* Silver Burdett
7/8 (3+2+2)	"Donkey Cart"	*Music Around the World,* Silver Burdett
7/8 (3+2+2)	"Gerakina"	*Toward World Understanding With Song,* Wadsworth
5/4, 7/8 2/8, 3/8	"4th Movement"	*Trio,* Ravel
(2+3+2+2)	"Little Bird, Go Through My Window"	*Together We Sing,* Lower Grades Book, Follett
3/4, 2/4	"The Quaker's Courtship"	*This Is Music, Book 5,* Allyn and Bacon
2/4, 3/4	"Second Movement"	*Quartet in D,* Tschaikowsky
3/4, 2/4	"The Miller's Daughter"	*Making Music Your Own,* Book 6, Silver Burdett
5/4, 6/4	"Promenade"	*Pictures at an Exhibition,* Moussorgsky
5/4, 3/4	"One May Morning"	Book Six, *Birchard Series*

3/4, 2/4, 5/4	"My Corn Is Now Stretching Out Its Hands"	*Music Now and Long Ago*, Silver Burdett
9/8, 2/4	"A Jogging Along"	*This Is Music*, Book 5, Allyn and Bacon
6/8, 3/4, 2/8	"Mexican Hat Dance"	*Music in Our Country*, Silver Burdett
4/4, 3/4	"Twelve Days of Christmas"	*Toward World Understanding With Song*, Wadsworth
5/8, 6/8, 2/4	"Summer Has Come"	*Voices of the World*, Follett
6/8, 3/4, 4/8, 3/4, 2/4		
	Pop! Goes the Weasel!	Variations, Cailliet Adventures in Music 4, v. 2

Other recordings for further exploration are:

Wheat Dance	Ginastera	Adventures in Music, 4, v. 1
"Hoe-Down" from *Rodeo*	Copland	Adventures in Music 5, v. 2
Brazilian Dance	Guarnieri	Adventures in Music 6, v. 2
Time Out	Brubeck	Columbia CL 1397
Time Farther Out	Brubeck	Columbia CL 1690

(Selected jazz records are particularly suitable for rhythmic study because of the regularity of the beat.)

"Street in a Frontier Town" from *Billy the Kid* (polyrhythms[4])	Copland	Adventures in Music 6, v. 1
Six Dances in Bulgarian Rhythm	Bartók	Columbia SL 229; VBX 425
Le Marteau sans Maître	Boulez	Columbia ML 5275

Experiments in Music Creativity, Contemporary Music Project, MENC, Washington, D.C., 1966, lists rhythmic recordings recommended for classroom study on page 23. Currently, some record jackets of Ravi Shankar's Indian music explain the metrical organization of that music.

The older children enjoy experimenting with the less common meters, composing percussion pieces and songs having such beat group-

---

[4] For further study of polyrhythms, see *The Study of Music in the Elementary School: A Conceptual Approach*, Charles L. Gary, ed. (Music Educators National Conference, Washington, D.C., 1967), pp. 47–50.

ings. All asymmetrical meters are combinations of 2 and 3 beat groups. 5/4 is either 3 + 2 or 2 + 3; 7/8 and 7/4 is either 2 + 2 + 3, 2 + 3 +2, or 3 + 2 + 2. An interesting challenge for the class is to devise a logical conductor's beat for 7-beat and other less standard beat groups. A possible assignment for small groups or individuals might be structured as shown in the blank score to be filled in. The children should be free to alter the instrumentation and number of measures to suit their purposes. The first experience with this should be very simple, using only two or three instruments for four measures. By means of an opaque projector the entire class can study, read, perform, and evaluate such scores.

Percussion Score in 5/4 Meter

	1 2 3 4 5	1 2 3 4 5	1 2 3 4 5	etc.
Triangle				
Tambourine				
Wood block				
Bongo drums (or small drum)				
Conga drum (or large drum)				

Alla breve meter (¢) is really 2/2 meter. It could also be considered as 2/4 written in 4/4 so as to be more easily read, the notation being "less black" in that it has fewer eighths and sixteenth notes to decipher. 3/2 is not uncommon; songs such as "Kum Ba Ya" are written in that meter, and 9/8 is the meter for "Down in the Valley." Familiar songs can and do change meter, as testified by "Goodbye, My Lover, Goodbye," and "We Three Kings of Orient Are." The indexes of some of the series books will guide the teacher to activities involving the study of different meters. The most common meters according to elementary school use are shown on the next page.

Number of Beats	Duple Meter	Triple Meter
1		3/8 3/4 (tempo di valse)
2	2/4 2/2	6/8 6/4
3		3/8 3/4 9/8
4	4/8 4/4 4/2	12/8

Combinations of 2's and 3's
5	5/4 (3+2 or 2+3)
6	6/8 6/4 (3+3 or the less common 2+2+2)
7	7/8 7/4 (2+2+3, 2+3+2, 3+2+2)

What do meter signatures mean? They tell us only how many of a certain kind of note or its equivalent can be found in one measure. If the signature is 3/4, there are three quarter notes or their equivalent value in the measure. Whether each receives one beat or not is usually not revealed by the meter signature alone. Most of the time they will receive one beat, but when the tempo is very rapid the entire measure would receive only one beat. If the meter is 6/8, we know that there are six eighth notes or their equivalent in each measure, but we do not know from the meter signature whether there are two or six beats in those measures—whether each eighth note receives one beat or one third of a beat. Thus, the upper figure does *not* always tell us the number of beats in a measure, and the lower figure does *not* always tell us the kind of note that receives one beat. Meter signatures tell us only the number of a certain kind of note or its equivalent that can be written into one measure.

There is a possibility that in stressing meter accent teachers limit the capacity of children to think beyond its regularity. One way to begin to overcome this is to have them listen for accent in an excellent rendition of "America" from a recording or played on the piano by the teacher. The correct performance will reveal little or no meter accent. To add a definite accent to the first beat of each measure would destroy the solemnity and dignity of this melody. Hearing recordings of Gregorian chant will reveal no regular recurring beat or accent. Aspects of music which tend to make rhythm more free— less bound to the rigidity of regular beats and accents—include *rallentando* and *ritardando* (gradually slower) and *accelerando* (gradually faster). *Rubato* is a term which implies that the performer treats the tempo and note values very flexibly, employing many slight accelerandos and ritardandos. This may be done in two ways, either by applying this freedom to the melody while the beat remains stable, or by applying it to the music as a whole. Many jazz players illustrate the former; Liszt and Chopin, among many other nineteenth century composers, employed the latter. Recorded examples of their piano music illustrate it. There is some Oriental, Indian, and Hungarian music which has no metrical beat. Syncopation upsets the normal meter and accent by deviating from the regular recurring accent; it shifts accents to normally weak beats. The familiar "Hokey-Pokey," "Dry Bones," and "Rock Island Line," all in *Exploring Music with Children* and in many series books, are among the many songs from which older children can learn about syncopation. Again, the teacher should examine the indexes of series books for the heading "syncopation." Recorded selections such as Gershwin's "I Got Rhythm" and "Anything Goes," and many selected popular and jazz tunes of the day can be useful, as are standard selections such as Gottschalk's "Grand Walkaround" (Adventures in Music 5 vol. 1). When possible, the rhythmic notation should be written on the chalkboard to help children analyze syncopation. The *beat points*—the place or note in the measure where the metric beat falls— should be indicated, and the accents clearly marked.

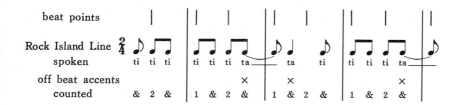

Latin-American music is usually a useful source of music in studying syncopation, and percussion patterns will add interest. Some Negro spirituals are excellent sources. An important thing about performing syncopated music is that the performer relax and permit himself to be a natural medium for transmitting the rhythm. The more one tenses himself and "tries very hard," the less success he is apt to have.

RHYTHM PATTERNS

One way children become conscious of definite rhythm patterns is by means of an activity such as echo-clapping, which was described earlier. Teachers guide children to recognize the patterns found in selected songs.

For example, they can discover three rhythm patterns in "Jingle at the Window"[5] from which the entire rhythmic structure of the song is built.

 three times

ten times

three times

"Au Clair de la Lune" consists of a four-measure phrase rhythm pattern which is used four times; it is the rhythmic unifying element for the entire song.

 - four times

All of "Ten Little Indians" except the concluding two measures consists of the pattern:

 - three times

With the exception of the final three measures, "I Love the Mountains" is constructed upon two rhythm patterns:

 - two times

- four times

Younger children can identify patterns and teachers can write them on the chalkboard if the children are unable to notate the rhythm of what they hear. Older children can look for these repeated patterns in notation, as well as identifying them when listening to songs and recordings.

All songs do not contain such distinct patterns. Teachers must seek songs and recorded music which are best suited to build specific musical concepts. Words of songs can assist in performing rhythm patterns. A simple example is the song "Sally Go Round," in which seven-

[5] All the songs referred to under this side head are found in *Exploring Music With Children,* Wadsworth Publishing Company, and many series books.

year-olds decide they want to use the rhythm of the first four notes as an ostinato (repeated pattern) played by sticks throughout the song.

English Singing Game

Sal-ly go round the sun.____ Sal-ly go round the moon,____

Sal-ly go round the chim - ney pot on a Sun - day af - ter - noon.____

The children can remember the rhythm of the pattern by repeating silently the words "Sally go round" ( ). They might decide to have a wood block play the rhythm of the last two measures over and over along with the one the sticks play. It could be remembered by the rhythm of the words "Sunday afternoon" ( ). A rhythm pattern has been defined as a specific grouping of sounds related to an underlying beat.

Some of the many songs usable for the identification and study of rhythm patterns are "When Johnny Comes Marching Home," "Jingle Bells," "Over the River and Through the Woods," "Hanukkah," "The Old Brass Wagon," and "Skip to My Lou." Examples of the many recordings which serve the same purpose are "Country Gardens," arranged by Grainger, RCA Rhythm Album 6, "The Little White Donkey," Ibert, Adventures in Music 2, "Habañera," from *Carmen,* Bizet, Bowmar Orchestral Album #56, and "Golliwog's Cakewalk," Debussy, Bowmar #63.

RHYTHM-RELATED COMPOSITIONAL DEVICES

In today's music education children are composing as a regular part of their study. As they compose, they have an interest in and a need for some of the devices utilized by the adult composer. The terminology may seem complex at first, but it is all rather simple when once explained. Consider the terms *augmentation* and *diminution*. To augment something, one makes it bigger; to diminish something, one makes it smaller. This is what happens in rhythm. If a young composer is writing a score for percussion instruments and selects the pattern to begin with, he finds that he can, if he chooses, apply diminution by making this pattern one half its original value and repeating it. Writing this down, it looks like this:

The extension of the original pattern adds considerably to the feeling of tension he wants to create. He might follow this with an application of augmentation by making the original twice its size in time. He then would have constructed a four-measure composition from one pattern, a composition which built up to a climax, then produced a feeling of release. Next he utilizes a canon treatment of his pattern to add more to his composition, and assigns this to the woodblock. He decides that a continuous eighth-note pattern played by maracas would add a certain stability and help unify his piece further. He then choses to be daring enough to experiment with polyrhythms by adding a hand drum playing quarter note beats in 3/4 meter. Now his composition is complete. He has done as many adult composers would do—used diminution, augmentation, canon, and polyrhythms. All he needs now is a group of his classmates to read, perform, and evaluate it. Learning *can* be exciting, creative, experimental, and intellectual—all at one time.

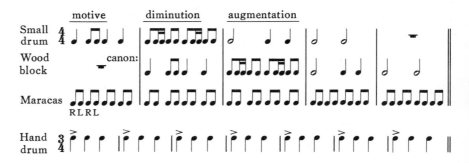

The above 3/4 part could be written in 4/4 meter by using the bar lines of the other parts. The accent would still dictate the true meter.

Characteristic Rhythm Patterns and Dances

There are rhythms and dances characteristic of peoples of the world, often related to their historical origins. We need to know more about them than we now do; the current interest in the rhythms of Africa and Asia will inevitably produce new materials of instruction.

Latin-American Patterns

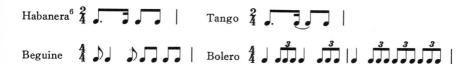

Habanera[6] $\frac{2}{4}$ | Tango $\frac{2}{4}$ |

Beguine $\frac{4}{4}$ | Bolero $\frac{4}{4}$ |

> *Basic Rhythms* (combine the three)
> 1. Timbales (paired single-head drums)

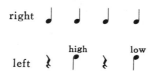

right   ♩   ♩   ♩   ♩

left   high   low

> 2. Maracas

right
left

> 3. Claves

Traditional Dances

Waltz $\frac{3}{4}$
slow   walk   walk   walk   walk   walk   walk
fast   run   run   run   run   run   run

Polka $\frac{2}{4}$
hop   walk walk walk   hop   walk walk walk

Scottische $\text{¢}\left(\frac{2}{2}\right)$
run   run   run   hop   run   run   run   hop

Mazurka $\frac{3}{4}$
walk   walk   hop   walk   walk   hop

[6] Recorded examples include "Habañera" from *Carmen* (Bizet) and *Jamaican Rumba* (Benjamin), both in Bowmar 56, and *Grand Walkaround* (Gottschalk) in Adventures in Music, V. 5–1.

When dances are used in music class, they serve musical objectives; when they are used in physical education classes the teacher utilizes them to realize the objectives of physical education. Sometimes these objectives are related; sometimes they are not. Only by asking himself, "Toward what musical objectives am I working in my lesson plan?" can the teacher be certain that he is using dances in the study of music. They can be useful in the study of beat, meter, pattern, notation, instruments, syncopation, and in relation to dance rhythms utilized by composers. For example, the waltz and Johann Strauss, the mazurka and Chopin, the bolero and Ravel, the polka and Dvorak, Weinberger, and Shostakovitch.

Most of the formal dances are taught in the intermediate grades, although the simple waltz and minuet are sometimes introduced in the third grade. The waltz is first presented as a type of walk in which a large step then two smaller steps are made as dancers move in a circle. The teacher can learn how to teach dances from readily-available sources— the music series books, physical education books, record jackets, and from courses of study. In situations where children are reluctant to have only one partner throughout a dance, mixer-types are useful. Examples of these found in many of the books are "The Old Brass Wagon," "Red River Valley," (both in *Singing With Children,* Wadsworth Publishing Company) and "The Caller's Song" in *Music for Young Americans,* Book 6.

Examples of familiar dance songs are "Holla Hi, Holla Ho," "Stodola Pumpa," "Du, Du Liegst Mir im Herzen," and the American songs "Buffalo Gals," "Four in a Boat," "Goin' to Boston," "Sourwood Mountain," and "Turkey in the Straw." Recordings include the RCA Victor Series *The World of Folk Dances,* Bowmar Records' *Singing Games, Singing Games and Folk Dances, Folk Dances, Singing Square Dances,* and *Play Party Games,* and many more from other sources.

TEACHING FOLK DANCES

There are folk dances from all over the world. The four American types are (1) play-party games, (2) round dances, (3) long-ways and circular formation dances, and (4) square dances. The origin of the *play-party game* is interesting; at a time in American history when dancing and musical instruments were sometimes frowned upon, people sang dance accompaniments instead of playing them, and called the dance a game, thus getting around the restrictions of those days. *Round dances* are done with partners. They were "round" because to move easily about a crowded hall, the partners danced in the same circular direction.

Examples of this type include the waltz, polka, schottische, rye waltz, and the varsovienne ("Put Your Little Foot . . ."). *Long-ways* and *circular* formation dances include the Virginia Reel. The *square dance* is one in which eight dancers (four couples) salute, curtsy, and change partners in a square formation while performing many interesting figures. Possible steps in teaching a folk dance follow:

1. In preparation, study the directions of the selected dance. It should be one of which the children already know the basic movements required, but if they do not, be sure to teach these as separate rhythms as a preparatory step to their learning the dance.

2. As you study the dance, practice the steps without the music. Then listen to the music or learn the music, and do the steps in rhythm to it.

3. If necessary, write any difficult part of the directions on a small pad or card that can be carried inconspicuously in the hand.

4. Teach the song (if it is a dance song) so that the children know the melody and words well before attempting to learn the dance.

5. Direct the children into the proper dance formation.

6. Have the children practice the first set of steps with no music. Then have them do these steps while speaking the rhythm of the words of the song, and guide them to associate the word-rhythm with the steps. Repeat until the steps are learned.

7. Do this much of the dance with the music.

8. Repeat Steps 6 and 7 with the next set of steps. Continue this process until the entire dance is learned.

9. Do the entire dance with the music.

An Expanding Concept of Rhythm

Besides expanding their concept of rhythm in music, children should be helped to find rhythm in other areas of living. There is rhythm all about us—in the waves of the ocean, day and night, life cycles of plants and animals, the heart beat, moving oars, the grain of wood, in machinery, poetry, speech, dance, and when we walk. How does Debussy compose music that reflects the rhythm of the ocean? Hear his *La Mer.* How does the composer of an art song manage the rhythm of the poem he sets to music? Might there be a relation between the beat, its divisions, and certain architecture? Are there evidences of unity, balance, and variety in man's many experiences with rhythm? There is a world of rhythm to be explored.

Percussion Instruments

Percussion instruments can be considered to be extensions of the body. The body can produce sounds of rhythmic value. Hand clapping of various kinds (flat-palmed for loud, cup-palmed for lower pitches, and fingers only for soft) provide some possibilities. The sound made in pulling the tongue away from the roof of the mouth can be done in ways to produce high and low-pitched "clicks" which imitate the ticking of a clock. Stamping feet, tapping toes, hands slapping thighs, and snapping fingers contribute their sounds too, and all of these can be done with a beat and with accents to form beat groups. Although making such sounds or using rhythmic speech help to build a real feeling for rhythm, they are limited in tone quality, and children are happy to explore and use the sounds of the many percussion instruments, usually with great interest.

THE EARLY YEARS

Children in nursery school, kindergarten, and first grade should be helped to experiment with the sounds made by miscellaneous objects of wood, metal, glass, and stone when they are tapped, shaken, and struck. The teacher who is encouraging concept formation of high and low pitch will group the sound producers accordingly at either end of a table. Later the children will play the ear training game of sorting these out according to different classifications. One will be high and low pitch. Others could be types of tone quality such as ringing, scratching, rattling, jingling, and booming. After handling, sounding, and naming all these sound producers and instruments, the children can face away from the table and piano while the teacher tests their ability to identify and describe the different sounds. They may also identify instruments that have short and long duration of sound.

The classroom might have the following instruments:

5 jingle bells	3 triangles	1 pair coconut shells
3 jingle sticks	5 pairs sticks	2 tambourines
1 large drum	1 pair cymbals	3 pairs sandblocks
1 small drum	2 pairs finger cymbals	1 wood block

A first-grade teacher made these comments concerning activities in her room that culminated in the successful use of this equipment:

The children are given many opportunities to initiate their own rhythmic activities. Duration, volume, accent, tempo, and moods are felt with hands, fingers, feet, and moving bodies. Percussion instruments are but extensions of tapping feet and clapping hands. Thus the children *gradually* use drums, bells, woodblocks and sticks to accompany or to create rhythm patterns. By careful listening children find one drum lower or higher in pitch than another. They discover differences in quality as well as in pitch by tapping different places on their instruments. They suggest that part of a song reminds them of a bell or a gong. Tambourines and other instruments can be used for spontaneous self-expression and interpretation during story time.

In this first grade the children had done "drum talk"—beating out the rhythm of words in drum language; they had walked, run, or tapped instruments as they spoke their names in rhythm; they had used scarves, streamers, and balloons to help them to feel and see other rhythms. Instruments were introduced slowly over several weeks, one at a time. Clapping generally preceded playing at first. Early playing was informal; each child played each instrument at one time or another. Songs such as "Little Miss Muffet" were used in which the light-sounding instruments played first, then the heavier-sounding wooden instruments took their turn as the climax of the song approached, and the two were combined in the concluding climax. Among the many other steps in learning to play the instruments was having those holding wooden instruments play on the primary accents and those holding metal instruments play on the other beats. After this, further discriminations between instruments were made, sometimes selecting those that seemed best to play with a piano piece, a song, or a recording. When the music changed, a need for a change in instrumentation developed. Some children made suggestions concerning the use of specific instruments.

It is not until the second grade that most children can perform either the metric beat *or* the melody-rhythm of a piece when asked. Prior to this time these two rhythms are worked with separately.

Children are guided to find that percussion instruments can substitute for body movements such as walking, marching, and skipping. They can sound them to feel the beat. They find out that chopsticks can make a sound suggestive of rain falling on a roof, that sand blocks can imitate a train, that rattles and drums seem quite necessary to make some American Indian songs sound complete, and that words of songs sometimes suggest certain accompanying instruments or percussion sound effects. They find that instruments can be played to produce accents which will eventually outline the meter, and that instruments can reproduce the rhythm of the melody—usually the rhythm of the words. As they grow older, by keeping their toes on the floor they can make the *heel-clap* sound for two-beat meters, the heels sounding the down-beat and the hands clapping the up-beat. Dances are sometimes accompanied in this way. Transfer can be made to low drum—high drum for the same rhythm; other less heavy-sounding instruments can substitute for the high drum. Notation is brought in to explain what has taken place only after the young child has first heard and felt the rhythm pattern he is to see. After his experience with it, a picture of it (the notation) helps him visualize the concept.

In the early years the instruments are introduced slowly in connection with small or large group work, one or two at a time. This initial group work with the instruments is of necessity teacher-directed. Series books for these levels contain songs with which to introduce instruments. Since the emphasis today is upon children's growth in creative ability and in musical discrimination, fully written published scores for percussion instruments that the teacher dictates to the children are rarely used. It should be made clear that there is nothing wrong with a teacher using such scores to introduce children to the potentialities of group instrumental performance; it is wrong only when this is continued to the exclusion of opportunities for children to grow in listening, discriminating, and in analyzing music in order to create their own scores. One logical approach to such scores is found in the series books where in place of standard notation, tiny drawings of the particular instrument tell the child when to play it.

Swanson[7] believes that the mass rhythm band activity for kindergarten and first grade which was once popular, was never appropriate for that age group. Children at this age level are individualistic rather than fully cooperating members of a large group; the score had to be dictated by the teacher, which meant children's creativity and discrimination were practically absent; and there were sometimes aspects of exploiting little children for the entertainment of adults.

LATER YEARS: AGES 9-12

By the third grade children can create their own percussion scores for small and large ensemble use, based upon their growing understanding of rhythm, playing instruments, the tone qualities of instruments, notation, form and general musical taste. To add intruments to recorded music, the children first listen carefully, discuss what they have heard, theorize on what tone qualities and dynamics may be appropriate,

---

[7] Swanson, Bessie, *Music in the Education of Children,* 2nd ed. (Belmont, Calif.: Wadsworth Publishing Company, 1964), p. 93.

experiment by performing with the instruments, and finally decide upon the completed score. Certain criteria should be developed, such as:

Is the effect musical?
Can the recorded music be clearly heard when the instruments play?
Are there musical reasons for the selection of the instruments?
Is the form of the music reflected in the choice and use of the instruments —when they play and when they are silent?
Is the general effect of the music—heavy, light, thick, thin, high, low— reflected in the choice of the instruments?

There is opportunity in this activity to utilize rhythmic music of all types, from selected music by "name" composers to ethnic music of the world and to jazz.

Using percussion instruments to contribute to the interpretation of songs continues through the elementary school into junior high school. Sound effects heard on radio, television, and in the movies form a very real part of everyday living. Children in *every* grade enjoy the challenge of adding or creating descriptive sound effects to help communicate the message of certain songs. One or two drums can add immeasurably to an American Indian song; a tambourine or two can lend atmosphere to a Gypsy song; a combination of tambourine, drums, claves, and maracas can vitalize a Latin American song. A rhythm pattern drawn from the music at hand can be both experimental and creative to the children who are guided to discover it. This experience can relate to note reading skill when the pattern is written on the chalkboard in notation to be analyzed—so that "we can see what we did" or so that "our work can be saved and remembered for tomorrow's lesson." This develops associations between playing instruments, feeling rhythm, and visualizing it. Percussion accompaniments may be constructed from part of the melody rhythm, from the meter, or from a combination of these. Two or three simple patterns may sound complex when combined. Contrasting rhythms can be played on two or more different instruments or groups of instruments and the combinations of two or more patterns with the rhythm of the meter can be challenging, interesting, and tests of rhythmic growth. *Polyrhythms* may be either two contrasting rhythms within the same meter, or two different meters used at the same time, sometimes called "polymetric."

PERCUSSION INSTRUMENTS DESCRIBED

The successful use of percussion instruments demands knowledge of a variety of sounds. The teacher of music needs to know the tone qualities that can be produced by each instrument, and how to play each of them. In general, commercially made instruments are superior to those made by teachers and children, although some of the latter can be quite suitable for temporary use, and a few can be of permanent value.

Percussion Instrument Sound Chart

Wooden instruments that "click" and have short duration	*Types of tone*
Sticks	Light
Claves	Not as light
Castanets	Not as light
Coconut shells	Heavier
Wood blocks	Heavier
Tone block	Depends on size
Xylophone	Depends on size and pitch
Metal instruments that ring or jingle and have longer duration	
Finger cymbals	Delicate
Triangle	Light
Jingle bells	Light
Jingle clogs	Not as light
Tambourine	Varied, depending on way it is played
Gong	Heavy
Cymbals	Heavy
Instruments that swish or rattle	
Sandblocks	Light
Strip rattles	Light
Maracas and other rattles	Varied
Instruments that "scratch"	
Sticks	Light (when grooves are scratched)
Guiro (notched gourd)	Not as light
Hawaiian instruments	
Pu'ili (slit bamboo sticks)	Light
'Illi-ili (stones)	Not as light
'I pu (large gourd)	Heavier, depending on size
Instruments that "boom"	
Drums	Varied, depending upon size and method of striking

WOODEN INSTRUMENTS

Rhythm sticks can be made from dowel rods of from 3/8" to 5/8" in diameter, purchased from lumber yards. They are usually cut in 12" lengths. Hardwood produces the most resonant sounds and will not break as easily as softwood. Ends can be smoothed with sandpaper; they can be enameled any desired color. Children hold one in each hand and strike them together. They should explore differences in pitch and sound by tapping different places on the sticks, and by tapping the sticks on suitable objects such as the floor and desk.

Claves are paired resonant sticks about an inch in diameter. They can sometimes be satisfactorily made from six-inch lengths of a broom stick or from doweling that is an inch in diameter. While the professional method of playing is to hold one clave loosely in the partly closed left hand, resting on the heel of the hand with the other end resting on the fingernails and on the thumb and index finger, and to strike this one with the other clave held stick-like in the right hand, many play them in a manner similar to rhythm sticks, by simply holding them stick-like in each hand. This instrument is seldom used in primary grades. It has its major place in Cuban songs and Latin American dances of the intermediate grades. A favorite example of claves rhythm that can be learned through speaking the rhythm of words is:

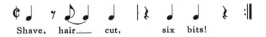

Shave, hair—— cut, six bits!

A more intricate claves rhythm is played in 4/4 meter on the underlined numbers representing eighth notes: 1 2 3 4 5 6 7 8 1 2 3 4 5 6 7 8.

Castanets used by children and by adult orchestra players are mounted on a handle. The instrument is made of a pair of cupped pieces of resonant hardwood, usually chestnut, attached by a cord. Of Spanish origin, the adult Spanish dancer holds a pair of unmounted castanets, one in each hand. The skilled dancer-player produces a variety of exciting effects from a sharp click to a sustained muffled rattle. Those played by children will produce only the sharp click. One castanet is sufficient, because of its penetrating sound. A recording of Chabrier's *España* rhapsody will illustrate its use in the adult orchestra.

Coconut shells are useful to imitate hoofbeats of horses. Ripe coconuts can be purchased at food stores and the outside fibers can be removed, if desired, by a coarse kitchen "scratcher." They are then cut in half with a saw and the meat is scraped out. The two halves are then struck together to make a "clip-clop" sound. Children should explore the variety of sounds possible by striking them together in different ways including inside out, and striking them with sticks. Two paper cups can imitate coconut shells with a softer sound.

Woodblocks are best obtained from commercial sources, although imitations can be made from sections of old baseball bats. Woodblocks are sometimes held suspended by a cord to increase vibration. They are

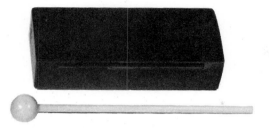

struck lightly with a hard rubber mallet at the hollow side near the edge over the slot. They can be played resting on a desk, preferably on a piece of felt, or held in the palm of the adult hand.

Children should experiment by striking them at other places, and with different beaters. They are useful to enhance songs about such subjects as ponies, cowboys, and clocks.

The *tone block* is produced commercially. The instrument is held in the left hand with the cut side toward the player. It is struck lightly on top with a stick, above the cut opening. Different sizes have different pitches, and this fact can be useful in song accompaniments.

The *xylophone,* a keyboard melody instrument, should be purchased for best results although it has been made experimentally by teachers and students in upper grades from redwood strips or one-inch doweling resting on ropes. In early primary grades it is often used for a special *glissando* effect to describe such incidents in songs as "The mouse ran up the clock," in "Hickory Dickory Dock." Later on it is used as a melody instrument. The *marimba* is a xylophone of Latin American origin that has metal tube resonators. (Illustrations of these instruments are shown in Chapter 9.)

METAL INSTRUMENTS

Finger cymbals are tiny replicas of the larger cymbal, and are usually obtained commercially rather than made by teachers. One is usually held in each hand, and they are struck together lightly at the edge or flat together for different effects. They can also be played with one hand, with the two cymbals fastened to fingers that can strike the instruments together. This latter way enables a dancer to accompany his own dancing with delicate metallic punctuations. Finger cymbals are useful for subtle effects in Oriental songs and to portray elves or angels.

The *triangle* is struck lightly by a metal rod on the inside corner of the base of the instrument. A large nail or spike will sometimes make a satisfactory substitute. It is held suspended by a cord. The tone can be continued by moving the beater back and forth rapidly on the inside edges of the two sides. It can be silenced by touching it.

Jingle bells are purchased. They are played by shaking them vigorously. Some are mounted on sticks while others are worn around the wrist or ankle. A small tinkling sound can be produced by holding

them toward the floor and moving them back and forth with a gentle motion of the wrist.

Jingle clogs are more easily purchased than made. Their major use is in primary grades. They are held in one hand and tapped against the palm of the other hand in a manner that leaves the jingles free to sound. When teachers make them from metal discs used in roofing, fastened loosely on a stick, they will gain added resonance if the discs are bent slightly. Sometimes the discs are alternated with bottle caps.

The commercially produced *tambourine* is best. It is held at the place on the instrument where there are no metal jingles. To play it, the head is struck against the heel of the hand, or it is shaken. The instrument strikes the hand; the hand does not strike the instrument. Experimental effects can be produced by tapping it on the knee, tapping it with fingers, and using a rubbing motion with the thumb followed by striking, tapping, or shaking. The head is coated with shellac and powdered rosin when professional drummers use the thumb roll. Tambourines lend atmosphere to Gypsy, Hebrew, Spanish, and Italian songs.

The true *gong* is relatively expensive. A large one could be borrowed from the high school band, perhaps. A gong can be made from German silver about one foot square. Cut a circle from this. Drill holes for the cord that will suspend it. Then hammer the edges, testing the sound

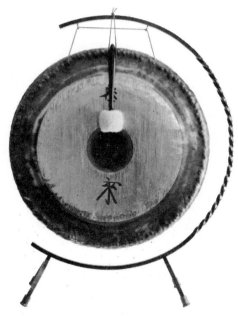

from time to time, until the edges curve inward about two inches. A substitute can be found in the metal lid of the heavy barrel-like cardboard containers often used as waste baskets in schools. Ask the school custodian to save one of the containers (to use as a drum) and the lid to use as a gong. Drill a hole by which to suspend it. A suspended length of iron pipe can be another substitute. This instrument is used with songs about cathedral bells, huge clocks, and the Orient.

Cymbals of the best tone are commercially made, although some teachers have found good tones in aluminum pan lids. They are held one in each hand and struck together in a glancing blow with hands moving up and down in contrary directions. Other effects can be found by striking the cymbal on its edge, and with different beaters or sticks.

INSTRUMENTS THAT SWISH OR RATTLE

Sandblocks, used largely in primary grades, can be made from any soft wood from 3/4″ to 1″ thick and about 3″ by 3″ square. Handles can be door or drawer pulls, spools, leather, or small pieces of wood. Fasten the handle with screws, and place No. 1–0 sandpaper or emery cloth (this lasts longer) on the rubbing side of the block with thumb tacks. Hold a block in each hand and rub the rough surfaces together. Some teachers believe that the motion of the arms required to play sandblocks is a superior means by which the five-and six-year-olds can achieve rhythmic control in a very short time.

Maracas can be purchased or made from a pair of gourds by placing in them a suitable amount of dry seeds, pebbles, or bird shot. They are necessary for many Latin American dance songs. Maracas are held either by handles or by the neck of an elongated gourd, and are usually shaken in a steady eighth-note rhythm. The arms move back and forth;

the wrists are stiff. For a soft effect they can be tapped by the fingers rather than shaken. Gourds from which to make maracas and guiros can be purchased from the Pearson Gourd Farm, 1409 North Merced Avenue, Box 310, El Monte, California. The catalog of this firm gives directions for the construction of these instruments. A single maraca on a long handle is used as an American Indian rattle. It can be decorated with feathers and furs. The *cabaca* is a large enameled gourd that has small wooden beads strung loosely around it. This form of rattle is a Latin American instrument. *Strip rattles* can be made from walnut shells and bottle caps suspended alternately on 3″ to 4″ cords suspended from a band. They are worn on the wrist or ankle in American Indian dances. *Other rattles* can be made from spice cans, typewriter ribbon cans, pill boxes, ice cream and cottage cheese cartons, salt boxes, etc. A maraca-like rattle can be made from a large electric light bulb. Cover it with papier mâché: when dry, break glass.

INSTRUMENTS THAT "SCRATCH"

Rhythm sticks make a light scratching sound when they are stroked across notches. The notches appear in most commercially made sticks, and can be added to teacher-made ones by making a row of shallow saw cuts on one of each pair of sticks. These can be filed to the proper depth and smoothness, and the smooth stick is then stroked over the notched stick.

A *guiro* is a large gourd with ridges cut along its side. It is played with a small stick or a wire scratcher scraped back and forth across the ridges. It is a Latin American instrument. Besides the scratching sound it can be made to produce a tap-scrape-tap rhythm.

HAWAIIAN INSTRUMENTS

Pu 'ili are slit bamboo sticks. They can be made from two 18″ bamboo sticks that are 1″ to 2″ in diameter. The lowest large joint is the handle. It can be drilled out and sanded. Holes 1/4″ to 3/8″ in diameter are drilled above this joint to serve as guides for cutting out corresponding slices from the holes to the tip. The sticks are struck softly together and used in graceful motions as an extension of the arm. *'Illi-ili* are pairs of small rounded volcanic rocks to be held in the palm of the hand and clapped or rubbed together. Using many players gives an interesting effect. The

'*I pu* is a "drum" made from a wide, jar-shaped gourd. The top of the stem end is cut off and the seeds and pulp are removed. It is played by slapping the side of the gourd with the palm of the hand.

DRUMS

There are many kinds and sizes of drums, manufactured and teacher-made. Some have one head, others two. They come singly and by two's and even three's. For different effects they can be struck off-center or in the center, with the fingertips, the heel of the hand, or with various types of padded beaters. There should be at least two drums in every classroom; one of low pitch and one of high pitch. The many types of commercial drums include the tom-tom, tunable drums, bongo, and conga drums. Homemade drums of varying quality may be devised from chopping bowls, wooden kegs, lard cans, and wastebaskets with goatskin (soaked 24 hours), real calfskin or heavy rubber thumbtacked, nailed, or laced on. Old drumheads can be used, salvaged from stores or from the high school bandroom. To paint skin drumheads, use water-color paint applied on the *wet* head. Color is an important element in constructing any of the instruments because it makes them more attractive to children. Smaller drums can be devised from oatmeal boxes or other cardboard containers, used as they are or with ends covered with a rubber sheet or very heavy paper. Flowerpot "drums" can be made by stretching and taping wet heavy paper across the opening; the paper tightens as it dries. Ready-made drums of fair quality are found in the very heavy cardboard barrel-like cartons used to ship chinaware, seed, ice cream mix, and sweeping compound. These are stood open-end-down on two books (to raise them off the floor in order to increase resonance) and pounded. They can be useful as drums, and have added utility in that the metal cover can be used as a gong. These potential drums are often found as wastebaskets in school corridors.

Drum beaters can be purchased. They can be made from sticks of doweling of sufficient diameter cut to proper length, and soft rubber balls. The doweling is glued into a hole made in the ball. Instead of the rubber ball, a ball of cotton, covered with muslin and tied, can be used, or a ball can be made of aluminum foil covered with muslin and painted with two or three coats of the nitrate liquid used by airplane manufacturers.

The *conga drum* is a large long Cuban drum played with the palms of the hands, usually with the left hand with flat fingers striking the edge of the head and the right hand also with flat fingers striking the center of the head.

The *bongo drum,* another Latin American instrument, is a double drum; one is larger than the other. Held between the knees with the small drum on the right, it is played with the tips of the fingers and the

thumbs. The bongo is used in Latin American music.

Some of the many possible songs for introducing and expanding the use of percussion instruments are the familiar "Hickory, Dickory, Dock," "Jingle Bells," "Jingle at the Window," "Ten Little Indians," various songs about trains, "This Old Man," "Toodola," "When the Saints Go Marching In," "Mister Banjo," "Down the River," "Sandy Land," and "Tinga Layo."

SUMMARY We have described some of the contributions that percussion instruments can make to children's explorations of tone qualities, dynamics, pitch, form, rhythm, and the interpretations of songs in which their use is appropriate. Concepts of the phrase, repetition, and contrast can be enhanced by creating percussion scores which reflect these aspects of form. Feelings for mood can be reflected in the choice of and the manner of playing the instruments. Notation can be learned and understood better when children find it useful to them in playing and composing percussion scores. Every concept of rhythm may be strengthened at times by the use of these instruments.

Examples of music for various rhythmic uses including body movement, listening-analysis, and creating percussion scores are on pages 236–238.

Bowmar Orchestral Library, Marches # 54; Dances # 55, # 56, # 84
Bowmar Records Albums:

Holiday Rhythms	1–5
Mexican Folk Dances	4–6
Rhythm Is Fun	K–2
Rhythm Time	1–3
Singing Games and Folk Dances (6 albums)	K–6
Singing Square Dances—Album 1	4–5
Album 2	6–7

Capitol Records Distributing Corporation
1750 North Vine St., Hollywood, California 90028

Listen, Move, and Dance, Vols. 1 and 2
Vol. 1, side one: "Moving Percussion"
    side two: "Electronic Sound Pictures"
Vol. 2, side one: "Music for Quick and Light, Quick and Strong, and Slow
      and Light Movements"
    side two: "Electronic Sound Patterns

Children's Record Guild and Young People's Records	*Suggested*
The Greystone Corporation	*Grade Levels*
100 Sixth Avenue, New York 13, N.Y.	
"Do This, Do That!"	K–1
"Drummer Boy"	K–3
"Eensie Beensie Spider"	K–2
"Folk Songs for Singing and Dancing"	2–5
"I Am a Circus"	K–2
"Let's Dance"	1–4
"Little Indian Drum" ("drum talk")	K–2
"Little Red Wagon"	K–2
"Merry Toy Shop"	K–3
"My Playful Scarf" (creative)	K–3
"My Playmate the Wind" (creative)	1–4
"Nothing To Do" (fundamental movements)	K–2
"Out of Doors"	K–3
"Ride 'Em Cowboy"	K–3
"Skittery Skattery"	K–2
"Slow Joe" (fast and slow)	K–2
"Strike Up the Band" (percussion)	K–3
"Swing Your Partner" (create dances)	2–6
"Sunday in the Park"	K–2
"Trains and Planes"	N–1
"When I Was Very Young"	N–2
"Visit to My Little Friend" (fundamental movements)	K–3

The following albums contain many of the above:

EAD 2005: *Things To Do*	K–3
EAD 2006: *More Things To Do*	K–3
EAD 2017: *Let's Play Rhythms*	K–3
EAD 2027: *Rhythm, Fun, and Songs*	K–2

Classroom Materials, Inc.
93 Myrtle Drive
Great Neck, New York 11020

"Introducing the Rhythm Instruments"	K–1

Columbia Records, Inc.
Educational Department
799 Seventh Avenue
New York 19, N.Y.

Participation Records

"Jum-A-Jingles" (rope skipping, ball bouncing)	1–3
"Lead a Little Orchestra" (conducting)	1–3
"Let's Have a Rhythm Band"	1–3

World Library of Folk and Primitive Music
    (ethnic recordings)

Folkways Records

"Adventures in Rhythm" (Ella Jenkins)	4–6
"American Play-Parties"	3–6
"Calypsos for Children"	3–6
"Dance Along"	K–3
"Folk Songs for Young Folks" (animals)	K–3
"Jamaica Songs and Games" (calypso)	3–6
"Rhythms for Children"	K–3
"Skip Rope Games"	K–3

    (Note: The Folkways Catalog contains ethnic recordings from all
       over the world.)

Methodist Church Publishing House
417 Church St.
Nashville 2, Tennessee

World of Fun Folk Dances
New World of Fun Series
    (Booklets of dance instructions available.)

RCA Victor Dance-A-Story Records (storybook record combination)

	Age Level
"Little Duck"	3–7
"Noah's Ark"	3–9
"Magic Mountain"	5–12
"Balloons"	4–12
"The Brave Hunter"	5–8
"Flappy and Floppy"	3–7
"The Toy Tree"	3–7
"At the Beach"	5–12

RCA Victor Basic Record Library for Elementary Schools

The Rhythm Program Six albums, one for each grade,	1–6
	Grade Level
Music of American Indians (album)	1–6
Music for Rhythm Bands (album)	1–3

Miscellaneous

"Arkansas Traveler"		Bowmar #56
"Brazilian Dance"	Guarnieri	Adventures in Music 6, v. 2
"Country Garden"	Grainger arr.	RCA Rhythm 6
"Farandole"	Bizet	Adventures in Music 6, v. 6
"Gavotte in D Minor"	Grétry	RCA Rhythm 5
"Golliwog's Cakewalk"	Debussy	Bowmar #63
"Jamaican Rumba"	Benjamin	Bowmar #56
"Juba Dance," "Turkey in the Straw," "War Dance of the Cheyenne," "Gossip"		Music Sound Books 8024
"La Czarine" (Mazurka)	Ganne	RCA Rhythm 6
"March Past of the Kitchen Utensils"	Vaughan-Williams	Adventures in Music 3, v. 1
"Minuet" from *Don Giovanni*	Mozart	RCA Rhythm 5
"Shepherds' Dance"	German	RCA Rhythm 5
"Spanish Dance No. 1"	Falla	Adventures in Music 6, v. 1
"Wedding Day at Troldhaugen"	Grieg	Bowmar #62

(For specific suggestions, study the Teachers Guides for the *Adventures in Music* Albums.)

INDIVIDUAL DIFFERENCES

Since children are different in physical make-up, the teacher can expect that what is an easy rhythmic response for one child may be a difficult one for another. To assist the child who finds rhythm difficult, the teacher seeks to guide him to success either in the same rhythm at a slower tempo, or with a different and more simple rhythmic action to which he can respond at his own natural tempo. When he succeeds, the child should then be helped to synchronize his movement with gradually slower and faster tempos. It helps some children to produce the sound of the rhythm by clapping, singing, speaking, chanting, or making up sounds; their sounds and actions are then more easily synchronized and a habit of doing an action with a sound begins to develop.

Sometimes a six-year-old does not understand that there is supposed to be a definite relation between the sound he hears and what his muscles are to do. Therefore, he cannot march in time with music until he is guided to discover this relation, possibly by the example of other children. Teachers should remember that when children are asked to move in time with music, they are being expected to (1) control a specific movement, (2) listen to the music, and (3) synchronize the two. It is natural that some children find the teacher's request to do three things at once confusing, and that the teacher must help the child by permitting him to learn the movement well before asking him to add the two other aspects. Sometimes the use of a paper streamer or a scarf will help a child to comprehend a motion that he cannot understand by use of the arm alone. The teacher should remember to emphasize use of the large muscles, for such children are probably not sufficiently developed physically to control the small muscles well.

When some children cannot clap their hands in time with music, they can sometimes succeed by striking both hands on the thighs. Some teachers slow the speed of recordings for action-responses of subnormal children. When this is done with songs, it should be remembered that this also lowers the pitch. Thus, the pitch can not be lowered out of the natural vocal range if the recordng is to be used for singing with the action. For children who are above average in physical control, the teacher encourages responses of a creative nature of which they are physically capable. Body movements and playing percussion instruments can provide means for successful participation other than singing for children who need to experience success.

Normal Expectations

EARLY CHILDHOOD

Rhythmic activities are free and informal; they emphasize use of the big muscles in large, free motions. The children do imaginative and creative play in imitation of men, animals, and things. They become able to respond to simple patterns played on the drum, piano, tone block, or record player with actions such as walking, marching, running, jumping, hopping, skipping, galloping, and tiptoeing. Concepts of high-low, heavy-light, long-short, and soft-loud can be acquired. Simple directed action songs and singing games are played, such as "The Elephants," "Eensy Weensy Spider," and "Hey Diddle Diddle." Such songs are found in quantity in nursery and kindergarten series books. Dramatizations, finger plays, and hand movements are done. Children learn to use some percussion instruments to tap in time with music and for sound effects that add interest and variety to musical experiences.

LEVELS ONE AND TWO

Ability to respond to fundamental movements with large free motions: walking, running, jumping, hopping, skipping, and combinations of these.

Performance and enjoyment of action songs (such as "If You're Happy") and singing game songs (such as "Wee Little Man," "My Pretty Little Miss," "Looby Lou," "Clapping Land," and "Pony Land").

Ability to respond to rhythm with movements such as swinging, bending, twisting, swaying, stretching, pushing, pulling.

Creative response to rhythm (rhythmic dramatization).

Ability to do simple dance steps, skills, and formations including galloping, sliding, skipping, bowing, circling, singing games, circle with partner on the right.

Understanding of the relation of rhythmic movement to quarter, eighth, and half notes (walking, running, and step-bending or bowing), and ability to use these rhythms by playing them on percussion instruments.

Growth in ability to suggest suitable percussion accompaniments for piano pieces and for recorded music.

Comprehension of whether the music "swings" in two's or three's (duple or triple meter).

Ability to combine movement and some percussion instruments with greater skill and for more specific purposes in level two.

Awareness of repeated rhythm patterns and repeated and contrasting phrases or sections of music in level two.

LEVELS THREE AND FOUR

Mastery of rhythmic concepts and skills taught in kindergarten through levels one and two.

Knowledge of many action songs, singing games, and simple play-party games and dances.

Ability to create and notate simple percussion scores.

The transfer of rhythmic understanding gained from body responses to note and rest values, including the dotted note.

Continued development in understanding beat, patterns, accent, meter, and form through body responses.

Development of increased awareness of the differences between descriptive music and pure ("pattern") music through creative rhythmic dramatization.

Knowledge of conductor's patterns for 2, 3, and 4 beat meters.

Ability to perform combined movements of walk-step, step-hop, skip-hop, step-slide, slide-hop, and to use these movements in dances and dramatizations.

Ability to march to duple and quadruple measures, accenting the first beat of each measure.

Recognition and identification of 2, 3, and 4 beat meters in recordings or in the singing and playing of the teacher.

Ability to step the melody rhythm of selected familiar songs.

Ability to clap, step, and write in notation simple rhythm patterns played by the teacher.

Recognition of the musical phrase through body movement.

Ability to create and notate percussion scores to songs and recordings.

Ability to interpret songs and recordings with rhythmic movement.

Ability to use percussion instruments to play both metric and melody rhythms.

Ability to use percussion instruments with discrimination.

LEVELS FIVE AND SIX

Mastery of rhythmic concepts and skills of the earlier levels.

Ability to dramatize work songs and ballads.

Ability to notate more complex rhythm patterns.

Knowledge of meter, notation, and melody rhythm in relation to the beat.

Creative interpretation of music's emotion and structure through movement.

Ability to use conductor's beat patterns in all common meters.

Ability to create more complex and tasteful percussion scores and to use percussion instruments with discrimination for sound effects with music.

Understanding the concept of syncopation through movement and the use of percussion instruments.

Increased skill in moving to and in reading the notation of more complex patterns.

Growth in comprehension and use of asymmetrical meters.

A repertoire of many American play party games and dances and folk dances of the world; an understanding of the place of these in the world of music.

Ability to play and enjoy Latin-American percussion instruments.

Selected Songs

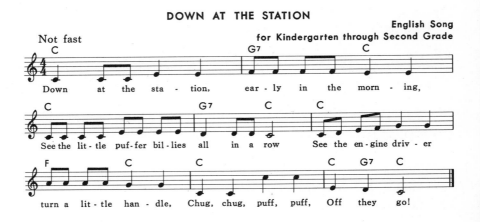

DOWN AT THE STATION

English Song
for Kindergarten through Second Grade

SOME SUGGESTED RHYTHMIC ACTIVITIES

Children

1. Clap the meter, four beats to the measure, as in measure 7; say "Chug, chug, puff, puff."
2. Clap the word-rhythm as you say the words.
3. Combine 1 and 2 by selecting appropriate percussion instruments for these rhythms.

Teacher

4. Select a rhythm pattern such as the note values in the first measure and have this played on a percussion instrument throughout the song. Children can learn it by repeating the words "Down by the station" in the rhythm of the first measure.
5. Nine-year-olds can step the note values, first of selected measures, then in two-measure parts until the entire song can be stepped.
6. Older children can identify each rhythm pattern, step it, and notate it.

SAILING

Italian Melody
for Grades Two and Three

SOME SUGGESTED RHYTHMIC ACTIVITIES

Children

1. Sway in time with the music.
2. Clap hands or use percussion instruments on the first beat of each measure and in the rhythm of the meter in three beats to the measure.

Teacher

3. Guide the children to invent with hand clapping or percussion instruments an appropriate way to mark the end of each of the four phrases, thus teaching phrase awareness.
4. Have the class conduct 3/4 meter.
5. Teach a simple waltz run or step. Example:

OLD MACDONALD

American Song

SOME SUGGESTED RHYTHMIC ACTIVITIES

Children

1. Sing the song, discuss aspects of it that may influence a percussion accompaniment, then create a percussion score and notate it.
2. Invent actions each time "Ee-i-ee-i-o" is sung. Dramatize the song.

Teacher

3. Review the basic beat by having the class conduct the meter.

THE PAW-PAW PATCH

Kentucky Singing Game for Grades Three through Five

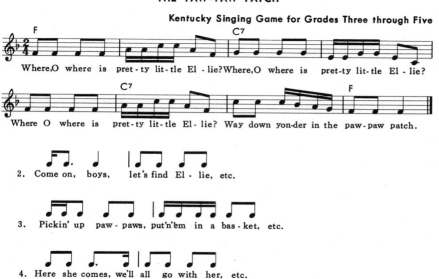

SOME SUGGESTED RHYTHMIC ACTIVITIES

Children

1. Create a dance-dramatization of the song.

Teacher

2. Use the song to teach the relation of word-rhythms to note values; use the different word-rhythms of the verses in a percussion score for the song.

RIG - A - JIG - JIG

SOME SUGGESTED RHYTHMIC ACTIVITIES

Children

1. Create a dance; learn and compare 2/4 and fast 6/8 meters in the process.
2. With percussion instruments, enhance the leisurely walking effect of the verse and the excited skipping effect of the refrain.

TO PUERTO RICO

SOME SUGGESTED RHYTHMIC ACTIVITIES

Children

1. Devise a Latin American percussion score and notate it. Possibilities
    include:

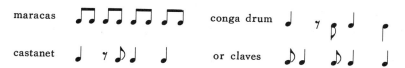

maracas   conga drum

castanet   or claves

Teacher

2. Teach for the concept of syncopation.

THE COUNT

Brazilian Song for Grades Five and Six

1. He wrote me a let-ter, ca-ram - ba! It asked for my
2. This he told my fa-ther, ca-ram - ba! Fa - ther shook with

hand.   I wrote him my an-swer, ca - ram - ba!
wrath.   He broke ev - 'ry pot in the kich - en;

Said, "No wed - ding band."   I ran down the path!

SOME SUGGESTED RHYTHMIC ACTIVITIES

Children

1. Devise a Latin American percussion score.

Teacher

2. Teach the ♪ ♩ ♩ rhythm pattern through use of the word "caramba,"
    which children enjoy emphasizing in the song.

3. Teach ♫ ♫ by comparing it with ♪♩ ♪♩ ♩ in "To Puerto
    Rico"; it is the same rhythm twice as fast. The generalization is that the
    same pattern can occur in lesser or greater note values (in diminution or
    augmentation).

Some Activities and Suggestions for Lesson Plans

A primary problem with music lesson plans is how to guide children toward the learning of musical facts and skills, the forming of concepts and generalizations in ways that truly attract children to music. It is the intent of every good teacher that children *enjoy* their experiences with music. Perhaps we can learn from the Manhattanville Music Curriculum Program (USEO 6–1999) ideas which help music lessons become both interesting and fascinating to the learners. This program deals more with ways of learning than with specific strategies. Its concept of the music class is that of a laboratory for discovery, dealing with sounds and skills. It is a place where children can explore music on their own terms and on their level of understanding by performing, composing, and evaluating music. The teacher is assumed to be a guide who creates problems for children to solve. He stimulates rather than dominates; he encourages rather than dictates; he questions more than he answers; and he is as sensitive to the learner as he is to the subject matter he wants children to learn. Every student is involved at times as a composer, a performer, a conductor, and a critic. Every student makes musical judgments at some time which are often hypotheses he must test through creative exploration and then evaluate. Some part of most lesson plans should reflect aspects of the Manhattanville exploratory approach.

The learner may imitate, explore, discover, recognize, identify, inquire, contrast, differentiate, classify, verbalize, recall, and evaluate. He may utilize one or more of the following activities to do these things: singing, playing instruments, moving his body, creating, reading, dramatizing, impersonating, and discussing. Remember to utilize all the appropriate senses in a lesson plan: hearing, seeing, and feeling with body muscles. Plan so that children listen before they attempt to respond with movement or with their voices. Avoid presenting too much in one lesson.

The teacher should help children sense the beat by sounding some type of clearly stated rhythmic introduction to performance-type activities. This can be done with hand clapping, with the Autoharp, with percussion instruments, with counting, and with the teacher's singing or playing.

In the following pages the reader will find a large number of activities listed which are related to the Structure of Music Outline in Chapter 6. He should not feel responsible for knowing how to work with each of these; they are presented as a list from which to choose. Some of them will require teaching experience to do well. Therefore, these activities and suggestions can be dealt with in part in the college class, in part during student teaching, and in part during later years of professional teaching. They combine both American and European teaching strategies and are listed in order of increasing difficulty. However, to relate these to specific levels of instruction, refer to the Scope and Sequence Chart in Appendix A, which deals with kindergarten through grade six.

Tempo

A Developmental Plan

The child discovers his natural tempo

The teacher adapts drum or piano accompaniment to the natural tempo of the individual learner.

The child recognizes relative fast and slow in songs, drum beats, and in recorded music.

The teacher provides the opportunity for the child to compare two songs, one fast and one slow; and two recordings, one fast and one slow.

The child discovers the concept of tempos appropriate for imitating animals or describing activities. The eye aids the ear.

The teacher uses songs and recordings that suggest appropriate rhythms for the movements of animals and man. The teacher draws chart-pictures of tempo vocabulary: a marching soldier —Di Marcia; a turtle—Adagio; a sleeping baby—Largo; a jet liner— Presto; a spinning top slowing down —Rallentando; a rocket taking off— Accelerando, and so on.

The child sees and identifies tempo designations in the musical score and understands them.

The teacher selects music which encourages such identification.

The child is able to provide appropriate tempo names for music sung and heard.

"What would happen if the tempo of this song is slowed down?" "Let's try it." "Is the result better, or worse?" "Why do you think so?" "Can you think of ways to vary the tempo that might improve this song?" "What terminology can you use to describe the changes in tempo?"

Behavioral Objective: The child reveals his understanding of concepts of degrees of fast and slow by . . . . . (what specific performance).

Dynamics

A Developmental Plan

The child begins to understand the difference between soft and loud and degrees of softer and louder by hearing and by acting this out in body movements. The comprehension of variations in dynamics increase; the child is able to express these in creative ways such as in body movement and in drawings.

piano (p)—soft
forte (f)—loud
The teacher plans experiences in which the children find these terms useful. Songs and recorded music offer experiences to build increasing comprehension of the variations in dynamics.

Vocabulary additions become useful to the learners in their own compositions.

Accent, crescendo (cres.), decrescendo (decres.), mezzo piano (mp), pianissimo (pp), mezzo forte (mf), fortissimo (ff).

Increasing ability to enter into a deeper analysis of music with respect to dynamics.

The children will suggest dynamics for their musical interpretations, and they will experiment with dynamic levels for the purpose of communicating ideas by means of music.

Behavioral Objective: The child reveals his understanding of concepts of loud and soft by . . . . . (what specific performance).

Rhythm

Basic Rhythmic Responses Beginning with the Beat

The child discovers his natural tempo; the teacher adapts drum or piano accompaniment to the natural tempo of the individual learner.

The teacher improvises on the beat with drum or piano and the children respond with walking, running, skipping, galloping, as they are able. (When the piano is used, the black keys provide an easy way to improvise.)

Use word rhythms of names, sayings, and poems; clap hands, march, step, or play percussion instruments in order to feel the rhythm. Limericks can be fun.

One child creates a rhythm pattern within the notational limits set by the teacher; a second child creates a different one that "fits" with the first one. The two patterns may be written on the chalkboard; the class then plays them in sequence, then in combination.

Dramatize the beat. "How many ways can you act it out?" (chopping a tree down, shoveling snow, hammering, sawing, etc.)

Dramatize the beat through walking. "How many different ways can we walk?" (tired, slow, lightly, fast, heavily like an elephant, like a toy soldier, etc.)

After young children have learned to walk in time with the beat, ask them to draw their own original notation or picturing of the quarter note beat pattern. Guide this to eventually relate to the regular quarter note notation.

Dramatize running. "How many ways can we run?" (as in a race, fast, slow, as if we are tired, quietly so no one will see or hear us.)

Use songs appropriate for rhythmic dramatizing or impersonating.

Imitative clapping; the teacher claps rhythm patterns for the children to imitate in order that they may learn about accent, meter, measure, slow-fast, long-short. This activity leads to canon clapping. See the Orff-Keetman *Music for Children I—Pentatonic* for suggestions.

Word-rhythm clapping; use rhythms of names of people, geographical places, flowers, animals, foods, etc., as well as nursery rhymes and poetry.

Use question and answer clapping for study of beat, accent, meter, and phrase.

The teacher plays a steady beat while children take turns performing a different note value that "fits with it."

Experiment with clapping one note value or rhythm pattern while doing another one with the feet.

Experiment with combining two or three patterns. The melody rhythms of two songs can be used for this also; example: *Are You Sleeping?* and *Row, Row, Row Your Boat* even though one is in 6/8 meter and the other is in 2/4 meter.

Perform after-beats with heels and clapping, perhaps to accompany a dance song. Keep toes on the floor; use heels for beat one and clap on two. Eventually do this at a faster tempo, with heels on the beat and clapping on and: 1 *and* 2 *and* 3 *and* 4 *and.*

Experiment with beats and after-beats; try clapping or walking on first the beat, then on the after-beat; try alternating phrases this way, then try alternating measures.

Make a unit study of different kinds of marches; include one grand march in the gymnasium. See Bowmar #54 *Marches* and RCA Rhythm Program VI.

Make a unit study of the waltz. Find different types of waltzes in *Adventures in Music.*

Make a unit study of dance which relates clearly to music learning.

The Study of Meter

Use selected words to discover accent. Examples: a-rith-me-tic, ge-og-ra-phy.

Ask children to invent ways to respond to the beats in every common meter.

Examples: 2/4—touch knees, then head.

3/4—touch knees, hip, forehead.

4/4—clap above head for first beat, clap opposite chest for second beat, slap thighs for third beat, touch knees for fourth beat.

5/4—walking, except for a jump on the first beat.

For all meters: push both hands into the air for the first beat and pull back for the other beats.

Conduct the meter while singing the song; discover that two rhythms are in evidence, the meter rhythm and the melody rhythm.

Divide the class and experiment with clapping the rhythm of one melody at the same time as that of another melody; select tunes of the same tempo and meter. Later, combine different meters having the same tempo.

Experiment with well-known songs to find answers to challenging questions: "What would happen if C became ¢ in this song?" "If slow 6/8 became fast 6/8?" "If 3/4 became 3/8?"

When working with 3/4 meter with older children, play or sing "When Irish Eyes Are Smiling" in its appropriately fast tempo. Ask the class to identify the beat and its grouping. They should discover two beats of three divisions each—and in sets of two's. Then proceed to a recording of a fast waltz such as "The Blue Danube" and explore the beats in it. The learners should discover that a quarter note does not always receive one beat and that the meter signature signifies units of measure, not beats. They should find that the lower number of the signature represents a note (not a beat), and that the upper number tells the number of those notes or their equivalent in one measure. Test the relationship of beat and meter further by playing a recording—and showing the score—of the beginning of Mendelssohn's *Italian Symphony*. They will find that there is but one beat for each 6/8 measure.

Ask children to compose a piece with an unusual, but organized, meter pattern such as one measure each of 3/4, 2/4, and 2/4 in repeated succession.

Experiment with writing a familiar song in a number of different meters including some less common ones such as 5/4 and 7/8.

The Study of Rhythm Patterns

Utilize words whenever they can assist children to feel and comprehend the pattern. Examples:

violets, daffodils, chocolate,

peppermint, tumblebug, bumblebee

marigold

water-lily

lilies of the valley

"Sit in a circle and clap your hands."

wisteria

Use long-short line notation to picture duration and pitch.

Use the Young People's Record *Little Indian Drum* to encourage a creative study of sending word-rhythm messages by drumming.

Let children manipulate colored sticks or colored sheets of paper cut in proper sizes to represent whole, half, quarter, and eighth notes. Students arrange sticks or paper in various combinations with the stipulation that no combination can be of larger size than the biggest stick or sheet. Then they clap or speak the resulting note-value arrangements. Students can also place these on the floor and walk or step them as they count the measure beats. More advanced students can chart entire short songs in this manner.

Use *Threshold To Music* Experience Charts, First Year, 1–11. These are useful in assisting the understanding of the beat and quarter note, eighth note and quarter rest values.

The teacher plays measures of drum beats or plays selected measures of standard "classical" music on the piano; the children respond by translating these to the *ti-ti-ta's*.

"Which is the one I clap?" The teacher asks children which of the following measures on the chalkboard or chart he claps:

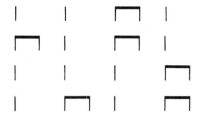

"Which one did I play?" The children select the correct rhythmic grouping from six different small cards or charts at their desks, or from six large charts on the wall. These can be done in adult notation.

Use flashcards with simple rhythm patterns. The teacher shows a card, then conceals it; then he asks the class to clap it, promoting note memory.

The children tap a steady beat while the teacher plays a tune to this beat. The game is for the children to remember the tune and write it in rhythmic notation. A Hungarian third grade wrote this one correctly:

The teacher writes a clapping performance test with two objectives —note reading and introducing an aspect of the style of some contemporary music. Notice that the eighth note group is every other measure; this gives some stability to the exercise. Older children are to establish the beat, then clap this:

Alter familiar melodies by changing note values or meters; let the children make the suggestions and do the experimenting.

Ask the children to devise a notated rhythm pattern to use as an ostinato throughout a familiar song. Let them evaluate its degree of success.

Encourage the composition of rhythmic pieces. Children can clap hands, snap fingers, slap thighs, stamp feet, and play percussion instruments. Use simple note values and patterns at first. Eventually employ all common meters; later on use uncommon meters for advanced students or classes. Utilize both original and planned forms such as minuet and gavotte. Set selected poems to rhythmic notation of various percussive effects.

Challenge the children to read rhythm patterns from chalkboard, overhead projector, or chart. Encourage them to write patterns for the class to read. Challenge the older children with patterns in less common meter signatures.

Ask the children to clap a notated pattern while singing "Lightly Row." They will be doing two things at once, singing the melody and clapping

the rhythmic ostinato. Example: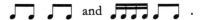

Ask the children to write similar patterns to try with other songs. Have them evaluate the suitability.

Use repetitious rhythmic variations of common tunes to help children learn specific patterns. Example: With the tune of "Twinkle, Twinkle, Little Star," sing (with *la*) or play the melody throughout with one pattern, altering the number of melody tones to fit the selected pattern, such as

♫ ♩ ♫ ♩ and ♬♬ ♫ ♩ .

Ask children to listen carefully to selected songs, find outstanding rhythm patterns, and write them.

Challenge the children to listen to Milhaud's "Copacabana," Adventures in Music 4 v. 2, to find and identify the four major rhythm patterns used by the composer.

Conduct the meter while singing designated patterns. The children conduct a meter (3/4) while they sing different patterns from the chalkboard, each

time on an ascending or descending scale tone. For example, ♩. ♪♩

would be sung with Latin or neutral syllables for a few scale degrees, then

♫ ♩ ♫ ♩ ♫ ♩ for several pitches, then ♩ ♩ , ♩.♫♫ ♩ and

others. The entire pattern would be sung on *one* pitch at a time. The teacher has a series of such patterns written on the chalkboard before the class begins.

Draw Creative Responses to Relative Duration,
Accent, Meter, Patterns, Dynamics and Tempo.

Utilize Percussion Instruments

Proceed from body movement and word rhythms to the same beats and accents
with percussion instruments. Introduce instruments one or two at a time.

Try using Children's Record Guild recording "Strike Up the Band," in which
percussion instruments are *reviewed*. Their order is drum, cymbal, wood
block, jingle bells, sticks, triangle, tambourine. Evaluate this approach.

Encourage children to select percussion instruments for specific purposes—
to accompany fundamental movements, to provide sound effects for stories,
for accompaniments to songs or recordings. Tape results for student evaluation.

Use percussion instruments for specific purposes such as to help children learn
concepts of the beat, measure, question-and-answer, slow-fast, accent,
long-short, loud-soft, crescendo-decrescendo.

Use the instruments to build concepts of the phrase, balance, form, instrumentation. Looking at the scores in *This Is Music,* Book 4, Allyn and Bacon, will
be helpful.

Provide opportunities for the children to suggest and write percussion accompaniments at their level of capability.

Use the instruments to help children learn the concepts of AB, ABA, and rondo
forms.

Utilize the instruments to help children build concepts of experimental music;
the children will first compose experimental compositions according to the
teacher's established limits of the piece, then later on with their own free
planning. Tape these compositions, then replay for student evaluation.

Utilize Recordings; Other Listening Experiences

Try using the Children's Record Guild recording "A Visit to My Little Friend"
to review simple fundamental movements.

Study similar and contrasting phrases by body movement, using appropriate
recordings from *Adventures in Music,* the *RCA Rhythm Program,* and other
educational collections and albums. Draw from the children how they might
"act out" the music when it is the same and when it is different. Possibilities
will include reversing directions and changing steps to reflect phrases that
are the same and those that are different.

Relate physical movements or feelings with recorded music to build concepts of
staccato and legato articulation in recorded music. *Legato* relates to such
feelings as stroking a cat, stroking velvet, and walking slowly in deep
water. *Staccato* relates to such physical sensations as putting a finger quickly
in and out of boiling water, walking on a hot sidewalk, and touching
prickles.

To encourage sensitivity to fundamental movements, assign groups of children a basic movement to express physically whenever it occurs rhythmically in selected recorded music. This activity is described in detail in *New Approaches to Music in the Elementary School,* Raebeck and Wheeler, W. C. Brown Company Publishers, Dubuque, Iowa, 1964, p. 112.

Children's free movement in response to recordings is described in detail in Raebeck and Wheeler, p. 114.

To develop tonal memory in the "inner ear," clap or play the rhythm of familiar songs and ask children to identify the songs. Have very young children choose between two or three songs. Older children can play a game of such song identification by each in turn clapping a rhythm for the class.

Listen to selected recordings to discover and notate distinctive rhythm patterns. These can be simple ones from songs in recordings for the music series at first. Older children can do this with established patterns such as the habanera or bolero. Examples of recordings for these older children are Cui's *Orientale,* Porter's *Begin the Beguine,* and Ravel's *Bolero.*

Listen to recordings to discover and notate syncopation.

Use selected recordings to teach concepts of the beat, phrase, a b, a b a, A B, A B A, and rondo forms. Percussion instruments and body movements may be employed to reinforce these concepts.

Listen to recordings to determine meter.

Listen in order to reflect in body movement all that the learner hears in the music. This means a total analysis of the music in movement at the learner's level of musical sensitivity. A book that describes this in detail is *Interpreting Music Through Movement* by Louise Humphreys and Jerrold Ross, Prentice-Hall, Inc., 1964.

Utilize Dance to Teach Music Concepts

The children create dances based upon accents, meters, rhythm patterns and forms. Songs or recordings may be used.

Children do free dance improvisations to songs and recordings, often by couples with hands on each other's shoulders. Such improvisations are based upon accents, meter, phrases, and rhythm patterns.

Traditional dances are learned and their notated rhythm patterns are observed and related to the body movement.

SOME BEHAVIORAL OBJECTIVES

Behavioral objectives are generally written in two different ways. If the lesson plan clearly describes the activity through which the children's ability is to be tested, the form is written simply: "The children will be able to distinguish between the beat and the rhythm of the melody or words of the song." If the lesson plan does not explain this, then the form that follows is used.

The child

can distinguish between the beat and the rhythm of the melody or words of a song by . . . . . (state the performance activity here)
can differentiate between even and uneven rhythm patterns by: . . . . .
reveals awareness of metrical divisions in two's and three's by:
can understand 2-to-1 notational relationships such as

$$\half + \half = \whole \qquad \quarter + \quarter = \half \qquad \eighth\eighth = \quarter \quad by: \ldots$$

finds relationships between accent patterns and common meters by: . . . . .
can understand 3-to-1 notational relationships such as

$$\quarter\,\quarter\,\quarter = \dottedhalf \qquad \eighth\eighth\eighth = \dottedhalf \qquad by: \ldots$$

reveals his understanding of 4-to-1 notational relationships such as

$$\eighth\eighth\eighth\eighth = \half \qquad \sixteenth\sixteenth\sixteenth\sixteenth = \quarter \qquad by: \ldots$$

demonstrates his comprehension of any specific common meter by: . . . . .
identifies syncopated patterns by: . . . . .
reveals his comprehension of more complex rhythm patterns by: . . . . .
reveals his comprehension of less common meters by: . . . . .
is able to relate rhythm patterns in songs and recorded music to the principles of unity and variety by: . . . . .
can identify distinctive rhythm patterns in national songs and dances by: . . . . .
is able to employ and understand accent pattern in unusual meters as combinations of those previously learned by: . . . . .
is able to comprehend rhythmic devices utilized by composers by: . . . . .

For writing lesson plans, refer to the following as needed:

1. the Developmental Characteristics and Implications Chart in Chapter 3.

2. the Structure of Music Chart, tempo, dynamics, and rhythm sections, and plans for teaching music in Chapter 6.

3. types of thinking, types of questions, principles of learning in Chapter 4.

4. the environment for learning and necessary routines for teaching in Chapter 5.

5. the Scope and Sequence Chart in the Appendix.

Some generalizations in addition to those found in the Structure of Music Chart are:

Rhythm is ordered (made orderly or organized) by stronger and weaker accents.

Rhythm is ordered by rhythm patterns in melodies.

Meter measures beats and rhythm mathematically.

The beat and rhythm patterns are unifying influences.

Melody-rhythm is as important to melodic individuality as is melodic contour (pitch levels).

When longer and shorter sounds and silences are grouped, rhythm is the outcome.

Polyrhythms result when different rhythm patterns or groupings sound at the same time.

INQUIRY AND SELECTED ACTIVITIES

1. Miss Smith is teaching rhythm to her class today. First she tells the children that she is going to play walking music and they are to walk to it. Next she tells them to listen to the running music she will play, and instructs them that they are to do tip-toe running. After this the children are informed that they will skip to the teacher's playing. The last activity is a more complex one in which the children are told that the music tells them to walk for eight steps, skip for eight counts, then walk for eight steps. After practicing several times, the class does quite well. Rewrite this lesson so that it becomes a creative-exploratory one for the children.

2. Observe a lesson in rhythm in an elementary school. Identify the concepts being taught, determine which are being stressed and ascertain what strategies are used to develop them. How would you develop these concepts if you were the teacher?

3. Develop a resource unit on rhythm for a specific achievement level. Include the following: generalizations, concepts, typical data, behavioral objectives, types of questions, teaching strategies and activities, and materials.

4. List all the ways you can think of to encourage children to create rhythm.

5. In every song there are ordinarily three distinct aspects of rhythm: the rhythm of the first beat of the measure (primary accent), the rhythm of the beat, and the rhythm of the melody or words. Try writing a percussion score for a familiar song on this basis. Select instruments to play on the rhythm of the first beat and select others to play on the other two rhythms. Experiment by dividing instruments into groups of similar pitches and

into groups of similar type. Find out which of the instruments are most appropriate for each rhythm.

6. Compile a file of recordings for use in teaching concepts of rhythm.

7. Appoint class committees to investigate the origin of folk and traditional dances in which they are interested. Each committee will report its findings, demonstrate the dance, play related music, and present ways to use this knowledge with children.

8. If you were in a classroom that contained no percussion instruments, what potentialities for sound could you find in the materials around you? Examples: the sound of paper held in the air and tapped with a pencil, buckles or heavy jewelry struck with another object, the waste basket, and sounds made with the body. Use these to create an interesting percussion score.

9. "Orchestrate" the following words with speech and percussion instruments:

> 6/8 *Life pays in kind,*
> *Life pays in kind; A*
> *song for a song, a blow for a blow,*
> *Life pays in kind.*

10. Make up a story and use percussion instruments for sound effects. Example: The alarm clock (triangle) wakens us in the morning. The clock (gong or finger cymbals) strikes eight. Mother calls, "Are You Sleeping?" (sing the song to the accompaniment of the clock ticking—woodblock, rhythm sticks). On the way to school we hear a train (sandblocks) and horses (coconut shells). Such a story is another way to help children learn the appropriateness of specific percussion instruments.

REFERENCES

ANDREWS, GLADYS, *Creative Rhythmic Movement for Children*. Englewood Cliffs, New Jersey: Prentice-Hall, Inc., 1954.

COLE, NATALIE R., *The Arts in the Classroom*. New York: The John Day Company, Inc., 1940. Chapter 4.

COLEMAN, SATIS, *The Drum Book*. New York: The John Day Company, Inc., 1931.

DOLL, EDNA, AND MARY J. NELSON, *Rhythms Today*. Morristown, N.J.: Silver Burdett Co, 1965.

DRIVER, ANN, *Music and Movement*. New York: Oxford University Press, 1947.

DRIVER, ETHEL, *A Pathway to Dalcroze Eurythmics*. New York: Thomas Nelson & Sons, 1951.

GARY, CHARLES L. ED., *The Study of Music in the Elementary School: A Conceptual Approach*. Music Educators National Conference, Washington, D.C., 1967. pp. 11–50.

HOOD, MARGUERITE V. AND E. J. SCHULTZ, *Learning Music Through Rhythm.* Boston: Ginn & Company, 1949.

HUMPHREYS, LOUISE, AND JERROLD ROSS, *Interpreting Music Through Movement.* Englewood Cliffs, New Jersey: Prentice-Hall, Inc., 1964.

JACQUES-DALCROZE, EMILE, *Rhythm, Music, and Education.* New York: G. P. Putnam's Sons, 1921.

KRAUS, RICHARD, *A Pocket Guide of Folk and Square Dances and Singing Games for the Elementary School,* Prentice-Hall, Inc., 1966. Recordings to use with this book may be obtained from Educational Dance Recordings, Inc., Box 6062, Bridgeport, Connecticut.

MACE, KATHRINE, *Let's Dance a Story.* New York: Abelard-Schuman, 1955.

MANDELL, MURIEL AND ROBERT E. WOOD, *Make Your Own Musical Instruments.* New York: Sterling Publishing Company, 1957.

MARSH, MARY VAL, "An Exploration in Percussion," *Music Educators Journal,* (June-July, 1962), pp. 37–40.

MASON, BERNARD S., *Drums, Tomtoms, Rattles.* New York: A. S. Barnes & Co., 1938.

MORALES, HUMBERT, *Latin American Instruments.* New York: H. Adler Publishers Corp., 1954.

MORGAN, E., AND H. GRUBBS, "An Approach to Rhythms for Children," *Childhood Education,* XXIX (April, 1953) pp. 383–7.

MUKERJI, ROSE, "The Arts: Repetitive or Creative," in *Creative Teaching in the Elementary School* by Abraham Shumsky, (Appleton-Century-Crofts, New York, 1965,) pp. 210–27.

MURRAY, RUTH L., *Dance in Elementary Education.* New York: Harper and Row, 1953.

MURSELL, JAMES L., *Music Education, Principles and Programs.* Morristown, New Jersey: Silver Burdett Company, 1956. Chapter 9.

ORFF, CARL, AND GUNILD KEETMAN, *Music for Children, I-Pentatonic,* English adaptation by Doreen Hall and Arnold Walter, New York, Associated Music Publishers, 1956, pp. 66–87. Also see *Music for Children* recording, Angel Records 3582 B, and *Music for Children* film, Contemporary Films, New York.

RAEBECK, LOIS, AND LAWRENCE WHEELER, *New Approaches to Music in the Elementary School.* Dubuque, Iowa: Wm. C. Brown Company Publishers, 1964, Chapter 4.

RICHARDS, MARY HELEN, *Threshold to Music:* Experience Charts for the First Year, Teachers Text/Manual *The First Three Years,* Harper and Row, Publishers, Evanston, Illinois.

ROHRBOUGH, LYNN, *Handy Play Party Book.* Delaware, Ohio: Cooperative Recreation Service. Also *Handy Square Dance Book* and *Handy Folk Dance Book.*

SAFFRAN, ROSANNA B., *First Book of Rhythms.* New York: Holt, Rinehart & Winston, Inc., 1963.

SHEEHY, EMMA DICKSON, *Children Discover Music and Dance*. New York: Holt, Rinehart & Winston, Inc., 1959. Chapters 7, 8.

SWANSON, BESSIE, *Music in the Education of Children*. Wadsworth Publishing Company, Inc., 1964, Chapters 3, 4.

Films

Building Children's Personalities with Creative Dancing, University of California Extension Division Film 5844. For teachers.

Developing Skills in Music, Group One, Society for Visual Education, Inc., Chicago. Four filmstrips with records for primary-intermediate grades.

Discovering Rhythm, United World Films, Universal Education and Visual Arts, 221 Park Ave. South, New York City 10003. Concepts in rhythm for children from pre-school to seven years.

Let's Begin With the Beat, EMC Corporation, St. Paul, Minn. A sound-filmstrip.

Pantomimes, Brandon Films, New York. How the body may be used to communicate ideas.

Percussion, Churchill Films, 662 N. Robertson Blvd., Los Angeles, Cal. 90069. Includes children playing Indonesian instruments.

Percussion, the Pulse of Music, National Educational Television, Audio-Visual Center, Indiana University, Bloomington, Indiana. Three professional percussionists demonstrate instruments and involve children in playing them.

Rhythm Instruments and Movement, Encyclopaedia Britannica Films, Wilmette, Ill.

9

pitch, melody, and singing

In Chapter 8 it was stated that there are relationships
between body movement in response to music and learning concepts of pitch and melody. By means of such movement the
learner can improve his ability to listen to music and to grasp
tonal and other expressive relationships. From this foundation
the teacher assists children to further their learning to hear pitch
accurately and to reproduce vocally what they hear. He also
helps them to sing with understanding and to use their singing
voices for self-expression in daily living.

RECENT RESEARCH

An opinion survey included as part of *An Interim Report* of
Cooperative Research Project No. 5-0241,* by A. Oren Gould
of Western Illinois University agrees with earlier estimates of the
approximate percentage of children that teachers classify as "non-
singers"; it was 50% for the first grade with a steady reduction

---

*A publication produced from the completed project is *Finding and
Learning to Use the Singing Voice: A Manual for Teachers* by A. Oren Gould
(Washington, D. C.: Office of Education (Ditew), Bureau of Research, OEC
6–10–016, 1968).

to 5% in the sixth grade. However, the percentage of children that teachers classified as "problem singers" was 36.6% in the first grade with a gradual reduction to 11% in the sixth grade. This study claims to have established two basic principles of learning to sing: 1) the child must *learn to hear his own voice* in speaking and singing and to control high and low pitch levels with it, and 2) the child must experience unison with another voice or instrument and *learn the sound and feeling of his voice as it matches the pitches which he hears*. Both visual and tonal associations are needed to develop the concepts of high and low in speaking and singing. (The use of the tape recorder would be valuable in helping the child hear his own voice.) Recommended activities include speech-to-song activities; repeated patterns in play or game songs such as found in echo songs, songs about animals, and roll call songs, use of humming and neutral syllables, body movements of many types which dramatize pitch and tonal direction, and mechanical devices such as bells and piano keyboard to hear and visualize pitch changes. The survey, which was sent to 578 teachers in every state, nine European countries, Canada, South America, and Australia, revealed "a certain amount of consensus" in the following:

1. All children can be helped to participate to some extent in singing activities with enjoyment and success.

2. Inability to sing a prescribed pitch does not prove that the child cannot hear pitch differences; it may mean only that he has not yet learned "what it feels like" to use his voice in unison with another.

3. The most common vocal problem is that of the low speaking voice coupled with the child's inability to sing comfortably at the higher pitch the teacher prescribes for the class.

4. Many of the children's psychological inhibitions toward singing can be traced to attitudes and remarks of parents and teachers.

5. Remedial measures in the group are more easily employed during kindergarten through grade three; in later grade levels more individual attention is necessary.

A study now in progress by Dr. Robert B. Smith at the University of Illinois, *The Effect of Group Nursery School Music Training on Later Achievement and Interest in Music: A Ten Year Progress Report,* began with teaching three- and four-year-old children in groups of twenty. The study plans to follow these children through the secondary school. After one year, the nursery school children were able to sing more accurately than older groups. They were also more advanced in rhythmic and listening skills. It was found that in general the children sang lower pitches more easily than high pitches—"low" meaning the range from middle C up to A, and "high" meaning the range from G above middle C to D a fifth above G. Furthermore, experimental subjects demonstrated far greater interest in music than those in the control groups, and girls were more advanced than boys, as a group, in all grade levels. However, the experimental group boys appeared to close the gap at the fifth grade level. With the exception of the experimental group girls, the children experienced a slump in pitch accuracy at the third grade level which has not been explained. Tentative conclusions in the ninth year of the study include:

1. Lower tones should be used in those songs selected for younger children. (The control group boys found relatively good pitch accuracy only in the "extreme lower range" of low B♭ to first space F.)

2. It is possible that songs emphasizing the upper range pitches should not be a major part of the song repertoire until the intermediate grades. (All boys were improving at the fifth-grade level.)

3. Teachers should be conscious of sex differences as they plan singing programs for young children. Boys are usually slow beginners and make less progress than girls in the early years. It was indicated that boys who have nursery school music training can "catch up" to the girls in pitch accuracy at about the fifth grade level if vocal ranges appropriate for them are used.

It was believed that evidence to date suggests that children who have nursery school experience display, during the years which follow, a greater interest in music and a higher level of achievement than children who do not have this experience. Among the most significant implications of this incomplete study are: 1) boys are not able to progress as rapidly as girls, and teacher plans should reflect this, and 2) the range of most songs for young children should tend to be low rather than high in order to achieve maximum success in matching tones. However, there will be exceptions to these implications.

The Child Voice

The child voice is often described as light in quality as well as in volume. It is also an extremely flexible mechanism, as illustrated by the strident cries of the playground. The teacher, then, is confronted by a voice that is capable of expressing many moods in song. Since there are many moods to express, this child voice can be sweetly soft and ethereal as it sings "Lullaby and goodnight" and can be momentarily harsh as it sings "David *killed* Goliath!" A logical way of deciding upon the voice quality desired in any song is for the teacher and children to discuss what manner of voice should be used to express the meaning of the words properly and to evaluate this continually when they sing. Although the child voice is light in quality, it should not sound weak or overly soft.

Many of the problems related to singing are soon solved when one adds to the above idea the following:

1. To make a generally pleasing sound (simple, natural, and clear).

2. To sing in a manner that avoids strain and tenseness.

3. To take breaths where one does when speaking the words (usually as the punctuation indicates); do not interrupt the phrase by breathing in unnatural places.

4. To enunciate clearly, but pronounce r's as Southerners do [ah(r)], and sound final consonants distinctly and in unison.

VOICE RANGE AND PRODUCTION

Classroom teachers insisted for years that songs in the older series books demanded too high a range for a great many of the children's voices. As the years passed, these teachers observed a gradual lowering of the ranges in later books. However, individual voices vary greatly in range, particularly in the ability to sing high pitches. A minority of children can sing well above the top line of the staff, but in *group* singing this line is probably the upper limit for most classrooms. Three-year-olds generally sing in a range of three to five notes; four-year-olds sing in a range of five to six notes; five-year-olds can expand this to an octave. Because most pre-school children sing within the following range, it follows that it will be useful *at the beginning* of the first grade for group singing.

The range within which most songs in series books are written is the following:

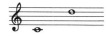

This range seems to be a basic one: it suits most adult voices well, and is also the playing range of many of the small wind instruments to be discussed later in this chapter. The one that most children are able to sing by the sixth grade follows. (However, some of the boys cannot sing this high because their voices may be in the first stages of change.)

Ranges that some of the children can sing successfully and yet include many "problem singers" are:

The authors observed no hesitancy on the part of Hungarian teachers to use these ranges for all of the children *some* of the time. It is obvious that there are different ranges for different age groups and for boys and girls at some levels. However, all children, even in kindergarten and first grade, should be encouraged to use all of their comfortable range, especially that of middle C to fourth line D or fifth line F.

The concept of range of voices and instruments is part of the expanding concepts of degrees of high and low in pitch. This study of high and low continues by observing and experiencing the ranges of the different bell sets, the piano, and of all the adult instruments. By the sixth grade high and low can be related to charts such as one provided by the Conn Corporation, Elkhart, Indiana. "Range Chart for Band and Orchestra Instruments Showing Practical Ranges Commonly Used." This chart compares the ranges of the piano, voices, and instruments as well as the vibrations per second for each pitch. The questions "How high?" and "How low?" have scientific implications for this study by older children.

Teachers often search for songs of limited range with which to initiate easy singing experiences. Examples follow:

3-*note range:*	Hot Cross Buns
	Merrily We Roll Along
4-*note range:*	A-Hunting We Will Go
	Sally Go Round
5-*note range:*	Go Tell Aunt Rhody
	Cradle Song (Rousseau)

Lightly Row
Sleep Baby Sleep
Mary Had a Little Lamb
Oats Peas Beans and Barley
Flowing River
Green Gravel
Whistle Daughter Whistle
Grandria Grunts
Old Woman (some versions)
When the Saints Come Marching In
Jingle Bells (refrain)

6-note range: This Old Man
Baa Baa Black Sheep
Old MacDonald
London Bridge
Lovely Evening
Hey Betty Martin
Skip To My Lou
Goodbye My Lover Goodbye
O Susanna
Old Brass Wagon
Pop! Goes the Weasel
Hickory Dickory Dock
Looby Lou
Caisson Song
Jolly Old St. Nicholas
Up On The Housetop
Au Claire de la Lune
Susy, Little Susy
Cindy
The Mocking Bird

When series books present a song in a particular key, the writers have selected that key with the vocal range in mind. While it is indicative of a proper range for children's voices, there are considerations that lead teachers to change this range. Most of the songs in recent books are pitched in an easy, fairly low range. Therefore, after a song has been learned, the teacher should pitch it and other songs gradually higher, by half-steps, until teacher and children have extended their range into that considered normal for voices that have had help in developing the range to its natural span. Other songs will be printed in keys that demand a high range. Should a class be as yet unable to reach this range, the teacher will pitch these songs somewhat lower—usually not more than two whole steps at the most—then gradually pitch them higher as the singing range

of the children improves. In today's music fundamentals classes for classroom teachers, simple transposition of the key by building the tonic
chord (135) on the new keynote on bells or piano or singing it from a
note sounded on a pitchpipe is commonly taught. Teachers of music
need to be able to change the key of a song when the stage of development of the children's voice range makes this advisable.

The matter of correct pitching of songs becomes more complex in
the sixth grade, where some of the boys may be in the first stage of voice
change. The full range of these voices will normally fall approximately
a fourth; thus a well-developed singing range of B♭ below middle C up
to top line F will drop to a range of from F on the bass staff extending up
to an octave above middle C.

Since the highest and lowest pitches of any range are somewhat more
difficult to sing than the middle pitches, teachers select music that does
not stress these extremes. The implications of this are two: first, that
many of the melodies in sixth-grade song books cannot be sung by
these boys in the range in which they are written, and second, that part-
singing thus becomes a necessity. To sustain interest in singing, the
teacher plans vocal parts these boys can sing easily in their range and takes
special care to provide for this type of individual difference. Low harmony parts and chord root parts are helpful in this instance; these will
be discussed in the next chapter.

A successful music specialist declares that the natural range of the
voice—both the children's and the classroom teacher's—is fairly high
when properly developed, and that normal voices should be able to sing
the F on the top line of the staff with ease. She states that vocal range is
largely a matter of correct breathing, breath support, and voice production. In her intermediate grade classes, the children enjoy standing,
then bending deeply with arms hanging limply, taking breaths—inhaling
and exhaling—while noting the fact that the diaphragm, not the chest,
is primarily involved in breathing. Then, remembering to breathe with
the diaphragm, they stand erect, closed fists held near the shoulders with
arm muscles taut, inhale, then pretend to "chew" the air while slowly
exhaling at the teacher's signal. At other times, instead of "chewing" air,

they place the index finger of the right hand on the lips and slowly and steadily exhale against the finger. These and other exercises, such as holding a piece of thin paper against a wall with the breath for gradually longer periods of time, are done to develop breath control. The teacher's approach appeals to the boys, for she emphasizes that they should take part in sports and in physical development to acquire the muscles they need in order to sing! There is truth in this, and the trained vocalist will not use the word "relax" that is employed in this chapter, but substitute "flexibility" instead, a word having somewhat different connotations.

To extend the range further, this teacher has the children vocalize up and down the first five tones of the major scale with vowels such as "ah", "oh," and "oo," one-half step higher each time, as one hears adult vocalists practice. When the higher range is reached, the children are instructed to relax their faces to look as if they "had no sense at all," with the jaw held naturally and loose. The teacher takes special care not to injure voices by vocalizing them too high or too low, and she can tell by the facial expression when a child attempts pitches beyond his range at a given stage in his vocal development. In this way, this teacher extends the vocal range of her students to one believed suitable by the vocally trained.

A problem of some classroom teachers is that they have not learned to use their singing voices properly, and therefore hesitate to sing pitches they consider high. Many have used only a chest voice which they try to force upward in an attempt to sing higher pitches. They need to learn how to sing in their high voice. Usually when these teachers try singing high pitches softly in what can be termed a "half-voice" (i.e., it feels as though one is using only half the voice he is accustomed to using; it is the head voice without the chest voice), they find that they can soon sing in a high voice that is very comparable to the child voice, and that eventually they will sing the high pitches with ease.

The classroom teacher needs a clear, natural voice. Children are attracted by singing that sounds natural and normal. The male teacher's voice is no longer as rare as it once was in elementary school music. Most children are well-oriented to listening to and singing with this octave-lower voice on recordings, television, and radio as well as at home with their fathers. Once in a while a child will be confused by it and try to match its pitch. When this occurs, the male teacher should explain that his voice changed, and that he cannot sing as high as the children. He should play the song on an instrument that gives proper pitch, or have a child who knows the song sing it. In instances where teachers believe they cannot sing well enough to use their singing voices in teaching music, they can employ substitutions such as recordings, musical instruments, and children who sing well.

The following are physical requirements for good singing:

1. *Posture*. Place feet on the floor with the weight of the body somewhat forward, not on the back of the chair. Sit up straight, but not in a stiff or tense way. If standing, place the weight of the body toward the toes, not on the heels.

2. *Breathing*. Fill the abdominal region with air first (i.e., breathe "low," not high in the chest). This is the kind of breathing we do when lying flat on the floor or flat in bed. The goal in breathing is a controlled, continuous flow of breath. A husky or breathy sound indicates wasted breath.

3. *Open Throat*. Use the open, relaxed throat one has when about to yawn. Sing with the mouth open wide, but not so wide that it causes tension. Use "oo" and "ah" to relax the throat.

4. *Good Enunciation*. Open the mouth and use lips *generously* in pronouncing words. Be sure to pronounce final consonants distinctly.

Poor results often come from singing too loud, singing too soft, not opening the mouth sufficiently, a slouching posture, a stiff and tense posture, a lack of interest, an unhealthy room temperature, and failure of the teacher to let the children comprehend the pitch and harmonic background of a song before asking them to sing it. The above physical requirements for good singing require that children are seated on chairs most of the time, rather than on a rug, because of the effect of posture on the proper use of lungs and diaphragm.

Pitch Discrimination and Learning to Sing

THE OUT-OF-TUNE SINGER

To adults who learned about high and low long ago, these concepts which are vital to listening and singing appear to be extremely simple. Yet, some seven-year-olds will confuse them. Young children often confuse *high* with *loud* and *fast* and *low* with *soft* and *slow*. When adults analyze this they find that high and low in pitch are abstractions; the association of high and low pitch with high and low physical levels is artificial, however necessary for understanding. To make these experiences concrete for children it is essential that they be made "real" in terms of high and low physical position both with the body and with objects, in pictures, and by relating to things in the child's world such as airplanes, trees, and stars (high), floor, rug, and grass (low). Step bells and ordinary bells held on end with the large bars down can relate high in pitch with the high bars and low in pitch with the low bars; this is effective because bells serve as audio-visual aids. Teachers employ songs in the kindergarten which children dramatize and later relate by discussion to high and low. One of them is "Red Birds Flying."

RED BIRDS FLYING

Children are taught to play little action games in first grade such as:

The above example relates high and low to widely spaced pitches illustrating these words and dramatizing them in terms of physical movement. The following example is relatively more complex:

Many simple examples of song material useful in teaching these basic concepts are to be found in the series books and in other supplementary books, particularly those on the kindergarten and first-grade levels. However, any teacher can improvise his own songs for this purpose.

Acting out the melody line of songs in terms of pitch levels is a device that aids people of all ages to be more conscious of differences in pitch. The hand is used with a generous motion to move up, down, or to stay the same according to differences in pitch. When children are guided to respond in this manner their concepts of pitch relationships often improve to a remarkable degree. In the above example the hand would move vertically as follows to reflect the melodic contour.

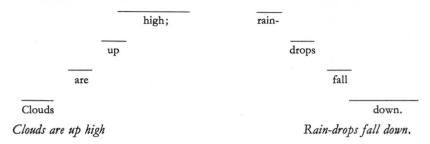

Clouds are up high   Rain-drops fall down.

The fact that at a certain stage of development a child does not sing in tune in no way proves that he is not musical. Instances can be cited to illustrate that it is possible for an out-of-tune singer to be an excellent musician. Among examples known to the authors are the concert master of a symphony orchestra and an eight-year old boy pianist who played Bach with understanding, composed music of some quality, and who was an opera enthusiast. There is also the story of the secondary school music specialist who assumed his superintendent could not hear how his music groups sounded because the man could not match tones. He was wrong; the superintendent listened to them with critical judgment. Apparently these people never learned to relate their vocal mechanisms to what their ears heard; they did not know how this felt. Other reasons for people being unable to match tones with their singing voices are said to be general immaturity, a deprived musical environment, psychological blocks imposed by adults who tell them they cannot sing, lack of interest, failure to try as a result of fear, boredom, or of deprived cultural background, and physical abnormalities which require attention of physicians. At another stage of musical development the child is something of a borderline case. If the teacher establishes a favorable environment, he can sing in tune. However, if the teacher does not establish the pitch firmly before asking him to sing, if there is an accompaniment that confuses the child, or if the psychological situation is one in which his muscles become tense, he will probably fail to match tones.

In theory, inability to sing in tune should disappear during the elementary school years if children are given consistent help. There are skilled music specialists who insist that there should be no out-of-tune singers by the end of the second grade. However, in today's schools there are often a few children who cannot match tones well in each of the upper elementary grades. Teachers should be ready to assist these students toward pleasurable and accurate singing at whatever level they find them.

Occasionally a child does not find his singing voice, or cannot control its pitch, until he is in high school. Teachers sustain the musical interest of these children through a program of varied activities—rhythmic responses, listening, playing instruments, creating music, reading about music and musicians, plus continuing to try to sing. There should be three major points of emphasis in helping the child: he should be a participant in music activities that are happy, interesting, challenging, and satisfying; he should have many experiences in which he will listen carefully to pitches and to pitch differences; and because he learns to sing by singing, he should be encouraged to try.

During some stages of development, these children do not hear the pitch of their own voices and often sing loudly (and happily) off key. There arise the following problems: (1) how to help them to listen, (2) how to keep these voices from hindering other children who are trying to keep on pitch, (3) how to help them to make as real a contribution to the group as the children who sing well, and (4) in the intermediate grades, how to help them with their errors in such a way that they are encouraged to try and remain confident of eventual success.

For young children who have not yet learned how to sing, the chanting of old rhymes such as "Humpty Dumpty," "Mary Mary Quite Contrary" and "Rub-a-Dub-Dub, Three Men in a Tub" can be helpful. Children like the *feel* of rhythmic or repetitious words; they enjoy saying them together. If the teacher will establish the pitch of a low note such as middle C and help them to *chant* the words on that pitch, a beginning can be made in singing such one-pitch songs. In a few days the words can be sung to the pitches of two tones, C and D, as follows:

To accomplish this, the teacher may conduct in pitch levels, helping by the ups and downs of the arm to indicate the low pitch and the higher pitch. Next, this might be done on three pitches—and soon the children will have learned not only to find their singing voices but to sing a song as well.

Many of the children who cannot match tones try to sing with the same voice they use when they speak. Therefore, it is the task of the teacher to help such children find their "high" or singing voices. This may be done in a game situation. A favorite device is to have the children pretend to be the wind, a bird, or a siren. Children often sense pitch differences more keenly through actions such as the teacher's lifting a child's hand up high, or the children's starting from a squatting position (low) and moving to a standing position (high). Another popular device is to have a child pretend he is calling someone who is far away, or pretend he is someone's mother calling him to come home from a great distance. When this is done, a sustained speech results—and when speech is thus sustained (vowels held out) singing takes place.

When a child sings, but sings low and does not match the pitch expected of him, *if the teacher and class will match the child's pitch* and sing the song with him in the key of his own choosing, there often begins a procedure that brings success with the gradual raising of the pitch by singing this song in successively higher keys.

The term "tone-matching" is not intended to convey emphasis upon an isolated drill technique. It is the authors' intention that it be thought of as "songs and games for helping uncertain singers." Such a song or game may be sung by a class and a child may be selected to sing his part at the correct time. The part will be sung at the right time because the teacher will sing with him in case he is not ready to sing independently. Little or no attempt is made to correct faulty pitch or rhythm while the song is being sung. It takes patience and faith on the part of a teacher to wait weeks and months for some children to sing correctly.

A commonly used device for listening and tone-matching is the calling of the roll in song and having each child sing his answer on the same pitches. If someone is absent, the entire class responds by singing "absent," thus adding variety to this game. The teacher varies the pitch of these conversations-in-song, singing to each child in the range in which he will be most likely to succeed. Later, the purpose of the teacher will vary according to the progress of each child, and for some he will be working to extend the range of already successful singers. Some successful singers may begin to improvise answers on pitches other than those the teacher sings; little question-and-answer tunes are created in this manner.

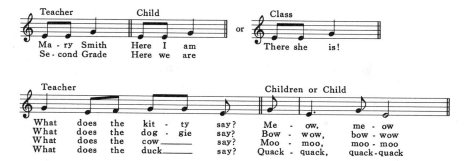

Another well-known tone-matching game is one in which the teacher places various objects in the hands of the children, who may be told to put their heads down on their desks and close their eyes. The game is played by the teacher singing, "Who has the ———?" and the child who possesses the object sitting up and singing, "I have the ———." An additional listening experience is to ask the class to identify an unseen child by the sound of his singing voice.

After learning to play this type of song-game, the teacher can sing questions such as, "What did you do last Sunday?" and "What did you have for breakfast?" and the child can create his own answer with rhythmic and melodic variety. When a child has difficulty in matching tones with the teacher in any of these tone games, matching tones to another child's singing may do the trick. It is not wise to remain working with any one child too long in any of these procedures. To do so would make the other children restless because the progress of the game would be stopped, and it would unduly draw the child's attention to the fact that he is somehow not as successful as others in his class. This refers to primary grades. A further aid to listening is the suggestion that the children "tune in" their voices just as they tune in radio stations. This is a concept children can understand because they know that the dial must be in exactly the right place for the station to "come in" properly. Another suggestion is to sing a familiar grouping of tones (or even a single pitch) for the children while they listen. Then ask them to listen with their "inner ears" while this is repeated for them. Next, ask the children to sing it. Finally, ask them if they sang exactly what they heard. Some of the children who cannot yet match tones will know that they have not sung what they heard. This process when repeated over weeks and months has notably improved the ability to listen and to match tones, especially when the teacher organizes his presentation so that part of the class listens to and evaluates the singing of groups of children within the class, thus involving every child in the room with either singing or listening. Spontaneous tone games such as creating a "song" from children's words—i.e., "Johnny has a hair cut, a crew cut, too,"—and having children sing these words or additional words of their own in turn can sometimes help.

Picking out melodies or parts of melodies on the bells or piano can be a listening experience of value. These instruments can be used with songs that contain tones or tone patterns which are both played and sung. Listening for the proper time to play the instrument, and being sure the correct pitches have been sounded constitute a good listening experience in a situation of challenge and interest, and it helps build the background that leads to eventual singing on pitch.

There are certain tonal groups that are particularly easy for children to sing. It follows that if the teacher selects songs that contain these tonal groups, especially if they are repeated in the songs, and if these songs are pitched in easy singing range, there should result more than average success in group singing.

Among these are:

Number 1 is the easiest interval for children to sing; it is the descending minor third (5–3 or 1–6₁). Number 2 is an extension of number 1; it is sung by children all over the world in their natural, undirected play. Number 3, a descending series of three tones in whole-step arrangement, and Number 4, the ascending fourth, are easy to sing. Number 4 is often found in the 5–8 position in major and minor scales. Number 5, the pentatonic mode, is an important aspect of music children create spontaneously; songs based on it are easy to sing because no half-steps are involved. "This Old Man" and "The Caisson Song" emphasize the minor third. "Three Blind Mice" and "Mary Had a Little Lamb" stress the 3–2–1 note group, with the ascending fourth also stressed in "Three Blind Mice." The popularity of many songs can be traced to their utilization of these easily sung tonal groups. It follows that if easy-to-sing songs are pitched in easy-to-sing keys for the individual child as well as for the class, they can speed the progress of children in becoming more skilled in tone-matching, which is hearing what is sounded, and reproducing this with the voice.

At times it is impossible to prevent the voices of out-of-tuners from hindering to some extent the progress of those children who are farther advanced in singing skills. A decision that is only of temporary value is to select out-of-tuners to make such contributions as the "zz" of a bee, the "tick tock" of a clock, the "ding dong" and other sound effects instead of singing. However, since faulty singers learn to sing by singing, this device is no solution to their problem. Furthermore it would be unwise to make any obvious division of a class into singers and those who do something else. Careful listening is essential, but listening and never singing will not produce singers. Out-of-tuners should have many opportunities to listen to good examples of singing. Safeguards in this include the use of small groups or solo singers as examples to be listened to and constructively evaluated so that there is no obvious division of the class into singers and out-of-tuners, and the inclusion of some good singers with the out-of-tuners when such temporary groupings are made. When out-of-tuners respond rhythmically to music, when they play the Autoharp, bells, and percussion instruments, and when they offer ideas for interpretation, dramatization and experimentation, they are making real contributions to group music even though they do not yet sing well. Teachers should give them full credit for what they contribute so that they feel they are first-class members of the group.

The traditional seating arrangement for music classes, much in vogue years ago, was dictated by concern for the out-of-tuners. They were seated in a group in front of the room, with the good singing voices of other children behind them and with the good singing voice of the teacher in front of them. It was supposed that this seating arrangement, which gave them correct pitches from both behind and in front, was of great aid to them. Its disadvantage seems to have been that the obvious segregation of the out-of-tuners was a greater psychological block than the seating was an aid. It has been largely abandoned today. If children are seated in this manner, such seating is done in some way that presumably makes the children unaware of its purpose. Actually, the increasing informality of seating in today's classrooms tends to make any rigid seating plans for music work unlikely. The seating arrangement should permit the teacher to move freely through the class, so as to listen to each singer.

In the intermediate grades a problem may be how to continue to help the out-of-tuners without discouraging them. One teacher begins each year with what she terms "making a joyful noise." Her entire emphasis is upon the joyous participation of every child with no regard as to whether or not he is in tune, although she is learning and studying the capabilities and problems of each child during this time. As soon as her first objective is achieved, she begins her work of helping every child to sing on pitch. She walks among the children as they sing, helping the ones who need her. While the singing is in progress she unobtrusively tells Jimmy that he is singing lower than the song is sounding, and to listen to her as she sings. She may tell him to sit with his good friend Billy and tell Billy to help him. All of this is done in good spirit, without setting anyone apart from the group and always emphasizing to Jimmy that he is going to sing in tune soon—to listen hard and to keep on trying. Usually this teacher has eliminated the out-of-tune singer by January.

Older children who cannot sing in tune know very well that they cannot, and they appreciate any help that adults can give them as long as they are not embarrassed before their peers. Therefore small-group work apart from the class is desirable. A plan that has proved helpful is for the teacher to work with out-of-tuners in groups of two or four, with each child paired with another of like voice quality and range. With four, the teacher will place each child at a far corner of the room. He may begin with a story of children who have become separated in the woods or in the hills, and who are trying to find (call to) each other. One out-of-tune singer is then asked to call in sustained speech (which is singing) to his partner across the room as though he were a city block away. He will ordinarily call his partner's name in the two pitches of the descending minor third pattern (number 1 on page 276). Then his partner will answer on the same pitches; this is the "game." When this contact through tone matching has been established, they next begin singing other information back and forth, such as "Where are you?" "I'm over here," "Are you hungry?" and so on. The two children in the other corners of the room first listen to the pitches sung by the first two, then take their turn. Most of these children will find that they can hear the pitch given them in this way, and that they can answer it with surprising accuracy. After this introduction comes the repetition and extension of this singing back and forth, then eventually the singing of easy-to-sing songs pitched in a range comfortable to the voices, and soon four more accurate singers have been added to classroom music.

Individual work with bells, including step bells, trying to match tones with the pitch of different metal bars in experimental fashion, can help. Time and relative privacy should be provided for such individual learning.

Time in which to practice hearing only one voice seems necessary for some as a prerequisite for group singing. That this has not already occurred may indicate a lack of singing in the home. The singing of a mother to her baby and to her young children is highly important in musical development. Music education begins at home, in the cradle.

Some boys have psychological difficulty that stems from attempting to imitate their father's low voices and wanting to sound like men, not like their mothers, their female teachers, or girls. This can be overcome by explaining to the boys that their voices ordinarily change in grades seven through nine, and that shortly before the change begins, they will have better high voices than the girls, a soprano voice that signals the change to come. In fifth and sixth grades this is important to boys, and their understanding of this may determine whether they will use their still unchanged voices naturally or whether they will attempt to sing "down in their shoes." It is best to avoid using the adult terms "soprano" and "alto" and use instead "high" and "low." In three-part singing the parts are "high, middle, and low" rather than the terms descriptive of adult voices.

ESTABLISHING PITCH FOR SINGING   One of the most common failings of teachers of music is that of not giving the children sufficient time in which to hear the beginning pitch of songs a class is reviewing. This is because the teacher will "hear with his inner ear" the song in its proper harmonic setting, but will forget that the children, or many of them, are not hearing this. Too often these teachers sound a pitch and start the singing long before children have had time to orient themselves to this pitch, its relation to the scale in which the song is to be sung, and the harmonic setting of the first tones of the melody. This failure of teachers to help the children sense the pitch fully places some of the children at such a disadvantage that they are out-of-tune singers when they need not be. When reviewing a song with a class, the following procedure is recommended:

1. Sound the 1 3 5 chord built from the keynote[1] of the song by means of the piano, the bells, or by singing it. Sound 1 3 5 3 1. This is to establish a feeling for the key, that is, a feeling for the home tone in relation to the scale. The playing of the chord sequence I V_7 I on the piano or Autoharp does this excellently.

2. Sound at some length the keynote of the song. This should be sounded on an accurate instrument such as the piano, bells, or pitch pipe.

3. Sing the keynote with the neutral syllable "loo."

4. Ask the children to sing this pitch, helping those who have difficulty. They can also sing 1 3 5 3 1 and 1 5₁ 1 if the range permits.

5. Sing or otherwise sound the first note of the song if it is a note other than the keynote.

6. Ask the children to sing it and help them to match it.

7. Set the tempo by counting, directing, or clapping the rhythm of the meter and saying "Sing!" or, in rhythm, "Ready, sing!", after which the singing begins on the beat following the instruction "sing." Another way is for the teacher to sing the first two or four measures of the song, and say "Sing!" as stated above. Doing this establishes the tempo and spirit of the song.

[1] The keynote or home tone is found in major keys having sharps in the key signature by calling the last sharp to the right "7" and counting up to the next line or space. This will be "8" (1), the keynote. The keynote or home tone is found in major keys having flats in the key signature by calling the last flat to the right "4" and counting up or down to "8" or "1". Also, in keys having two or more flats in the key signature, the next to the last flat to the right *is* the keynote.

The home tone of the relative minor is on the sixth step of the major scale. Call this step "1" and the above procedure to establish pitch for singing is operative in minor keys, beginning with the 1–3–5 chord in minor.

SELECTING SONGS FOR TONE-MATCHING

The teacher finds that he must analyze the melodies of songs to determine whether or not they may be useful in "listen-then-sing" activities. When selecting songs of genuine appeal to children, he looks for easily sung repeated-note patterns and phrases that are obvious and clear. He seeks songs with parts that can be echoed, songs from which he can extract tone calls. songs with a limited range, and songs with final measures that can be repeated to create aesthetically satisfying codas. He also seeks question-and-answer songs, and dialogue songs. These permit the children to take turns in singing and in constructive critical listening to the singing of others. He will use these songs to help children sing on pitch, with good tone quality, and with good taste.

Three song examples follow, the first two for primary level and the third for intermediate level. The third example, "When the Saints Come Marching In," has a tone pattern repeated twice in the original melody, and can be used in this form. However, it is printed here in a specially arranged form to repeat the pattern four times, and to add another repeated pattern near the end. It is an example of how teachers arrange songs to adapt them to tone matching. The song has a small range, with rhythm and spirit that children enjoy. The second group must listen carefully to the first group, and is challenged to echo the tone pattern perfectly. Other examples include "Old Texas," page 378, which is an echo-type song when sung as a canon, and "The Keeper," page 375. These and others are in many of the series books. See the Appendix for a song sources chart.

I HAVE A LITTLE BIRD

Peggy Burgess

Elementary Education Class
University of Oregon
Arr. R. E. N.

I have a lit-tle bird, who is well-known to you. He
lives with-in a clock, and each hour he sings cuck-oo.

CODA
Class or Group   Teacher   Group   Child

Each hour he sings cuck-oo.   Cuck-oo   cuck-oo   cuck-oo.

THE ECHO

Kate Forman   Old Children's Air

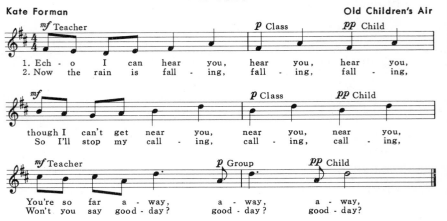

1. Ech - o I can hear you, hear you, hear you,
2. Now the rain is fall - ing, fall - ing, fall - ing,

though I can't get near you, near you, near you,
So I'll stop my call - ing, call - ing, call - ing,

You're so far a - way, a - way, a - way,
Won't you say good - day? good - day? good - day?

WHEN THE SAINTS COME MARCHING IN

New Orleans Song
Arr. R. E. N.

March tempo

Group One
Oh when the saints come march - ing

Group Two Oh when the saints

in Everyone

come march - ing in, Oh when the saints come march - ing

in Lord, I want to be in that num - ber.

Group One When the saints march in,

Group Two When the saints march

Everyone

in, When the saints come march - ing in.

Examples of other echo-type songs are:

Are You Sleeping?	How Do You Do?
By'm Bye	If I Ask You
Barnyard Song	Getting Acquainted
Roll Over	What Did You Do Last Summer?
Today Is Monday	John the Rabbit
Who Did?	The Sparrow's School (Chichipapa)
Echo Carol	Hoo Hoo!
Long John	Follow On
(all in *Exploring Music With Children*)	(all in *Singing With Children*)

Examples of repetitious songs helpful in tone matching are:

Ding Dong Bell
Where Are You Going, My Good Old Man?
Hey, Betty Martin
Deaf Woman's Courtship
Hey Lidee
Goodbye, Old Paint

(all in *Exploring Music With Children*)

TONAL MEMORY is necessary for the singer. Teachers can assist the development of tonal memory by such activities as:

1. Humming a familiar tune and asking the children to identify it; then asking children to hum it back to the teacher.

2. Arranging a signal whereby children stop singing during the performance of a familiar song, but continue to *think* the tune for a phrase or two. Then the teacher signals them to change from thinking the tune to singing it, and so on.

3. Playing a game in which children hum a tune for the class to identify.

4. Having the class sing songs with neutral syllables (*la, loo*) rather than the words so that the singers can concentrate on the melody.

5. Challenging individual children to explore the black keys of the piano—to work alone to find the melodies of pentatonic tunes they know such as "Old MacDonald," "All Night, All Day," "Get On Board," "Auld Lang Syne," "Land of the Silver Birch," "The Campbells Are Coming," and "Swing Low, Sweet Chariot." They can also create and try to remember tunes of their own.

6. Asking children to notate parts of well-known tunes from memory when they are sufficiently advanced for this activity.

Pitch discrimination and the concepts of high and low are often explored by beginning with the descending minor third interval, 5–3 (*so-mi*). First, many names, nursery rhymes and other poems or words are sung on the two pitches. Next, hand signals may be performed by the children in response to them. The teacher sings *so* or *mi* and the children learn to identify both as high or low and with the hand signs. After children have learned the hand signals individual children can "think" the pitches and give hand signals to the class to be translated into pitch. Next, *la* (6) is added, and the three pitches are used in many ways in improvising short songs, setting poems to them, learning the hand signals, devising ear training games with them as described for *so* and *mi* above, and seeing the relation of the pitches in notation. Notice that the eye, ear, and body are all involved in learning pitch discrimination. Eventually

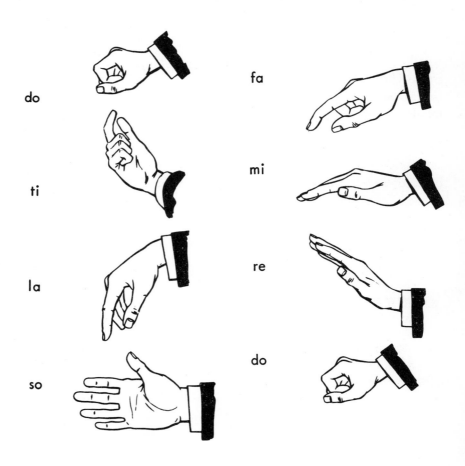

do

ti

la

so

fa

mi

re

do

re and *do* are added, and there are the hand signals, notation, improvisation of little melodies, playing of the pitches and the tunes on bells and xylophones, and using the five pitches of the pentatonic scale. Rhythm patterns performed with the body and with percussion instruments can be utilized all the way through this process; the learning of notation and its description of the *duration* of pitch (note values), which was discussed in the previous chapter, can be applied throughout this developmental experience with pitch. Children can be guided to discover that rhythm and melody are integrally related; that one cannot have a melody unless the pitches are assigned duration which is basic to rhythm.

TENSION, CLIMAX, AND RELEASE

Referring to the next item on the structure of music outline, p. 120, the teacher may guide children to form concepts and generalizations based upon the relation of pitch to tension, climax, and release. This study is relatively complex because dynamics and other factors are contributing influences. Repetition of tone and rhythm patterns often builds tension to be relieved by a change in the melody or rhythm. Sometimes tension and climax are brought about by successively higher pitches, and release accomplished by descending pitches. Duration of pitch—shorter or longer note values—can be another factor. The learning is based upon *how children feel* in response to the music or the song and how the teacher guides them to search for the causes of this feeling. This knowledge can then be useful in the individual child's composing of music.

HOW DO MELODY TONES MOVE?

Young children can discover that the tones of melodies move in three ways: they can repeat, they can move in steps (scalewise), and they can move in skips or leaps (often chordwise and octavewise). When these concepts are being built, the teacher selects songs and recorded music that most clearly reveal these tonal movements. Prior to this the children's first discovery may be that melodies move in single lines, horizontally. While the contour of a melody may move up and down or stay the same for a while, there is a steady linear progression. In songs such as "That's the Way Tunes Go" and "Space Ship" the concepts of both repeated tones and stepwise progression can be studied by the children in response to the teacher's question, "In what different ways do you think this melody moves?"

THAT'S THE WAY TUNES GO

Tunes may go up a step or two, or on one note they stay a while, They skip some-times to high and low! That's the way tunes go.

From *Exploring Music with Children* by Robert E. Nye and Vernice T. Nye. © 1966 by Wadsworth Publishing Company, Inc., Belmont, California. Reprinted by permission of the publisher.

SPACE SHIP

Wilma Wittemeyer
Arr. R. E. N.

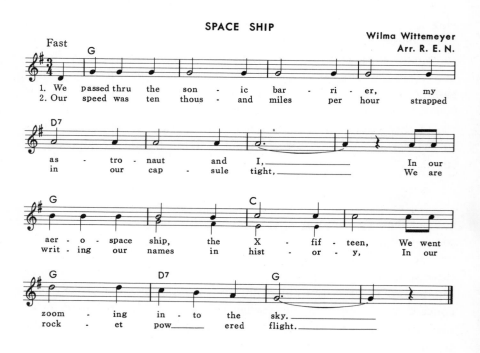

1. We passed thru the son - ic bar - ri - er, my
2. Our speed was ten thous - and miles per hour strapped

as - tro - naut and I,_____ In our
in our cap - sule tight,_____ We are

aer - o - space ship, the X - fif - teen, We went
writ - ing our names in hist - or - y, In our

zoom - ing in - to the sky._____
rock - et pow_____ ered flight._____

"Taffy" is another scaleline song with repeated notes; it is also useful for experience with the octave leap.

From *Singing With Children* by Robert and Vernice Nye, Neva Aubin, and George Kyme. © 1970 by Wadsworth Publishing Company, Inc., Belmont, California. Reprinted by permission of the publisher.

Suggestions for use: "Taffy" can be used to introduce children to the C scale. Children find the C scale easy to play on the piano because of the consecutive white keys.

After the song is learned, one child can sing the first measure, another the second measure, another the third and fourth measures, and so on. Children enjoy this method, which also serves to strengthen tonal memory.

"The Hat" exemplifies a chordline song; it contains skips and leaps besides repeated notes. By experimenting, older children can find that F, A, and C are notes that can be played together on bells or piano to accompany the song, and thus begin to relate chordline melodies with accompanying chords.

THE HAT

From *Birchard Music Series,* Book 3, copyright © 1962 by Summy-Birchard Company, Evanston, Illinois. All rights reserved. Used by permission.

A World of Scales to Explore

WHAT IS A SCALE, AND HOW MANY DIFFERENT KINDS CAN YOU FIND ?

The term *scale* means "ladder." It refers to an arrangement of rising pitches. Children soon become familiar with the major scale through experiences with scale songs and playing the C scale on bells and xylophone. They quickly find that one can sing or play down the scale as well as up. The bells and piano keyboard are effective audio-visual devices for children to use in determining a definition or description of the C major scale as consisting of both whole steps and half steps, and for the eventual discovery of their precise arrangement. Following this could be "trying out" the major scale pattern, beginning on notes other than C to find if it sounds the same. Although F and G are often the notes tried next, there are eleven black and white keys other than C with which to experiment. The fact that the major scale can be played from any black or white key is an important discovery. The children may find that the major scale consists of one repeated pattern: whole-step, whole-step, half-step, (whole-step) whole-step, whole-step, half-step. There should be provision in the classroom for independent study of this scale (diatonic) pattern. Some teachers use so-fa hand signals to explore the scale and its intervals. The advantage is said to be that it has somewhat the same function as fingering on an instrument, and it is assumed that it makes scale tones less abstract to the learner; a disadvantage is that pitch movements expressed in hand signals must be done rather slowly to be seen and understood.

Major Scale	1	2	3	4	5	6	7	8
	d	r	m	f	s	l	t	d

Pentatonic Scale	1	2	3	5	6	8
	d	r	m	s	l	d

Visual Spacing
of the
Major Scale

8	d
7	t
6	l
5	s
4	f
3	m
2	r
1	d

Where are the half
steps?

The major scale should be compared with the pentatonic scale— the scale in which there are no half-steps. Both the keyboard and charts are needed to explore and explain these scale patterns. A large chart of the keyboard, placed in a commanding position in the classroom, is considered an essential piece of equipment by a great many teachers. They refer to it frequently during music class to explain tonal relationships visually.

In any study of scales there should be an immediate association with song materials to explore how a scale is used in music. Because so many of American children's songs are in major keys, this association is fairly obvious. However, the less commonly used tonalities need to be sensed in like fashion through songs that employ their scale structures. In working with a song built on a scale which is strange, the children might first determine on which note the tonal center (key note) seems to be, then try to construct the scale from that note, utilizing notes from the melody to complete it. The minor keys are not "strange" to the children; they should have heard them many times from their environment. Eight-year-olds can begin to learn their precise structures through additional experiences with songs which are built on them. There are two ways to conceptualize the relationship of minor scales to major scales. (Since adults argue about them, it should be interesting for the teacher to watch how the children's thinking about them evolves.) One way is to consider every minor scale a relative of a major scale, that is, every minor scale can be thought of as beginning on the sixth step (*la*) of a major scale. Thus, it would be sung from *la* to *la* or from 6 to 6. This way of thinking has adherents because the syllables and numbers seem to remain stable— attached to the major scale concept. Another way is to think only of the pattern of the particular form of minor scale, call the home tone *1* or *do*, and sing it as though it began on the same scale step as a major scale does. This is of advantage when it comes to piano chording because the I-chord corresponds by number to scale tone one. Either way can be used. Most adults believe that the "best" way is the one they have been taught. Let the children explore both ways and decide which seems to be the most logical to them.

With selected song material (see the indexes of the series books), the three kinds of minor scales in common use can be worked with, and the children should use them to write their own compositions. Sometimes recordings will initiate an exciting exploration of a minor scale; Cui's *Orientale* is one example. A problem for children to solve is "What feelings are communicated by use of minor tonalities in music?" They should find that there are at least as many communicated by minor keys as by major keys, and that minor is not necessarily associated with "sad."

By the teacher's creating an environment in which children are stimulated to discover and explore these scales for themselves, the same subject matter that under other conditions can be a rather frightening, puzzling, and teacher-pressured memorization of three kinds of minor scales (natural or pure, harmonic and melodic) can be part of a thrilling adventure in expanding the concept of "scale." The learner can discover for himself the truly fascinating ways in which man has structured many different kinds of scales for expressing himself and communicating his feelings to others.

B♭	F		C	G

B♭ A	F E	do ti	C B	G F♯
G	D	la	A	E
F	C	so	G	D
E♭ D	B♭ A	fa mi	F E	C B
C	G	re	D	A
B♭	F	do	C	G

How are syllables and letter names related?
Play these on the bells. Find the same scale
starting on a note not written here; play it.

PASSIVE AND ACTIVE SCALE TONES; CHARTS OF MINOR SCALES

A typical scale involves a specific tonality. Children learn easily to identify the home tone as the most important pitch to which all the other scale members are related. Through expanding musical experiences, children will rate scale tone 5 as the next most influential, and scale tone 4 would be third in general importance. However, when persons sense the tonality of scales thoroughly, they come to feel that certain of the pitches tend to give them a sense of satisfaction and stability, while certain other pitches give them the feeling that they should move on to an adjacent pitch above or below. Using the major scale as an example, the *passive* tones are those of the tonic (I) chord, 1, 3, 5, and 8. The active tones are 2, which tends to move down to 1 or up to 3; 4, which tends to move down to 3 or up to 5; 6, which tends to move down to 5 or up to 7; and 7, which pulls strongly to 8, and is called the *leading tone* because of this. These qualities of scale members can be discerned by children. Older children feel them more strongly than young children because their harmonic sense is more developed. To explore the passive and active qualities of scale members, ask the children to sing slowly up and down the scale, directing them to stop at different scale tones. Then ask them which way they feel the pitch should move—up, down, or stay the same. The natural movement of melodies with regard to active and passive scale tones relates to the beauty of melodies, the ease of singing them, note reading, the children's use of them in their own compositions, and their expanding concepts of scale and tonality.

ONE MAY MORNING

From *Birchard Music Series*, Book 6, copyright © 1962 by Summy-Birchard Company, Evanston, Illinois. All rights reserved. Used by permission.

What scale is this? Find it on the bells.
2 whole steps, 1 half step, 3 whole steps, 1 half step

1	2		3 4	5	6		7 8
1	2 3		4	5 6		7	8
1	2 3		4	5 6			7 8
1	2 3		4	5	6		7 8

Try to play these on the bells. What are the names of these scales?
How would you sing them with the syllables?

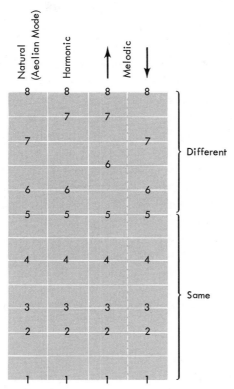

Find these minor scales on the bells and play them.

MINOR SCALES

Compare this scale chart with the others. Which suits you best? Why?

MAJOR		do	re	mi	fa	so		la	ti	do
PENTATONIC		do	re	mi		so		la		do
MINOR natural la	ti	do	re	mi	fa	so		la		
MINOR harmonic la	ti	do	re	mi	fa		si	la		
MINOR melodic la	ti	do	re	mi	fi		si	la		

How are minor scales alike? How are they different?
How would you sing them with numbers?

PENTATONIC MELODIES The term "pentatonic melody" is sometimes puzzling because there are several kinds which may be classified into four types. The first is the tune which is clearly pentatonic in both melody and any accompanying pitches and in which no harmonization (chord changes) is desired. Second is the melody which has been harmonized; tunes in this classification can be treated successfully as either those in which no chord change takes place or as those in which harmonization can be applied. Third is a melody which contains a few non-pentatonic tones—such as major scale steps 4 and/or 7; these appear in unimportant places in the melody (not on the beat) so that no harmonization need take place. Fourth is the type which has a melody within the pentatonic scale but in which harmonization seems essential. Each type is useful in one or more ways in teaching. Pentatonic songs will be found listed in classified indexes of the series books. Examples not mentioned earlier include "Goodbye, Old Paint," "Grandma Grunts," "The Riddle Son," "Nobody Knows the Trouble I've Seen," and "Night Herding Song." As stated earlier, they can be played on the black keys of the piano, an activity which assists the development of tonal memory.

PENTATONIC SCALES

Tonal center ↑

KEY SIGNATURES Children who have explored the scales and understand their organization will have no difficulty in determining why key signatures are necessary. When they fit the major scale pattern to different places on the keyboard they find black keys essential. From these, key signatures can be derived. Unless children find use for scales and key signatures, they will soon forget them. One logical use is in their own compositions. Another is in the performance of instrumental music; one must use the key signature in order to know what note to play and what fingering to use. Children who play the bells and small wind instruments will learn practical applications for key signatures. Vocal music does not demand the same analysis of key signatures that instrumental music does; all the singer needs to know is the beginning pitch and *where that pitch is in the scale.* However, in order to know where the pitch of a new song is in the scale, one needs to know the key signature. If the teacher knows this, the children hardly need to, for the teacher can then give them the pitch and tell them where it is in the scale by having them sing first 1–3–5–3–1, then up or down the scale to the beginning note. Thus, in a purely vocal approach the teacher must invent situations in which the signature is of use to the learner. One is to select a student to be the teacher of a new song and ask the class to help the teacher plan what to do. Usually the need to know where the beginning note is in relation to the scale will appear early in the process. It is best to use two or more songs, each beginning on a different scale tone. For how to identify the key from the key signature, see p. 314, this chapter.

THE LESS COMMON MODES

Some scales were used more frequently in earlier centuries than recently. Today both contemporary composers and folk singers have brought them to a more prominent position in the music that surrounds us. They can be utilized to compose songs and instrumental pieces with a "different" flavor and to reflect older periods. For example, a troubadour song could be written with both words and melody that communicate feelings from that time in world history. Indexes in series books guide teachers to modal songs. The Ionian mode is the major scale pattern; the Aeolian is the pure minor scale pattern. The less common modes are the following scales:

Dorian	Phrygian	Lydian	Mixolydian
8	8	8	8
		7	
7	7		7
6		6	6
	6		
5	5	5	5
		4	
4	4		4
		3	3
3	3		
2		2	2
	2		
1	1	1	1

For a different "flavor", compose in the old modes.

Some examples of songs written in less common modes are the folk songs "I Wonder as I Wander," "Every Night When the Sun Goes In," "The Shanty Boys in the Pine," "The Days of '49," and "Ground Hog." Plain chants from church sources which exemplify the older use of the modes are in some of the series books.

ACCIDENTALS, CHROMATIC, AND WHOLE-TONE SCALES

Accidentals (sharps, flats, or cancel signs not stipulated by the key signature) are to be found in two of the minor scales, songs written both in these minor keys, and in major keys as well. A song such as "I Heard the Bells on Christmas Day," contains some half-steps with accidentals. This can lead to exploring the *chromatic* scale which consists entirely of half-steps. Another approach to this scale can be through a recording of "Flight of the Bumblebee" by Rimsky-Korsakoff (Bowmar #52).

CHROMATIC SCALE

do	di	re	ri	mi	fa	fi	so	si	la	li	ti	do
C	C♯	D	D♯	E	F	F♯	G	G♯	A	A♯	B	C

do	ti	te	la	le	so	se	fa	mi	me	re	rah	do
C	B	B♭	A	A♭	G	G♭	F	E	E♭	D	D♭	C

WHOLE-TONE SCALE

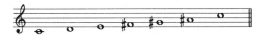

The chromatic and whole-tone scales can be used as "discrepant events" following the study of active and passive scale tones. These scales lack the feeling of tonality characteristic of major and minor scales. When children analyze why songs based on major and minor scales have home tones, they will find that the half-steps have something to do with this feeling of tonality. When they analyze the chromatic scale they will find nothing but half-steps; neither the whole-tone scale nor the pentatonic scale has half-steps. Interesting generalizations may come from this. When would a composer not desire a feeling of tonality? What kinds of feelings would he be trying to communicate? *Mists,* by Howard Hanson, is a composition which utilizes the whole-tone scale.[1] The whole-tone scale can be compared to the pentatonic, and children can determine which has the larger degree of key feeling. (The authors always assume that when they write of scales or any other of the "music fundamentals," the teacher will be utilizing related songs and recordings which bring the study of the concept to musical life, and that the children will be using these in their own compositions for specific reasons. The good teacher knows that unless these aspects of music are truly interesting or useful to the learner, little will be gained from studying them.)

ETHNIC SCALES

The concept of *scale* is further expanded when ethnic scales are discovered or introduced. There are many of these scales; music education is only at the threshold of beginning to recognize them. They relate very well to some aspects of social studies. For example, in the study of Japan, children can listen to music and compose music based upon ethnic scales of that country. One is the already-known pentatonic scale. Another is the scale used in the song "Sakura" (Bowmar #66). Beautiful "Japanese" songs can be composed by children who use this scale.

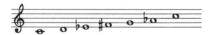

Much of the popular music of Japan is based on this scale:

A gypsy scale:

A scale of American Negro origin:

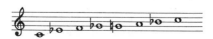

[1] From *For the First Time*, Mercury Recording.

A source of some selected ethnic scales is Gertrude Wollner's *Improvisation in Music,* Doubleday & Company, Inc., Garden City, New York, 1963, Chapter Five, "Adventures in Unusual Scales." Pentatonic, whole-tone, four-tone, chromatic, Hungarian, Arabian, Hindu, Asiatic Indian, Egyptian, Irish, and modal scales are notated. Currently the explanations on some of the record jackets of Ravi Shankar's Indian music explains the scale structure utilized in this music. To invent an *original* scale upon which to base songs and instrumental compositions, the learner can plan to have either an irregular arrangement of whole-steps, half-steps, and other intervals as in the above examples, or a regular arrangement such as a consistent alternating of whole and half-steps or a consistent use of an interval such as the minor or major third.

THE TONE ROW

This scale is an invented one, often based on the 12 steps of the chromatic scale. The elementary school learner can use resonator bells. Place the bars in an order that when sounded will not remind the listener of any tonality; this will require moving the bars about until the new scale sounds "atonal,"—that is, without any definite tonal center. The row will include all 12 tones, but not in the original consecutive order. Experiment with this arrangement of scale tones by playing familiar melody rhythms such as "Three Blind Mice" to discover new melodic sounds. Then attempt composition with your new scale, using the succession of pitches over and over again in different ways. (Your scale can also be constructed with fewer than 12 tones.) When one listens to this type of music from recordings, he will find that certain compositional techniques of long standing are employed to manipulate melodies. Manipulation of traditional melodies will be discussed later in this chapter; the same techniques apply to tone row music. Composers have used some of them for centuries. With the tone row, traditional harmony is absent; a new concept of harmonization is constructed, often being built from the vertical "happenings" of multiple melodic lines instead of the chords of old.

Tone Patterns and Intervals

Understanding and being able to use tone patterns and intervals relate to learning to read music effectively. When children can comprehend tonal and rhythmic groups, as they comprehend words of English, they are learning to read music. Rhythm patterns were discussed in the previous chapter. Tonal patterns found in songs can be taught as parts of those songs. Tone patterns common to many songs include the following:

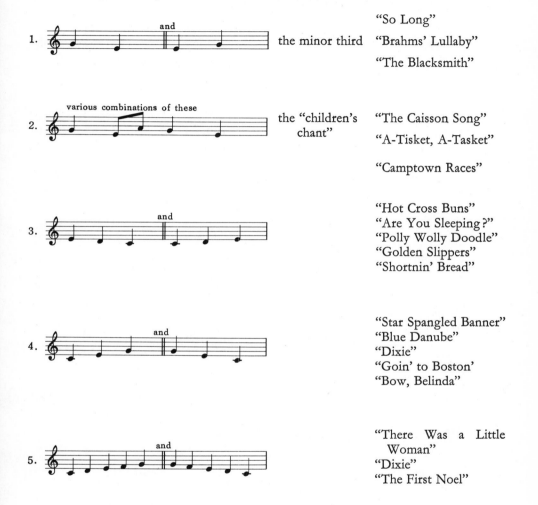

1.   the minor third   "So Long"
                                "Brahms' Lullaby"
                                "The Blacksmith"

2.   the "children's chant"   "The Caisson Song"
                                "A-Tisket, A-Tasket"
                                "Camptown Races"

3.   "Hot Cross Buns"
                                "Are You Sleeping?"
                                "Polly Wolly Doodle"
                                "Golden Slippers"
                                "Shortnin' Bread"

4.   "Star Spangled Banner"
                                "Blue Danube"
                                "Dixie"
                                "Goin' to Boston'"
                                "Bow, Belinda"

5.   "There Was a Little Woman"
                                "Dixie"
                                "The First Noel"

When the children have identified these and other tone patterns and can find them in songs and hear them from recordings, the next step is to identify variant uses of the patterns. For example, with reference to pattern number 5 above, the teacher may ask, "Find out how this scaleline pattern is used differently in 'Twinkle, Twinkle, Little Star,'" and "Look for it in 'Joshua Fought the Battle of Jericho'; how is it different in that minor song?"

INTERVALS

Although these are presented in music fundamentals courses, it may be appropriate to review them now. The illustrations below explain them:

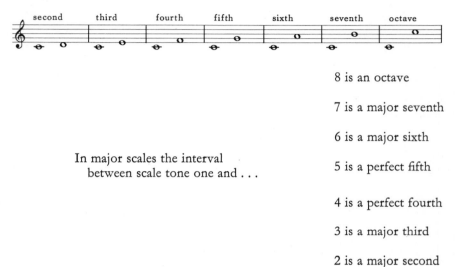

In major scales the interval
between scale tone one and . . .

8 is an octave

7 is a major seventh

6 is a major sixth

5 is a perfect fifth

4 is a perfect fourth

3 is a major third

2 is a major second

Relate these to the less common intervals below:

THE C MAJOR SCALE INTERVALS

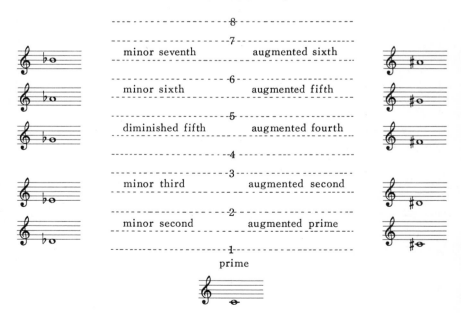

Notice that the notes illustrated at either end of the horizontal lines are the same keys on the keyboard; that is, D flat is the same black key as C sharp, and so on. These are *enharmonic* tones—those which are the same degree of the chromatic scale, but written differently on the staff. The augmented and diminished intervals are very seldom used in the elementary school. They may appear, however, in children's experimental compositions.

In order of using and learning melodic intervals, the young learner usually begins with the descending minor third. The second is part of any scale-line pattern; the octave, the fourth, and the fifth are commonly used in children's songs. The sixth, then the seventh, would probably come next in order of usage. They are learned through associations with their use in familiar songs, followed by "guessing" games of interval identification. To be certain they have identified the interval correctly, children can test their decision by beginning with 1 or *do* and "singing up to it."

The minor third is exemplified in "Brahms' Lullaby," "The Caisson Song," and "Lightly Row"; the major third in "Mary and Martha," "Little David," and "Swing Low, Sweet Chariot"; the fourth in "Taps," "I've Been Working on the Railroad," "Auld Lang Syne," and "Hark! the Herald Angels Sing"; the fifth in "Twinkle, Twinke, Little Star," and "Baa, Baa, Black Sheep"; the sixth in "My Bonnie," "Bendemeer's Stream," and "It Came Upon the Midnight Clear"; and the octave with "Annie Laurie," and "Wait for the Wagon." The minor sixth is often identified by thinking the major sixth first, then comparing it with the half-step smaller interval. The minor and major sevenths are often identified by comparing them with the octave.

Ability to read music through knowledge of intervals becomes essential in the instance of contemporary melodies that do not move in the scalewise and chordwise manner of traditional melodies. If syllables are used with this music, the teacher should consider using the *fixed do* system in which C is always *do*.

The usefulness of tone patterns and intervals in reading music can be understood when songs are analyzed with these aspects in mind. For example, "Love Somebody" contains tone patterns one, three, and four, the interval of a perfect fourth numerous times, and the interval of a perfect fifth once. Anyone knowing these and the rhythm patterns discussed in the previous chapter can sight-sing the song. How many times do each of the tone patterns occur? How many times is the interval of the fourth used?

LOVE SOMEBODY

Chord-line melody patterns are another helpful factor in note reading; this will be referred to in the next chapter. Tone pattern four and its inversions is one such pattern. "Love Somebody" contains this pattern in G and D chord-lines and an inversion of the G chord appears in the last two phrases. Analyze "Alouette" in terms of tone patterns and intervals.

ALOUETTE (Skylark)

1. { Et la tête,   Et la tête.
    A - lou-ette,   A - lou-ette.   Oh!
2. { Et le bec,   Et le bec.
    Et la tête,   Et la tête.   Oh!
    A - lou-ette,   A - lou-ette.

3. Le nez   4. Le dos   5. Les pattes   6. Le cou
(the nose)   *(the back)*   *(the claws)*   *(the neck)*

Forms of Melodies

The answers to the questions, "Is the tune the same or is it different now?" and "How is it different?" guide children into learning concepts of the different ways melodies are put together. Very young children can answer these questions. The mind seeks a sense of order, and music is one of the better ways to foster the concept of form. Children can listen for form, hear it, analyze it, and apply it in their own compositions. The concepts of same, different, repetition, contrast, and variety can grow through finding the phrases of songs and comparing them. This is done first through the ear; later it can be seen in notation. In the preceding chapter body movement was shown to be a means of discovering these similarities and differences, and percussion instruments were used to emphasize them.

It is important to remember that one-part (unary), two-part (binary), and three-part (ternary) song forms have many variants. Teacher and class should expect to find songs with phrase orders which are modifications of these model forms, and songs with different forms. For a simple example, "Whistle, Daughter, Whistle," has a unary form in which the same phrase is repeated note for note; it could be described as *a a*. "Hole in the Bucket" is also unary, but the phrase ends differently, hence it could be described as *a a'*.

HOLE IN THE BUCKET

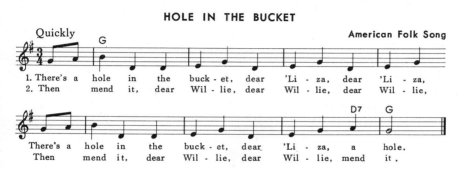

American Folk Song

1. There's a hole in the buck-et, dear 'Li - za, dear 'Li - za,
2. Then mend it, dear Wil - lie, dear Wil - lie, dear Wil - lie,

There's a hole in the buck-et, dear 'Li - za, a hole.
Then mend it, dear Wil - lie, dear Wil - lie, mend it.

"Go Tell Aunt Rhodie" is an example of binary form in which there are two unlike phrases, thus *a b*. "Li'l 'Liza Jane" is a variant of this, with four phrases, *a a' b b'*.

GO TELL AUNT RHODY

There are many examples of ternary (three-part) form, of which "O Tannenbaum" is one, *a a b a*. The important aspect is a melodic statement, contrast, then a return to the beginning. Theorists ignore the first repetition of *a*, consider the form to be *a b a*, and compare it to an arch in architecture. "O Tannenbaum" includes another aspect of melody structure, the *sequence,* part of the melody repeated at a higher or lower pitch level. This is a device children can use in their compositions. "I Love the Mountains" is a song which is sequential in character.

O TANNENBAUM (O Christmas Tree)

O, Tannenbaum, O, Tannenbaum,   Du Grünst nicht nur zur Sommerzeit,
Wie treu sind deine Blätter !   Nein auch im Winter, wenn es schneit.
O, Tannenbaum, O, Tannenbaum,   O, Tannenbaum, O, Tannenbaum,
Wie treu sind deine Blätter !   Wie treu sind deine Blätter !

Exploring the Manipulation of Melodies

In the preceding chapter certain aspects of music composition were explored with percussion instruments in a non-melodic situation. These were augmentation, diminution, and canonic treatment. See p. 215, "Rhythm-Related Compositional Devices." These can be applied to melodies in the same way as described there, and older children can experiment with them in their compositions. Other composer's techniques which children can learn to utilize include *transposition,* placing the melody in another key, *inversion,* writing it upside down, *retrograde,* writing it backwards, giving it a *variations* treatment by altering it rhythmically, melodically, or harmonically, and using *octave displacement,* which is distorting the melody with octave leaps. Octave displacement, inversion, and retrograde are illustrated below with "London Bridge." Stravinsky's

LONDON BRIDGE

Singing Game

Lon - don Bridge is fall - ing down, fall - ing down, fall - ing down.

Lon - don Bridge is fall - ing down, My fair la - dy. ____

Inverted

(complete it)

Retrograde

(complete it)

Octave Displacement

(complete it)

"Greeting Prelude" exemplifies octave displacement with the familiar tune, "Happy Birthday to You," and it is useful at every elementary school level. One series, *Exploring Music,* 1966 edition, has it recorded for the first grade book, and page 73 of the Teacher's Book suggests treating "Hot Cross Buns" this way. "Greeting Prelude" is included on the Columbia Record *Instrumental Miniatures,* a group of short pieces by Stravinsky. Materials useful in exploring variation form include *Hot Cross Buns.* Young People's Record 5005, Lucien Calliet's *Variations on Pop Goes the Weasel,* Adventures in Music 4, vol. 1, excerpts from variations Mozart wrote on a French folk tune we know as "Twinkle, Twinkle, Little Star," presented for piano in *Exploring Music With Children,* the *Second Movement* of Haydn's *C Major* (Emperor) *Quartet,* which uses a familiar hymn tune, and Charles Ives' *Variations on America.*

The most popular approach in introducing the manipulation of melodies is by means of very simple and well-known songs. Some additional examples include "Baa, Baa, Black Sheep," "Three Blind Mice," "Are You Sleeping?" and "Mary Had a Little Lamb."

What Do Melodies Communicate?

Songs are the union of poetry and melody; their words describe rather clearly the thought being communicated. Children should be encouraged to form judgments about how well the melody reflects the message of the words. "This song is said to be a lullaby." "How does the melody suggest that it is a lullaby?" "How well does it succeed in communicating this idea?" A song such as "Sleep, Baby, Sleep" could be used for an example. When such questions are stated, the teacher is relating man and music in recognition that at least 90% of the music of the world is functionally used rather than set apart as an art for the connoisseur. How does the melody of a work song, a street vendor's song, a dance song, suggest the message of the words? How well does it do it? The first question stimulates analysis and the second a value judgment which might also further analysis. Analyze "Sleep, Baby, Sleep" to find how the relative instance or absence of fast, slow, note values, range, form, repetition, contrast, climax, release, and other aspects affect the communication of the song's message.

Melodies can reflect a mood, describe something, be an exercise similar to a puzzle, or suggest beauty for its own sake. Children can,

SLEEP, BABY, SLEEP

2. Sleep, baby, sleep! The large stars are the sheep.
   The little ones, the lambs, I guess,
   The gentle moon, the shepherdess,
   Sleep, baby, sleep! Sleep, baby, sleep!

at their own level of musical growth, analyze many famed recorded melodies and make value judgments about them. Of the numerous possibilities, the following are a few examples:

Bach	Air for the G String
Barber	Adagio for Strings
Cage, Cowell, etc.	*Sounds of New Music* (Folkways FX 6160)
Dvorák	Humoresque
Gounod	Avé Maria
Ghys	Amaryllis
McDowell	To a Water Lily
Mendelssohn	Spring Song
Paderewski	Minuet
Ravel	La Valse
Rubenstein	Melody in F
Saint-Saëns	The Swan
Schumann	Träumerei (Dreams)
Tschaikovsky	March Slav
Villa-Lobos	Bachianas Brasileiras No. 5
Wagner	Ride of the Valkyries
Waldteufel	Skaters Waltz

Teaching Rote Songs

SELECTING FIRST SONGS FOR ROTE TEACHING

When one tries to describe the teaching of rote songs he is tempted to say that there are almost as many approaches as there are songs. Many short songs can be taught as complete songs rather than in sections. However, one of the easiest types to begin with is the song which calls for an answer. "John the Rabbit" is one in which children reply, singing the words "Yes, ma'am." "Old MacDonald" is another. Children want to sing "Ee-i-ee-i-o" while the teacher sings the rest of it.

OLD MACDONALD

American Song

After they have learned to sing the three-pitch "Ee-i-ee-i-o" part, the teacher may suggest that they learn the one-pitch "Here a chick, there a chick, ev'rywhere a chick chick" section. Soon part of the class can sing the first two measures, "Old MacDonald had a farm," and another part can sing "Ee-i-ee-i-o"—and everyone will sing "Here a chick, etc." As the learning progresses, the teacher will ask questions which assist the children in reviewing or learning the words. "What did Old MacDonald have?" (A farm) "Sing it: Old MacDonald had a farm." (They sing.) "What did he have on his farm?" (He had some chicks.) "Sing that part." (They sing.) "Where were those chicks?" (A chick chick here and a chick chick there.) "Sing it." Soon the entire song can be sung by the class. However, it is always fun—and it adds variety—to have different groups sing different parts. "Girls, you sing the parts about Old MacDonald and what he had on his farm. Boys, you sing 'Ee-i-ee-i-o.' All of you sing the 'chick chick' parts." Sometimes all the girls with red dresses can sing a part, or all children with brown eyes or white shoes; this adds to the pleasure of the occasion.

Young children will react in individual ways. Some may want to begin singing too soon, before they have listened to what they are to sing, and an understanding must be made that they are to listen carefully "before their turn comes." Some may not sing; they need to listen longer, or their interest needs to be further stirred. Most of them will want to contribute actively as soon as possible; this is why songs with easy answering parts or parts suggesting simple physical responses are enjoyed and usually learned rather quickly. The logical procedure is to always work from the easiest parts first.

The echo-type song is one in which children sing parts which repeat pitch for pitch what the teacher has sung. "Are You Sleeping?" is one of this type. Every measure of this song is followed by an exact repetition. Thus the teacher presents it as a complete song first, then eventually asks the class to sing each part after her. A signal is developed such as the teacher's pointing to herself when it is her turn to sing, and to the children when it is their turn. "Follow On" is another echo song. Later on some of the children will sing with the teacher in "Follow On," and ultimately the class can be divided into two groups, one of which will sing the teacher's part. "Old Texas" can be sung in the same general way; six-year-olds who can sing on pitch will sing it well.

FOLLOW ON!

Old Song

Repetitious songs are easily taught by rote. "A-Tisket, A-Tasket" is a young children's song centered about the 5–3–6–5 tone pattern. Its sing-song repetitiveness makes it easy for children to learn. Other songs of this type include "Tideo," "Rig-A-Jig-Jig," "Pick a Bale of Cotton," "Hole in the Bucket," and "Standin' in the Need of Prayer." "Trampin'" is also an example.

After the teacher introduces "Trampin'" by singing it all the way through, the children may begin entering on the chorus part, "Tryin' to make heaven my home." In reviewing the words and meaning of the song the teacher may ask, "What is the singer doing?" (trampin') "What does that mean?" "What is he trying to do?" "Has he ever been to heaven?" "What has he been told about it?" Later on, a child or group of children will sing the teacher's solo part, with everyone singing the chorus.

TRAMPIN'

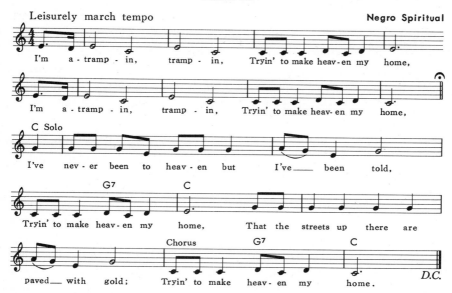

Songs such as "O Tannenbaum" and "Lightly Row" which have a phrase organization of *a a b a*, and other songs of longer length than these, are commonly taught by phrase-echoing. The teacher sings the song or plays a recording of it, then discusses its meaning with the children, endeavoring to increase comprehension and interest. He then sings the first phrase; the children echo this. Then he sings the second phrase; the children repeat this phrase also. He then asks them to sing both phrases and they do. The teacher next sings the *b* phrase, which seems more difficult because it is different; the children echo this. The process continues, phrase by phrase until the song is learned. More complex songs may require a combination of these different approaches. Teachers need to study each song, analyze each thoroughly, then plan the best strategy for learning the particular melody.

MUSIC CONCEPTS AND ROTE TEACHING

While rote singing is a necessary step in musical growth—and it is an honored procedure from the standpoint of the history of man—if teachers go no farther than this type of teaching, the result can be only a form of music illiteracy. Phyllis E. Dorman writes, "There is a certain dignity and logic in the simplest song. A song, any song, makes use of the same tools present in the most complicated of the musical classics.

Every element is there: rhythm, melody, form, tonality, texture, dynamics, color, and aesthetics. Yet the students are allowed to remain almost totally unaware of these. Songs should be used to teach musical concepts."[2] She recommends that *music* be taught instead of only songs.

Although singing of rote songs may take place at any level and at any age, more of this type of learning is necessarily used with young children who can do little or no reading of notation. However, every song contains elements of music the teacher can use in some way to prepare for or begin work with understanding music and learning about notation. The following can be considered steps in teaching young children rote songs, keeping music concepts in mind while doing so.

ESTABLISHING THE PITCH   Because the range of any song is a crucial matter, the teacher *must* establish the key and the beginning pitch accurately. This means using pitchpipe, bells, Autoharp (in tune), piano, or some other reliable instrument. At any level of instruction the teacher should hum the tonic chord (1–3–5–3–1; *do mi so mi do*) or play it on the bells. In keys such as D, E♭, E, F, G, and A♭ the low 5 (5_1) can be sung or played to further reinforce the key feeling (1–3–5–3–1–5,–1; *do mi so mi do so do.*). In minor keys this process begins on *la,* the sixth step of the major scale according to the key signature. Older children should be able to do this after the teacher gives them the key note; it is an ear training experience and it is good to involve the class in establishing the pitch. In this process concepts of pitch, tone pattern, and key feeling are being nurtured. Furthermore, this care in establishing key and the beginning pitch (for the next step is to sing up or down the scale to the beginning note of the song if it does not begin on the key note) marks the difference between success or failure in some of the children's singing on pitch.

MOTIVATING INTEREST   There are many possible ways to motivate songs. Sometimes the teacher announces the title and tells briefly with what it is concerned. Sometimes it is all a surprise—the children listen to find out what it is about. It is wise to take very little time for this because the school day is too short, and every minute counts; no time should be wasted. Pictures may help. After the teacher sings the song he should ask the children what its story or message is in a series of questions illustrated earlier in this section of the chapter.

[2] Dorman, Phyllis E., "A Protest Against Musical Illiteracy," *Music Educators Journal,* November, 1967, p. 99.

BEAT AND METER   As the teacher sings the song again he might walk quietly in place to the beat while the children do likewise or imitate his walk with creative adaptations, such as walking with the hands in the air, with fingers on desks, or with silently clapping hands. Accents may call attention to the meter, whether or not children understand what meter is at the earliest levels.

PHRASE   As the teacher sings the song again, the phrase order can be stressed. For young children, the teacher may ask them to stand and imitate what he does—move arms to depict a phrase ⌒ , step the beat while turning the body, reversing directions for a contrasting phrase, holding up a finger for phrase one, adding a finger for each subsequent phrase, and so on. Some of this can be done with older children; however, those with good music backgrounds can sense the phrase order by listening, using their better-developed tonal memory. Logical questions to ask include, "How many phrases did you hear?" "Are there any that are the same?" "Similar?" "Different?" "Which ones?"

MELODIC DIRECTION: CONTOUR.   The teacher can ask the children to show by their hand positions what they think is the up and down direction of the melody. In a later lesson their analysis can give them answers to questions regarding steps and skips in the melody line and if certain phrases conclude up or down.

INDEPENDENT SINGING   After the children have heard a song several times with this kind of analytical guidance, (and perhaps after some of the techniques suggested under *Selecting First Songs for Rote Teaching* have been used) they should sing it without the teacher's voice. The teacher can assist by high and low hand positions, but he will join in singing only if absolutely necessary. A goal is to assure the children's independence of both the teacher's voice and the piano. Also, teachers cannot listen to children's singing if they too are singing. The children may then repeat the song, sometimes using the hand positions with the teacher.

TEXTURE   The next time the children sing the song, the teacher may use accompanying instruments to provide different textures. If the piano sounds exactly the same as the melody the children sing, it is sounding only the melody in unison with their voices. It is an example of monophony. If the Autoharp or guitar sounds a chordal accompaniment which supports the melody, there is homophony, a quite different texture. "Did it sound the same or different this time?" "What made it sound different?" comprise a way to begin a discussion of texture even though the children may not know the adult terminology. Different types of accompaniments can be discussed, described, analyzed, and evaluated for their suitability for the melody. The accompaniments of recorded songs can contribute to the study of texture.

TONE QUALITY   Tone qualities of voices and of accompanying instruments can be evaluated in terms of their suitability to express the meaning of the song or in terms of beauty.

DYNAMICS   The children can be encouraged to try to sing the song at different dynamic levels—loud, soft, crescendo, decrescendo, with accents, and so on. They should determine the dynamics most suited to the song, thus learning about interpretation and aesthetic discrimination.

Thus the teaching of rote songs can become "rote-note" teaching because it can expand children's music concepts to the place when what they already have sensed and worked with is described in notation which, after all, is only a kind of picture-description of the melody.

GENERAL DIRECTIONS

FINDING THE KEYNOTE IN MAJOR TONALITIES   This is necessary to enable the teacher and children to establish the pitch and key feeling (tonality) of a song. In review, the ways to find the keynote (home tone) from key signatures are:

1.   The sharp farthest to the right is scale tone 7 or *ti*. Count up to 8 or *do*, or down to 1 or *do*. The letter name of 8 or 1 is the name of the key.

2.   The flat farthest to the right is scale tone 4 or *fa*. Count down to 1 or up to 8; the letter name of 8 or 1 is the name of the key. A quicker way for key signatures containing two or more flats is: the next-to-the-last flat on the right is the keynote.

Songs in major tonalities ordinarily end on 1, 3, or 5.

FINDING THE KEY IN MINOR TONALITIES

1.   Find the major tonality indicated by the key signature.

2.   Find the sixth degree of the major scale (6 or *la*). This note is the keynote of the relative minor tonality.

Songs in minor usually end on *la*, and rarely on *do* or *mi*.

Learn the song thoroughly before attempting to teach it.
Have the children participate actively in some way as soon as possible.
Don't plan too much to do with the same song on the same day; this can
become boring.

One of the better ways to signal the children to begin singing (when
it is their turn to sing the entire song) is to sing the first two or four
measures and say "Sing!" on the beat *before* the children are to begin
singing. For example, when a teacher sings "Old MacDonald had a farm,
Ee-i-ee-i-o SING!" the tempo has been established, the children have
sensed the rhythm, tonality, and spirit of the song, and they can come
in all together at the beginning. Part of good group singing is to begin
together, and this singing introduction by the teacher is one way to
make this possible. Other ways to start children singing include counting
the meter and saying "Sing!" on the beat before the children are to begin,
and by competent conducting.

Possible activities for children to do while they listen to a teacher
introduce a new rote song by singing it to them include:

Clapping hands (tips of fingers) soundlessly to the beat;
Clapping hands soundlessly to the rhythm of the words or melody;
Standing in place and trying to discern phrases by making heart-shaped
    movements with the hands and arms;
Conducting the meter or determining the meter by trying to conduct it;
Determining whether the music swings in two's or three's;
Acting out pitch levels and/or melodic contour with hands and arms;
Analyzing what is heard in terms of scalewise and skipwise patterns;
Listening for outstanding rhythm patterns;
Listening for outstanding tone patterns.

Playing the I V_7 I chord sequence on Autoharp, guitar, or piano is
another good way to establish key feeling. Then ask the children to sing
the home tone.

Take breaths generally at the end of phrases. People do not "break
a phrase" by taking a breath during it when speaking; neither should
this be done when singing. Periods, commas, and semicolons often point
out the proper places to breathe.

Encourage children to suggest ways for better interpretation of the
song.

SEEING WHAT WE HEAR

The above discussion has considered the teaching of songs by means of guided repetitions. The teacher's plans lead from purely rote singing to understanding music concepts that help children toward reading notation. Some activities that build notational concepts include having children:

1. Compare the notation of two familiar songs of the same tempo, one which uses many eighth and sixteenth notes and another which has whole notes, half notes, and quarter notes. Guide them to discover that the "whiteness" of notation relates to long note duration and the "blackness" of notation relates to short note duration.

2. Look for familiar rhythm patterns and note patterns in the notation of selected songs.

3. Look at the notation of phrases of known songs to find out that when phrases sound the same they look the same, and when they sound different, they look different.

4. Watch the notated melody line and follow it on the page with an index finger, all the while relating high and low in pitch with high and low on the staff.

5. Relate the keyboard to notation by providing easy songs to play on the bells by number, by the note names stamped on the bars, and eventually by notation. (See Using "Melody Instruments" in this chapter.)

USING RECORDINGS OF SONGS

Recordings can be substituted for teachers' voices in teaching songs. It is well known that children learn some songs automatically from children's recordings they play at home, and from radio and television programs. Singing commercials are frequently learned also. However, when recordings are used, many of the flexible techniques suggested above cannot be employed.

The children must sing softly in order to hear the recording. The volume of the record player can be gradually turned down as the children learn a song so that they will become increasingly independent of the recording. Another test to determine how well the children have learned a song is to have them begin singing with the recording, then lift up the needle and have them continue without its help.

It is well to emphasize teaching the words when songs are learned by rote from recordings; they are frequently written on the chalkboard.

Another technique, useful as a later step in the learning process, is to have small groups of children, no more than six, stand by the record player and sing with it while the remainder of the class listens to evaluate their efforts constructively and awaits their turn at doing the same thing.

The recordings that accompany the series books as well as some other song books can be of genuine value in teaching songs. They usually provide worthy examples for children to hear and imitate: they often bring to the classroom fascinating instrumental accompaniments that could be provided in no other way. They aid the teacher who studies them even though he may prefer not to use them in the classroom, because with their assistance he learns songs correctly, both rhythmically and melodically. Beginning teachers should study the recordings that accompany the series books they are to use in their classrooms. Before the fall term begins, if they hear these recordings over a period of days they will have absorbed a repertoire of songs they need to know, and will have saved time by not having to pick out each song on a keyboard instrument and learn it without a model to follow. When a child tends the record player the teacher is free to move about the room to listen to individual voices and to direct class activities. The teacher can stop singing and listen to the children—something every teacher of music needs to do. No matter how well qualified a music specialist may be, there are times when a recording will provide an effective way to teach some songs. However, recordings cannot completely take the place of the teacher's voice; younger children sometimes find it difficult to understand the diction of voices strange to them. In all of the grades, a machine is no substitute for the personality of a teacher who sings.

THE USE OF THE PIANO AND OTHER VOICE SUBSTITUTES

The piano or bells may be substituted for the voice or recording by teachers who lack confidence in their singing voices and do not have recordings of songs they need to teach. Words for such songs may be learned by rote or written on the chalkboard. The teacher will then play the melody of the song. This may be repeated while the children do several of the activities of the rote singing process already described in this chapter, the instrument thus taking the place of the voice or recording. For a song of some length the phrase method may be desirable. After the playing of the entire song, the melody of the first phrase will be played; the children will mouth the words silently as it is played again. Then the children may sing this phrase with the piano; and next, sing without its support. This can be continued throughout the remaining phrase, combining some of them along the way. As the song is learned, the support of the instrument is gradually withdrawn to gain independence from it. If a child in the class is a good natural musician and has a pleasing voice, he may be an excellent teacher's assistant by singing to the class phrases or entire songs that he has learned from the teacher's playing the piano or bells. Recorder- and flute-type instruments are sometimes employed also in this approach to teaching singing.

Although it is highly desirable to have a piano in every classroom, the piano is not essential in teaching or in accompanying songs. In a normal situation where the teacher uses his singing voice, the piano has its greatest use at the end of the learning process. A song may be introduced by playing it on the piano in a simple manner. Since younger children find it difficult to hear a melody when an elaborate accompaniment is played, a simple accompaniment, permitting the melody to predominate clearly, is the most effective style of playing. During most of the learning process involved in teaching songs the piano has little use, for two reasons: (1) when the teacher is playing the piano he cannot hear the children well enough to tell if each child is singing correctly, and (2) he is in a stationary position and is unable to move through the class to hear and to help individual children with their problems. Another reason for not using the piano at this time is that if it is used constantly the children cannot sing independently and may become semi-helpless without it. However, after a song has been learned, the addition of a piano accompaniment can be a thrilling and satisfying experience, adding greatly to the singer's enjoyment and to the musical effect of the performance.

Although the piano is not an absolute necessity, it is an important means of enrichment. It is also a very important tool for learning many things about music. Thus, the piano has its rightful place in the well-equipped classroom along with the radio, record player, Autoharp, bells, percussion instruments, projectors and tape recorders—but not as a dominating instrument.

Using Melody Instruments

A characteristic of children of the United States is their interest in mechanical things. Making music by playing an instrument, no matter how simple the instrument, attracts them. It follows that if teachers guide this interest along the lines of learning both the skills of playing and the understanding of the elements of music, it can yield great benefits.

When melody instruments are employed to invent introductions, codas, interludes, and to play tone patterns, concepts of melody and form are being expanded. The concept of *interval* can be made clear by seeing intervals on keyboard instruments, by seeing and feeling them on blowing-type (small wind) instruments, and by comparing what is seen, felt, and heard with written intervals on the staff. The key signature is relatively unimpressive to the singer, but of undeniable significance to the player of melody instruments. Note reading becomes clearly practical and functional when the player must relate notation to the keyboard or to fingerings on a wind instrument. Instruments are also useful in studying aspects of music such as scale-line, chord-line, legato, staccato, and a host of others related to analysis and performance. Flute-type instruments lend atmosphere to American Indian music; the individually-plucked strings of the psaltery, Autoharp, guitar, and ukulele can produce imitation Oriental melodies; and the marimba contributes in an authentic manner to Latin American music. Children can use melody instruments to compose melodies. They are easy to play; they can be taught by the classroom teacher. Their use combines auditory, tactile, and visual perception to build music concepts. It is theorized that some children will be more interested in trying to match tones with their voices when they produce pitches themselves on a melody instrument. Children who cannot sing well should be able to make their own music by means of instruments. Furthermore, the more experienced and gifted children can have additional musical experiences from their opportunities with instruments.

WATER GLASSES AND BOTTLES

Some teachers use water glasses and bottles as introductory experiences to keyboard instruments such as bells, xylophone, and piano. There are tuned glasses that can be used without water, obtainable from various sources on order, even from some variety stores. Other teachers employ glasses with water, knowing that this probably means some spilling and evaporation, both of which necessitate retuning because of the change in water levels. Some teachers use bottles with water, often corked or capped to keep retuning at a minimum.

One of the first listening activities in primary grades is experimenting with sounds made with metal, wood, glass, and stone. These early experiences lead to experiments with water glasses and bottles. By striking glasses and bottles when they are empty and when they contain water, children can make certain scientific observations. They discover that the pitch and tone quality are affected by the size and thickness of the glass or bottle. They may also discover that decreasing the amount of water raises the pitch and increasing the amount of water lowers the pitch—except in some glasses and bottles that will not tune lower no matter how much water is added. They may also discover that striking glasses or bottles with soft objects such as felt-covered mallets produces soft tones. Let the children generalize from their experimentation that: The more water one pours into a glass or bottle, the lower the pitch is. The lowest pitch is made by filling glasses and bottles full of water. The highest pitch is produced when a glass or bottle is empty. The best tone quality is produced when a soft mallet strikes the glass as if pulling the sound out, not hitting it in.

After experimenting with glasses and bottles, children and teacher may decide that bottles are superior because if one can seal them, the pitch will remain stable. However, the most important element of comparison should be the beauty of the sound, which could be determined by the quality of the glass in either of these instruments. Paint or paper strips can be placed on them to show the water level that produces the desired pitch. Numeral names, note names, or syllable names can be painted on or written on paper stickers. Some teachers put vegetable dyes or other coloring in the water to add interest. Placing glasses on a thick cloth will result in a better tone.

Interest in playing melodies on bottles may prompt the teacher or the children to make or obtain a rack from which to suspend the bottles. When this is done, each bottle is suspended by two loops of string, one on each side of the bottle neck, to help it to hang with more stability.

The first experience in playing songs on glasses or bottles is generally with only three pitches: 3–2–1 (mi-re-do). However, it is good to compose a song with only one pitch, that of 1 (do); then a song with scale tone 1 and 2; and finally, a song with tones 1, 2, and 3, arriving at the three-pitch stage in a logical way. Known songs in the three-tone category are "Hot Cross Buns" and "Merrily We Roll Along." After this, the next step is to use four-and five-tone melodies. Teachers often devise their own three-, four-, and five-tone songs as examples, then encourage the children to compose others with scale-tones 1–2–3–4–5. After this experience has been digested, more scale tones are added until melodies are created on all eight pitches of the major scale. The pentatonic tonal organization can be used also, beginning with songs based on scale tones 5–3, then 5–6–3, then 1–2–3–5–6. It is advantageous to transfer skills acquired on glasses and bottles to bells and xylophones. Bells provide a good introduction to the piano keyboard. Some teachers prefer to go directly to them rather than introduce them by means of experimental glasses and bottles.

BELLS AND XYLOPHONES

When children have had opportunities to explore the bells for themselves, they can make a number of discoveries:

Long bars sound low pitches.
Short bars sound high pitches.
The arrangement of white keys and black keys is the same as that of the piano except that the piano has more keys.
To play a scale going up, one plays from left to right.
To play a scale going down, one plays from right to left.

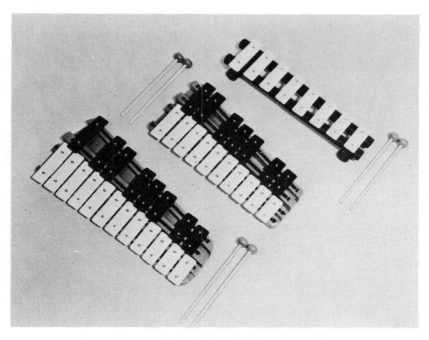

Penguin Song Bells
PERIPOLE, INC.

A five-note (pentatonic) scale can be played on the black keys.

White keys played from C to C sound the C major scale.

If a standard bell set can be stood on end, with large bars down, and held against the chalkboard or chart paper, staff lines can be drawn from the bars to relate the keyboard to the staff.

To produce the best tone, one strikes the middle of the bar and draws the tone out rather than hitting it in.

The same sequence of pitches is used to initiate playing the bells as was described for glasses and bottles. *Resonator* bells are made of individual tone bars that can be taken from the carrying case if desired. For example, if children are to compose tunes with only three or four pitches, those particular bars can be removed from the set, placed in order, and played apart from the other bars to prevent possible confusion of young children when they would try to play those bars when placed in keyboard position among all the other bars. When they are removed from the set, there can be no doubt as to which ones are to be used for creating tunes.

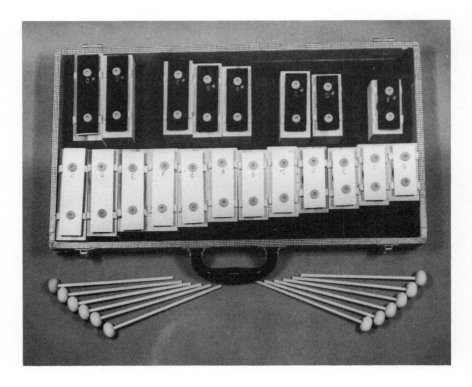

Resonator Bells

B. F. KITCHING CO., INC.

Before children understand music notation, teachers guide them to play by ear and by numeral notation.[3] The scale-tone numbers can be written on the white metal keys with black crayon. or they can be placed on tagboard in back of the bells. Numeral notation could appear as follows. Notice that the "fast notes" are circled.

Hot Cross Buns
3 2　1 –　3 2 1–
⟨1111⟩⟨2222⟩ 3 2 1–

Mary Had a Little Lamb
3212 333– 222– 333–
3212 3333 2232 1—

five-note tune

six-note tune

Jingle Bells
333– 333– 3512 3—
4444 433⟨33⟩3223 2–5–
333– 333– 3512 3—
4444 433⟨33⟩5542 1—

Are You Sleeping?
1 2 3 1 1 2 3 1 345–345–
⟨6543⟩ 1 ⟨6543⟩ 1 1⟨5⟩1–1⟨5⟩1–

Use C major or G major to avoid black keys. Use F major to introduce one black key (B♭). *Hot Cross Buns* and *Mary Had a Little Lamb* can be played on the group of three black keys. Some teachers prefer to introduce the piano keyboard in this way to overcome possible hesitation about the black keys later. With guidance and careful listening, young children can play songs or parts of songs in keys such as F and G major where one black key is necessary. The general procedure at first is to learn a song well by rote before attempting to play it (*listen, sing,* then *play*).

Although children may begin playing songs with the aid of numerals, they are soon looking at notation the teacher has prepared for them that includes the numerals written beneath (or above) the note they represent. Later, teachers prepare notation in which the numerals appear only with the beginning note of each measure, then only with the beginning note of each phrase, and finally they are abandoned altogether because the children have made the transition from numerals to the notes on the staff.

The bells have many uses. If a classroom teacher has difficulty with his singing voice, the instrument can be used to teach rote songs. Difficult tonal patterns in songs can be isolated and studied by means of the bells. They are often employed to establish the pitch of songs by sounding the keynote, playing tones of the tonic chord (I), then playing the starting pitch. Special sound effects such as chimes, church bells, and sleigh bells

[3] A well-known book that introduces numeral notation in kindergarten and first grade is *Timothy's Tunes* by Adeline McCall (Boston Music Company). The *Psaltery Book* by Satis Coleman (John Day Company) is another. *Fun with the Melody-bells* by Rj Staples (Follett) further develops the use of numeral notation.

can be produced to enhance songs. Children can play simple parts of songs involving a single tone up to an entire scale, and they can play complete songs. Introductions, codas, and interludes—all created on the bells—can be added. Older children can write descants and other added parts to songs and play them on the bells. Bells can assist part-singing.

The "suggestions to the teacher" in one of the music series states that if children had access to keyboard instruments, many of the problems in teaching understanding of pitch differences, of the interval relationship of tones, and of music notation generally would be minimized. The reason is that the keyboard constitutes a highly significant *audio-visual* tool for learning. Children enjoy "picking out tunes" and in doing so on the bells or piano they *see* and *feel* and *hear* the interval relationships of tones. This can lead to a real comprehension of the meaning of the notes on the staff—a comprehension frequently lacking in children whose musical experiences have been confined to a singing approach. In every elementary classroom there should be a music corner that includes bells and easy music to play on them. Some teachers have a "song of the week" which children learn to play before school, after school, and during the school day. When played with a padded mallet or a pencil with a rubber eraser, this soft-toned instrument seldom disturbs other classroom activities.

The *xylophone* is similar to the bells, but made of wood instead of metal. *Xylo* is the Greek word for wood. Because its wood strips do not vibrate as long as the metal bars of the bells, it has a more percussive quality. A more attractive xylophone is the *marimba,* which has resonators, usually metal tubes, beneath the wood strips. German music educators use the term xylophone, but prefer the terms *glockenspiel* or *metallophone* to bells. The metallophone is often lower pitched than the glockenspiel.

EAR TRAINING WITH BELLS   Some ear training-tonal memory activities with bells include:

> The teacher plays a few consecutive scale tones on the bells; a child is asked to come to the bells and play what he has heard.
>
> A child can make up a short tune; he then asks another child to play what he has heard. If this child does it correctly, he then has the privilege of making up a tune and calling on another classmate to remember it and play it. If a child cannot recall the tune, another is called on. The class listens and judges. (This needs to be a game, not "pressure.")

Xylophone
EDUCATIONAL MUSIC BUREAU

The teacher asks a child to play an easy, well-known song. At first the
teacher will give the starting pitch. Later, as the game grows more
demanding, the child will have to find the beginning pitch.

Later, older children can "take dictation" from the teacher's playing the
bells. The teacher will give the name of the first note and the key in
which the dictation is to be given. Then the children will write the pitches
they hear on the staff in notation, either individually on paper or collec-
tively with a flannel or magnetic board.

Other forms of bells are the step bells, which are made in the form of
stair steps illustrating the ascending and descending pitches of the scale,
and the *glockenturm,* a German instrument which is played vertically and
reveals visually the relationship of keyboard and staff.

THE PIANO AS A MELODY INSTRUMENT

The piano can be used by children in connection with songs in the
same informal ways the percussion instruments and bells are used. Like
the bells, the keyboard provides an audio-visual tool. The piano can be
used as an instrument of percussion, melody, harmony, and as any
combination of these. It is therefore a superior means by which to gain
concepts in music study.

Classroom teachers do not need to be pianists to teach music through
keyboard experience. They need only to be introduced to it so that they
can proceed in the same way the children do. In the beginning a child

can play a tone that sounds "one" when the clock strikes "one" in *Hickory Dickory Dock,* as he may have done earlier on the bells. In a song that has words of importance on one or two tones, children may play these at the time they occur in the melody. The same little three-note melodies played on glasses, bottles, and bells can be played on the piano keyboard. As time goes on, four-and five-finger patterns can be used in an incidental way in both ascending and descending forms. Here are some examples of such usage:

ONE FINGER
The child plays repeated single tones such as the beginning of *Jingle Bells.* He can play a tone-matching game by striking a pitch that is within his voice range, then trying to match it vocally.

TWO FINGERS
The child plays repeated motives in songs and can also match tones, playing as well as singing such scale tones as 5 and 3 ("so" and "mi").

THREE FINGERS
The scale tones 3 2 1 can be played whenever the words "three blind mice" occur in the song of that name. The tonal pattern 1 2 3 1 can be played with the words "Are you sleeping?" in the song of that name.

FOUR FINGERS
Scale tones 4 4 3 3 2 2 1 in *Twinkle, Twinkle, Little Star* can be played when the following words appear: "How I wonder what you are," and "Twinkle, twinkle all the night." Scale tones 5 5 4 4 3 3 2 can be played along with the words, "Up above the world so high," and "Like a diamond in the sky."

FIVE FINGERS
Scale tones 5 43 21 are used at the end of *Row Your Boat* with the words, "Life is but a dream," and the scale tones 5 443 2 1 are used with the words "Ten little Indian boys" at the end of that song. Songs requiring only five fingers can easily be played. Such songs are listed near the beginning of this chapter.

SCALES
Many songs are based on scales and parts of scales that can readily be played on the keyboard.

A natural outgrowth of such piano-song relationships is the composing of little songs within the limitations of three, four, and five scale tones—songs that children can both sing and play. Eventually this activity will lead to the use of more scale tones in song composition.

The resourceful teacher will gain pleasure and satisfaction in finding songs to which these simple uses of the piano are suited, knowing that by such processes children learn to listen and thus improve their singing ability at the same time. This type of keyboard experience merges with the listening process of tone-matching and makes it more of a game because of the added variety.

Another simple use of the piano is the playing of the notes according to the chord names to provide an easy added part to songs. Example: play F with the F chord, G with the G chord, and so on. (See *Chord Roots*, Chapter Ten). Still more for children to do with the keyboard instruments include playing the rhythm of children's names with one tone or a series of tones; playing two tones that illustrate in correct pitch the concepts of high and low pitch in connection with songs; playing short tone patterns for tone-matching purposes or to add interest to songs; playing octave intervals in songs that emphasize this interval; playing other intervals in songs that feature them; playing different note values and rhythm patterns for children to respond to; playing entire characteristic phrases such as the beginning of "The Caisson Song."

Playing the bells, a small instrument, logically comes before playing the piano, a very large instrument. Whatever is done on the bells, however, applies directly to the piano because the keyboard is virtually the same.

Electric organs are used in some schools. These vary in size from small two-octave instruments to the type people purchase for home use. The larger ones can be played without disturbing others by use of earphones through which only the player can hear what is being sounded.

Organa 12
M. HOHNER, INC.

Such instruments provide an additional type of tone quality for the classroom. The large ones have stops which produce a number of different tone qualities. Certain experiences in dynamics can be studied with the organ, and its sustained and accurate pitch is an advantage. The older (non-electric) reed organ often has a pleasant tone that blends well with voices.

SMALL WINDS AS MELODY INSTRUMENTS

Experts in this field recommend that young children have individual experience with the six-hole tin whistle or fife before using instruments such as the Song Flute, Tonette, Flutophone, and Melody Flute. This early beginning would be experimental and without the use of notation. Simple familiar songs could be found on it, and children would naturally make up their own tunes by playing it. Playing small winds by notation would then be introduced at the third or fourth grade level, with the Melody Flute following these. Its superior tone is similar to that of the real flute. The *recorder* is often played in the intermediate grades. Its period of greatest popularity was between the 15th and 18th centuries. In recent years there has been a strong revival of interest in it because: 1) it is an adult instrument played by adults with pleasure; 2) there is a substantial amount of excellent solo and ensemble music available to play on it, including music by "name" composers of both the past and the present; 3) it is easily mastered, although more difficult than the Song

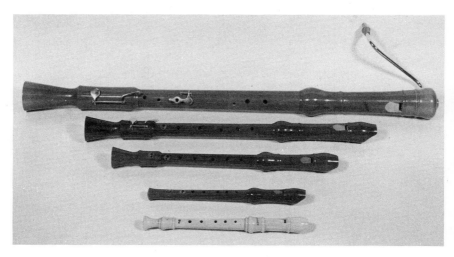

A Family of Recorders
RHYTHM BAND, INC.

Flute, Tonette, Flutophone, and Melody Flute; and 4) it is comparatively inexpensive.

Acceptance of the recorder for upper elementary and junior high school use has been speeded by reductions in price to a low figure when purchased by schools in quanity. The range of the soprano instrument permits sounding middle C as the lowest pitch and continuing upward as high as the normal vocal range. The soprano is widely used because it is built in the key of C, thus having immediate use in playing the music children sing directly from series books; also, it costs less than the larger recorders. The alto is practical to use; it is believed easier to play than the popular soprano. Helpful information can be obtained from music dealers and companies that specialize in the recorder, such as the Hargail Music Press, 157 West 57th Street, New York City 10019, a concern that imports recorders and publishes recorder music.[4] Some teachers suggest requesting special tips on recorder mouthpieces because the wooden mouthpieces sometimes fray. The baroque recorder is preferred to the German, despite the somewhat easier fingering of the latter, because of better pitch accuracy. The best recorders are made of wood, and the best of these are higher priced. Acceptable plastic instruments are available from firms such as Empire Music Company, 3216 44th Avenue S.W., Seattle, Washington 98116 and Trophy Music Company, 1278 West 9th Street, Cleveland, Ohio 44113. Plastic models are less expensive.

While music programs in some European and American schools include playing recorders on a mass basis by young children, some American music educators believe it to be unwise to begin small wind instruction with this instrument. Their reasons include the comparative difficulty of playing it and the psychological consideration that using recorders in the primary school levels tends to brand them as childish toys in the minds of older children who might otherwise enjoy them and realize these are serious adult instruments.

Now let us discuss some problems involved with the other small winds.

Song Flute

CONN CORPOLATION

---

[4] Hargail offers teachers complimentary copies of *New Hargail Recorder Curriculum for Teachers* and *The Recorder in Our Schools*.

Tonette

CHICAGO MUSICAL INSTRUMENT CO.

Flutophone

TROPHY PRODUCTS CO.

These instruments have a range of a ninth:

The Tonette can be tuned by adjusting the mouthpiece. Advantages of tuning are offset by the fact that the plastic material wears when the mouthpiece is pulled in and out frequently, and that the teacher must be sure that all Tonettes are tuned alike when they are played by a group. After a mouthpiece has become worn, it can be kept from falling out by placing a thin strip of paper between the mouthpiece and the body of the instrument where they join. Some teachers use tape to hold the parts together. The Song Flute cannot be tuned. This disadvantage is offset by having all instruments in the same pitch, and by the assurance that no mouthpiece will fall out. Both the Song Flute and the Tonette are constructed so that children's fingers fall naturally in place on the finger-holes, which are set in a curved line, while the Flutophone has finger-holes that are set in a straight line.

The sound of these instruments is essentially soft, as is necessary for classroom use. Because all three instruments are limited to the range previously mentioned, their most common use is in connection with songs within the range of the ninth beginning on middle C. A ninth is the interval of an octave plus one whole-step. Two frequently used instruments having a larger range—each of about two octaves beginning on middle C—are the Symphonette and the Melody Flute. These are somewhat more difficult to play than those of smaller range and, in the opinion of the authors, should seldom be used below fifth grade. Of all these simple instruments, the one with the most pleasing tone is the Melody Flute. All except the Melody Flute finger like the saxophone, the flute, and the upper register of the clarinet. The Melody Flute's fingering is one finger removed from that of the standard instruments. This does not bother children who later change to a real flute, clarinet, or saxophone which, for example, fingers G with three fingers while the Melody Flute fingering for the same note requires only two fingers.

Melody Flute

MELODY FLUTE COMPANY

There are music supervisors who object to the use of these instruments in the classroom. Their major objections are: (1) the children enjoy them so much that unless a teacher knows how to control the situation they may be overemphasized to the neglect of other aspects of the music program—particularly singing; (2) when they are played out of tune their use constitutes a poor musical experience. It follows, then, that the teacher who uses the instruments must avoid these pitfalls. It is suggested that three rules be followed:

1. Use such instruments on a mass basis no more than once a week.

2. On the day the instruments are used the children should be using their singing voices *in connection with playing the instruments* approximately one-half of the time, as will be explained below.

3. The teacher will devise ways for the children to play the instruments in tune.

Although out-of-tune playing is a grave disadvantage, this need not occur. A convention of music educators was startled by the perfection of pitch and the beauty of tone exhibited on the Flutophone by primary grade children under the direction of a classroom teacher. When the musicians asked her how she had achieved this excellent result, she replied that she had instructed the children in blowing through soda straws into glasses of water before she had given them the instruments to play. The children blew bubbles in the water at her direction, starting and stopping them at her signal, and they had taken the straws home with them to continue such exercises. Other teachers have agreed that breath control is the "secret" in gaining mastery of pitch and tone quality with these little instruments. Some have used exercises employed by teachers of wind band instruments, such as having children hold sheets of thin paper on a wall with their exhaled breath for increasing lengths of time. Others have profited from suggestions of vocal music supervisors who learned certain breath control exercises in their voice training. The teaching procedure described below in connection with the *Modern Musical Fun* book includes another approach to the problem of playing in tune that should be considered in the serious study of the small winds.

If a teacher can learn to teach these instruments properly, he will find that through this playing experience he can teach listening, note-reading, sight-singing, part-singing, and music composition as well as playing.

After the teacher decides to use the instruments, his first task is to choose the one best suited to his group. If possible, the children should participate in the choice by experimenting with several of them. Of course, when two or more children blow the same instrument the teacher should have available a sterilizing agent.[5] The teacher should learn to play the chosen instrument well before attempting to teach the class how to play it. Skill on any of them is easy to acquire, so this is not an obstacle. Tonguing is learned by starting to blow as if to say "Too."

A good beginning book for elementary classroom use should contain many well-known songs to sing and play, including some to sing and play in parts. A book that fills these requirements is *Modern Musical Fun*, distributed by the Lyons Band Instrument Company, 688 Industrial Drive, Elmhurst, Ill. 60126. Its subtitle is "For Singing and Playing with the Tonette." This implies that the playing should supplement the singing —not dominate it or obstruct it.

The following teaching procedure is implied by the subtitle. The standard procedure in teaching any of the small winds is to begin with the notes B, A, and G on the staff. On page two of this book we find the first fingering to be learned by the children, the note B on the middle line of the staff. Before attempting to play this note the children should first *hear* the pitch and *sing* it. The teacher plays the note several times wihle the class listens to the pitch and to the tone quality. Then the teacher sings the pitch. The class sings the pitch—singing the note

[5] A variety of disinfectants is available at drug stores. One should be selected that will not affect plastics adversely.

name B, for the children are going to learn the note names in a purposeful setting. There may follow more answering back and forth from the teacher to the class (teacher plays and sings B) and from the class to the teacher (class sings B until everyone has matched the pitch vocally and has really "absorbed" it). Thus, when the children finally play B on their instruments, they will tend to match the pitch they have heard to the extent of adjusting their lips and mouths automatically to produce it with some accuracy. Next, this book presents the note A, and we recommend that it be taught in the same manner that B was taught. Following the presentation of B and A is a little song constructed on these two pitches. Here the teacher asks the children to sing B and A again. When this is accomplished (i.e., when the children have matched tones again and remember each pitch distinctly), they are asked to sing the song "On Tip Toe" using the note names as words. This done, they next sing the song with the words. Then they play the song on the instruments. Thus the children have had, first, meaningful experiences in listening (tone matching), then in sightsinging, and finally in playing the instruments. Some of them will be concentrating on notation for the first time in their lives.

On page three the note G should be learned in the same manner that B and A were learned. The children then sight-sing the next song, "A Safety Song," which employs the three pitches. They sing them first with the note names, then with the words. Lastly, they play the song. These same three notes can now be played in songs that emphasize the three-note pattern: "Hot Cross Buns," "Old MacDonald," "Trampin'," and "Yankee Doodle."

FINGERING
(For Small Winds Such as Tonette, Song Flute, and Flutophone)

At the bottom of page three there is a song called "Melody." Words can be invented by the children when they have learned to sing it with note names and to play it. It can be sung one line at a time and as a rudimentary duet introducing part-singing. It is then played a line at a time and as a duet. To aid the part-singing, one instrument can remain on each part when the class sings.

Proceeding from this very simple introduction with the above method, B♭, F♯, and the other tones of the C scale are learned. Keen listening for proper pitch, sight-singing, music notation study, and part-singing are combined in this type of instrumental experience. Appropriate songs to play can be found in the series books, and listening and singing based on the instrumental activity can be continued from this source of material.

The Melodica, which uses metal reeds like the harmonica, is a small wind instrument built in the form of a keyboard. Some teachers use it to play melodies to substitute for singing or to guard against over-use of their singing voices. A special mouthpiece attachment permits the child to see the keyboard when he plays it to better understand intervals, note patterns, chords, and scalewise melodies. The instrument sounds chords as well as melodies.

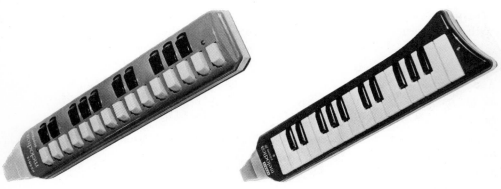

Melodica

M. HOHNER, INC.

Melodica Piano

M. HOHNER, INC.

Creating Melodies

Teachers at all elementary levels are alert to children's spontaneous creating of songs and calls. They notate or tape record those believed to be of value to the child or to the class so they can be saved for later use.

Jumping-rope verses can be set to music; original songs from the playground can be taken indoors.

One sunny morning a little girl in first grade was holding her teacher's hand as she left the building to go to directed play. Deeply affected by the beauty of the day, she sang:

A BEAUTIFUL DAY

First Grade, Washington School
Eugene, Oregon

The teacher asked the child to repeat her song and they sang it together so that they could remember it when they returned to the classroom and share it with the others. Another teacher of a first-grade group had just concluded a reading lesson in which children had learned new words. It was shortly before lunch, and the children suddenly related the new words to their interest in food:

The above examples illustrate the point that creating simple songs is an ability children possess and one that grows under the guidance of good teachers. It is only a short step from spontaneous creative activity to the point where a teacher says of a well-known poem, "Let's sing it today instead of speaking it," and the setting of poetry to music becomes a classroom activity.

The classroom teacher is in the most strategic position to establish an environment in which children can create music. He knows the interests of the children, and he has most to do with encouraging creative responses as normal aspects of the entire school day. Children are *normally* creative, and when they find they have the ability and skill to compose simple songs or instrumental pieces, they will frequently do this at home as a play activity, bringing their compositions to school.

Short verse that has a clearly defined rhythm may be used for a type of song improvisation that emphasizes this rhythm. As a background for this activity children should have sung many short poems and simple word rhythms. The words are spoken by the children in a regular beat pattern set by the teacher. The teacher establishes key feeling by chording the familiar I V₇ I sequence in a key of his choice, and when introducing this activity he will sing the first word of the poem, thus suggesting to the children the beginning note of the song-to-be. While he beats time (it is basic to the method that the rhythm never be interrupted) individual children are asked to sing the poem. The other children may be urged to continue to speak the words softly while they listen to the song being born. The rhythm is stressed, the assumption being that if the rhythm is maintained, a melody will appear from each child which can be as spontaneous and uninhibited as speech. It is further assumed that it is as natural for children to have many musical ideas as it is for them to have many ideas expressed in language. This approach to song creation can be effective on any level and is believed by some to possess virtues that are superior, from the standpoint of creativeness, to the phrase approach, which will be described later. One finds supposedly well-trained musicians who have little feeling for the onward movement of music; they often "break" the rhythm. It is believed that if children experience this type of creative expression, which keeps the rhythmic flow proceeding without interruption, there might be fewer adult musicians who lack a feeling for rhythmic consistency.

Instruments such as the bells and piano are sometimes of aid in stimulating the creative process. A special music teacher used four tone bars from a set of resonator bells with a first-grade class. The children were interested in new shoes, which several of them wore that day, and with the aid of the four tones they created a song on the subject called "New Shoes," which they also learned to play on the bells. Its repetitious words are typical of first-grade children. This song was sung throughout the term whenever one of the children came to school with new shoes.

NEW SHOES

Laboratory School
University of Wisconsin
Milwaukee

New shoes, new shoes, nice, new clean shoes.

New shoes, new shoes, nice, new shoes.

Melodies without words are created by children who have opportunities to experiment with tuned water bottles, xylophones, bells, piano,
recorder-type instruments, and the instruments of the band and orchestra.

Teachers save worthy compositions by writing them down in music
notation. If a teacher has had special music training, he can "take dictation" when the children create a song—that is, associate at once the
tones he hears with degrees of the scale. For instance, several song examples in this chapter are based on the same note pattern—the familiar
1–3–5 chord or the *tonic* chord. The recognition of this fact makes notating such songs a simple matter. Since few classroom teachers have had
this kind of training, most of them rely on other means to notate these
songs. For example, the teacher who heard Ann sing "A Beautiful Day"
sang it with her so that when she returned to the classroom she could
find the song on the bells or piano. To help remember the melody of a
child's song, the inexperienced teacher can invent pictorial ways to
record melodies by such means as drawing a continuous or a broken
line showing the directions of the pitches and by drawing short and long
dashes to represent comparative note values. Some teachers write melodies
with numerals or syllables and determine the notation later. Some use
tape recorders and "take it off" the tape later. Others have the children
help them remember the song until a special music teacher or another
chassroom teacher has time to help notate it. Some children in the intermediate grades can be of help. There is always a way to notate these songs,
and any teacher who tries will improve in skill with practice.

An activity that deserves respect is adding original verses to songs.
When children do this, they must feel the fundamental rhythm and
accomodate words and melody to this rhythm. It is good preparation
for later activities in which poems are set to music. Words must be set
to music so that accents we use naturally in speech fall on musically-
accented beats. For example, "the" and "a" are normally quite unimportant
words; they will be sung on parts of the measure of little rhythmic
importance—almost never on accented parts of the measure or notes of
long duration, since this would give them importance to which they are
not entitled.

As soon as children understand and can use notation, the song-
creating process in the classroom should include the notating of the song
on the chalkboard where everyone can participate to some degree in seeing
that it is written in such a manner that it correctly pictures what was created.
Also, when good songs are notated in or transposed to keys that children
find easy to use when playing recorder-type instruments, such songs may

be duplicated and given to the children. When children take such songs home to play for their parents on these instruments or on the piano, they are learning about music notation as a by-product of their creative activity.

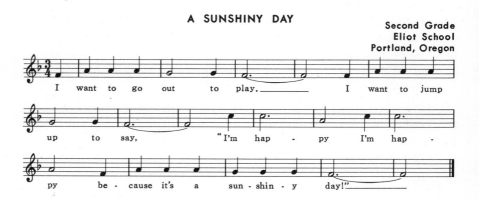

A SUNSHINY DAY

Second Grade
Eliot School
Portland, Oregon

I want to go out to play.___ I want to jump up to say, "I'm hap - py I'm hap - py be - cause it's a sun - shin - y day!"___

The following excerpt from the *Alabama Education Journal*[6] concerns the writing of poetry and music on the intermediate grade level. The teacher had enriched the children's background for this activity by developing vocabulary through increasing awareness to beauty in the classroom, in nature, and by reading appropriate poetry for the class.

Until the time when the writing of poetry was found to be an enjoyable activity there had been no particular relation between poetry and music. However, when the time came to try to set some of the poetry to music, the students were eager to try. At the beginning, poems with a very simple and direct rhythm were read by the class so that everyone felt the same rhythmic flow of the words. The children moved at their desks to the rhythm of the words, and they tapped the rhythm. While there was some early hesitance because of the newness of the procedure, this disappeared abruptly after the first experience with it. Children tried "walking out" the rhythm of their poems by walking while they spoke them. As a consequence, the rhythm of the words was a dominant feature of the first songs composed. Later on, the more subtle meanings of words, and the varying moods of the poems became of increasing importance and shared an equal emphasis with rhythm. All that was done with creative music was an outgrowth of the earlier and continuing efforts of the classroom teacher to guide activities in such a way that the children were free to develop their sensitivity to visual impressions, to word meanings, and to sounds.

[6] Vernice Trousdale and Robert E. Nye, "The Fourth Grade Writes Music," *Alabama Educational Journal*, December, 1950.

At first, the children selected from their store of poems they had written those which they felt would be easiest to set to music. The music teacher discussed these with the class and together they examined and experimented to find those with the clearest rhythmic patterns. Then the staff was placed on the blackboard and the words were written beneath it. The music teacher chose the key in which the song would be written and played the tonic chord (1 3 5) on a bell set. This gave the children a harmonic setting in which to start to think tonally. Later on in the year this was abandoned.

No one knew in what way the class would compose its song. Sometimes everyone sang phrases together and the music teacher wrote on the chalk-board what he heard as majority opinion. At other times individuals volunteered phrases of the song, one after another, until it was completed. The group judged the suitability of these musical thoughts, and frequently had to discriminate between two or more versions of the same phrase. When the song was completed to the satisfaction of all, the correct meter signature was added, and bar lines and note values were determined. Here was the learning of music fundamentals in a "real" situation. Even so, the music teacher was always ready to hurry this part of the procedure whenever he felt that an overemphasis on the mechanical details was beginning to detract from the enjoyment of the creative experience. These songs were often reproduced so the children could take them home to show to their parents and play them on the piano and on instruments such as bell sets and Tonettes. While at the beginning the children had to be encouraged to sing their musical ideas to the class, this early stage of reluctance changed rapidly to one of nearly 100 per cent participation in which the music teacher found it necessary to stress self-control in waiting one's turn. In order to express more completely the meaning of the words, the boys and girls experimented with choric reading in various combinations with singing. Almost from the first they began bringing to the class poems they had written at home, and sharing with the group their musical ideas which had been born along with the words.

Near the end of the year, a college class asked to observe the composition of songs in the fourth grade. The music teacher selected three poems of varying types. The children were not satisfied with their setting of a poem written in strict rhythm. One girl objected that it "sounded too much alike," while a boy stated flatly that "it was monotonous." This led to a revision of the last half of the song which satisfied the group's feeling of what was musically suitable. This discussion and revision revealed aesthetic discrimination at the fourth-grade level. The second song was a little jingle, "The Funny Instrument." The group found this to be of such obvious tonal suggestibility that everyone began to sing together, and they sang it in unison as though they had known it always.

The third and last poem had no strong rhythm or rhyme to guide the composers. They solved this problem by contributing ideas phrase by phrase. This song seemed to give the children a greater feeling of accomplishment and aesthetic appreciation than any they had done before. After it was completed and on the chalkboard, one of the girls suggested repeating the last four notes softly. This was tried and proved to be very effective. A boy contributed the practical thought that putting repeat marks in the right places would eliminate having to write more notes, so this was done.

MOONLIGHT

Fourth Grade
Kilby Training Scool
Florence State College
Florence, Alabama

Dark is the night as I lie in my bed: The stars and the moon give light. As I lie in my bed rest - ing my head. I go to sleep_____ I

In the course of this creative work each child developed more respect for the worth of each of the other children. The ability to contribute successfully to group action led to a feeling of security which gave, in turn, poise and self-assurance. Some who had not been able to succeed in other things found in the composition of poetry and music the satisfaction of those basic needs so frequently listed by educators: success, acceptance, belonging, and security. Some children wrote poems which showed evidence of giving emotional outlets for their worries and troubles.[7]

The class had become more conscious of those intangible elements of beauty inherent in all art. They learned to enjoy many different types of poetry, not only their own, but the poems in the many books which they read voluntarily.

The improvement in the skills of English composition was apparent. The practical use of music notation made music symbols more easily understood.[8]

As culminating activities of some units of work, programs were presented. The original poems and songs made these programs more vital to both students and their parents.

[7] "Little Brother"
    My little brother, as you can see,
    Is just as cute as cute can be.
    My little brother makes me mad,
    And that's why I am always sad.
[8] One of the favorite pastimes during free periods was going to the blackboard, drawing a staff, and writing tunes.

This use of poetry and music was considered successful by those who were in contact with the fourth grade. The teachers believe that knowing the child and providing opportunity and encouragement for him to develop his powers of expression comprise the foundation on which love and enjoyment of poetry and music can be built.

The goal of such group work is not fully accomplished with the successful co-operative composition of songs exhibited by this fourth grade; *the ultimate goal is to develop this creative activity into the successful writing of music by individuals.* In other words, this group process should be a stimulus for each child to write his own songs in the same way that he paints his own pictures. In the situation described in the above article, it would be expected that during the fifth- and sixth-grade years of this same group of children, the bringing to school of songs and instrumental tunes written at home would be commonplace, and that these children would do this because they had acquired the skills of a creative act that is fun, challenging, and satisfying to do.

When children can compose poetry and songs, the writing of simple operettas is not beyond the possibilities of the intermediate grades. Another opportunity is more teaching about musical form. Since the form of most of the songs children compose is simple in structure, often being a question-and-answer type with repeated phrases, teachers can guide children to discover elements of form in music by having them examine their own compositions. To analyze song form is interesting to children when it concerns a song they have written.

The procedure many teachers follow when they guide children in song writing in grades three and above is as follows:

1. Choose words that are simple, have steady rhythmic flow, and are understood by children.

2. Write the words on the chalkboard under the staff. Discuss the meaning of the words, seeking ideas that will influence the song writing. Such ideas will include mood and anything that may reflect descending or ascending pitch.

3. Have the class read the words in unison so that a definite rhythm is established. Use clapping or stepping if necessary. The most heavily accented words or word syllables can be underlined. Measure bars can be drawn before (to the left of) these words or word syllables.

4. If this activity is comparatively new to the children, sound the tonic chord by singing 1 3 5 3 1 (do-mi-sol-mi-do), or by playing it on Autoharp or piano. If these instruments are used, it is better to play the chord

sequence I V₇ I to establish a definite key feeling. If the children are experienced in song writing, this step is not necessary because they "hear with their inner ears" what they create, and the arbitrary setting of a key may interfere with the creative process.

5. Ask for suggestions to start the song. There are several approaches. In the earliest stages of learning to compose, a teacher may have all or part of the first phrase written and ask the class to finish that section of the song. This can be done by the class *thinking* what the rest of the song might be (after singing the first part several times) and finally singing it, the teacher accepting the majority opinion. Soon individuals will have melodic suggestions to offer, and the process becomes one of both group and individual contribution. The group is the controlling force, however, and exercises discrimination in choosing between versions of parts of the song that are volunteered by individuals. The composition generally proceeds phrase by phrase with the group singing frequently from the beginning of the song. The teacher notates the song as it grows in length. Those teachers who can take musical dictation will write stemless notes on the staff. Since it is necessary to proceed with rapidity to avoid lagging interest, these are usually little lines (/) instead of filled out notes (♩). Some teachers will prefer to use numerals or syllables and "figure" from these. Others will use the keyboard directly, and still others will employ lines on the chalkboard that indicate high and low in pitch and tonal duration.

6. Have the class decide what the meter signature is. If the bar lines have not already been placed, they can be written before the heavily accented notes. Sometimes the song will need to be transposed to a more suitable key for the voices. The key signature will be determined, as will note values. Stems, flags, beams, and dots will be added wherever necessary.

7. Autoharp or piano chords can be added as desired.

8. The children can now evaluate their song. Does it reflect the meaning of the words suitably? Does it communicate the mood desired? Can the song be improved? Is it notated correctly?

9. If the song is of good quality, it should be saved by placing it in a class notebook. If it is in a key in which children can play recorder-type instruments, reproduce it on a duplicating machine so that the children may use notation at home in playing the song for their parents.

The good teacher knows that the major purpose of this activity is not to produce composers, but rather to gain the joy and confidence that come from a creative process. Below are some poems to be used in building skill and confidence in song writing. This is a satisfying activity that is fun to do. One should forget real or imagined musical deficiencies of the moment and enjoy it!

When children write their own music, they are personally concerned with melody, form, tempo, dynamics, and correct notation. They are further concerned with tension and release, repetition and contrast, range, and how the tones move. Creating music is a superior means of acquiring music concepts.

POEMS THAT MAY BE SET TO MUSIC BY YOUNG CHILDREN

"Early to Bed"

Early to bed and early to rise,
Makes a man healthy and wealthy and wise.

Old Rhyme

"Choo Choo Train"

Choo choo train, choo choo train,
Chugging down the track.
Choo choo train, choo choo train,
Clank, clank, clack, clack, clack!

"Robins"

Three baby robins
Have learned a new song;
It's "Tweet-a-tweet, tweet-a-tweet"
All the day long.

"The Snowman"

I'm a little snowman fat and white,
Here is my hat and here is my pipe.
When the sun comes out to play
Then I'll melt and go away.

POEMS THAT MAY BE SET TO MUSIC BY OLDER CHILDREN

"The Tree"

The tree outside my window
Is cold and dark and brown.
All the pretty colored leaves
Have fallen to the ground.

"Pioneer Mother"

Mother was singing a lullaby
To quiet her tiny babe.
The night was cool and calm and clear;
The child was peacefully sleeping.

*Composed by a fifth-grade
class for their Westward
Movement Unit*

"Autumn Leaves"

Pretty leaves of red and yellow,
Colors all so warm and mellow.
Blow, wind, blow, and leaves will scatter
Before the rain comes pitter-patter.

"Dreaming"

As twilight draws her curtain and pins it with a star,
Two sleepy, nodding children that view it from afar,
Are whisked away to dreamland, where streets are paved with gold,
Where trees are ever silver green, and all is safe from cold.

"The River"

Dark brown is the river; golden is the sand.
It flows along forever, with trees on either hand.

Robert Louis Stevenson

Songs in Symphonic Music

Familiar melodies comprise one successful approach to the study of
symphonic music. When a song is well known by children, they thrill
to its discovery in symphonic works, and interest in listening is stimulated.
However, identifying the melody is only the first step. Because the essence
of symphonic music is *thematic development* (which is what a composer
does with and to his tunes), the answer to the question, "What does the
composer do with his tune?" can bring forth exciting explorations. How
fully children are able to answer the question will depend upon their
stage of musical development. Such inquiry will encourage individual
listening and the identification of forms such as rondo and variations,
as well as knowledge of compositional devices.

Composer	Title	Song or Themes
BARLOW	The Winter's Passed	"Wayfaring Stranger," "Black Is the Color of My True Love's Hair"
BEETHOVEN	String Quartet Op. 59, No. 2	Russian hymn "Praise to God" (*This Is Music* Book 4)
	Symphony 8, Second Movement, Theme	"The Metronome" (Adventures in Music 6 v. 1)
	Symphony 9, Fourth Movement	"United Nations Hymn" ("World Anthem") *This Is Music* Book 6
	Wellington's Victory	"For He's a Jolly Good Fellow"
BLOCH	America	"Yankee Doodle," "Old Folks at Home," "Hail Columbia."
BRAHMS	Academic Festival Overture	"Guadeamus Igitur" (student song often found in series books for grades 7–8) (Bowmar #76)
CAILLIET	Variations on Pop Goes the Weasel	"Pop Goes the Weasel" (Bowmar #65) (Adventures in Music 4 v. 1)
CHOPIN	Fantasy Impromptu	"I'm Always Chasing Rainbows"
COPLAND	Appalachian Spring	"Simple Gifts" (Bowmar #75)
	Billy the Kid, Fourth Theme	"Goodbye, Old Paint"
	Lincoln Portrait	"Camptown Races," "Springfield Mountain" ("Pesky Sarpent")
	Rodeo	"Hoe-Down" (Adventures in Music 5 v. 2) (Bowmar #55)
DVORAK	Symphony 5	"Swing Low, Sweet Chariot" (First Movement, Third Theme) "Going Home" (Second Movement, First Theme)
DOHNANYI	Variations on a Nursery Tune	"Twinkle, Twinkle, Little Star" (piano and orchestra)

Composer	Title	Song or Themes
GOULD	American Salute	"When Johnny Comes Marching Home" (Adventures in Music 5 v. 1) (Bowmar #65)
	Cowboy Rhapsody	"Goodbye, Old Paint," "Home on the Range"
	Variations on When Johnny Comes Marching Home	"When Johnny Comes Marching Home"
GRAINGER	Londonderry Air	"Londonderry Air" (Adventures in Music 4 v. 2)
GROFE	Death Valley Suite	"O Susanna" (Adventures in Music 4 v. 1)
GUION	Turkey in the Straw	"Old Zip Coon" (same tune)
HARRIS	Folk Song Symphony	"Irish Washerwoman," "Bury Me Not on the Lone Prarie," "Streets of Laredo," "Turkey in the Straw," "When Johnny Comes Marching Home."
HAYDN	"Emperor" Quartet in C Major	"Glorious Things of Thee Are Spoken" ("Austrian National Hymn") Appears in several of the music series.
HUMPERDINCK	Hansel and Gretel, Prelude to Act 1	"Prayer," "Song of the Gingerbread Children," "Partner, Come and Dance With Me."
IVES	Second Symphony	"Columbia, Gem of the Ocean," "Camptown Races," "Reveille," "Joy to the World," "Long Long Ago," "Old Folks at Home"
KAY	Western Symphony	"Red River Valley," "The Girl I Left Behind Me," "Golden Slippers," "Jim Along Josie" (Vox Recording)

Composer	Work	Titles
McBride	Mexican Rhapsody	"Hat Dance," "Rancho Grande," "La Cucaracha"
	Pumpkineaters Little Fugue	"Peter, Peter, Pumpkin Eater" (Bowmar #65)
McDonald	Children's Symphony	"Farmer in the Dell," "Jingle Bells" (Adventures in Music 3 v. 2)
Mahler	First Symphony, Third Movement	"Are You Sleeping?"
Mussorgsky	Boris Godunov, Coronation Scene	"Praise to God" (*This Is Music* Book 4)
Nelson	Kentucky Mountain Portraits	"Cindy," "Skip to My Lou," "Paw Paw Patch"
Rossini	William Tell Overture	"Lone Ranger Theme" (Bowmar #76) (Adventures in Music 3 v. 1)
Sibelius	Finlandia	"Song of Peace" and other titles
Sowerby	Irish Washerwoman	"Lane County Bachelor" and other titles
Stravinsky	Greeting Prelude	"Happy Birthday to You" (Columbia Record *Instrumental Miniatures*)
Tschaikovsky	1812 Overture	"Russian National Hymn" and other titles
	Symphony 4, Fourth Movement	"The Birch Tree" (Adventures in Music 6 v. 2)
Vardell	Joe Clark Steps Out	"Old Joe Clark" (Mercury Recording)
Vaughan-Williams	Fantasia on Greensleeves	"What Child Is This?" ("Greensleeves") (Adventures in Music 6 v. 2)
Quilter	A Children's Overture	"Girls and Boys Come Out to Play," "St. Paul's Steeple," "Dame Get Up and Bake Your Pies," "Over the Hills and Far Away," "The Frog and the Crow," "The Frog He Would A-Wooing Go," "Oranges and Lemons," "Baa Baa Black Sheep"

Assembly Singing and Cumulative Song Lists

Many elementary schools compile cumulative song lists[9] which suggest that certain songs be taught at various levels. These lists are compiled for the purpose of providing the students with a commonly known body of song material that is part of their cultural heritage. Teachers plan co-operatively which songs should be on such lists, taking careful consideration of the songs most enjoyed by children. These lists should be under constant revision. The songs they include are ordinarily used in student assemblies and at other times when mass singing is of value to school morale. They are divided into classifications that assure variety, such as *patriotic and service songs* (important in the national tradition), *songs of religious and ethical value* (important in character development), *fun songs* (for group morale), *special-day songs* (Christmas, Thanksgiving), *American folk songs* (our nation at work and play), *folk songs of other lands* (the lands of our forefathers). There are many other possible classifications. Care should be taken to keep the list sufficiently flexible so that songs of immediate and temporary value can be used.

Nothing is as effective as group singing in building group spirit and the feeling of unity every school needs. It is, therefore, an essential element in the total school program. Singing in conjunction with assemblies should be planned carefully so that the children as a group know many songs they can sing well together. However, pleasing variety is attained when the primary children sing a new song for the older children and vice versa, or when one class sings and dramatizes "something special" for the assembly in an informal way.[10]

Individual Differences and Normal Expectations with Emphasis on Skills

As stated earlier, individual differences must be expected, identified, and accommodated at all levels of instruction. The following statements concerning normal expectations do not identify many of the variants present in every classroom. Teachers at all levels should be ready to assist the out-of-tune singer to become a confident in-tune singer through

[9] A suggested list for classroom, assembly, and community use is found in *Music in American Education* published by the Music Educators National Conference, Chicago (1955), p. 319.

[10] The article "Everyone Sings Together," *Music Educators Journal,* January, 1956, pp. 46–48, describes the organization of assembly sings in a Massachusetts elementary school.

specially planned listening experiences, planned uses of song materials in the large group, in the small group, and in individual instruction. Experience in singing—alone, in small groups, and in large groups—is needed at all levels, provided the child can do this in a situation where he does not lose status with his peers.

The variety of possible instrumental music experiences in the general music class can accommodate all the types of individual differences resulting from physical development in normal children that affect the manipulation of instruments, as well as variations in physical co-ordination resulting from deviant growth patterns or disease, and degrees of musical ability. For some children, manipulating an instrument is an important physical release. For others it is an intellectual challenge. For those unable to sing well it is an opportunity to succeed in another important aspect of music. Since instrumental music experiences can range from the very simple to the complex, they constitute activities suited to satisfy certain needs of every child.

As always, it requires an inventive teacher to accommodate individual differences within the music class. For example, let us imagine a situation in which a teacher has brought older children to the point where they can write the notation of melodies the teacher plays for them (take music dictation). It can be expected that there will be a few musically advanced children who do this so well that they will be bored with the moderate level of difficulty suited for most of the children. To provide for the needs of these few children, the teacher might:

1. have them write the notes in the bass as well as in the treble clef.

2. have them take dictation in retrograde (backwards).

3. have them create melodies suitable for this purpose, and present them to the class.

NORMAL EXPECTATIONS, AGES 5 AND 6

Many children need help in learning to listen. Some need help in developing concepts of high and low pitch; others need help in finding their singing voices. Some need to learn to match tones. Ordinarily all songs are taught by rote, an exception being pre-notational experiences from large charts. There should be much use of the descending minor third, easy tone patterns, and pentatonic melodies. Much of this comes from singing conversations and spontaneously-created song fragments, songs, and chants. Careful listening to good examples is necessary.

Playing melody instruments in kindergarten is on a very easy level because five-year-olds have poor control of small muscles. There is exploration of the sound, pitch, and feel of bells, piano, wood, metal, and stretched skin. There can be simple rote playing experiences on the bells, such as sounding only one resonator bar or one specifically marked bar on the bells, or a few tones in a scale line. Bells constructed in the form of steps help teach concepts of high and low scale tones. At the six-year level, exploratory activities broaden. *Timothy's Tunes,* by Adeline McCall (Boston Music Co.) presents an introduction to the keyboard via the bells for this level. After numbers are comprehended and associated with scale steps on bells, some children will be able to play simple parts written in numeral notation.

AGES 7 AND 8

With a good background of music experiences on the earlier levels, only a small minority will be unable to match tones. However, in situations where music experience has been meager, this minority may be large. Even in good situations, after summer vacation many children need a period of review and reorientation in careful listening to pitch and to singing. They will make rapid improvement after a slow beginning. Music books are in the hands of children when they are ready for them in terms of their musical growth and their physical maturity. While many songs are learned by rote, others are learned with the books in hand. The teacher guides ear and eye co-ordination for comprehending the picture of the music, which is notation. When the children on any level learn to sing well on pitch, rounds can be introduced. Some children may lead singing. By age 8 nearly all children who have good music backgrounds should be able to sing on pitch most of the time. Therefore, the singing of chants, descants, and rounds (see next chapter) assumes increasing importance. These children are interested in anything new, and they ordinarily enjoy learning to understand and use notation, which can be emphasized at this level. Tone quality and range improve under guidance of the teacher and through listening and evaluation by the children.

Seven-year-olds are able to play bells; they enjoy seeing and touching band and orchestra instruments, and can learn to identify nearly all of them by sight and by sound. Some children can play a small wind instrument, and some will be taking piano lessons. Eight-year-olds are more capable of learning the above skills. Some classes at this level will have mass instruction on a small wind instrument, although nine-year-olds can learn them more rapidly. They should be able to play the bells from notation, and be able to improvise introductions and codas for appropriate songs. They can learn to recognize any instrument by its tone quality.

AGES 9, 10, 11

Tone quality, vocal range, and song interpretation should show continuing improvement. Comprehension of characteristics of melody should be revealed in many ways, such as use of tone patterns and intervals in reading notation, relationships of dynamics, note duration, and melodic contour to tension, climax, and release. Phrase arrangements should be easily analyzed and the concept of song forms and their many variants should grow rapidly. Voice blending will be a goal; children should try to blend voices until they sound like one voice. At age eleven most boys will have unchanged voices, but some may be in the early stage of voice change, their voices dropping about an interval of a fourth in range. This places their voices in a range from the middle of the treble staff down to the highest part of the bass staff. These voices must be accommodated by assigning or writing parts in this new range. There is sight-singing of songs both from series books and special books written for this purpose, such as those from the Handy-Folio Music Company, Minneapolis, Minnesota.

By ages 10 and 11 nearly all common band and orchestra instruments can be played by most of the children.

Analyzing Melodies

When children analyze melodies, they should seek answers to such questions as:

How do tones move? (scalewise, stepwise, repeated tones)
What is the phrase arrangement?
What is the type of tonal organization? (major, minor, modal, pentatonic, tone row, ethnic scale, etc.)
What is the range?
Is there evidence of tension and release? If so, how is this achieved?
Is there evidence of a climax? If so, how is this achieved?
Are there other significant aspects? (such as rhythm patterns, tone patterns, dynamics, sequence).

Some Activities and Suggestions for Lesson Plans

Review this same heading in Chapter 8.

As in the previous chapter, there follows a large number of activities which relate to the Structure of Music Outline in Chapter 6. They are presented as a list from which to select. The reader should not feel responsible for knowing how to deal with all of these. Some may require teaching experience to do well. Some can be dealt with in the college class, some in student teaching, and some in later years of professional teaching. They include both American and European strategies.

Melody

Activities that teachers may use to realize their objectives:

Pitch Recognition

Play a listening game to increase sensitivity to sound by identifying sources of sound. Children close eyes; teacher taps various objects and instruments in the room; children identify.

The teacher of young children groups simple instruments on a table according to high and low in pitch. The children, one, two, or three at a time, experiment with them and compare their high and low sounds. Later the teacher mixes the instruments, and the children will group them into those that produce high pitches and those that produce low pitches.

Test young children's comprehension of high and low sounds by playing a commercial recording or specially-made tape of common sounds from their environment. Examples of low sounds: fog horn, truck motor, man's voice, tuba, low pitches on the piano. High sounds: a whistle, a bird chirping, a woman's voice, a flute, high pitches on the piano. Children can make a mark high on a paper for a high pitch and low on the paper for a low pitch. One child in front of the room can place dashes on a flannel board in a similar way.

Have children relate high and low in pitch to relative high-low positions of the body and of objects. Reach high and low in relation to obvious high and low in pitch. Use other body movements, marks on the chalkboard, the glockenturm, step bells, standard bell sets placed in vertical position with large bars down. Find or discover high and low in speaking voices, bars on resonator bells, and different sized drums.

A pitch game can be played with three pitches: middle C, the octave above, and the G in between. When children hear the highest pitch, they place their hands over their heads; when they hear the middle pitch they place their hands in front of them; when they hear middle C they place their hands on their thighs.

Compare two scale songs. The children are to determine which one begins high and goes down in pitch and which one begins low and goes up in pitch.

Identify high and low instruments of the orchestra as they play melodies on recordings or as they are played on instruments by older children.

Relate pitch to melodic contour; use chalkboard, body movement, and dramatization to reflect scale and chord tonal patterns.

Use exemplary songs to discover that pitches can move in three ways: up, down, or stay the same.

Write the major scale vertically on the chalkboard in numbers or syllables. The class will sing as the teacher points.

Relate melodic contour to tension, climax, and release; use songs and instrumental music that portray these aspects clearly; dramatize.

Provide opportunities for children to explore properties of sound: pitch, tone quality, intensity, and duration by means of Peripole Sound Kits. They can discover that vibrations make sound, how sound travels, how different instruments produce musical sound in different ways when struck, bowed, or plucked, and how sound is reproduced. (Peripole, Inc., 51–17 Rockaway Beach Blvd., Far Rockaway, N.Y. 11691.)

Notation of Pitch

Relate high-low concepts to the staff; use step bells, glockenturm, or standard bell sets placed on end in low-high position, chalkboard staff, or magnetic or flannel board. Utilize known songs or parts of songs.

Relate melodic direction (contour) to notation; use common tonal patterns and known songs.

Relate rhythm and pitch in notation; use known songs.

Relate numerals and/or syllables to pitch notation; See *Singing and Associated Activities*.

Bells and other melody instruments can be used to relate pitch notation to note names.

Use a game for general comprehension of notation: teacher makes four two-measure charts of an eight-measure song and arranges them out of order before the class; he then sings or plays the song, and the children arrange the charts in correct order according to what they hear.

Study basic note patterns and find them in songs: such as 321; 135; 5678; 54321; 531; 12345; 565; 5653.

Manipulate a tune rhythmically. Teacher writes a short melody on the chalkboard with all or most of the notes quarter notes; the children are to use eighth notes (and make changes with them) to make the tune more interesting. Later with other melodies, they will use other note values such as dotted notes, in increasing complexity of note values.

Have children demonstrate their command of pitch and rhythm notation by making a familiar song eccentric by manipulating the meter. Challenge them to change the meter and the note values in accordance with that meter if necessary. Every measure could be a different meter; however, having every other measure the same meter might provide some unity. The children are to use their judgment. Sing the altered song from the notation. Evaluate the result.

Scales and Their Relation to Melody

Learn to hear and to sing the home tone (key note or tonal center). The teacher sings or plays a melody, but stops before it is complete. Children are to sing the home tone or to make up an ending that concludes with the home tone.

Have young children listen to the Young People's Record *Music Listening Game* for scalewise movement.

Relate numerals and/or syllables to major scale tones. See *Singing and Associated Activities*.

Examine the major scale with step bells, with drawings, then see it on the staff ascending and descending. Dramatize it. Sing songs emphasizing the major scale; see it pictured as steps or a ladder.

Find whole steps and half-steps in the major scale; discover the two whole-whole-half step patterns (the two tetrachords). Try this both by ear and by observing the pitches on the keyboard. Draw the two tetrachord patterns and have children play them on bells and piano. 1 2 34 5 6 78 .If standard bell sets are used, children need to understand that from low to high is from left to right on the keyboard.

Relate pentatonic scales to the black keys of keyboard instruments; then transpose this scale pattern to white keys in what we think of as major keys C, F, and G. Compare this scale to the major scale; then use the form of pentatonic scale that is similar to the natural minor—6–1–2–3–5–6. Compose pentatonic songs and tunes; sing and play pentatonic songs. Listen to a recording of pentatonic music such as Bartók's *An Evening in the Village* (Adventures in Music 5, v. 2).

Discover minor tonality; compare major melody with minor melody.

Find the natural minor scale pattern—the whole and half step design of it. Use songs in natural minor (Aeolian mode); let children compose songs in this tonality. Write the scale on the staff; compare it with the major scale. Play scale and songs on the bells.

Discover the harmonic minor scale through songs; repeat the process regarding the natural minor above; compare this scale with the natural minor.

Discover the melodic minor scale through selected songs; repeat the above process of natural and harmonic minor scales.

Identify passive and active scale tones. Utilize melodies that illustrate natural tone movement tendencies; analyze melodies with this in mind. Dramatize tone movements with body movements. Children can compose tunes to illustrate passive and active scale tones, explaining why they may choose to "violate" the most normal movement of scale tones. For example, tone pattern 12345 seems to be "wrong" in some aspects, yet it is entirely correct. From this, the children should generalize that the active-passive scale tone concept is a partial guide only, and that while it is worthy of some consideration, it would be an impractical handicap if followed blindly. Older children can be challenged to investigate under what specific conditions this concept does not apply.

Explore the chromatic scale tones at the beginning of the carol, "I Heard the Bells on Christmas Day," and in the recording, "Flight of the

Bumblebee," by Rimsky-Korsakov. Listen to the lion's roar in the recording of Saint Saëns' *Carnival of the Animals*. Have children theorize on the uses composers make of chromatic scale steps. Play this 12-tone scale on keyboard instruments. Why are accidentals used? Write the scale on the chalkboard ascending and descending.

Construct a tone row from the pitches of the chromatic scale. The 12 resonator bells within the scale of C can be used. To add interest, a child who is blindfolded can mix up the bars and arrange them in a row. Then without the blindfold he can play the resulting sequence of tones. If three or more pitches remind the class of a melody moving toward a tonal center, these must be changed so that no tonal center is suggested. A child can now play the row from left to right, then from right to left (retrograde) so the class can try to keep the order of pitches in mind. Next the class can select the rhythm in which these tones are to be sounded in their composition. Write the tone row on the staff. Then the class, or each child in the class, can take this row and write a composition with it, using such techniques as diminution, augmentation, inversion, retrograde, retrograde inversion, and canon. *Making Music Your Own,* Book 6, p. 202, is an example of how a series book introduces the tone row. Remember that the composer does not always use all twelve tones; he may choose to write a row with fewer tones.

Several children can improvise on a written tone row. Example: one might begin playing on a recorder or other small wind instrument; he could be joined by another playing the row on the bells; later a third could join them, playing on a xylophone. The piano might substitute for the xylophone. The class should evaluate the experiment. How might the effect be improved or changed?

Study and compare ethnic scales. Sources: Gertrude P. Wollner's *Improvisation in Music,* Doubleday, 1963, Chapter Five, and *Toward World Understanding With Song,* Wadsworth Publishing Company, 1967, pp. 156–7. Children can use these scales to compose songs and instrumental pieces.

Invent original scales; write melodies based on these scales; use them with familiar songs to discover what happens when a familiar song is placed in a new scale setting.

Explore the reasons for key signatures. Play songs with arbitrarily changed key signatures. What is the result? Why are key signatures used by composers?

Intervals and Their Relation to Melody

Examine the concept of interval as the distance between the home tone and other major scale members, counting up. Count from 1 or *do* up to each scale tone to find the interval. Arrange for children to discover how each interval is named. What does a third look like on the staff? (line-line or space-space). What does a fifth look like? A second?

Examine intervals as the distances between the home tone and other scale members, counting down the scale. Children can make a generalization about how to identify intervals.

Arrange for children to discover by means of the keyboard two kinds of seconds, thirds, sixths, and sevenths (major and minor) intervals. What is the difference between them? What might an *augmented* interval be? (expand by another halfstep). What might a *diminished* interval be? (contract by another halfstep). Why do you suppose that fourths and fifths and octaves are called "perfect" intervals? Use the keyboard, then the staff to answer these questions and to picture examples. Children should play these on keyboard instruments to see, hear, and feel the distances involved; they should find them in songs and use them in their compositions.

Compare horizontal (melodic) intervals with vertical (harmonic) intervals. The first type is found in melodies and the second in chords.

Relate thirds, fifths, and fourths to common chords. Why is a seventh chord called a seventh chord? (Examine the seventh chord in root position to answer this.) Use melodies that relate to chord tones. Examples include the beginning of *The Blue Danube, Aloha Oe, Dixie,* and *The Star-Spangled Banner*. Find other melodic chord tone intervals and realize the chords.

Relate specific intervals to song melodies as described in this chapter.

Singing and Associated Activities

To progress toward establishing the singing voice, teach for tonal perception. Use many different tone qualities such as that of the voice, piano, bells, large and small bottles, small wind instruments, different percussion instruments. After the first identification by sound and sight, the children are to turn their backs and play the game of telling what made the sound and if it was high or low in pitch.

Later, if such sounds are in vocal range, they may be asked to try to match the pitch with their voices.

Have children imitate vocally the sounds of birds, animals, musical instruments, train whistles, and other environmental pitch sounds.

Establish and utilize the rhythm of selected words, then relate these to the descending minor third in a vocal range comfortable for the child. Have children improvise tonal fragments with these words and pitches. Relate to high and low. Have children in turn sing such things as months of the year, children's names, etc., with this 5–3 pattern. The entire class can listen, then echo what an individual child sings. Also use short verses such as "Rain, rain, go away; come again some other day."

Utilize tonal conversations in which the teacher sings questions, comments, or directions to which children improvise singing answers. They may use any pitch they like. Examples: "Come in," (5–1); "Shut the door." (5–5–8)

Relate *so-mi* (5–3) to rhythmic responses and hand signals. Have children first clap hands on hearing 5 and slap thighs on hearing 3. Later, hold palms together for 5 and hold hands out straight with palms down for 3. Eventually show these pitches on the staff and relate chants and tonal fragments to the Kodály abbreviated rhythmic notation: l l Π l

Use *la, so, mi* (5–3–6–5–3) in many creative combinations. Show these on the staff as a picture of the music. Examples: "I am bigger than you are," "Johnny has a quarter," and "I like chocolate cake and pie."

Teach the hand signal for *la* and have children describe their calls with the three signals. Play games by singing in response to hand signals.

Practice tonal memory. The class first sings a familiar song. The game takes place when the teacher turns his back at times during the singing; when he does this the class does not sing, but instead *thinks* the song as it continues in their minds. When the teacher again faces the class, the children sing as usual. Words, syllables, or numbers can be used.

The teacher or a child sings a melody with "la," "loo," or hums it; the children try to identify it.

Teach the hand signals for *re* and *do* and use scale tones 1–2–3–5–6 for song-like drills and for the creation of tunes and songs by the children. Eventually show these pitches on the staff. "This is what it looks like when it sounds that way."

Teacher provides the first two measures of a four-measure phrase; individual children improvise the final two measures to make an ending. Example:

The teacher makes silent hand signals. The children remember them and then sing the signaled tune. At first the teacher repeats his signals as the children sing; later he does not.

Discover and identify phrases; use songs with clearly defined phrases.

Pitch game: the teacher sings at random the pitches *so, mi, do*; children use hand signals to identify which of the three pitches they hear.

The teacher sings in syllables or numbers the pitches 1–2–3–5–6 in songlike drills; children make hand signals to match the pitches. Later the teacher sings with *loo* or *la* and the children continue to identify the pitches by hand signals.

Children use body movements to dramatize the direction of tone patterns, scale lines, and skips heard in selected songs or recorded music. (This is applicable to many of the above activities.)

Children sing appropriate tonal patterns from chalkboard or magnetic board.

The baseball game: The class is divided into two teams; each has an interesting name. Corners of the room are the four bases. A scorekeeper is appointed. At first the teacher uses scale tones 1–2–3–4–5 and later increases this to the full major scale. He plays on an instrument short successions of notes that always begin on *do*. At first there are no skips—only scale lines and repeated notes. After careful listening, the players sing what was played. If each one "up to bat" reproduces each pitch accurately, he advances to the next base. After three players strike out, the other team goes to bat. Score is kept on the chalkboard. The game's difficulty is increased as the players' skill grows. A variant of the game adds a flannel or magnetic board on which to notate what is played.

Employ the following scale patterns in song-like drills using hand signals and notation:

$$5\ 4\ 3\ 2\ 1$$
$$3\ 2\ 1\ \underline{7}\ \underline{6}$$
$$6\ 5\ 4\ 3\ 2\ 1\ \underline{7}\ \underline{6}$$
$$8\ 7\ 6\ 5\ 4\ 3\ 2\ 1$$

Add low *so* and *la* to the above and create song-like drills with scale tones
5₁ 6₁ 1 2 3 5 6; children will use these pentatonic tones to create
tunes and songs.

For ear training, write a scale on the chalkboard. Have the children sing
it. Then eliminate one note. Have the children sing the scale again
as they "think" (not sing) the missing pitch. Continue this with
other missing notes, and eventually with multiple missing notes.

Identify songs from charts of their untitled notation.

Compare tone patterns in songs as to stepwise or chordwise structure.
Relate to specific scales or chords if possible.

Discover and identify sequences in songs by ear and by eye; utilize songs
in which sequences are a significant aspect.

Present some rhythm patterns to the class. Ask the children to create
melodies based on these patterns.

Use symphony themes for note reading exercises. The Bowmar Charts
are a handy device for this; they accompany the Bowmar Orchestral
Library; Series Three includes a transparency of themes.

Compare and analyze each phrase ending in a selected song.

Ear training experiment: There are hand signals used by men working
in the lumber mills of Washington and Oregon to designate the
number of inches to be cut from a log. These can be used in place
of the European hand signals. An advantage is that these signals
can be made more rapidly.

1	2	3	4	5	6	7	8
index finger	index finger and middle finger	fingers 5 4 3	fingers 5 4 3 2	little finger	fist	close finger tips to thumb	thumb

Challenge the students to sing any familiar song in syllables or numbers.

Study melodies of great music. Analyze them in terms of scalelines and
chordlines, unity, variety, range, rhythm, tension, climax, and
release.

Melody Instruments

The use of individual resonator bars by children in relation to songs
gives a helpful indication of pitch and tone quality; a tone is *real*
when held in the hand and played with a mallet.

Let children play simple 3, 4, and 5 note tunes, tonal patterns, and repeated or other important easy parts of songs on water glasses, resonator bells, regular bell sets; older children may use the piano and small wind instruments.

Relate low and high (vertical relationships) with the keyboard left and right.

Let children invent tunes and songs on resonator bells, limited by the number of bars given them to work with.

Let children create pentatonic tunes on keyboard black keys or on other resonator bars selected by the teacher.

Build the major scale concept (and later on, other scales) by means of the keyboard (bells, Melodica, piano) and charts.

Relate bars of bell sets to lines and spaces on the staff. The glockenturm does this at once. A regular bell set can be placed in a vertical position and lines drawn from it on chalkboard or chart paper.

Let children play 3, 4, and 5 note songs on small wind instruments and the piano. Five-finger songs are appropriate for the piano.

Refer frequently to a large chart of the keyboard to help children understand interval relationships of tones; keep such a chart before the class at all times to stress visual understanding of pitch differences.

Let children use the keyboard in their analysis of scale patterns.

Develop the concept of transposition by playing a song in several keys on a melody instrument. Plan to permit children to "find" the tune by ear, beginning on different pitches.

Teach note names through learning fingering on small winds and playing tunes from notation on all melody instruments.

Establish a percussion rhythm; then have children improvise over this in turn on melody instruments.

Have children learn a song first; then have them play it on melody instruments. Singing it first establishes the tune to be played on the instruments.

Sing songs having sequences. Let children "discover" them. Notate a short composition of one of the children. Then ask each child to take any measure of his choice and come to the bell set and make up a sequence from that measure.

Guide children to discover the tetrachord by means of the keyboard. By playing the first four notes of the ascending five-finger piano patterns in the key of C major, and putting two of these patterns together (the second begins on G) one can build a C major scale.

Have children play descants from notation on keyboard and small wind instruments.

Create introductions and codas with melody instruments.

Emphasize some important intervalic aspect of melody by having children play these notes on the bells or small wind instrument each time they occur.

Provide for individual practice and experimentation on the keyboard by using a classroom organ with earphone attachment so that only the player hears the sound.

FORM

Children can discover and compare phrases in appropriate songs; they can discover one-part, two-part, and three-part song forms in the same way. They can form generalizations such as associating repetition with the concept or principle of unity, and contrast with variety. Sequences, tonal patterns and their alterations can be found by hearing them and by seeing them in notation. Recordings and percussion instruments can assist. Children can show comprehension of phrase endings by sounding finger cymbals; different phrases can be played or accompanied by different instruments or sung by different voices; breaths can be taken at the ends of phrases when singing and playing blowing instruments; body movements can reflect phrases.

Children can expand the concept that melodies can be manipulated by transposing tunes they know, and by applying techniques of diminution, augmentation, inversion, retrograde, and retrograde-inversion. (For more examples, see Mozart's "Alleluia," *Exploring Music With Children*, Wadsworth Publishing Company, p. 205, and suggestions on p. 84.) They can explore variation form by taking a familiar melody and applying rhythmic, melodic, (and later) harmonic variations. Use the Childrens Record Guild recording 5005 *Hot Cross Buns* to explain variations, and see *Exploring Music With Children*, pp. 210–215, for piano variations on "Twinkle, Twinkle, Little Star."

Unusual and Contemporary Melodies

Utilize the pentatonic idiom in song and in children's composition as the nearest we have to an internationally-understood tonal system.

Let children hear recordings of ethnic music that has melodies and scales different from most Western music. Folkways Records and the Columbia World Library of Folk and Primitive Music provide authentic examples. Read *Toward World Understanding With Song,* Wadsworth Publishing Company, pp. 9–13, for an introduction to this.

Use the tone row as a created scale and a compositional device. As early as the third grade a set of resonator bells can be distributed among the children, using the 12 chromatic tones within one octave. The challenge is to work out a series of pitches in which no tone is repeated and in which the triad (1–3–5) sound and obvious tonal sequences are avoided. When completed, the tone row should reveal no tonal center (home tone). Other sounds, such as those made from wood blocks, can be substituted for some of the bars if this makes the product more interesting. Write the row in notation. Have the children experiment with composing using this series— the rule being that every note has to be played in sequence during the composition. The row can be tried in retrograde, in inversion, and with rhythmic alterations. All these effects should be evaluated by the class.

Teach folk songs that are "different," from such places as Greece, Bulgaria, Albania, Yugoslavia, Arabia, Central Africa, and Asia. *Folk Songs of Europe* by Maud Karpeles is a good source of European music. Notice the irregularity of phrase lengths in exotic melodies; 3-, 5-, and 6-measure phrases are common.

Select songs constructed on modal scales which are different from the usual major and minor scales. Let the children use these scales in their composition.

Teach a plainsong melody; try singing it and playing it in vertical fourths, fifths, and seconds as experiments in sound.

Make a traditional song eccentric by manipulating the meter (and consequently, some note values).

Melodic improvisations can be done over unusual rhythm patterns played on percussion instruments.

Use the octave displacement device to alter familiar melodies and with tone row compositions. See the example in this chapter.

Challenge the class to learn to read modulating melodies with syllables, numbers, and hand signals. Example:

Read atonal melodies with the fixed *do* system in which middle C is always *do*.

Challenge the children to compose unusual melodies, testing principles of unity, variety, tension, climax, and release.

Examine electronic music on recordings; relate this sound to certain television programs; make a tape loop.

SOME CUMULATIVE BEHAVIORAL OBJECTIVES

The child can:

Identify pitch and/or melodic movement such as high, low, up, down, same, by . . . . .

recognize high and low associated with right and left on keyboard instruments by . . . . .

comprehend tonal movement in steps, skips, leaps, and scale lines by . . . . .

reveal general comprehension of the major scale by . . . . .

recognize melodic phrases as being the same, almost the same, or different by . . . . .

recognize scaleline and chordline tonal groupings by . . . . .

analyze major scales in terms of half and wholesteps by . . . . .

identify specific song forms by . . . . .

recognize tonal sequences by . . . . .

differentiate between major and minor by . . . . .

analyze and compare the structure of specific scales (major, minor, pentatonic, chromatic, modal) by . . . . .

identify specific common intervals by . . . . .

utilize modes other than major or minor by . . . . .

demonstrate ability to manipulate melodies by . . . . .

demonstrate ability to utilize the tone row concept by . . . . .

demonstrate understanding of melody in electronic music by . . . . .

For writing lesson plans, refer to the following as needed:

1. The Developmental Characteristics and Implications Chart in Chapter 3;

2. The Structure of Music Outline—melody section—and plans for teaching music in Chapter 6;

3. Types of thinking, types of questions, and principles of learning in Chapter 4;

4. Chapter 8, Tempo, Dynamics, and Rhythm, to relate to the study of melody;

5. The environment for learning and necessary routines for teaching in Chapter 5;

6. The Scope and Sequence Chart in the Appendix.

Plan to have surprises (sometimes discrepant events) in most lessons. No child should come to class thinking that he knows it all.

INQUIRY AND SELECTED ACTIVITIES

1. Make a collection of songs that can be taught in ways that give the out-of-tune singer pleasurable participation and experiences that lead to his eventual singing in tune.

2. The black keys of the piano form a pentatonic scale. Compose a song or piano piece on the black keys. Add a bagpipe (open-fifth) bass for an accompaniment.

3. Investigate ways other than numerals, syllables, and note names to help identify scale tones. The American shapenote system is one. Another is an idea of the late W. Otto Miessner which he stated in an article, "The Art of Tonal Thinking," *Music Educators Journal,* January, 1962.

4. Learn to identify songs that are in minor keys from the notation of the song. If the song's final note can be identified as scale tone six in the *major* scale derived from the key signature, then the song is in minor, and this note is the name of the minor key in which it is written.

5. A fifth-grade boy asks, "Why are there two flats in the key of B♭ major?" Ask him to answer his own question by using the bells. Clues: Remember the halfsteps between scale tones 3 and 4, and 7 and 8; build the scale beginning on B♭.

6. Make a collection of songs of limited range (3, 4, 5, and 6 notes) with which to help children learn to sing. Add to the songs suggested in this chapter others found in series books and other sources.

7. Listen to Mary Helen Richards' *Threshold to Music* Teacher Training Recording and identify more activities teachers use to attain their objectives.

REFERENCES

Articles and Books

DORMAN, PHYLLIS E., "A Protest Against Musical Illiteracy," *Music Educators Journal* (November, 1967) pp. 99–107.

GARY, CHARLES L., ED., *The Study of Music in the Elementary School—A Conceptual Approach.* Music Educators National Conference, Washington, D.C., 1967, pp. 51–65. Helpful in writing lesson plans.

INGRAM, MADELINE, AND WM. C. RICE, *Vocal Techniques for Children and Youth.* Nashville, Tenn. Abingdon Press.

NORDHOLM, HARRIET, *Singing in the Elementary Schools.* Englewood Cliffs, New Jersey: Prentice-Hall, Inc., 1966.

NYE, ROBERT E., "If You Don't Use Syllables, What Do You Use?" *Music Educators Journal* (April-May, 1953), pp. 41–2.

SLAUGHTER, C. H., "Those Dissonant Boys," *Music Educators Journal* (February-March, 1966), pp. 110–12. Sociological factors relating to boy disinterest in music.

SWANSON, BESSIE R., *Music in the Education of Children.* Belmont, California: Wadsworth Publishing Company, Inc., 1964. Chapters 2 and 6.

Songs for Young Children

BAILEY, CHARITY, *Sing a Song with Charity Bailey.* New York: Plymouth Music Company.

COLEMAN, SATIS N. AND ALICE G. THORN, *Singing Time; Another Singing Time; The Little Singing Time; A New Singing Time.* New York: The John Day Company.

CROWNINSHIELD, ETHEL, *Mother Goose Songs; Sing and Play Book; Stories That Sing; Songs and Stories About Animals.* Boston, Mass: Boston Music Company.

KODALY, ZOLTAN, *Fifty Nursery Songs Within the Range of Five Notes; 333 Elementary Exercises.* Oceanside, New York: Boosey & Hawkes, English by Percy M. Young.

LANDECK, BEATRICE, *Songs to Grow On; More Songs to Grow On.* New York: Marks and Sloane. Recorded by Folkways Records.

SCOTT, RICHARD, *Clap, Tap, and Sing Choral Method.* Minneapolis, Minn: Handy-Folio Music Company. For use in grades 2–5. Beginning with rhythm, this 48 page book takes children through the sight-singing of melodies to foundations of part singing. All songs are playable on small wind instruments.

SEEGER, RUTH CRAWFORD, *American Folk Songs for Children; Animal Folk Songs for Children; American Folk Songs for Christmas.* New York: Doubleday and Company, Inc.

Songs Children Like. Washington, D.C.: Association for Childhood Education.

VANDRE, CARL, *Easy Songs for Young Singers*. 309 5th Ave. South, Minneapolis, Minn. 55415. Handy-Folio Music Company.

WOOD, LUCILLE F. AND LOUISE B. SCOTT, *Singing Fun; More Singing Fun*. St. Louis, Mo: Webster Publishing Company. Recorded by Bowmar Records.

General Collections

ADES, HAWLEY, *One for the Melody*. Delaware Water Gap, Penna: Shawnee Press Inc. 26 unison songs by classic composers, with a story about each composer.

DALLIN, LEON, AND LYNN DALLIN, *Heritage Songster*. Dubuque, Iowa: Wm. C. Brown Company Publishers. Traditional songs Americans sing.

NYE, ROBERT, AND VERNICE NYE, *Exploring Music With Children*. Belmont, California: Wadsworth Publishing Company, Inc. A specialized song collection for teaching music to elementary school children.

NYE, ROBERT E., VERNICE T. NYE, NEVA AUBIN, AND GEORGE KYME, *Singing With Children*. Belmont, California: Wadsworth Publishing Company, Inc. Selected songs for teaching music to elementary school children.

NYE, VERNICE T., ROBERT E. NYE, AND H. VIRGINIA NYE, *Toward World Understanding With Song*. Belmont, California: Wadsworth Publishing Company, Inc. A collection to enhance both social studies and music.

RAEBECK, LOIS, AND LAWRENCE WHEELER, *New Approaches to Music in the Elementary School*. Dubuque, Iowa: Wm. C. Brown Publishers, 1964, Chapter 2.

RINDERER, LEO, ET. AL., *Sing a Song to Sight Read*. Park Ridge, Illinois: Neil A. Kjos, Publisher.

SMITH, FOWLER, AND HARRY ROBERT WILSON, *Songs We Sing*. Minneapolis, Minn.: Schmitt, Hall, and McCreary.

SNYDER, ALICE M., *Sing and Strum*. New York: Mills Music, Inc.

TOBITT, JANET E., *The Ditty Bag*. Box 97, Pleasantville, New York.

Recordings for Singing

BOWMAR RECORDS, INC., 622 Rodier Drive, Glendale, California 91201. *Bowmar Records Catalog*. Lists approximately 20 albums for singing, including three for children "with special needs."

CAPITOL RECORDS DISTRIBUTING CORPORATION, 1750 North Vine St., Hollywood, California, 90019. *Music For Children* Album. English children demonstrate rhythm and melody through the methods of Carl Orff on an Angel Recording.

CHILDRENS MUSIC CENTER, 5373 West Pico Blvd., Los Angeles, California, 90019. *The Best Records and Books for the School Curriculum* Catalog. Lists selected recordings for school use.

CLASSROOM MATERIALS CO., 93 Myrtle Drive, Great Neck, New York 11020.
    Johnny Can Sing Too. (K-3) Vol. 1, 2. For discovering singing voices and
    helping them develop.
    You Too Can Sing! (4–6) For children with singing problems.
    Classroom Sing Along (4–6) To aid the teacher in teaching songs.
FOLKWAYS RECORDS, 121 W. 47th St., New York, N. Y. 10011.
    You'll Sing a Song and I'll Sing a Song (Ella Jenkins) FC 7664
    See the Folkways Catalog for many more.
GREYSTONE CORPORATION, 100 Sixth Avenue, New York. Children's Record
    Guild and Young People's Records.
    Albums: *Let's Sing* (1–5)
             Folk Songs (1–5)
             Songs to Sing (1–4) activity songs
RCA VICTOR EDUCATIONAL SALES, 155 E. 24th Street, New York, N.Y. 10010.
    RCA Victor Basic Record Library for Elementary Schools: *The Singing
    Program.* One album each for primary grades, fourth, fifth, and sixth
    grades.
    RCA Victor Educational and Library Record Catalog. Issued annually.
STANLEY BOWMAR CO., Inc., Valhalla, New York.
    Records, Tapes, and Instructional Materials for the Classroom Catalog. Lists
    many records for singing activities.

Instruction Books for Melody Instruments

BECKMAN, FREDERICK, *Classroom Method for Melody Flute,* Melody Flute Company,
    Laurel, Maryland. Contains melodies but no words to sing; a very good
    piano accompaniment book is available.
BUCHTEL, FORREST L., *Buchtel Recorder Method,* Book 1, Neil A. Kjos Music Co.,
    Park Ridge, Illinois. Baroque system for C recorders—soprano and tenor.
BURGETT, ELAINE, ET. AL., *Modern Musical Fun for Singing and Playing With the
    Tonette.* Lyons Band Instrument Company, 688 Industrial Drive, Elmhurst,
    Ill. 60126.
EARLE, FREDERICK, *Trophy Elementary Recorder Method, Baroque System,* Trophy
    Music Company, 1278 W. 9th St., Cleveland, Ohio 44113.
JAMES, MARGARET, *The Pipers' Guild Handbook,* J. B. Cramer & Co., Ltd., 139
    Bond Street, London W1, England. Concerns bamboo pipes.
LANAHAN, WALTER D., *Melody Method for the Recorder,* Melody Flute Company,
    Laurel, Maryland.
NEWMAN, HAROLD, AND GRACE W. NEWMAN, *Music Shall Live—Singing and
    Playing with the Recorder,* Hargail Music Press, 157 West 57th Street, New
    York. N.Y.
ROWE, A. W., *The New Melodica Tutor,* M. Hohner, Ltd., Hicksville, N.Y.
WOELFLIN, LESLIE, *Classroom Melody Instruments: A Programmed Text,* Scott,

Foresman and Company, Chicago, Illinois. College students teach themselves to play the Tonette, Song Flute, Flutophone, and recorder.

Films and Filmstrips

BELL TELEPHONE COMPANY, inquire at nearest office about free loan.
Musical Atoms—A Study of Intervals, Young People's Concert Series, Leonard Bernstein. (age 10 and up) Wagner, Brahms, and Vaughan-Williams. (one hour)

CLASSROOM MATERIALS CO., 93 Myrtle Drive, Great Neck, N. Y. 11020.
Introduction to Music Reading (Grades 1–3) 33 1/3 RPM recording and color filmstrip. Rhythm, singing, and playing.
Exploring Music Reading (grades 1–3) 33 1/3 RPM recording and color filmstrip. Steps, skips, 4/4 meter, C scale.

CONTEMPORARY FILMS, 267 West 25th Street, New York, N.Y.
Music For Children. A presentation of Orff methods. For teachers.

EMC CORPORATION, Educational Materials Division, 180 E. 6th Street, St. Paul, Minn., 55101.
Listen to My Line (for age 10 and up). A sound filmstrip dealing with melody.

McGRAW-HILL BOOK COMPANY, Text-Film Dept., 330 West 42st Street, New York, N.Y.
What Is Melody? Young People's Concert Series, Leonard Bernstein. (age 10 and up) Beethoven, Wagner, Hindemith, Mozart, and Brahms. One hour.
What Makes Music Symphonic? Young People's Concert Series, Leonard Bernstein. (age 10 and up) Mozart, Beethoven, Tchaikovsky, Gershwin. One hour.
What Does Music Mean? Young People's Concert Series, Leonard Bernstein. (age 10 and up) Resolves the problem of understanding music versus extra-musical stories. One hour.

SHETLER, DONALD J., *Film Guide for Music Educators,* Music Educators National Conference, Washington, D.C. A must for music educators.

SOCIETY FOR VISUAL EDUCATION, INC., 1345 Diversey Parkway, Chicago, Ill. 60614.
Developing Skills in Music, Group Two. A sound-filmstrip dealing with staff, notes, major and minor scales, accidentals, chromatics, key signatures, intervals, phrases.

UNITED WORLD FILMS, INC., Universal Education and Visual Arts, 221 Park Avenue South, New York, N.Y., 10003.
Discovering Melody. (ages 5–7) An 11-minute film dealing with high, low, scale, melody, staff, notes, lines, spaces.

YOUNG AMERICA FILMS, INC., 18 E. 41st Street, New York, N.Y. 10017.
Songs to Sing Series. Four filmstrips in color with Mother Goose songs.

Other Materials

Educom Song Transparencies, Educom, Ltd., Box 388, Mount Kisco, N.Y. 10549.

Keyboard Scale and Chord Finder, Carl Van Roy Co., 51–17 Rockaway Beach Blvd., Far Rockaway, New York, 11691. A small cardboard device.

Magnetic Note Board, Martin Tolchin Music, Inc., 147 Scranton Ave., Lynbrook, N.Y. 11563.

Melodies of the Masters, Capital Record A–8569. Useful for the study of recorded melodies.

Movsesian Music Reading Method, Viking Company, 113 E. Edgmont Street, Los Angeles, California. A guide with 14 charts of songs to read, sing, and play.

Mysto Music Master, Maggie Magnetic Visual Aids Corporation, 11 W. 42nd Street, N.Y. 10036. A steel board with an easel back painted with treble and bass clefs and a section of the piano keyboard. Magnetized sharps, flats, and note symbols are placed on the board.

New Introduction to Music; by Howard Doolin, General Words and Music, 525 Busse Highway, Park Ridge, Ill. 60068. Level One: *Pitch and Duration of Tone;* Level Two: *Pitch and Duration of Tone Using Notation;* Level Three: *Modes and Form.* Children sing and play American folk songs in a method designed for the classroom teacher.

Vandre Interlocking Keyboard, Mills Music, Inc., New York. Plastic, with raised black keys.

3M Brand Packets for Overhead Projectors, Number 4: *Assembly Singing,* Minnesota Mining and Manufacturing Company, St. Paul, Minn.

10

polyphony, harmony, and texture

The reader has noticed the order of recent chapters—
rhythm, melody, and now harmony. This reflects to some degree
the order in which these basic elements of music are comprehended by children. The development of the harmonic sense
follows the comprehension of rhythm and melody. This development is characteristic of western cultures. It is either not as evident
or is absent in other cultures, although the mass audio media of
our times is tending to produce a world music consisting of an
amalgamation of the contributions of all peoples. While Western
music evolved to emphasize harmony, music of Asia and Africa
emphasized rhythmic and melodic developments, more complex
than those of the West. In the ethnic music of Asia and Africa,
harmony is incidental to the interrelation of rhythm and melody,
although the octave, the fifth, and the fourth appear vertically
in much of it, as does some simple tonic-dominant harmony.

Polyphony is another word for counterpoint. Its earliest
definition had to do with point against point (note against note).
For our purposes we will regard it as a combining of melodic
lines into a unified musical fabric. In the traditional Western
music, polyphony operates in accordance with certain harmonic
principles. However, in some contemporary music it operates

by disregarding traditional harmony. Thus, there can be said to be two general types of polyphony, harmonic and non-harmonic. According to traditional standards, harmonic polyphony sounds well; it is consonant. Non-harmonic polyphony does not sound the same; it is apt to be dissonant. The music of Johann Sebastian Bach is polyphonic; it can be viewed as horizontal threads of melody moving along together. At the same time, when this music is viewed vertically, chords and chord changes appear at certain places. We find it is a texture woven of threads moving in both vertical and horizontal ways. A common example of this combination of the horizontal and vertical aspects of music is the round. Teachers should occasionally write a round in full on the chalkboard, each entry written on a staff beneath the previous entry. Children can then see, as well as hear, how the polyphony fits together harmonically.

Children first learn melody, the monophonic (one-voice) horizontal line. It is believed they are able to sense next the moving of two or more melody lines together. This is reflected in the classroom in the use of canons, rounds, chants, ostinati, and descants that they can perform after they have learned to sing in tune or to play a melody instrument with a group. For most children the ability to hear and sing harmonically develops between the ages of nine and thirteen. In the elementary school this growing harmonic sense is reflected by an emphasis on part-singing for the ten and eleven-year-olds.

Among western nations there are differences in the degree of emphasis given to harmonic music by music educators. In the United States it has been emphasized throughout all levels of instruction to a greater degree than in most other nations. It is possible that young children like the sound of harmony even though most of them cannot hear it analytically and, on the other hand, harmony may be overused; it can confuse some children who are trying to comprehend and sing melodies. Research is needed to determine the suitability of harmonic music for young children. It seems logical that the young child should first be helped to comprehend rhythm and melody, and that this should be done with as little interference from other sounds (such as harmony) as possible. Second, the child should be assisted in developing his ability to comprehend two or more melodic lines functioning at once and relating to each other. Third, this interaction of melodic lines should lead rather quickly into learning about harmony. It should also develop a certain independence in thinking and composing melodic lines, which may or may not be harmonically related. Thus, the child will be able to deal both with traditional harmony and with some of the music of today which avoids such harmony; the eleven-year-old should understand both types of music. It is our task to help him achieve this.

EXPLORING COMBINATIONS OF PITCHES

Among the first experiences children have with harmony in the classroom are the accompaniments of songs they have learned as monophonic (unaccompanied) melodies. From this, the thinnest of textures, they are transported into a different world of sound by accompaniments played by the teacher on Autoharp, guitar, piano or by means of recordings. This is usually homophonic music (melody with accompaniment). Many different textures can be produced in accompaniments, and children should be guided to discern what types they are. Thin, thick, heavy, and light are simple descriptive terms for textures, but there should be a good many other adjectives in use as time goes by. As soon as they are able, children should be helped to find out how music is organized to produce these various effects. An interesting question to ask when using the piano is, "What would happen if the melody (in the treble clef) and the harmony (in the bass clef) were inverted?" and then proceed to find out by experimenting. Older children can find chords in chordline melodies and relate these to chords they can build on the bells and piano, or play on the Autoharp to accompany these melodies.

Some teachers make it possible for children to experiment with combining all sorts of pitches and sounds, both as isolated "chords" and as a series of chord sound effects.

The methods of Carl Orff include the addition of instrumental *ostinati* (recurring melodic fragments) to pentatonic melodies to provide a polyphonic texture. Accompaniments to melodies may begin with a *bourdon* (open fifth in most instances) in the bass. From this can develop "moving bourdons" produced by alternating the two tones; both growing from this and adding to it are the repeated tonal fragments, the ostinati. It is assumed that within these limitations children can create music that is truly children's music, rather than music which is basically too adult and too harmonically complex for children to comprehend fully.

Lit - tle   Miss   Muf - fet   sat   on   a   tuf - fet,   etc.

Possible bourdons that would sound one octave lower are played on the alto glockenspiel. Two mallets are used.

The possible combinations of these tones seem almost inexhaustible, and the above are only a beginning. The reader is referred to three references for further study, each having essentially the same title. The film, *Music for Children,* is available from Contemporary Films, 267 West 25th Street, New York, N.Y. 10001; a record album of the same title (recorded in England by Angel and marketed in this country by Capitol Records) is available at any record shop. The book *Music for Children I Pentatonic* can be obtained from Associated Music Publishers, 609 Fifth Avenue, New York. N.Y. 10017, in an English adaptation by Doreen Hall and Arnold Walter, Canadian musicians. Books II and III refer to major and minor, respectively. Orff-inspired instruments can be obtained from M. Hohner, Inc., Andrews Road, Hicksville, N.Y., Rhythm Band Incorporated, 407–409 Throckmorton Street, Fort Worth, Texas 76102, and Lyons Band Instrument Company, 688 Industrial Drive, Elmhurst, Illinois 60126. Orff methods include canonic treatment of melody lines, another type of ployphony which will be discussed shortly.

Among the several theories about progressing toward comprehension of the vertical aspects of music (hearing more than one part at a time) is one that begins with the dialogue song, a type of song in which children are divided into two groups which take turns at singing the sections. While this is not part-singing in the harmonic sense, it is assumed that the classroom singers will become oriented to the idea of being assigned to groups which are responsible for singing their respective parts at the proper time in relation to the other parts. An example of a dialogue song for intermediate grades is "The Keeper."

THE KEEPER

Unknown

Old English
Dialogue Song

The keep-er did a-shoot-ing go, And under his cloak he car-ried a bow, All for to shoot at a mer-ry lit-tle doe, A-mong the leaves so__ green, O!

Jack-ie boy! Sing ye well! Hey down,
Mas-ter! Ve-ry well! Ho down,

Der-ry der-ry down, A-mong the leaves so__ green, O! To my
A-mong the leaves so__ green, O!

hey, down, down! Hey down,
To my ho, down, down! Ho down,

der-ry der-ry down, A-mong the leaves so__ green, O!
A-mong the leaves so__ green, O!

ROUNDS AND CANONS

The singing of rounds and canons[1] is believed to be a step toward the comprehension of harmony. Whether this opinion can be justified depends upon how such songs are taught. If children are taught to sing them in a manner that leads them to out-shout other parts, or to put their hands over their ears so that they cannot hear the other parts, then no real part-singing is taking place. If, on the other hand, they are taught in a manner that leads the singers to hear how the other parts join with theirs, then the experience can justifiably be called a form of part-singing. The teaching procedure may be outlined as follows:

1. The children learn the melody well.

2. The children learn to hear the harmony upon which the melody is based. The teacher chords this harmony on the Autoharp or piano, or uses a recording that provides a clear and simple harmonization. He tells the children how many times they are to sing the song.

3. The hearing of the new part (second entrance) of the round is accomplished by the teacher singing or playing this part while the class is softly singing the first part and is listening to how the parts join together to make interesting music.

4. Some children join with the teacher on the new part. Listening to all the parts and how they join together in the harmonic setting is stressed. Balance of the parts so that all singers can hear all of the parts is essential.

5. If the round is of more than two parts, the new parts are added in the same general manner as above.

6. Rounds can be ended in three different ways: each part can finish separately, all parts can end on a chord together (each part stopping wherever it may be in the round), and each part can sustain the final note of that part until all parts are finished.

After children have learned to sing rounds in this way and have acquired a good understanding of this type of singing, a procedure can be used that repeats the first two points above. Then the children can be divided into two groups, and a leader who sings well is selected for each group. Each group practices singing the song while the other group listens and evaluates. Then the round is sung according to the teacher's instructions, with careful attention directed to tone quality and balance.

[1] Rounds and canons are similar. The difference is that a round repeats (goes back to the beginning) whereas a canon does not. A round is a "circle canon."

Using a tape recorder can focus attention on listening to both parts and how they relate vertically.

Rounds and canons are emphasized in fourth and fifth grades and are used less frequently in the primary grades because many of the children are not of sufficient musical maturity to be able to sing them well and to hear with understanding what they are doing. It is possible, however, for exceptional first-grade children to sing canons like "Old Texas" because they are echo-type songs.

Frequently sung rounds include "Are You Sleeping?", "Three Blind Mice," "Little Tom Tinker," "Row Your Boat," "Scotland's Burning," "Sweetly Sings the Donkey," "Kookaburra," and "The Canoe Song."

NÖEL, NÖEL (Canon)

Old French Carol
Translated and Arranged by Robert E. Nye

OLD TEXAS

Canon

I'm goin' to leave ol' Tex-as now They've got no

I'm goin' to leave ol' Tex-as now

use for the long-horn cow.

They've got no use for the long-horn cow.

From *This Is Music,* Book *V,* by William R. Sur, Robert E. Nye, William R. Fisher, and Mary R. Tolbert, Copyright © 1967 and 1962 by Allyn and Bacon, Inc. Used by permission.

ROUND OF THANKS

Traditional   Four-part round

For health and strength and dai - ly food we

give Thee thanks, O Lord!

PRAY GOD BLESS

Four-part round

Pray God bless all friends here, A

mer - ry mer - ry Christ - mas and a hap - py New Year.

CHANTS

Chants have been defined as recurring melodic patterns or figures. As in the case of chord roots, knowledge of the harmony forms the basis for understanding chants. These added parts have value as creative and part-singing activities as well as being music that some immature singers can sing in tune. Easy chants can be sung in the primary grades.

Initial experiences in writing simple chants may be gained through the use of well-known songs that can be accompanied by only one chord such as "Row Your Boat," "Are You Sleeping?" and "Little Tom Tinker." The first tone to be used would be the chord root. Using this tone, invent a rhythm pattern that contrasts with the melody. The regular recurrence of this rhythmic pattern is sung on the pitch of the chord root (i.e., the home tone, "1," or "do"). For example, in the case of "Row Your Boat" the patterns that can be composed to be sung in conjunction with the melody are myriad. A few of them are:

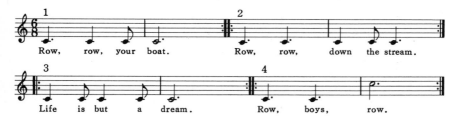

Percussion instruments are frequently used to accentuate the rhythm of a chant, and melody instruments are sometimes of aid in keeping some children on pitch. For dramatic effect those children singing the chant often begin about four measures before the melody begins, thus adding an *introduction* to the song. They also may continue for a few measures after the melody is finished, thus adding a *coda*. "Row Your Boat" may be sung as a melody with an added chant. When sung as a two-part round, addition of the chant results in a form of three-part singing, and when extended to be a four-part round, the chant adds a fifth part. With such simple song material, three- and four-part singing of this type can be done in fourth grade. Furthermore, the chant itself can be extended so that still more parts result.

For example, the above chants are pitched on "1" (C) of the 1–3–5 (tonic) chord. The chanters can be divided into two groups with one group singing on scale tone 3 at the same time the other sings on 1.

When this is learned, the chanters can be divided further into three groups singing the chant on scale tones 1, 3, and 5 respectively. This is an example of vocal chording done in the rhythm of a chant. The melody adds a part. If the chant now consists of three parts and the round is sung in four parts, a seven-part song results. The teacher is, of course, limited in the number of possible parts by the musical maturity and size of his group. However, the possibilities present in this simple music are surprising. Chording instruments can be a natural companion activity to this type of part singing. Melody instruments may be used also.

Thus far we have been concerned with the one-note chant. There are other possiblities. For example, "Are You Sleeping?" could have chants as follows:

"Little Tom Tinker" could have these:

SOME CHANT PATTERNS FOR

I-Chord Harmonization	V$_7$-Chord Harmonization
5 5 5	5 5 5
5 6 5	5 6 5
5 3 5	5 2 5,5 4 5
3 5 3	2 5 2,4 5 4
1 3 5,5 3 1	5 4 2,2 4 5
1 8,8 1	5, 5,5 5,
8 5 8	2 5 2,7 5 7
8 7 6 5	7 7 6 5,7 6 5 5
8 5 6 7	5 5 6 7,7 6 5 5
8 5 6 5	7 5 6 5,2 5 6 5
8 7 6 5,5 6 7 8	5 4 3 2

Multiple chants (two or more different ones) could conceivably be employed in the same song. However, if too many different words are sung at one time, the meaning is lost and the effect ceases to be very musical. Experimenting by substituting neutral syllables or melody instruments may be worthwhile.

When chants are sung with two-chord songs, the initial experiences are usually with scale tone 5 because that tone is common to two chords, I and V_7. This is the only tone of the scale on which it is possible to create a one-tone chant in such songs. Such rhythmic chants for "Three Blind Mice" might be:

Children often alter the final repetition of such chants in order that the last pitch sung will be the home tone.

Another commonly used chant is one based on the scale tones 5 and 6. Scale tone 6 is a member of neither the I nor the V_7 chord yet it has the unusual quality of not interfering with the harmony as long as it is placed on an unaccented part of the measure. This kind of a chant for "Looby Loo" could be:

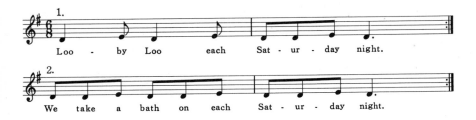

This 5–6–5 pattern works very well with songs like "Old Texas," "Ten Little Indians" and "Skip to My Lou"; children can invent many rhythmic variants of it.

LOOBY LOO

American Singing Game

2. left hand   3. right foot   4. left foot   5. whole self

This song describes an old American custom before the days of plumbing. The children are taking a bath in a washtub near the kitchen stove which burned wood or coal. They are testing the temperature of the water before getting into the tub.

Although all good chants are essentially simple, slightly more complex chants can be written for songs like "Looby Loo." One way to proceed with writing such a chant is to analyze the harmony of "Looby Loo" and chart it to find what this harmony demands of a four-measure-long chant. Looking at the song, we find that it consists of four four-measure phrases. The problem is to find what chords harmonize each of the meaures, and view this in a vertical fashion to find how to write a chant that will fit this harmonic arrangement. We find:

measure	1	2	3	4(*of each phrase*)
phrase 1......	G	G	G	D_7
phrase 2......	G	G	D_7	G
phrase 3......	G	G	G	G
phrase 4......	G	G	GD_7	G
	$\overline{G}$	$\overline{G}$	$\overline{G\&D_7}$	$\overline{G\&D_7}$

Looking down the columns it can be seen that a chant for "Looby Loo" must be written in the following harmonic scheme: the first measure of the chant requires a pattern related to the G chord (I); the second measure requires a pattern related to the G chord; the third and fourth measures require patterns related to *both* G and D_7 (V_7) chords. This means that during measures three and four, the chant is restricted to patterns such as those made up of scale tone 5, or scale tones 5 and 6— simple patterns that sound well with *either* chord I or V_7.

The following chart is included for those who wish to pursue more fully the writing of chants and other added parts to songs. It endeavors to picture some of the simple movements of tones possible during common chord changes. It will assist in the writing of descants as well as chants.

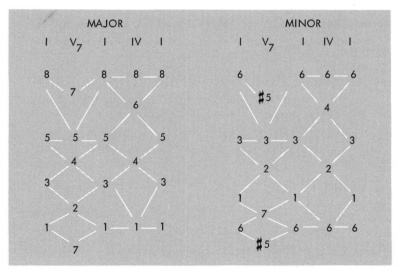

Chants may become monotonous because of their constant repetition. Therefore it is desirable that they be omitted from sections of some songs. Chants for three-chord songs are necessarily more complex, since they are based upon the tones of three chords rather than two.

COUNTERMELODIES AND DESCANTS

Singing countermelodies and descants constitutes another of the many approaches. A countermelody is an added melodic part, usually lower than the original melody, which often *imitates* it and often moves in *contrary motion* to it. Ideally, a descant is a melody in its own right although written to accompany another melody. In practice, the descant is subordinate to the melody. It is usually higher in pitch than the melody; a small group of children sing it while the majority of the children sing the melody. The reason for this is that high pitches sound relatively louder than low pitches when they are combined in part-singing; therefore a small group on a high part balances with a larger group on a low part.

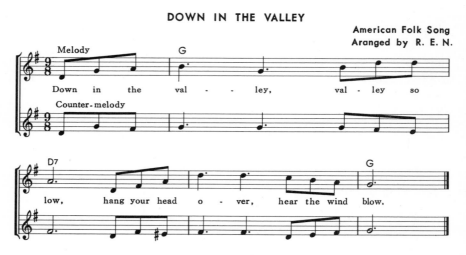

DOWN IN THE VALLEY

American Folk Song
Aranged by R. E. N.

From *Our Land of Song,* Copyright © 1942, 1956 by Summy-Birchard Company, Evanston, Illinois. All rights reserved. Used by permission.

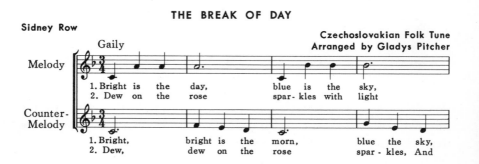

THE BREAK OF DAY

Sidney Row

Czechoslovakian Folk Tune
Arranged by Gladys Pitcher

From Beattie, Wolverton, Wilson, and Hinga, *The American Singer, Combined Grades.* Used by permission of American Book Company.

When the teacher understands the relation between countermelodies or descants, the chords and the original melodies, he can guide children to compose them. The first example is a countermelody to "Down in the Valley." In this case it is of such melodic nature in its own right that it is easier to sing than the real melody. Eight-year-olds can sing this simple polyphony.

A beautiful traditional-type descant, higher than the melody, and therefore to be sung by a small group, is one composed by Ewald Nolte to "Silent Night." It is designed for sixth grade.

SILENT NIGHT

Joseph Mohr

Franz Gruber
Descant by Ewald Nolte

Ideally, countermelodies and descants should be learned in integral relation to the original melody, because when they are learned as separate songs and then combined, many children fail to hear the harmonic relationship of the two parts. The melody should be well learned first of all, and a feeling for the harmony should be established with guitar, Autoharp, or piano.

The elementary school chorus may learn a descant or countermelody to be sung while the rest of the children sing a melody; and these may be combined in an assembly program. Likewise, children who are musically advanced may prepare descants out of school to be used in class with the melody sung by the other children. Another use for this type of added part is with certain melody instruments—from Song Flutes, Melody Flutes, Melodicas, and bells to violins and flutes. If done with discretion, employing a melody instrument is a way of strengthening either or both parts.

PARTNER SONGS

Some songs having identical harmonization can be sung simultaneously. A major value of this is recreational, because the attempt is fun. However, this has value in learning to sing in parts if it is taught in the same general manner suggested for rounds remembering that the children should hear both parts as they sing, and that aesthetic values should not be forgotten. "Three Blind Mice," "Row Your Boat," "Are Your Sleeping," and "The Farmer in the Dell" can be combined with each other. Other combinations are "Ten Little Indians" and "Skip to My Lou"; the choruses of "Blue-Tail Fly" and "Shoo Fly"; "Solomon Levi" and "A Spanish Cavalier"; "Darling Nellie Gray" and "When You and I Were Young, Maggie"; "Goodnight Ladies" and "When the Saints Come Marching In"; "Keep the Home Fires Burning" and "There's a Long, Long Trail"; "Humoresque" and "Old Folks at Home"; and "Ring the Banjo" and "The Girl I Left Behind Me." Frederick Beckman has developed this idea cleverly in his two collections, *Partner Songs* and *More Partner Songs,* published by Ginn and Company. They can be used in intermediate grades.

Children should be guided to answer the question, "Why do these songs sound acceptable when they are sung at the same time?" The answer should be found by conducting experiments. "Let's try 'America' and 'The Star-Spangled Banner' to find out how they sound together." "What happened?" "Why don't they sound well in certain places?" "Let's write those notes on the board to see what they are and how they combine." "How many different aspects of music must be the same when two songs can be combined?" "Let's try to list them." Older children may be able to make the generalization that when melodies have the same meter, tempo, and harmonic arrangement, they can be combined. An example of combining songs is the following, in which "Lone Star Trail" and "Leaving Old Texas" are arranged to "fit together."

THE LONE STAR TRAIL
(Descant: "Leavin' Old Texas")
American Cowboy Songs
Arranged by R. E. N.

From *This Is Music,* Book V, by William R, Sur, Robert E. Nye, William R. Fisher, and Mary R. Tolbert, Copyright © 1967 and 1962 by Allyn and Bacon, Inc. Used by permission.

ADDING HARMONIC ENDINGS

This simple and effective way to develop a feeling for harmony may be initiated in third grade, where two-part harmonic endings may be used, and expanded in the fourth grade to three-part endings. In this activity the teacher adds a part or parts to the final note or notes of a song. For example, "Three Blind Mice" ends with scale tones 3 2 1. The children would be told to sing or hum those tones softly while they listen to the teacher as she[2] sings the words on scale tones 3 2 3. Next, the children who believe they can sing the new part will join with the teacher while the others continue singing the melody. It has been the experience of many teachers that some children may never before have been conscious of their ability to hear two different pitches at one time in this fashion. These children may ask to sing such a harmonic ending again and again in order that they may fully enjoy what is to them a new comprehension of beauty.

This idea can be expanded as follows:

Harmonic endings can be easily created by teachers and children. It is recommended that these be taught first by rote, since the aim at this juncture is to develop harmonic feeling. Notation can then be used to show how the already experienced harmony looks. Eventually this can lead to an understanding and purposeful use of the notation of part-singing. This activity develops a helpful background for later improvising of parts ("barbershop harmony"), and for singing in thirds and sixths.

SINGING CHORD ROOTS

The singing of chord roots as an approach to learning to think harmonically is important, according to some music educators. They believe that the musical environment of elementary school children is quite different today than it once was. Children are brought into a world brimming with music with which they are in direct contact—almost from birth—due to the prevalence of radio, recordings, and television. Further-

---

[2] A woman teacher is referred to here because the female voice has the same pitch as the unchanged child voice. A man teacher would probably play the new part on an instrument to avoid using his octave-lower voice.

more, this music which they hear daily does not consist of a single melody line; it is built of rhythm and harmony as well as melody. Consequently, it can be theorized that children may find less interest in isolated melody than did the children of thirty years ago. All this leads to a belief that young children first need an emphasis on rhythm, then upon singing melodies to which simple harmony is later added by means of the teacher's voice, chording on Autoharp, guitar, or piano, and using selected recordings. It follows theoretically that if children have this rich background in rhythm and harmony they will be better able to understand, sing, and enjoy melody because of their comprehension of its place in combination with the other two major components of music. There may be logic in the claim that some older children are bored with music programs that are confined largely to melody because such music suffers by comparison to the more complete music heard outside the classroom. Some advise, "Let the children have *all* of the music, not only the melody." Another implication is that if children are taught rhythm, melody, and harmony, rather than mostly melody, part-singing will become a much more evident and successful part of the music program.

Chord roots constitute one of the easiest parts to add to a song because of the harmonic strength of the root, which is the foundation tone of each chord. Although this activity is primarily of intermediate grade level, it is possible for some younger children to take part in it. The songs employed are those that are best harmonized by only two or three chords. The following example can be harmonized by G and D_7 (I and V_7). First, the melody is learned; then the harmony is experienced by chording an accompaniment or from a recorded accompaniment; finally, the chord roots are added. The words can be sung in melody rhythm on the pitch of the chord root. Numerals, note names, or syllables are sometimes sung on the pitch indicated.

It seems undeniable that singing chord roots stresses the concept of chord change, especially since chord change is the essense of harmony. The singing or playing of melodies to which children "find" the roots by ear is another aspect of this study of harmony. It requires harmonic thinking without the aid of any type of notation. Because this thin texture of melody and chord root is not always aesthetically satisfying, success with the activity quickly prompts the addition of more parts in order that a richer texture will make the harmony more complete.

To provide for individual differences and to support the new chord root part, some children can play this part on bells, piano, and small winds. The viola and cello can provide a bass effect. Let us assume that

VARSOVIENNE
(Put Your Little Foot)

Traditional

Put your lit - tle foot, put your lit - tle foot, put your

Chord root

lit - tle foot right there, Put your lit - tle foot, put your

lit - tle foot, put your lit - tle foot right there.

the children are going to build a score for the singing and playing of "Put Your Little Foot," a score that will reveal their ideas about rhythm and harmony as well as about melody. The teacher has placed the melody on the chalkboard. He has also written the two "piano" chords that accompany this song. The children's first task is to find where in the song each of the chords is needed, if it is to be sounded on the piano or Autoharp to accompany the song. Since they have been taught that the note that receives the heavy accent or accents is ordinarily a tone of the required chord, they have an important clue on which to work. They know that the first beat of the measure in every meter signature is the most heavily accented beat, and that in 3/4 meter there is only one primary accent (the first beat) in each measure. (In 4/4 meter there are two— a primary accent on the first beat and a secondary accent on the third beat.) The children find that in the first three measures of "Put Your Little Foot" the note on the first beat is B. Looking at the chords, they notice that B is a member of the tones of the G (I) chord, but not of the D_7 (V_7) chord. Therefore, the chord needed for those three measures (or at least at the beginning of them) is the G chord. The note at the beginning of the fourth measure is A. The children find A to be a member of the D_7 chord; therefore this is the chord needed in the fourth measure. They proceed in this manner to the end of the song, then "try out" their harmony with the melody to see if it is correct. In some songs, the note D may be on the first beat of a measure. In this case, the children will decide by listening which of the chords is the right one to use. They can also tell by analyzing all the notes of any measure to find to which chord most of the notes belong. This is an important clue whenever students are determining chords for songs for which chords are not designated.

Now that the children have found the chords, they may write these on a staff below the melody, later creating a more interesting piano part derived from these chords. If one knows the chord, he knows the note that is the chord root, because the note G is the root of the G (I) chord and the note D is the root of the D_7 (V_7) chord. These notes are placed on a staff below the other music already written. Next, the children may invent rhythms for the song, which they will play on suitable percussion instruments. If they know how to write chants they may add one to their song. There will be continuous experimenting which will involve singing and playing of parts, a use and understanding of harmony, and different ways of presenting the melody. The beginning of the score may look like this:

Put Your Little Foot

To add to this simple melody, harmony, and rhythm, children may create more parts in the form of chants and simple countermelodies:

The opportunities for creative experiences are very great in this approach to music. Creating and experimenting with such a score can provide a basic experience for understanding harmony. Singing chord roots contributes markedly to the further comprehension of harmony because they form the foundation tones of the harmonic structure that supports the melody. Since understanding chord roots comes from understanding the chords (and chording) on the piano and Autoharp, it stimulates the addition of other rhythmic and harmonic parts.

LEARNING TO HEAR CHORD CHANGES

The experience with chord roots is basically an experience in sensing and identifying chord changes. The teacher plans similar experiences with chording on the piano and Autoharp. He contrives situations in which the sounding chord is "wrong," and the children are to notice this and want it corrected. The wrong and right chords are played; the children choose the one that "fits" the melody best. The experience commonly includes the teacher's selecting a familiar two-chord song (I and V_7 or I and IV) and playing the tonic chord all the way through, or until the children show in some way that the harmonic accompaniment should be corrected. He interests the children in searching for the best sounding chord. The measures of some songs have alternate harmonizations; the teacher lets the children select the Autoharp or piano chords which sound the best to them; he continues to help them be conscious of chord sounds and chord changes. After children have learned to play the Autoharp, he can let them improvise accompaniments to songs of simple harmonization "by ear"—listening to find when the melody demands a chord change, then choosing the chord that sounds best. With two-chord songs the children's problem is a simple one of deciding which of two chords should be used. When skill in this has been developed, the teacher selects three-chord songs for them to work with. Some children can become expert in chord selection on the Autoharp and develop extreme sensitivity to chord changes when their teachers have planned experiences which help them to develop this responsiveness to harmony.

The particular chords at the end of phrases form *cadences*. These pertain to a feeling of momentary or permanent conclusion. Children might analyze cadences, classify them accordingly, and apply them in their own compositions.

STUDYING THIRDS AND SIXTHS

An approach older from the standpoint of general use than singing chord roots is the employment of thirds and sixths. As in other approaches to harmony, children are assumed to know the melody very well, and to have heard the song on a recording or accompanied by the Autoharp or piano in a manner that helps them comprehend the integral relation of the melody and harmony. The singing of thirds was introduced in the section on harmonic endings. This use of thirds can be expanded to include parts of songs and eventually entire songs, providing the melodies accommodate this. For example. "London Bridge" can be sung in thirds except for near the end, where a sixth is necessary.

LONDON BRIDGE

The music series books include songs that rely heavily on thirds to introduce part-singing. A song that can be sung in its entirety in thirds is the well-known "Polly Wolly Doodle."

POLLY WOLLY DOODLE

American Song

An interval that sounds similar to the third is the sixth, which is the inversion of the third. After children have become accustomed to singing in parallel thirds, they can easily learn to sing in parallel sixths. Any song that can be sung in thirds can be sung in sixths. "Polly Wolly Doodle" illustrates this. However, when the interval is changed in this way the key must often change also to accommodate the voice range.

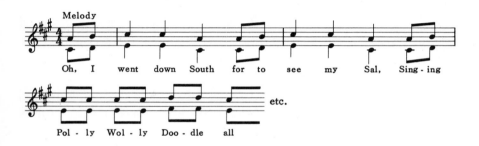

Songs such as "Lightly Row," "Goodbye My Love, Goodbye," "Yankee Doodle," "Hand Me Down My Walking Cane," "To Puerto Rico" (page 246), "Catch a Falling Star," and the refrain of "Marching to Pretoria" can be used to advantage in approaching part-singing through the use of thirds and sixths.

There are older methods of teaching part-singing which emphasize drilling on each part, then putting them together. Today the emphasis is upon helping children to hear a new part in relation to the melody and the harmony so that they hear all of the music. This principle is applicable no matter what type of part-singing is being done, whether it be round, descant, or traditional two- and three-part singing. The general outline of progress in part-singing in grades four, five, and six is as follows:

1. The learning of the melody.

2. The comprehension of the harmony (chord structure) that accompanies the melody by use of Autoharp, piano, or guitar chording, or a suitable recording.

3. The introduction of the new part in a manner that permits the children to hear the integral relation of the two parts. (Children hum the melody or sing it softly while the teacher sings or plays the new part.) Harmony must be *heard* before it is *made*.

4. The singing of the new part by those children who are ready for part-singing, always working for a balance in volume that permits the hearing of both parts by all of the children.

5. Introducing a third part by repeating Steps 3 and 4, adding the new part to the two parts previously learned.

6. When children have learned to feel secure in part-singing activities, then the sight-reading of part songs can be an interesting and challenging activity. When this skill is developed, Steps 1, 2, and 3 are eliminated. Since sight-singing is a complicated skill, neutral syllables instead of words are generally used at first so that the children can concentrate on the notation. The words are added when children feel secure on the parts.

In general, the voices of fifth- and sixth-grade children are unchanged and have approximately the same range, with the exception of boys in the first stage of the voice change. Technically, it is incorrect to call these immature voices "soprano" or "alto." It is more accurate to abandon these adult terms and to call the children's voice parts "high," "low," and "middle," rather than "first soprano," "alto," and "second soprano." It is the aim of the teacher that every child sing each of these parts, changing from one to another according to the directions of the moment or by being assigned them in different songs.

In each of the music series fifth grade books will be found songs that stress parallel thirds. Following songs in thirds will be those that include both thirds and sixths, then some fourths and fifths. Every teacher of the older children should know the sequence of songs through which part-singing skills are expected to be learned in the particular series books available in his school. Suggestions in the teacher's book must be studied carefully. Some two-part songs are included in the fourth-grade books in preparation for the emphasis on harmony in the fifth grade.

An interesting creative approach to singing thirds and sixths is one in which children compose songs confined within four pitches of the major scale, 3, 4, 5, and 6. After such a song has been composed and learned, a parallel third part can be added below. When this same new part is transposed one octave higher, parallel sixths result. Try this with "Sleep, Baby, Sleep."

The male teacher is at some disadvantage in teaching part-singing, since his voice sounds one octave lower than the child voice. Therefore, it is necessary for him to use some melody instrument instead of his voice when he wishes to illustrate part-singing of unchanged voices. His voice is excellent, however, in the singing of chord roots. There is seldom a changed voice among sixth-grade children, but in case there should be, the singing of special parts, such as chord roots by the male teacher along with the boy, will help the child adjust to his temporarily unique situation.

IMPROVISING HARMONY PARTS

The improvising of harmony parts has often been overlooked as one practical approach to part-singing. "Barber-shopping" or "singing harmony by ear" has had a definite carry-over into the natural musical expression of boys and girls when they are on field trips or picnics, at camp and at home. The writers know of an elementary school where the improvising of parts by volunteer neighborhood quartets was an activity of importance, even affecting school and community programs. A list of songs that have had use in this activity includes "Home on the Range," "Down by the Old Mill Stream," "There's a Long, Long Trail," "Moonlight and Roses," "Let the Rest of the World Go By," "Eyes of Texas" (I've Been Working on the Railroad"), "Red River Valley," "Oh My Darling Clementine," "A Bicycle Built for Two." This activity is usually most effective at sixth-grade level, where it develops into three-part singing, although some fifth grades can do well with it. *Exploring Music With Children* contains a sequence of songs by which to help older children develop skill in harmonic improvisation (pp. 184–200).

VOCAL CHORDING

An example of one type of vocal chording was mentioned on page 379 in connection with I-chord songs. Usually, chording of the vocal type consists of the same tones that are often used for piano chording in the treble clef. The children may be divided into four groups, with one assigned the melody and the other three assigned the three chord tones. This activity would logically begin with one-chord melodies and progress to three-chord melodies. It may start in a simple way in third or fourth grade. It is sometimes emphasized in fifth and sixth grades as an approach to three-part singing. The ease with which children can learn to chord vocally will be determined by their ability to hear harmony; their ability to learn harmony will be favorably influenced by successful experiences in instrumental chording and by guided listening activities that aid the hearing of chord changes. A chord root part can be added if the range is appropriate.

The chords to be sung can be arranged in several positions. This chart illustrates chord positions that are sometimes used as exercises to introduce children to this activity. Although numbers or syllables may be used to introduce this work, humming or the neutral syllable "loo" is used in performance.

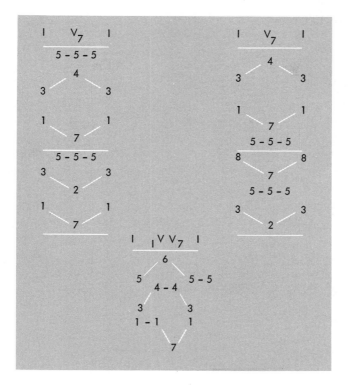

The following excerpt from "Silent Night" illustrates this activity:

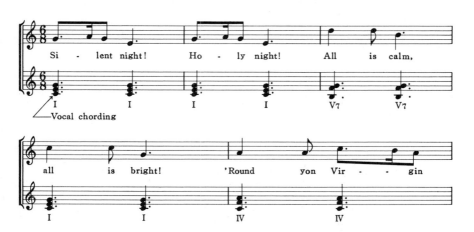

THE ELEMENTARY SCHOOL CHORUS

Among the special interest groups in the elementary school are the orchestra, band, and chorus. The instrumental groups are generally the responsibility of special music teachers but the chorus is frequently taught either by the music teacher or by a classroom teacher. Although some schools have a primary grades chorus which sings unison songs, the usual chorus is composed of fifth and sixth graders. Today's teachers are fortunate in having an improved selection of song materials to use, some of which are listed at the end of this chapter. Not only do the series books include chants, descants, and countermelodies in addition to the standard types of two- and three-part songs, but there are valuable supplementary materials. There is no standard seating arrangement for elementary choruses. However, it is best to have the lowest and highest parts seated so that each can hear the other well. In this way the group is able to keep more accurately on pitch. In chorus work which has a goal of public performance, the children are more or less permanently assigned to one of the parts (high, middle, or low).

Harmony Instruments

Chording instruments are useful in helping children to hear chord changes. They are also useful in introducing the study of certain aspects of music theory. Harmony instruments are used to accompany songs, dramatic play, and rhythmic movement. They are important to both music and social studies when they lend atmosphere to folk songs of Europe and the Americas. (Autoharp, guitar, concertina, and occasionally the ukulele.)

THE AUTOHARP

The Autoharp is an instrument of ancient lineage which has come to be popular in elementary and junior high schools, and is used by folk singers. The model most popular today has 15 push-button bars with felts that prevent the vibration of strings other than those that sound the chord tones desired. The 12 and 15 bar models are usually preferred to the five bar model, although it has some value in primary grades, since they can be played in more keys, making them generally more useful. The 12 bar model was once the standard instrument. Advantages of the 15 bar model are:

The addition of D major, E♭ major, and F₇ to the original 12 chords provides the primary chords for 7 keys instead of 5 keys on the 12 bar instrument.

The addition of the keys of B♭ major and D major to the original keys of C, F, and G major, and A and D minor offer forty per cent more latitude in key selection.

Five additional chords are provided in the keys of C, F, and B♭.

Autoharp

OSCAR SCHMIDT-INTERNATIONAL, INC.

Although some children in primary grades are able to play the instrument satisfactorily, it is not until the fourth grade that most children can do so. In early primary grades teachers often press the buttons while children strum the strings. It is believed that guiding children to listen carefully to Autoharp chording assists the development of a feeling for harmony, which is part of the preparation for part-singing in intermediate grades. It is something of a substitute for the piano in situations where no piano is available, as well as being valuable for enrichment in rooms that have pianos. Hearing chord changes and playing the correct chord at the proper time are valuable for ear-training purposes, and teachers should emphasize these as listening experiences in their efforts to develop children's musicianship. The act of chording is a rhythmic response. A child who is yet unable to sing beautifully may be able to make as beautiful music on the Autoharp as anyone else; thus success on this instrument can help individual children feel a sense of accomplishment essential to good social and emotional growth. Chording on the Autoharp is an effective way to stimulate interest in the study of chords on the piano and on the staff. Another use of the Autoharp is to establish the tempo of a song by playing introductory chords in the desired rhythm.

The Autoharp is placed on a desk or table, with the corner between the two straight ends of the instrument pointing somewhat toward the player. Fingers of the left hand press firmly on the appropriate button while the right hand strokes the full range of the strings from left to right with a pick. Sometimes the player may choose to stroke the strings on the left side of the bridge to produce a deeper-toned effect than is obtained on the right side. *Finger forms* are important, and the player needs to analyze the chord progressions he is to play, then plan the most simple and efficient way to place the correct finger on the button. In most of the music suggested for Autoharp chording there will be no more than three chords, the tonic (I), the dominant seventh (V_7), and the subdominant (IV). The finger form for these chords in the keys of C major, G major, F major, D minor, and A minor is as follows:

	IV	V_7	I
left hand			
	ring finger	middle finger	index finger

Try this finger form in the above keys, and find the straight position and the triangular position of the fingers in this basic finger form.

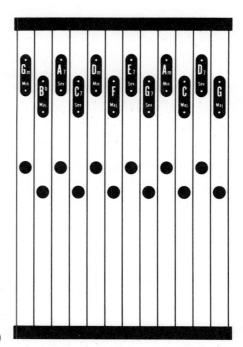

Autoharp Bridge (12-bar Model)

The strings are stroked with a pick held in the right hand, unless the player is left handed. The loud tone produced with a plastic pick is needed for most classroom singing, while the soft tone produced with a felt pick is best for solo and small ensemble singing. Picks are made in different shapes and sizes. Some are worn on a finger while others are held between thumb and index finger. Some teachers use the plastic fasteners from bread wrappers as substitutes. Men teachers often use their fingernails instead of a pick.

When teaching children to play the Autoharp, it is the usual practice to begin with songs that require only one chord to accompany, proceeding to those requiring two chords, then to songs in which three chords are necessary. It is desirable to play part of the time by rote to be sure that the children are *hearing* the chord changes, not simply pushing buttons mechanically. Such songs follow:

I-chord songs:	*key*
"Row Your Boat", "Little Tom Tinker"	C major
"Are You Sleeping?" "Farmer in the Dell," "For Health and Strength"	F major
"Canoe Song"	D minor
"Zum Gali Gali"	G minor

403

II-chord songs:

"Mary Had a Little Lamb," "Sandy Land," "Looby Loo,"	G major
"London Bridge," "Ten Little Indians," "Hush Little Baby," "Polly Wolly Doodle"	F major
"Old Smoky," "Oats, Peas, Beans, and Barley," "Little Red Caboose"	C major
"Down in the Valley," "Long Long Ago," "Bow Belinda," "Shoo Fly," "Susie Little Susie"	F major
"Nobody Home"	G minor
"Lovely Evening" (I-IV)	F major
"Wayfaring Stranger"	D minor

III-chord songs:

"Silent Night," Brahms' "Lullaby," "Marines' Hymn"	C major
"My Bonnie," "Jingle Bells," "Camptown Races," "Old Brass Wagon"	G major
"Red River Valley," "Twinkle Twinkle, Little Star," "This Old Man," "Hickory Dickory Dock," "Home on the Range"	F major
"Go Down, Moses"	A minor
"Old King Cole"	D minor

Since some two- and three-chord songs are not written in these common keys, using the Autoharp to accompany them requires *transposing* them into keys that will make it possible to play such songs on the instrument. This involves placing the the fingers in the finger form of the key nearest to the original key of the song and following the I, V_7, and IV designations, or their equivalent in letter names. The teacher should be certain that the range of pitches in the new key is suitable for children's voices. The 15 bar model permits playing in B♭ and D major also.

A problem in the use of Autoharps is tuning them.[3] There is no universally accepted method. Ordinarily, one tunes to a piano that is in proper pitch, although a pitch pipe can be used. The strings sounding the C major chord may be tuned first (all the C's, E's, and G's), then the strings of the G_7 chord (all B's, D's, and F's—the G's having been tuned as part of the C chord), and next the F major chord (all A's—the F's and C's having been tuned as pitches belonging to the other chords). These three chords should then be played slowly to hear whether any of the strings need further adjusting. After this, the other strings may be tuned

---

[3] The new Autoharps remain in tune much longer than the earlier models.

| E♭ Maj. | D Maj. | F⁷ Sev. | Gᵐ Min. | B♭ Maj. | A⁷ Sev. | C⁷ Sev. | Dᵐ Min. | F Maj. | E⁷ Sev. | G⁷ Sev. | Aᵐ Min. | C Maj. | D⁷ Sev. | G Maj. |

Autoharp Bridge (15-bar Model)

as individual tones of the chromatic scale (all the half-steps). Then every chord of the instrument is played slowly to determine possible need for further tuning. A child can play the pitches on the piano while the teacher adjusts the strings. As a general rule, the teacher must do the adjusting of the strings, not the children. The only cases the authors know where strings have been broken are those in which elementary school children tighten strings to the breaking point because they think they hear the pitch to which they are tuning one octave higher than it sounds. To keep the instrument in tune and to protect it, it should be kept either in the case it comes in or on a covered shelf, out of the sunlight and away from sources of heat, cold, or dampness. When the instrument is subject to changes in temperature, the expansion and contraction of the strings causes changes in their tension, hence changes in pitch.

Some European music educators do not look with favor on chording instruments such as the Autoharp at the primary level, claiming that children do not possess sufficient harmonic sense at this age to profit from it. However, many American educators believe that chording instruments can provide a valuable listening experience for this age group. Young children can learn to recognize the I-chord as the "home" chord, the V_7-chord as the "away-from-home" chord, and the IV-chord as the "longing-for-home" or "leaning" chord. They can identify them by appropriate motions: the "home" chord with folded arms, the "away-from-home" chord with outstretched arms, and the "leaning" chord by raising both arms to the left or to the right. Children can create other interpretations of the characteristic sound of each of these chords, and create their own related body responses.

Types of Autoharp accompaniments. Like any other musical instrument, the Autoharp should be played with good taste, and there should be logical reasons for the particular style of the accompaniment played.

The mood of the song indicates whether the player uses a slow relaxed stroke (as for lullabies and quiet songs), or a strong fast stroke (as for marches and rhythmic, exciting songs). For some waltzes, an um-pah-pah style is called for. This can be made by strumming the first beat of each measure with low-pitched strings and the other two beats with high-pitched strings. A deeper, richer effect is obtained by playing on the left side of the bridge. This brings out the sound of the lower strings and omits a few of the highest pitches. The player can make an appropriate accompaniment for some Spanish-type music by chording in the rhythm of ♩. ♪♩ ♩. A bagpipe or bourdon effect is made by holding down two buttons at the same time: G major and F minor, D_7 and D minor, and A_7 and A minor. This effect is useful for pentatonic music, for some Scottish music, and for folk songs based upon the open fifth of the bagpipe or musette. Individual strings can be plucked to simulate Oriental-type music. A zither or tamburitza effect that characterizes some Eastern European folk music can be produced by two players on the same instrument. One player presses the buttons while the other strokes the strings rapidly with wooden mallets. A metal bar or object placed across the strings will produce a steel guitar effect. Minor seventh chords can be sounded when two instruments are used. For example, G-minor and B♭-major chords played simultaneously will sound the G-minor seventh chord. A minor plus C major will sound the A-minor seventh chord, and D minor plus F major sounds the D-minor seventh chord. For songs of slow tempo, a skilled player can produce both the melody and the harmony. To obtain this effect, a chord is played for each tone of the melody, and the player strums the strings only as far as the melody pitch. A harp effect is obtained by reversing the usual stroke, the player beginning the stroke with the high strings and moving the pick toward the low strings.

"Autoharp chords" appear in many music books, and are commonly found in series books. Besides the many references to the instrument in such books, there are other helpful publications. Some examples are:

Autoharp Accompaniments to Favorite Songs, by Lillian Mohr Fox. Summy-Birchard Publishing Co., 1834 Ridge Ave., Evanston, Illinois.

Autoharp Song Folio, by Evelyn Waldrop. William J. Smith Music Company, 245 W. 31st St., New York, N.Y.

Fun with the Classroom Harps, by Rj Staples. Follett Publishing Company, 1010 W. Washington Blvd., Chicago, Illinois.

Golden Autoharp Melodies, by Sigmund Spaeth. National Autoharp Sales Co., 560 31st St., Des Moines, Iowa.

Harmony Fun with the Autoharp, by Beatrice Krone. Neil A. Kjos Music Co., 525 Busse Highway, Park Ridge, Illinois.

Many Ways to Play the Autoharp, Vols. 1, 2, Oscar Schmidt-International, Inc., Garden State Road, Union, New Jersey 07083. For adults. Vol. 2 includes advanced techniques. New.

Teachers Guide for the Golden Autoharp, by Lorrain Watters. National Autoharp Sales Co., 560 31st St., Des Moines, Iowa.

UKULELE AND GUITAR

If the desirability of chording experiences on the Autoharp has gained wide acceptance in elementary music education, it follows that there should be similar values in other chording instruments such as the ukulele and guitar. The ukulele has supporters from the fourth grade on, and chording on the guitar is done by some children who are ten and eleven years old. (The ukulele also has the doubtful distinction of being one of the most commonly misspelled words in music.)

Standard tuning on the ukulele was once G-C-E-A from low to high strings. In recent years a preference for tuning the instrument one whole step higher, to A-D-F♯-B, has developed. Thus, the ukulele

beginner finds two tunings in current use. Notice that if the teacher employs both tunings, the fingering for the common chords in G major and F major become the same, as does that for D major and C major.

Most ukuleles are made of wood, and need the same protection against dropping, cold, heat, and sun that the Autoharp needs. Extreme dampness, dryness, or temperature changes will change the tuning and could crack the body of the instrument. Children need to be informed about how to strum the instrument or they may break strings by pulling them.

Experts in ukulele playing state that while the baritone ukulele is superior in tone quality and many teachers prefer it to the soprano (standard) instrument, the soprano is best for elementary school children in terms of student hand size; it is easier for children to play. It is easily retuned in C, when this is desirable for a whole-step lower singing range,

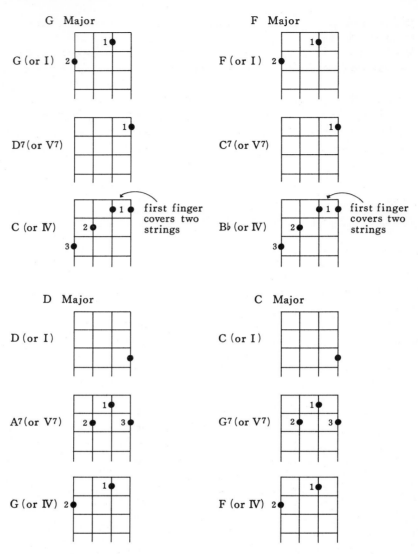

and it costs less than the baritone. Wood is preferred to plastic. Some teachers introduce the ukulele in a way that relates to the guitar and string bass. The following describes this approach, which begins with the D tuning of the soprano ukulele: A D F-sharp B.

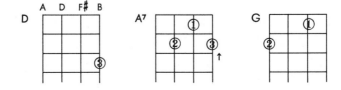

With the third finger as an anchor one can slide it up to the second fret and form:	The dominant 7th, A_7. The IV chord has one finger in common with the V_7;	One can use these fingers as pivots when he goes from one chord to another.

With these three primary chords one can play many folk songs.

The baritone, which is becoming a popular instrument for adults, is tuned a 5th below the soprano ukulele. Its first string, however, is an octave and a 5th below the soprano's first string, making its strings the same as the top four strings of the standard guitar;

Baritone Tuning:

This makes it a good instrument for beginners who may want to transfer to a standard guitar later on. The chords will be formed in the same way but will sound in different keys.

If one is using both instruments simultaneously, it is possible to stagger the teaching of these fingerings, permitting the advantage of being able to practice together. A system one teacher[4] devised to teach seven fingerings on each instrument makes possible playing all primary chords in two keys in common plus one extra key for each. Directly below these are the added fingerings for the other two strings on the guitar.

These seven fingerings are the easiest for the beginner to play. They comprise the primary triads of the keys of D, G, and C major for the ukulele, and G, C, and F major for the baritone ukulele. (See p. 408.)

Guitar chords that are easiest for the older child to play are those on page 410. They are not easily learned. One clever little girl removed the lower two strings on her guitar so she could practice the baritone fingerings until her fingers grew stronger.

Also to be noted is the fact that the lower four guitar strings are the same as those on the string bass. The chord-roots are plucked with the index finger when played with other folk instruments. These can be related to chords on the guitar; this would be useful only to a student knowing the guitar chords well. (See p. 408.)

Since the string bass does not have frets, small thin strips of masking tape can be used to mark the half steps for inexperienced players.

[4] Mrs. Erma Kleehammer.

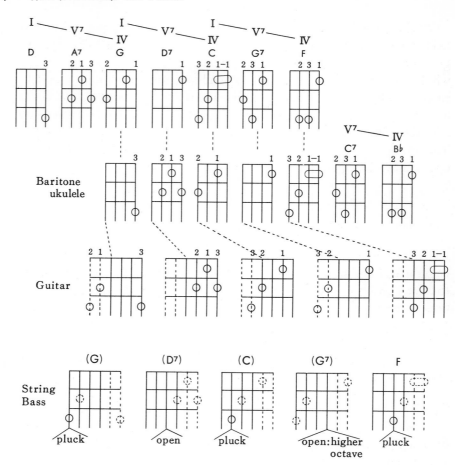

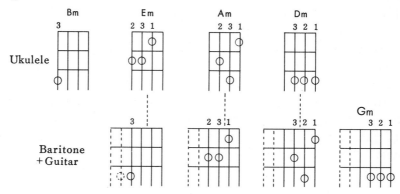

Some of the more common minor chords for the ukulele, baritone and guitar are:

The prevalence of folk instruments in popular entertainment has led many children to identify with this kind of music. The guitar-playing governess in "The Sound of Music" and the Singing Nun have provided wholesome prototypes. All ages of children are responding to folk-singers such as Peter, Paul and Mary and innovators in the folk-idiom like the Beatles. Burl Ives and Pete Seeger have for some time been recording folk tunes for children with guitar and banjo accompaniment. This music has great appeal to many children, and they respond to the opportunity to accompany themselves on folk instruments.

PIANO CHORDING

Since the 1 3 5 note pattern becomes a familiar one to children, being used both in their songs and in the procedure that enables the class to have a feeling for the key before singing, this is a logical note combination to use in the initial teaching of chording. This 1 3 5 chord (a major *triad* in *root position*) is also a basic concept in the study of music theory.

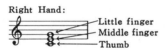

Right Hand:
— Little finger
— Middle finger
— Thumb

Should a child be unable to exert equal pressure through these three fingers or in any other way be unable to control them at first, he may use any combination of fingers of both hands to accomplish the playing of this chord, or he may play only the two highest notes of a three-note chord, a procedure often employed in primary grades. The teacher may help the child to play the chord in a steady walking-note rhythm, then while he continues playing in rhythm, have the class sing "Row, row, row your boat." To a child who has never played the piano, the discovery that he can accompany a well-known song in this simple manner is thrilling. There are few songs that can be accompanied by the lone 1 3 5 chord. Some were listed earlier in this chapter on page 403.

Songs that rightfully require two chords (I and V$_7$) but that might be usable as one-chord songs include "Old MacDonald," "Farmer in the Dell," "Three Blind Mice," "Goodbye Old Paint," "Swing Low Sweet Chariot," "Taps," and "Shortnin' Bread."

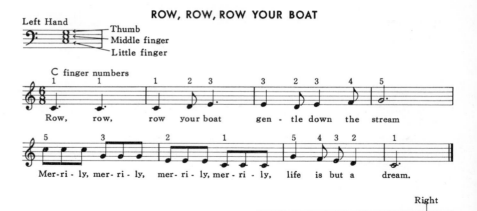

Summary of possibilities:

Play the melody with the right hand.
Play the melody with the left hand.
Play the chord with the left hand.
Play the chord with the right hand.
Play the chord with both hands.
Play the melody with the right hand and the chord with the left hand.
Play the melody with the left hand (in bass clef) and the chord with the right hand (in treble clef).
Play the chord in other forms, such as one note at a time.

How often the chord is sounded depends on how the individual feels about the song. One child may play a chord on every beat. Another may choose to sound the chord every other beat. Still another child may alter the steady pattern of chord-sounding by a pause at the end of a phrase. Children should be free to be as individually creative as possible in this simple way.

When a child has learned how to build 1 3 5 chords on different pitches such as C, F, G, and has learned to recognized the distinctive sound of the major chord, the 1 3 5 chord in minor may be easily taught. A child can soon learn that the minor chord has its own characteristic sound and that he can build both major and minor chords at will. Experience will expand the child's feeling for the difference in sound between major and minor. The mechanical difference between major and minor 1 3 5 chords is merely that the middle finger, which plays scale tone 3, is placed one half-step lower in minor than in major. Few commonly known songs can be accompanied by the lone minor 1 3 5 chord, but children can compose such songs easily. An example follows:

SLAVE SONG

Piano chording:

Suggested rhythmic responses:

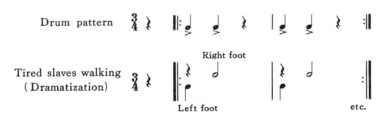

Singing and playing:
A piano part invented later which can be sung as a chant:

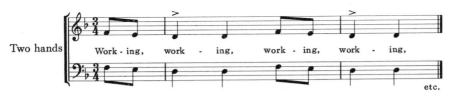

The children discovered that their song could be sung as a round.

A song of Israeli origin that can be accompanied by the G-minor chord is "Zum Gali Gali."

If children have used the Autoharp with songs requiring two or more different chords, the addition of the V_7 chord to permit improvising a piano accompaniment to many familiar songs is relatively easy. A simple form of the chord change from I to V_7 and back to I is as follows:

Using the hand position for the 1 3 5 *chord as a starting point,* the following directions apply in *all* major keys:

right hand: The little finger remains on the same key. The fourth finger is placed one half-step higher than the third finger was. The thumb is placed one half-step lower than before.

left hand: The thumb remains on the same key. The index finger is placed one half-step higher than the middle finger was. The little finger is placed one half-step lower than before.

Many songs can be harmonized with the I and V_7 chords. Some of the most familiar were listed earlier for Autoharp chording.

Since most songs in minor keys are based on a scale in which the seventh tone is raised one half-step, practically all minor I-V_7 chord songs will have the V_7 chord played exactly the same as it is played in the major keys of the same name, i.e., the V_7 chord in G minor is the same chord

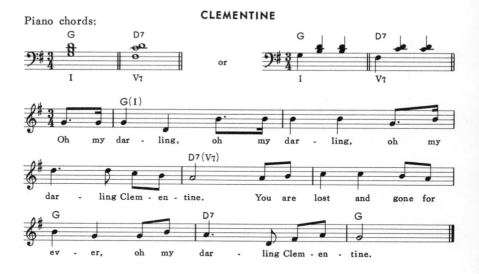

CLEMENTINE

as in G major. Thus, the only difference in chording would be in the I chord, which in minor would have its third (the middle note) one half-step lower than in the major chord. It is a simple matter, then, to play "Nobody Home" in G minor:[5]

[5] Some musicians abbreviate G minor by writing "g," and G major by "G."

NOBODY HOME

Piano chording:

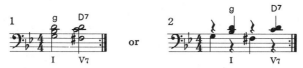

or yet another way:

Suggestion: Try making up an introduction using the style of Example 3. Also, improvise an ending for this round. Add suitable percussion instruments and hand clapping.

Other interesting songs in minor that use these same chords are the French carol "Pat-a-pan" and the English carol "Dame, Get Up." Percussion instruments go well with "Pat-a-pan."

The hand position for the IV chord is easier than the hand position for the V_7 chord. The "rule" for the change from I to IV is as follows:

left hand: The little finger remains on the same key. The index finger is placed one half-step higher than the middle finger was. The thumb moves up one whole step.

right hand: The thumb remains on the same key. The middle finger is placed one half-step higher than before. The little finger moves up one whole step.

The round "Christmas Bells" provides a good introduction to this chord change. Use the above chords as marked.

The familiar round "Lovely Evening" and the cowboy song "The Railroad Corral" (*This Is Music: Book 6*) are other examples of songs that require only the I and IV chords for their harmonization.

CHRISTMAS BELLS

The IV chord in minor is played by lowering the highest of the three tones of the major IV chord one half-step. An American folk song that can be harmonized with only I and IV chords is "Wayfaring Stranger":

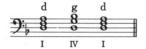

WAYFARING STRANGER

Examples of the many songs in major keys easily chorded with I, IV, and V₇ chords are "The Caisson Song," "Oh Susanna," "He's a Jolly Good Fellow," "The First Noel," "Night Herding Song," "Eyes of Texas (I've Been Working on the Railroad)," "All Through the Night," "Sing Your Way Home," "Deck the Halls," "Happy Birthday to You," "Old Oaken Bucket," "Auld Lang Syne," "Annie Laurie," "Old Folks at Home," "Reuben and Rachel," "Santa Lucia," "The Muffin Man." Others were listed earlier for Autoharp chording.

CINDY

This use of the piano in the classroom can result in a teacher's learning to play comparatively well. Should any teacher desire to hasten this learning process, there are beginning piano books that employ and expand the method of chording used in this chapter; by means of these an adult can teach himself to play with more skill. A list of such books is found at the end of the chapter.

Teachers should use the loud (sustaining) pedal of the piano sparingly. A common fault of piano players is overuse of this pedal, whch results in a blur of tones rather than in the clarity and distinctness children need to hear.

If one can chord with I, IV, and V_7 chords in major keys, it is not difficult to chord in minor keys with I, IV, and V_7. Incidentally, minor keys are not as important as major keys as far as common usage in the United States is concerned. While peoples of Eastern Europe find in minor tonality a natural expression, the people of the United States lean rather heavily toward the major tonality. American children should be able to identify minor and major and to enjoy hearing the changes from minor to major and vice versa in songs such as "We Three Kings of Orient Are," "When Johnny Comes Marching Home," and "Minka."

Children sometimes ask the question, "From where do the V_7 and IV chords come, and why are our fingers in the positions they are on the keyboard?"

A 1 3 5 chord can be built on every step of the scale. We could chord by using only 1 3 5 chords, but it would be very awkward to do, and it would not sound well. What we are trying to do with our chord positions at the piano is to move our fingers as little as possible. It is something like being "intelligently lazy"—which in this case is also being efficient. Here are the I, IV, and V chords in the 1 3 5 position in the C-major scale:

These chords can also be called C, F, and G, because they have two names, one being the Roman numeral that corresponds to the Arabic number name of the scale tone on which the chord is built, and the other being the letter name of the note that is "1" when the chord is in the 1 3 5 (root) position. Here is the V_7 chord in root position.

We are still in the key of C major. Compare the V₇ with the V above. This chord is called V₇ because a note has been added that is seven lines and spaces above G. The notes from the bottom to the top in this chord are G, B, D, and F, or 1 3 5 7. It is V₇ because G is the fifth step of the scale of C, and we are using that key in this illustration.

The following illustration shows where we obtain the simple three-finger hand position for chording:

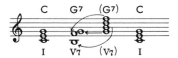

By rearranging the G 1 3 5 7 chord into another *position,* and by omitting the note D, which is the one we can most easily eliminate without injuring the sound of the chord, we can keep the hand in the same place as it the was in playing the I chord and move only the fingers.

The IV chord that we use in piano chording is another position of original 1 3 5 arrangement of the notes:

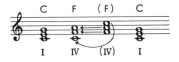

Common chord positions are:

The first inversion is called 6–3 because if one counts from the lowest note to the highest, numbering the lowest note "1", the *interval* is found to be that of a *sixth.* Counting in similar manner, from the lowest note to the middle one, reveals that this interval is a *third,* hence this is a 6–3 chord. The origin of the name of the 6–4 chord can be counted out in the same way. The two intervals here are a sixth and a *fourth,* hence the name 6–4 chord. See "The Blacksmith," p. 423, to find how these chords appear in a melody line.

CHORDING WITH BELLS

The "piano chords" can be played on resonator bells effectively. Teachers use these individual tone bars in many ways. The bars can be distributed among numbers of children, each having a bar and a mallet with which to strike it. In the key of C, for example, all children who hold bells marked C, E or G, will sound them when the C-major chord is needed, and when the F-major chord is required in the harmonization of the song, all children holding bars that sound F, A, and C will strike them. Of course, they must be struck at the same instant, and this demands the close attention of the players. To produce an interesting shimmering effect, the player needs two mallets with which he strikes the bell in rapid alternation. Playing chords in this manner with appropriate songs can make truly beautiful music. Motivating a fourth, fifth, or sixth-grade class to harmonize a song in this way can initiate a study of chord structure that includes learning note names and their relation to the staff and key signature.

Hand bells can be used also, and the Melodica was mentioned earlier as an instrument on which one can play both melody and harmony.

THE SINGING CLASSROOM ORCHESTRA

When children have learned to play small wind instruments, to chord on the piano and Autoharp, and to play the bells and percussion instruments, the possibility of the singing classroom orchestra presents itself. When the teacher finds a melody line in the range of the wind instruments with the chords named, there are opportunities for combining various instruments with voices, or alternating instruments and voices. Here is a creative activity developing musical discrimination—the children and the teacher will have to orchestrate the song according to their own judgment. Children can also have experiences in conducting such orchestras. Songs that are not found in books at hand can be presented by means of projector or can be drawn on large (two by three feet) sheets of heavy paper or light cardboard and placed where all the children can see. Music can be quickly drawn on such paper. A staff liner with chalk is used to mark the staff. These chalk lines are drawn over with black crayon, freehand. When two-part songs are written, the melody part may be in black crayon while the harmony part is in another color for easier reading. Examples follow:

Theme from NINTH SYMPHONY

The *Theme from the Ninth Symphony* is an example of the very simple beginning music a classroom orchestra uses. Ordinarily, themes from the great symphonies are not applicable to this type of work. This particular theme, however, has the simplicity of folk music and is understood easily by children. It can be extended to include more of the original melody than appears here. An interesting and thrilling event after words have been set to it and the song is learned, is the teacher's playing a recording of a section of the last movement of the *Ninth Symphony*. Watching the reaction, she will find children who are fascinated listeners to "their song" and who will be interested in what Beethoven does with it. Appreciation may be at an extremely high level at this point. The key of C was chosen because it is easiest for the playing of the instruments. The key of F is preferable as soon as the fingering of B♭ is learned, because it places the singing voice in a better range.

"Come, Ye Thankful People, Come" is much more difficult and represents a later experience in the development of the classroom orchestra.

COME, YE THANKFUL PEOPLE, COME

While some classroom teachers will be able to write their own classroom orchestra arrangements and make their own charts, others may not be able to do so. In these cases the music specialist becomes the helper, the arranger, and perhaps the chart-maker who assists the room teacher.

Instrumental music activities in the general music program constitute not an end in themselves but an important aid in the teaching of better listening, singing, musical discrimination, creativity, part-singing, and note-reading, and serve as an introduction to simple music theory—all in a setting that children enjoy, understand, and know to be purposeful. It is essential that instruments used in combination in the classroom be in tune with each other. It has been suggested that instruments be used en masse only one period during the week; on that day the teacher should so organize the lesson that the children are singing approximately half the time.

More Concepts of Polyphony and Harmony

Thus far in this chapter certain concepts of polyphony, harmony, texture, and related skills in vocal and instrumental performance have been dealt with. Polyphony was equated with counterpoint, and these terms meant a type of music in which melodic lines were combined in horizontal fashion in a kind of texture that can be described as polyphonic or contrapuntal. This texture could be thin or thick, according to the number of parts employed. A two-part round would be of thin texture, while the description of adding chants to one-chord songs implied that as one added other parts, one by one, to the other horizontal lines, the thicker the texture became. Teachers' well-planned questions should guide children to recognize these aspects of music.

The concept of *contrary motion* as a composer's device was mentioned in the discussion of countermelody and illustrated in a song. The fugue can be introduced as an extension of the concept of the round or canon as part of the study of texture. The Young People's Record 431, *Round and Round,* takes the listener from round and canon to the fugue. *Cat's Fugue* by Scarlatti (Music Sound Books Recording 78039; Keyboard Junior Recording K60A-2) and Bach's *Little Fugue in G Minor* (Adventures in Music 6, v. 1; Bowmar 86) are often used in this study. Unlike the round or canon, the fugue is a relatively free form. The listener can detect the theme, and the teacher should have it notated before the class. As far as this chapter is concerned, the important aspects of the fugue are polyphonic texture, repeated appearances of the theme, imitation as a composer's device, the fugal entry (like a canon—one voice at a time), and the relationships between the polyphony and the harmony. Children may discover that unlike the round, the second voice to enter (called the *answer*) is in a different key, usually a fifth above or a fourth below the theme (called the *subject*). Some advanced students may be interested in the vocal fugue in *This Is Music,* Book 8, pp. 48–52, which is analyzed in the book and recorded. They may notice that a *stretto* is a matter of voices entering with the subject in rapid succession, overlapping each other. Music of Palestrina and Bach can be heard and their types of polyphony described and discussed by the older children.

A WORLD OF CHORDS

Conventional harmony (chord structure) which dominated the European music of 1450 to 1900 is based upon triads and their inversions.

THE BLACKSMITH

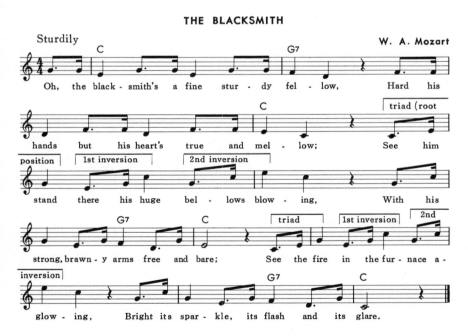

2. Blow the fire, stir the coals, heaping more on,
   Till the iron is aglow, let it roar on !
   As the smith high his hammer keeps swinging,
   Fiery sparks fall in showers all around ;
   And the sledge on the anvil keeps ringing,
   Giving out its loud clanging sound.

These inversions, some of which were written in the section on piano chording, appear in the melody of many songs. For elementary school children, the names of the inversions are not particularly vital; the important factor is the comprehension that the same notes in these different positions form the same chord. An example of inversions appearing in a melody line is a song from Mozart's opera *The Marriage of Figaro* which acquired words years ago identifying it as "The Blacksmith." Another version of it appears as "My Opera" in *Singing With Children.* Compare these horizontal chords with the vertical chords in the piano chording section, and plan similar experiences for children. Try using the chords indicated in the melody for accompanying those measures. Another song to use in the same study is "My Home's in Montana." The children's generalization resulting from a series of such experiments could be, "When tones of specific chords appear in melodies, those chords form a suitable accompaniment." Other possible generalizations might include, "A chord is a vertical arrangement of three or more tones," and "When there are changes in a melody, there are usually changes in the harmony."

A triad or root position chord is a 1–3–5 tonal structure; another third is added to form a seventh chord, a 1–3–5–7 arrangement of tones. The relation of the I and V_7 chords to the major scale is as follows:

Seventh chords, or parts of them, are commonly found in melody lines. Find some in "The Blacksmith," "The Lone Star Trail," and "Down in the Valley," all in this chapter. Children should rediscover that the I-chord yields a feeling of stability, whereas the V_7-chord is restless and seems to demand change (resolution). The IV-chord is another three-note chord with the same pattern of inversions as the I-chord; its only difference is that it is constructed on the fourth degree of the scale while the I-chord is built on the first degree.

For studying chords in vertical position, some three-part songs in fifth- and sixth-grade series books are helpful. One of these is "Jarabe," in which *passing tones* and *non-chord* tones can be discovered and in which contrary motion can be reviewed.

JARABE

Melody and words from *Spanish-American Folksongs,* collected by Eleanore Hague; published by the American Folklore Society, Inc. Used by permission. Found in This Is Music, Book V, by William R. Sur, Robert E. Nye, William R. Fisher, and Mary R. Tolbert. Copyright © 1967 and 1962 by Allyn and Bacon, Inc. Used by permission.

The attention of older children can be drawn to songs in which there are key changes in order to solve the problem of how a composer *modulates* (changes) from one key to another. Two such songs are "The Erie Canal," and "We Three Kings of Orient Are," in which both major and minor tonalities occur. Relationships between the minor scales on which the songs are based and the minor chords used to accompany them can be examined, then compared with the relationships between major scales and major melodies. If there is sufficient interest, some questions might be, "What happens when triads are built on every degree of the major scale?" "What would happen if we built triads on every degree of the minor scale?" "Do you find any unusual chords?" "What might they be?" "How would you write them?" The harmonizations of "Ma Belle Bimba" and "We Wish You a Merry Christmas" require both major and minor chords; older children can create their own harmonizations, making aesthetic judgments as to which chords are the most pleasing.

CONTEMPORARY HARMONY

One possible approach to contemporary harmony would take place after the children have found that chords in traditional harmony are constructed in thirds. The teacher could ask, "What would happen if chords were built of fourths rather than thirds?" and let the children find out by their experimenting with fourths. Then the teacher might ask the same question about fifths, sevenths, and seconds. Another beginning could be in response to the teacher's question, "What kinds of chords are needed to harmonize a composition written in the whole-tone scale? Write one and be ready to tell the class about those chords."

Music of today is in a period of unlimited experimentation. It is described by some as involving deliberate violation of the traditional harmonic system of chords and chord resolutions by the employment of parallel chords, chords built with fourths, other arrangements leading to abandonment of former restrictions, and toward the absence of tonal centers. This does not mean that the music of the future is necessarily what the results of experimental composition seem to indicate, but it is likely that some of this will be a genuine part of it. It appears that music educators have the responsibility of helping children think musically in the two generally defined areas of traditional harmony and its opposite, and in the great area in between these two extremes. This area in between the extremes may be the most important when the future reveals itself in this time of rapid change.

In tone row composition tones of the row are combined as chords. In atonal polyphony the chords "happen" when horizontal lines of melody sound at one time. The pen of the less talented experimenter is likely to produce less artistic music; the more talented will use new harmonic resources with discretion and taste. The composers most likely to live in the history of music will do what the great ones have always done—find some way to integrate the new with the old in a pleasing way. In the elementary schools our duty is to expose children to all types of music, including the current experimentation. Experience with the tone row and its type of harmony can begin as early as the third grade. The fifth and sixth grades can sing a folk song in one key while chording it in another, record this bitonality on tape, play it back and evaluate the effect. They can also sing songs in parallel fourths and fifths for experimental purposes and evaluate them the same way. *Children like to experiment* and to evaluate what happens—and this seems to be one of the best times in history to experiment with music. They can experiment with traditional harmony by finding different harmonizations for the same song. Improvisation can be done on the black keys while chording in the key of C major. Authentic recorded music of Africa and Asia can be listened to, studied, and its harmonic qualities can be examined and compared to Western harmony. In some of this music, harmony may be absent, in some it may be present but different from Western harmony, and in some the harmony may resemble that of the West.

Recordings useful in exploring contemporary harmony include:

"Laranjeires" from *Saudades do Brazil,* Milhaud   Adventures in Music
    dissonance, bitonality   4 v. 2

"Copacabana" from *Saudades do Brazil,* Milhaud   Adventures in Music
    bitonality, dissonance   4 v. 2

Mathis der Maler, Hindemith   Columbia
    harmony constructed of fourths and fifths

Folk-Song Symphony, Harris   Vanguard
    contemporary harmonizations of U.S. folk
     songs

"March" (Number 5) from *King David,* Honneger   Vanguard
    polytonality, three keys at one time

"Putnam's Camp" from *Three Places in New*
   England, Ives   Columbia; Mercury
    bitonality; describes two bands playing in
    different keys

"Circus Music" from *The Red Pony,* Copland   Adventures in Music
     3 v. 1

Bachianas Brasilieras No. 2, Villa-Lobos   Capitol

The Complete Music, Webern   Columbia
    tone row music

Sounds of New Music   Folkways FX 6160
    electronic music

Children's exploration of harmony and polyphony should deepen their insight into how melody and harmony interrelate. There is no better way to learn about music than to compose it. Although few children will be professional composers, every child can benefit from writing his own melody and harmony, regardless of how modest the level may be. Music paper should be standard equipment in the classroom.

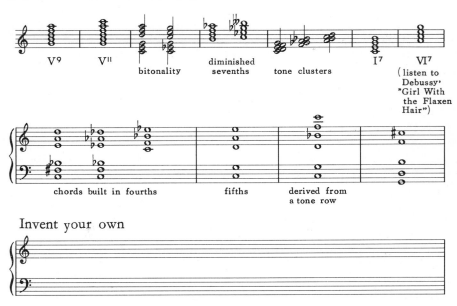

Invent your own

Some Activities and Suggestions for Lesson Plans

Polyphony

Learning to listen to more than one part: One half of the class sustains one pitch, *do* or 1, while the other half sings other pitches guided by the teacher's hand signs or by his pointing to scale degrees indicated by numbers or syllables written vertically on the chalkboard. Later, both *do* and *so* and *la* and *mi* are used alternately as sustaining tones. This activity progresses until both groups are singing moving parts, following two-hand signals by the teacher, or by advanced children, and eventually from a chart or chalkboard with notation.

Encourage children to create chants and ostinati to add variety to songs of simple harmonization. Measures from some rounds can be used in the same way, sung or played with the melody.

When the large majority of the class has learned to sing in tune, sing pentatonic melodies as two-part rounds. Sing other two-part rounds, being sure to make this an experience in hearing both parts at once. When the class is secure in singing two-part rounds, try three and four-part rounds.

Devise ways to call the children's attention to the horizontal character of rounds; this is *polyphonic music,* or *polyphony;* work toward the children's eventual generalization that when there are two or more melodic lines moving together in horizontal fashion, polyphony results. Write a short traditional round with all parts notated on the chalkboard so that the children can see this.

Plan questions to help children develop a vocabulary of terms descriptive of polyphonic texture such as light, heavy, thick, thin, and degrees of these. Use selected recordings. Have the children compare thin polyphonic texture with rich, thick homophonic texture, for example. Compare the melodic lines of polyphony with threads in the weaving of tapestry.

Invent simple bell parts for songs that permit each measure to be harmonized by only one chord. One example is the Danish "Han Skal Leve," ("The Birthday Song" in Birchard Music Series Book 4). Have bell players play the first note of each measure to produce a simple added part. Parts of many songs can be used this way, one example being the familiar "Weggis Song."

Sing and play countermelodies and descants as an extension of the above experiences. Ask the children to find for themselves the differences between rounds and added parts of this type, and present their findings to the class.

Small groups can improvise in the pentatonic idiom. Example: with five children, three might play different-toned percussion instruments while one might play the bells and the other a small wind instrument to create two-voiced polyphony.

To introduce dissonance as an aspect of contemporary music, experiment with singing any known song as a round, regardless of possible dissonances. When this is performed satisfactorily, tape it and let the children analyze and evaluate it.

Let the children discover the composer's device of imitation by listening to selected recordings exemplifying it.

Explore Sousa's *Semper Fidelis March* to discover the melodies and how he combines them. Find out if the children can explain the plan he used to make them "fit together."

Let the children discover the fugue and some aspects of its texture and style by listening to recordings and reading references. Later on, test their knowledge of "fugal entries" by finding if they recognize them in other music.

Harmony

Basic to comprehending the chord changes which are characteristic of harmony, is much experience in non-harmonic music—that music in which are no there chord changes. This type of music includes short tonal fragments and calls, pentatonic music, I-chord songs, and unaccompanied music which has melodies that are not strongly suggestive of harmony. Later, one chord on the Autoharp suffices to accompany songs such as "The Farmer in the Dell" and "Old MacDonald." The teacher can finger the Autoharp while young children stroke the strings.

Create and sing songs based on the two most common forms of the pentatonic scale and guide children to hear the difference between them. While many songs are composed on major scale tones 123568, others such as "The Canoe Song" use scale tones 612356. The first implies major tonality; the second implies minor tonality.

After a melody has been learned by a class, the teacher accompanies it with rhythmic and melodic patterns different from the melody. The challenge to the child is to continue hearing and singing the melody despite the addition of harmony and contrasting rhythms and melodic patterns.

The teacher plays I, V_7, and IV chords on the Autoharp, guitar, or piano. The children are to describe, identify, and compare these chords in some inventive way. When this has been done, an identification game can be played. For example, some children have identified the tonic chord as the "at home" chord, the dominant as the "away from home" chord, and the subdominant as the "leaning" chord. Another approach is to ask them to identify the chords with their arms. Example: V_7 may be arms up; I may be arms down. They can be asked to describe major and minor chords in some creative way. Some children have decided that palms up denotes major and palms down represents minor.

Arrange to have children experience the difference between major and minor tonalities through the use of familiar songs. Example: first sing and play "Merrily We Roll Along" in major, then in minor. Ask children to describe the difference they hear.

After a song is well-learned, make a harmonic ending (a harmonized
cadence) by adding a few harmonizing notes to be sung by part of
the class. Example:

There are songs and parts of songs that can be sung and played in parallel
thirds. Utilize those such as "Hot Cross Buns," "Sally Go Round,"
"Polly Wolly Doodle," and the first phrase of "Au Claire de la
Lune." First the melody is reviewed thoroughly with a strongly
harmonic accompaniment. Then either part of the class or the
teacher—alone at first—will sing (at the same time as the melody) the
tune at the interval of a third. Because the harmony has been comprehended, some automatic adjustments of whole and half steps
will take place in the new part. When the teacher does this, the class
can discover by ear what is different about the new part. The children
should see the related parts in notation in order to see "what it
looks like when it sounds this way." The interval of a third should
be identified by sight and sound. On the staff it will be space-space
or line-line. In subsequent lessons the teacher can help the children
to formulate the following ideas: 1) Melody with harmonic accompaniment is homophonic music; 2) The interval of a third is in this
instance a vertical (harmonic) interval as compared to the third
which is horizontal (melodic) and appears in the melody; 3) Both
types of thirds might be found in a two-part song.
Have children analyze the textures of different harmonic accompaniments:
sustained chords, broken chords, repeated patterns, frequently-
sounded chords. Use piano, Autoharp, recordings.
The children can compose songs using only major scale tones 234567
(avoiding the home tone). Such songs can be sung in two parts, the
added part being either a sixth higher or a third lower.
Thirds can be inverted to form sixths, and these can be sung and played.
Utilize songs such as those mentioned above, but transpose them
when necessary into keys suitable for the range of the children's
voices. Follow the same procedure as in the study of the third—
seeing the sixth in notation and identifying both melodic and
harmonic intervals. The sixth appears as a melodic interval in
"My Bonnie."

Words of songs can be sung on the pitches of the chord roots to form a harmonic part to add to simple melodies. Begin with two-chord songs, then proceed to three-chord songs. The letter name of the chord reveals the notes to be used, and those pitches suggest the harmony of the song (the chord changes).

Sing two-part songs that require thirds and sixths in their harmonization. Use notation from charts, transparencies, or books.

Challenge the children to identify the I, V_7, and IV chords by holding up the appropriate number of fingers as they listen to recorded music such as the "Romanze" from *Eine kleine Nachtmusik,* by Mozart. (Adventures in Music 4 v. 1).

Sing the I, IV, and V_7 "piano chords" to accompany certain three-chord songs. After the class is divided into four groups, the melody and three chord-tone parts (high, low, and middle) are assigned. This simple procedure gives the effect of four-part harmony. "Silent Night" and "Brahms' Lullaby" are often used.

Continue to have children explore and identify characteristics of the tonic, dominant, and subdominant chords. Examine these both in their relation to melodies and in relation to each other as chords without the melody. Find prominent chord sequences in songs, such as V_7 I IV I and IV V_7 I.

Plan to have children analyze melodies to seek relationships between tonal patterns of chord-line character in melodies and the chords accompanying those melodies. Guide them to find the line-line-line and space-space-space appearance of the tonic chord. The children should eventually make the generalization that when a chord is prominent in the melody, it is very likely to be the one needed in the accompaniment.

Arrange for children to create their own Autoharp or piano chord accompaniments to easy two- and three-chord songs that have no chord designations. Have them discover how they will decide which chords to use. (They must use ear and eye.)

Expand the children's concept of a chord from three pitches sounding simultaneously to one sounded on the Autoharp. Have children write the C major chord shown on the Autoharp on the grand staff. Ask them what chord tones repeat, how this might affect their definition of "chord," and how it might relate to their future compositions. Let them try playing the notes of the Autoharp chord on the piano. Can the chord be extended further in range?

Write the major scale vertically in numbers or syllables. Divide the class into two groups—left hand and right hand; each group sings according to which hand the teacher uses as a pointer. Then the teacher points to scale degrees that will produce either unison and two-part singing or both. Later on, do the same with minor scales and other modes.

Produce charts showing vertical chords that will be matched with charts of melodies in which the same chords appear horizontally. This is to further emphasize the relationship of chords and melodies.

The teacher can create a canon and write it in numbers or syllables for the class to sing. *Example:*

$$1\ 1\ 2\ 3\ 4\ 5\ -\ 5\ 4\ 3\ 4\ 3\ 2\ 1\ -$$
$$1\ 1\ 2\ 3\ 4\ 5\ -\ 5\ 4\ 3\ 4\ 3\ 2\ 1\ -$$

Review the partner songs suggested in the discussion of polyphony in this chapter. Ask the children to solve the puzzle of why these songs can be combined.

Improvise harmony: The teacher plays loudly on the Autoharp a slowly changing succession of chords. The children will listen carefully and hum pitches to "fit" the chords.

One way to introduce part-singing is to divide a class into thirds. The teacher sings the new part while one group sings the melody very softly. The other groups listen to the two parts while waiting for their turn. Then the teacher will ask some children to join with her on the new part.

Dramatize the relation of chords to scales by forming a major scale of eight children standing before the class, each with a resonator bar representing the correctly-ordered note of that scale from 1 through 8. The teacher asks students holding bars 1, 3, and 5 to step out of the scale (in front of it, but remaining in their approximate positions) and to play their tones together as a chord in tremulo style so that it can be sustained. From this point on, experiments can take place. "How can we make a minor chord?" "Can we make a chord based on scale step two?" "How can we find the V_7 chord?" "What positions of the V_7 chord are possible when we have only these eight pitches to work with?" "How does this appear in notation?" When notes are needed that are not in the eight scale tones, others from the class can be called up in front, given his tone bar, and placed in keyboard position with the others. For example, the problem may be to act out the whole tone scale in this way. "What other bars will be necessary?" "What does it sound like?" "How can it be notated?" "How is a triad formed in this scale?" "How many different chords are possible in this scale?"

Show a short traditional round with *all* parts written out, with each stave in correct vertical relation so that each note is shown in vertical relation to the other notes. Have this on a transparency or on the chalkboard so the learners can analyze it to find out how melody and harmony are interrelated in a round. Older children who comprehend this fully can write rounds.

Suggest to the class that they improvise a second part to "Streets of Laredo," using only pitches 3, 4, and 5 of the scale. After this has been accomplished, add a third part—the interval of a third lower than the second part. This would consist of scale tones 1, 2, and 3. The class should evaluate the result and analyze what made it possible.

Discover chord inversions by extracting vertical chords from chordline sections of melodies.

Discover modulation in songs such as "The Erie Canal" and "We Three Kings of Orient Are" and identify the modulating chord.

Improvise harmony by ear with such songs as "Hot Cross Buns" and many others listed in the index of *Exploring Music With Children,* p, 292, "Part songs (creating parts)."

Study the relation between traditional polyphony and harmony such as found in the polyphony of J. S. Bach. Use selected recordings and scores. Project a section of a score on a screen and have the students analyze it (at their level) horizontally and vertically. The chords will be found vertically, on the beat in most instances.

To understand experiments in contemporary music, the children will sing a familiar song such as "Twinkle, Twinkle, Little Star" while the teacher first plays an eccentric harmonization, then plays the traditional harmony, but in a key other than the one in which the melody is being sung. When these can be done reasonably well, tape them and play them back for analysis and discussion.

Use chord sequences as the basis for melodic improvisation. Begin with I IV V_7 I in familiar keys. Place the chords on the chalkboard, a transparency, or a chart. One child can play the chords while another improvises on bells, a small wind instrument, or with his voice.

For individual practice in part-singing, provide two tape recorders, placing them in either a sound-resistant cubicle in the classroom or space in another room. Have chord sequences establishing the tonality on each tape, also the beginning pitches of the melody and of the harmony part of a two-part song. One tape would follow this with the melody, the other tape with the harmony part. A child, using notation to help him, sings the missing part along with each machine. When the child wants to listen to himself for evaluation, another tape can be placed on one of the machines and he can record his duet to play back and analyze.

SOME CUMULATIVE BEHAVIORAL OBJECTIVES

The child

    can recognize the tonal center of a song by . . . . .

    is conscious of chord changes, and reveals this by . . . . .

    can identify chord patterns in the melody line by . . . . .

    can differentiate between major and minor tonality by . . . . .

    is conscious of the need for chord changes, and reveals this by . . . . .

    is aware of the combination of melodic lines in rounds and in added ostinati and chants, and reveals this by . . . . .

    demonstrates ability to perform chants or ostinati by . . . . .

    demonstrates uses of chords on Autoharp or piano by . . . . .

    is able to identify I, IV, and V_7 chords in major keys by . . . . .
        (One way is to be able to play Autoharp accompaniments by ear.)

    will demonstrate ability to recognize and utilize thirds and sixths intervals by . . . . .

    is able to secure his feeling of tonality by . . . . . .
        (Some ways include singing or playing the tonic chord and playing I V_7 I chord sequences.)

    identifies I, IV, and V_7 chords in minor keys by . . . . .

    reveals increasing comprehension of harmony by . . . .
        (Some ways are by singing harmony parts, creating harmonic accompaniments, and creating chants and descants.)

    is able to construct chords built on intervals such as seconds, fourths, fifths, and sevenths by . . . . .

    reveals comprehension of homophonic and polyphonic textures by . . . . .

    reveals ability to identify contemporary harmonizations by . . . . .

For writing lesson plans, refer to the following as needed:

1. The Developmental Characteristics and Implications Chart in Chapter 3.

2. The Structure of Music Outline—polyphony, harmony, and texture section—and plans for teaching music in Chapter 6.

3. Types of thinking, types of questions, and principles of learning in Chapter 4.

4. Chapter 9, to relate aspects of melody to harmony.

5. The environment for learning and necessary routines for teaching in Chapter 5.

6. The Scope and Sequence Chart in Appendix A in the envelope at the back of the book.

Some generalizations, conclusions, and findings for children to discover are:

Harmony is a vertical arrangement of pitches.

Tonality (key feeling) results when the harmony of a piece of music indicates a tonal center to which its other tones are attracted or related.

When two tones are on adjacent lines or spaces, they form the interval of a third.

Thirds (and other intervals) may be found vertically in harmonies and horizontally in melodies.

The tones of the dominant seventh chord (V_7) resolve naturally to the tonic chord; this fixes the tonality.

The tones of the subdominant (IV) chord resolve naturally to either the tonic chord or follow a progression to the dominant seventh chord followed by the tonic chord.

When at the end of a succession of chords in a phrase a feeling of repose is suggested, the chords which communicate this feeling comprise a cadence.[8]

The IV   I cadence sounds like "Amen."

---

[8] *Cadence* may be explored if the teacher deems it worthwhile. The cadence is the melodic and/or harmonic aspect of the phrase ending, which conveys the impression of momentary or full conclusion. The *perfect* cadence occurs normally at the end of a composition, when the keynote is sounded in the highest voice (harmonically as part of the tonic chord). When harmonized, either the dominant or subdominant chord precedes the final tonic chord. The *authentic* cadence is the result of a V-I chord sequence, and the *plagal* cadence is the result of a IV-I chord sequence. There are others: *mixed, imperfect,* and *deceptive.*

INQUIRY AND SELECTED ACTIVITIES

1. Collect and compose songs that can be accompanied by one chord only, and compile them in a music notebook. They are to be used for introducing chording on the Autoharp, piano, and ukulele. Demonstrate how to use such songs for introductory part-singing.

2. Learn to identify songs that are in minor keys from the notation of the song. If the song's final note can be identified as scale tone six in the *major* scale derived from the key signature, then the song is in minor, and this note's letter name is the name of the minor key in which the song is written. The most important clue is how the song sounds, for it is more important to be able to recognize minor tonalities by the ear than to have to depend upon notation.

3. Select a two-chord melody and develop a score that provides melody, rhythm, and harmony as suggested in this chapter. Add chord roots.

4. Examine music series books to seek a sequence of songs you could use to help children learn to sing in parts at the fifth grade level. Add some techniques of your own learned in this chapter.

5. Inquire into chants, ostinati, and bourdons. Write some.

6. Some radio and television programs utilize electronic and other types of contemporary music. Tape record sections of these and bring them into the classroom for analysis by the class.

REFERENCES

Articles and Books

FRANK, PAUL L., "Orff and Bresgen as Music Educators," *Music Educators Journal,* (Feb-March, 1964), pp. 58–64.

GARY, CHARLES L., ED., *The Study of Music in the Elementary School—A Conceptual Approach,* Music Educators National Conference, Washington, D.C., 1967, pp. 67–81, harmony.

JONES ARCHIE, ED., *Music Education in Action.* Dubuque, Iowa: Wm. C. Brown Company, Publishers, pp. 51–56.

NYE, ROBERT E., "The Elementary Classroom Orchestra," *Educational Music Magazine,* (Nov-Dec., 1946).

TUFTS, NANCY P., *The Children's Choir,* Vol. 2. Philadelphia, Pa: Fortress Press. The children's choir, the boy choir, the handbell choir.

Autoharp and Guitar

Bay, Mel, *Mel Bay Guitar Series*. Kirkwood, Mo.: Mel Bay Publishing Company. Begins at the elementary school level; fourth grade and up.

The Many Ways to Play the Autoharp, Vols. 1, 2. Garden State Road, Union, New Jersey. New Oscar Schmidt-International, Inc. New.

Schearer, Aaron, Vol. I, *Classic Guitar*. New York: Franko Columbo, Publisher.

Silverman, Jerry, *Beginning the Folk Guitar*. New York: Oak Publishing Co.

60 Songs with 6 Chords for Guitar, Books I, II., New York, N.Y.: Consolidated Music Publishers.

Films

Elements of Composition (New York Wind Ensemble) melody, harmony, rhythm, and counterpoint, NET Film Service, Bloomington, Indiana.

Harmony in Music, Coronet Instructional Films, Chicago, Ill. Introduces harmony and chords. Grades 5–8. 12 minutes. Also from Craig Corporation.

Let's Get Together (harmony), EMC Corporation, St. Paul, Minn 55101. For age 10 and up.

Music, The Expressive Language, Sutherland Productions, 201 N. Occidental Blvd.. Los Angeles, Calif. 90026. Rhythm, melody, harmony, and learning to read music, Grades 4–6.

Two-Part Singing, Johnson Hunt Productions, Hollywood Calif. Grades 4–6. 20 minutes.

Refer to *Film Guide for Music Educators,* by Donald J. Shetler, Music Educators National Conference, Washington, D.C. for an annotated listing of films.

Making Music

BAMPTON, RUTH, *Sing With Me,* Theodore Presser Company, Bryn Mawr, Pa. For grades 4–6.

BECKMAN, FREDERICK, *Partner Songs; More Partner Songs,* Ginn and Company, New York. Combinable songs for grades 5–7.

BELL, LESLIE, *The Festival Song Book: One,* Mills Music, Inc., New York. For unaccompanied voices.

BURAKOFF, GERALD, AND LAWRENCE WHEELER, *Music Making in the Elementary School,* Hargail Music, Inc., New York, N.Y. 10019. Student's and Teacher's Editions. Uses recorder, voice, bells, and rhythm instruments.

CHEYETTE, IRVING, AND ALBERT RENNA, *Songs to Sing with Recreational Instruments,* Theodore Presser Company, Philadelphia, Pa.

COOPER, IRVIN, *Songs for Pre-Teentime,* Carl Fischer, Inc., New York. For grades 6–7.

EHRET, WALTER, *The Youthful Chorister,* Marks Music Corporation, New York. SA.

EISENKRAMER HENRY E., *Strum and Sing: Guitar in the Classroom,* Summy-Birchard Company, Evanston, Illinois.

GARY, CHARLES L., *The Study of Music in the Elementary School—A Conceptual Approach,* Music Educators National Conference, Washington, D.C. See the list of choral compositions pp. 162–3.

GEARHART, LIVINGSTON, *A Christmas Singing Bee,* Shawnee Press, Delaware Water Gap, Pa.

GOLDING, SALLY, EUGENE LONSTEIN AND JERROLD ROSS, *Melodies for Music Makers,* Carl Van Roy Co., Far Rockaway, N.Y. Part songs with melody and percussion instruments.

JUREY, EDWARD B., *Mills First Chorus Album,* Mills Music, Inc., New York, N.Y.

KENT, WILLYS PECK, *A Book of Descants,* Vantage Press, New York, N.Y. For grades 5–8.

KODALY, ZOLTAN, *Bicinia Hungarica* I, II; *Let Us Sing Correctly:* 101 exercises in intonation, Boosey & Hawkes, Oceanside, N.Y.

KRONE, BEATRICE, AND MAX KRONE, *Our First Songs to Sing with Descants* (for upper primary grades); *Very Easy Descants; Songs to Sing with Descants; Descants for Christmas; Our Third Book of Descants; From Descants to Trios; Descants and Rounds for Special Days,* Neil A. Kjos Music Company, Park Ridge, Illinois.

MARAIS, JOSEPH, *Marais and Miranda Two-Part Singing,* Charles Hansen Music Corporation, New York, N.Y. With optional obligato.

RHEA, LOIS, *Singing Is Fun,* Bourne, Inc., New York, N.Y.

SCOTT, RICHARD, *Clap, Tap and Sing* (for grades 2–5); *Sevenfold Choral Method* (for grades 5–7, Handy-Folio Music Company, Minneapolis, Minn.

SLIND, LLOYD H., *Melody, Rhythm, and Harmony; More Melody, Rhythm, and Harmony,* Mills Music, Inc., New York, N.Y.

SNYDER, ALICE M., *Sing and Strum,* Mills Music, Inc., New York, N.Y.

VANDRE, CARL, *Adventures in Harmony, Rhythm, and Song,* Handy-Folio Music Company, Minneapolis, Minn.

WIEDINMEYER, CLEMENT, *Play-Sing-Chord Along,* Shawnee Press, Delaware Water Gap, Pa.

Organ

Adventure in Keyboard, Lowrey Organ Company, Chicago, Ill. A ten-week program for elementary school students.

The Pointer System School Program, Pointer System, Inc., Winona, Minn. Includes instructional films.

Piano Books for Chording

Easy:

ECKSTEIN, MAXWELL, *Play It Now.* Carl Fisher.

FRISCH, FAY TEMPLETON, *The Play-Way to Music, Book Two*. Amsco Music Publications, Inc.

NEVIN, MARK, *Tunes You Like,* Books 1, 2, 3, 4. Schroeder and Gunther, Inc.

NEVIN, MARK, *Repertoire Album,* Book 1. Belwin, Inc.

STEINER, ERIC. *One, Four, Five*. Mills Music, Inc.; *Repertoire Album Book I,* Belwin, Inc.

Slightly more difficult:

BERMONT, GEORGES, *Play That Tune,* Books 1, 2. 3, 4. Musicord Publications.

115 Easy Piano Pieces and Folk Songs, Hansen Publications.

RICHTER, ADA, *Songs I Can Play*. M. Witmark and Sons.

STICKLES, WILLIAM, *Easy Hymns and Sacred Songs for the Piano*. Hansen Publications.

Recordings

Growing Up With Music, Bowmar Records, Glendale, Calif. Five albums based on the descant books of Beatrice and Max Krone.

Let's Sing a Round, Bowmar Records, Glendale, Calif.

Tune Your Autoharp, Rhythm Band, Inc., Fort Worth, Texas

Miscellaneous

DOOLIN, HOWARD, *A New Introduction to Music, Level Four:* Harmony, General Words and Music, Park Ridge, Ill.

11

tone qualities

When discussing tone qualities, the terms *tone color* and *timbre* (tam-bur) are often used. Tone color is a term borrowed from art; it implies that tone qualities are accomplished in music in the same general way the artist selects and combines colors in painting. Timbre is the French word for tone quality. Thus, tone quality, tone color, and timbre mean the same thing: the difference in sound between tones of the same pitch when produced by different instruments or voices. For example, the same pitch played on a violin, a trumpet, or a flute varies greatly in tone quality.

In music education of the past there was emphasis on identification of the sources of tone—the specific instrument or voice that produced it. Research has shown that very young children can learn to do such identification. However, merely trying to identify sources of tone has apparently been an unsuccessful approach to learning, since the majority of adults are surprisingly lacking in knowledge of musical instruments, and few can identify many with accuracy. The child's curiosity should be encouraged—what is there in the construction of a given instrument that produces its particular tone quality; how the player of the instrument can affect tone quality by his manner of playing; why particular tone qualities are selected by composers as the most suitable to enhance melodies and harmonies; the effect of range on tone quality; how tone quality interrelates with melody, harmony, texture, and form to make music more attractive. If the study of tone quality can be based on the reasons for the employment of certain instruments in a composition, the mechanical construction and the method of playing them, then the identification of the instrument or combinations of instruments should become part of a logical scheme of things rather than the memorizing of isolated facts that may be soon forgotten.

When a composer selects certain instruments or voices to convey the meaning of a composition, one of his reasons may be to imitate a sound of nature. Children should decide why the clarinet, flute, and piccolo are often chosen to imitate a bird by comparing these tones with those of other instruments. It should be obvious why a composer would choose the tympani rather than a tambourine to imitate a clap of thunder. There are interesting psychological associations that man has acquired in his listening experiences. When the French horn plays a certain type of melody, hunting may be brought to mind; when the oboe plays another type of melody, a pastoral scene, possibly with sheep and shepherd, is suggested. However, there is a vast amount of music that has no such associative meanings. When dealing with this, the study becomes one of discovery—why great composers select certain instruments to perform certain melodies, why these instruments suit these melodies better than other instruments, and how poorly some would sound if assigned the same melodies. Of course teachers know that once in a while children may disagree with great composers, yet when the children have logical reasons for their point of view, their judgment is respected. The Leonard Bernstein film, *What Does Orchestration Mean?* (McGraw-Hill Films, 1 hour, grades 5-up) deals with choosing "the right instruments at the right time in the right combination." Sometimes the sound of certain instruments and combinations of instruments can unite with melodies, harmonies, and textures to produce music suggestive of particular nations and localities. One example is music used on television and in films which is written to suggest the open spaces of the American West. This fascinating study requires ability to analyze, and it is complex for adults to manage. Therefore the teacher must keep his expectations within the limits of the musical background of his class and not expect more than this. However, every student should acquire some appreciation for the great contribution tone qualities supply to satisfying the need for contrast and variety in music. In fact, the very first attraction to music may come from beautiful tones that infants hear; parents are wise to plan these experiences in music for very young children.

In the primary grades there is an emphasis on the function of percussion instruments to produce sound effects, and the children are helped to explore the different types of tone qualities they can find by playing the instruments in different and experimental ways. This was discussed in Chapter 8; Selected Activity 10 at the end of that chapter illustrates this. Classification of percussion instruments according to their tone qualities, also suggested in Chapter 8, is part of the process of learning concepts relating to why and how certain sounds are produced by instruments and objects. This inquiry might not take place unless the teacher plans questions such as, "Does the woodblock sound the same as the rhythm sticks?" "Why do you suppose the sound is different?" "Look at each to see how it is made." "Yes, the woodblock is hollow; what difference might that make?" The ways of producing several different tone qualities on each instrument stress the importance of the method used to play them. For example, if a player uses two rapidly alternating mallets on a resonator bar, the continuous effect will be different from striking it once with one mallet; if three players each use two mallets in this way to produce a continuous-sounding chord, there will be a shimmering effect. From such beginnings, other instruments are introduced in relation to their sound and function. Several different ways of playing the Autoharp were presented in Chapter 10; children can find that playing on either side of the bars yields a difference in tone quality. The enjoyment of beauty of tone is good in itself, and should be experienced often. Then there should come a time when attention is called to how this beauty is produced. When children enter the fourth grade they should be ready for more specific analyses of tone qualities and their functions.

WHAT MAKES SOUND?

For sound to occur, something must vibrate. Young children can experiment with a rubber band stretched across an open-top box. When they pluck it, they can see it quiver at a fast rate, and they can hear that this vibration makes a sound. Every time the rubber band moves back and forth, a sound-wave (cycle) is formed of molecules of air. The sound waves go through the air to reach our eardrums, causing them to vibrate.

Nerves carry this sensation to the brain, and our stored experiences usually tell us what kind of a sound we are hearing. The children will find that if the rubber band is pulled out far, then let go, the vibration is wide and the sound is louder; if the band is pulled a short distance, the vibration is less and the sound is soft. Through further experimentation it will be found that the lowest pitch will be sounded when the entire band vibrates, and that higher pitches will be sounded when a finger is placed on the band to shorten the vibrating portion. Thus, children may be able to generalize that the length of a vibrating object influences its pitch; the longer, the lower; the shorter, the higher. It should also be discovered that a shorter length vibrates more rapidly than a longer length.

In some woodwind instruments—the flute and piccolo—the sound is produced by a vibrating column of air, while in others—the clarinet, oboe, and bassoon—the sound is produced by a vibrating reed. By taking a bottle, and blowing across its open top, a sound can be made that comes from vibrating air. By pouring water into the bottle, the children can discover that the longer the vibrating air column, the lower the pitch is; and the shorter the vibrating air column, the higher the pitch. To imitate the vibration of the double reed of the oboe and bassoon children can flatten one end of a soda straw, cut off the corners, and practice blowing into the straw through this flattened end. When brass instruments sound, the players' lips are the vibrating agent. Some children will be able to make a circular cup "mouthpiece" with their thumb and index finger, put their lips together on it and blow into it to produce a sound with their vibrating lips. They can watch large drumheads to see that striking them causes vibrations. They can examine a piano to discover that hammers strike the strings and cause them to vibrate. When string instruments are made to vibrate, the player either plucks the strings, as the children did the rubber band, or draws a bow across them. Perhaps the children can learn from a violinist that rosin is rubbed on the horse hair in the bow to increase the friction to make the strings vibrate. Perhaps they can answer the question, "Why is it that the player is never supposed to touch the horse hair of the bow?" (Because the oil in the skin transferred to the horse hair reduces the friction needed to make the string vibrate.) As this study continues with many different instruments, consideration should be given to the material the instrument is made of, the length of the instrument, the length of the vibrating section, and the existence of *resonating chambers,* such as those of the woodblock and the violin; all of these may affect tone quality. It might be noted that science tells us it should not matter what kind of material is used for instruments having vibrating air columns. However, many musicians continue to want recorders made of wood rather than of plastic, frequently arguing about the virtues of wood and metal versus synthetic materials. Other topics of scientific or historical interest include the *vibrato* as it is used by instrumentalists and singers, the overtone series and its relation to tone quality, and the historical development of modern instruments; these topics can be investigated by older children. Some may be interested in the relation between the clavichord, harpsichord, and piano, in the relation of the viols and the modern string family, and in the evolution of the valve instruments.

There are teachers who plan experiences for children with such stress on qualities of sound and dynamics that temporarily it is necessary to exclude melody and rhythm. Children are encouraged to create new sounds with familiar instruments, such as placing materials of different types (pieces of metal, paper, felt pads) on piano wires, and combining these experimental tone qualities with percussion instruments like the gong and woodblock to create a background for a poem or choric reading. Some teachers challenge children to create new tone qualities by taking sounds from their environment, taping these, and arranging them in a suitable order. An example might be lunchroom sounds, in which a short piece would utilize the sound of feet, talking, trays being stacked, the bell, and so on. These could be varied by playing the tape at different speeds and retaping them. Another way might be to have children create a plan for using such sounds, then have the class imitate or reproduce them from an experimental score in the same general way that orchestra instruments imitate. Other ideas for children to work with could include sounds in the morning on the way to school, sounds of a shopping trip, sounds of the city, sounds of the country, and sounds of interesting tone qualities with no story.

Such an approach is used to involve children in the sounds of experimental composition. Electronic sounds are included, often using the assistance of a tape recorder; tone generators borrowed from the science department contribute to the many types of tone qualities composers use today. Continuing the emphasis on contemporary music, these teachers may prefer *Variations for Orchestra* by the contemporary composer Ginastera to the more traditional materials for later experiences in instrument identification.

Voices and Instruments

VOICES

Earlier in this book, an activity was recommended in which young children learned to listen to the speaking and singing voices of their unseen classmates to identify them in a game situation. Children will notice that some voices are higher or lower pitched than others, and that some are clearer in tone quality than others. They can generalize that every person has a different, and perhaps unique, quality in his voice. While the voices of older children are best identified in terms of high, medium, and low, the terms for adult voices—soprano, alto, tenor, baritone and bass—can be introduced to them as high and low in the instance of women and men, respectively. Suitable recordings may be used to compare the qualities of each. If possible, the children should hear a soprano and an alto sing the same song in the same range, then discuss the difference in tone quality that will be revealed. The same can be done with a tenor and a bass. They will be interested when a man and a woman sing the same song an octave apart, and they should try to describe the tone quality in each of the above experiences. For eleven-year-olds these adult classifications may be subdivided further. For example, there are subdivisions of the soprano voice: *coloratura* (the highest), *dramatic, lyric,* and *mezzo*—which is another term for alto.[1] The *contralto* is a low alto, the lowest female voice. The male voice falls into three major classifications, tenor, baritone, and bass. The baritone is the middle range male voice. There are subdivisions of the male voices, but there is little need to enlarge upon this. Perhaps the essential knowledge consists of knowing the five major classifications and that each of these can be further subdivided. Each voice type has a characteristic tone quality.

The tone qualities of combinations of voices are studied by ten and eleven-year-olds. They should know the duet, trio, quartet, and quintet (and possibly the sextette, octette, and nonette), as well as the different types of choral groups—men's, women's, and mixed—and be able to recognize the sound of choral music, choruses singing sacred music, and choruses singing secular music. These small and large ensembles should be compared to instrumental groups; for example, children should be aware of similarities and differences between a vocal quartet of soprano,

---

[1] Some consider the alto range to be one wholestep lower than the mezzo.

alto, tenor, and bass, and the string quartet of first violin, second violin, viola, and cello.

After the children learn that each child has a somewhat unique voice, unlike anyone else's, it is a challenge for them to work to blend their voices—to try to sound together more like one voice than many. They can select a child whose voice is pleasing to them, and one which they agree is a type of tone quality worthy for the entire class to imitate. Then this child will sing a tone or a few tones alone. After this, one other child joins the first, and the game is to make the two voices sound as much as possible like one voice. Then another child joins the first two, and this continues until all the class is trying to blend in an attempt to unify the tone quality.

Recordings to illustrate voices are usually not found in the educational collections. Examples of arias from operas are often used. The following are a few examples:

"Bell Song" from *Lakmé* (Delibes)	Coloratura Soprano
"Queen of the Night Arias" from *The Magic Flute* (Mozart)	
Bachianas Brasilieras No. 5 (Villa-Lobos)	Lyric Soprano
"Depuis le jour" from *Louise* (Charpentier)	
"Habanera" from *Carmen* (Bizet)	Mezzo Soprano (Alto)
"Barcarolle" from *Tales of Hoffman* (Offenbach)	
"He Was Despised" from the *Messiah* (Handel)	Contralto
"Dido's Lament" from *Dido and Aeneas* (Purcell)	
"Song of India" from *Sadko* (Rimsky-Korsakoff)	Tenor
"Celeste Aida" from *Aida* (Verdi)	
"Largo al factotum" from *Barber of Seville* (Rossini)	Baritone
(see Making Music Your Own, Book 6, recorded)	
"Toreador Song" from *Carmen* (Bizet)	Bass
"Mephisto's Serenade" from *Faust* (Gounod)	

The children should compare the different voices, verbalize about the tone qualities, and in the process expand their descriptive vocabularies. The teacher's role is to have the children explore, discover, identify, compare, evaluate, and describe tone qualities, telling them only what is necessary to help them learn for themselves.

STRINGS

The string family of the orchestra is made up of the violin, viola, cello, and double bass (string bass, bass viol). They are approximately the same shape except that the violin is the smallest, the viola somewhat larger, the cello so large that the player must sit in a chair and rest the instrument on the floor, and the double bass so very large that the player ordinarily stands up to play it. These instruments are called "the first family of the orchestra." Study of the seating plan of an orchestra will explain one reason why. Listening carefully to symphonic music will reveal that the strings are truly the backbone of the orchestra, with the brass, woodwinds, and percussion sections assisting by adding many contrasting tone qualities.

The string instruments produce a variety of tone qualities within their family. The violin, viola, and cello use *vibrato,* a slight varying of pitch produced by rapid movement of the left hand while pressing down on a string. The term *con sordino* means with a mute; when the mute is attached to the bridge, the device that supports the strings, the tone becomes smaller and more nasal. These instruments produce *harmonics,* higher pitches of reduced resonance with flute-like tones that occur when the player touches, but does not press down on a string, and bows very lightly on that string. When these instruments are played by plucking strings, this is called *pizzicato*; it produces still another tone quality. A short, fast stroke played in the middle of the bow with a slight bounce from the string is *spiccato* bowing. Double stops, the playing and bowing of two strings at once, gives another effect. The *tremulo* produces a rather tense impression; it is done by moving the bow back and forth a short distance at an extremely fast rate. A flute-like effect is made by *sur la touche,* a slight bowing over the finger board, and a glassy effect, *sul ponticello,* is made by bowing very close to the bridge. An unusual orchestral effect is the *col legno,* which means using the wood of the bow rather than the hair. The *glissando* is produced by playing scale passages with many tiny movements of the left hand to change the pitch in almost a sliding effect. The normal tone qualities of these instruments can be described in various ways. A beginning can be made with these:

violin: The string instrument that most resembles the qualities of the human voice; great versatility in range of expression; extremely sensitive tone qualities.

viola: a veiled and nasal quality; darker in color than the violin.

cello: the bass violin; a deep masculine voice of soulful quality.

double bass: very low, heavy tone quality; it often sounds one octave lower than the cello.

Children, older students, and adults should be asked to demonstrate these instruments. While films and recordings are helpful, nothing takes the place of a good, well-qualified, live performer.

The harp is another string instrument; the player is seated with the string section of the orchestra. It can be compared to the piano in some ways; it has a range of six octaves and a fifth. There are seven foot pedals, each of which can be pressed down two notches, each notch representing one halfstep. The harp makes splashing, cascading effects. The *glissando* is used frequently to produce these. Harmonics are sounded by placing the palm of the hand in the middle of the strings; this places the pitch one octave higher than normal, making possible a quality of mystery. A different effect is made by plucking strings close to the sounding board.

The keyboard instruments include the piano, harpsichord, and celesta. The tone qualities of the piano should be thoroughly explored; special experimental effects can be made. In the piano, felt hammers strike the strings; the harpsichord strings are made to vibrate by means of a plucking mechanism. The celesta is basically a percussion instrument. Its keyboard causes hammers to strike the steel bars of what approximates a type of glockenspiel (bell set). The tone is of unusual light quality; a famed celesta piece is "Dance of the Sugar Plum Fairy" from the *Nutcracker Suite* of Tschaikovsky. The harpsichord—older than the piano—was the favorite keyboard instrument at the time of Haydn and Mozart. Its tone quality is considerably lighter than the piano, and it has less expressive capability. The Young People's Record 411, *Said the Piano to the Harpsichord,* is informative, and it communicates to children.

Stringed instruments not part of the symphony orchestra include the guitar, banjo, ukulele, mandolin, lyre, zither, Autoharp, and others. These should be explored to identify the tone qualities they produce. There is excellent guitar literature, much of it from Spanish sources; children should know of Segovia and others who play the classical guitar. Bowmar 84 includes a guitar selection.

Examples of recordings portraying tone qualities of the symphony strings include:

Scheherazade Suite, Rimsky-Korsakov	violin cadenzas
Flight of the Bumblebee, Rimsky-Korsakov, Bowmar 53	violin
Eine kleine Nachtmusik, Mozart, Adventures in Music 4 v. 1	strings
The Wonderful Violin, Moore, Young People's Record 311	violin
Danse Macabre, Saint-Saens, Bowmar 59	viola plays second theme

"The Swan," *Carnival of the Animals,* Saint-Saëns, Bowmar 59, Adventures in Music 3 v. 2 — cello

"Elephants," *Carnival of the Animals,* Saint-Saëns, Bowmar 51 — double bass

"Jimbo's Lullaby," Debussy, Bowmar 51 — double bass

Suggested films include:

Listening to Good Music: The String Quartet	Encyclopaedia Britannica Films
The String Choir	Encyclopaedia Britannica Films
The String Trio	Coronet Instructional Films
The Trio	World Artists, Inc.
String Sounds	Churchill Films

WOODWINDS

The woodwind instruments not only blend well with the strings of the orchestra, but they add other interesting tone qualities which can be used in the performance of melodies or subsidiary parts that contribute to the effect the composer plans to achieve. It is of interest that the wood-winds in the concert band seem to take the place of the strings in the orchestra; for example, when one looks at a concert band, he finds many clarinets instead of many violins.

The modern flute is a descendant of the recorder. It is a *transverse* flute, which means that one holds it at right angles to the mouth and blows across a hole in the side of it. The recorder is an end-blown flute. While it is said that the best recorders are made of wood, the modern flute is generally made of silver. Its tone quality varies with the range. Low pitches are relatively big and somewhat breathy, while higher tones become increasingly bright and penetrating with ascending pitches. An impressive flute solo at the beginning of a composition that emphasizes tone qualities is in Debussy's *Afternoon of a Faun,* followed by colorful effects on a harp. (Remember that a *faun* is a creature from rural Roman mythology, a man principally human, but with a goat's tail, pointed ears, short horns, and sometimes cloven feet.) Another favorite composition featuring flutes is Tschaikovsky's "Dance of the Toy Flutes," from the *Nutcracker Suite,* Bowmar 58. The piccolo is a small flute, half as long, and pitched one octave higher. It plays the highest pitches of any instrument in the woodwind family, and its tone quality is exceedingly brilliant and penetrating. A favorite piccolo solo is in Sousa's *Stars and Stripes Forever,* Bowmar 54. Others are found in the "Chinese Dance" from Tschaikovsky's *Nutcracker Suite,* Bowmar 59, and "Entrance of the Little Fauns" by Pierné, Bowmar 54.

The most commonly found clarinet is the B♭ instrument; some of the children who are studying this single reed instrument can demonstrate it. There is a family of clarinets, with the E♭ being smaller and higher in pitch, and the alto and bass being lower, as would be expected. There are other less common clarinets, including the clarinet in A and the double bass in B♭, the latter being an octave lower than the bass clarinet. The B♭ clarinet has three registers, each with a different tone quality. The lowest is rich and full-bodied, the middle is sometimes breathy and is the most difficult to make sound well; the highest is brilliant and versatile. This variety of tone qualities gives the clarinet a good deal of breadth of expression. Examples include Prokofiev's *Peter and the Wolf,* Saint-Saëns' "Cuckoo in the Deep Woods," from *Carnival of the Animals,* Bowmar 51, and the second movement of Rimsky-Korsakov's *Scheherazade Suite.* Clarinets are made of wood, ebonite, and occasionally of metal.

The saxophone is seldom used in orchestras, but widely used in bands and dance bands. There is a family of saxophones, including soprano, alto, tenor, baritone, and bass. The most commonly seen are in the following order, alto, tenor, and baritone. These are in most school bands and in many dance bands. Although they have cane reeds like clarinets, they are made of metal. The tone quality of the instrument is such that it blends with other woodwinds or brass instruments. This tone quality can be changed markedly by the player, thus can be sweet, raucous, or brusque as desired in certain types of jazz and dance music.

The oboe family includes all the double reed instruments. The oboe is about the same size as the B♭ clarinet. The English horn is an alto oboe and the bassoon is the bass instrument of the family. The contrabassoon is an octave lower than the ordinary bassoon. The oboe tone quality is often described as nasal, pastoral, oriental, and plaintive. *Peter and the Wolf* demonstrates the oboe tone quality, as does the second movement of Tschaikovsky's *Symphony No. 4* and his "Puss in Boots and the White Cat," from the *Sleeping Beauty,* Adventures in Music 3 v. 1. The English horn has a pear-shaped bell which is one source of its melancholy tone quality. Examples of its sound appear in the "Largo" of Dvořák's *New World Symphony,* Sibelius' *Swan of Tuonela,* and "Puss in Boots and the White Cat," mentioned above. Children should discover how the bassoon is built, since the design permits it to have a great length of tube. (The contra-bassoon has over sixteen feet.) Besides serving as a bass instrument, its tone blends well with the French horn and enables it to play solo passages of distinction. While its tone quality is rather even except at extreme high and low ranges, it has a certain versatility which enables it to project plaintive, gruff, and humorous impressions. It can play over a wide range with legato and staccato articulation. Examples are found in "In the Hall of the Mountain King," from *Peer Gynt Suite*, by Grieg, Adventures in Music 3 v. 2, and Bowmar 59; "Berceuse" from Stravinsky's *Firebird Suite*; the second movement of Tschaikovsky's *Symphony No. 4*; and in *Rondo for Bassoon and Orchestra*, Children's Record Guild 1009. The grandfather theme in *Peter and the Wolf* is played by a contra-bassoon.

Additional variety in the performance of woodwind instruments is attained by legato and staccato tonguing, as well as double, triple, and flutter tonguing. Double tonguing can be explained by letting out the breath with a series of repeated "t-t" tonguings; triple tonguing is a repeated "t-k-t." These are of particular importance in flute playing.

The film *Introducing the Woodwinds,* Indiana University, introduces the instruments of the woodwind quintet to children. These are flute (and piccolo), clarinet, oboe, bassoon, and French horn—the brass instrument that possesses a tone quality which blends with both the woodwinds and the brasses. *Wind Sounds,* Churchill Films, treats of woodwinds and brasses.

BRASSES

Children can quickly find a major difference between a bugle and a trumpet, or cornet, in that the bugle lacks valves. They can then discern why the bugle can play only bugle calls whereas the other instruments can play both bugle calls and melodies. They should study the valve and its length of tubing to find what valves do to the length of the air column, and how much each valve lowers a pitch. They will see that the cornet is shorter than the trumpet, and they will hear that its tone quality is less brilliant. The player has a great deal to do with the sound of these instruments; he can produce tones of both coarse and pleasing qualities at will. The baritone is a larger instrument found in bands; the melophone is an instrument about the size of a French horn but which lacks the golden quality of the French horn tone; it is used for marching bands and for students who may later progress to the more difficult French horn. The tubing of the French horn should be examined to try to determine how long the instrument would be if it were a straight horn like the alphorn, a folk instrument from the Alps. Both tone quality and pitch are influenced by a practice called *stopping,* which is the insertion of the hand into the bell. Mutes made of metal, wood, or cardboard change the tone qualities of the cornet, trumpet, French horn, and trombone. Both school band and dance band players of trumpet and trombone can demonstrate their several types of mutes in the classroom. While the cornet and trumpet have the most commanding tones, the French horn has the tone that blends with other instruments the best, although it can be bold and brassy when this is desired. The tones of these instruments can be varied by legato and staccato tonguing, double and triple tonguing, flutter tonguing, and the use of mutes. Four sizes of trombones are used in the symphony orchestra, the most common being the tenor. This instrument and an occasional bass trombone will be seen in school bands. The trombone and baritone have larger mouthpieces than those of the cornet, trumpet, and French horn; this results in a tone quality of less brilliance, but of more dignity and solemnity. Children will be interested in how the trombone's slide shortens or lengthens the air column in place of the valve mechanism. Because of the slide, trombones can produce a *portamento,* which is a gliding from one tone to another through all degrees of pitches. The lowest pitched instruments of the brass family are the tubas and sousaphones. The sousaphone is the instrument carried on the shoulder of its players in marching bands; its huge shiny bell makes an impressive appearance. New plastic materials are being used today in place of metal in order to reduce the weight the player must carry. The tuba player is seated in the orchestra and appears occasionally in the band. As expected, these bass instruments have the largest mouthpieces. As told in the children's recording, *Tubby the Tuba,* Decca Records, the tuba seldom plays melodies. Instead, it normally supports the band as the primary low bass instrument, and it assists the double basses of the orchestra. Its tone is deep and its execution somewhat ponderous.

Examples of brass instrument tone qualities include:

"Finale," *William Tell Overture,* Rossini, Adventures in Music 3 v. 1; Bowmar 76	Trumpet
"Changing of the Guard," *Carmen Suite,* Bizet, Adventures in Music 3 v. 2	
The King's Trumpet, Children's Record Guild 5040	
Peter and the Wolf, Prokofiev	French horn

"Nocturne," *Midsummer Night's Dream,* Mendelssohn

"Third Movement," *Symphony No. 3,* Brahms

"Prelude to Act 3," *Lohengrin,* Wagner   Trombone

Stars and Stripes Forever, Sousa, Adventures in Music
    4 v. 2; Bowmar 54

"Bydlo," *Pictures at an Exhibition,* Moussorgsky,
    Adventures in Music 2; Bowmar 82   Tuba

"Departure," *Winter Holiday,* Prokofiev, Adventures
    in Music 2

PERCUSSION

Example of percussion instrument tone qualities include:

Danse Macabre, Saint-Saëns

"Dagger Dance," *Natoma,* Herbert, Adventures in
    Music 3 v. 1   Cymbals, Drums

Semper Fidelis, Sousa, Adventures in Music 3 v. 2   Cymbals, Drums

"In the Hall of the Mountain King," *Per Gynt Suite,*
    Grieg Adventures in Music 3 v. 2; Bowmar 59   Drums, Timpani

"Tarantella," *Fantastic Toy Shop,* Rossini, Adventures
    in Music 3 v. 2; Bowmar 56   Tambourine

The Alligator and the Coon, Thomson, Adventures in
    Music 3 v. 2   Xylophone

Said the Piano to the Harpsichord, Young People's   Piano, Harpsi-
    Record 411   chord

"Pianists," *Carnival of the Animals,* Saint-Saëns,
    Bowmar 51   Piano

Chopin, Liszt, Debussy piano pieces; Grieg and
    Rachmaninoff concertos   Piano

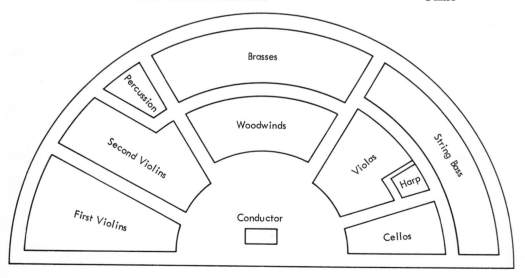

Films:

Percussion Group	Encyclopaedia Britannica Films
Percussion, Pulse of Music	Indiana University
Percussion Sounds	Churchill Films

Band and Orchestra Instruments in the Elementary School

Clarinets, trombones, cornets, saxophones, and other large instruments can be played by children in the intermediate grades. However, their tones are too powerful to blend with the light voices of children, thus they are ill-suited for inclusion in a classroom orchestra that is associated with the singing program. The authors of some of the music series books have nonetheless included some interesting uses for these instruments. These include instrumental solos, duets, descants, and true orchestrations of some of the songs. It appears that the best use for these orchestrations is in the playing of instrumental introductions and/or accompaniments for songs on special programs or for large vocal groups.

Lessons given on these instruments by the teacher of instrumental music should be scheduled in the special interest period when possible. The temporary withdrawal of some children from the classroom may be a disruption unless the teacher can make plans in accordance with it. Much of the irritation that sometimes comes when children leave the classroom for these lessons can be avoided if all teachers concerned have an opportunity to plan the instrumental music schedule co-operatively.

Teachers of general music in grades four, five, and six can encourage membership in band and orchestra classes. Preliminary steps toward this end can include bulletin board displays of instruments and instrumentalists; presenting recordings, films, and film strips that illustrate instruments and families of instruments in ways that attract the interest of the age group; displaying attractive catalogues obtained from instrument manufacturers; displaying commercially produced charts of orchestra instruments; and making available to the children books that include pictures of children playing instruments, such as *Tune Up: Instruments of the Orchestra and Their Players,* by Harriett Huntington (Doubleday and Company). The general music teacher and the specialist in instrumental music should plan together times when the specialist can speak to the class and when he and children can demonstrate instruments. The sending of notices to parents and the planning for parent-teacher conferences about the selection, rental, or purchase of instruments should also be done by joint consideration of the general teacher and the specialist. A time should be decided upon when the specialist will bring instruments to the class and permit children to try them. (This will necessitate use of a germicide.) The specialist should explain to the class why certain children are suited to the playing of certain instruments, but not for others. He should demonstrate the importance of finger size, length, and flexibility in playing the clarinet, for example, and the importance of being able to "buzz" the lips in playing the trumpet. Teeth formation should be revealed as important. For instance, a small overbite is preferable for small brass instruments while a large overbite is acceptable for bass and baritone. The instrumental teacher should avoid teaching fingering in a way that confuses "finger numbers" with scale-tone numbers. To say that A is played with the first and second fingers is correct, but to say that "A is two" is confusing to the child who is learning numeral names of scale tones. Both the general music teacher and the specialist can utilize instrumental scores in series books, and they can plan some of these correlated activities together. Singing in the instrumental class can assist in pitch accuracy on the instruments and in the growth of balanced musicianship. To sing, then play rote melodies demands and teaches musical skills. The instrumental score can at times be sung.

The child most likely to succeed in band and orchestra will be one who is sufficiently mature physically to play the instrument, who is generally musical, and who possesses reliability and perseverance.

Some Activities and Suggestions for Lesson Plans

General

The many recordings, pictures, and films that assist in the study of instruments can be utilized for teachers' specific purposes.

Children can identify and compare the recorded tone qualities of the orchestra, band, and chorus.

When studying the tone quality of any instrument, the children should be helped to explore the physical characteristics of that instrument in order to discern the effect of its mechanical features on that tone quality.

Emphasize the *function* of various tone qualities in communicating moods and ideas.

Study the many folk instruments and their tone qualities. One reference is Album L 24, *Folk Instruments of the World,* Follett Publishing Company, with an explanatory folder that includes drawings of the instruments.

Identify and compare the tone qualities and the make-up of various vocal and instrumental ensembles: duets, trios, quartets, quintets, sextets, etc.

Investigate the seating arrangement of a band. Draw it, and compare this plan with that of the orchestra.

Research the organ as a class of instruments. Listen to masterworks for the organ; describe the tone qualities of organs and compare them with other instruments.

Select four instruments or sound producers, each of distinctive tone quality. Have groups of children combine them in a musical score to experiment with their sounds singly and in combination. It may be necessary to devise an original notation system if the sounds are unusual.

Discuss and theorize differences between tone and noise in relation to listening to examples planned (perhaps on tape) by the teacher. Suggest that some children research the difference; discuss possible functions of tone and noise.

When children examine a band or orchestra score that they borrow from the instrumental music teacher, they will find that instrument parts are written in different keys. They may find that some instruments are built in different keys. By experimenting with playing written notes on instruments and comparing the resulting pitch with the piano or bells, they can discover that when B♭ instruments play written C, the pitch is that of B♭, and when E♭ instruments play C, the pitch sounded is E♭. The teacher could plan a discrepant event by asking children who play instruments to all play the same song from a series book. This would be one way to discover which instruments are "transposing" instruments and which are not.

Plan for advanced older children to explore acoustics. Help them study resonance, harmonics, the overtone series, partials, and vibrato. Relate music and science.

Arrange to have children hear some electronic music. Have them discuss the tone qualities they hear, and try to determine the function of this type of music in some television programs.

Children can either contrast or compare the tone qualities and the instrumentation of the military band, the symphonic band, and the dance band.

Arrange for a group of children to create a dance based upon the various instruments heard in a colorful symphonic recording.

If possible, let children work with an *oscilloscope,* an electric machine which pictures the sound waves produced by tone qualities. Let them compare the sound waves of the flute, violin, and trumpet.

Percussion

In order to increase sensitivity to tone qualities, have young children identify sources of sound in tone games. Later, the teacher can make the game more complex by producing somewhat different qualities of sound from the same object; different sounds can come from the same percussion instrument by striking it or holding it in different ways. Children may discover that instruments should normally be held in such a way that they are free to vibrate.

Children can classify percussion instruments in accordance with the type of sound. Which instruments click? Ring? Jingle? Swish? Rattle? Boom? Which have sounds that are light? Heavy? Medium? Can we arrange the instruments according to how light and how heavy their sounds are? This activity leads to relating instruments to their functions in accompanying songs and recordings.

Children can decide upon the suitability of specific instruments for sound effects. They can be selected by young children to correspond to characters in stories such as *The Three Bears, Three Billy Goats Gruff,* and MacDowell's composition, *Of a Tailor and a Bear.*

Older children can use adult classifications, and might decide to group instruments as follows:

membrane:	tympani (kettledrum)	*solid:*	cymbals, regular and antique
	snare drum (side drum)		triangle
	hand drum		tuning fork
	tambourine		castanets
	bass drum		claves
hollow:	wood block	*keyboard:*	glockenspiel and bells
	tubular bells		celesta
	marimba		xylophone
	bottles		piano
	glass and pottery bowls		chimes

Let children suggest possible classifications; there are many more.

Listen to a recording of a gamelan orchestra from Indonesia. Then create an imitation which will require a conductor to bring in different sections and to have other sections stop playing at times. Groups of children select, or are assigned percussion instruments of contrasting tone qualities. Each group will repeat a very short rhythm pattern as long as the conductor desires. For example, long-short-long could be one such pattern. A bell set or other melody instrument could be used to improvise a tune to sound along with various combinations of the groups. Have children evaluate the experiment.

Voices

Plan for young children to listen to different speaking and singing voices in the class. With eyes closed, can individuals in the class identify these voices? Play listening games such as this, emphasizing the uniqueness in the vocal sounds of each person. Let children classify the speaking voices and relate these to choric reading with dark, medium and light voices speaking their appropriate lines.

Involve the class in vocal tone blending as described in this chapter.

Combinations of singing voices produce different tone qualities. Challenge children to identify types of choruses, and ensembles such as duets, trios, and quartets from recorded examples.

Interest older children in studying the assignment of parts in part-singing. They will soon meet the problem of range versus tone quality in the cases of some children.

The preceding activity may lead to a study of the mature voice and its classifications.

Strings

Plan that children discover the relation of length and thickness of strings to pitch and tone quality. Compare the sounds made by plucking and bowing a string.

Plan that children learn to identify the sound of the string quartet. Have them compare its instruments and parts to the soprano, alto, tenor, and bass in vocal music.

Have the class explore the piano and harp; have them compare the instruments in appearance and in tone quality. Ask the children to solve the problem of why they do not sound alike.

Have a player, either live or on a recording or film, demonstrate staccato, legato, and spiccato as matters of tone duration, and have the class discuss these with relation to tone quality.

Involve the children with comparing the piano and the harpsichord, both from the standpoints of tone quality and the mechanical features which produce the differences in quality. Challenge them to identify them in recorded music.

Have the children answer the question of the relative importance of the strings in the orchestra.

Have the children classify string instruments. First they will decide on the possible classifications. These may include bowed, plucked, stroked or strummed, and keyboard. Include folk instruments.

Ask the children to answer puzzles such as, "Why do you think that Saint-Saëns chose the cello to play the melody of "The Swan?" "Can you think of another instrument that would do equally as well or even better with that melody?" Plan similar experiences involving other instruments.

Woodwinds, Flute Type

Young children should have opportunity for limited exploration of simple types of blowing instruments. One, two, or three well-sounded tones can be unilized with some songs and very simple improvisations.

Older children can learn to play nearly all simple blowing instruments such as the Song Flute, Tonette, Flutophone, Symphonette, and Melody Flute; the latter two are slightly more difficult to play than the first three. The Melody Flute sounds much like the real flute when played well.

The recorder, the easiest to play of the adult instruments, can be played by some. Eventually, the family of recorders can be explained through picture, recorded sound, and real-life viewing, if possible.

The flute and piccolo can be introduced by sight and sound, and by the function each has in selected music. Example: Is there any other instrument that can play the piccolo part in Sousa's *Stars and Stripes Forever*? The tone qualities of these instruments can be compared with those of the children's small winds. Ask the children to describe the difference in sound of the flute and piccolo. (The flute is said to have the "coolest" tone of any of the instruments.)

Woodwinds, Reed Type

Reed instruments possess powerful tone colors that can either blend with other instruments or be used in solo passages. Have children continue to explore the function of each instument, and especially when a composer selects it for an important part of a composition.

Have children describe the various tone colors resulting from combinations of these instruments both within the woodwind family and with other instruments.

Brasses

Use appropriate suggestions from the preceding pages for the study of these instruments and their tone qualities which make them unique. Compare their tone qualities with those of the other instruments. Have children find out which are transposing instruments and which are not; emphasize the functions of each in communicating moods and ideas. Continue to ask why a composer selected the brasses or a particular brass instrument for a prominent part in a composition. Study the effect of valves, slides, and the tension and relaxing of the lip muscles on pitch. Remember that some of Wagner's music displays brass tone colors well. Be sure children find out why composers often have the French horn play in combination with the woodwinds while they do not use other brass instruments in this manner. Have them listen to recordings in which this instrument plays with woodwinds to seek their answer.

SOME CUMULATIVE BEHAVIORAL OBJECTIVES

The child

selects percussion instruments for his accompaniments which have tone qualities appropriate to the music, as shown by . . . . .

identifies common musical instruments by sight and sound by . . . . .

relates tone qualities to communicative and expressive ideas by . . . . .

utilizes tone color in playing instruments, as shown by . . . . .

identifies orchestral instruments by . . . . .

identifies characteristic instrumental and vocal groups by . . . . .

associates specific tone qualities with some cultural, national, or composer's style by . . . . .

shows his understanding of the scientific basis for the difference in tone qualities by . . . . .

shows his understanding of the communicative functions of various tone qualities by . . . . .

can classify voices and instruments according to tone quality and range, as shown by . . . . .

For writing lesson plans, refer to the following as needed:

1. The Developmental Characteristics and Implications Chart in Chapter 3.
2. The Structure of Music Chart, Tone Qualities section, in Chapter 6.
3. Types of thinking and questions, principles of learning in Chapter 4.
4. The Scope and Sequence Chart in the Appendix.
5. The environment for learning and necessary routines for teaching in Chapter 5.

SOME ADDITIONAL GENERALIZATIONS

The ways in which instruments are played result in different tone qualities from the same instrument.

Applying different tone qualities to the same melody produces variety and contrast.

Instruments can be played in combination to create a vast variety of tone qualities.

REFERENCES

Books for Teachers

COPLAND, AARON, *What to Listen for in Music,* rev. ed. New York, N.Y.: Mentor Books, 1964, Chapter 7.

GARY, CHARLES L., *The Study of Music in the Elementary School—A Conceptual Approach,* Music Educators National Conference, Washington D.C., 1967, pp. 136–56.

SWANSON, BESSIE R., *Planning Music in the Education of Children.* Belmont, Calif.: Wadsworth Publishing Company, Inc., 1965, pp. 62–67.

WALTON, CHARLES, *Teaching Guide* (for Instruments of the Orchestra Recordings), RCA-Victor, Camden, New Jersey.

Books for Children

BALET, JAN, *What Makes an Orchestra*. New York, N.Y.: Oxford University Press, 1951. A book to use in preparation for concerts.

BRITTEN, BENJAMIN, AND IMOGENE HOLST, *The Wonderful World of Music*. New York, N.Y.: Garden City Books, 1958. An unusually attractive book.

BUNCHE, JANE, *Introduction to the Instruments of the Orchestra*. New York, N.Y.: Golden Press, 1962.

EDGERLY, BEATRICE, *From the Hunter's Bow*. New York, N.Y.: G. P. Putnam's Sons, 1942. A child's reference book on instruments.

FROST, BRUNO, *A Child's Book of Music Makers*. Chicago, Ill.: Maxton Publishing Company, 1957.

HUNTINGTON, HARRIET E., *Tune Up*. New York, N.Y.: Doubleday & Company, Inc., 1952. Includes illustrations of children playing instruments.

LACEY, MARION, *Picture Book of Musical Instruments,* Lothrop, Lee & Shepard Co., 1952. Includes historical sketches.

LAPRADE, ERNEST, *Alice in Orchestralia,* Doubleday & Company, Inc., 1948.

MONTGOMERY, ELIZABETH RIDER, *The Story Behind Musical Instruments*. New York, N.Y.: Dodd, Mead & Co., 1953.

POSELL, ELSA, *This Is An Orchestra*. Boston, Mass.: Houghton Mifflin, 1950.

RICHARDSON, ALLEN L., *Tooters, Tweeters, Strings, & Beaters*. New York, N.Y.: Grosset & Dunlap. 1964. Amusing for all grades; suitable for primary children.

SMITH, PETER, *First Book of the Orchestra,* Franklin Watts, New York, N.Y., 1963.

Films

Refer to SHETLER, DONALD J., *Film Guide for Music Educators,* Music Educators National Conference, Washington, D.C.

Move To Music, Modern Talking Picture Service, 1212 Avenue of the Americas, New York, N.Y. 10036. A motivational film to interest elementary school children in studying instruments. 25 minutes. Free.

Toot, Whistle, Boom, and Plunk, Walt Disney Productions, Educational Film Division, Burbank, Calif. A cartoon about the origin and development of instruments. For all elementary grades.

What Does Orchestration Mean? Leonard Bernstein, McGraw-Hill Films. Grade 5-up. One hour. Haydn, Brahms, Debussy, Stravinsky, Gershwin, Copland. Also inquire of nearest Bell Telephone Office.

Filmstrips (with recordings)

Instruments of the Symphony Orchestra, a series of six filmstrips, Jam Handy Organization, 2821 East Grand Blvd., Detroit, Mich.

Listen to a Rainbow, EMC Corporation, St. Paul, Minn. 55101. Deals with tone color. For age 10 and up.

Meet the Instruments, Bowmar Records, Inc., 622 Rodier Drive, Glendale, Calif. 91201. Two filmstrips. 25 laminated pictures available.

Musical Books for Young People, a series of six filmstrips, Society for Visual Education, Chicago, Ill. Strings, brass, woodwinds, percussion, keyboard, and folk instruments. Intermediate and junior high.

Pictures and Charts

Construction of the Grand Piano; Evolution of the Grand Piano, Baldwin Piano Company, Cincinnati, Ohio. Also pamphlet, Story of the Baldwin Piano.

Instruments of the Band and Orchestra, F. A. Owen Publishing Co. (publishers of *Instructor Magazine*). Pictures of children playing instruments.

Instruments of the Orchestra Charts, J. W. Pepper and Son, 1423 Vine Street, Philadelphia, Pa. 22 charts for use with RCA recordings.

Meet the Instruments, Bowmar Records, 622 Rodier Drive, Glendale, Calif. 91201. 25 laminated posters.

Musical Instrument Pictures, C. G. Conn, Ltd., Elkhart, Indiana.

Musical Instruments, York Band Instrument Company, Grand Rapids, Michigan.

Range Chart for Band and Orchestra Instruments, C. G. Conn, Ltd., Elkhart, Indiana.

Recordings

BOWMAR ORCHESTRAL LIBRARY

Ensembles, Large and Small, Album 83. Includes Britten's *Young Person's Guide to the Orchestra,* a string quartet, percussion ensemble, brass ensemble, and chorale.

COLUMBIA RECORDS, 799 Seventh Ave., New York, N.Y.

Carnival of the Animals, Saint-Saëns, and *Young Person's Guide to the Orchestra,* Britten. ML 5768.

First Chair, ML 4629. Features bassoon, cello, clarinet, flute, French horn, oboe, trumpet, and violin. For upper elementary.

The Military Band, Col. 1056.

Peter and the Wolf, Tubby the Tuba, and *Pan the Piper,* all on CL 671.

Piccolo, Saxie and Co., CL 1233.

GREYSTONE CORPORATION, 100 Sixth Ave., New York, N.Y., Children's Record Guild and Young People's Records.

Billy Rings a Bell

Drummer Boy

Four Bears

Golden Goose

Hunter's Horn, The

King's Trumpet, The

Licorice Stick (clarinet)

Little Brass Band
Mr. Grump and *The Dingle School Band*
Neighbor's Band
On Lemmer Lemmer Street (violin)
Rondo for Bassoon and Orchestra
Runaway Sheep (wind instruments)
Said the Piano to the Harpsichord
Strike up the Band
Walk in the Forest
Wonderful Violin
MERCURY RECORD CORPORATION
The Composer and His Orchestra, Vol. 1. Howard Hanson tells how he uses
    instruments.
Guitar Music from the Courts of Spain, Caledonia Romera plays.
MUSIC EDUCATION RECORD CORPORATION, Box 445, Englewood, N.J.
The Complete Orchestra. 5 records, 33 instruments featured. For age 10-up.
RCA VICTOR
Popular Classics for Spanish Guitar, Julian Breen plays.
WONDERLAND RECORDS
A Child's Introduction to Instruments of the Orchestra, Wonderland 1443.

Magazine and Teaching Supplies

Young Keyboard Junior Magazine: pictures, thematic charts, lesson plans, radio
    and television guide, recordings (produced annually), and "Build Your
    Own Orchestra" cardboard set. 1346 Chapel Street, New Haven, Con-
    necticut.
Free brochure on handbells, Schulmerich Carillons, Inc., Carillon Hill, Sellers-
    ville, Pa.
3M Brand Packets for Overhead Projectors. No. 2, *Families of Musical Instru-
    ments,* Minnesota Mining and Manufacturing Co., St. Paul, Minn.

form

It is the practice today to consider two kinds of form. One is form *in* music; the other concerns forms *of* music. The first consists of aspects of music relating to generalizations such as: melodies can be divided into logical parts; melodies can be extended and altered. The second is concerned with the larger forms of music such as song forms, suites, and symphonies.

Children can discover natural divisions of melodies comparable to a sentence in speech in answer to the questions, "Is the tune the same now or is it different?" and "Is it different or is it almost the same?" This division is called the phrase. Phrases are often thought of as being four measures in length, and while most of the songs in the series books seem to demonstrate this, phrases can be found in these books that vary from two to eight measures. Richard Strauss, the composer, once spoke of expanding a phrase of two or four measures into one of sixteen to thirty-two measures. Thus, while four-measure phrases are the most common, natural divisions of melodies encountered by elementary-school children may be from two to eight measures long. The important idea is not their length as much as it is that melodies can be divided into logical parts called phrases. This, of course, is the generalization teachers want children to make. Sometimes two phrases relate to each other in a special way; these two phrases are called a *period*. They can be improvised in the classroom by the teacher singing the first phrase and children taking turns improvising the second phrase; the teacher sings a "question", and the child sings an "answering" phrase.

Sometimes an entire phrase or a part of the melody within a phrase is found to be repeated on a different degree of the scale, either higher or lower than the first appearance of the phrase or note pattern. This was identified as the *sequence* in the analysis of melody in Chapter 9.

Identifying *same* or *different* is the key to understanding form. Young children's experience with this is at first more physical than it is intellectual. The teacher suggests that they move their bodies in relation to what they hear in the music. Among the suggestions for lesson plans in Chapter 8 was to draw from children how they might "act out" the music to show when it was the same and when it was different. In learning to recognize different phrases or larger contrasting sections of music, children may change movements or steps, reverse directions, and play different kinds of percussion instruments. Phrase repetition and difference are found in the songs children sing and in recorded music to which they listen. As in all aspects of teaching music, teachers select very clear examples of the phrase or larger sections of music when their objective is to help children distinguish "same" and "different." Very young children can compare Bartók's *Bear Dance,* which consists of repeated A sections separated by interludes, with Prokofiev's *Waltz on Ice,* (both in Adventures in Music 3 v. 2), which has three different sections in simple rondo form—ABACA. Their discoveries may include that music is made of different tunes or parts; sometimes these are the same, sometimes they are different, and some music has more parts than other music. Teachers can use visual aids, such as hats, costumes, streamers, masks, dancers, and colors, to dramatize same and different parts of music. To emphasize this in phrases, one group of children can be asked to sing phrases that are alike and another group those that contrast—boys and girls, those with black hair and those with brown hair, those with rubber-soled shoes and those with leather-soled shoes, and so on. Children can play finger cymbals to mark the ends of phrases; this gives them a purpose for listening carefully. Older children can classify phrases as being alike, different, and almost alike; they can study the notation of recorded music or familiar songs to form the generalization that when phrases look alike, they sound alike.

Suggestions in the booklets that accompany the *Adventures in Music* Albums are helpful. Review chapter 8 in this book; the *Forms of Melodies* section includes examples of phrase arrangements in songs.

Children are sometimes guided to "act out" phrases in ways such as the following arm movements:

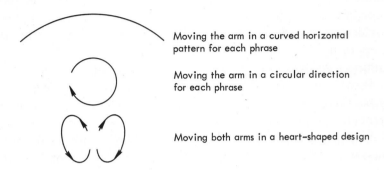

Moving the arm in a curved horizontal pattern for each phrase

Moving the arm in a circular direction for each phrase

Moving both arms in a heart-shaped design

Children do not always agree in their physical responses to a phrase, some feeling the phrase to be half the length that others may feel it to be. In certain songs it is interesting to note that adults are more apt to feel long phrases than are children, who often feel twice the number of phrases that the adults do. When this occurs, the children usually divide each long phrase into two shorter ones. In the opinion of the authors, this is not of particular importance, the real point being that children learn to sense that music is divided into logical sections. In view of individual differences in musical background, unanimity of response to phrase length cannot be expected. However, the simplicity of most of the songs found in music series books makes for fairly obvious phrase lengths.

In some songs, recordings, and piano selections there are obviously contrasting sections of the music, each of which may be composed of a number of phrases. These contrasting sections call for differences in the percussion score.

Teachers have learned that some older children are not usually greatly interested in phrases and some other structural aspects of music. While from an artistic point of view form is highly important because all works of art have form, and while scholars have written that understanding form is the most fundamental aspect of music learning, children of elementary-school age do not always find themselves in agreement with the scholars. These children are practical people, and they are not impressed unless they can understand the *function* of phenomena like form. The function of form seems to be to provide in different ways for two opposing concepts, *unity* and *contrast* or variety. Children who have acquired concepts of unity and contrast may find meaning in form. For example, when children are confronted with a phrase order such as *a a b a*, or *a b a c a*, and the teacher asks, "What is there in this tune that gives us a feeling of variety or contrast?" and "What is there that gives us a feeling of unity?" the function of form is made clear. Phrases *b* and *c* provide variety, and phrase *a* provides unity with its repetitions. Understanding this brings added meaning to the form of their own compositions. There are a number of interesting discoveries when they apply the principles of unity and contrast. Perhaps they will decide that the sequence serves both; it offers unity because it is a repetition, but it offers variety because the pitch is different.

Another generalization which concerns form is that melodies can be extended and altered by composers in various ways. By listening to music, making music, and creating music, children discover and use introductions, codas, and interludes. Introductions and codas are usually derived from melodies, but an interlude is often a contrasting section. Repetition is an obvious way to extend melodies. *Thematic development* is a term that describes what composers do with themes (tunes) they use in their larger compositions. When themes are developed they are extended or altered in many ways, including those presented in *Exploring the Manipulation of Melodies* in Chapter 9: augmentation, diminution, canon, inversion, retrograde, and octave displacement. These are only a sampling of what composers do with the two themes in the middle (development) section of sonata-allegro form.

Before we leave forms *in* music, we should again refer to unity and variety. Aspects of form should be tested and analyzed by children in these terms. The various forms of melodic alteration sometimes contain both elements. For example, an inverted melody has a natural relation with the original melody; because of this there should be some degree of unity found in it. The children can discover that the rhythm remains the same, providing rhythmic unity. The inverted melody sounds different, however, so variety is also achieved by the inversion. Eventually children will discover that they must analyze unity and variety in terms of the elements of music. Unity may be attained by *repetition* of rhythm, melody, harmony, texture, tempo, dynamics, and tone quality. Variety may be attained by *changes* in rhythm, melody, harmony, texture, tempo, dynamics, and tone quality. When the form *of* music is understood, form can be added to the above list of musical elements. This infers that teachers' questions can be quite to the point. "How is unity achieved in this composition?" "Was there repetition of (any of the above elements of music)?" "How was contrast achieved?" "Was there a change in (any of the above elements of music)?" "How did it change?" In this way analytical listening is guided, and the function of these aspects of form is made clear to the learner. Form becomes a logical scheme of things.

FORMS OF MUSIC

The songs in the series books have been identified as being made of phrases, some repeated note-for-note, some repeated with changes, and some contrasting and different. These are placed in an order that makes musical sense. Songs such as "At Pierrot's Door," (Au Claire de la Lune), "The Blue Bell of Scotland," "The Marines' Hymn," "0 Susanna," and "Long, Long Ago," have clearly defined phrases, both repeated and contrasting. Most of the songs are printed with one phrase on each line of a page. When songs are not printed that way, commas, semicolons, and periods in the texts, or rests in the melody offer semi-reliable clues as to the length of phrases. Song forms presented in Chapter 9, *Forms of Melodies,* were one-part (unary) with a phrase arrangement of *a a*; two-part (binary) with a phrase arrangement of *a b* or *a a b b*; and three-part (ternary) with a phrase arrangement of *a b a* or *a a b a*. It was stated that there are many variants of these forms; this section of Chapter 9 should be reviewed at this time.

Examples of one-part songs are Bach's "Cradle Hymn," and the folk song "Whistle, Daughter, Whistle." Other commonly used examples include:

Two-Part Song Form	*Three-Part Song Form*
"Du, Du, Liegst Mir im Herzen"	"Cradle Song" (French folk song)
"Go Tell Aunt Rhody"	"Lightly Row" (includes sequence)
"Li'l 'Liza Jane"	"Rosa, Come and Go Dancing" (includes sequence)
"Shortnin' Bread"	"Shoo Fly" (includes sequence)
	"Twinkle, Twinkle, Little Star"
	"Drink To Me Only With Thine Eyes"

The following examples of binary and ternary instrumental forms are to be found in *Adventures in Music* Albums: Binary: "Wheat Dance," Ginastera, 4 v. 1; "Bourée and Menuetto," Handel, 3 v. 2, also Bowmar 62; "Copacabana," Milhaud, 4 v. 2; Ternary: "Hungarian Dance No. 1," 5 v. 2; "Circus Music," Copland, 3 v. 1.

From the child's point of view, identifying phrases and larger sections in terms of letters of the alphabet is not very appealing or even as logical as some other ways. To dramatize phrase differences, some teachers find that freeing the children to draw the form in their own creative ways can attract interest and induce far more learning. For example, phrases *a b a* might be:

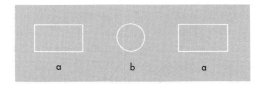

The sections of a rondo could be:

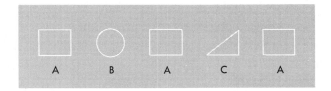

Another form might be drawn as:

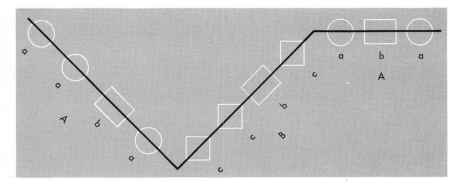

Using colors adds more interest too, because color highlights the contrasts. Some children will draw objects rather than the geometric designs illustrated here. The evaluative criterion is, "Does this drawing tell us clearly what the form is?" or "Does it show us all the different parts in their true order?"

The A B A sectional form is common to many larger forms. It is the same principle as the *a b a* phrase arrangement of a two-part song except that the idea is expanded into large sections—A B A— rather than only several phrases. Schumann's *Traumerei,* Adventures in Music 4 v. 2; Bowmar 63, and Debussy's *En Bateau,* Bowmar 53, are among the numerous examples of this form.

The principle of the *rondo* is a basic theme or section, A, which is alternated with two or more contrasting themes. Children sometimes compare its scheme with a sandwich. The shortest rondo is A B A C A. If one compares A to a slice of bread and B and C to different sandwich fillings, the result is a special kind of double-decker sandwich. Longer rondos may be A B A C A B A or A B A C A D A. The rondeau is similar; it is an extension of the latter example using a different contrasting section each time—only the A section repeats. A beginning concept of the rondo is acquired by young children in simple ways. This might begin with establishing a beat, then having the class say the name of the school, "Oak Ridge School," followed by the first and last name of a child, then the name of the school followed by the name of another child, and so on. The teacher's questions help the class realize the scheme of what they are doing—what is the same and what is different. Next, the same rondo principle is done with percussion instruments and even with rows of objects in the room. From here, the class applies this scheme to short melodies, and eventually they are composing rondos. This is related to recorded rondos such as Mozart's "Romanza," from *Eine Kleine Nachtmusik* (A B A C A coda), Adventures in Music 4 v. 1, Bowmar 86, Musical Sound Books 78004, Prokofiev's "Waltz on Ice," from *Winter Holiday,* Adventures in Music 6 v. 2, and Young People's Record *Rondo for Bassoon and Orchestra.* Other recorded rondos include Haydn's *Gypsy Rondo,* Bowmar 64, and Kodály's "Viennese Musical Clock," Adventures in Music 2, Bowmar 81.

Some teachers may question how much responsibility they have in including the larger forms of music in the curriculum. In an adequate music program the teacher takes advantage of the contacts children have with these forms both in their out-of-school environment and in the planned school environment. Such contacts are made through radio, television, live concerts, recordings, tapes, video-tapes, and films. The school environment provides these as part of a planned, spiral, and sequential music program for children at each level of interest and understanding. There will be planned exploratory listening to help children find what is meant by theme and variations, fugue, sonata-allegro, suite, sonata, symphony, concerto, opera, oratorio, and cantata. The limits of the experience will be determined by the child's level of understanding and interest. When children are engaged in exploration and inquiry, they need and want to know about these forms, and the teacher helps them by guiding their discovery process with questions, recordings, films, and helpful library references. In most instances, the theme or themes of the music under study are on the chalkboard, shown on a screen, or present in chart form.

The variation form is an extension of the concept of altering melodies. However, as the learner's concept of *variation* grows, he finds that music can be varied in terms of its melody, rhythm, harmony, texture, tempo, dynamics, form, tone quality, and its general style. This can make listening to variations an adventure somewhat like a mystery which gradually resolves itself as the listener detects which musical element or elements the composer changes in order to create the variation. Generally there is a theme, followed by the different treatments of it. Unity is provided by the theme, which is always present in some form; variety is provided by the changing of any of the musical elements. There is another form of variations which is of a continuous type. In it, a melody or a chord progression is repeated over and over, with variety coming from changes in the other elements. In Calliet's *Variations on Pop Goes the Weasel,* Adventures in Music 4 v. 1, Bowmar 65, Music Sound Books 78114, the theme is presented first. This is followed by Variation One, a fugue in which contrast is provided by the polyphonic texture. Variation Two is a minuet, which contributes variety with its change in meter, two tunes sounding at once, and the augmentation of one of the tunes. Variation Three, "Adagio," differs by means of a slow tempo, a change to a minor key, and the introduction of a different tune. Variation Four adds to the variety by changes in tone qualities and texture to imitate the sound of a music box. Variation Five changes the style to jazz, and the children can hear the trumpet produce a "Wah Wah" sound with a mute which alters the usual trumpet tone quality. In all these variations, contrasts are made by using different instruments to sound various tone qualities.

Children can be sure that composers find both pleasure and challenge in working with the variation form, and that listeners have both pleasure and challenge in trying to hear what was done to the music to vary it. Children can use the techniques explained in *Exploring the Manipulation of Melodies* in Chapter 9 to make some variations of their own on familiar, simple songs, then apply other possibilities in terms of rhythm, harmony, texture, tempo, dynamics, tone quality, form, or general style, as their knowledge of music expands.

Other variations recorded in the educational collections include the Young People's Record, *Hot Cross Buns*; Anderson's *The Girl I Left Behind Me,* Adventures in Music 5 v. 2; Copland's "Simple Gifts," from *Appalachian Spring,* Bowmar 65, Musical Sound Books 7852, Guarnieri's *Brazilian Dance,* Adventures in Music 6 v. 2, Bowmar 55; and *Theme and Variations for Percussion Instruments,* by Kraft, Bowmar 83. *Variations on "America,"* by Ives, Louisville Records, is interesting to work with.

The round, canon, and fugue are more a matter of polyphonic texture than of form, but they are customarily included in discussions such as this, and are classified as polyphonic forms. The last movement of the Franck *Violin Sonata* is an attractive example of a canon, which is similar to a round but does not repeat as rounds do. The round is a type of canon —a "circle canon." There are different types of canons; this could be a research project for an advanced student interested in the subject.

As stated earlier, the fugue is a rather free form. A theme (subject) is introduced by two or more voices in turn, developed in what can be considered another section, then restated in the final part of the form. If children should describe a fugue after listening to it carefully, they might say that when one voice or instrument states a theme, and then continues playing another melody while a second voice states the theme a fourth lower or a fifth higher, the beginning of a fugue has been created. The melody the first voice plays or sings when the second voice sounds the theme is called the "countersubject." This process may continue with the entrance of other voices, each beginning with the subject. This first section is called an exposition. It is followed by a free section consisting of statements of the subject, often in altered forms, and "episodes," something akin to interludes, based on tone patterns or rhythm patterns found in the subject and countersubject. Sometimes there is a *stretto* near the end, when the voices sound the subject in a way that there is overlapping of the entrances. The subject is restated clearly to establish unity again at the end.

The fugue may appear somewhat complicated by its description, and the teacher must use good judgment in knowing how far to expect a class of eleven-year-olds to proceed with it. Depending on the group, going into fine detail may be something only some advanced children will find interesting. However, the entire class can detect the unique beginning and the texture of the fugue; even young children can do this. Fugues useful in the classroom include:

Little Fugue in G Minor, Bach	Adventures in Music 6 v. 1, Bowmar 86
Pumpkineater's Little Fugue, McBride	Bowmar 65
Fugue and Chorale on "Yankee Doodle," Thomson	Bowmar 65

Elementary school children are usually not greatly concerned about the details of some of the larger forms of music, but they are genuinely interested in being able to identify them and comprehend them in a general way. Individual children may become highly interested in the symphony, the opera, and the ballet, and will want to read about them and experience them by means of films, concerts, and recordings.

The sonata-allegro form is an expanded A B A form. Its plan is a statement of two different themes followed by the development of those themes as a contrasting section, then a restatement of the themes to provide unity. Sometimes one of the themes will be in a familiar song-form. The first theme is apt to be masculine and vigorous while the second theme may be feminine and lyrical, thus providing contrast. There are often transitional passages between this first part of the form (Exposition) and the second part (Development). In the development section the themes and parts of the themes are treated in many different ways, and the listener may identify inversion, rhythmic alteration, sequence, change of key, and many other techniques composers use in creating variety. The final section is the Recapitulation, in which there is a restatement of the themes, often followed by a coda. This form is often used as the first movement of a symphony, sonata, concerto, quartet, and quintet, as well as appearing in some overtures and other types of composition. Clear examples are provided in the following first movements of symphonies: Schubert's *Unfinished Symphony,* Mozart's *Symphony No. 40 in G Minor,* and Prokofiev's *Classical Symphony* (Bowmar 73).

The *suite* has an interesting history which some advanced children may want to research. The suites we hear today are often dance suites (in which a series of related dances constitute the composition), the ballet suite, the opera suite, and suites based on dramatic stage works. Dance suites are usually made of dances of the sixteenth and seventeenth centuries, the allemand, courante, saraband, gigue, and a number of others. The suites based on stage works such as opera, ballet, and drama, are selections taken from the music written for these events and arranged for concert performance. Still other suites are written on ideas based on philosophy, psychology, and even sections of a country, as testified by Grofé's *Grand Canyon Suite* and *Mississippi River Suite,* Bowmar 61.

Dance Suites	English Suites, Bach	
	Harpsichord Suites, Handel	
Ballet Suites	*Nutcracker Suite,* Tchaikovsky	Bowmar 58
	Petrushka Suite, Stravinsky	
	Daphnis and Chloe Suite No. 2, Ravel	Bowmar 86
	Scheherazade Suite, Rimsky-Korsakov	Bowmar 77
Suites based on other	*Peer Gynt Suite,* Grieg	Bowmar 59
stage works	*Facade Suite,* Walton	
		Bowmar 55
Opera Suites	*Carmen Suite,* Bizet	
	Suite from *Amahl and*	
	the Night Visitors, Menotti	Bowmar 58

The symphony is a large work for orchestra which is usually, but not always, in four movements, one of which is in sonata-allegro form. The overture is a composition used to introduce an opera, ballet, or stage play, or it can be an independent concert work. Some are in sonata-allegro form while others are medleys of melodies from the work being introduced. Still others are in a free form which reflects a story.

The opera, oratorio, and cantata are large vocal works. The opera is a stage play in which the words are sung rather than spoken, in which the singers are accompanied by an orchestra, in which there may be duets, trios, sextets, and other ensembles, a chorus, and even a ballet. The *recitative* is a rather declamatory vocal style which attempts to imitate natural speech; an *aria* is a solo; an *arioso* is midway between the recitative and aria. Menotti's *Amahl and the Night Visitors* is a favorite of children, as is Humperdinck's *Hansel and Gretel.* Other operas used at the elementary school level include *Aida,* by Verdi; *The Little Sweep,* by Britten; *La Boheme,* by Puccini; *Carmen,* by Bizet; and *The Magic Flute,* by Mozart. The oratorio is usually of religious nature, somewhat dramatic in character, but having no stage action. Chorus, orchestra, and soloists are present, but without costumes and stage scenery. Some arias from oratorios can be found in the series books. The cantata is similar to the oratorio, having chorus and orchestra with optional solos. Song forms, chorale, rondo, aria, and recitative may be present.

Some forms are based on poems and stories. The art song is a musical setting of a poem in which melody and accompaniment combine to interpret the mood and meaning of the text. Some art songs by famed composers and poets are to be found in the series books, for example, Schubert's "The Linden Tree" in *This Is Music* Book 5. The symphonic poem, or tone poem, is a work for symphony orchestra in which the form is dictated by a story, a description, or a character. Operas, oratorios, and cantatas are based on stories, and their forms are influenced by them.

Children can write their own little operas by choosing a story and using both songs they know and songs they will compose. They can plan solos, duets, trios, and choruses, write an accompanying instrumental score, and add their version of a ballet. Such creative activity can lead children to identify with opera rather than to regard it as a somewhat alien form, as some may do. Every year in the Christmas season, Menotti's *Amahl and the Night Visitors* is presented over one of the television networks. Teachers should prepare the children for their viewing of it in their homes. Summy-Birchard publishes short children's versions of many well-known operas.

Some Suggestions for Lesson Plans

The teacher's question, "Is the tune the same as it was, or is it different now?" is important when children listen to songs or recorded instrumental music. "Did the music change, or did it stay the same?" is another way to state it. It centers attention on the phrases of songs and on sections of larger forms. It focuses attention on repetition (unity provided by repeating the phrase or section) and variety (contrast provided by the phrase or section being different). Older children will discover that rhythmic and harmonic repetition and contrast become part of the concepts of unity and variety. These should be reinforced by studying the notation of music. Percussion scores can emphasize the different phrases or sections by differences in the created instrumentation. Body movements can express these. To expand the concept that melodies can be extended, introductions and codas, both instrumental and vocal, can be added to known songs, and interludes can be improvised between repetitions of songs by percussion and/or melody instruments.

The rondo, as an expansion of the concept of same-different, can be introduced with percussion instruments. The A section or *a* phrase can be agreed upon; it may be suggested by the teacher or created by the class. Then individual children will improvise the B, C, and D parts of the rondo. Thus, in accordance with the teacher's plan, the form would be A B A C A D A—or some variant or extension of this. Eventually the class can listen to rondos and chart their forms, possibly with designs as well as letters.

The sequence can be discovered in songs and instrumental pieces and by studying the score; it can be used as a device in composition when the children create their own music.

Phrase improvisation: The teacher plays or sings a phrase that seems to ask a question; individual children improvise phrases that answer it.

The teacher writes the first phrase of a composition on the chalkboard; the children complete the composition.

The teacher writes the recurring section of a rondo on the chalkboard; the children extend the composition by writing the other parts of the form.

Phrase plans: The teacher and children agree on a phrase plan for a composition; the children individually write the piece according to plan.

The words of a clearly phrase-wise poem is taken from literature or from words of an unfamiliar song and placed on the chalkboard. Individual children improvise melodies to suit the words.

Ask piano students in the class to play pieces they know from operas and symphonies. Such pieces are found in many piano books.

Older children are grouped in fours. They number off from one to four. Number one improvises and sings phrase *a* by numbers or syllables; numbers two and three must sing different phrases *b* and *c*, respectively. Number four may either repeat phrase *a* or continue with a concluding phrase *d*. Then each child advances a number, and the process continues.

Variations: The teacher writes a self-contained phrase, one that sounds complete, on the chalkboard. It is of four or five measures; all measures but the last consist of quarter notes; the final measure has but one long note in it. The task of the children is to vary this phrase with different patterns of note values—rhythmic alteration.

Variations: The teacher writes a four or five measure melody on the chalkboard. The children's task is to vary it as they wish in terms of melody, rhythm, and meter.

Variations: The children are assigned a simple, familiar tune. They will try to answer the question, "In how many different ways might this tune be varied?"

Thematic development as a means of extending a short melodic-rhythmic idea can be studied by having children explore such music as the beginning of Beethoven's *Fifth Symphony*. "What different things did the composer do with his melodic idea?" List them.

Children should be guided to recognize repetitions of tonal and rhythmic patterns by eye (in notation) as well as by ear, and to discover these patterns in altered forms.

Children should be guided to discover that the phrases in some songs are not always arranged in the neatly-designed two- and three-part song forms often sketched on chalkboards. Instead, composers demonstrate variety in concept and freedom to create phrase plans beyond these standard forms. Children can discover free forms in which composers place sections of larger compositions in no common order. These are called free sectional forms.

REFERENCES

Books

BULLA, CLYDE R., *The Ring and the Fire*. New York, N.Y.: Thomas Y. Crowell Company, 1962. Stories of the operas of Wagner's *Ring of the Nibelung* cycle; includes major themes. For children.

———, *Stories of Favorite Operas*. New York, N.Y.: Thomas Y. Crowell Company, 1959. Stories of 23 well-known operas; useful for children and teachers.

COMMINS, DOROTHY BERLINER, *All About the Symphony Orchestra and What It Plays*. Eau Claire, Wis.: E. M. Hale and Company, 1961. The instruments, conductor, large instrumental forms, and some composers. For older children and teachers.

CROSS, DONZELLA, *Music Stories for Boys and Girls*. Boston: Ginn and Company, 1926. Legends, myths, and stories in opera, suite, ballet. For intermediate grades and teachers.

DISNEY, WALT, *The Nutcracker Suite*. Boston: Little, Brown & Co., 1941. For children.

GARY, CHARLES L, *The Study of Music in the Elementary School—A Conceptual Approach,* Music Educators National Conference, Washington, D.C., 1967, pp. 85–112. For teacher's lesson plans.

GOULDEN, SHIRLEY, *The Royal Book of Ballet.* Chicago: Follett Publishing Company, 1962. For all ages.

SIEGMEISTER, ELIE, *Invitation to Music.* Irvington-on-Hudson, New York: Harvey House, Inc., 1961. For more mature children. A companion recording of the same name is available from Folkways Records.

SWANSON, BESSIE R., *Planning Music in the Education of Children.* Belmont, Calif.: Wadsworth Publishing Company, 1965, pp. 70–73. For teachers.

WHEELER, OPAL, *Adventures of Richard Wagner.* New York, N.Y.: E. P. Dutton and Company, Inc., 1960. For intermediate grade children.

Films

Forms of Music: Instrumental, Coronet Instructional Films, 16 min. Traces historical development of sonata, concerto, symphony, and tone poem. For advanced children.

Let's Discover the Design, EMC Corporation, St. Paul, Minn. 55101. For age 10 and up.

Music Stories, filmstrips in color with recordings. *Hansel and Gretel, The Nutcracker Suite, Peer Gynt Suite, The Firebird Suite, The Sorcerer's Apprentice,* Jam Handy Organization, 2821 East Grand Avenue, Detroit, Mich.

Opera and Ballet Stories, filmstrips in color with recordings. *Lohengrin, The Magic Flute, Aida, The Barber of Seville, Die Meistersinger, Coppelia,* Jam Handy Organization.

Symphony Orchestra, The, Encyclopaedia Britannica Films, 14 min. Traces growth of symphony orchestra from string quintet to the modern orchestra. Enjoyable for grades 4–6.

Young People's Concert Series (Leonard Bernstein) *What Makes Music Symphonic?; What Is a Concerto?; What Is Sonata Form?"* McGraw-Hill Films. Each one hour. For age ten and up.

Recordings

Child's Introduction to Opera, Childcraft Records Album 38. Includes *Barber of Seville, Amahl and the Night Visitors, Hansel and Gretel.*

History of Music in Sound, Vol. 5, "Opera and Church Music," RCA-Victor. For adults; to be adapted for class use by the teacher.

Musical Forms for Boys and Girls; World of Ballet for Boys and Girls; Opera for Boys and Girls; Symphonies for Boys and Girls; Chamber Music for Boys and Girls (Mozart sonatas for violin), Peter Pan Records, 461 Eighth Ave., New York City.

Also see various *Bowmar Orchestral Library* Albums which relate to the study of form.

13

styles and listening

STYLE* AS IDENTIFICATION AND CLASSIFICATION

The reader has noticed that beginning with Chapter 8 each succeeding chapter has added one or more musical elements until we have by now considered all the basic ones. Knowledge of these is necessary when one considers style. The concept of style also has reference to identifying and classifying. A recorded piece might be said to be in "symphony orchestra" style. This may mean only that the listener heard music that sounded typically like that played by a symphony orchestra rather than that played by a military band or a dance band. There is a generally understood operatic style—the type of music most often composed for opera; this can be listened to analytically to find what the factors are that tend to produce this style. There are characteristic national styles in which certain rhythm patterns, melody-types, and harmonies tend to reflect nations or peoples in some unique way; for example, Spanish rhythm, German chorale style, and the gamelan music of the Indonesian people. Polyphonic style refers to a style of contrapuntal writing. When style is used in these ways

* The reader is referred to the definition of style in the Harvard Dictionary of Music.

it may be associated with such varied types of music as those of historical periods, folk music, instrumental, march, vocal, national, Viennese waltz, a specific dance, 12-tone, atonal, jazz, popular, religious, secular, ceremonial, blues, musical comedy, operetta, opera, patriotic, symphonic, polyphonic, homophonic, monophonic, military band, symphonic band, rock, piano, boogie-woogie, and so on.

Teachers' questions lead students to consider style in both comparative and analytical ways. One of the important objectives of music teaching is to help the learner think musically. Thinking about style is an effective way to do this because it leads children to draw upon their knowledge of all the elements of music. It also invites comparisons. Thus, when children are trying to identify some music new to them, and one remarks that it has a folk quality about it, the teacher might ask, "What is there about this music that leads you to identify it as folk music?" The class may then propose theories regarding beat, tone quality, type of accompaniment, harmony, and form which together may give them the impression that the music has or has not a folk music style. Some of the many styles come from functional music which is used to meet specific needs of man, such as ceremonial music. When children analyze such music they may find that it includes sections where the tone quality of certain brass instruments is used to attract attention, where the tempo is (for good reason) that of a dignified walk, where the harmony may be blocky, solid, and resolves with assurance into the tonic, and where the texture may be rich and full, giving the impression of power, dignity, and grandeur.

While young children can deal with simple aspects of style, a more complete study requires a background of knowledge that is usually not gained until the age of ten or eleven; therefore this part of the chapter refers largely to these older children who should have the opportunity to explore in depth the style of a few carefully chosen selections or composers.

STYLE AS ANALYSIS AND MUSIC IN HISTORY

Turning from the more simple kinds of styles above, we will now consider style in a higher intellectual sense. This definition requires more than a knowledge of music. Hans Tichler writes, "Style is the result of the interweaving of all the primary elements of music—rhythm, melody, harmony, counterpoint, instrumentation, expression, non-musical associations, and structure—combined with historical, social, and biographical elements."[1] Such a definition calls upon knowledge of all the elements of music, of all types of musical expression and forms, of music in its social-historical context, and of the life and character of the individual composer. This seems to tax the resources of adults and at first impression may seem beyond the capacities of elementary-school children. Maynard Anderson defines style in music as "the special arrangement of the component elements of the art combined with the distillation of relevant attributes of an era."[2] If ten and eleven year old children are able to discern the combination of musical elements described in the previous chapter on form, they are dealing with music analysis that relates to style. If they were to add "historical, social, and biographical elements," and "the distillation of relevant attributes of an era," they could consider problems of style on adult terms. Thus, inasmuch as children study these things and apply them in combination, they can work with style so defined. If the music specialist deals with this element, he must guide the study so that both music elements and non-music elements which influence the music are related. If the classroom teacher is already dealing with historical, social, and biographical elements, he has a ready-made situation in which to inject a consideration of the music of that time and place. There is opportunity here for team planning and teaching by classroom teacher and specialist. No matter who is teaching music, if the teacher is guiding the learning of music as an expression of humanity, he will probably be involved in aspects of style in accordance with the definitions of Tichler and Anderson.

Older elementary school children can quickly identify music as being "ancient," "old," "traditional," and "modern." This music might be a Gregorian plainsong, a Bach concerto grosso, a nineteenth-century romantic piece, and a piece with twentieth century harmonization. They willhear and identify the monophony of the plainsong, the polyphony, rhythm, harmony, and tone quality of the Bach orchestra piece, the more or less traditional harmony and melodic emphasis of the romantic music, and the contrasting harmony and dissonant qualities of the contemporary music. To continue their study in depth they need to know the people of those times, the historical setting, and the composer as a person—in order to understand more about how that style of music came to be. This

[1] Tichler, Hans, "The Teaching of Music Appreciation," *Journal of Research in Music Education,* Fall, 1959, p. 169.
[2] Anderson, Maynard C., "On Teaching Musical Style," *Music Educators Journal,* Feb-March, 1966, p. 89.

involves a great deal of conceptual learning. It involves relationships with other arts, and with history, sociology, and psychology—all on the elementary-school level and in terms that children can deal with. When a teacher is consciously concerned with helping children grow in their understanding of style, he will tend to be more precise in his planning, and he will tend to select music of quality to use. This approach to music has some relationships with the humanities course in high school, and is preparatory for it.

INFLUENCES AFFECTING STYLE

The personality of a composer is reflected in his music; children need to know about the man in order to understand his style. His general personality, his particular temperament, and the age he was when he wrote a specific composition are factors which influence his music. For example, they may discover that Haydn's personality was warm and genial, and that Beethoven's was serious and at times brooding.

Children may further find that national musical traits influence style. French music is likely to be buoyant, rhythmic, of light beat (not heavy like the German beat), and sophisticated. German music is apt to be sober, vigorous, of sturdy rhythm, thick texture (Brahms' music is an example), occupied with working out problems, and subjective. Italian music is usually vital, rhythmic, with a more marked beat, emphasizes melody and the beauty of the human voice, and frequently has embellishments. English music is often refreshing, harmonious, cool in tone, and quite matter of fact. Russian music is likely to go to extremes of loud, soft, fast, and slow, to have rhythmic tension, to be emotional, to have mixed and less common meters, is harmonious, and is not much concerned with polyphony. The technical equipment of composers influences their styles. Some are skilled in counterpoint; others are not. Some excel at being ingenious with harmony, some with their clarity of form, and some with their skill at using a vocal-type melody line.

As a rule the period in which composers live influences their style. When children discover this they may generalize that they must know about the people of those times in order to better understand the music written then.

BAROQUE PERIOD (1600–1750) This was an age of exploration, discovery, and expansion, and music reflected this exuberance with impressiveness and grandeur. Opera came into being as a new large form and was presented with a lavishness unknown in our time. Other new forms were created, including the concerto grosso, fugue, the dance suite, trio sonata, overture, cantata, and oratorio. Men making history in other areas were Newton and Harvey in science, Molière and Milton in literature, and Rubens and Rembrandt in art. The orchestra was not yet standardized, and the harpsichord was an important basic instrument in many ensembles. It was often played from a "figured bass" score from which the player improvised his harmony from numbers (figures). Polyphony was integrated into the harmonic system we know. Dynamics were on levels of loud and soft; the crescendo and decrescendo were either not known or not used, perhaps because the instruments of that day were not very flexible. The music of Bach and others had a strong and clear beat which was a contrast to the preceding Renaissance Period in which the feeling of meter was either not that distinct or not that simple. Major and minor tonalities predominated, as did polyphony. Baroque period composers whose music appears in the school music collections include Bach, Corelli, and Handel.

VIENNESE CLASSICAL PERIOD (1750–1810)   Cultural life was dominated by the aristocracy—the ruling class. In service to this group, the arts became formalized, restrained, elegant, and impersonal. Many composers were employed to write music for the aristocratic establishment rather than the church, which had been the chief employer of musicians in the past. Melodies were often folk-like in their simplicity, but what seems simple and rather child-like to today's ears was in reality the restrained sophistication of that day, and should not be misunderstood as being "child-like." (However, today's children like them and can comprehend them.) Melodic development was skillfully employed. The texture of this music was thin and clear. The sonata-allegro form was developed; it is one of man's greatest intellectual achievements. The modern orchestra took shape, as did the symphony, quartet, and concerto forms. Form was an important element. The beat was lighter than the vigorous baroque beat, and the music seems to be more refined. Polyphony was relegated to the background, and homophony, with two and four-measure phrase lengths, was the rule. The dominant stylistic concepts of music of this period are considered *classical* elements of style no matter at what time in history they may appear. They are: clarity, restraint, objectivity, conformity, and balance. The music of the following classical composers is found in the school music collections: Gluck, Haydn, Mozart, Schubert, and early Beethoven. Beethoven stands as a musical giant who began composing in classical style, then gradually became an early romantic composer. His position is like that of a bridge between the classical and romantic periods.

THE ROMANTIC PERIOD (1810–1890)   With the French Revolution, the power of the aristocracy was broken, and a period followed which reflected the rejection of the old order. It was a time of freedom to explore and to break away from the conformity, restraint, and objectivity of the classical period. It can be compared to the expansion that took place in the baroque period. When the royal courts dwindled, the composers who had depended on them for a living were set free to write as they pleased, but in the process they lost their economic security. This trend has continued into the present day when most composers earn their living in some other occupation. The concert hall became the center of musical interest, taking the place of the church and court of the past. This was a time when a spirit of freedom for the common man swept European thought. Music reflected this by freeing rhythm from its classical regularity—*tempo rubato, accelerando,* and *ritardando* reached their full development and use. Extremes in tempo and dynamics became common as opposed to the restraint of the classicists. Chromaticism, dissonance, and a richer texture tended to replace the more simple harmony and the clear, thin texture of the classical period. Neither did the composers accept the restrictions of classical forms; they felt free to modify them and to invent new ones such as the romantic art song, the rhapsody, and the tone poem, all free forms. As the piano was improved mechanically to produce more volume and a bigger tone, composers wrote a great deal of music for it, and the harpsichord declined in importance. The piano could fill a concert hall with sound; the harpsichord could not. The music was predominantly homophonic; polyphony was not popular. Because composers were free to be different, some concentrated upon expressing national styles by emphasizing aspects of music associated with certain nations. Instrumental tone qualities were employed as valued tools in composition; there was an increasing emphasis on tone color as an element of music. Long, flowing melodies that could be sung were popular. This music was apt to be subjective, personal, emotional, and nationalistic in its reflection of the age. Most of the best-known music today is from this period. Among the many romantic period composers represented in the school music collections are Bizet, Brahms, Chabrier, Dvořák, Grieg, Schumann, Sibelius, Tchaikovsky, and Wagner.

THE IMPRESSIONIST PERIOD (1890–1910) Although other composers continued to write in late romantic style, the impressionists wearied of this emotional and thick-textured music. They also felt that the traditional harmonic system was approaching exhaustion. Thus they set about to produce unusual tone qualities and to de-emphasize the romantic melody by breaking it up into fragments of its former length. They did not seek description as much as they did an impression of things; there seemed to be in their music an almost pagan return to a worship of nature. They employed tone colors which included exploiting instrumental ranges not commonly used before (such as high trombone and low flute), harmonies that freely broke the old rules by employing old modes, whole-tone scales, the pentatonic scale, parallel fourths, fifths, and octaves, all used in tasteful ways. This gave much of their music a hazy and dream-like quality that relates to impressionism in art. Muted instruments and the harp added special effects. Thematic development was practically absent, and the tonic-dominant harmony weakened in favor of unexpected and often unresolved chords. The texture is luminous and transparent rather than heavy and turgid as found in some romantic music. Form was de-emphasized; much of this music is only a series of episodes. This tendency away from earlier concepts of melody and harmony point toward the experimentalism of the contemporary period. Impressionist composers whose music is found in school music collections are Debussy, Falla, Griffes, Ravel, and Respighi.

THE CONTEMPORARY PERIOD (1910–   ) While all manner of music has been and is being written in our own time, certain tendencies are rather clear. These are believed to reflect the general character of the turbulent and rapidly-changing world in which we live. A gradual abandonment of traditional harmony has taken place. The tone-row abandons it completely, and old modes and overlooked folk scales from all over the world are exploited in the effort to create new or different music. Dissonance is utilized to an extreme, according to classical standards. Polytonality and polyrhythms are boldly used. Composers are frequently employed as teachers, librarians, and in occupations other than composing. There are few economic ties to encourage them to write music for specific social purposes. Instead, there is a vast amount of experimentation rather than creating music for specific use, such as Bach did for his church services. At the same time, there is much contemporary music being written for religious use. There is sometimes a return to aspects of earlier periods—the objectivity and thin texture of the classical period, and the polyphonic techniques of the baroque. Such polyphony is usually dissonant in contrast to the harmonic polyphony of the earlier period. Rhythm and meter sometimes seem to have aspects in common with pre-baroque music; rhythmic freedom and complexity is a leading feature of much contemporary music. At times there is strong rhythm, an emphasis on unrelieved tension, and a mechanical style which may reflect the impersonal civilization of the day. New sources of tone have been found. These include synthetic tones produced by machines such as tone generators, and sounds of the world about us which are treated in different ways (musique concrete). Both types are placed on tape in electronic composition. Music of the following composers is found in the educational collections: Bartók, Copland, Ginastera, Guarnieri, Ives, Kabalevsky, Khatchaturian, Kodály, Menotti, Milhaud, Prokofiev, Shostakovitch, Stravinsky, Villa-Lobos, and Walton. None are considered avant garde; none are electronic composers. Thus, teachers select recordings such as Folkways Records' *Twelve-Tone Music, Sounds of New Music* and *Electronic Music* to supplement the school music collections. However, later collections will include some of this music. Composers of experimental music include Mossolov, Cage, Varese, Cowell, Ussachevsky, Luening, Schuller, and Stockhausen.

When children have sufficient experience in music so that they are able to analyze it according to the elements which comprise it, they can gradually discover dominant stylistic characteristics for themselves, and this is as it should be. The teacher should select music that is clearly representative of each period, if his objective is to help children learn about them. Only after they are secure in their knowledge of one style period should contrasting characteristics of another period be introduced. Also, only after children are secure in identifying separate styles—classical and romantic music, for example—should music be used which has elements of each. In such an instance the children should seek to find out which characteristics, classical or romantic, are the strongest, and attempt to classify it in this way. The teacher's function is not as a lecturer on music styles; it is to arrange situations in which children find for themselves what the style is through their own exploration, discovery, and inquiry.

Some Suggestions for Lesson Plans

Find ways to call children's attention to national, folk, and ethnic styles. Spanish, Latin-American, Arabian, Central African, Indian, Chinese, Japanese, and Indonesian songs as well as other recorded music have recognizable styles in terms of the elements which comprise music. There are many variations within those styles. For example, in the music of Central Africa, there are differences in musics of East, Middle, and West regions.

Arrange to study march styles, involving eight to eleven-year-olds in comparing and analyzing recorded marches. Young children might compare military band marches with *March of the Little Lead Soldiers, Parade of the Wooden Soldiers, March of the Toys, March of the Dwarfs,* and *Funeral March of a Marionette.* Older children could add to these the march movements from Beethoven's *Third Symphony* and Tchaikovsky's *Sixth Symphony* as well as "March" from Prokofiev's *Love of Three Oranges,* an opera. "March and Cortege" from Gounod's opera, *The Queen of Sheba,* is another type of march.

Select two different national music styles such as those of Spain and England. Have children compare selected music to find similarities and differences. Have them theorize on the reasons for these differences.

After older children have considerable knowledge of certain composers' music, have them contrast the music of two radically different composers and attempt to describe their styles in terms of how each manages the elements of music.

As an outgrowth of knowledge of many folk songs and of characteristic music of nations such as Spain, Cuba, Germany, France, Italy, and Russia, play recorded instrumental and vocal selections that typify the music of the selected countries. The game is to identify the country by the characteristics of the music. Have a map in front of the room. Sometimes children will recognize a specific song or melody; other times they must seek clues from unfamiliar music.

Adapt the preceding activity to make an identification game from style periods of music history. Even when children do not know the various styles well, they are able to group music in categories they can invent—very old, old, not very old, new, and very new.

For a related activity using notation, take four to eight Bowmar thematic charts or teacher-made charts of themes, number them, and have a game-quiz on identification of the notation by listening to the melodies of the matching recorded music.

Select a familiar tune. Let children re-write it to make its style similar to or imitative of that of *Blue Danube Waltz,* a Sousa march, jazz, and others that come to mind. Let the children report to the class on their efforts and discuss what one must do with certain of the elements of music to reflect the styles of such familiar compositions.

Assign children a melodic pattern or a phrase and let them alter it by treating it with aspects of contemporary style. They may try changes of register, alternating meters, and other departures from traditional music.

Compare music of similar type from different style periods; ask children to discover similarities and differences. Examples may be extracted from music such as the following: Bach's *Air for the G String* and Villa-Lobos' *Bachianas Brasileiras No. 5* in which Villa-Lobos sets about the task of reflecting Bach in twentieth century Brazil; Bach's *Brandenburg Concerto No. 2 in F Major* and Bartók's *Concerto for Orchestra*; the first movement of Haydn's *Symphony 101* (The Clock) and the first movement of Prokofiev's *Classical Symphony*; and a representative part of any romantic symphony with part of Stravinsky's *Symphony in Three Movements.*

Let children listen to Milton Babbit's presentation of electronic music in a record which accompanies the sixth grade book of the Holt, Rinchart and Winston's *Exploring Music* Series. Also let them hear and evaluate Hugh LeCaine's "Dripsody" in Folkways Records' *Electronic Music* (FM 3436/FMS 3436), which is based on the sound of a drop of water.

Have children explore descriptive music to interest them in discovering the musical means a composer uses to give the impression or a description of a place, some geographical feature, or a country. Examples: Grofé's *Grand Canyon Suite* and *Death Valley Suite;* Coate's *London Suite;* Ives' *Three Places in New England,* Chabrier's *España Rhapsodie,* Copland's *El Salon Mexico,* Debussy's *Nuage* (Clouds) and *La Mer* (The Sea), and Gershwin's *An American in Paris.*

Involve older children in answering questions such as, "If you were a composer who wanted to write some music representing a particular time and place in history, what are some of the things you might do in your music to give the feeling of that time and place?" "If you wanted to write music that described a specific geographical place, how might you do it?" "If you composed a piece about the United States, what would you do in that music to let the listener know that you were reflecting your ideas about your country?" ("How did Ives, Gershwin, Copland, Grofé, and others do it?")

WRITING LESSON PLANS

By now the reader may have discovered for himself that the experienced teacher is almost continually assisting children toward their formulation of several or many generalizations even while the emphasis in a lesson may be on only one of them. In fact, discoveries, inferences, and remarks concerning form, style, and tone quality can be logical parts of the experience children have in a lesson that emphasizes none of these. If the reader has thought of his lesson plans as being somewhat cumulative, beginning with rhythm, then adding melody to rhythm, then adding harmony to these, and so on, even though he may be emphasizing the subject of a given chapter in his plan, he has included aspects of other elements of music in it. Studying the chapters concerned with form and style should assist in expanding the concepts of music as a union of a number of its basic elements, and as a reflection of humanity at a given time and place.

SOME CUMULATIVE BEHAVIORAL OBJECTIVES

The child

concerns himself with changes in dynamics and tempo, and relates them logically to the music, as shown by . . . . .

reveals awareness of major and minor tonalities related to feelings and expressiveness by . . . . .

associates simple stylistic aspects of music with nations or cultures (includes choice of instrument, characteristic rhythm pattern), by . . . . .

reveals growth in ability to analyze cultural, national, or composers' styles by their rhythmic, melodic, harmonic, and form aspects, as well as by their use of instruments and vocal tone quality as shown by . . . . .

can analyze and identify styles in terms of popular music, jazz, various cultures, historical periods, and individual composers by . . . . .

reveals sensitivity to stylistic aspects in his musical performance by . . . . .

reveals increasing understanding of historical styles by executing dances of a particular time, as shown by . . . . .

reveals increasing understanding that style is a synthesis of musical elements by . . . . .

Listening

Since listening to recordings, to voices, to instruments, and to a variety of sounds has been emphasized in this book, the reader has already found that listening is the basic music activity. By this time he has had a good measure of experience studying the elements of music by listening to the rhythm, pitch, melody, tempo, dynamics, harmony, texture, tone quality, and form found in music of many types. He has used recordings as part or as parts of his lesson plans to help children discover many things about music and to solve many musical problems. Thus, this section need include only information about listening which has not been introduced in earlier chapters.

THE TEACHER ANALYZES RECORDINGS FOR CLASS USE

Recordings are usually selected in terms of their clarity of presentation of the specific aspects of music the children are studying. The teacher needs to choose recordings which emphasize the musical elements he wants the children to find while listening. The conceptual approach to teaching music provides its own clear outline by which teachers can analyze recordings for class use. One teacher[3] made a large chart that can be used with any recording or with an entire collection of educational recordings. Her headings, which were written horizontally across the top of the chart, were as follows: composer, title, sources, general feeling, rhythm, dynamics-tempo, melody, harmony, texture, tone quality, national origin, style period, additional comments. These headings served as criteria as she listened to each recording. She wrote only in the spaces beneath the headings that named outstanding characteristics of the music. For example, in the instance of Anderson's *The Girl I Left Behind Me,* she found the general feeling *lively,* the rhythm featured by *march rhythm and syncopation,* the melody contained *augmentation and diminution,* the form was *theme and variations,* the national origin was *Irish folk,* and the style *20th century.* The other spaces were left blank because she found nothing out-

---

[3] Mrs. Madeline Tews, Springfield Schools, Oregon.

standing relating to those headings. Later, when she searched for music featuring a specific musical element, she could look down a column on her chart and select from the compositions accordingly. For example, she could choose recordings for quiet listening (under general feeling), for studying polyphony (under texture), for studying woodwind tone qualities (under tone qualities), and for studying accents (under dynamics and tempo). She continued working with her chart until it consisted of a number of long sheets of paper and it contained every record in one collection of recordings.

Such information might be condensed in a card file. There are a number of ways in which entries can be made on cards, one of which appears below. By making duplicate cards, the teacher can have a file at his desk and a central file available to all.

Composer	Number of Record or Album
Title	Sources of information about the music
Music Elements Emphasized	Comments:

In selecting recordings and films, authenticity is an important criterion. This is not always easy to determine, and it often requires some reference reading to obtain necessary information. The teacher needs authentic music of a given time. Sometimes he will be confronted with versions which are not genuine. Some music has been distorted or altered to render it ill-suited for the classroom. Examples are choral and other arrangements of the *Nutcracker Suite,* which is instrumental music from a ballet, and spoken versions of *Carnival of the Animals,* another instrumental composition which has no words written for it by the composer, and none are intended. There is another kind of music which needs some explanation by the teacher; this is stylized music based upon authentic sources but purposely altered by the composer. For example, some so-called American Indian music is based to a degree upon Indian sources, but the melodies are transposed into major or minor tonality, and they are harmonized in the traditional European manner. Since most authentic Indian music is not in our scale system, and harmony as we know it did not exist in Indian music, the teacher needs to explain that while inspiration may have come from authentic sources, the music has been rewritten into our tonal and harmonic system. In so doing, it has been altered. Sometimes a composer idealizes older forms or characteristic types of music such as Ravel did in his *La Valse,* which idealizes the nineteenth century waltz, and his *Tzigane,* which idealizes Gypsy music. Children can theorize and investigate to the extent of their ability upon what the composer based his concept, and to what degree his music resembles the authentic stimulus of his creativity.

Catalogs offer assistance to teachers who are seeking recordings of certain uses. They are published by concerns such as the Children's Music Center, Folkways, Bowmar Records, and RCA-Victor. (The catalog of the Children's Music Center classifies recordings in relation to all commonly taught units of school work.) Further assistance is provided by teacher's guides which accompany the school record collections, and the books of Lillian Baldwin, *Tiny Masterpieces for Very Young Listeners,* (Theodore Presser, Bryn Mawr, Penna.); and Music for Young Listeners: *The Green Book* (for fourth grade); *The Crimson Book* (fifth grade); *The Blue Book* (sixth grade); and *Music to Remember* (grades seven and eight), all published by the Silver Burdett Company. These books are written in an appropriate vocabulary for the age levels; both children and teachers can read them. Recordings to use with the books are obtained from the Sound Book Press Society, Inc., Scarsdale, New York, or from Silver Burdett. The *Bowmar Orchestral Library* consists of three series comprising 36 ungraded albums, accompanied by wall charts of themes printed on heavy cardboard; Series Three adds themes on transparencies, lesson plans, and record grove spreads for ease in finding places on the discs.

Other aids include pictures of instruments, composers, and subjects related to the content of the music being studied. Some sources are listed at the end of this chapter. One is Keyboard Junior, a concern that publishes the magazine *Young Keyboard Junior* for grades four through six, available at bundle subscription rates. Supplementary materials are provided to assist the classroom use of the magazine. These cover recordings, lesson plans, charts of themes, radio and television guides, as well as pictures—conductors, composers, instruments, and operas.

The tape recorder, opaque and overhead projectors should not be neglected as helpful aids. Recording a class performance on tape, then listening to it and evaluating the performance, can provide excellent motivation. The tape recorder can be used to record music excerpts from many sources for classroom use; sometimes this means taping personally-owned recordings rather than taking these to school. When music is taped, it offers the advantage of enabling the teacher to stop the sound to ask questions or to comment, then start it again without the trouble of seeking the correct groove on a disc recording.

Films are helpfully indexed and described in *Film Guide for Music Educators,* published in 1968 by the Music Educators National Conference, 1201 Sixteenth St. N.W., Washington, D.C. 20036. They are classified under many headings.

There can be some assistance from related art activities. It was mentioned in the chapter on form that children can find satisfaction in communicating by means of geometric or figure designs what they hear of the form of music. Other relationships between painting and music can be cool and warm colors as related to cool and warm style, and straight or curved lines as related to the rhythmic feeling or the melodic contour.

Incidental playing of recordings outside the music class creates familiarity with music of quality. The classroom teacher is the one most able to provide this. There is a repertoire of good music with which all children should be familiar; it can be enjoyed and assimilated in part by playing it when background music is in order. This music should be of a type that promotes relaxation and emotional stability, as the famed article by Katherine Scott Taylor[4] states. She used such music as Bach's *Air for the G String,* and uncomplicated chamber music of Beethoven, Haydn, Schubert, and Schumann to create a calm environment for a first-grade group of children of migrant workers. Discipline problems dwindled while the children learned to enjoy fine music. Types of listening differ in accordance with the function of the particular recording. For instance, some recordings that include music are not designed for musical listening, but only to tell a story that is made more enjoyable through the addition of background music. They may be useful in language arts. Some that include music with story-telling may be purely for recreation, while others may offer much learning about music and musicians. The good teacher studies a recording, analyzes its true function, and uses it in accordance with that function—if he finds it worth using.

During class-time listening, the teacher is always an example of an interested listener, illustrating by his actions and attitude the concentration necessary for listening. He listens attentively to hear the things for which he has prepared his class to listen. When this is properly planned, there will be no talking while the recording is being played; attention is centered on the music, not on the teacher's talking. If there is an over-all

[4] Taylor, Katherine Scott, "An Autochthonous Approach to Music Education," *Music Educators Journal,* February-March, 1949, pp. 17–19, 50–52; September-October, 1959, pp. 35–39.

principle involved, it is that the teacher and class are always listening for some definite purpose.

EMOTIONAL AND INTELLECTUAL ENJOYMENT

The following illustration is an attempt to show the growing amount of analytical listening a child should experience as he progresses from kindergarten through sixth grade. Notice that enjoyment in listening develops from nonintellectual foundations, and that these bases for nonintellectual listening remain present even though the amount of intellectual listening increases. Since music is based upon physical responses, feelings, and emotions, these "nonintellectual" aspects should never be forgotten nor neglected. However, if the teaching of listening is poorly guided, and serves only nonintellectual purposes, intellectual enjoyment and understanding can never be achieved.

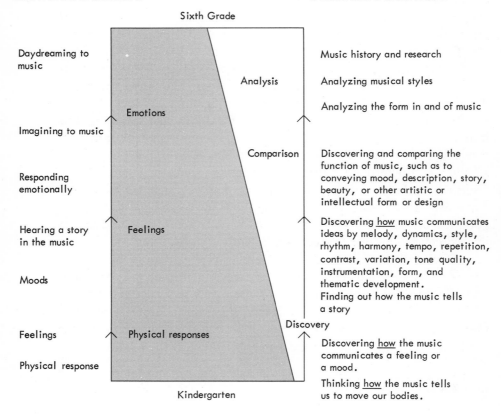

EMOTIONAL ENJOYMENT   INTELLECTUAL ENJOYMENT

Sixth Grade

Daydreaming to music

Analysis

Music history and research

Analyzing musical styles

Analyzing the form in and of music

Emotions

Imagining to music

Comparison

Discovering and comparing the function of music, such as to conveying mood, description, story, beauty, or other artistic or intellectual form or design

Responding emotionally

Hearing a story in the music

Feelings

Discovering how music communicates ideas by melody, dynamics, style, rhythm, harmony, tempo, repetition, contrast, variation, tone quality, instrumentation, form, and thematic development.
Finding out how the music tells a story

Moods

Feelings

Physical responses

Discovery

Discovering how the music communicates a feeling or a mood.

Physical response

Thinking how the music tells us to move our bodies.

Kindergarten

READINESS FOR LISTENING

Before children are asked to listen, there are physical factors to be considered. These include having the record player in proper position in the room and set with the correct turntable speed, the record placed on the machine, the children seated in a way that will promote attention to listening, healthy room temperature, and appropriate lighting. There should be freedom from interference—competing noises, interest-catching articles, and irrelevant activities of some children that can distract the attention of others.

The teacher should remember that a sizable vocabulary is necessary for verbalizing about music, and that this vocabulary should be gradually acquired by children. New words, both descriptive and musical, should be listed on the board as they are needed or as they appear in discussion. Motivation sometimes begins with interesting new words. The teacher can "set the stage" by relating certain aspects of the classroom environment to the general mood or type of the music. These include lighting, objects and their placement, and the teacher's tone of voice and facial expression. For example, if Sibelius' *Swan of Tuonela* is studied in a sixth grade class, the lighting could be darkened in keeping with the somber mood of the music, a picture of the dark waters of Finland's lakes might occupy a central location, and the teacher's voice and facial expression could match the solemn overtones of this legend of the ancient past. He might tell part of the story, keeping this tone of voice and facial expression throughout. When children come to realize that such listening is "staged" for their benefit and enjoyment, they can become intrigued with what they are about to hear. To increase interest and speed in the learning process, visual aids are used: pictures, slides, and scores shown on opaque projectors, thematic material drawn on the chalkboard or charts, and commercially available or teacher or child-made transparencies and time lines.

Readiness to listen to music is influenced by a child's maturity level and by the music listening he has had in his out-of-school environment. The teacher plans with these in mind. A child's interest in listening is more likely to be keen when he can understand a large part of what he hears. Therefore, he is more ready to respond when the content of the music relates to his past experiences, and when the music contains familiar elements, particularly rhythmic and melodic. Recognizing familiar melodies in new settings assists motivation. A list of recorded music of this type based on familiar songs is found in Chapter 9. Further motivation comes from teachers' plans that include asking the children to answer specific questions and to solve specific problems by listening carefully to what they are to hear.

RECORDINGS FOR VARIOUS LEVELS OF INSTRUCTION

All children are likely to enjoy listening to recordings that possess some of the following characteristics: (1) potential for active physical response; (2) a distinct mood; (3) songlike melodies; (4) beautiful tone qualities; (5) a story or message in the music; (6) content that relates to their experience and interest; (7) length in relation to their genuine interest. Older children with musical experience background have the ability to be more analytical in their responses to music than younger children. While some recordings are made to appeal to specific age levels, music in general is not; it is a communication by a composer for anyone who can grasp its meaning. A movement from a symphony is generally too lengthy, and when used will be reduced to an excerpt. However, length must be measured in terms of interest; children can listen for long periods of time if they are truly interested. For young children this may mean physical responses; for children of all ages, music can be used as a background to other activities if the mood is one that is not distracting or disturbing. In the long run, whether or not a particular recording should be used on a particular level depends upon its appropriateness on that level in terms of the teacher's objectives. Besides exemplifying music concepts, other purposes may include presenting beauty for its own sake without comment, use for quality background listening before and after school, during rest periods, and during some other activity when such music adds aesthetic quality to the environment. The same recorded music may serve one purpose, such as rhythmic response, at lower levels and another purpose, such as the study of tone quality, form, or style, at a higher level.

LISTENING TO PROGRAM MUSIC

In the primary levels children often listen to stories from recordings which are told with music in the background to add interest and color. Older children listen to recordings of historical or literary nature which include background music. While music is present, neither of these situations is centered on learning about music; they are examples of music being used to enhance another subject. The educational objectives are not concerned with music.

When program music is used in music classes, attention is eventually centered on *how* the music suggests the story, description, or mood. In preparation for a more extended experience in listening to this type of music, the teacher studies the selection and analyzes it in terms of the musical elements discussed in this book. He will then relate these elements to the story or description. He will also be familiar with information about the composer, his life and times. He will plan questions, may place a list of guiding statements or words on the chalkboard, or plan some other way to guide the listening of the class to help them discover the musical meaning of the work. He will have questions planned for use after the class has heard the recording.

There are many different types of program music, and they demand different approaches. In some instances it is necessary to tell the children the story before they hear the music; in others they can be free to make up their own stories (which may be as good or better than the composer's), but in all cases they are to explain how the elements of music are used to describe the mood, description, or story. Obviously, the older children will be able to give the more precise analysis, while young children will express these ideas in more simple terms. The teacher encourages the children to explain the music to the extent they are able, later supplying whatever information is necessary. As in other aspects of music, the lesson is planned in a way that results in general success, not bewilderment or frustration. The teacher knows the children's capabilities and he can challenge them to grow in their ability to hear music, thus stimulating a feeling of accomplishment.

Sometimes it adds variety and encourages divergent thinking to tell the name of a recording before the children hear it, and ask them, "If you composed a piece of music with this title, what would you do to convey the idea to the listener?" "How would you use the music elements to help the listener understand your meaning?"

If a teacher asks children to imagine a story suggested to them by an unnamed composition, there are no wrong answers; the thinking is again divergent. Their imagined stories may be entirely different from the composer's story. However, the child has the responsibility to explain what happens in the music to justify his story. It is this that makes the experience a musical one rather than one in story-telling. Some children may not hear a story. It will then be their responsibility to tell what they did hear, and their answers should be in terms of the elements of music.

LISTENING TO ABSOLUTE MUSIC

Absolute or "pure" music is that which has no extra-musical meaning. It exists for its own sake as a work of art. With this type of music the teacher and children work directly with the elements of music—the melodies, tone and rhythm patterns, tone qualities, form, and so on. Repetition and contrast, tension and release, cool and warm, will be listened for. The function of form and tone qualities will be examined and discussed free of any program. A large amount of music has no story aspect, and children need to be clear in their classification of music into the two types—program and absolute. Thus, "story music" must not be over-emphasized.

Remember that children need the opportunity to compare and analyze music in order to develop ability to discriminate and to make value judgments. They do not fully accept value judgments made by adults; they need to be helped to make their own.

THE RECORD PLAYER

In any listening, children are attracted by beauty of tone, therefore the record player and the record need to be of a quality that produces this beauty. Scratched records and poor-sounding players have no place in a situation where children are to be helped to enjoy, learn about, and appreciate music. Records should be kept in their jackets to protect them from dust. They should be handled so that the grooves are not touched by the hand, which can soil them. To protect them from warping, they should be stood up straight on edge, not stacked flat or placed in a slanting position. The needles should be in good condition because a worn needle will damage records and distort the tone. It is good practice to begin playing a recording at low volume, then turn it up rather than to risk accidentally "blasting" the listeners.

LISTENING TO CONTEMPORARY MUSIC

Contemporary music sometimes provides marked contrasts with other music. Some constitutes "discrepant events." For example, the children have learned that music always communicates something, which may be a mood, description, story, beauty for its own sake, the working out of a particular form or some challenge the composer assigned himself, or the conscious or unconscious reflection of a period or nation in historical context, or the personality of the composer. Against this concept of communicating something, the children may be challenged by a contemporary work that is claimed by its composer to communicate nothing; it is to be recognized only for what it is. The children's minds are then pitted against the composer's with the question, "Can a composer write music which does not in some way reflect the age in which he lives?" "Is there something about this music that may communicate something about the decade in which he composed it?" "Is there something about this music that can be recognized as ageless or timeless, thus acceptable in any age?" "Is there something about this music that exists only for itself and nothing else?" Again, older children can be challenged with this type of divergent thinking which has its convergent possibilities also.

Today's children are conditioned to the sounds of electronic music they hear while watching certain television programs, and the concept of the tape recorder as a source of musical sounds should be well understood and practiced in classroom composition. Children now work with small computers and may be able to understand better than many older people that they can be used in composition, that the major problem is how the computer is programed, and that the number of possibilities is incredible. The point of view of the music educator is that children need to be exposed to every type of music. This does not mean that they are expected to *like* every type of music. To understand something about every type of music gives the child knowledge by means of which he can decide whether or not he likes it; this is his personal business. He needs to explore the different kinds of music somewhat like the scientist examines classifications of plant and animal life under a microscope. Contemporary music takes its rightful place with all the other types of music as part of the world of organized sound. An interesting aspect of composing with a tape recorder is that notation can be by-passed; this makes it easy for children to do. No one knows with certainty the future of electronic music; its possible position in music history has been compared with that of the beginnings of opera in 1600. In some teacher education programs, a laboratory course in electronic music is required. Experimental music seems to be a reflection of our time. Picasso said, "Strangeness was what we wanted the people to think about, because we were aware that the world was becoming very strange and not exactly reassuring." Contemporary music has tended to reject emotion as a necessary component of art; this is in part a reaction against the emotion-filled romantic music of the nineteenth century. The concept that art is beauty is rejected by many contemporary composers, painters, and sculptors; these people try to portray concepts of reality as they see it, whether this is inspiring or degrading. In music, this results in some radically changed concepts of tonality, harmony, melody, consonance, and dissonance from those held for centuries before. People who do not or cannot accept such changes criticise this music as being overintellectual, mechanical in nature, and lacking in emotional meaning. Whether the listener likes this music or not seems not to be the question. It is here, it exists, and each listener is called upon to examine it in a situation in which final judgment is not yet possible. Children can be helped by letting them discuss what they like and do not like about it without trying to lead them into a final judgment. Experience with contemporary music has been a part of the study of every musical element in this book. If this approach is followed, contemporary music will take its place as one type of music among all the other types, and children should be relatively open-minded about it.

Some bridges can be built between the music of today and that of the past. For example, the following aspects of form in music can be found in both contemporary and baroque music: ostinato figures, bourdon bass, pedal point (one long-held pitch usually in the bass above which changing harmonies take place), and improvisation. There are forms of music common to all periods, such as two-part, three-part, variation and rondo. If we go back far enough in music history we find the use of tonalities other than major and minor. The non-western music of Asia and Africa lead in some ways toward contemporary music because they are different from most of the music we know best. Baroque-style music of contemporary groups like the Beatles and the Swingle Singers is helpful when comparing it with authentic baroque music; it helps children to associate the present with the past. Orff, Bartók, Hindemith, Britten, and Kodály are contemporary composers who have written music for children which teachers should study and evaluate for classroom use. Included in listening in the primary grades to instrumental music, and in singing activities, there should be recordings and songs with expanded tonality (so that the children are not restricted in their classroom experience to only major-minor tonality), free rhythm, and asymmetrical forms. These are gradually appearing in later series books. Improvisation by children can be extended to include twelve-tone and serial improvisation as suggested earlier. Composition with a tape recorder can be a vital listening experience.

PURPOSES FOR LISTENING

Listening is more than hearing; the teacher must establish the necessity of listening attentively for some good and logical reason. It may be to discover, to verify, to define, to follow a sequence of events, to answer a question, to relate, to compare, to examine music critically, or to seek entertainment or relaxed enjoyment. Listening activities require courtesy because no one should have the right to interfere with another's listening. To motivate listening and to make it a creative experience, teachers plan questions that stimulate divergent thinking whenever this is appropriate. The highest levels of listening require inductive and deductive thinking.

The following list of some possible purposes for listening is from *Music Eduction in Oregon Schools,* a 1960 publication of the State Department of Education, Salem, Oregón. It is reprinted from the second edition of this book by the request of a number of music educators.

KINDERGARTEN AND GRADES 1–3

General Purpose	*Specific Purpose*
To find pleasure	By preparing for physical responses to music By enjoying sheer beauty of sound By resting and relaxing to music
To develop skills	By recognizing pitch changes By learning to match pitch with voice or instrument By learning to sing a song By learning to improve tone quality in singing By learning to recognize melodies By learning to respond by physical movement By learning to recognize specific instruments By learning concert-audience manners
To develop creative capacities	By planning responses by body movements and drawing By creating dramatizations and stories
To develop knowledge of music literature	By listening to recordings of significant songs By listening to recordings of significant instrumental music

	By evaluating recordings brought from home by children By listening to school and community concerts By listening to selected radio and television music
To develop understanding of music symbols and vocabulary	By hearing high and low and associating these with notation By hearing pitches of long and short duration and associating these with note values By hearing scale and chord patterns and associating these with notation By hearing such things as slurs, repeats, accents, ritards, accelerandos, pauses, and associating these with the term or symbol as soon as the maturity level permits
To develop understanding of musical form	By hearing and identifying phrases; by hearing phrases that are the same and that are different By hearing and identifying introductions, interludes, codas By finding out how music communicates ideas and concepts
To develop understanding of humanity	By hearing and identifying childhood emotions expressed in music By hearing interests common to humanity expressed in music of various peoples of the world By learning to co-operate to achieve good musical results

GRADES 4–6

To find pleasure	By preparing for physical responses to music By enjoying sheer beauty of sound By resting and relaxing to music By listening to performances of classmates and others By sharing interesting music with others
To develop skills	By identifying the more unusual instruments

	By identifying major, minor, pentatonic and other modes By recognizing common pitch intervals By hearing harmony parts in part-singing By becoming increasingly aware of all the component parts of musical form through listening By responding to rhythmic aspects of music with increasing accuracy
To develop creative capacities	By listening in order to respond to music with bodily movement By listening in order to devise an appropriate accompaniment By listening in order to improvise another vocal or instrumental part to a song By listening in order to respond with art media By listening in order to respond with written descriptions or stories
To develop knowledge of music literature	By listening to program music By listening to music that has no story By listening to music of great composers By learning to recognize folk and national characteristics in music By relating music to world history and events
To develop understanding of musical symbols and vocabulary	By identifying by notation the themes that are heard in the music By following notation as children listen to a harmony part sung by the teacher By hearing scale and chord patterns and associating these with notation By hearing such aspects as slurs, repeats, accents, ritards, accelerandos, pauses, and associating these with the term or symbol
To develop understanding of musical form	By identifying two- and three-part song forms when these are heard By identifying forms such as rondo, variation, and fugue when heard

By hearing and identifying such aspects as contrast, tension and release, polyphony, homophony, and instrumentation

By becoming aware of larger musical forms such as classic dance suites, orchestral suites, tone poems, concertos, operas, symphonies

To develop understanding of humanity

By learning of humanity's common needs through listening to music

By learning to appreciate through music the characteristic differences in humanity that add interest in and appreciation of other peoples of the world

By learning how mankind has used music as a form of communication throughout history

Some Suggestions to Assist Listening

Devote only a part of the music period to listening to recordings. Plan a variety of music activities, combining different kinds of listening experiences with singing, rhythmic responses, and playing instruments. Remember that children are normally unable to sit still and listen for very long.

Use *good quality recordings* on a *good quality machine*. Even the loveliest music cannot succeed if distorted by poor equipment. Records should be stored vertically in folders to protect them from scratches and dust. The needle should be of high quality and the correct type for the machine. The tone arm should be placed on the record very gently. Because the human skin is oily, and oil damages records, the record should be touched only on the edge and in the center, never on the grooves. Dust should be removed with something clean and lint-free, such as a damp sponge.

Bring *live performers* into the classroom from school and community —but be sure before they are invited that they can perform suitably. Let the young children touch and feel the instruments used, for it is through physical contact that they gain in comprehension.

Use visual aids: an attractive *bulletin board* with pictures, newspaper and magazine write-ups, concert and recital programs, and clever cartoons about music and musicians. If the teacher changes the content of the bulletin board regularly, the children will read it with interest. *Films* and *filmstrips* have an important place. *Write music themes* on the chalkboard or use charts if the children do not have them to follow in their books while listening. Sing these themes before playing the recordings, if they are singable. Use charts of altered themes and rhythms.

Bring listening to life by relating it to current events, motion pictures, radio and television programs outside the classroom, local concerts, and to newspaper and magazine feature stories.

Use appropriate *radio and television* programs in the classroom, taking care to prepare the children for them fully and to follow up afterwards.

Add a *Listening Post* to the classroom music center. This is a control box with headphones which may be attached to any record player, thus permitting several children to listen without disturbing the class. It is manufactured by A. M. Brooks Company, 1222 West Washington Blvd., Los Angeles, California. There are other similar teaching tools. One is The Listening Corner, devised for both music listening and speech training and accommodating eight sets of headphones and a microphone input. It is manufactured by Caliphone Corporation, 1041 North Sycamore Ave., Hollywood, California. These can sometimes be made in high school manual arts classes.

To help direct listening, place a list of key words on the chalkboard before the recording is played. Example: mood, instruments heard, meter, form, sounds of nature.

Prepare the children to understand the music of *concerts and recitals* given at the school or in the community.

Request that special *concerts and programs* for children be given at school and prepare the children to listen to them. (See Chapter 18)

Employ *music notebooks and scrap books* in grades five and six—but use discretion. Children can put into them all the things listed above for the bulletin board. However, if children feel compelled to assemble bulk without true interest, such a project can defeat its purpose. Maybe all of this belongs on a lively bulletin board after all!

Provide a time when children can bring favorite *recordings from home* to share with the class, explaining why they like them.

Give children the opportunity to play appropriate thematic material on piano, bells, and other instruments.

Children can plan with the teacher a *pretend concert* of recorded music. Such programs can be organized around ideas such as music of other lands, marches of many kinds, musical instruments and soloists, music of certain composers, and American music. Concert behavior is studied and planned. A variant of this was done by a student teacher in music who substituted himself and his school-of-music friends for the recordings, and substituted the school auditorium for the classroom. The children "sold" themselves tickets, provided ushers, and planned what their behavior was to be in the intermission. The university students entered wholeheartedly into the idea, dressing in formal clothes. This program was planned so that the children joined with the performers in singing at the close of the concert.

Place appropriate books about composers and music in the music corner and in the school library.

Organize listening sessions by grouping the recordings around unifying themes such as types of instruments (percussion, woodwind, brass, string), elements of music, dances, marches, different composers' concepts of sunrise, sunset, seasons, the sea, day and night, plant and animal life.

Read or tell stories about composers to make them live in children's minds. Especially appropriate are stories about these men in their childhood, and about composers' relations with children. For example, Bach, Mozart, and Mendelssohn composed music when they were very young. Dioramas and puppetry may be employed.

In primary grades a lengthy recording such as *Tubby the Tuba* is too long for playing at one sitting. Make it a continued story and play one or two sides a day, reviewing them before playing another side the next day. In intermediate grades, the *Nutcracker* Suite (Tchaikovsky) is too long for one listening lesson. Therefore, play a section of it a day. Really long compositions have little or no place in elementary school music.

The piano can be used effectively for some listening experiences, particularly in the kindergarten and first grade.

By all means use the tape recorder to record children's singing and playing. Nothing stimulates interest in listening to recorded music as much as *making* recordings.

Children need *vocabulary* in order to discuss music they hear. This vocabulary is of two types: (1) musical terms such as *ballet* and *suite,* and (2) descriptive words. Musical terms can be written on the chalkboard and explained by the teacher before a recording is played. After the children have listened to a recording, descriptive words can be drawn from them through class discussion and written on the chalkboard as an activity in both music and language arts.

Allow children to respond to music physically when they are listening, as long as this response is of a type that does not interfere with the listening of others. Remember that it is normal to want to move to music. Discover and notate rhythm patterns.

For an activity in language arts classroom teachers can encourage children to write creative plays concerning lives of composers. These plays might be performed by the class and include playing and singing music of the particular composer.

Play "music detective." Present an unfamiliar recording. The game is for the class to tell what it hears. List the findings. Can any generalizations be formed from the findings?

INQUIRY AND SELECTED ACTIVITIES

1. Listen to the third movement of Ferde Grofé's *Death Valley Suite*. List the experiences you think are described in the music when the pioneers' wagon train crosses the Valley. Listen to the recording again, and explain how the music suggests these experiences by means of melody, rhythm, harmony, tone quality, contrast, repetition, tempo, and dynamics.
2. Examine a music series book of your choice to find listening activities. Prepare a short listening lesson for that grade level based in part on suggestions in the teacher's book.
3. Make a comparative study of two or more music series to assess their assistance to the teacher in listening activities.
4. Plan (with children, if possible) a "pretend concert" for an elementary classroom, using recordings. On what kind of plan will it be organized? How can children help plan it? What considerations not primarily musical may be taught by means of this activity?
5. Select recordings of worthwhile music for use in the classroom at times when quiet background music is appropriate.
6. Investigate the services your state university or state system of higher education offers teachers in supplying 16 mm. films to enrich listening studies in elementary-school music.

REFERENCES

Books

BALDWIN, LILLIAN, *Music for Young Listeners: The Green Book, The Blue Book, The Crimson Book.* Morristown, New Jersey: Silver Burdett Company, 1951. Also *Tiny Masterpieces for Very Young Listeners.* Bryn Mawr, Pennsylvania: Theodore Presser Company, 1958. These books can be read by both teachers and children; they are written in children's vocabulary. Recordings for each book are obtainable from Music Sound Book Press, Box 444, Scarsdale, N.Y.

BARLOW, HAROLD AND SAM MORGENSTERN, *A Dictionary of Musical Themes.* New York: Crown Publishers, Inc., 1948.

FABER, VIRGINIA, *Musical Adventures,* Books One, Two, and Three. Hollywood, California 90028: Highland Music Company. A music listening series for elementary classrooms; contains stories of compositions, teacher's information sheet, and student's biography of the composer.

HARTSHORN, WILLIAM C. AND HELEN S. LEAVITT, *The Mentor; New Horizons; The Pilot; Prelude;* and *Progress.* Boston, Mass: Ginn and Company, 1940.

KINSCELLA, HAZEL, *The Kinscella Readers,* 2nd ed., 8 vols. University Publishing Company, Lincoln, Nebraska, 1949. Vol. 8, *History Sings,* has particular value in upper grades. For children and teachers.

McMILLAN, L. EILEEN, *Guiding Children's Growth Through Music.* Boston, Mass: Ginn and Company, 1959. Chapter 5 and Appendix B.

MYERS, LOUISE, *Teaching Children Music in the Elementary School.* Englewood Cliffs, N.J.: Prentice-Hall, Inc., 1961. Chapters 6 and 12.

PIERCE, ANNE E., *Teaching Music in the Elementary School.* Holt, Rinehart, & Winston, Inc., 1959. Classified list of recordings pp. 183–91.

SWANSON, BESSIE R., *Music in the Education of Children.* Wadsworth Publishing Company, Inc., 1964. Chapter 8.

TIPTON, GLADYS AND ELEANOR TIPTON, *Teachers' Guides* for Adventures in Music recordings, RCA-Victor, New York, N.Y.

Music History

BUCHANAN, FRANCIS, *How Man Made Music.* Chicago, Ill.: Follett Publishing Company, 1951.

COMMINS, DOROTHY BERLINER, *All About the Symphony Orchestra and What It Plays.* Eau Claire, Wis.: E. M. Hale and Company, 1961. The instruments, conductor, large instrumental forms, and some composers.

COPLAND, AARON, *What to Listen for in Music,* rev. ed., McGraw-Hill Book Co., Inc., 1957.

KINSKY, GEORGE, ET AL., *A History of Music in Pictures.* New York, N.Y.: Dover Publications, 1951. Useful with an opaque projector.

MACHLIS, JOSEPH, *The Enjoyment of Music,* shorter edition, W. W. Norton & Company, Inc., 1957.

MILLER, HUGH, *An Outline History of Music.* New York, N.Y.: Barnes and Noble, Inc.

RATNER, LEONARD G., *Music—The Listener's Art.* McGraw-Hill Book Company, Inc., 1957.

STRINGHAM, EDWIN J., *Listening to Music Creatively,* 2nd ed., Englewood Cliffs, N.J.: Prentice-Hall, Inc., 1959.

WOLD, MILO AND EDMUND CYKLER, *An Introduction to Music and Art in the Western World,* 2nd ed., Dubuque, Iowa: William C. Brown, 1965.

Books for Children About Composers

Collective:

GREEMAN, WARREN S. AND RUTH WITTAKER, *Great Composers.* New York: Abelard, 1952.

HUGHES, LANGSTON, *Famous Negro Music Makers.* New York, N.Y.: Dodd Mead, 1955. Junior high school level.

WICKER, IREENE, *Young Music Makers: Boyhoods of Famous Composers.* New York, N.Y.: Bobbs Merrill, 1961. Eight European and four American composers.

Individual:

BACH, JOHANN SEBASTIAN	Albus, Harry, *Music Maker, Johann Sebastian Bach,* Grand Rapids, Mich.: Wm. B. Eerdmans Publishing Co., 1950.
	Goss, Madeleine B., *Deep-flowing Brook: The Story of Johann Sebastian Bach,* Holt, Rinehart & Winston, New York, N.Y., 1938.
	Manton, Jo, *A Portrait of Bach.* New York, N.Y.: Abelard, 1957.
	Wheeler, Opal and Sybil Deucher, *Sebastian Bach: Boy from Thuringia,* E. P. Dutton Co., New York, N.Y., 1937.
BEETHOVEN, LUDWIG VAN	Kaufman, Helen L., *The Story of Beethoven,* New York, N.Y.: Grosset and Dunlap, 1957.
	Komroff, Manuel, *Beethoven and the World of Music,* New York, N.Y.: Dodd, Mead and Co., 1961.
	Mirsky, Reba P., *Beethoven,* Chicago, Ill.: Follett Publishing Company, 1958.
	Wheeler, Opal, *Ludwig van Beethoven and the Chiming Tower Bells.* New York, N.Y.: E. P. Dutton.

BERNSTEIN, LEONARD

Briggs, John, *Leonard Bernstein: the Man, His Work, and His World,* World Publishing Co., 1961.

Ewen, David, *Leonard Bernstein, a Biography for Young People,* Simon & Schuster, 1959.

BRAHMS, JOHANNES

Deucher, Sybil, *Young Brahms,* E. P. Dutton, 1949.

CHOPIN, FREDERIC

Wheeler, Opal, *Frederic Chopin, Son of Poland, Early Years,* and *Frederic Chopin, Son of Poland, Later Years,* E. P. Dutton.

FOSTER, STEPHEN

Douty, Esther, *The Story of Stephen Foster,* Grosset and Dunlap, 1954.

Higgins, Helen Boyd, *Stephen Foster: Boy Minstrel,* Bobbs Merrill, 1962.

Howard, John T., *Stephen Foster, America's Troubadour,* Apollo, Smith and Peter, 1962.

Peere, Catherine O., *Stephen Foster: His Life,* Holt, Rinehart and Winston, 1952.

Wheeler, Opal, *Stephen Foster and His Little Dog Tray,* E. P. Dutton.

GILBERT, W.S.

Pearson, Hesketh, *Gilbert: His Life and Strife,* Harper and Row, 1958.

Purdy, Claire Lee, *Gilbert and Sullivan: Masters of Mirth and Melody,* Messner, 1946. For older readers.

Wymer, Norman, *Gilbert and Sullivan,* E. P. Dutton, 1962.

GRIEG, EDVARD

Deucher, Sybil, *Edvard Grieg, Boy of the North-land,* E. P. Dutton, 1946.

Purdy, Claire Lee, *Song of the North: the Story of Edvard Grieg,* Messner, 1941.

HANDEL, JOSEPH

Barne, Kitty, *Introducing Handel,* Roy, 1957.

Wheeler, Opal, *Handel at the Court of Kings,* E. P. Dutton, 1962.

HAYDN, JOSEPH

Kaufman, Helen L., *The Story of Haydn,* Grosset and Dunlap, 1962.

Wheeler, Opal and Sybil Deucher, *Joseph Haydn: the Merry Little Peasant,* E. P. Dutton, 1936.

KEY, FRANCIS SCOTT

Stevenson, Augusta, *Francis Scott Key: Maryland Boy,* Bobbs Merrill, 1960.

MACDOWELL, EDWARD

Wheeler, Opal and Sybil Deucher, *Edward MacDowell and His Cabin in the Pines,* E. P. Dutton, 1940.

MOZART, WOLFGANG	Kaufman, Helen L., *The Story of Mozart,* Grosset and Dunlap, 1955. Komroff, Manuel, *Mozart,* Knopf, 1956. Mirsky, Reba P., *Mozart,* Follett Publishing Co., 1960. Wheeler, Opal, and Sybil Deucher, *Curtain Calls for Wolfgang Mozart,* and *Mozart, the Wonder Boy,* E. P. Dutton, 1934.
SCHUBERT, FRANZ	Wheeler, Opal, and Sybil Deucher, *Curtain Calls for Franz Schubert,* E. P. Dutton, 1941. ———, *Franz Schubert and His Merry Friends,* E. P. Dutton, 1939.
SCHUMANN, ROBERT	Wheeler, Opal, *Robert Schumann and His Mascot Ziff,* E. P. Dutton.
SOUSA, JOHN PHILIP	Weil, Ann, *John Philip Sousa: Marching Boy,* Bobbs-Merrill, 1962.
TCHAIKOVSKY, PETER	Wheeler, Opal, *The Story of Peter Tchaikovsky,* E. P. Dutton. ———, *Peter Tchaikovsky and the Nutcracker Ballet,* E. P. Dutton, 1959.
WAGNER, RICHARD	Wheeler, Opal, *Adventures of Richard Wagner,* E. P. Dutton, 1960.

Filmstrips with Recordings

Biographies of Great Composers, each 30 minutes: *Haydn, Mozart, Beethoven, Schubert, Verdi, Puccini,* Bowmar Records, Inc., 10515 Burbank Blvd., North Hollywood, California 91601.

Famous Composers and Their Music: Chopin, Schumann, Mendelssohn, Tchaikovsky, Grieg, Brahms, The Jam Handy Organization, 2821 E. Grand Blvd., Detroit, Mich., 48211.

Great Composers and Their Music: Bach, Handel, Haydn, Mozart, Beethoven, Schubert, The Jam Handy Organization.

The Story of Handel's "Messiah," Society for Visual Education, Inc., 1345 Diversey Parkway, Chicago, Ill. 60614. 20 minutes.

The Story of Johann Sebastian Bach and His Christmas Oratorio, Society for Visual Education. 35 minutes.

The Story of the Nutcracker, Society for Visual Education. 32 minutes. Adapted from the Nutcracker legend and Tchaikovsky's musical score.

Films

(Refer to *Film Guide for Music Educators,* by Donald J. Shetler, Music Educators National Conference, 1201 Sixteenth St. N.W., Washington, D.C.)

Composers: The American Tradition (Copland, Harris, Thomson, Piston, Sessions, Ives), National Educational Television, Indiana University, Bloomington, Indiana 47401.

Composers: Electronic Music (Milton Babbitt), National Educational Television.

Music in Motion: The Enchanted Lake (Liadov), Musilog Corporation, P.O. Box 1199, Santa Barbara, California 93102. A pictorial interpretation of the music; impressionist music; a twelve-page manual accompanies the film. Similar films interpreting the music of 15 other composers are available.

Music of Williamsburg, Film Distribution Section, Colonial Williamsburg, Inc., Box C, Williamsburg, Virginia 23185. Depicts music's place in the everyday life of the Virginia colonists. Two versions, 29 minutes and 40 minutes.

The Peter Tchaikovsky Story, Walt Disney 16 mm Films, 350 South Buena Vista St., Burbank, California 91503. 30 minutes.

Young People's Concert Series: What Does Classical Music Mean?; What Is American Music?; What Is Impressionism?; Humor in Music; Folk Music in the Concert Hall; Jazz in the Concert Hall, McGraw-Hill Films, 330 West 42 Street, New York, N.Y. 10036. One hour, for age 10 and up.

Recordings

Baroque Beatles Book, Elektra Records, 51 W. 51st St., New York, N.Y. 10019.

Child's Introduction to Folk Music, Wonderland Records 1436.

Child's Introduction to Jazz, Wonderland Records 1435.

Clock Went Backwards, The (History of Music), Greystone Corporation.

Humor in Music—"Till Eulenspiegel's Merry Pranks," Columbia Records. Leonard Bernstein discusses and conducts.

Music Master Series 1, 2, Educational Audio Visual, Inc., 57 Wheeler Ave., Pleasantville, N.Y. Series One: 10 records with program notes, Bach, Mozart, Chopin, Mendelssohn, Schubert, Grieg, Tchaikovsky, Strauss, Beethoven. Series Two: Brahms, Foster, Haydn, Liszt, Berlioz, Paganini.

Music Masters, VOX Records. A series of 21 records, for composers, their stories and their music: Bach, Mozart, Chopin, Mendelssohn, Schubert, Schumann & Grieg, Handel, Tchaikovsky, Brahms, Johann Strauss, Beethoven, Haydn, Foster & Sousa, Liszt & Paganini, Berlioz, Rossini, Wagner, Vivaldi & Corelli, Verdi, Rachmaninoff & Prokofiev, Gershwin.

Music of Aaron Copland; Music of Igor Stravinsky, Greystone Corporation.

Period Albums, each on the Life, Times, and Music of Bach, Beethoven, Haydn, Brahms, Chopin, Honegger, Mozart, Schubert, Schumann, Tchaikovsky.

Story of Jazz, Folkways Records FC 7312.

Symphonic Fantasies for Listening and Learning in the Elementary Grades: "The Old King and His Fiddlers Four," and "Brother John and the Village Orchestra," Bowmar Records, Inc.

Time Out, Columbia Records. The Dave Brubeck Quartet.

Charts and Pictures

Famous Composers, RCA-Victor Record Division, 155 East 24th St., New York, N.Y.

Great Composers, Willis Music Company, 124 East 4th Street, Cincinnati, Ohio.

Historical Panorama, Schmitt, Hall & McCreary Company, Park Ave. and 6th St., Minneapolis, Minn. Time line relates music and world history.

Music in Europe Map, Denoyer Geppert Company.

Portraits of Composers, Bowmar Educational Records. Two sets of 20 reproductions or folio of 20 sheets of portrait miniatures, each.

Portraits of Great Composers, Schmitt, Hall & McCreary Company.

Portraits of Great Composers, RCA-Victor Record Division.

Miscellaneous

PROGRAM NOTE SERVICE, 210 West 101 Street, New York, N.Y. 10025. Writes notes for youth concerts.

Young Keyboard Junior Magazine, 1346 Chapel St., New Haven 11, Connecticut. Also provides pictures, thematic charts, lesson plans, radio and television guide, and recordings.

14

creativity, more about notation

One of the inconsistencies of music teaching in the past was that although music was claimed to be one of the creative arts, it was not taught that way. James A. Smith writes, "Although we have associated the development of creativity with the creative arts in the past, the teaching in this area has done more to 'kill off' creativity than to foster it. . . . The lack of creative people in our modern world and the crying need for them is living testimony to the ineffectiveness of the art, music, and literature teaching of the past."[1] Other writers have claimed that their experience in school music stressed prescriptive skills and the imitative reproducing of music, rather than permitting creativity to grow and flourish.

E. Paul Torrance defines creativity as "the process of becoming sensitive to problems, deficiencies, gaps in knowledge, missing elements, disharmonies, and so on; identifying the difficulty; searching for solutions, making guesses or formulating hypotheses about the deficiencies; testing and retesting these hypotheses and possibly modifying and retesting them; and finally communi-

---

[1] Smith, James A., *Setting Conditions for Creative Teaching in the Elementary School* (Boston, Mass.: Allyn and Bacon, 1966), p. 176.

516

cating results."[2] B. Bernard Fitzgerald writes, "In terms of education generally . . . creativity is a *process* which combines *learning and thinking* in a way which might be called learning through discovery. Creativity as a learning process provides the motivation and opportunity for *all* children to learn more effectively than they would with traditional approaches which stress acquisition of facts rather than the development of ideas."[3]

Alex S. Osburn[4] puts all this in a practical setting, and has the creator ask himself a number of questions to which the authors of this book have supplied some of the possible answers:

Q.	*Can it be put to new uses?*	A.	Can it make different sounds?
	Can I adapt it to another use?		How about tape recorders, computers and musical instruments?
	Can I modify it?		Can I change the rhythm, melody, harmony, tone quality, form, etc?
	Can I magnify it?		Let's try increasing the volume, augmentation, a wider range, a thicker texture.
	Can I minify it?		Let's try decreasing the volume, diminution, a lesser range, a thinner texture.
	Can I substitute?		Try other voices, tone qualities, textures, harmonies.
	Can I rearrange it?		Alter the elements of music.
	Can I revise it?		Can I write it backwards, upside-down, in other styles?
	Can I combine it?		Can I combine it with another song, a descant, rhythm, ostinato, harmony, instrument, meter, rhythm pattern, etc.?

[2] Torrance, E. Paul, "Scientific Views of Creativity and Factors Affecting Its Growth," *Daedalus,* Summer, 1965, pp. 663–4.

[3] Fitzgerald, B. Bernard, "Creative Music Teaching in the Elementary School," *NEA Journal,* December, 1964.

[4] Osburn, Alex S., *Applied Imagination,* 3rd ed. (New York, N.Y.: Charles Scribner's Sons, 1963).

In this book creativity has been what the authors intended as a consistent thread throughout. The classroom as a laboratory in which children can explore, discover, and create music has been stressed. The teacher is to be a helpful guide who asks more questions than he answers. This little section is added to further define creativity and to stress it as a part of the learning process that every child needs to experience.

Inquiry and Suggested Activities

1. Put yourself in the role of an intelligent observer of either your college music class or a music class in an elementary school. What elements of genuine creativity do you find? What elements do you find that are definitely not creative? Is it logical to expect a teacher to be creative at all times? Explain.

2. What conditions are necessary in school music for creativity to take place?

3. Identify one *new* thing or activity you would like to try each day for a week. Evaluate the effect of this on you as a teacher and on the children as learners.

4. Read a biography of a composer you regard as being particularly creative. Identify what was especially creative in his work, and try to find what there was in his life which resulted in his creativity.

5. Read the article, "A Blossom Song: A Project in Creative Poetry and Art," in *Musart,* April-May, 1967. It concerns team teaching in music and English in which children wrote *haiku* poetry in the manner of the Japanese poeple, and set the poetry to music using Japanese scales, adding percussion instruments to some. Write your own *haiku* and set it to music.

More About Notation

Learning to read notation fluently is learning to master a skill which can be used in many ways by the learner as he explores, inquires and creates.

The symbols of music, like words of a language, convey man's thoughts and feelings. These symbols are a means to communicate ideas. Music reading assists the learner to grasp the nature and character of music through understanding its symbols, not merely the ability to identify detail. If music is taught fully, learning to read music is an integral part of it. If music reading is taught rightly, it always has an immediate functional or interesting purpose for children. Since children differ in the ways they learn to understand notation, and since music reading is a complex skill, a variety of approaches should be employed. Every normal child should gain reasonable skill in reading music for social and cultural reasons, as well as for musical purposes.

Notation has been referred to many times in this book. There will be no effort here to review each of the ways it has had a part in the study of every element of music. The reader has already seen that the understanding of notation can be taught in a gradual, informative, and purposeful way when teachers and pupils use it to explain and analyze what is heard, sung, and played. In this approach, knowledge of music symbols grows primarily from the study of music itself, rather than from other activities isolated from teaching objectives concerned with developing responsiveness to the elements of music. Every music series has an approach to note reading similar to this. The reader should study them to find out how a given series assists the teacher in helping children in creative ways to use and understand notation. The suggestions should be evaluated in terms of their suitability to specific groups of boys and girls at their current stage of musical growth.

While the the majority of teachers plan the teaching of notation in terms of the above discussion, a minority claim that while integrating notation into the study of music concepts is proper and commendable, it is not enough. These teachers are convinced that some extra effort must be made if children are to gain necessary skill in the use of notation.

The teachers' first point concerns the series books. They claim that these books are multi-purpose books, and that multi-purpose books cannot be expected to teach notation in a very orderly, sequential, or thorough way. They also claim that series books are written in terms of what children's voices can sing rather than in terms of what children's minds are doing in learning notation. Thus, they add, rote singing is overemphasized and the comprehension of notation is correspondingly neglected. Skill in sight-singing develops gradually through use of a large amount of music so simple that children can grasp it quickly. The series books fail to provide this music in sufficient quantity; using them can promote frustration and slow reading habits from placing before children notation that is too complex for them to utilize.

To provide simple music for this purpose generally means the temporary use of music that does not have much musical worth—a choice most music educators are reluctant to make. A popular theory is that selection of music from folk or art sources is mandatory, and that music written for specific notational problems is usually unworthy for school use. Furthermore, this is disturbing to another theory that all music learning should come from a study of good music. The answer made to this problem is derived from a comparison of the usual music-reading approach in the elementary classroom with the approach of the beginning instrumentalist. It is widely acknowledged that instrumentalists as a group are far better music readers than are vocalists. This is attributed to the fact that when a person begins to play an instrument he learns to play only a note or two at a time, and each new note is added gradually along with simple tunes and exercises based on these few notes. It follows theoretically that if this instrumental approach is practiced in vocal classes, the children may become good note readers in the way the instrumentalist does, and would then be able to use notation in the reading of much more music than is the common practice.

The reader should remember that this viewpoint does not mean abandoning the approaches to understanding and using notation stressed throughout this book. It implies the *addition* of other materials of instruction to this approach. These materials come from three sources: commercial, teacher-made, and from research projects undertaken to find appropriate folk and art music.

One publisher has specialized in publishing easy vocal materials based on the above described instrumental approach. This is the Handy-Folio Music Company, 309 5th Avenue South, Minneapolis, Minnesota 55415. The author is Carl Vandre, who uses Victor Carlton and Richard Scott as pen names.

However, teachers can plan and organize material of their own in chart form, and use such charts sequentially. They can be mounted on easels or hung on walls. A few have developed mimeographed booklets for specific note-reading purposes. Others are doing research in library books, manuscripts and microfilms to attempt to find music of some stature for reading purposes. Both commercial and teacher-made efforts are based on the principle that the child needs simple music in which groups of notes can be seen at a glance, and that these note patterns should be used repeatedly by the children until they are learned. Such a pattern is scale tones 1, 2, 3. Another could be 3, 2, 1. When these are mastered, they could be combined in a song or tune that uses these notes in both ascending and descending forms. Rhythmic groupings of notes are stressed, as in the concept of identical rhythmic relationships in different tempos, such as ♩ ♩ ♩ ♩ , ♫♫ , and ♬♬ , and various rhythmic combinations such as ♩ ♩ ♩ , ♫ ♩ , and ♫♩ . The dotted note can be taught in the same comparative way. One basic rhythm or tonal combination is taught at a time. Music is found or written that uses the rhythm, tone pattern, or interval consistently, and relationships are then found in songs in the series books. Dull drill should play no part in this, and success in note reading should be ever present. In one school system the music supervisor's charts are a popular feature. The classroom teachers evaluate them regularly and suggest changes when they believe improvements can be made. The children in the several elementary schools ask each other the number of the chart hanging in their room; they know that to have learned the content of one and thus gain a new one is visible evidence of their progress. In another school the music supervisor's collection of songs has been mimeographed to form several specialized song books that assist a step-by-step approach to understanding and using notation. She is doing research to add folk and art songs to her collections that relate to specific problems in understanding notation.

Four guiding principles appear in this type of work that are applicable in all methods of teaching this aspect of music:

1. Begin note reading with *very* simple material, avoiding any difficult rhythm or interval, and teach only one rhythm or note pattern at a time.

2. Use many different materials in which these same patterns appear, including songs in the series books.

3. Present new rhythm patterns, note patterns, and intervals only after the first ones have been learned.

4. Include the review of previously learned notation with the introduction of new material. Use notation consistently, but do not permit it to unbalance a music program. Keep materials for notation study sufficiently simple so that all normal children can read them and find genuine success in doing so.

NUMBERS, LETTER NAMES, AND SYLLABLES

Men have long attempted to find practical ways of learning to read music notation. Roughly one thousand years ago two monks sought to improve the skill of their respective choirs in this regard. One of them, Guido d'Arezzo, invented a system of Latin syllables used as a measuring stick to identify scale tones. This system has evolved to become the *do re me fa sol la ti do* of today. In the United States this is called the *moveable do* system because *do* represents the keynote of all major keys. In France is it called the *fixed do* system because middle C is always *do*. The other monk, Odo of Clugny, chose an instrumental approach. He had his choir learn to play the monochord, a one-stringed Greek instrument, then apply this understanding of tone relationships to singing by notation. These approaches to teaching music reading, the Latin-syllable and the instrumental, are both very much alive today.

Lowell Mason, who was appointed to teach music in the schools of Boston in 1838, was the first officially appointed American school music teacher. His method of teaching music reading was a three-fold approach which began with associating the numbers 1, 2, 3, 4, 5, 6, 7, 8 with the degrees of the scale, using the Latin syllables also, and including the regular note names as a third aspect. Mason used numbers in all initial explanations of tonal relationship; the tonic chord and all the intervals were taught by extensive numeral drills, often from charts. The syllables came to be emphasized by music teachers, partly because of their use in ear-training and sight-singing on the college level.

In 1845[5] and 1883[6] methods of teaching music reading were published that represented revolts against the use of Latin syllables, and that unsuccessfully attempted to eliminate syllables by substituting numerals. The preface of Jordan's *New Method of Sight-Singing* stated that methods of sight-singing with syllables were too intricate, explaining:

> While some persons overcome the difficulties thus presented [by syllables] in reading music, the larger number are left as much in the dark as ever. ... The distinctive features of this [numeral] method ... are the separating of the two mental processes necessarily employed by the persons reading at sight. These processes are, 1st. Reading or comprehending the scale number of each tone. ... 2nd. The production of the tone read. The usual custom of using the syllables Do, Re, Mi, etc., is dropped, not because it is impossible to teach a person by that method but because experience has shown that while a few learn, many fail.

The Jordan Method began with the numbered C scale, then soon transposed the numeral concept to other common keys. Finally, the neutral syllable *la* was sung while the student *thought* the numbers. Chromatics were avoided.

    [5] H. M. Beal, *The Boston Numeral Harmony; or Day and Beal's Phonography of Music* (Boston: 1845).
    [6] Julian Jordan, *New Method of Sight-Singing* (New York: Bigelow and Main, 1883).

C - Major scale

1[7]	2	3	4	5	6	7	8
do	re	mi	fa	so	la	ti	do

A - Minor scale (relative minor, harmonic form)

1	2	3	4	5	6	#7	8
la	ti	do	re	mi	fa	si	la

C - Minor scale (parallel minor, harmonic form)

1	2	3	4	5	6	7	8
la	ti	do	re	mi	fa	si	la

In the early twentieth century the names of Samuel Cole and Alfred White stand out as music educators who taught and advocated the use of numerals rather than syllables. Still later Howard Hinga discarded both syllables and numbers in the teaching of music reading in the schools of Rochester, New York. A study made by one of the authors of the present book at Highland Park, Illinois, yielded evidence that interest in devices such as syllables and numerals was highest in the third grade, indicating that if teachers chose to employ them, they might consider emphasizing them on that grade level. Another in-service study made at the same school yielded evidence that an approach to music reading consisting of a minimal use of numbers combined with an emphasis on easy-to-play instruments was much more effective than an approach consisting almost exclusively of the use of Latin syllables. Although the children, in this instance, preferred numbers to syllables, slightly more than half of them stated their dislike of singing with either. Their natural inclination was

---

[7] When numerals are used in music theory, the first tone of every scale, whether major or minor, is *1*. However, it is common practice in many schools to teach the concept of minor in terms of the *relative* minor in a way that equates the Latin syllable *la* with the numeral *6*, thus beginning every minor scale with *6*. An advantage in so doing is that all scales relate to the major tonality as indicated by the key signature. Another is that the numerals relate directly to the Latin syllable names. A disadvantage is that the chords I, IV, and V_7 in minor then appear to be based on scale tones *6, 2,* and *3*, which is confusing. Thus, one of the less important issues in teaching the notation of minor scales and chords is whether to do this from the standpoint of the parallel minor or the relative minor. The authors believe in the use of both as each is needed to explain scale, chord, and key relationships.

Ascending:

do	di	re	ri	mi	fa	fi	sol	si	la	li	ti	do
1	♯1	2	♯2	3	4	♯4	5	♯5	6	♯6	7	8

Descending:

do	ti	te	la	le	sol	se	fa	mi	me	re	rah	do
8	7	♭7	6	♭6	5	♭5	4	3	♭3	2	♭2	1

to sing songs with meaningful words, and they had a normal dislike of any substitute unless there was a game aspect to the teacher's presentation.

Numerals and syllables are similar devices. They represent the same idea in that both are "measuring sticks" to help one understand the relationship of the tones of the scale. "1" and "do" are two ways of naming the same thing—the key note in major keys (the home tone). Because numbers are already familiar, they are often preferred by elementary school teachers and children to the Latin syllables, which are unfamiliar. Either device may be introduced in connection with songs that are already well known to children. When syllables are used, many teachers believe that the first grade is the place to begin teaching them. Gradually *do* or *1* is recognized by the children as the home tone, and other syllables or numbers acquire meaning and position in relation to *do* or *1*. After children have been guided to think tonal relationships accurately in terms of numbers or syllables, the teacher usually has them sight-sing with a neutral syllable such as "loo" while they *think* numbers or syllables. Theoretically, *these devices should be employed only when their use can solve a problem and when they are needed to make music activities more meaningful.* The letter names are learned also, whether the teacher is employing numerals, syllables, or both. Letter names assume real significance when easy-to-play instruments are used by the children. A comparative analysis of numerals and syllables follows:

Numerals	*Syllables*
familiar terminology; logical to children	unfamiliar terminology; meaningless when introduced
poor from standpoint of voice production	excellent from standpoint of voice production
favored by music theorists; numbers apply to harmony	not favored by music theorists; syllables do not apply to harmony

chromatics very awkward and are avoided	chromatics easily sung (but elementary school music rarely uses them)
excellent in explaining intervals	poor in explaining intervals
harmful to enjoyment if overused	harmful to enjoyment if overused

Whether or not the prospective public school teacher will employ numbers and/or syllables in his music teaching depends upon a number of circumstances. The person who can best interpret these is the teacher of the college music education class who has the opportunity to study the trends and traditions of the area served by his institution. The college teacher and his students are faced with a number of circumstances, trends, and facts: (a) among authors of series books are found those who neither believe in nor practice the use of syllables in their own teaching even though the books they write endorse syllables; (b) musicians who play musical instruments have no need of syllables or numbers in order to become sight-readers of music; (c) American music educators disagree on the value and use of syllables and numbers, and (d) many European music educators favor the use of syllables.

This state of confusion is not as serious as it first appears and may be resolved by the knowledge that most of the activities mentioned in this book can be accomplished without the aid of syllables, and that should a teacher find himself in a teaching situation in which syllables must be employed, he can learn them along with the children. Perhaps most important is the fact that many teachers use a combination of numbers, syllables, and letter names because they have found each to be of value in helping children understand the relationship of tones.

EVALUATION OF NOTE READING

A simple type of written test can be used before young children understand the staff. For example, if the teacher's purpose has been to expand concepts of how pitches move in scale-line patterns, he can use the first three notes of "Three Blind Mice" and similar repeated patterns in songs the children have come to know well. Written correctly, this particular pattern could be drawn:

o   o   o— | o   o   o—

On the test paper, however, it might appear with one misplaced note, and the children would be asked to find and circle the error:

o   o   o— | o   ⊚   o—

Later in the year, this type of test can be written on the staff when children are able to understand its function. A test that is usable in grades three and above assumes knowledge of the staff. The test paper is so designed that the first two measures of a four-measure phrase are followed by from two to four versions of the final two measures, only one of which is correct. If familiar song material is used, the children may or may not be expected to write the test *thinking* the pitches from the notation with no assistance of any kind. If unfamiliar phrases are used, the teacher must play or sing the phrase and the children would be asked to check the phrase ending that is the one sounded by the teacher. Other questions that might be answered in written tests might include "How many measures are there in the song?" (Teacher plays song again). "How many eighth notes do you hear in the example I will play now?" "Now listen for the number of dotted-eighth and sixteenth-note patterns in what I will play next." When children understand the function of the key signature and why the key signature is important, they can be asked to identify key signatures and key notes in music. An exciting type of test can come from the taping by the children of a familiar song, then the analysis of what is heard when it is played back. In such a test, items could refer to the meter signature, phrase structure, and the notation of important rhythmic and melodic patterns. Recordings can be used this same way. A useful way to test ability to hear and write melody is based upon a numeral or syllable system that can be expanded to include more scale tones than illustrated below. Children can write the melody by circling the appropriate numerals. After this, they might transfer the melody to the staff.

2 2 ② 2 2 2

①① 1 ① 1 ①

7 7 7 7 ⑦ 7

Other possibilities for evaluation of learning notation include observing children's use of notation as they play songs on the bells; using flash cards to find the extent of recognition of terms and symbols, and the speed of this recognition; ascertaining the degree of success in sight-reading easy note patterns and songs; testing ability to recognize phrases that are the same and those that are different by examining the notation of songs; asking individuals to clap or sing notated rhythm patterns;

asking children to analyze and explain meter signatures; testing ability to differentiate between two notated rhythm patterns by tapping or clapping them; attempting to notate the rhythm of familiar songs; and attempting to notate parts or all of the melodies of selected familiar songs. Standardized tests should be studied carefully before using them. The teacher should know the purpose of the test and what use will be made of the findings if it is given. The Knuth Achievement Tests in Music, Educational Test Bureau, Inc., 720 Washington Ave., S. E. Minneapolis, Minnesota, have as their purpose the testing of ability to recognize rhythmic and melodic elements of music. They can be used in grades three-eight, with different versions for grades three-four, five-six, and seven-eight.

Other Suggestions

1. Remember that line notation is a step toward learning note values, and that rhythmic movement such as stepping the melody rhythm assists learning to read notes. These were discussed in Chapter 8.
2. A common formula for introducing note reading is: *hear it* sung by the teacher or played on a recording; learn to *sing it* by rote and to *act it out* in pitch levels; *play it* on the keyboard or other instruments by ear; *see it* on the chalkboard, chart, or printed page. Remember that music notation is essentially a *picture* of what the ear has heard and the body has felt.
3. Music reading is seldom a separate and special study; it is an integral part of listening, moving to music, singing, and playing instruments. When it is taught in relation to these, it takes on meaning and purpose that motivate the learning of notation.
4. Beginning experiences in music reading should be so simple that success is virtually assured.
5. Emphasize only one aspect of note reading at a time.
6. Children see the five lines of the staff but sometimes fail to comprehend the concept of *space*. The function of the spaces should be made clear.
7. Some teachers begin note reading using only a one-line staff. They place notes on, above, and below this line (*do, re,* and *ti,* or *1, 2,* and *7*). They gradually add more lines as they need them until the five-line staff emerges.

8. Music terms and symbols should be learned in context, i.e., in connection with the music with which the children are working.

9. "When phrases sound alike they look alike" is a valuable generalization for children to make.

10. When the interval of a third appears in a melody, the note moves either from a line to the next line, or from a space to the next space (line-line, space-space). When a 1–3–5 chord pattern occurs in a melody, the notes are either line-line-line or space-space-space. Concepts such as this help children to visualize intervals and note patterns.

11. Progress from rote singing to note singing should be so gradual that the child never feels that note reading is a new activity. In other words, he should always have an adequate background for the next step undertaken in understanding notation.

12. The answer to the question "When should I teach children to understand notation?" is "When they have need of it in their daily music activities." If a teacher plans a rich and varied program of music activities, the children are certain to have need of notation, and they will try to learn it because it will have functions that are useful to them and understood by them.

13. Teach first the comprehension of phrases and patterns of notes. After these are grasped, teach the smaller details. Good note reading is based upon the recognition of patterns of notes or note groupings rather than seeing one note at a time.

14. Use a variety of approaches to music reading because of the many individual differences among children and because there is no *one* right way to teach it.

15. The goal is to teach children to "see with their ears" and to "hear with their eyes."

16. The simultaneous reading of words and notes is extremely difficult. Seeing the words distracts children from seeing the notes. Therefore when emphasizing note reading, sing often without words; use neutral syllables such as "loo" so that attention can be centered on the notation. When preparing to read both words and music at the same time, it is a good idea for the children first to speak the words rhythmically so that they will have a good feeling for the meter and note values.

17. When themes of recorded music are placed on the chalkboard or chart during listening activities, the eye can help the ear, and

something about notation may be learned. If the themes are singable, sing them from notation before the recording is played.

18. When children observe notation while listening to a recording or to the teacher's singing, find out if they are following the notation by stopping the music and seeing if their fingers are pointing to the last note sounded. Some teachers ask children to "frame" measures with their two index fingers, moving the fingers along as the music progresses.

19. Classroom teachers can organize group and individual instruction in note reading. Some children are ready for understanding notation while others may not be. Some of the failures of the past stem from trying to teach any given aspect of notation to every child in the same way at the same time.

20. Emphasize the instrumental approach to note reading, relating this to singing as described in Chapter 9.

21. Challenge the children to "think" familiar melodies first with numbers, then with syllables, and finally writing them in notation.

22. Let the children use notation to experiment with arbitrary tonal sequences derived from telephone numbers, street numbers on houses, and a picture of birds resting on five horizontal telephone wires.

TECHNIQUES AND DEVICES

1. Playing on bells that have been turned on end reveals how ups and downs in pitch look. This can be related to the ups and downs of notes on the staff.

2. A flannel board can be made by stretching and taping outing flannel over heavy cardboard. Lines of the staff can be drawn with a Flo-master Pen, and notes made of black felt. Children enjoy manipulating the notes, and the appearance of the flannel board notation is superior to that of notation drawn on a chalkboard. Some teachers prefer to use no cardboard but instead fasten the top and bottom of the flannel to slender wooden rods. With this construction the device can be rolled up and stored when not in use.

3. The scale can be written vertically on the chalkboard either in

numbers, in regular notation, or in syllables. The class sings various scale tones as the teacher points to them.

4. "Singing from the hand" is useful for drill on difficult passages from song material and for intervals. The teacher uses the right hand to point to the scale tones the class sings. (Some European teachers use this.)

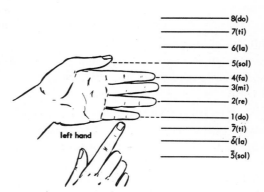

5. The hand is also useful when the fingers are used to represent the staff. Ear-training drills can be done, and some intervals can be practiced when the children sing the "notes" to which the teacher's right index finger points.

6. The "mystery tune" game can be played by placing a few measures of a familiar song on the chalkboard and hiding these by pulling a map down over it. Or this can be written on a chart and its contents concealed by turning its face to the wall. When the children are ready, reveal the notation. The game is to name the tune by studying the notation without humming or playing it.

7. In the intermediate grades it can be fun as well as challenging to read familiar songs that have been notated in humorously distorted rhythm. Example:

AUNT RHODY

8. An ear-training exercise relating physical responses to degrees of the scale can be done while standing.

   Scale tone 1 = arms down at sides
   2 = hands on hips
   3 = fingers on outside of shoulders
   4 = fingers on top of shoulders
   5 = fingers above ears on sides of head
   6 = hands somewhat above head
   7 = arms stretched high above head
   8 = stand on toes with arms stretched high above head

   The teacher may ask the children to close their eyes and respond to scale tones as he plays them on the bells.

9. European teachers use hand signs to indicate degrees of the scale, and have children sing the scale tones "from the hand." They plan ear-training drills with this visual method, emphasizing scale and chord patterns. Hand signs are also used to assist learning difficult parts of songs. (See p. 532.)

10. Some Swiss teachers use a metal half note on a stem, which they move on the lines and spaces of a large staff drawn on the chalkboard. The students sight sing whatever the moving note indicates. Young children can use this device to draw notes on the chalkboard by writing in the hollow note head. A substitute for this device is a bell mallet which has a white or red rubber ball to serve as the note head.

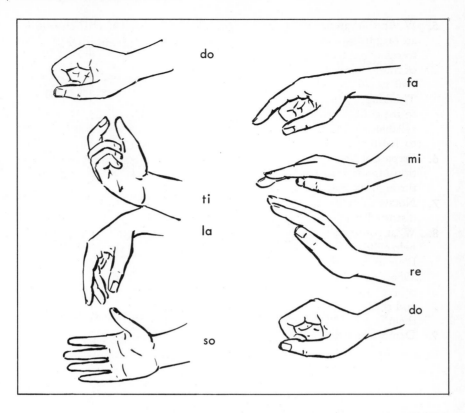

INQUIRY AND SELECTED ACTIVITIES

1. Select a song from a series book and analyze it in terms of possible use for note reading in intermediate grades. Consider the key, the beginning note, note values, scale lines and chord lines in the melody, other note patterns, difficult intervals and rhythms, and measures and phrases that are alike and different.

2. Make a flannel board and demonstrate its use to the class.

3. Evaluate from your own experience the playing of keyboard and blowing-type instruments in learning to understand notation and its use.

4. Construct the following audio-visual aid to help children understand the staff. Hang a solidly constructed bell set vertically so that it is over the chalkboard or on free wall space. The large bars are downward. Draw a staff on either the chalkboard or light cardboard, the staff having lines that lead horizontally from the appropriate bars of the bells. From bottom to top they will be, E, G, B, D, F. This helps the children visualize the relation between tones sounded on the bells and the notes that represent these pitches on the staff.

5. W. Otto Miessner, American music educator and innovator, introduced an original system to use in teaching tonal relationships. Its purpose is to remove the conflict in syllable and numeral systems in which the reader of music must deal with a relative tonal system operating in a fixed pitch staff notation system. Read Mr. Miessner's article, "The Art of Tonal Thinking," *Music Educators Journal* for January, 1962. Explain this system to the college class. Ask the class to sing simple tunes with the Miessner syllables. Ask the class to try to determine whether this system is superior to Latin syllables or numerals.

6. Prepare a short, simple test to measure understanding of tonal relationships and notation to be given in a grade of your choice from three through six.

7. Notate a familiar song in several different meters to produce rhythmically distorted versions that are both fun and challenging to sing.

8. What concepts and generalizations does a teacher need to know—and to help children form when they study notation? The second page of Chapter Four in *Exploring Music With Children,* Wadsworth Publishing Company, 1966, lists some concepts and generalizations for teacher and learner; others can be gleaned from this book, particularly from Chapters 8, 9, and this one. Find these concepts and generalizations and list or group them in a way to reflect an order of difficulty from easy to complex.

9. Demonstrate using the magnetic board.

REFERENCES AND MATERIALS

Articles and Books

BENTLEY, ARNOLD, *Aural Foundations of Music Reading.* London: Novello and Company, Ltd.. U.S. agent for Novello is H. W. Gray, 159 E. 48 St., N.Y. 10017. The English approach, stressing hand signs.

FLAGG, MARION, *Musical Learning.* Evanston, Ill.: Summy-Birchard Publishing Company, 1949. Chapter 10.

HEFFERNAN, CHARLES W., *Teaching Children to Read Music.* New York: Appleton-Century-Crofts, 1968.

LANDECK, BEATRICE, *Children and Music.* New York: William Sloane Associates, Inc., 1952. Appendix I.

MYERS, LOUISE, *Teaching Children Music in the Elementary School* (3rd ed.). Englewood Cliffs, N.J.: Prentice-Hall, Inc., 1961. Chapter 7.

NYE, ROBERT E., "If You Don't Use Syllables, What Do You Use?" *Music Educators Journal,* April-May, 1953, pp. 41–2.

NYE, ROBERT E., VERNICE NYE, *Exploring Music With Children.* Belmont, California: Wadsworth Publishing Company, 1966. Chapter 4.

PIERCE, ANNE E., *Teaching Music in the Elementary School*. New York: Holt, Rinehart and Winston, Inc., 1959. Chapter 7.

RINDERER, LEO, ET AL., *Music Education*. Park Ridge, Ill.: Neil A. Kjos Music Co., 1961.

————, *Sing a Song to Sight Read*. Park Ridge, Ill.: Neil A. Kjos Music Co., 1961.

Song Books

RUFF, EDNA AND HERMAN SMITH, *It's Fun to Sing!* Minneapolis: Schmitt, Hall and McCreary. First steps in sight-singing.

———— *High Low—Together Go!* Minneapolis: Schmitt, Hall and McCreary. Two-part sight-singing.

SCOTT, RICHARD, *Sing at Sight Series*. Minneapolis: Handy Folio Music Company.

VANDRE, CARL, *Clap, Tap and Sing Choral Method*. Minneapolis: Handy Folio Music Company. For grades 2–5.

———— *Sevenfold Choral Method*. Handy Folio Music Company. For grades 6–12.

Films and Filmstrips

JOHNSON HUNT PRODUCTIONS, 6509 De Longpre Ave., Hollywood, Cal. *Music Reading*. 20 minutes. Grades 4–6.

McGRAW-HILL BOOK COMPANY, INC., 330 W. 42nd St., New York 36, N.Y. *Young America Sings*. Teaching filmstrips. Double-faced 12-inch LP recordings with correlated filmstrips. Rote to note singing. Units for grades 3, 4, 5.

SOCIETY FOR VISUAL EDUCATION, INC., 1345 Diversey Parkway, Chicago 14, Ill.

Developing Skills in Music (Group One). All elementary grades. Filmstrips, teacher's guides, and recordings: "Rhythm, the Quarter Note and the Half Note"; "Measures, Whole Notes and Eighth Notes"; "Dotted Notes and Rest"; and "Time Signatures and the Accent." *Developing Skills in Music* (Group Two): "The Staff and Its Notes"; "Major and Minor Scales, Accidentals, and Chromatics"; "Key Signatures"; "Intervals and Phrases."

Special Materials

Children Should Know Music. Wilkinsburg, Penna.: Hayes School Publishing Company. Master carbons for spirit or liquid duplicators. Book 1: Primary; Book 2: Intermediate; Book 3: Middle and Upper. Notation, Theory, Appreciation, History.

Educöm Music Transparencies, Educom Ltd., Box 388, Mt. Kisco, New York 10549. Staff transparencies for teacher and student use.

Glockenturm (bell tower). Wilhelm Monke, Köln-Ehrenfeld, Gutenburg Strasse 61, Germany. The U.S. representative is M. Hohner, Andrews Road, Hicksville, N.Y.

Keyway Theory Guide. Match-a-Tach, Box 72, Mentor, Ohio. Display boards, 67 musical characters, 51 symbols, 16 red nodes. Magnetic.

Music Tutor. Felton, Calif.: Teeter Industries. An electric device operated by the teacher, which "flashes" notes to be sung to stimulate the see/react process in note reading.

Reading and Writing Music, Book 1, Tibor Bachmann. Continental Press, Inc., Elizabethtown, Penna. 17022. For primary grades, based on the Kodály method and designed to teach children to read music and to sing by reading.

Songs for Our Small World, Georgia E. Garlid and Lynn Freeman Olson. Schmitt, Hall & McCreary Company, 527 Park Avenue, Minneapolis, Minn. 55415. Original songs and correlated activities for reading readiness in primary school classrooms. Teacher's Book, Child's Book, and two L.P. records.

music in early childhood

Music in Early Childhood

The importance of education for young children has been emphasized in the experience our nation has had with such programs as Head Start, and in music education by recent research such as that of Dr. Robert Smith and others at the University of Illinois. It has been learned that by providing these children with worth-while and appropriate experiences in the early years their later musical growth can be enhanced.

The research and writings of Piaget, Bruner, Bloom and others reveal that young children can learn rapidly and acquire knowledge quickly. In the 1960's it was acknowledged that the children of the poor were suffering a severe educational disadvantage. The federal government began at that time to finance special programs for young children, and the educators of the nation began to examine not only the education of the very young, but to re-examine the customary education of the primary years to find if all young children might not be deprived of some educational experiences they need as bases for realizing their full potential as receiving and contributing members of society.

Bloom suggests that "the first four years of life are critical in mental growth." In short, he suggests that

> intelligence, the capacity to learn, grows as much during the first four years as in the next thirteen. After age seventeen intelligence continues to develop but at a comparatively slow pace. Failure to develop proper learning patterns in the pre-primary years is likely to lead to continued failure or near failure throughout the remainder of the individual's school career.[1]

It is true that many children are growing up deficient in experiences basic to their optimum musical development, and that the first four years of a child's life are just as crucial, if not more so, to his musical growth in attitudes, appreciations and understanding as they are to his intellectual development. In fact, the two cannot be separated since the young child naturally interprets his intellectual world through his use of body movement and the imitation of sounds. As a result of his limited vocabulary at this age, musical expression through rhythmic movement and through singing about objects and events becomes his best vehicle for communicating his thoughts.

MUSIC CONTRIBUTES TO GROWTH

> Children should sing ten times as much as is now the custom in our schools, just as they should talk ten times as much as now is permitted in most schools. The old-time speechless school is thought to have thwarted the child's intellectual growth; the songless school probably stunts the child's emotional growth. Undoubtedly music should play a larger part in the life of the child in nursery school, kindergarten, and the primary grades than it now does.[2]

Most young children are bombarded daily by a world of sound and different types and forms of music through television, radio, performing groups in the community, movies, recordings and, in some of the more fortunate situations, the discussion of music, singing, and playing of instruments by members of the family. These many exposures can be advantageous, if understanding and qualified adults assist the child in comparing various types of music and in becoming discriminating in his choices. All of this early exposure to music has tended to increase the

[1] Bloom, Benjamin S., Allison Davis, and Robert Hess, *Compensatory Education for Cultural Deprivation* (New York: Holt, Rinehart & Winston, Inc., 1965), p. 16.

[2] Logan, Lillian M., *Teaching the Young Child* (Boston, Mass.: Houghton Mifflin Company, 1960), p. 324.

young child's attention span and interest in music, especially where he has received adequate guidance in developing musical attitudes, appreciations, understandings, judgments and discriminations. It is obvious that precise and specific planning for and guidance of these children is necessary if they are to grow in the ability to enjoy and skillfully and creatively participate in music activities.

Music should become an integral part of every area of the curriculum. It should be related to and result from simple, concrete and first-hand experiences. Music can assist each child in the realization of his physical, social, emotional, aesthetic and intellectual potentialities. Children grow by moving their bodies and reacting to sound; music provides fascinating opportunities for them to do this in creative ways.

Man has utilized music all through history to comment upon his experiences and children do this naturally and easily in the normal process of development. To grow emotionally and socially, children need to feel worthy and confident. Freedom to experiment and to respond in creative ways to music can produce these feelings. Music properly taught can provide opportunity for children to learn appropriate ways of relating to others; it can provide ways of doing this with little or no fear or threat. Through music, children can be led progressively to find more meaning in life about them, if they are guided in the effective use of their senses of hearing, seeing, and feeling as tools for exploring their surrounding environment. As they inquire through the use of these senses, their concepts of such terms as fast, slow, loud, light and soft, high and low, quiet, still, skipping, running, walking, creeping, waddling, squirming, crawling, zooming, gliding, soaring, fluttering, sad, happy, and many others, are expanded, becoming a part of their language development which in turn becomes a vehicle of thought that enhances the children's learning in all areas.

Leeper emphasizes the importance of music in the lives of young children in the statement

> Music can contribute in many ways by offering opportunities for listening, creating, singing, rhythmic responses, and playing instruments. Through these activities, the child experiences pleasure, joy, and creative expression; develops listening skills and auditory discrimination; gains in physical development and use of his body; and increases the range and flexibility of his voice. The child grows in his appreciation of music and can learn to be discriminating in his choices.[3]

[3] Leeper, Sarah Hammond, et al., *Good Schools for Young Children,* 2nd ed. (New York: The Macmillan Company, 1968), p. 360.

MUSIC IN THE SCHOOL DAY

Music for these children is not left to chance. The teacher provides an environment conducive to the optimum learning of musical expression. Careful planning and preparation are necessary if spontaneous and creative musical responses are to result. Some guidance on the part of the teacher is essential but too much direction and emphasis on unrelated or meaningless musical skills and terminology will deaden the children's interest and response.

Young children naturally enjoy sound and movement. They personally express the world through the use of their voice and body. They spontaneously chant self-created tunes about objects, people and events surrounding them. A teacher of the very young must look to the spontaneous, individual expressions of these children for her clues or beginning points in expanding and enriching their musical experiences. Through her acceptance and sensitivity to each child's movement, action, creative chants, comments, and rhythms, the child is encouraged to explore and experiment with movement, rhythm, and sound at his own level of understanding. She responds to the child by singing with him; having him answer her singing question, or he sings musical questions and she sings answers; she accompanies his creative movements and songs. Thus their music is given structure and the children learn skills in a meaningful context at their level of comprehension.

The teacher establishes by her example that music is an accepted and enjoyed means of human expression; because of this the children are more apt to utilize music to satisfy their needs for communication, movement and self-expression. *The teacher knows both the children and music;* unless she understands both she will be unable to help them to attain the value and skills of music.

Leavitt discusses the place of music in the young child's daily program. He says that music for this age

cannot be blocked off into isolated periods of the day. Music is so closely tied in with the emotions that it springs forth spontaneously as the child plays. While this spontaneous overflow is a nucleus of musical expression, it does not preclude setting a time apart for re-creating and extending these experiences. The important thing is to keep a balance between the spontaneous musical creation and thoughtful musical re-creation. Balance does not necessarily mean equal lengths of time. Balance is dependent on the maturity of the child. The two-year-old may spend his time exclusively with spontaneous musical response, while the more mature five-year-old will demand more time for re-creating and extending musical experiences with his classmates.[4]

THE MUSICAL ENVIRONMENT OF THE HOME AND SCHOOL

It is a truism that children are inclined to be more interested in music and to possess more positive attitudes toward and appreciations for music when they are reared in homes in which there is singing, in which various types and qualities of music are heard, performed, discussed and enjoyed, and in which they are guided and encouraged to respond. The musical understandings, skills, attitudes and appreciations possessed by the parents, or concerned adults, have a pronounced influence upon the musical interest and growth of the child. The parent's, or concerned adult's, musical aspirations for the child, the encouragement and incentives offered for musical development, the emphasis placed on the values of music and its performance, the accessibility of music books, instruments, recordings, musical performing groups—solos, concerts, opera, bands, and musical performance on television, radio and in movies—further enhance children's understanding of and desire to perform music.

Teachers need to solicit the interest and assistance of parents in developing musical experiences for children. They should be invited to: take part in discussions of music programs; to observe the children perform in music; ask questions; and to participate in evening music classes in order to improve their own music skills and understandings.

Concerned adults and the parents of young children, and particularly those in disadvantaged homes and communities, should be encouraged to join together as a group and be recognized as a significant aspect of the teaching staff—not merely as "teacher's aides in the classroom" but "teacher's aides of music" in the home and community.

THE VERY YOUNG CHILD AND MUSIC—BIRTH TO THREE YEARS

Most children from birth to age three are educated at home. The mother or nurse takes individual care of the child. Her words, her playful gestures accompanied by rhythmic sayings, and her singing, give the child its first impressions of music. During the first year of life the child absorbs musical impressions from its home environment. The beat of melodies it is listening to inspires it to move and it follows singing attentively. Singing

[4] Leavitt, Jerome E., *Nursery-Kindergarten Education* (New York: McGraw-Hill Book Company, 1958), p. 132.

and rhythmic response do not take place at one fixed time of the day but occasionally as natural opportunities occur. However, the mother or nurse should sing and hum to it often throughout the day.

From the age of 12 to 26 months the child begins to speak; he begins to imitate syllables, intonation, and the pitch of tunes. With frequent attempts and much repetition his accuracy develops gradually. He sometimes sings a motive from small melodies; he can sing the end of a phrase or hum without words.

The age of 26 to 36 months is marked by more advanced experimentation with speech sounds and forming sentences. The joy resulting from the reproduction of syllables and from identifying and producing high and low sounds often inspires the child to create little melodies and rhythmic body movement. The use of nursery rhymes and limericks develops his sense of rhythm, his pronunciation and enunciation of words, and his body response to rhythm.

Approximately at this age he is able to talk in a higher voice or sing small melodies with words in a range of three or four notes—seldom more than the range of the sixth. These small tunes are clustered about the pitches *so-mi* and *so-la-mi* in accordance with the natural intonation of speech.

MUSIC FOR NURSERY AND KINDERGARTEN CHILDREN—AGES 3–5

An important aim in music teaching of children aged 3, 4, and 5 is to help them sing clearly and with pleasure and enjoyment by the time they leave kindergarten for the first year in primary school, age 6. The children should understand the concepts of high and low in pitch, loud and soft in volume, and fast and slow in tempo. They learn to sing songs taught by rote by the mother, the teacher, and by hearing some on radio, television, or recordings.

One of the common beliefs concerning the attention span of this age child is that it is short, ranging from five to ten minutes for sustained musical effort for the age of three and approximately fifteen minutes for those of four and five. This belief remains valid for most of these children but recent research indicates that this is an individual matter and can vary widely from child to child in terms of his interest and over-all maturity, and of his previous exposure to and experience with music. Therefore the teacher will need to determine the interest span of each child and provide music experiences accordingly.

Many of the nursery school children behave as individuals rather than as persons belonging to a group, and the observer of a nursery school class should not be startled if one child leaves the group to do something else—such as to paint what he feels or to get up and dance or dramatize, while the group may be singing. Within the group, part of the children might, at the suggestion of the teacher, do some type of simple body response while the other children sing. Singing is a matter of imitating the teacher, and a major aim of the teacher is to build a classroom environment that fosters children's spontaneous use of singing. These children are often uncertain about knowing words to songs, and sometimes substitute other words. They enjoy the ego-centered pleasure of the teacher's singing of short songs they create in their play or in their concern about some other aspect of school or experience outside of school. Sometimes they choose to paint what they feel as they listen to recorded music.

Never are all of the children of any chronological age group ready for the same types and levels of music experiences. Leeper warns:

> because the child is not ready to participate in one activity (such as clapping in time to music) the teacher may decide that he should not be forced and leave him alone. . . . He should not be forced but activities can be paced to his development and he can be helped to take the next step. Not forcing does not mean leaving the child alone unchallenged. . . . the teacher can arrange many worth-while experiences. There should be opportunities to climb, run and jump which can help the child gain control of the large muscles. As he experiments with body movement he will set his own tempo.[5]

The young child experiments with interpreting music in logical and feasible ways for him. He uses his big muscles and body movements as he claps, walks, runs, jumps, rolls, bounces, and crawls. Through such movements he gradually discovers relationships between his movements and the beat and tempo of music. In like manner, as he imitates the sounds found in his environment, he begins to make associations of high and low pitches with the sounds of his voice.

Young children compose or chant creative songs or tonal fragments about such activities as planting seeds, chasing a butterfly, flying a kite, rolling down a hill, baking a cake, washing the dishes, setting the table, rocking the baby. The teacher records their tunes and assists them in

[5] Leeper, Sarah Hammond, et. al., *Good Schools for Young Children*, rev. ed., (New York: The Macmillan Company, 1968), p. 360.

singing them again at a later time. But in addition to singing their songs, the teacher selects songs of high interest and appeal, teaching them by rote. They may listen to the recordings of some. She often carries on singing conversations with the children—singing greetings, directions, and suggestions while the children improvise replies in song. At times the teacher sings humorous songs as well as those having artistic value; she may play these melodies on instruments such as bells, xylophone, violin, flute and piano. The children of this age enjoy and need much repetition.

By the time the children who have attended nursery school are of kindergarten age, they should have learned how to sing in loosely organized groups and how to sing alone without being helped by the teacher. Their singing should be secure within the range of the sixth from middle C to A and some will have progressed to a wider range. As young children explore music on their own level of understanding they develop a sense of individual worth and accomplishment that increases their ability to express themselves. They learn that there are many different types of music that communicate many thoughts and ideas to us and for us. We sing when we are happy, when we play and work; we sing about things that happen to us, using music to tell people how we feel. We can express ourselves by singing, dramatizing, playing instruments, and by rhythmic responses.

Simple percussion instruments can be used in the nursery school and kindergarten with rhythm experiences. The child's natural response to music is often to first respond by some body movement, sing it, then play it with the instruments. The teacher plans ways to encourage listening carefully to the music to be worked with—listen first, then respond. When a new song is introduced, the children learn to listen to the teacher. It is possible to learn concepts of rhythmic notation from large charts and the ti-ti-ta's mentioned in previous chapters.

Regular and systematic music experiences in the early years provide a solid basis for further education in the primary and intermediate grades. In planning and providing music experiences for these children the *process* of learning must receive more attention than the *product*. Gans comments that, "in the past there has been undue emphasis on music as a product rather than a process. Children—ordinary children—have considerably more power to make music than the traditional music curriculum for young children would suggest."[6]

[6] Gans, Roma, et al., *Teaching Young Children* (New York: World Book Company, 1952), p. 306.

Experiences in Music

RHYTHM

Edna Buttalph says:

> The natural sequence with children of nursery and primary years is from motion to song, rather than from song to motion. Full, free use of the body not only relaxes the children, but makes them ready and eager for singing time. Yet too often in special music periods, children are gathered in small chairs in a circle, and the very first procedure is the singing of songs. The children's urge to move, almost invariably strong, is criticized by the eager specialist, convinced she has something beautiful to give. She may become annoyed when the children do not give her their immediate and quiet attention and she creates for herself some totally unnecessary problems.[7]

The teacher provides space for the young child's random movements, since these are the large muscle type. At first she provides the child many opportunities to explore movement; more formal and complex rhythmic learnings are presented later. Soon the child will be able to move to his own beat for brief periods; the teacher observes this and accompanies the child's beat with drum, piano, or clapping. The child learns to recognize that the teacher is playing what he is performing with his body. He usually tries faster tempos before being able to control slower ones. The teacher works to help the child grow toward being able to keep time with the teacher's beat. He reviews what they have done together thus far—the teacher conforms to the child's tempo—and suggests that something new be tried. He will beat first with the child, then slightly faster or slightly slower; can the child listen to this and walk the way the drum does?

To explore rhythmic movement with children ask them to:

Stand tall like a tree.
Let your arms move like the branches on a tree.
Move like the leaves on the tree. (tremble)
Be a cat creeping toward a mouse.
See if you can move like a snake.
Be as still as smoke.

[7] Edna G. Buttalph, *Music for the Classroom Teacher,* (New York: Bank Street College, 1958), p. 15.

Be as quiet as a mouse.
Crawl like a worm.
Move like a feather in the breeze.
Hop like a toad.
Trot like a pony.
Sail like a boat.
Zoom like an airplane.
Flit like a bee.
Gallop like a horse.
Walk like an elephant.

SINGING

Early childhood singing programs should be planned in accordance with sex differences. In general, girls are superior to boys in their ability to match pitch. By the age of ten, boys who have had early singing experiences in nursery school and kindergarten tend to equal the ability of girls if songs are pitched in ranges appropriate for them.

The child listens to songs sung by the teacher and others; he responds with physical actions. He eventually sings a word or short section of a song with another voice. He next sings with another voice or with the group, but not always at the same time, often being a measure or so behind and not always with the same words. The teacher should be alert to this and expect great individual differences; he should not force children into the music activities, but try to entice them by creatively inventing relationships between what they are doing and the music. The teacher plans ways to help the child listen carefully and to be aware of relative high and low pitches. The descending minor third, then added tones of the pentatonic scale, are emphasized in many early singing experiences (See Chapter 9). Echo-type songs are often used in which the children have opportunity to listen to part of the melody they will repeat as the song progresses. Melodies without accompaniment or with very minimal accompaniment are used because these children need to hear many melodies without the complications of other pitches at this stage of their development. The child becomes able to sing along with the group and to match tones; he enjoys singing alone, requests favorite songs, and identifies songs he knows. The teacher does not expect the same of all the children, and seldom directs *everyone* to sing; she finds some way to encourage each child and to give him some measure of success in at least one of the areas of music each day. He selects songs of varying length and subject content. Most children's voices center around G above middle C; however, a very easy beginning range to use initially is from middle C to the A above, with a five-note range recommended. Singing occurs throughout the day, often incidentally. Comments about certain happenings or items may be sung as short fragments. Songs are selected about subjects familiar to the children; the children's spontaneous songs are "caught" by the teacher and used by the group, if appropriate; most songs are simple, short, and have repeated parts or phrases. Tone matching drills are played like games. There are echo games with children's names and those in which children play the part of street vendors selling such things as newspapers and ice cream. Sometimes the child will hum a pitch and the teacher tries to find it on piano or bells; then the children listen to decide if the teacher matched it. The teacher hums part of a song and the children identify it; a child first thinks a tune, then hums it for the children to see if they can recognize it. Concepts of high and low are worked with in a game climate. Children often confuse high and low with loud and soft; teachers should be prepared to help them eliminate this error.

Children need to experiment with their voices; some of them need this to learn to sing. They like to invent imitations of the sound of a duck, a bird, a cow, a calf, a pig, a horse, a dog, a fire siren, and the wind.

SELECTION AND TEACHING SONGS

SELECTING SONGS In selecting songs the teacher should choose those which are simple, short and contain conversation and repetition. Repetitive words and phrases appeal to this age and are usually easy to learn. Even though most young children need short simple songs, some children vary widely from this norm depending on physical, social, intellectual and musical maturity and exposure to various types and levels of music. Therefore the teacher must study each child's level of maturity and interests, selecting songs which challenge and interest him as an individual. More difficult musical concepts and performance are provided spirally and progressively.

Both the text and music of the songs selected for children should be emotionally satisfying and appealing. The establishment of a rigid "norm" for all children to achieve in musical skills, understandings and appreciations is not advocated. It is generally accepted today that a child must be set free to explore, inquire, experiment, analyze, hypothesize and generalize on his own level of performance and in terms of his unique ways of learning. However, the teacher should establish a set of general criteria to use as a guide in the selection of appropriate song material. Her list could include such criteria as follows:

The song:

1. Is easy to sing and is not too long but contains a complete musical idea.

2. Is of suitable range for most of the children and contains charm and lasting quality.

3. Has rhythm that flows but is also appropriate and child-like in appeal.

4. Contains sufficient repetition in both melodic and rhythmic patterns and is lyrical.

5. Contains words which relate to the child's interest and experience background and which express his concerns and emotions.

6. Contains words and music which agree in conveying the same message.

7. Contributes to the realization of identified general and behavioral objectives and to the development of musical concepts and generalizations.

The rhythmic and song materials for nursery school and kindergarten are selected in accordance with the musical abilities of the children and the degree of difficulty in rhythm, words, melody, vocabulary, and concepts.

The teacher uses three main sources in selecting songs for children: (1) suitable folk song collections; (2) songs composed by noted children's composers; and (3) those from the works of the masters. However, if children are singing songs that they have learned in the home from adults, radio, recordings or television, the teacher accepts this music and begins to build on the present level and interest of the children. Gradually she expands and deepens the child's musical understanding and appreciation.

TEACHING A SONG

Teaching of a new song is usually done when the children are rested and ready for a new learning experience. Appropriate times to present a new song are at the first group activity of the day, coming usually soon after they arrive in the morning or just after a rest period.

A new song is thoroughly learned and memorized by the teacher. A recording of it may be played, listened to and analyzed. If an Autoharp, guitar or piano accompaniment is to be used she must learn to play it well and softly so as not to detract from hearing the melody. She determines her over-all objectives for teaching the song, identifies and specifies the pupil's behavioral objectives to be realized, selects appropriate materials needed for teaching the song, finds ways of introducing it to the children, devises means of evaluating each child's progress, and she thinks of possible creative and enrichment types of related activities in which to involve children following the learning of the words and melody.

To introduce the song and to build a background and readiness for it, the teacher may read a short related story and discuss it with the children; they may dramatize the story. Some other time during the day or the next day she may tell the children the title of the song and relate its content to the story read previously. The song is then sung in its entirety by the teacher. After she sings it to the children one or two times she may repeat the words to be sure that they understand them. The children who are sufficiently interested are encouraged to begin to sing with her. As the song progresses toward completion others are invited to join in until finally most of the children may be singing. They learn the proper interpretation of the mood, the phrasing, enunciation and correct pitch by imitating the singing style of the teacher. She teaches the song over a period of days by singing the complete song one or two times each day. After the children learn the melody they may be assisted in improving the quality of singing certain parts of the song.

Children may be involved in creative and enrichment types of musical activities appropriately related to the song they are learning. Such activities as dramatization of the song, creating a rhythmic response or selecting, deciding when and how to play an instrument to create certain effects for certain parts of the song may be employed. The teacher may also relate the song to other activities or experiences at school or home.

The teacher watches the children and takes clues from them as to how long to engage them at one time in the learning of a song, as well as how long to prolong a related follow-up activity. Continuous and analytical attention is given to the selection of songs appropriate for the children in terms of interest, maturity and experience. Records are kept of each child's progress and needs.

The young child enjoys having his songs recorded on tape; he listens to his singing repeatedly as he plays the tape. The teacher uses these recordings to analyze the child's musical growth and needs; then she plans specific learning activities for each child's musical development based upon the needs indicated by the tape.

LISTENING

At first the child is apt to listen while doing something else, listening only enough to be merely aware of the music. For listening the teacher selects a variety of music which includes different moods and interesting and aesthetically attractive sounds. Music is sometimes listened to in relation to stories. The child learns to enjoy short songs, instrumental selections and recordings alone or with an older person; later he does this with small, then large groups. He becomes able to analyze music to the extent of using concepts such as loud, soft, fast, slow, heavy, light, happy, sad, high, low. He can listen to music to answer questions about it, and listen to his own playing or singing and correct errors. He can also listen to simple rhythm patterns and then reproduce them or interpret them through dramatics, rhythmic movement and interpretation.

PLAYING INSTRUMENTS

The child first manipulates and explores percussion instruments, discovering differences in sounds and ways of playing them. He advances from noise to more musical sounds as the teacher asks him which of the ways he plays sounds best to him. The teacher provides opportunities for individual experimentation and study of the instruments by the child. He plays rhythm sticks when he marches, but not yet in time with his feet. He continues to explore high, low, wood, metal, and various pitches and tone qualities of the instruments; he becomes able to recognize instruments by their sound. He next is able to play an instrument in time with the beats of a recording, piano, or drum; he becomes able to perform on instruments with a group of children. His interest expands to those which adults play, and he learns to identify several by ear and by sight. The teacher plays selected recordings while the child listens; he asks what manner of percussion tone quality is best for the music. The child then selects the instrument he believes appropriate and his power of discrimination continues to develop. Sensitivity to the form, texture, and mood of the music grow as the child is encouraged to listen, then respond creatively. This process is later applied to the group. Adult instruments are brought to school to be examined; older children or adults may perform on them. A field trip may be planned to visit a band or orchestra rehearsal.

CREATING

The child experiments with body movements, sound of percussion instruments, and chants he sings during his individual play. He learns that he may change the words of songs, and he does this; eventually he creates new verses. He learns through experimentation and helpful questions from the teacher to select appropriate instruments with which to accompany songs. He can act out in rhythmic movement the mood of a song and actions implied by the song; he dramatizes. He can make up tunes vocally and on the bells. The teacher provides a learning environment that permits children to chant as they play and to experiment with sound in general. Songs are learned which provide opportunities for changing the words—such as animal songs, substituting a different animal and the sound he makes or the way he moves. Providing hats, scarves, balloons and other items help to creatively interpret aspects of characters or the music itself.

The teacher is alert to songs the child makes up on the playground or when he is alone, absorbed in some other activity. She evaluates these for possible use. She employs songs with words which suggest action; she lets the child or children suggest and plan the action. There can be group composition followed by individual composition. The teacher finds the tune on the piano and notates it, tape records it, or she writes it in syllables, numbers or other musical shorthand to notate later.

SUMMARY

Concepts of rhythm, pitch, tone quality, simple form, melody, tempo, and dynamics are worked with at the level of each child. Vocal control and range grow and expand; enjoyment builds the foundation for these and for growth in discrimination, sensitivity, motor control, and ability to hear music accurately.

INQUIRY AND SUGGESTED ACTIVITIES

1. Observe in a nursery school or kindergarten to see:
   a. How music is integrated into all of the activities of the curriculum.
   b. How music is presented to stimulate and encourage thinking and creativity.

    c.   What basic music principles and concepts are being developed? How?

    d.   How music is used to build cultural understanding and values.

    e.   What teaching strategies is the teacher using with these children? What kinds of comments is she making; what kinds of questions is she asking?

2. Determine the role of the teacher in her assistance in the development of aesthetic appreciation.

3. Specifically determine what you would need to know about each child in order to teach music in an effective way to him. How would you obtain this information? How would you design a music program for a child based on this information?

4. Explore and outline the types of musical experiences young children should encounter during their pre-primary years.

5. Determine and state the necessary physical conditions, types of materials and media for a good music program for young children; what would be necessary to produce a desirable social, emotional and aesthetic environment for encouraging the development of musical appreciations, concepts, and understandings?

6. Explore possible ways of working with parents and interested adults in the home and community to further musical interest and growth in children.

7. What musical values can be derived by the children from listening to selected records and then having them join in with the singing or respond physically to the music?

8. Visit an early childhood class (ages 3, 4, and 5) during a free activity period to observe the following:

    a.   Instances of children singing familiar songs as they work or play.

    b.   Children's creative musical improvisation.

9. Examine and list the song books found in the classroom for early childhood. Explore how they are used or how they could be used.

10. How would you arrange kindergarten children in a group singing situation period? How long would you usually involve this age in musical group activities? What types of songs could you use? How would you attempt to raise the quality of their performance?

11. List as many ways as you can think of that songs and rhythmic response can be used to develop creativity in children.

12. Do research on the Montessori method of teaching music and determine its creative and non-creative implications.

13. Use your creative capabilities by

    a.   Indicating all the ways you can teach a song, dance, improvisation of songs, dances and instrumentation to young children.

    b.   Explore and record creative ways to use audio-visual materials in the teaching of music to young children (tapes, charts, pictures, demonstrations, observation of performing people, experimenting with instruments and sound materials).

14. Select a folk song suitable for young children; teach it to the class or if possible to a young child. Analyze your results.
15. How would you attempt to develop in young children the ability to listen carefully in the rhythms and appreciation period?
16. Observe a young child and record at least 12 occasions in which he becomes involved in rhythm in activities not pertaining directly to music.
17. Identify objects or articles that could be used to produce rhythm. Bring four or five to class and compare them with those brought by other students. Experiment with instruments and materials to produce sounds. Then formulate a list of possible materials to provide for children to experiment with and discover sound qualities and rhythm.
18. Observe a child's rhythmic movement and his tempo. Accompany him with an appropriate percussion instrument. Allow the child to set the tempo.
19. Evaluate three or four children's recordings to use in teaching young children music. Share them with other college students for selecting songs for young children. Select a song you consider to be appropriate for this age and prepare to teach this song to a group of young children if possible; if it is not possible to teach it to children, teach to your classmates. Use the criteria stated in this chapter or formulate your own list of criteria and evaluate your song choice in terms of them.

SONG BOOKS, CHARTS, RECORDINGS, AND FILMS

SONG BOOKS Some of the publishers of music textbooks include books for nursery school and kindergarten in their series. These books are addressed to the teacher; the indexes provide quick references to songs classified under such headings as animals; machines such as airplanes, cars, boats and trains; seasons; special days and holidays; folk songs; fun; nursery rhymes; action songs, dramatization and pantomime; singing games; lullabies; toys; playthings and play; songs about children and adults. Rhythm is usually subclassified into walking, tip-toeing, marching, running, jumping, swaying, rolling, hopping, trotting and so on.

Teachers should remember to transpose songs to lower or higher keys when necessary. They should also use and adapt songs, piano selections and other suggestions found in series books written for first grade use. Several nursery, kindergarten and first grade books are needed in a classroom.

Gunild Keetman's *Music for Children I Pentatonic* book contains nursery rhymes, songs and other music activities for the young child. The books compiled by Beatrice Landeck, *Songs to Grow On* and *More Songs to Grow On,* and those by Ruth Crawford Seeger, *American Folk*

Songs for Children, Animal Folk Songs for Children, and *American Folk Songs for Christmas* include songs both charming and useful for early childhood.

CHARTS Appropriate and useful charts are available for use in teaching music to the very young. Mary Helen Richards' *Threshold to Music* materials include experience charts for kindergarten. Hand signals for so, la, and mi (5, 6, 3) and rudimentary notation for quarter and eighth notes are introduced. Peg Hoenack's materials for pre-school and primary children, *Songs I Can Play* series, and *Let's Sing and Play Together* series, may be purchased from Ellsworth Studios, 4611 Willow Lane, Chevy Chase, Maryland 20015. Howard Doolin has produced charts for use in kindergarten through third grade entitled *A New Introduction to Music, Level One: Pitch and Duration of Tone* (Park Ridge, Ill.: General Words and Music Company, 1966). Systems for Education, Inc. at 612 North Michigan Avenue, Chicago, 60611 has produced *The Headstart With Music Program* which is a program consisting of musical activities and listening songs designed for children in kindergarten and primary grades. The program's two 12″ LP records contain 27 selections; there are 16 large (18″ × 24″) colored easel cards; on one side of the card is a picture which evokes mood or the story of song and on the other side the musical notation and words of the song are printed in large easy to read type.

RECORDINGS—DISC AND TAPE The teacher of young children should select and evaluate recordings to be certain that the pitch of the song is suited to the children's vocal range; that the melody line is sufficiently simple; and that the presentation is conducive to the development of appropriate musical concepts, skills, appreciations and realization of specific musical objectives.

Recordings accompanying the series books are the most readily accessible. Other recordings are found in the catalogs of the Greystone Corporation (Young Peoples Records and Children's Record Guild), Bowmar, Folkways, Decca, Capital, RCA Victor, Columbia and other educational supply houses. Recordings from standard collections such as *Adventures in Music* can be used.

Some recent recordings recommended for this age are:

BOWMAR RECORDS, INC.
> The Small Musicians Series by Lucille Wood
> Another Mother Goose and Nursery—1–12″ LP

> Rope Jumping and Ball Handling—1–12″ LP
> The Rainy Day Record (ideal for indoors)—1–12″ LP
> Folk Songs for Little Singers—1–12″ LP

LYONS, INC., 688 Industrial Drive, Elmhurst, Illinois, 60126
> LP 506–Finger Games—1–12″ 33 1/3 RPM Kindergarten—2nd Grade
> LP 507–Singing Action Games—1–12″ 33 1/3 RPM Grades 1–3
> LP 508–Action Songs and Rounds—1–12″ 33 1/3 RPM Grades 1–3

KINDER COLLEGE, INC., 2504 N.E. 34th Avenue, Portland, Oregon 97212
> Singing Our Way Through School—A Teacher's Guide and 9 Records.

THE UNITED WORLD FILMS' *Discovering Music* Series is designed for pre-primary and primary grades; Teacher's Guides are available for the two films currently available—*Discovering Rhythm* and *Discovering Melody*. United World is a division of Universal Education and Visual Arts.

Films

Discovering Melody. Universal Education and Visual Arts, 221 Park Avenue South, New York, N.Y. 10003.

Discovering Rhythm.

Music in Motion No. 11 "The Enchanted Lake" (Liadov). Musilog Corporation, 1600 Anacapa Street, Santa Barbara, Calif. 93102. A pictorial-sound impression of a beautiful lake and its environs; an aesthetic experience.

Piano Books

McCALL, ADELINE, *Timothy's Tunes*. Boston: Boston Music Company. The child can begin with the bells and progress to the piano keyboard in an introductory way.

MEIER, GUY, AND MARY JARMAN NELSON, *The Two of Us*. Evanston, Ill.: Summy-Birchard Company. A child and an adult play piano together.

NELSON, MARY JARMAN, *Piano Music for Early Childhood*. New York: Charles Hanson Music Company.

REFERENCES

Selected Books

ANDREWS, GLADYS, *Creative Rhythms for Children*. Englewood Cliffs, N.J.: Prentice-Hall, Inc., 1954.

BLEY, EDGAR S., *The Best Singing Games for Children of All Ages*. New York: Sterling Publishing Company, 1957.

BROWN, MARGARET WISE, *The Little Brass Band*. New York: Harper and Row, Publishers, 1955. Read the story to the children; have them identify instruments as they listen to the recording with the same title; then they experiment with playing the instruments and observe others play band instruments.

————, *Indoor Noisy Book;* also *Country Noisy Book* and *Seashore Noisy Book*. New York: William Scott, Inc., 1946.

CLEVELAND ASSOCIATION FOR NURSERY EDUCATION, *Cane Review*. Biannual publication containing songs, stories, and games. 2084 Cornell Road, Cleveland, Ohio.

COLEMAN, SATIS N., *Creative Music*. New York: The John Day Company, 1940. Also *Creative Music in the Home,* 1939, and *Singing Time* by same author and publisher.

ELLING, MARY, *Wheels and Noises*. New York: Wonder Book, Inc., 1950. Describes the noises of machines with wheels. Children enjoy imitating the sounds.

FOSTER, JOSEPHINE, AND NEITH E. HEADLEY, "Creative Self-Expression," *Education in the Kindergarten* (4th ed.). New York: American Book Company, 1966. Chapter 8.

FREILICOFF, NAOMI, *The Magic of Music*. New York: New York State Association for Nursery Education, May, 1953. Describes vividly the effect of rhythms on children.

HOBAN, RUSSELL, *The Songs in My Drum*. New York: Harper and Row, Publishers, 1962.

HOOD, MARGUERITE V., AND E. J. SHULZ, *Learning Music Through Rhythm*. Boston: Ginn and Company, 1949.

HORWICH, FRANCES R., *Here Comes the Band*. Chicago: Rand McNally & Co., 1956. Children improvise instruments to form a band like the one described in the book.

HUEY, J. FRANCIS, "Enjoying and Producing Music," *Teaching Primary Children*. New York: Holt, Rinehart and Winston, 1965. Chapter 13.

HUGHES, LANGSTON, *The First Book of Rhythms*. New York: Franklin Watts, Inc., 1954.

HUNT, EVELYN, *Music Time*. New York: The Viking Press, 1942.

JENKINS, ELLA, *The Ella Jenkins Song Book for Children*. New York: Oak Publications.

JONES, BETTY JENSEN, *What Is Music for Young Children?* Kingston, Rhode Island: National Association for Nursery Education, College of Home Economics, University of Rhode Island, 1959.

KODÁLY, ZOLTAN, *Fifty Nursery Songs within the Range of Five Notes,* trans. Percy M. Young. Oceanside, N.Y.: Boosey and Hawkes, 1963.

LAMBERT, HAZEL M., "Music Activities," *Early Childhood Education*. Boston: Allyn & Bacon, Inc., 1960. Chapter 17.

LANDECK, BEATRICE, *Children and Music*. New York: William Sloane Associates, Inc., 1952.

LEAVITT, JEROME, "Story and Music Time," *Nursery-Kindergarten Education*. New York: McGraw-Hill Book Company, Inc., 1958. Chapter 7.

LOGAN, LILLIAN M., "Rhythm and the Dance" and "Music," *Teaching the Young Child*. Boston: Houghton Mifflin Company. Pp. 311–36.

MacCARTNEY, L. P., *Songs for the Nursery School and the Kindergarten*. Cincinnati: Wills Music Company.

MACE, KATHERINE, *Let's Dance a Story*. New York: Abelard-Schuman, Inc., 1955.

MACHERONI, ANNA MARIA, *Developing the Musical Senses: The Montessori Approach to Music for the Ear, Voice, Eye, and Hand*. Cincinnati: Greenwood Press, 1967.

MEHL, MARIE, ET AL., "Creative Music," *Teaching in the Elementary School*. New York: The Ronald Press Company, 1958. Pp. 352–55.

MONTESSORI, MARIA, *The Montessori Elementary Material*. Cambridge, Mass.: Robert Bentley, Inc., 1964.

NEW YORK STATE EDUCATION DEPARTMENT, BUREAU OF ELEMENTARY CURRICULUM DEVELOPMENT, *Children the Music Makers*. Albany: The Bureau, 1953.

NORTON, JUNE, *Sing and Be Happy*. New York: The John Day Company, Inc., 1957.

READ, KATHERINE, "Through Creative Expression—the Inner World," *The Nursery School* (4th ed.). Philadelphia: W. B. Saunders Company, 1966. Chapter 12.

RUDOLPH, MARGUERITA, AND DOROTHY COHEN, "Music and Rhythms in School," *Kindergarten—A Year of Learning*. New York: Appleton-Century-Crofts, 1964. Chapter 11.

SANDOR, FRIGYES, ED., "Music Teaching in Nursery Schools," *Musical Education in Hungary*. London: Barrie and Rockliff, 1966. Chapter 3.

SEEGER, RUTH, *American Folk Songs for Children*. Garden City, New York: Doubleday & Company, Inc.

SHEEHY, EMMA DICKSON, *There's Music in Children* (2nd ed.). New York: Holt, Rinehart and Winston, Inc., 1968.

SHOWERS, PAUL, *The Listening Walk*. New York: Thomas Y. Crowell Company, 1961. As children listen to this story, they imitate the sounds they hear.

SMITH, JAMES A., *Creative Teaching of the Creative Arts in the Elementary School*. Boston: Allyn & Bacon, 1967.

Songs Children Like: Folk Songs from Many Lands. Washington, D. C.: The Association for Childhood Education, 1954.

STEINER, CHARLOTTE, *Kiki Loves Music*. Garden City, New York: Doubleday & Company, Inc., 1954. Kiki learns the difference between the sounds of noise and those of music and distinguishes the sounds of several instruments.

STEPHENS, ADA D., ED., *Toward the Development of Creativity in Early Childhood*. Toledo, Ohio: College of Education, University of Toledo, 1963.

TALLMAGE, LYDIA FERN, WILLIAM H. TALLMAGE, AND FRANCIS M. WILSON, *Sing Trouble Away*. 1790 Broadway, New York: New York Teachers Library, 1957. Contains songs and suggestions to aid children in freeing their emotions and frustrations through music.

TODD, VIVIAN E., AND HELEN HEFFERNAN, "Enjoying Musical Sounds," *The Years Before School*. New York: The Macmillan Company, 1964. Chapter 14.

TRIPP, PAUL, *Tubby the Tuba*. New York: Treasure Books, 1954.

WILKIN, ESTHER, *Baby Listens*. New York: The Golden Press, 1960. The baby listens to many sounds in his environment—bells, raindrops and others.

WOOD, LUCILLE, *Songs for Singing Fun*. St. Louis: Webster Publications. Also *More Singing Fun* is a book by the same author and publisher. A 78 rpm record with the same title is available from Bowmar.

Selected Articles

BAILEY, CHARITY, "Music and the Beginning School Child," *Young Children*, XXI, No. 4 (1966), 200–204.

EDWARDS, ESTHER P., "Kindergarten Is Too Late," *Saturday Review*, June 15, 1968.

FOSTER, E. P., "Song Within: Music and the Disadvantaged Preschool Child," *Young Children*, XX, No. 6 (1965), 373–76.

HALL, M. E., "The Guitar in the Classroom," *Music Journal*, XXIV, No. 3 (1966), 121–23.

HATTWICK, MELVIN S., "The Role of Pitch Level and Range in Singing of Preschool, First Grade and Second Grade Children," *Child Development*, IV, No. 4 (1933), 281–91.

HUNT, J. M., "The Psychological Basis for Using Preschool Enrichment as an Antidote for Cultural Deprivation," *Merrill-Palmer Quarterly*, X, No. 3 (July, 1964), 209–43.

JERSILD, A. T., AND SYLVIA F. BEINSTOCK, "The Influence of Training on the Vocal Ability of Three-Year-Old Children," *Child Development*, XI, No. 4 (1931), 272–91.

MERRILL, L., "Where Do Our Children Lose Their Ears?" *Music Journal*, XXIV, No. 3 (1966), 57, 116–17.

ROSENBERG, MARTHA, "Let Creative Music Unlock Their Imaginations," *Journal of Nursery Education*, XVII, No. 3 (1962), 126–27.

———, "Making Music Pictures with Rhythm Instruments," *Journal of Nursery Education*, XVIII, No. 3 (1963), 189–90.

SMITH, ROBERT B., "Effect of Group Vocal Training on the Singing Ability of Nursery School Children," *Journal Research in Music Education*, XI, No. 2 (1963), 137–41.

TAYLOR, KATHERINE S., "An Autochthonous Approach to Music Education," *Music Educators Journal*, (February-March, 1949), pp. 17–19, 50–52; (September-October, 1959), pp. 35–39. The story of 25 migrant first-graders and their teacher.

16

music for the disadvantaged and the handicapped

Music and the Disadvantaged

In a quotation from the book *The Disadvantaged: Challenge to Education,* by Mario D. Fantini and Gerald Weinstein in the publication *Education, USA,* it is stated that:

> The meaning of disadvantaged must be broadened to include all those who are blocked in any way from fulfilling their human potential. This blocking can take place anywhere: in a slum, or in an affluent suburb where children may also be neglected, overprotected, ruled by iron-handed parents, or guided by no rules at all. . . . The disadvantaged poor, who find the conventional education system 'phoney' have helped us to understand better why it may be considered 'phoney' by all children. . . . What educators are learning about teaching the economically disadvantaged can be applied to all other classes of disadvantaged in schools.

Thus, before we discuss ways of providing music programs for the disadvantaged we must first identify who the disadvantaged are.

The children usually considered to be disadvantaged are those who suffer from poverty which results from unemployed or physically, emotionally, or mentally handicapped parents, broken homes, lack of love and appropriate attention, and from an impoverished learning experience background. These children often suffer from feelings of inferiority, confusion, hostility, distrust or apathy. Gertrude Noar writes that the disadvantaged are:

> children of the unassimilated lowest class Caucasians, Negroes, Puerto Ricans, American Indians, Mexican Americans. They are one of every three city children who have too little of everything: too little living space, too little (and poor quality) food and sleep, too little personal attention, too little medical and nursing care when sick and too little correction of defects, too little energy and endurance, too little information about themselves and their world, too little curiosity (why ask when no one answers?), too little success, too little self confidence, too little reason to try, too little money and clothing, too little to play with and read, and too little happiness."[1]

Disadvantaged children is a term which describes individuals who come from diverse social and cultural environments about whom teachers of music must become informed in order to be able to understand and empathize. Until a teacher can speak the child's kind of language, know his problems, and begin to see the world through the eyes of such a child, he will be unable to stimulate him to learn music. Effort should be made to accept these children's speech dialects, vocabulary, and language, whether these be illiterate or foreign. Deprived children are made to feel different and inferior if the teacher and their classmates are constantly attempting to change their language, and if they refuse to accept the music these children have learned in their deprived environments which reflects the only life and security they know.

BEHAVIOR OF THE DISADVANTAGED

It is always dangerous to generalize and to risk constructing stereotypes because, as with all children, each is an individual and as such is different from, yet similar to, everyone else. For example, some economically disadvantaged may possess the highest moral standards, strongest family ties and healthiest self-concepts. However, generalized descriptions may be helpful in trying to understand these children.

[1] Noar, Gertrude, *Teaching the Disadvantaged,* Pamphlet 33, *What Research Says to the Teacher,* Dept. of Classroom Teachers, National Education Association, Washington, D.C., 1967, p. 3.

Frustrations and anxieties of children who come from certain types of severe deprivation tend to create classroom behavior of a disruptive nature. Their answers to a teacher's questions may be given in angry or impudent tones; this may reflect fear or lack of confidence. Many of these children are underachievers; this may come from an atmosphere of hopelessness resulting from discrimination and rejection, or from a lack of encouragement from parents and adults for attempting achievement, or from fearing failure or ridicule. Some seem to lack any idea of organization, neatness, or cleanliness in the way they handle their desks and school equipment. As a result of such problems arising from their immediate home and community environments, the teachers of these children must be prepared to work in classrooms with a much higher noise level than is customarily found in the classrooms of a middle class community. They will need to seek suitable and effective teaching strategies to be used in this type of environment until more organized ways of working are explored and implemented cooperatively by the learners and the teacher.

Many of these children have never owned anything of consequence; in their own families they take whatever they need from whatever supply exists in the home. Therefore it can seem normal to them to take whatever they need from any source of supply in a school. While this is called stealing in higher social strata, these children may be doing only what they always do at home. Sometimes if a friendly-intentioned white teacher touches a Negro child, the child's reaction may be one of anger. This is not unusual when many Negro children have been taught to fear white people as enemies. Sometimes Negro teachers who represent the middle class are as likely to be rejected as white teachers. Many deprived children seem lazy, inactive, and appear to have little concept of promptness or the value of time. This usually results from a home environment where there is no reason to hurry, meet appointments, or to compete with anyone.

Most of these children have poor self concepts. In their own minds failure is almost certain. When the teacher reveals in different ways that he, too, doubts their chances for success, the danger of becoming listless non-learners is compounded. The teacher of music can, through music's many facets, make success possible, and begin to change the feeling that success is impossible, to a feeling of knowing that it is almost assured.

Deprived children are ultra-sensitive to words which the middle class seldom thinks about. Analyze "A whole note is worth four quarter notes." A whole note is *white*; quarter notes are *black*. To the disadvantaged

Negro child this can mean that somebody thinks one white person is worth four black persons. Thus, teachers should be careful about the possible inferences of *black* and *brown*. If some of these children use pro-fanity as normal everyday speech, the teacher should not be shocked when it comes out in the school room. Instead of shock, the teacher must, by his example, gradually expand the child's vocabulary with desire to include more effective words for precise and polished expression of ideas. He should reinforce and reward socially and intellectually acceptable behavior, but in most cases ignore the unacceptable types of behavior.

INFLUENCE OF THE HOME AND COMMUNITY

For too long it has been a common belief that musical talent and skill are innate. Now we have adequate research to prove that children who live in musically impoverished environments, especially during the earlier years of life, are more retarded and ineffective in the area of music than are those with enriched musical environments. Music appreciation and competency are environmentally as well as hereditarily determined.

Joseph Froomkin[2] writes, "Most compensatory education programs are not strong enough to insulate the child from the failure and detri-mental effects of his home environment. This is a must, if we expect real achievement. . . . ." He also states that new methods of working with families must be developed. The Child Development Center is an institu-tion developed in connection with the Head Start Project. It is one of several community action programs operated under the United States Office of Health, Education, and Welfare. In concept this program at-tempts to draw together all resources—family, community and profes-sionals—which can assist in the total development of the child, music being one of the important areas of development. It is recognized in this program that both professionals and non-professionals can make needed and meaningful contributions. It draws upon the professional skills of persons in nutrition, health, education, psychology, social work, and recreation. Finally, the Center emphasizes that the family is funda-mental to the child's development and that parents should play an important role in developing policies, working in the Center, and par-ticipating in the programs. Parents are more easily involved when children are at the nursery school level; this leads most naturally to

[2] As quoted in *Education USA,* Washington Monitor, National School Public Association, Washington, D.C., March 18, 1968, p. 1.

visits to the home by personnel from the Center. Parents whose only contact with the school has been when the child has done something wrong may have to be convinced by clergymen or other community leaders that they are wanted and needed at the Center in order to work together to secure better things for their children. The Center has programs for parents as well as for children—it attempts to assist the entire family. The programs are organized around the needs of the children and parents; the children and parents are not to be fitted to preconceived programs. Parents participate in many ways, both as part or full-time employees or as volunteers. There are myriad possibilities, from driving buses, maintenance and repair, food services, teaching media services, teaching and nursing services, cleaning, decorating, and painting. Parents who are musicians, or who know folk songs, foreign language songs, and dances can make musical contributions to both children's music classes and family recreational events. Music teachers might emulate some of the Suzuki methods in which the parent learns with the child. However, the beginning is, as usual, where the child is in music. The music teacher needs to know the songs the child knows and make the initial contacts in these terms; then gradually the repertoire can be expanded into related, but less familiar ground. If the child should not know any songs, the teacher begins with those that relate to familiar activities and the environment of the child. The teacher and children often create their own songs about things they understand, then they progress to interesting and challenging folk songs and art songs.

THE TEACHER OF ECONOMICALLY AND EDUCATIONALLY DISADVANTAGED CHILDREN

There is a major communication and cultural gap between teachers prepared in most teacher preparatory institutions and disadvantaged children, which some believe to be extremely damaging to these children. Clark describes this conflict of cultures as being "essentially a class war, a socioeconomic and racial warfare being waged on the battleground of our schools, with middle-class and middle-class aspiring teachers provided with a powerful arsenal of half-truths, prejudices, and rationalizations, arrayed against hopelessly outclassed working-class youngsters. This is an uneven balance, particularly since, like most battles, it comes under the guise of righteousness."[3]

[3] Clark, Kenneth B., *Dark Ghetto: Dilemmas of Social Power* (New York: Harper & Row, Publishers, 1965), p. 129.

Martin Deutsch thinks that the minority group and class status is harming the lower-class child since he "enters the school situation so poorly prepared to produce what the school demands that initial failures are almost inevitable, and the school experience becomes negatively rather than positively reinforced." Deutsch sees experiential differentials as crucial, teachers poorly trained to understand and cope with cultural variations.[4]

According to Davis 95% of teachers are from middle-class origins, a way of life that differs drastically from that of the majority of these students. When beginning teaching they usually undergo a noticeable emotional upset when they confront lower-class pupils.

"Many middle-class teachers, particularly at first, find it impossible to understand the attitudes and values of these pupils; they are puzzled by the students' reactions to the material and to the instructor, and by their often sullen, resentful behavior—the result in many cases is bewilderment followed by disillusionment and apathy."[5]

These teachers who are ill-prepared to teach the deprived—the very children who need the most skilled and talented teachers—usually resort to accepting and expecting lower standards than could be realized by most of these children under the direction of capable teachers. As a result these pupils usually find school so dull, unchallenging, and unproductive that they withdraw from school mentally if not physically.

The competent teacher of disadvantaged children realizes their importance to the nation and has faith in their ability to learn. He knows how to work with parents and the community. He has an open mind with no preconceived ideas about these children, and he does not think of them as stereotypes. Academic goals that are unrealistically high are avoided; goals are realistic, yet challenging, and children are encouraged by small successes. This teacher begins with the concrete and moves to the abstract. He finds ways to involve the children in the process of learning; this is one way discipline problems are reduced. Unorthodox strategies for encouraging learning are sought; he does not try to build programs on I.Q. scores because I.Q. scores reflect experience as well as

---

[4] Deutsch, Martin, *Minority Group and Class Status as Related to Social and Personality Factors in Scholastic Achievement* (Ithaca, New York: Society for Applied Anthropology, Monograph No. 2, 1960), p. 3.

[5] Davis, Allison, "Society, the School and the Culturally Deprived Student," *Improving English Skills of Culturally Different Youth in Large Cities,* eds. Arno Jewett, Joseph Mersand, and Doris V. Gunderson (Washington, D.C.: U.S. Government Printing Office, 1964), p. 15.

innate mental capacity. He is democratic in his behavior, fosters creativity, encourages questions, exploration, experimentation, consultation, and discovery. He seeks and respects the ideas of the children and holds different expectations for each of them.

Frances Andrews writes that this teacher of music will not make mass application of the traditional materials of instruction, and he will not assume that the children will like any given music because he does. Andrews concludes that the preparation of such teachers will include:

(a) The development of an understanding of the depressed conditions in which many of the disadvantaged exist, conditions that may create not only complete indifference to the musical values accepted by the average teacher, but a lack of interest in musical experiences and materials.

(b) A heavy emphasis on the properties of music as a common means of expression that has always existed in many cultures and at many levels.[6]

In some situations it is believed that male teachers can be particularly helpful when boys are without suitable male models in the home or community. In disadvantaged families, the father may be either absent, incapacitated, or in an inferior economic situation to the mother. It is assumed that the female teacher is more apt to denounce physically aggressive tendencies in children. Since these children are very likely to be physically aggressive because their environment has compelled them to be, it is further assumed that male teachers can be more understanding of this tendency. While this may not always be true, it tends to underline the fact that these schools should have a sufficiently large proportion of male teachers to keep them from being female-centered.

The teacher knows that being disadvantaged has nothing to do with race; it arises from lower-class origin. These children have been influenced by their environment to respond to the immediate and the concrete; they are able to do little with concept formation or generalizing. Unless helped to do otherwise, their learning will be an accumulation of facts dealing with the immediate rather than learning to think in abstractions, hypothesizing, and involving themselves with types of active and inquisitive learning. They are strongly inclined to repeat and accept, rather than to strike out into the unknown because they doubt their ability to control or direct their learning. Thus, the music teacher must provide a succession of experiences in music which will gradually

---

[6] Andrews, Frances, "The Preparation of Music Educators for the Culturally Disadvantaged," *Music Educators Journal* (February, 1967), p. 43.

take these learners out of their passive and repetitive habits, leading them into types of active participation until they become involved in the various facets and processes of learning. As in the teaching of middle class children, the teacher must ask himself whether he is merely transmitting information or encouraging the development of concept formation and generalizing. The difference will be in the learners themselves, and the understanding and adjustments made by the teacher to help these particular learners. For example, the music teacher will encourage questions from the children about a musical instrument, tone qualities and what produces them, why drums sound different when they are struck in different places, and he will encourage explorations such as to discover how many different types of sound can be made to come from a piano. If the music teacher can utilize the numerous possibilities presented by music to involve the learner in types of learning that place him in a commanding position, music can be of great assistance in changing his ways of thinking. It can enable him to form concepts, generalizations, abstractions, theories, and an understanding of the aesthetic values of music.

Music does not carry with it the fear that is sometimes present when certain other subjects are studied. Its very nature assists the teacher and makes it easier for the child to become active—as long as the teacher does not place him in an "exposed" or embarrassing position among his peers.

In summary it must be realized that the teacher's role is not one of an all-seeing individual who possesses all answers and knowledge. He will assume the position of a director of learning as he diagnoses errors, consults with the learner, and suggests new approaches.

MATERIALS, RESOURCES AND TEACHING STRATEGIES

When the teacher's role and strategies of teaching are changed, he must likewise change the types of materials used in the classroom. His initial emphasis will be on musical performance instead of verbal presentations.

One of the outstanding weaknesses in teaching this type of student has been the teacher's inclination to over-verbalize to students who, through lack of experience with words, conceptual ideas, and abstractions, are left frustrated and thwarted. The traditional middle-class oriented music books have been found to be inappropriate in many situations. New music books will have to be written for the use of the educationally deprived child. However, much can be accomplished with audio-visual materials and techniques.

Examples:

> Tape the singing of the class at two-month intervals.
> Play back if the teacher finds significant progress.
> Listen to small excerpts; discuss.
> Use pictures which explain.
> "Notate" by any means meaningful to the class.

The educationally deprived child must be challenged to learn by means of direct experiences. Ray suggests that,

"Some of the learning problems of children who fit into the category often labeled 'educationally deprived' will be lessened if their experience background is enlarged and enriched through selected visual and aural experiences."[7]

Music teachers need to learn varied uses of available audio-visual technology. This may need to be done in an inservice program whereby they can share ideas and explore the utilization of teaching media for disadvantaged children. Teachers are not using to the best advantage the instructional media which are available. Not until teachers become more actively aware of the magnitude of opportunity to expand these children's understanding of themselves, creating a new world through assisting them in the experiencing of music physically, aurally and visually, will they use these audio-visual media with unqualified success.

"There is an evident need in the teaching profession to examine and re-evaluate the pre-service and inservice education of teachers, with particular emphasis on assessing learning resources. Teachers need to be prepared psychologically to explore the resources and to utilize them in a positive constructive fashion in their everyday classroom instruction. Once the basic fundamentals of audio-visual media have been assimilated by the teacher, the specific application to culturally deprived students becomes the next question which needs to be explored."[8]

Little instructional media to date has been designed for the deprived child. Teachers and local systems will therefore need to prepare appropriate materials. More materials for these children will eventually be commercially available but teachers will always need to prepare some materials to suit the unique abilities and interests of some children.

---

[7] Ray, Henry W., "Environment-Enrichment Program in Pennsylvania," *Audio-Visual Instruction*, X (January 1965), 35.

[8] Vairo, Philip D., and Frank Whittaker, "Needed: Learning Tools for the Deprived Child," *Peabody Journal of Education*, XLV, No. 2 (September 1967), p. 122.

The paramount tasks confronting the (music) teacher of the culturally deprived are: (1) to determine the materials to prepare; and (2) to decide how to use them effectively.

It is generally believed that deprived children need a learning environment in which they can associate their daily lives outside the school with the activities in the classroom.

Most schools will have equipment for the preparation of overhead transparencies and 35 mm slides. The deprived child will find security in lessons prepared with visual material taken from his immediate environment.

The teacher uses instructional aids not as a substitute for teaching, but as an enrichment and supplement. The children use sight and hearing, in addition to their minds, to provide depth, meaning and understanding to life.

MOTIVATING THE EDUCATIONALLY DISADVANTAGED CHILD TO LEARN MUSIC

With the educationally deprived, as with all types of children, the most important incentive and motivation to learn originates with becoming involved in a task in which one sees meaning, purpose, and value. When one is permitted to become personally and intrinsically involved in solving pertinent and challenging problems, external motivation is seldom needed.

The goals for the disadvantaged and handicapped must be defined in very specific language. These children identify their educational goals in more definite terms than do their teachers. They usually want to learn music. It is only after they have met innumerable failures and after confidence in their ability to learn has been shattered by the type of instruction received that they eventually cease to try.

Slow learners are present in all classrooms in any school. However, according to many authorities there is a greater percentage of children from socially and educationally deprived environments who are slow learners, than from the less deprived areas. In a severely deprived group of children, from 80 to 90% of them have been found to be slow learners. Therefore, the teacher of the economically and educationally disadvantaged must be clearly aware of the problems confronting slow learners, their learning capabilities and potentials, rates of growth, methods of instruction and motivation. The most capable teachers (not the weakest) should be assigned to schools attended by disadvantaged learners. It is obvious that these children need more individualized programs and attention, and an enriched learning environment appropriate for extending their limited experience backgrounds. There are no unique methods for obtaining success with slow learners.

In the beginning, at least, slow learners will need to be exposed to developmental materials where skill and instruction are systematic. Systematic instruction is essential for a slow learner since his achievement of new skills is dependent upon the mastery of successive steps. Means whereby the learner can see some type of growth and success each day, helped by the teacher to build on these successes sequentially and consistently, are a necessity for the slow learner.

Teachers will need to begin with the specific kinds of music the children know. They may use songs such as those including names to teach identity and self-recognition. Experiences with these familiar musical encounters should be so organized and spaced that the pupils enjoy and successfully learn them. By beginning on their understanding and achievement level, they can accomplish that "quick" success they so badly need. The teacher must plan a curriculum according to where the children are at present.

Young children and children from deprived environments need many opportunities to express themselves through physical and kinesthetic involvement in music (psycho motor). Soon their thinking and their rhythmic responses are prompted by the music. These children enjoy repeating the same songs many times, if they can create slight variations of interpretations from time to time. Repetition of satisfying musical experiences is a natural source of interest and enjoyment for the young or immature learner. This repetition gives them a feeling of mastery and security. As they feel secure with the experimentation and mastery of certain parts of music, they feel less inhibited in creating new interpretations through performance and experimenting. Children in a relaxed environment improvise freely.

From performance and concrete experiences children can be led to discuss or verbalize. Since disadvantaged children usually possess extremely deficient vocabularies and language facility, verbalization and discussions related to firsthand experiences should be used as soon as profitable. They should be gradually led to discuss, explore, experiment, analyze, compare, create and perform on their level. The teacher and child should grow in ability to question not so much *What* and *When* but instead *Imagine that—What if—? Why—?* This style leads gradually into improved ability to verbalize, to solve problems, to infer meaning and to imagine and create.

In summary, some specific points to consider in teaching music to the disadvantaged are as follows:

1. Teachers working with disadvantaged children need to be carefully selected and prepared to teach the deprived. They need to be persons who can understand the problems of the economically and educationally disadvantaged children, as well as the adults of the area. Skills in communicating effectively with both the children and adults are necessary. They must truly believe in the individual worth and dignity of each child involved, be able to plan, implement and evaluate appropriate and effective programs and teaching strategies for these learners.

2. These teachers will need to be able to devise ways to involve parents in the music program of the school, in the learning experiences of their child and in becoming positive consumers of and contributors to music in the community. They will need to see that parents are assisted in becoming aware of the various musical experiences available to them in the community, selecting different types of musical programs to view and attend in addition to many types of music to listen to. Assistance with the selection of instruments is often appreciated. Parents' interest and concern in music, like that of children, are expanded in direct proportion to the amount and types of personal involvement in music.

3. Examine and analyze carefully the child's background and what he is capable of doing musically; then begin by engaging him as a co-worker in planning, exploring and evaluating his progress in the learning of music. These children need to be actively involved in exploring, experimenting, discussing, and participating at their level in various musical experiences. They must be given an opportunity to learn—mainly in concrete and non-verbal ways at first. They should participate in making as many individual decisions as possible. This might include what songs they would like to sing or listen to; what instruments to use in accompanying a song; how they could interpret the song or musical selection through rhythmic response; how they could alter the tempo and dynamics to improve their performance; how to change the melody when this is desirable; what new parts to add to the song; evaluation of their progress; or the planning of a musical presentation for parent groups or another class group or the entire school. Decision-making is a cooperative and equally shared endeavor between pupils and teacher. Pupils will be allowed to try out their decisions and adjust their learning activities and procedures accordingly; they will learn to act on their decisions, to face the consequences in constructive and positive ways and in turn profit from former mistakes. This is a great need of most disadvantaged learners.

4. Gradually and consistently the standards and goals of each child are adjusted and elevated to a higher and more challenging level in keeping with his interests and abilities. He must not be hurried, and the learning environment must be one of purpose, free from anxiety, pressure and threat; each child will be respected because of his uniqueness and individual worth. The teacher is a relaxed, warm and accepting person; he utilizes positive and constructive procedures.

5. Pupils are involved in exploration and inquiry that include the use of the different types and levels of questions, observing, analyzing, hypothesizing, conceptualizing and generalizing, which at first will likely be at a very elementary level. These children need to master some basic social skills also, which will enhance their chances for building wholesome human relationships with peers and adults. Even though most of their learning experiences should be individualized, they also need opportunities to work in small peer groups. When possible they should be placed in a group of more normal and verbal students; but the size of the class group should be kept small enough to give individual attention and assistance to each child. Of course at the appropriate time when older children feel successful, they should have opportunity to participate in a larger performing group. This serves to enhance interest and motivation in learning, in building their feeling of acceptance and self-esteem, and to develop ability to appreciate and respect others. Throughout their musical experience during the elementary school years, the children should have opportunity to read about and listen to members of their own cultural group who are successful in various aspects of music. They can listen to them in person, on television and radio or from recordings. These children, who usually have given up hope of ever being able to succeed and lack incentive to try, need to see that those from similar disadvantaged backgrounds who have tried have been successful.

6. Schools for disadvantaged children should prepare and select materials in terms of objectives for a program of this type and formulate specific teaching procedures suited to the learning problems of these children.

7. Many opportunities for children to become involved in divergent and creative ways in the improvisation and interpretation of music should be provided. They should be encouraged to listen creatively, then to interpret the music through painting, dramatization, dance and movement and instrumental accompaniments. The creation of words and music are encouraged. The children should be invited to create different endings to music, or where appropriate, to add or delete parts. As a forerunner to creativity these learners will need assistance in observing the various aspects of the immediate environment—the sounds and rhythm in nature; i.e. sounds and movements of man and beasts, movement and sound of water, leaf in the breeze, machines, insects. As they describe these sounds and movements in creative ways, they develop observation skills, vocab-

ulary, and sensitiveness to artistic subjects. Through such experiences these children achieve new openness to experience, wanting to know the whys as well as the essential details. The dimensions of human dignity are extended.

8. The children are encouraged and guided in the use of self-evaluation. Self-analysis and evaluation is conducive to the building of sound motivation and incentives to learn. Self-evaluation and analysis skills in music can be developed through the use of appropriate questions which cause self-criticism by the students. For example: what caused the drum to sound different this time from the last time you hit it? What can you do to improve the singing of this song? Why do you like this recording? How could you change the ending of the song to—? What do you like most about this type of music?

    The use of well selected programed learning materials which are designed around specific behavioral objectives are valuable—the learner receives quick feedback regarding his success and is able to use this success as an incentive and basis for elevating his next level of achievement. Children also profit from taping their music performance and then listening to the tape to analyze and plan ways of improvement. They then perform again and listen to this tape. This process may be repeated many times if necessary.

9. The teachers of the disadvantaged must devise adequate, effective and exacting ways to evaluate each child's progress in music. These are needed not only as incentives and motivations for these children, but the teachers will also need these data in order to build a logical, sequential and spirally effective program for each student. In working with disadvantaged children it is concluded that these learners need to be helped to become open to musical experiences; they need to enjoy music fully and to arrange, design and clarify musical values, concepts and skills through careful analysis, and creative production and performance of music.

    It should be realized that even though most of these children have records of failure, they can succeed at difficult tasks if they are involved in activities they really want to do.

The Handicapped Children

Because there are different kinds of handicaps endured by humanity, a great many of these children will have much in common with "normal" children. Another way of looking at the handicapped is that every human being is probably handicapped in some way or other, either physically, mentally, emotionally, or culturally. However, this section is concerned only with types of handicaps which tend to set children apart from the norm. Some of these children will be able to learn as much about music as any other children. For all of these children, however, music can make a substantial contribution to their growth, their lives, and their happiness. For many of them, music will serve non-musical goals at the same time the teacher plans experiences to expand music concepts. The teacher will find extreme differences of ability. Some will have speech and other communication problems; music may be the only way they can satisfy their need to communicate with others. It has been found that when handicapped children feel success and satisfaction in music, there is a tendency to enjoy and learn more in other areas of study.

There is the belief that the less severely handicapped child should remain in the home and in the regular public school. His learning can be enhanced by the normalcy of his environment, if this environment is educationally productive for the normal child. Music teachers need to understand these children, to develop effective ways to plan experiences appropriate for their specific abilities and handicaps, and to help them to develop ways of gaining full acceptance into the social and emotional climate of the school room. If music is taught by a specialist, it is of paramount importance that the classroom teacher and the specialist cooperatively plan and teach these children. As the trend toward teaching the less severely handicapped children in the regular school continues, the demand for music therapists will grow. The therapist would work with classroom teachers, music specialists, and parents of the children in community mental health and child centers. Therefore, he should be trained in music education, music in therapy, clinical techniques relating to music education, and in special education. Problems of the past have resulted from teachers who have known music education for normal children but not for children with special physical, emotional, and social problems—a variant of knowing music but not the child. On the other hand, persons trained for teaching the handicapped have seldom been prepared to work with music.

One of the reactions college students have when they look at songs, recordings, and other music materials for the handicapped is, "There seems to be little or no difference between these songs and those we use in any normal classroom." It is true that there are great similarities and even duplications of materials for the normal and for the handicapped of some types. The great differences are found in the style and strategies of teaching employed in the learning and use of music, and sometimes in the goals of music teaching for some types of handicapped children. Harriet Nordholm writes,

Many exceptional children have apparent musical talents that need to be nurtured and developed. These children, because they represent a deviation from the norm, need music in their lives for enrichment and fulfillment. Through music, such a child will develop feelings of belonging, sharing, and contributing. Music will bring him something that nothing else in the curriculum can do. The very fact that a child is different means that he will inevitably have lonely hours. Here is where music . . . can help him through those forlorn, despondent moments.[9]

THE VISUALLY HANDICAPPED

Because the blind have lost one of the most important five physical senses, developing the powers of the other senses is crucially important. They often have little feeling of security, and are troubled when routine is altered or when they are moved to places strange to them. It is not easy for the blind to convey feelings to others through their facial expressions. These expressions are learned in large part through imitation— since they cannot see, they cannot imitate. They are inclined to develop mannerisms they are not aware of and to become egocentric, tending to live within themselves rather than communicating well with the world about them. A common admonition among those who work with the blind is, "Don't take the child by the hand and lead him; let him hold on to your arm. Help him to be as independent as possible."

Music can be of tremendous importance to the blind child because it offers means of self-expression, communication with others, and social integration. Because of dependence on hearing which substitutes in part for the lack of seeing, the world of sound is a very real one. He may be able to sing well and in tune before the average normal child can, because he concentrates more completely on the sounds he hears. He listens to and enjoys rhythm in music and responds to it well; tone qualities are highly interesting and attractive; dynamics and different tempos can be exciting and entertaining. He may react to moods in music with emotions of higher calibre than the average normal child, and he may feel spiritual qualities in music more completely.

The sense of touch is highly significant to the blind child. This relates well to the playing of musical instruments. Thus the blind child usually can learn to play well. His voice is also more important to him than to a normal child who can see as well as sing and speak. Through his voice,

[9] Nordholm, Harriet, *Singing in the Elementary Schools* (Englewood Cliffs, N.J.: Prentice-Hall, Inc., 1966), p. 61.

he can communicate in song as well as anyone. It is the teacher's responsibility to adapt his teaching strategies to assist the child in learning to sing and play well. (There are blind teachers of music and blind piano tuners who have been successful in their professions.) The child's sense of touch also applies to learning to read music in Braille so that he need not depend entirely upon rote learning of music. The sheet should be placed securely beneath his hand. This is difficult when playing an instrument from notation because one hand must be touching the sheet. Some percussion instruments can be equipped with foot pedals to compensate for the hand's being occupied, but instruments requiring the use of two hands demand another approach. In reading music with such instruments, the child would have to first read and understand the notation, then pick up the instrument and play what he had felt. He should learn to write Braille to become independent in working with music. This frees him to take music dictation and to write music of his own creation. He can read books about music in Braille, thus partake of the same intellectual nourishment as other children.

Blind children can be competent members of singing groups; in fact, schools for the blind often have excellent children's choirs. The favorable psychology of pleasurable group activity is present here as with any group of normal children. When teachers help a blind child to play an instrument, a duplicate of the same instrument, no matter what it may be, is very helpful since the child needs to hear someone else sound the tones so that he can imitate them. As in the teaching of any other children, musical activities and goals should be carefully graduated in difficulty to avoid frustration. The child should be treated in general like a normal child, except that the teacher must be very much aware of the special sensitivities of the blind. Again, plan for success, satisfaction, and security; avoid frustration. Remember the joys music can give to children.

THE AURALLY HANDICAPPED

To speak of an aural art in relation to children who cannot hear would at first seem to be an anomaly. It is true that a deaf child can never experience music in the same way as a normal child, because he is deprived of hearing tone qualities and harmony. However, he can feel through his skin, muscles, and bones the vibrations of music, and this is his substitute for a hearing apparatus. This puts him in contact with sound that moves through time, and he can identify some elements of music such as rhythm, accent, duration, and pitch, although to a limited extent. New types of hearing aids can assist children who are not 100% deaf—and few are in this category—and other devices which amplify sound can be placed in rooms for group work with the deaf. Floors made of materials which transmit vibrations help these children to feel them. Since low pitches are much more easily "heard," these are emphasized. However, the children can identify high and low to some degree. The piano is useful in feeling vibrations; children can place both hands on it as the teacher plays. Teachers relate the usual visual aids to explain the different feel of the vibrations of high and low pitches; even the conventional sense of touch can be used, with high vibrations associated with the feel of fine-textured cloth and low vibrations with the feel of coarse-textured material. At one school for the deaf in The Netherlands the study of vibrations over a four year period led children to identify the pitches of the major scale. This was accomplished through the use of colored blocks of different sizes, the large ones being the lower pitches; an identification game was played with them. Accompanying this was the analysis by the children of each pitch of the scale with an agreed-upon gesture to go with the pitch. The major importance of this is not as much the skill of pitch identification as it is being in communication with aspects of what the rest of the world hears, thus feeling psychologically a part of the world of normal humanity.

When deaf children feel vibrations they can organize sound in the same way normal children can. Therefore, rhythm can be understood through touching the piano, the Autoharp (which can be held by the child), the tambourine (which can be placed against different parts of the body and even walked or danced with); hand drums and other percussion instruments can be used to create rhythm patterns. Therefore, body movement in rhythm such as walking, running, and skipping can be imitated on vibrating instruments. When deaf children have rooms equipped with amplifiers and special floors, they can learn to dance to vibrations; they feel degrees of loud and soft.

When deaf children learn to feel rhythm patterns and accents, their ability to learn to speak is greatly facilitated. Through rhythm accentuation the natural accents and syllabic duration in word pronunciation can be explained by means of rhythmic patterns played on tambourine, drum, or by a succession of chords at the piano. This is obviously one of the major values of this type of music teaching. As with other types of exceptional children, the primary value of music for the deaf is to counteract feelings of inferiority, of being inhibited and apart. Thus mental health and personality development are important outcomes of working with the deaf in music. The teacher needs to be one who respects the potential of each child and who has the infinite patience and creative skill to help each one grow as a person.

THE ORTHOPEDICALLY HANDICAPPED

The music education of this type of physically handicapped children is not basically different from that of normal children, with the important exception that the music experience must be planned in accordance with the infirmity of the individual. The significance of the teacher knowing each child's problems thoroughly and the need for special planning is exemplified in the story told by a music teacher who was at that time inexperienced in working with handicapped children. In a too-sudden exposure to them she tried a familiar song:

> "One, two, three, four, five little fingers," I sang with enthusiasm. . . . Around this seemingly innocent beginning revolved profound experiences as I began my first day of music teaching in my new position. As we sang and counted, one child held up six little fingers. Another held up a mitten-like hand, with fingers webbed together. Another could not lift his hand, for it was hopelessly paralyzed and withered.[10]

Enjoyment, appreciation and enthusiasm for music are goals to strive for in teaching these children. Modifications in planning are always present because of the different physical limitations of individual children; each child is to learn to perform musically at his highest potential, and each child is to grow as far as possible in his knowledge of and responsiveness to music.

Children who cannot walk with their feet can "walk" by using their hands in the air or by playing on a drum in time to the marching feet of others. Children on crutches and in wheelchairs can dance within similar limitations. A child in a wheelchair can turn round and round to a waltz, for example. These problems call for many creative solutions by the teacher and eventually by the children. Each lesson may include many substitutions and compromises while the basic music program remains the same as for the normal child. Within their limitations these children can sing in a chorus and play musical instruments. Many times it is found

[10] Deaver, Mary Jo, "Teaching Music in Special Education Classes," *Lyons Music News,* 1967.

that the spastic child can sing better than he speaks and may enjoy solo singing before an understanding audience.

Music books are used when they have need of them, and notation, ear training, pitch, and rhythm in addition to other aspects of music education are taught, but always as a related music experience or game rather than drills which imply pressure. Sometimes the teacher's expectations in rhythmic work must be cautious because some of the children will be unable to match with precision the exact responses rhythm demands. In such instances, music with a strong melodic line may provide more freedom, permitting such children to make those responses in movement which they are able to do.

THE MENTALLY HANDICAPPED

The mentally handicapped have been classified into three groups, the untrainable, the trainable, and the mentally handicapped. It is the latter group we are dealing with here. These children are the slow learners; they are educable. Hershell Rowland raises the question of how these children should be approached. Are they different in musical aptitude from the normal child?[11] He found that the opinion of the majority of music teachers seemed to be that these children probably could not advance beyond the instructional materials designed for third or fourth grade. He then had to decide what his basic premise would be. Should he accept this verdict, or should he simply teach music as he would to any other group of the same chronological age—but with more ingenuity because of their particular handicap? He decided upon the latter. It was his experience that children had the same music interests that the "normal" children had. He concludes:

So the children loved music from *South Pacific*. Bobby couldn't carry a tune in a basket, but he could beat a tom-tom to make a musical background for "Bali Hai." Patty had a speech problem, so she was a palm tree swaying in the tropical breezes. As the storm hit the beach, John made the sound of thunder with a piece of tin.

Mr. Rowland does not identify the age group, but the reader will get the message and be able to adapt it to the older mentally handicapped children in elementary music classes.

[11] Rowland, Hershel, "Much Alike: A Little Different," *Music Educators Journal* (January, 1965), pp. 93–4.

Characteristics to look for among the mentally handicapped children include:

1. Speech problems
2. Poor motor skills
3. Low ability to adapt
4. Low capacity for mental imagery
5. Visual difficulties
6. Social difficulties
7. Poor retention
8. Limited appreciation
9. Low capacity for transfer of training
10. Low frustration level

In most instances these children need much experience with concrete objects, much visualizing, positive reinforcement, much repetition, frequent review, and frequent successes. Their music includes a repertoire of short songs of limited range with repeated phrases, which have a simple vocabulary of known words. In a research project at Teachers College, Columbia University, Richard Weber found that he could teach severely retarded children on standard band and orchestra instruments by means of individual lessons in which he used melodies of songs of only six note range (within the interval of a sixth). It was found that success with this performance aided the personality because it earned respect from other children, lengthened the attention span, and speeded the educational process.[12]

Writers on the subject of music and the mentally handicapped state two ideas that seem at first to be at variance. They write of the simple, repetitious songs that need to be used; they may write as do Paul Nordoff and Clive Robbins, "The standards of performance generally expected . . . are, in our experience, too low. Most of these children possess good musical intelligence; in many it is surprisingly advanced. Music therapy depends upon this musical intelligence being engaged to the full, drawing the whole child into concentrated activity."[13]

Dobbs suggests that, "A carefully selected music activity need not demand more of a child than he can give, but it does create situations in

---

[12] Vernazza, Marcelle, "What Are We Doing About Music in Special Education?" *Music Educators Journal* (April, 1967), p. 56.

[13] Nordoff, Paul, and Clive Robbins, "The Scope of Music Therapy with Handicapped Children," *Music in Education,* (May-June, 1967), 465.

which he can be stretched to his limit and enjoys being stretched if he is really absorbed in what he is doing. We must avoid any competitive element in the activity we choose . . . . Fortunately, the logical series of steps and dovetailed processes required for the progressive understanding of some subjects are not essential in many of the simpler musical activities."[14] From these quotations it appears that the teacher of the mentally handicapped must be prepared for a wide range of musical accomplishment from these children, with substantial accomplishment possible for some of them.

Dobbs adds that the emotional needs of these children are very great, and this is the strength of music. Music produces emotional responses and it can also express emotions within the person. "By awakening in us positive emotions it can stimulate us to more purposeful living and by acting as a channel for the release of our emotions, both positive and negative, it can contribute to the re-creation of our personalities." He advises that the music lesson be not only a daily occurrence but that music be used to add color and excitement to a variety of occasions such as birthdays, good morning, good-bye, welcome, and informal community singing. Arvin states that the value of music to a subnormal child resides in the fact that it can be treated as a non-academic subject at different levels of intelligence. "We should consider music as a help to his general development, not in terms of musical achievement, since his deficiency will prevent him from rising above a certain standard."[15]

MUSIC ACTIVITIES   It is important to this group of children that they feel the social unity of a music group, which must be one of the aims of the teacher. He must expect, however, a larger number of low voices (growlers) than in a group of normal children. Sometimes special lower parts written for such a child will solve part of the problem. Some cases will be solved through use of the kazoo. When this rudimentary instrument is sounded, the child must use his lungs, vocal cords, tongue, and lips—quite an exciting experience to one who has not been able to make a musical sound with the voice, and one that activates the various physical elements which will ultimately produce the singing tone without the instrument. A larger number of boys will have voices in the process of

[14] Dobbs, J. P. B., *The Slow Learner and Music* (London: Oxford University Press, 1966), pp. 9–10.
[15] Arvin, Juliette, *Music for the Handicapped Child* (New York: Oxford University Press, 1965), p. 68.

change than boys in a normal group. The songs should be of varied nature. While these children enjoy lively tunes just as normal children do, they also like the contrast of other types. Negro spirituals, carols, and even selected music of Bach and Handel can be part of this variety.

The instruments all require some kind of technical facility to play—even rhythm sticks, thus the teacher seeks instruments to match the capabilities of the child. The percussion instruments are the most commonly selected, followed by bells, xylophone, and Autoharp. The recorder is too difficult for these children because of the relatively complex fingering; a simple blowing instrument like a Song Flute might do for some.

Richard Weber published some results of his research mentioned earlier, naming it *Musicall*, 39 familiar melodies using only six different notes.[16] It is based on songs and tunes the child is assumed to know before he attempts to relate it to an instrument, and claims to assure much success. Key signatures and meter signatures are omitted. This method is recommended as a "pre-method" for normal children also. Weber claims that any standard instrument can be learned by mentally handicapped children within the limits of the 39 melodies, which are all in one key. While authorities do not recommend the standard string instruments, Weber claims they can be learned within these limitations. The band instruments can be played together, but the strings are not to be combined with band instruments in this method.

A few highly motivated children may be able to learn several chords on the ukulele and guitar with which to accompany singing. It is interesting that more girls than boys favor singing, and more boys than girls enjoy playing instruments.

As with normal children, describing listening experiences assists in enlarging vocabulary, and this is an important aspect of expanding mental powers. Use of the body to reflect the character of the music being listened to will help children focus attention on the music. The first listening experiences are only a minute or two in length. As the child extends his capacity to concentrate, the length gradually increases. If the teacher asks for more than the child can do, the child stops listening and becomes restless.

Rhythmic responses of these children are basically simple and elementary since many of them have poorly developed motor skills. For example, some may be unable to reproduce a skipping rhythm by clapping

[16] Musicall, Inc., Suite 611, 1841 Broadway, New York, N.Y.

or with percussion instruments, but they will learn to sound the beat with that rhythm. The children can move to music in response to variations in pitch. Fortunately, movements can be created which suit all stages of experience and intelligence, so creativity can play an important part and the teacher must watch each child for clues and ideas. As in normal children, these children must first acquire a repertoire of movements and learn to respond spontaneously to different types and characteristics of music. After this, progressively more complex music and rhythmic tasks can be expected. When simple dance steps are learned, the world of folk dance is opened, at least in part, to these children.

As a part of music experiences designed to give happiness to these children, many music concepts, such as high-low, loud-soft, fast-slow, beat, rhythm pattern, scale, skips and steps, tone qualities, and harmony, are introduced. As far as note reading is concerned, teachers have experimented with the children's playing melodies with Swiss Melode Bells from charts which had the notes in colors corresponding to those of the bells. The *Threshold to Music Charts* for kindergarten and first grade have been used successfully in introducing rhythmic and simple staff notation.

The reader should refer to the chapters concerned with the elements of music and select appropriate activities from the many suggested there.

INQUIRY AND SUGGESTED ACTIVITIES

1. Observe children in a music class for the handicapped to note the following:
   a. The music curriculum in use.
   b. Physical surroundings; the amount of space for the various types of handicapped children to move freely and with ease; types of equipment and instruments.
   c. The psychological and social atmosphere present in the classroom; is the teacher accepting and reinforcing or is he negative and rejecting; how do pupils relate to each other and to the teacher?
   d. The teaching strategies used.
   e. The nature of the handicaps present in the group.
   f. The teacher's provision for individual differences.
   g. The special capabilities and qualities of the teacher.
   h. The number of teacher's aides and how they are employed in the music class.

2. Observe a regular music class. Identify the number of children who possess noticeable handicaps. How are the mentally retarded and slow learners provided for? How does the music teacher deal with the special handicaps of these children? How would you deal with their problems?
3. Identify ways you believe to be effective in providing for individual differences in a particular music class.
4. What strategies might you use in teaching the slow learner?

REFERENCES

The Disadvantaged

ANDREWS, FRANCES, "The Preparation of Music Educators for the Culturally Disadvantaged," *Music Educators Journal* (February, 1967), pp. 40–43.

BEREITER, CARL AND SIEGFRIED ENGELMANN, "Music for the Preschool," *Teaching Disadvantaged Children in the Preschool*. Englewood Cliffs, N.J.: Prentice-Hall, Inc., 1966. Chapter Nine.

BIBER, BARBARA, "Educational Needs of Young Deprived Children," *Childhood Education* (September, 1967), p. 30.

"Coping with the Socially Different in the Social Sciences," *Education* (November, 1967), pp. 126–29.

DAWSON, HELAINE S., *On the Outskirts of Hope*. New York: McGraw-Hill Book Company, 1968.

FANTINI, MARIO D., AND GERALD WEINSTEIN, *The Disadvantaged: Challenge to Education*. New York: Harper and Row, Publishers, 1968.

"Home-School Relationships," Journal of Negro Education (Fall, 1967), pp. 349–52.

JENKINS, ELLA, *The Ella Jenkins Song Book*. 701 Seventh Ave., New York 10036: Oak Publications. Designed for Head Start Programs.

"Music's Part in Social Integration," *Etude* (March, 1957).

"Needed: a New Kind of School for the Slums," *Education Digest* (January, 1968).

NOAR, GERTRUDE, *What Research Says to the Teacher Series: Teaching the Disadvantaged*. Washington, D. C.: National Education Association, 1968.

"Relationship of Simple Audio-Visual Techniques to the Arts and the Disadvantaged," *AV Instructor* (January, 1968).

Films

Portrait of a Disadvantaged Child: Tommy Knight. Vision Associates, 1965, 16 min.

Portrait of the Inner City. Vision Associates, 1965, 15 min.

The Handicapped

ANTEY, JOHN W., *Sing and Learn*. New York: John Day Books, Inc.

BREINHOLT, BERNA, AND IRENE SCHOEPFLE, "Music Experiences for the Child With Speech Limitations," *Music Educators Journal,* XLVI (Sept.-Oct., 1960), pp. 49–50.

CAREY, MARGAREITA, "Music for the Educable Mentally Retarded," *Music Educators Journal,* XLVI (Feb.-March, 1960), pp. 72–74.

CATALOG: *The Best Records and Books for the School Curriculum.* Children's Music Center, 5373 W. Pico Blvd., Los Angeles, California, 90019. See pp. 70–72 of recent catalog, or "Special Needs" section.

COLE, FRANCES, ET. AL., *Music for Children with Special Needs.* Evanston, Ill.: Summy-Birchard, 1964.

DOBBS, J. P. B., *The Slow Learner and Music.* London: Oxford University Press, 1966.

GASTON, THAYER, *Music in Therapy.* New York: The Macmillan Company, 1968.

KONDOROSSY, ELIZABETH, "Let Their Music Speak for the Handicapped," *Music Educators Journal* (Feb.-March, 1966), pp. 115–19.

"Music Serves the Exceptional Child," *California Journal of Education* (May, 1956), pp. 233–34.

NEWACHECK, VIVIAN, "Music and the Slow Learner," *Music Educators Journal* (Nov.-Dec., 1953), pp. 48–50.

NORDHOLM, HARRIET, *Singing in the Elementary Schools.* Englewood Cliffs, N.J.: Prentice-Hall, Inc., 1966.

NORDOFF, PAUL, AND CLIVE ROBBINS, *Music Therapy for Handicapped Children.* Blouvelt, New York: Rudolph Steiner Publications.

————, AND CLIVE ROBBINS, "The Scope of Music Therapy with Handicapped Children," *Music in Education* (London), (May-June, 1967).

O'TOOLE, CATHERINE, "Music for the Handicapped Child," *Music Educators Journal,* XLVIII (June-July, 1962), pp. 73–76.

SCHNEIDER, ERWIN H., "Music Therapy and Music Education," *Perspectives in Music Education: Source Book III.* MENC, 1966, pp. 504–8.

SHEERENBERGER, RICHARD C., "Presenting Music to the Mentally Retarded," *Music Educators Journal,* XL (Nov.-Dec., 1954).

ROBINS, FERRIS AND JENNET, *Educational Rhythms for Mentally and Physically Handicapped.* New York: Associated Press, 291 Broadway, 1968.

ROLAND, HERSHEL, "Much Alike and Different," *Music Educators Journal* (January, 1965), pp. 93–94.

VERNAZZA, MARCELLE, "What are We Doing About Music in Special Education?" *Music Educators Journal* (April, 1967), pp. 55–58.

Film

A Song for Michael. Produced by F. Bornef for the Music Therapy Center (FN); distributed by Center, 18 West 74th Street, New York 10023.

17

relating with other areas

A beautiful song that possesses emotional values and that describes experiences meaningful to children has universal appeal. These aesthetic, emotional, and cultural qualities point toward this song's possible use for adding interest, meaning, and enjoyment to other areas of the curriculum. It is also true that the subject matter of other areas can make music study more interesting, meaningful, and enjoyable. Thus, while the skills in any area are not to be neglected, neither the learning of music nor learning in other areas can, in many instances, approach completeness without each aiding the other. Music has always been man's most natural artistic medium of expression, and through its use he continually interprets his civilizations, past and present. When music assumes its rightful place in the core of the curriculum, marked emphasis is given to it because of its real functions. On the other hand, relationships with other areas of instruction can assist the formulation of music concepts and generalizations.

Music and Other Areas

Generalizations to be worked toward in relating the arts include: any work of art has a plan or form; the arts provide a

584

type of pleasure for man; when people work creatively with the arts they arrange their materials in various combinations—words in literature, color, forms, and spaces in painting, elements of music in creating music, tempos and movements in dance; combinations of the materials of art provide interest and variety; everyone can experiment with original expressions by arranging and combining the materials of the arts; art relates to everyday living; an artist may view topics in special ways; man expresses his universal and unique concerns through the arts; the arts have some common elements; the arts have some marked differences.

The following outline consists of some of the more obvious bases for interrelating music and other areas.

ART

Rhythm is an element common to music, art, dance, poetry, and architecture.

Appropriate recordings stimulate creative art.

Songs can be illustrated by children's drawings.

Song creation can be inspired by pictures.

Pictures can motivate listening to descriptive music.

The making and decorating of simple musical instruments is in the area of arts and crafts.

Some ideas can be expressed in several media: art, music, dance, creative dramatics and writing.

Certain artistic styles are common to both art and music. Examples: impressionism and classicism.

Both art and music can be analyzed in terms of rhythm, balance, contrast, concreteness, and other aesthetic elements they have in common.

Certain concepts of form are common to both art and music.

Scenery and costumes can be made for musical programs.

PHYSICAL EDUCATION

Singing games and dances are activities considered to be in the areas both of music and physical education.

Music can be created for a known dance.

Dance can be created for known music.

Basic understanding of note values and meter signatures comes from body response.

Rhythm can be expressed in the dance, in music, in poetry, and in art.

Instrumental accompaniments can be created for body movement.
Interpretation of form in and of music can be reflected by creative dance.

SCIENCE

Some music concerns aspects of nature such as clouds, rain, the sea, the
seasons, stars.
Aspects of electronics include radio, television, amplifiers, recording and
reproducing sound, and composing with electronic media.
There are many scientists who have music as an enjoyable avocation.
Making and playing musical instruments and experimenting with sound-
producing materials motivate the study of acoustics, the science of
sound.
Correct posture and breathing in singing relates to health.

ARITHMETIC

The study of beats, note values, and meter signatures relates to the
understanding of number concepts.

LANGUAGE ARTS

Poetry and music are closely related; meters, phrases, word rhythms and
melody rhythms are often similar or identical.
Appropriate recordings can be employed to stimulate creative writing.
Poetry can be composed; music can be written to make songs based on
this poetry; poetry can be composed for melodies.
Some song interpretations can be developed into creative dramatizations.
There are many books to read about music, instruments, and musicians.
Music can be composed and recordings can be selected for use with
dramatizations, plays, and puppet shows.
Many songs, operatic and symphonic works are based upon literature
and drama.
Aspects of choric reading can relate to the process of learning songs.
Reading and singing words of songs can be an experience in the process
of improving comprehension, pronunciation and enunciation.
Music can be selected that relates to children's literature.
Music, dance, and language are communicative arts.
Using symbols of notation is a communicative skill.
Both music and language arts are concerned with listening, performing,
reading, and writing.

SOCIAL STUDIES

(This can include problems in science, health, safety, language arts, history, geography, citizenship, art, music, and rhythms.)

Music aids in understanding ideals, religions, and traditions of contemporary and past civilizations, cultures, nations, and times.

Music reveals mankind's common likenesses, differences, and concerns.

Music describes geographical and climatic conditions of various countries.

Music aids in teaching history and patriotism through study of appropriate music and composers.

Music is a unifying factor and morale builder; it aids personality development; it can relieve tensions and alleviate fatigue.

Dances, instrumental compositions, songs, and music plays can be created by children in connection with units of work in social studies.

Children can make musical instruments and costumes to portray the life of people of the past and present; they can study these people through songs and recorded music.

Adults from foreign countries may be invited to discuss and illustrate some aspects of their music and customs.

Music is frequently an important aspect of culminating activities of units of work.

Today more educators are finding the need to draw relationships from several different areas to free children to understand the interrelated world in which they live. For example, Thomson questions, "Why has not the study of elementary acoustics been a staple of the elementary music class of the past? It is basic, and children are fascinated by the sound-producing capabilities of all manner of machines, including musical instruments. . . . Children are also easily engaged in discussion about sound reflection and echoes, and this topic readily leads to a discussion of the way sound moves as a pressure wave through the air (or any other medium) and can be caused to bounce, like a rubber ball, away from any reflective surface."[1] Thomson further states that one does not have to go beyond the six-year-old's level of comprehension for him to discover how the slide of the trombone or the valve of the trumpet can alter pitch, and he can easily explore the relationship that exists between long strings or air columns and low pitches, or short strings or air columns and high pitches.

[1] Thomson, William, "New Math, New Science, New Music," *Music Educators Journal* (March, 1967), 82–3.

Correlation and Inter-relation of Music in the Curriculum

	CITIZENSHIP	SOCIAL RELATIONSHIPS	LANGUAGE ARTS	SCIENCE
SINGING	Patriotic songs inspire good citizenship, regard for country, emulation of great national figures.	Many songs inspire worldwide regard for other peoples. Songs of our own people broaden appreciation of our own country.	Good singing improves speech and diction. Foreign songs are a practical use of foreign languages.	Vocal techniques depend upon the understanding of some physiology and the physics of sound.
RHYTHMIC ACTIVITIES	Group planning, teamwork and individual expression are training for citizenship.	Folk dances and rhythmic activities are characteristic of many countries. They enhance social studies.	Folk dancing is enhanced greatly when songs are sung and social graces are expressed in their native tongue.	A study of the elements affecting movement, i.e., level, range, focus. Rhythm and mathematics are related.
CREATIVE ACTIVITIES	Teaching children to be creative stimulates critical thinking, problem-solving, and wise use of leisure time.	Creative activities invite the study of other cultures as well as our own.	Creative activities related to music and to the spoken word make for practical application of proper English.	Making instruments (water glasses, etc.) is more a science study than a study of music.
RHYTHM INSTRUMENTS	Working in unity is a lesson in democracy-in-action.	Characteristics of peoples are often revealed in rhythms. The instruments are a means of emphasizing this.	An opportunity to study rhythms as they were used in communication—native drums, etc.	A cursive study of sounds and sound effects—a study in physics.
MELODY FLUTES	All group effort requires the cooperation of the class. A lesson in good citizenship.	Flute, pipes have played an important part in the ceremonial life of early culture.	Listening to pitch is an aspect of language arts; symbols of notation constitute a language.	A study of the mathematical ratios of high and low tones produced by pipes is a practical approach to the study of sounds.
LISTENING	Appreciation of things cultural carries over in adult and community life.	The mores and folkways of many periods are reflected in music; thus correlating social studies.	Listening makes use of foreign words. It piques the interest of students for further study of languages.	The principle of tone production on each instrument is a part of appreciation and science of music.

Single copies of this chart, enlarged to 11″ × 17″, are available free of charge from

History	The Arts	Reading	Physical Education	Personality Development
Many songs enhance the study of all periods of history. These songs relate to heroes or great historic events.	Efforts toward artistic expression in music make for appreciation of beauty in all art.	The technique of good singing is carried over to good reading —phrasing, etc.	The action song or singing game has long been a part of physical education.	Expressive singing is emotional experience that broadens personality and dulls undesirable inhibitions.
The evolution of rhythmic expression coincides with the development of civilization.	Develops awareness of the elements of movement in related arts.	A feeling of the rhythmic flow in singing improves reading ability. Choral speaking is a combination of singing and reading.	Rhythmic activities can bring relaxation through a classroom day.	Bodily expression unshackles the spirit and draws personality into view.
Unit studies can include various applications of music, with wide creative opportunities.	Creative work is a medium through which music is correlated with the other arts.	Dramatizing the song helps to give a feeling for the dramatic in reading. This helps in developing the imagination.	Music's creative activities calling for motion are also physical education.	Self-expression is part of personality development. Creativeness is a part of developing self-confidence.
The development of percussion instruments is parallel to the development of civilization.	These instruments emphasize musical form. There is a relationship of musical form to painting, poetry, literature, and the dance.	Using music notation is a form of reading.	Precision marching and walking enter into many instrumental activities, all of which aid in development of coordination.	The group activities of music help to develop poise.
The flute, being one of the older instruments, was a part of tribal ceremonies, and used in courts of kings.	Ensemble playing is an art form better appreciated when an individual has the opportunity to participate.	Using music notation is a form of reading.	Breath control and good posture are developed by music training, both vocal and instrumental.	Musical skills develop confidence and build an extroverted personality.
Great music has been influenced in its creation by historical events, such as the War of 1812, the settling of "America."	Appreciation of fine music is a basis upon which a discriminating taste may be developed for all the arts.	Contributes to the intellectual aspect of literature. Music is often related to great literature and drama.	Active as well as passive body activity enter into listening, particularly in the primary grades.	Developing taste for beauty influences the personality characteristics of the individual favorably.

the American Music Conference, 332 South Michigan Avenue, Chicago, Illinois.

There are basic relationships between music and the other areas of the curriculum. However, the area that best lends itself to the combining of subject matter of all types is the social studies.

Music in Social Studies

The purpose of the social studies program is to help the society it represents provide for the immediate and long-time needs of young people. In some schools specific units are planned by the classroom teacher in terms of a chosen theme for each grade suited to the stage of development of that age group. In developing the theme, subject matter is drawn from the various social science disciplines. Social studies, science, and language arts make up the core of the program while arithmetic, health, physical education, music, and art are drawn upon to aid in the understanding and in the solution of the problems being studied. However, it should be kept in mind that in most schools having this type of program, additional time is allotted for the development of skills in arithmetic, physical education, music, and art.

The primary concern in the introduction of music into such units is not how much and what specific music can be used in this connection, but how music can contribute to a better understanding and realization of the problems and generalizations under consideration. The teacher of social studies selects specific concepts and generalizations in that area, then he and the pupils choose whatever music will help in the solution of the problems under study. The variety of musical experiences possible in such units is almost limitless, and can range from song interpretation and simple dramatization to writing original song plays.

From the standpoint of social studies, songs can be used to introduce a unit of study, to add meaning to an event or period of history, to add interest and variety, to reflect the thinking of people at a particular time, to explain what people were doing at a particular time, to stress similarities and differences in modes of living and working, to help children develop an understanding of needs, hopes, and fears common to all mankind, and to reveal relationships between nations and cultures.

A SUGGESTED UNIT FOR PRIMARY-AGE CHILDREN: "CHILDREN'S PETS"

It is logical that the study of any unit of work should begin with what children know from their own experience, thus the accepted order of learning proceeds from the *here, now* and *known* to the *there, far away,* and *unknown*. After becoming acquainted with the different pets in their immediate environment, children can then compare these with the pets of children in another country. In order to study pets in depth, the teacher guides the learners to examine all types of information which is pertinent, using scientific and social science data illuminated by literature, art, music, and dance—all on the children's level of comprehension. By examining the different aspects of problems concerning pets, children gain sufficient data to formulate understandings, concepts, and generalizations of significance. In keeping with the idea of depth studies and the importance of data in the construction of generalizations, it is suggested that after children study their own pets, they select one country, such as Japan, and compare their pets with those of Japanese children. Concepts involved with world understanding are formed by children of this age in the same manner; they first study problems of living in their immediate environment, then compare these with those of another country.

The teacher will include in her plans the major generalizations she hopes will evolve from this study. Among these may be:

1. Children all over the world have pets.

2. There are many different kinds of pets.

3. All pets need homes.

4. Pets eat different kinds of food.

5. Pets have ways of protecting themselves.

6. Pets must have love and kindness.

7. Japanese children have some pets that are the same as ours.

8. Japanese children have some pets that are different from ours.

In this book we are primarily concerned with indicating some of the music learnings which could assist children in formulating in their own terms significant generalizations comparable to those listed above. Some of these might be:

1. All pets have some way of moving their bodies; these can be imitated, dramatized, and played on certain instruments. (rhythm)

2. Most pets have some way of making sounds; these can be imitated with voices and instruments. (pitch and melody)

3. Songs have been written about pets; we can find some and sing them. (pitch, melody, dynamics)

4. We can make up poems about pets and write our own songs; we can sing and play these songs. (pitch, melody, dynamics, notation)

The creative teacher will include part of the music study as a logical way of using music to help realize the social studies objectives. Tone matching, impersonations, dramatization, fundamental rhythmic movements, the use of percussion and other instruments, will take place. Concepts of high and low, fast and slow, heavy and light can be worked with in a logical setting when pets are studied. Free rhythmic expression and improvised music may be created as the study develops. Some physical education guides provide suggestions for the movements of prancing horses, walking cats, and hopping rabbits. Appropriate singing games concerning pets may be found in series books. However, many of the best movements and games are those created by the children. Examples of recordings which may have value are Decca's *Animal Pictures in Music*, Phoebe James' album, *Animal Rhythms,* and the often-used *Carnival of the Animals*. Piano selections in books for nursery school, kindergarten, and first grade should be examined for possible use.

A SUGGESTED UNIT FOR INTERMEDIATE-AGE CHILDREN: "LIFE IN THE UNITED STATES AND MEXICO"

In such a unit there will be a number of major social science generalizations to be developed. One that involves music is, "The music of any country reflects the people's concerns in every aspect and area of life—historical, physical and geographical, political, economic, religious, emotional, social and aesthetic." After exploring and comparing nationalistic music of the United States and Mexico, children should be able to state this generalization, or one similar, in their own vocabulary.

Questions children might have that relate to music are as follows: What do the Mexican people do for entertainment? What types of entertainers are there in Mexico, and how might we demonstrate their activities? In what ways can we express work in Mexico? What is a fiesta? What fiestas, political and religious ceremonies and celebrations do they have in Mexico? How can we find out about these? What do people wear to fiestas? Could we dramatize activities of worship such as pilgrimages to shrines and lighting candles? What are some native dances and their origins? Why do some dancers wear masks? Where do they get their ideas for the designs on their costumes? What films and recordings would help us to understand music and dance in Mexico? Can we have a fiesta? Can we collect or make Mexican instruments such as castanets, tambourines, drums, flutes, and maracas? Can we dramatize breaking the piñata and *Las Posadas*[2] (the re-enactment of Mary and Joseph going from house to house seeking shelter)? Who are some famous Mexican musicians, composers, and artists? Is Mexican music different from ours? In what ways?

Songs from the series books and other sources should be used when they serve to enrich activities of the unit. For example, in the study of the fiesta, appropriate music and dances are essential and integral parts of the study. When the Mexican Christmas is taken up, a piñata can be constructed in arts and crafts, and a song and dance found or created to be used with it. Authentic Mexican folk songs depict the Mexican way of life in the same way that other authentic folk songs depict life in other parts of the world. Songs can be found or created that tell of the Mexican's food, clothing, transportation, holidays, love, customs, occupations, religion, superstitions, poverty, recreation, feelings and emotions. Mexican dance, music, and art are related in their color, rhythm, and spirited character. Songs and dances have significant meaning when they are a part of the problem-solving activities of the unit.

Songs such as "Carmen Carmela," "The Jarabe," "Cielito Lindo," "La Raspe," "La Cucaracha," and others are commonly found in series books. "La Golondrina" ("The Swallow") is a particular favorite of the Mexican people, and is often used to close meetings. With these songs, the series books suggest activities such as dancing from stated directions or with modified or created steps, making instruments, playing rhythms, part-singing, chording on guitar or Autoharp, developing percussion scores, singing descants, creating harmony parts, listening to related recordings, and studying Mexican Christmas and fiesta music and customs. Other activities could include painting colorful pictures to illustrate selected recordings of authentic Mexican music, listening to the music of Carlos Chavez and other Mexican composers, dramatizing a Mexican legend (including authentic or original rhythm patterns, flute playing, and dances), and studying and evaluating the guitar as an important Mexican and Spanish instrument, including listening to recordings of famed concert guitarists.

Characteristic Mexican dances include the following: "Chiapanecas" has as its subject the beauties in nature. Girls' costumes are embroidered with flowers and colorful fruits; boys wear sashes and brilliantly colored

[2] *Toward World Understanding With Song* (Belmont, Calif.: Wadsworth Publishing Company, 1967), p. 130.

neckerchiefs on white suits. "La Cucaracha" has as its leading figure a poor cockroach who cannot walk fast because of his lack of spending money. "Dance of the Little Old Men" ("Los Viejecitos") requires endurance and control of muscles. It is danced by strong young men who wear masks to make them appear old. "La Huapanga" is the most popular dance. It is a major recreational outlet for working people, who plan to dance it every eight days in larger cities. "El Jarabe" has courtship as its subject. The costumes are elaborately Spanish. It is featured in Mexican Independence Day celebrations and all Mexican school children know it. "La Pluma" derives its name from a headdress of feathers worn by the dancers, who reflect the warlike days of the conquistadors and Montezuma.

WORLD UNDERSTANDING

One of the most important aspects and major trends in the teaching of social studies today is an emphasis on world understanding. In regard to music as a subject, there are related generalizations such as follow:

1. The early history of the development of music in any country has a direct influence on the present and future types of music in that country.

2. The music of any country is undergoing more or less constant change.

3. The music of any country reflects the people's concerns in every aspect and area of life—social, aesthetic, religious, political, and economic.

4. The music of most cultures has been altered and influenced by music from another or other cultures.

5. Folk songs in all societies undergo constant change which reflects the changes taking place in those societies; both words and melodies may change over the years. (Example: Songs about "choo-choo" trains are not written today because the modern diesel engine does not make that sound.)

6. The music of a particular culture has a distinctive style that differentiates it from all other cultures.

7. Every society, no matter how primitive, has found a need for music, and has created its own types of music to serve its purposes.

8. The music, art, language, literature, architecture, recreation, food, clothing, and political and social customs of a people serve to bind them together into a national or cultural unit.

Music is sometimes considered solely as an art to be studied, and sometimes considered solely as an art that reflects humanity. This implied division is in many respects artificial, since music as an art is rooted in the lives of people. Both social studies and ethnomusicology demand that music be studied *in the context* of the society and times of which it is an expression. An example is the minuet, which became an official French court dance in 1650, and eventually became an expression of a courtly and aristocratic society. Its restraint and sophisticated artificiality reflected the patterned dignity and courtesies of the eighteenth-century ruling class. As this aristocratic society began to weaken, the minuet began to decline in importance as a dance, but became a movement in symphonies of Haydn and Mozart at a faster tempo, not danceable. This finally evolved to become the *scherzo* (literally joke) movement of Beethoven symphonies. Music is always communicating something, whether it is feelings of restraint or of freedom, a folk singer's reaction to his environment, aspects of a specific culture, or a sophisticated reflection by a professional composer of that culture.

Songs, dances, and instruments yield data about people's beliefs, values, and how they live or lived. Through the music of various people and times, children can discover *who they are,* and can find their places in the cultural stream that began in the past and will flow into the future. New songs, such as today's songs of protest, explain the concerns of the present day, while old songs are a means of understanding the past and its influence on the present. The historian and the anthropologist find music an essential ingredient of a culture, society, or tribal organization; thus it is one of the essentials of a civilized state of being. Music is not necessary for mere physical survival, but it is an ingredient which helps make survival worthwhile; it is a quality factor for living which indicates degrees of cultural sophistication.

Exploring the music of the world is a recent trend in both music education and in social studies. Children need to know the different kinds of music in the world if they are to understand other cultures. Composers need to know the music of the world in order to understand the music of today, which utilizes styles and unique uses of the elements of music from everywhere.

The school music of Japanese children is similar to that of American children, while the original, authentic Japanese music occupies a minority position. The native Japanese music stems historically from Chinese culture, causing the Japanese child to find himself amid two cultural streams of music. The excellent film, *Folk Songs of Japan,* useful for age eight and up, can be obtained from the nearest Japanese consulate (color, 29 min.). It portrays the beauty of the Japanese countryside while taking the listener through examples of all types of folk music including a contemporary popular song performed at a ski resort by young people. The combination of Japanese and American influences in this song encourages children's analyses of the music..

As children explore Asiatic music by means of television, recordings, films, and books, they will discover that concepts of music which differ from our common scales and harmonizations have a utility, charm, and worth of their own. Rhythm and melody, often accompanied by a simple drone, characterizes the music of India. The scale and melodic structure is found in the *raga*, of which there are hundreds. Each of these has from five to seven pitches and one or two secondary pitches. The performer elaborates and improvises on the raga of his choice. Each raga has non-musical implications which could be some feeling or emotion, a season, or a time of day. This music is horizontally conceived; there is no harmony as we know it—only the drone. Both melody and rhythm are more sophisticated than their counterparts in western music, although our composers are being increasingly influenced by Indian concepts of melody and rhythm. The *tala* is the rhythmic structure, organized into a number of beats with recurring accents. Approximately thirty talas are in common use. Some are regular in meter, such as $4 + 4 + 4 + 4$ beats, while others are irregular, such as the eleven-beat $7 + 2 + 2$. The musician improvises rhythmically on the basis of the tala. Three popular instruments are the *sitar,* a many-stringed fretted instrument, the *tabla,* a double drum, and the *tamboura,* a long-necked unfretted instrument with drone strings.

The mixing of eastern and western music has taken place in the popular music field with the raga-rock concept. Arabic music is a worthy study, as is the *gamelan* music of Indonesia which influenced Debussy and other composers. Something to avoid is thinking of nonwestern music as stereotypes. It is infinitely varied. For example, there are many differences in the music of one section of a country like Nigeria from other sections; the same is true of China and almost every country. The music of Africa has been influenced by music of Asia, Arabian music, music of the West, with Central Africa providing music more indigenous than other sections of that continent. American Indian and Hawaiian music are of special interest to people of the United States. American Indian music, generally speaking, utilizes steps smaller than our half-steps, uses a percussion accompaniment of drums, rasps, and rattles, employs the flute as a solo instrument, has no structured harmony, and has chant-like melodies which do not conform to the European scales. Original Hawaiian music has been practically destroyed by European musical influences, but researchers have managed to reconstruct some of it.

Native Hawaiian music was largely chant, centered about one pitch. Harmony was absent; the form was mainly of short repeated chants with instrumental interludes to provide contrast. The modern Hawaiian style resulted when missionary hymns and the Portuguese guitar were introduced. The guitar evolved to become the modern ukulele. Stylistic differences within the music of the West were discussed in Chapter 13. Recordings are available for classroom use which take the listener to the culture, nation, region, or even tribe, and permit him to study the authentic music of the selected people, place, or in some instances, time.

As educators are becoming more involved with conceptual learning, and as they strive to place the child in the center of the "teacher-learner process," they are devising teaching strategies that involve children in exploration and inquiry which enables them to formulate for themselves such generalizations as those to follow. They are often guided in exploring and inquiring into the life and problems of a country in such a manner as to develop major concepts and generalizations that apply to *all* cultures. Some of the generalizations which might be used as guides in developing an emphasis on the major common problems of any society are:

1. People of all countries have some form of home, family, and country which present problems and call forth emotional responses.

2. In all countries people need some form of clothing for protecting them from the weather and/or for decoration and social purposes.

3. People of all societies need foods which are obtained in similar or different ways.

4. People of all countries do some form of work.

5. People of every country engage in humor and recreation which may be similar or different from that of other countries.

6. All societies have some types of transportation and communication in order to exist.

7. People of every country have their own pets and animals.

8. Each nation has its special days which hold particular significance for its people.

9. Each country has music which may be unique in its employment and organization of the elements of music.

A recent book which provides a foundation for this approach at all elementary school levels is *Toward World Understanding With Song*.[3] Besides songs which relate to all of the above generalizations, there are reference lists for each unit of work, exhaustive classified lists of suggestions for pupil inquiry, suggested films, filmstrips, and recordings, annotated bibliographies of children's books, and an international calendar of special days. Folkways Album FD 5720 of the same name is available to present approximately thirty of the songs in several languages, and to sample authentic music of the Zuni Indians, the Chinese Classical Theater, an Iranian native orchestra, a Javenese gamelan orchestra, drums of the Yoruba people of Africa, a Puerto Rican orchestra, the alphorn and cowbells of Switzerland on a festive day.

In the study of world understanding it is essential that children realize that it is through the arts and literature that we know how man has thought and how he has felt about the common problems of men everywhere. Music has a major contribution to make in this study.

REFERENCES

Articles

KABALEVSKI, DIMITRI, "Mutual Enrichment of Children of Various Countries," *Music Educators Journal* (February, 1967), pp. 45–47.

KASILAG, LUCRECIA, "Asian Music in Education," *Music Educators Journal* (May, 1967), pp. 71–73.

MAY, ELIZABETH, "An Experiment with Australian Aboriginal Music," *Music Educators Journal* (December, 1967), pp. 47–50.

——, AND MANTLE HOOD, "Javanese Music for American Children," *Music Educators Journal* (April-May, 1962), pp. 40–41.

RED, VIRGINIA STROH, "The Sounds of India," *House Beautiful* (July, 1968), p. 61—.

WOOTEN, JEAN B., "The Delmarva Educational Television Project," *Perspectives in Music Education: Source Book III*. Washington, D.C.: Music Educators National Conference, 1966, pp. 498–503. Includes art experiences to assist understanding of form in music.

[3] Nye, Vernice T., Robert E. Nye, and H. Virginia Nye, *Toward World Understanding With Song* Belmont, Calif.: Wadsworth Publishing Company, Inc., 1967.

Books

ABRAHMS, ROGER D., AND GEORGE FOSS, *Anglo-American Folk Song Style*. Englewood Cliffs, N.J.: Prentice-Hall, Inc., 1968.

COOPERATIVE RECREATION SERVICE, *Little Book of Carols,* 43 Christmas songs from 16 countries. Delaware, Ohio: Cooperative Recreation Service.

DIETZ, BETTY WARNER, AND THOMAS C. PARK, *Folk Songs of China, Japan, Korea*. New York: John Day Company. For Grades K-5.

DIETZ, BETTY WARNER, AND MICHAEL B. OLATUNJI, *Musical Instruments of Africa*. New York: John Day Company. For grades 7–12.

ELLIOTT, RAYMOND, *Learning and Teaching Music*. Columbus, Ohio: Charles E. Merrill Books, Inc. 1966. pp. 269–359 relate to U.S. history in grades 5 and 6.

JAROLIMEK, JOHN, *Social Studies in Elementary Education*. New York: The Macmillan Company, 1967. Chapter 15, "Teaching for International Understanding."

KARPELES, MAUD, ED., *Folk Songs of Europe*. London: Novello, 1956. Authentic folksongs edited for the International Folk Music Council.

KELLY, JOHN M., JR., *Folk Songs Hawaii Sings*. Rutland, Vermont: Charles E. Tuttle.

KINSCELLA, HAZEL, *The Kinscella Readers* (2nd ed.). Lincoln, Nebraska: University Publishing Company, 1949. Books from second to eighth grade levels.

KRONE, BEATRICE PERHAM, *Janet and Jerry on the Farm; Come, Let Us Make a Garden; Songs of Travel and Transport*. Park Ridge, Ill.: Neil A. Kjos Music Company.

LANDECK, BEATRICE, *Echoes of Africa in Folk Songs of the Americas*. New York: Marks Music Corporation.

LOMAX, ALAN, *Folk Songs of North America*. New York: Doubleday & Company. Includes historical backgrounds.

LYONS, JOHN H., *Stories of Our American Patriotic Songs*. New York: Vanguard Press, Inc., 1942.

METCALF, LEON V., *Phonics in Song*. Leon V. Metcalf, 2521 11th Ave. West, Seattle, Washington 98119; also Pro Art, New York, N.Y. The association of letter symbol, song, and sound.

MICHAELIS, JOHN, *Social Studies for Children in a Democracy*. Englewood Cliffs, N.J.: Prentice-Hall, Inc., 1968. Music activities for social studies are described in pp. 492–500.

MYERS, LOUISE, *Teaching Children Music in the Elementary School,* 3rd ed., Englewood Cliffs, N.J.: Prentice-Hall, Inc., 1961. Chapter 12.

NETTL, BRUNO, *Folk and Traditional Music of the Western Continents*. Englewood Cliffs, N.J.: Prentice-Hall, Inc., 1968.

NYE, VERNICE T., ROBERT E. NYE, AND H. VIRGINIA NYE, *Toward World Understanding With Song*. Belmont, Calif. 94002: Wadsworth Publishing Company, 1967. Includes extensive reference lists; Folkways Album FD 5720 is available for use with the book.

OXFORD UNIVERSITY PRESS catalog includes a series of books titled *Children's Songs* (of Czechoslovakia, Denmark, France, Iceland, Italy, Russia, Spain), 200 Madison Avenue, New York, N.Y. 10016.

PETERSON, FREDERICK A., *Ancient Mexico*. New York: G. P. Putnam's Sons, 1959. Chapter 9, "Song and Dance," describes ancient musical instruments.

SCHIMMERLING, H. A., *Memories of Czechoslovakia*, 136 West 52 St., New York, N.Y. 10019: Marks Music Corporation. Insight into history and customs by means of 22 songs. See the Marks catalog for other national song collections.

SHUMSKY, ABRAHAM, *Creative Teaching in the Elementary School*. New York: Appleton-Century-Crofts, 1965, pp. 215–27.

SHUSTER, ALBERT H., AND MILTON E. PLOGHOFT, *The Emerging Elementary Curriculum for All Children*. Columbus, Ohio: Charles E. Merrill Books, Inc., 1963. Chapter 11, pp. 337–46.

STEVENSON, ROBERT M., *Music in Mexico*. New York: Thomas Y. Crowell Co., 1953.

SUR, WILLIAM R. et. al., *This Is Music*, Book Five. Boston: Allyn & Bacon, Inc., 1967. Pages 18–161 reflect the history of the United States in song.

TANABE, HISAO, *Japanese Music*. Tokyo: The Society for International Relations, 1936.

TOOZE, RUTH, AND BEATRICE KRONE, *Literature and Music as Resources for Social Studies*. Englewood Cliffs, N.J.: Prentice-Hall, Inc., 1955.

UNICEF, *Food Wonders of the World; Wonderful World of Clothes, Hi Neighbor* Series of books about nations of the world, with a recording of folk songs and dances for each book, U.S. Committee for UNICEF, P.O. Box 22, Church Street Station, New York, N.Y. 10008.

WHITE, FLORENCE, AND KAZUO AKIYAMA, *Children's Songs from Japan*. New York: Marks Music Corporation, 1960. 50 Japanese songs which tell American children how Japanese boys and girls live.

Films and Filmstrips

Discovering Texture; Discovering Color. Film Associates of California, 11024 Santa Monica Blvd., West Los Angeles, Calif. These films concern art; they can be used in comparing these elements in art and in music.

Folk Songs in American History. Six Filmstrips and Six Records, WASP Filmstrips, Palmer Lane West, Pleasantville, New York. 1. Early Colony Days, 2. Revolutionary War, 3. Workers of America, 4. In Search of Gold, 5. The South, 6. Civil War.

Folk Songs of Japan; Children's Songs of Japan. From nearest Japanese consulate.

Music in Motion, fifteen films, Musilog Corporation, P.O. Box 1199, 1600 Anacapa St., Santa Barbara, Calif. 93102. A series; each film has a study guide which includes a description of the film, the composer's life, and suggestions for relating to other subject areas. 1968.

Our American Heritage of Folk Music (social studies correlation). Twelve Film-strips, Society for Visual Education, Inc., 1345 Diversey Parkway, Chicago, Ill. 60614. Group One: Songs of the Sea, Songs of the Cowboy, Songs of the Mountains, Songs of the Plains, Songs of the Railroad, Songs of the Civil War. Group Two: Songs of the American Revolution, Songs of the Old South, Songs of Pioneer Mid-America, Songs of the Western Frontier, Songs of the Mississippi Valley, Songs of the Old Southwest.

Recordings, Examples of

BOWMAR RECORDS, 10515 Burbank Blvd., *Indicated*
North Hollywood, California *Grade Level*

Dance

Mexican Folk Dances, Canadian Folk Dances, Album 4 (*Around*   4–8
the World), Album 5 (*American*), Album 6 (*Latin American*)

Foreign Language Study

Songs for the Spanish Class, Songs for the French Class, Songs for the   3–6
Russian Class, Songs for the German Class, etc. Seven books
and record albums.

Orchestral Library

Album 51: *Animals and Circus;* Album 75: *U.S. History in Music*

Social Studies

Songs of Home, Neighborhood and Community, Holidays and
Seasons, Folk Songs of the U.S.A., Folk Songs of Many People,
Folk Songs of Latin America, Folk Songs of Canada, Folk Songs of
Our Pacific Neighbors, Folk Songs of California and the Old West,
North American Indian Songs, Children's Songs of Mexico, Folk
Songs of Africa, Favorite Songs of Japanese Children

CHILDREN'S MUSIC CENTER, INC., 5373 W. Pico Blvd., Los Angeles, Calif. 90019

The catalog of this company lists records and books that relate to foreign language study, social studies, physical education, literature, science and nature, U.S. history, and foreign lands.

COLUMBIA RECORDS, EDUCATION DEPARTMENT, 799 Seventh Ave., New York, N.Y. 10019

Columbia World Library of Folk and Primitive Music, Songs of the   5–12
North and South, Songs of the West, Songs of the Cowboy, The Revolution, The Union, The Confederacy.

DESOTO RECORDS (sponsored by the World Federation of the United Nations Association)

The Music and People of: *Indonesia, Thailand, Japan, India* (four albums as named).

ENRICHMENT RECORDS 246 Fifth Ave., New York, N.Y.

Albums

Pocahontas and Captain John Smith	4–6
Daniel Boone: The Opening of the Wilderness	
The Winter at Valley Forge	
Sam Houston: The Tallest Texan	
Voyages of Christopher Columbus	
Landing of the Pilgrims	
California Gold Rush	
Riding the Pony Express	
Paul Revere and the Minute Men	
Our Independence and the Constitution	
Building the First Transcontinental Railroad	
Wright Brothers: Pioneers of American Aviation	
Explorations of Père Marquette	
Lewis and Clark Expedition	
Monitor and the Merrimac	
Lee and Grant at Appomattox	

FOLKWAYS RECORDS, 121 West 47th St., New York, N.Y. 10036

The catalog *Folkways Records in Music Education* lists authentic folk music, ethnic music, and music history, with descriptive information with each album.

GREYSTONE CORPORATION (Children's Record Guild and Young People's Records), 100 Avenue of the Americas, New York, N.Y.

	Suggested Grade Level
Individual disks	
"Fog Boat Story" (transport)	1–3
"Jump Back, Little Toad" (safety)	K–3
"Ship Ahoy" (transport) (dramatization)	2–5
"Build Me a House" (social studies)	1–3
"Creepy Crawly Caterpillar (nature)	K–3
"Little Pedro in Brazil" (social studies)	4–6
"Pedro in Argentina" (social studies)	4–6
"Going West" (westward movement)	3–6
"Folk Songs for Orchestra" (social studies) (Russia)	3–6
"Chisholm Trail" (westward movement)	2–6
"Daniel Boone" (westward movement)	2–6
"Working on the Railroad" (transport)	2–5
"By Rocket to the Moon" (astronomy)	2–6
"Timber-r-r" (occupations)	3–6
"Pony Express" (westward movement)	3–6
"Christopher Columbus" (exploration)	1–6
"Around the World" (modes of travel)	N–1
"Yankee Doodle" (westward movement)	2–6

"Let's Be Policemen" (occupations)	K–2
"Peter the Pusher" (manners)	N–1
"The Singing Water" (nature and science)	1–4
"Let's Play Together" (co-operation)	N–2

Albums

Children's Almanac (12 disks on seasons)	1–8
America the Beautiful (history and legend)	2–6
Places and Things (science and social studies)	K–4
Cowboys and Indians	1–4
Trains, Planes and Ships (transportation)	K–3
Animals (The World Around Us)	K–3

McGRAW-HILL RECORDS (Argo Records) 327 West 41st St. New York, N.Y. 10036

The Living Tradition Series of field recordings of ethnic material. Music as a way of life.

PHOEBE JAMES, Box 904, Mentone, Calif.

Album 3: *Animal Rhythms;* Album 13: *Farm Animals*

RCA VICTOR, 155 E. 24th Street, New York, N.Y. 10010

CATALOG, see Physical Education, Language Arts, Social Science and World Culture, and Holidays in index.

UNIVERSITY OF WASHINGTON PRESS, Educational Services Dept., Seattle, Wash. 98105

African Song Stories. Told and sung by Abraham Dumisani Maraire.

Miscellaneous

"African Noel," by Allen G. Lewis, Plymouth Music Company, 1841 Broadway, New York 23, N.Y. Suitable for 5th-6th grades chorus; arranged from a Liberian folk song. SA or TB.

Art Color Reproductions to relate with the *Adventures in Music* Record Library (RCA-Victor), Artext Prints, Inc., Westport, Conn.

Songs of Hawaii, by Carol Rees, Mele Loke Publishing Co., P.O. Box 7142, Honolulu, Hawaii 96821. Send for catalog of song books and recordings.

Sound Kits; Musikits for the science program, Peripole, Inc., 51–17 Rockaway Beach Blvd., Far Rockaway, Long Island, New York.

18

performances

Many programs presented by elementary school children are comprised of related or inter-related activities that include or stress music as an important aspect. To make music for others is one of mankind's oldest interests and is a prime motivator for learning. The term "program" is used to denote many types of presentations from a unit-culminating activity done by boys and girls for themselves in their own classroom to a festival-type affair encompassing the entire school or groups of schools and presented before large public audiences. Other programs are school assemblies, concerts, special day programs, song plays (original or published), radio and television presentations, simple programs in which one class invites another to share its interests and accomplishments, and instrumental recitals.

Programs should be organized for specific educational purposes and therefore should have high educational value. They should be logical culminations of interesting daily activities, not something unrelated to normal experience. Children should enter into the planning along with teachers and administrators. Good programs inform parents of the purposes of the music program and the activities through which purposes are achieved. They should reveal the children's musical growth and development.

For example, one program presented to parents by a first-grade class was in five parts. The titles of the five sections were:

1. We *hear* and *sing* sounds and give them names and numbers.
2. We find sounds on a *staff*.
3. We do things with *rhythm*.
4. We find sounds on the *keyboard*.
5. We sing and *interpret*.

Under each of the headings were songs and activities selected from daily classroom experience through which the children could share their musical progress with their parents.[1]

It is entirely possible that pressures from school and community can result in programs that are contrary to good educational practice. Should this occur, the teacher should strive to orient parents and others to the types of programs that are justifiable from the standpoint of education. Neither children nor teachers should be exploited. Children's interests and development should come first; they should not be sacrificed for dubious entertainment or public relations values.

Since an important reason for the existence of programs is the value they have in building feelings of confidence, security, and belonging, all children should appear in them whenever possible. When it is impossible for every child to take part, perhaps scheduling two performances with alternate casts might remedy the difficulty. When there is no solution to this problem, the class should choose those of their number whom they wish to represent them.

To find songs relating to specific types of programs the teacher should refer to classified indexes of series books, and specialized song books dealing with Christmas, folk songs, singing games and dances, songs of specific nations and peoples, types of part-singing and music elements under study. Such books are often exhibited at professional conventions and can be purchased at educational supply houses. Public libraries are another source.

Costumes should be kept simple and inexpensive. Whenever possible, they should be made by the children in school. When parents are assigned this responsibility, unhappiness can result from some children being underdressed or overdressed by comparison with others. When the

[1] St. Frances Cabrini School, Tacoma, Washington.

children are dressed simply and identically (as much as the performance permits), this problem is minimized.

Large-scale programs are apt to interrupt the normal school day. When such programs are contemplated, teachers and administrators should decide whether their educational values are great enough to offset the losses due to interruption of normal class activities.

Although good performance is a worthy goal, too much emphasis on drill and "perfection" can destroy spontaneity and joy. Such programs are not worth the placing of children and teachers in an atmosphere of tension and emotional disturbance. A happier situation comes from an atmosphere of calm encouragement and relaxed enjoyment, stemming from well-laid plans organized by the children and teachers. After all, the major consideration should be what is happening to the boys and girls. This is often overlooked when adult standards of performance are mistakenly sought.

Programs presented for and by children in primary grades should be brief, with 30 minutes as a maximum length. Those presented for and by children in intermediate grades are ordinarily limited to not more than one hour. A trend has been in evidence toward shorter programs than were once presented in elementary schools, and it can be added that many parents are averse to lengthy presentations. Perhaps the example of television has spurred the trend toward brief and fast-moving programs for adults as well as for children. The most common faults of school presentations are (1) they are too lengthy, (2) the action is too slow-moving, (3) the children's speaking voices cannot be heard by the audience.

Although the emphasis today is to place educational values uppermost in school programs, entertainment values need not be shunned, for the one does not eliminate the other. The best programs are probably those in which educational and entertainment values are so well combined that they are inseparable.

Programs that include a number of classrooms require joint faculty planning and co-operation. One teacher explains,

> In our school the fifth-grade teacher, the art teacher and the music teacher plan a tentative program which is submitted at the next teachers' meeting for discussion. After changes have been made and it is acceptable to all concerned, each teacher selects a project or part of the program to plan with her class. The music teacher is the co-ordinator, the fifth grade teacher handles the speaking parts, and the art teacher takes

care of props and stage. Classroom teachers are responsible for their own class's part in the whole program. We try to let every child "in on the act" whether it be in the chorus, participating in pantomimes, stage-work, props, lighting, costumes, speaking parts, ushers, and publicity so that everyone feels that he has had a part. Parent help also aids in developing a closer tie with the home, and it can improve public relations.

The contemporary trend is toward programs that grow directly out of normal classroom study that convey to parents the learning that has taken place.

PROGRAMS FOR SPECIAL DAYS

Special-day programs include Thanksgiving, Christmas, Lincoln's Birthday, Valentine's Day, Washington's Birthday, Easter, and others.

HALLOWE'EN FUN

Ravinia Fifth Grade
Highland Park, Illinois

On the ee - rie night of Hal - lo - we'en, we are sure to meet a scar - y scene, the trees are sway - ing to and fro, the witch - es lan - terns are a - glow, it's beg - gar's night, you're sure to know! Boo!

Contributing to such programs are appropriate songs and dances from the music series books and from supplementary sources including those from among the songs and dances created by children. Original scripts and plays can be much more meaningful than set plans found in books and magazines, yet much good can come from the creative adapting of such material by children and teachers to better fill their own needs. The song above was written by a fifth-grade class for its Hallowe'en program.

The most important special-day programs are ordinarily those at Christmas time. They have two general aspects, the sacred and the secular, the latter having to do with the fun and gaiety of holiday good fellowship, Santa Claus, and the exchange or the giving of presents. The most common type of program is probably the one that relates the singing of Christmas songs to a script read by one or more readers. This has the advantage of being one of the easier types to prepare, but the disadvantage of being without action. It usually offers fewer opportunities for creative effort than some of the other types. An examination of the titles of Christmas programs presented over a period of years in a large city system yielded the following kinds of programs and titles of plays:

Those presented and attended by entire schools, by intermediate grades, by primary grades, or by individual rooms
Customs and carols of many lands
Original play with carols and dances
Tableau with choric reading, carols, and choral music (possible themes: Christmas around the world, Christmas cards)
Dramatized carols
Contrasting holy day and holiday
Carols and dances
Carols and shadow plays
Hanukkah and Christmas
Combined singing, instrumental music, and drama
The Nutcracker Suite with dances, singing, and orchestra
Christmas cantata
Operetta, "Santa Claus Is Coming to Town"
Band and choral music with tableau
A carol sing
Creative rhythms, songs, and dances
Favorite songs of the holiday season

Plays:
Why the Chimes Rang
Dickens' Christmas Carol
Birds' Christmas Carol
Night before Christmas
Spirit of Christmas
No Room at the Inn
Christmas Blessing
Magi's Gift
Littlest Angel
Melody of Christmas
Man Who Found the King

Elementary school music festivals are held most frequently in the spring, and thus are often considered a culminating project that is a logical outgrowth of the school year's work in music. A festival implies a large number of participants. Advantages of the festival include the thrill of participating in large groups, the uniting of many teachers and students in one project, and the opportunity to display progress in music to the school and community. Disadvantages include children tiring of the music in repeated rehearsals, the near absence (in many situations) of creative elements, and the lack of democratic elements due to dictatorial direction impossible to avoid in most large festivals. The selecting of songs is ordinarily done by the classroom teachers. For example, the third-grade teachers and their pupils agree upon the songs they want to sing, thus making a higher standard of co-operation likely than when a music director dictates the list of songs. However, no list of songs can suit every third-grade group and, while the majority of the children may be well served by the selection, there will always be those who find the songs too difficult or too easy. As in the case of other large-scale programs which sometimes disrupt the normal school day, teachers, children, and administrators should evaluate each festival carefully to determine whether the results are worth the effort involved. It is likely that the music festival's educational value for children is greater in small school systems than in large systems. For example, a four-room rural school or one city elementary school can conceivably produce a festival with many original and creative aspects, while a large city or county festival may become a routinized end within itself rather than an avenue that opens the door to further musical growth and creativity.

Many festivals bear no title except general ones such as "All City Music Festival" or "Spring Music Festival." Others have titles or even slogans or themes such as "This Is Music!" "Make Your Life More Musical," "Music Enriches Life," "A Montana Ranch Corral," "Pioneer Times," "Music, a Universal Language," "Music for Every Child, Every Child for Music," "The Old South," "Music Through History," and "Music of the Americas." In some localities, games are included with music to make the spring festival a "play day" for children.

OPERETTAS The elementary school operetta has the advantage of any activity that requires the working together of many teachers and children, such as developing a spirit of unity in the school, furthering the ability of children to work together in groups, and developing individual personalities—but the disadvantages have outweighed these if the frequency of programs of this type is a reliable criterion. Teachers have found a shortage of suitable material; few children's voices are capable of singing leading roles; there is often little opportunity found for creative aspects; the rehearsing of the leading parts can result in the neglect of the other children; and too much time may be required to prepare the operetta properly for public performance. Small original "operettas" are found today in some unit-culmination programs, thus illustrating the fact that it is possible for children to write their own small-form operettas.

When a teacher presents a program he must consider such aspects as the space necessary in which to present it; the space necessary for seating the expected audience; the time it will require to rehearse the program; the means of publicity; whether or not admission is to be charged, and if admission is charged, how the tickets are to be distributed and sold; whether there will be an announcer or a printed or mimeographed program; and if risers and other special equipment are necessary. The piano should be placed so that the accompanist and director can see each other and so the performers can hear it distinctly. After the program the teacher should evaluate it with the children.

CHILDREN'S CONCERTS

Concerts presented for children by adult musicians have become more frequent. These can be highly successful if they are well planned. When a local symphony orchestra or other group comes to an elementary school, the program will usually be from thirty to forty minutes in length. The school faculty plans *thoroughly* with the conductor or leader of the group; if this is not done, unexpected incidents are likely to occur. A true-life example is one in which a music staff either took for granted that the orchestra conductor understood young children or that he did not need to. (Planning a children's concert is much more complex than planning one for adults.) He was told that "it would be fine" to have a 30-minute program beginning at 3 o'clock, but he was not told *why* the concert must begin and end precisely on schedule. At this particular school, mothers drive to the building to take their children home at 3:30 and the children have strict orders to never keep mother waiting. The conductor did not begin the program at 3 o'clock, but leisurely started it at 3:10. He did not know that young children cannot sit quietly doing nothing, so his audience seemed unruly to him as little by little it became more restless and noisy as it waited for the orchestra to begin playing. When he had finished the program forty (not thirty) minutes later, he found that half of his audience had walked out in the middle of the program to meet the waiting mothers. The teachers were embarrassed and the conductor was confused and frustrated.

Besides planning the theme of the concert, which could concern specific elements of music and/or instruments of the orchestra, and which should relate logically to the study of music, the school faculty should explain all aspects of the timing and other arrangements with the conductor and the reasons for these. In the above example, the faculty did not make it clear why the concert was to be only 30 minutes in length. Planning needs to be done concerning which parts of a long selection will be performed and which parts will be omitted. Verbal explanations by the conductor and performers should be planned in advance. Featured players should stand where all the children can see them, coming to the front of the stage if necessary in order to show their instruments and manner of performance. The school faculty has the responsibility for the educational preparation of the children regarding the music to be performed, and for careful planning of audience manners. Local performing groups can be valuable resources. As in other educational planning, the objectives of the performance should be clear, and the planning precise.

In 1967 more than 5,000 concerts of various types were provided by Young Audiences, Inc., 115 East 92 Street, New York, N.Y. 10028, which started in Baltimore in 1949 and is now the largest concert agency in the world. Funds from the Ford Foundation and the Music Performance Trust Funds of the Recording Industries made the Young Audiences project possible. Funds from local communities will be necessary for its continuation. Its services should be investigated by school districts interested in children's concerts.

INQUIRY AND SUGGESTED ACTIVITIES

1. Select a type of public program, develop it, and list the administrative details involved in its presentation. How will you involve the children in its planning and execution? What is the learning you would expect to result from this program?

2. Attend elementary school music programs and evaluate them.

3. Plan a song-play with a music or social studies subject. Sketch the action and spoken lines; select and create the music.
4. Plan a special-day program to be presented by the children for themselves in their classroom. Then plan how it might be expanded to include parents as both audience and participants.
5. Listen to and evaluate children's concerts on radio and television.
6. Attend a children's concert given by a symphony orchestra or other adult professional group. Evaluate its effectiveness in terms of educational and social values.
7. When an excellent school program is scheduled, video-tape it for use in college classes, in PTA and school board meetings, and with community groups to explain the goals and achievements of the music offerings of the elementary school.
8. Obtain lists of recommended elementary school operettas from companies such as Keynote Music Service, Inc., 833 South Olive Street, Los Angeles, California 90014, and Educational Music Bureau, 434 South Wabash Avenue, Chicago, Illinois 60605.

REFERENCES

HOCHMAN, SYLVIA "A Concert With a Theme," *Music Educators Journal* (November, 1967), p. 109. An excellent example of planning with children and performers to build a concert based on concepts of forms of music.

MURRAY, JOSEPHINE, AND EFFIE BATHURST, *Creative Ways for Children's Programs*. Morristown, N.J.: Silver Burdett Company, 1938.

MURSELL, JAMES L., *Music in American Schools*. Morristown, N.J.: Silver Burdett Company, 1953. Chapter 11, "Public Performance."

PIERCE, ANNE E., *Teaching Music in the Elementary School*. New York: Holt, Rinehart & Winston, Inc., 1959. Chapter 12, "Special School Programs."

PLAVNIK, MAX, "From Passive Listening to Active Participation," *Music Educators Journal* (February-March, 1964).

Music for Christmas Programs

COLEMAN, SATIS N., AND ELIN JORGENSEN, *Christmas Carols from Many Countries*. New York: G. Schirmer, Inc., 1934.

DEARMER, PERCY, RALPH VAUGHAN-WILLIAMS, AND MARTIN SHAW, *Oxford Book of Carols*. New York: Oxford University Press, 1928.

GEARHART, LIVINGSTON, *A Christmas Singing Bee*. Delaware Water Gap, Pennsylvania: Shawnee Press.

GRIME, WILLIAM, *New Songs and Carols for Children*. New York: Carl Fischer, 1955.

HELLER, RUTH, *Christmas, Its Carols, Customs and Legends*. Minneapolis: Schmitt, Hall & McCreary Company, 1948.

———, *Christmas 'Round the World,* Books I and II. Evanston, Ill.: Summy-Birchard Company, 1962.

KRONE, BEATRICE AND MAX, *Descants for Christmas*. Park Ridge, Ill.: Neil A. Kjos Music Company, 1949.

KVAMME, TORSTEIN O., *The Christmas Carolers' Book in Song and Story*. Minneapolis: Schmitt, Hall & McCreary Company, 1935.

NYE, VIRGINIA, AND LOIS GURSKE, *Julenissen: The Christmas Elf,* and other authentic folk tales, customs, songs and dances from Norway, Holland, England, and Austria. Middleton, Wis.: Modern Productions, Inc., 1962. Also *A Folk Christmas,* a short operetta.

PERHAM, BEATRICE, *Christmas, Its Origins, Music & Traditions*. Park Ridge, Ill.: Neil A. Kjos Music Company, 1937.

SEEGER, RUTH CRAWFORD, *American Folk Songs for Christmas*. New York: Doubleday & Company, Inc., 1953.

SIMON, HENRY W., *A Treasury of Christmas Songs and Carols*. Boston: Houghton Mifflin Company, 1955.

VERNON, MARY STRAWN, ET AL., *Descants on Christmas Carols*. Minneapolis: Schmitt, Hall & McCreary Company, 1952.

Filmstrips

Christmas Celebrated in Song. 1345 Diversey Parkway, Chicago 14, Ill.: Society for Visual Education, Inc. Two filmstrips, recording, and teacher's manual. Useful for group singing.

Story of the Nutcracker. Same source. Filmstrip, recording, and guide. 32 minutes. Tchaikovsky's *Nutcracker* Suite.

19

evaluation

Evaluation is a means of discovering to what degree objectives have been attained. It must be made in terms of specific and immediate objectives as well as long range goals. Evaluation in music consists of assembling, interpreting, and using data to determine revisions in the learner's behavior as a result of his experience with music. Certain skills and knowledge of facts are rather easily measured by means of tests. Today the goals of music have expanded to include command of certain understandings, concepts, generalizations, skills, attitudes, values, and behaviors. These are more difficult to measure since less objective and more varied evaluative techniques must be employed. Evaluation is not an end in itself; it is a continuous process.

Suggested Guidelines to Be Used in the Evaluative Process

Any effective program of evaluation should be guided by several specific and significant criteria:

EVALUATION SHOULD BE MADE IN TERMS OF THE GOALS OF INSTRUCTION These goals are of several types and may include those for the year, those for short units of work, and those for daily plans. These goals are classified and stated as understandings, methods of inquiry (including various types of thinking) concepts, generalizations or "main ideas," skills, attitudes, and appreciations to be attained. Cognitive, affective, and psycho-motor aspects of music learning must be evaluated. The teacher plans his evaluative techniques when he plans his teaching. For example, he asks himself such questions as: To what extent do the children understand the relationship between vertical and horizontal chord tones? How successfully can the children play major scales on the bells which begin on several different pitches? To what extent is the class listening with interest at home to the televised Young People's Concerts?

EVALUATION IS MORE EFFECTIVE WHEN GOALS ARE STATED BEHAVIORALLY For example: The children indicate their understanding of the relationship between vertical and horizontal chord tones by arranging the horizontal tones found in melodies vertically, playing them on keyboard instruments, and singing them to accompany songs; the children demonstrate their understanding of the structure of the major scale by performing major scales without notation on the bells from several different pitches; the children reveal positive attitudes toward worthy music by listening with interest at home to the televised Young People's Concerts. The great value in stating goals behaviorally is that they are described in simple, direct, and realizable *performance* terms that point directly to evaluation. When children participate in this evaluation, the findings are *feedback* for them, which lead them consistently toward clear and valid perceptions that influence their choice of decisions and actions.

EVERYONE CONCERNED WITH THE LEARNING OF MUSIC SHOULD BE INVOLVED IN EVALUATION. The learning of music is facilitated when a receptive environment for inquiry into all aspects exists. Bringing about such an environment necessitates the co-operative formulation of a basic point of view, establishment of goals, means of realizing these goals, and ways of assessing to what extent the goals have been reached. Administrators, parents, other adults in the community, teachers, and pupils work together in this process. The teacher has the leading role, serving as a guide in this cooperative endeavor. Parents support educational programs when they become involved in them and understand them. Children learn best when they are given opportunities to identify what they need to learn, have some choice in what they are to learn, plan how they are going to learn it, and appraise how well they have done so.

Questions the learner might ask himself include: What do I already know about this problem? What does this goal or problem entail? What do I need to know? Where do I begin? What resources do I need? What is my next step? As a result of each bit of evaluative data collected, the teacher should become more secure and certain of what "next steps" should be taken. Through various means of evaluation the teacher constantly re-examines and revises the effectiveness of the music program and of the teaching-learning situation. Questions the teacher might ask include: Do the learners understand the goals? Are they of personal importance to the individual learners? How can I help the individual identify and analyze the various aspects of his goal and the difficulties entailed? What strategies can I use to help him become conscious of the next steps needed? How can I assist him in discovering other meanings and possibilities related to the problem?

DIAGNOSTIC TEACHING REQUIRES CONTINUOUS EVALUATION to assess the needs and capabilities of each learner implies what can be termed diagnostic teaching which itself is the essence of evaluation as a process. As part of this process, the teacher watches and listens to each learner with perception rather than only telling him or asking questions to be answered with memorized facts. This makes it necessary for the teacher to be always collecting evidence of degrees of competence and mastery in music in terms of the learner's musical behavior. It is essential that the teacher knows what concepts, generalizations, skills, knowledge, attitudes, and types of thinking are necessary for the learner to reach his goals. This process requires of the learner that he practice self-evaluation and accept responsibilities for the direction of his own learning. This is based upon his recognition of his needs and goals, which the teacher assists him to identify. It is necessary for the teacher to identify the concepts, skills, generalizations, and competence of each pupil, rather than holding to general levels of expectancy, since these levels are frequently not suited to the specific needs and capabilities of the individual learner. In this type of learning environment it is assumed that the learner will progress more effectively because he sees value and purpose for what he is doing. When he helps to establish goals, plans ways of working toward them, and carries out steps in *his* learning process, he has become involved in learning that has personal meaning for him. The inability of a child to fill his role in this type of environment may mean that he should have more experiences in music that can help him become aware of what he needs to learn.

Another implication of diagnostic teaching is that the teacher continually examine the music curriculum in light of how effectively it helps each child live in his world. This indicates continuous revision in terms of a changing world of man and music.

EVALUATION SHOULD BE RECOGNIZED AS NECESSARY FEEDBACK AND PUT TO USE A child requires feedback in order that he may adjust to the world about him, find reason to reorder or change the world about him, and to build his self-concept. The primary function of evaluation is to help the learner and the teacher improve the educational process for the individual. The school should provide a realistic, unbiased, and valid feedback to the learner so that he perceives his condition accurately, becoming better able to set goals and plan procedures to achieve them. The learner must be able to know, study, and assess the results of his attempts to learn; if he does not have this feedback, he does not know how to modify his behavior to improve his learning. This is the reason that evaluation is put to use in the classroom to plan next steps, select necessary materials, and to achieve higher levels of learning and performance. It is also put to use in restating goals of instruction and in making improvements in strategies, in materials, and in the techniques of evaluation.

RECORDS THAT ARE NECESSARY FOR FURTHERING THE QUALITY OF PUPIL LEARNING SHOULD EVOLVE FROM THE VARIOUS MEANS OF EVALUATION USED "The traditional system of marking and grading and credit granting is so inadequate and distorting, such a nuisance to good teaching and learning, that we simply have to throw it out and get ourselves something better."[1] Grading is increasingly seen as a report of doubtful accuracy created more for the benefit of parents and academic bookkeeping than for the teaching-learning process. The reason a grade symbol has little meaning is that it is rarely supported by an explanation of how it was determined. In order for a grade symbol to have meaning one must state the objectives, the type of evidence which indicates attainment of the objectives, and the analysis of the evidence. Most of what teachers are continually evaluating in their work in the classroom either cannot be summarized into a grade, or can be summarized only with extreme difficulty. In music there are many factors to consider. There can

[1] Fred T. Wilhelms, ed., *Evaluation as Feedback and Guide,* 1967 Yearbook, (Washington, D.C., Association for Supervision and Curriculum Development, 1967), p. 234.

be goals of progress in understanding and using the various elements of music, the various skills of the music program, types of musical thinking, and musical attitudes and behaviors. Even though a teacher analyzes each of these in relation to a specific child, the grade symbol may be as much a rating of the effectiveness of the teacher's strategies as it is of the child's progress. A principle of prime importance is that when grades must be given, the child should know what his grade means.

A teacher may find himself in a school in which grades are demanded; he then does the best he can to justify any grade he reports. He may be in a school in which a subject such as music is not graded, but where other subjects are. And he may find himself in a school in which letter or number grades are not given, but a checklist form with additional space for comment is provided. In some schools three spaces can be checked: superior, satisfactory, and unsatisfactory. Grades would seldom be reported if only teachers and children were concerned. Parents, colleges and universities, and future employers are those most interested in some kind of evaluative reporting. Of these, the employers are seldom interested in grades as such; they want to know the degree of skill the prospective employee has in the area of their concern, and this hardly concerns the elementary school child. Even colleges and universities have no real interest in music grades at the elementary-school level. This leaves only parents, who are usually more interested in progress reports, comment reports, and conferences with the teacher than in specific grade symbols. When grade symbols are analyzed in this way, it seems that while some kind of report to parents is worthwhile, this need not be in the form of a grade symbol. In many places where symbols are used, their meaning is restricted largely to a comparison of how well a child is doing in relation to the other children. If the child understands that this is only one way of looking at himself, and that certain other ways are more meaningful in terms of his personal growth and worth, little harm may result. What a child should want to know in music is his progress in one or more of the many facets of the study; a "C," "B," or "A" is simply not specifically meaningful. In situations in which the teacher reports a grade, then writes comments to explain it, the negative influence of the grade often offsets the intended constructive influence of the comments. Grade symbols can be particularly damaging in a subject such as music, because aspects of the affective domain cannot be meaningfully reported in that way.

Appropriate and accurate records should be available to supply whatever explicit information is needed by the teacher to assist him in his instruction and for his effective guidance of children. When a child transfers from one school to another, some form of professional record should accompany him to assist his new teacher. There is a need to communicate a child's progress through some form of record to parents. Records do not need to be exhaustive; they should include only necessary and pertinent data. Data and records can be effective in helping children become more self-directed and precise in their learning when these are organized into meaningful feedback that serves as a guide for them in making decisions and seeking understandings on their own.

Tests comprise one type of evaluative technique. They are no longer the major source of data. They have a place, however, in today's schools when they are used in conjunction with other techniques to help children evaluate their learning procedures and to help teachers evaluate their strategies.

MANY DIFFERENT TYPES OF EVALUATION ARE USED If all the different types of learning are to be assessed, there is cause to use varied evaluative devices and techniques. Evidences of children's musical growth can take place in their indidivual and group planning, individual and group performance, discussion, creative composition, and divergent thinking. Some possible types of evaluation follow:

Observation	Inventories	Case studies
Discussion	Samples of creative work	Tape recordings
Checklists	Teacher-made tests	Evaluative criteria
Diaries	Standardized tests	Cumulative records
Questionnaires	Group-made tests	Activity records
Charts	Anecdotal records	Attitude scales
Logs	Sociometric tests	Evaluative types of questions
Rating scales		Musical performance

Teachers decide what combination of devices they need to use in accordance with the types of evidence desired. For example, a teacher may decide he will evaluate ability to deal with data, concepts and generalizations, attitudes and interests, performance skills, and critical thinking; he will then select techniques of evaluation which will be used to gather this kind of data. Devices used to evaluate should have the following characteristics:

Validity. They measure what they profess to measure.

Reliability. They measure accurately and consistently.

Appropriateness. They are designed in accordance with the level of the individual or group to which they will be applied.

Practicality. They are easy to use, and are not unduly costly in terms of time or money.

Objectivity. They can be used by different persons with the same results.

Usefulness. They will reveal data that can be utilized.

Behaviorally-descriptive. They reveal data related to behavioral objectives and actions of the pupils.

Children practice self-evaluation by means of devices such as:

Group discussions

Folders containing samples of work, including creative composition

Tapes made of performances

Verbal feedback from teachers and peers

Standards decided upon by the group

Checklists

Diaries

Records on each child should be preserved so that subsequent teachers can plan more effectively. The interpretation of data in such a file must be made in terms of that child's progress as a unique individual. His position in the group, or score in relation to some national norm, is only one aspect of his relative progress.

EVALUATIVE CRITERIA

It is a popular procedure in education today to draw up check-lists of criteria by which to attempt to measure the degree of effectiveness of any given area of instruction. It is agreed that effective instructional programs are possible only when school personnel intelligently evaluate both the purposes of programs and the means by which these purposes are to be realized. In American education this evaluation may involve teachers, principals, supervisors, children, and parents. Many of the criteria suggested below are general, thus some will refer to all grade levels, while others will refer to some and not to others. Each criterion is to be followed by an evaluation of either *yes*, *no*, or *to some degree*, and these choices are to be followed by specific *plans for improvement*. (The original source of most of the following criteria is the Maryland State Department of Education.)

Activities and procedures in the classroom:	yes	no	to some degree	*plans for improvement*
are selected in terms of the developmental levels of the children and in terms of the identified objectives to be realized.				
are presented in a manner through which the children understand clearly the purposes of the activity.				
are developed in ways that actively involve the children.				
provide opportunities for children to "learn by doing."				
are sequentially planned so that children achieve the satisfaction of definite degrees of mastery of skills.				
foster enjoyment, understanding, and skills.				
provide for individual differences.				
relate to present-day life in the home, community, and world.				
provide for aesthetic, emotional, and intellectual development.				
sometimes have their origins in related areas of instruction, and sometimes stimulate interest in related areas.				
assist in developing good personalities.				
assist in understanding all mankind.				
The child's musical growth is measured by:				
his favorable attitude toward music.				

	yes	no	to some degree	plans for improvement
his musical discrimination and taste.				
his appreciation of aural beauty.				
his use of music out of school.				
his progress in singing.				
his progress in playing.				
his progress in rhythmic response.				
his progress in listening skills.				
his acquisition of a musical repertoire of value that is appropriate to his developmental level.				
the maximum development of his musical talents at a given time.				
his ability to analyze how music produces moods, emotions, descriptions, beauty, and intellectual concepts and forms.				
his ability to solve musical problems through understanding and using the components of music.				
his ability to use notation.				
his ability to evaluate his performance heard on a tape recorder.				
his ability to participate satisfactorily in group activities requiring co-operation and self-discipline.				
his ability to understand and use music vocabulary.				
his ability to sing his part in two, or three-part songs.				
his knowledge of instruments of the orchestra, their special characteristics and uses.				
his interest in outstanding performers, composers, and conductors.				
his knowledge of the larger musical forms.				
his ability to perform musically both individually and in small and large groups.				

The teacher of music:

is well prepared to teach the subject.

	yes	no	to some degree	plans for improvement
knows the purposes of music instruction and is able to select appropriate materials and activities to realize these.				
understands and enjoys music, and is enthusiastic about it.				
recognizes that children have varying interests and talents which are furthered through emotional, social, and intellectual contacts with music.				
participates professionally in efforts to improve both his teaching skills and the music program of the school.				
understands and utilizes a conceptual approach to teaching.				
emphasizes the process of learning.				
participates in community efforts to raise musical standards and to provide musical opportunities.				
has adequate facility on the piano.				
understands music as an important part of man's cultural heritage.				
can follow a logical sequential program of music instruction.				
can teach a balanced music program with its varied activities.				
continually evaluates the results of his teaching.				

The elementary school music program:

	yes	no	to some degree	plans for improvement
is accepted as an integral part of general education for every child.				
is a balanced program, with a variety of activities.				
is a well-planned and sequentially organized program.				
has a well-qualified staff.				
is supported by adequate materials of instruction.				
is recognized as basic to the secondary school music program.				
is being continuously evaluated in its scope, sequence, and balance by teachers, principals, supervisors, parents, and children.				
is a cooperative endeavor of classroom teachers, music specialists, principals, and parents who are working together to improve the musical education of children.				

	yes	no	to some degree	plans for improvement
has general and specific purposes that have been co-operatively established.				
utilizes community resources such as adult performers, concerts, television and radio.				
The elementary principal makes sure that:				
the teaching staff is well-qualified to teach music.				
the teaching staff is interested and enthusiastic in its music teaching.				
the teaching staff has a good knowledge of the materials, equipment, and activities involved in teaching music.				
the teaching staff has adequate piano facility.				
the teaching staff is constantly evaluating and improving its music teaching competency.				
the teaching staff co-operatively plans a music program that is organized logically, consistently, and sequentially.				
the music specialist is professionally oriented, is a member of the Music Educators National Conference, and attends its professional meetings.				
there are two or more sets of music series books available in each classroom.				
the record players are of a quality that reproduces music of maximum aesthetic appeal.				
an ample number of Autoharps, bell sets, pianos, percussion instruments and other items of equipment are supplied.				
each child has the opportunity to develop musically to his maximum capacity.				
the children demonstrate aesthetic quality in their musical performance.				
the children show evidence of discovery, creativity, and sensitivity in their approach to music.				
the children reveal evidence of using knowledge of the components of music to solve musical problems.				
the children learn to use musical terms and the symbols of notation.				

	yes	no	to some degree	plans for improvement
the children reveal ability to perform music individually, in small groups, and in large groups.				
the music room is acoustically adequate, has necessary storage space, is properly lighted, heated, ventilated, and has sufficient office facilities.				
adequate time is provided for music in the schedule.				
the music program reflects the enjoyment and enthusiasm of children, teachers, and parents.				
the music program reflects pride, dignity, and respect.				
the music program is doing its full share in fulfilling the educational purposes of the school.				
there is evidence that the program relates to music in the home and community, and that it is a positive force in raising the cultural level of the community.				
public musical performances are planned for educational purposes and values, not for exploiting children in the name of public relations.				

Examples of Evaluation[2]

Frances R. Link and Paul B. Diederich write about evaluation in music as follows:

A device we have projected for use in the near future is a questionnaire or checklist of what students can do in music at this stage, backed up by testing a sample of students on one or two tasks each to find out whether they can really do some of the harder things they have checked. If they know that they may be tested, few students will intentionally falsify what they can do, though some may be mistaken. A check of perhaps a random tenth of the students will then indicate the extent to which their replies may be taken at face value. A small number of typical items are reproduced below.

SURVEY OF MUSICAL ABILITY

Directions: Check all of the following that you can do. The list goes from easy to hard. You may be asked to do some of the harder things you check. Your score will be the number of the hardest task that you can do—not perfectly, but as well as is expected of students of your age.

1. You will hear a tape recording of a well-known song such as "Old Black Joe" and get a copy of the words. Can you sing it along with the recording?

2. You will hear a recording of a simple song that you have not heard before and get a copy of the words. After hearing it once, can you sing it along with the recording?

3. You will get a sheet of music with the opening bars of three well-known songs, without words. Below each of these the names of three songs will be listed. Can you read music well enough to recognize songs you know from the notes alone and pick out their names from the list?

4. The same sheet of music will have one line of notes of a song that you have not heard before. Certain points in this line will be lettered A, B, C, D, E. You will hear a recording that will stop at one of these points. Can you mark the point at which the recording stopped?

5. The next line of notes of the same song will be lettered in the same way. At one of these points the recording will not do what the notes say. Can you mark the point at which the recording differed from the notes?

---

[2] Frances R. Link and Paul B. Diederich, "A Cooperative Evaluation Program" from *Evaluation as Feedback and Guide,* 1967 Yearbook, Fred T. Wilhelms, editor. (Washington, D.C.: Association for Supervision and Curriculum Development, 1967), pp. 165–67. Copyright (c) 1967 by the Association for Supervision and Curriculum Development. Reprinted with permission of the Association and the authors.

6.   The next line of notes will be a familiar melody with words in two-part harmony, and you will hear a recording in which both parts are sung. Can you sing along with the part that is not the melody?

7.   The next line of notes will be the next line of the same song with words in two-part harmony, but the recording will have only the melody. Can you sing the other part from the notes without hearing it in the recording?

8.   The next line of notes will be a simple meloly with words that you have not heard before. The recording will play only the first bar. Can you sing the rest of this line (melody only) by sight-reading the notes?

9.   Can you sight-read a short, simple piece on a musical instrument that you have studied?

10.   Can you sight-read a part other than the melody on this instrument?

Any number of questions like these may be asked, but these will do as a sample. Remember that the subsequent testing will be feasible because only a random tenth of the students will be tested individually, and each will be asked to do only one or two of the harder tasks he has checked. The quality of performance will not be rated; the teacher will decide only whether the student can or cannot do the tasks that he has checked.

Listening. This will be a test based on short passages of tape-recorded music averaging about a minute in length. At the end there will be one or two complete selections lasting four or five minutes. Such questions as the following will be asked:

1.   Did you like this excerpt better than the last?_____ less?_____ about the same?_____

2.   What type of music was it? (march, waltz, symphony, concerto, opera, choral work, folk song, song from a musical comedy, etc.)

3.   Who or what was playing or singing? (tenor, baritone, violin, orchestra, etc.)

4.   What section of the orchestra (or what voice) carried the main melody?

5.   What other instruments or voices could you hear?

6.   Were there three beats per measure (as in a waltz) or four (as in a march)?

7.   Was the key major or minor?

8.   Was any part (or phrase) of this melody repeated? If so, how many times?

9.   Did you recognize the work from which this excerpt came? If so, which of the following was it? (three choices)

(Questions on the longer selection)

10.   Four musical phrases will be played. Indicate whether each phrase occurred or did not occur in the long selection you have just heard. (To get at attention span and musical memory.)

11.   Which of the following is the name of this musical form?

12. Check any of the following that you heard in this selection. (Variations, counterpoint, solo, duet, cadence, modulation, etc.)

(Questions on quality of performance)

Some excerpts may be played twice: once by professionals and once by amateurs, or once on a fine piano and again on a piano that is out of tune. Which was the better performance? First_____ Second_____ No difference_____ The same excerpts will be played again. Check any faults that you hear.

	First	Second
Wrong notes	_____	_____
Out of tune	_____	_____
Poor tone quality..........................	_____	_____
Some started or stopped later than others	_____	_____
Some parts drowned out more important parts ..	_____	_____

(Uneven rhythm, exaggerated emphasis, sliding into notes, etc.)

INQUIRY AND SUGGESTED ACTIVITIES

1. Examine courses of study in music published by city, county, and state educational agencies to learn what provisions are suggested for evaluation and to what extent evaluations are made in terms of purposes.
2. Indicate practical ways in which each of the criteria in the "Guidelines to Be Used in the Evaluative Process" in this chapter may be used in music teaching. At present, which ones do you believe should receive more attention? Which do you think are the most difficult to employ?
3. Invite a guest speaker who is a director of music, a music supervisor, or an elementary school principal to discuss how his music curriculum is evaluated and how improvements are made as a result of evaluations.
4. How can you aid children in using self-evaluation in the lessons and units of work you plan?
5. Arrange to observe a teacher teach a class in music, and discuss with him his evaluative techniques for improving his effectiveness as a music teacher.
6. Examine a cumulative record form used in a local school system. What music data is recorded? What additional entries, if any, are needed?
7. Prepare a sample check list, a guide for an observation, a questionnaire, and a chart that can be used in a music unit you plan to teach.
8. How can you use discussion as an evaluative technique in a unit or lesson you are planning? Anecdotal records? Tape recordings? Open-ended questions? Musical performance? Logs and diaries? Discuss these techniques critically with other students and with your teacher.
9. Prepare several objective-type test items to be used in measuring progress in the mastery of musical skills and concepts in a lesson or unit you plan to teach.

10. Examine standardized tests for appraising music. What outcomes of teaching are they designed to assess? How could they be used in relation to other evaluative techniques in a total program of evaluation?

11. Analyze and criticize the examples of evaluation suggested in this chapter by Link and Diederich. Then create devices of your own which you believe are more appropriate.

12. Formulate a lesson plan on the basis of pertinent objectives. Then devise ways to evaluate the success of the plan in terms of achieving these objectives.

REFERENCES

BENTLEY, ARNOLD, *Musical Ability in Children and its Measurement*. New York: October House, Inc., 1966. Explains the origin of Bentley's *Measures of Musical Abilities* tests.

BLOOM, BENJAMIN S., ED., *Taxonomy of Educational Objectives: Cognitive Domain*. New York: David McKay Company, Inc., 1956.

CAMPBELL, DONALD T., AND JULIAN C. STANLEY, *Experimental and Quasi-Experimental Designs for Research*. Chicago: Rand McNally & Company, 1963. For graduate students who are designing research projects.

COLWELL, RICHARD, *Elementary Music Achievement Tests*. Chicago: Follett Publishing Company, 1967. For grades 4–12.

GORDON, EDWIN, *The Musical Aptitude Profile*. Boston: Houghton Mifflin Company, 1965. Designed to assess musical aptitude in grades 4–12.

KRATHWOHL, DAVID R., BENJAMIN S. BLOOM, AND BERTRAM B. MESIA, *Taxonomy of Educational Objectives: Affective Domain*. New York: David McKay Company, Inc., 1964.

LEHMAN, PAUL R., *Tests and Measurements in Music*. Englewood Cliffs, N.J.: Prentice-Hall, Inc., 1968.

MICHAELIS, JOHN, *Social Studies for Children in a Democracy* (4th ed.). Englewood Cliffs, N.J.: Prentice-Hall, Inc., 1968. Chapter 17, "Evaluation."

WILHELMS, FRED T., ED., *Evaluation as Feedback and Guide*. Association for Supervision and Curriculum Development, 1201 Sixteenth Street N.W., Washington, D.C. 20036, 1967.

appendix b

Alphabetical Listing of Composers in Adventures in Music

Anderson: Irish Suite—THE GIRL I LEFT BEHIND ME, *GR. 5, Vol. 2*

Bach:
    Cantata No. 147—JESU, JOY OF MAN'S DESIRING, *GR. 5, Vol. 1*
    LITTLE FUGUE IN G MINOR (Arr. by L. Cailliet), *GR. 6, Vol. 1*
    Suite No. 2—BADINERIE, *GR. 3, Vol. 1*
    Suite No. 3—GIGUE, *GR. 1*

Bartok:
    Hungarian Sketches—BEAR DANCE, *GR. 3, Vol. 2*
    Hungarian Sketches—EVENING IN THE VILLAGE, *GR. 5, Vol. 2*
    Mikrokosmos Suite No. 2—JACK-IN-THE-BOX, *GR. 2*

Beethoven: Symphony No. 8—SECOND MOVEMENT, *GR. 6, Vol. 1*

Berlioz: The Damnation of Faust—BALLET OF THE SYLPHS, *GR. 1*

Bizet:
    Arlesienne Suite No. 1, L'—MINUETTO, *GR. 4, Vol. 2*
    Arlesienne Suite No. 2, L'—FARANDOLE, *GR. 6, Vol. 1*
    Carmen—CHANGING OF THE GUARD, *GR. 3, Vol. 2*
    Children's Games—THE BALL; CRADLE SONG; LEAP FROG, *GR. 1*

Borodin: ON THE STEPPES OF CENTRAL ASIA, *GR. 6, Vol. 1*

Brahms: HUNGARIAN DANCE NO. *1, GR. 5, Vol. 2*

Cailliet: POP! GOES THE WEASEL—Variations, *GR. 4, Vol. 1*

Carpenter: Adventures in a Perambulator—THE HURDY-GURDY, *GR. 5, Vol. 2*

Chabrier:
    ESPAÑA RAPSODIE, *GR. 5, Vol. 1*
    MARCHE JOYEUSE, *GR. 4, Vol. 1*

Charpentier: Impressions of Italy—ON MULE-BACK, *GR. 5, Vol. 1*

Coates: London Suite—KNIGHTSBRIDGE MARCH, *GR. 5, Vol. 2*

Copland:
    Billy the Kid Ballet Suite—STREET IN A FRONTIER TOWN, *GR. 6, Vol. 1*
    The Red Pony Suite—CIRCUS MUSIC, *GR. 3, Vol. 1*
    Rodeo—HOE-DOWN, *GR. 5, Vol. 2*

Corelli-Pinelli: Suite for Strings—SARABANDE, *GR. 6, Vol. 2*

Debussy:
    Children's Corner Suite—THE SNOW IS DANCING, *GR. 3, Vol. 1*
    La Mer—PLAY OF THE WAVES, *GR. 6, Vol. 2*

Delibes: Coppelia—WALTZ OF THE DOLL, *GR. 1*

Dvořák: SLAVONIC DANCE NO. 7, *GR. 4, Vol. 2*

Elgar:
    Wand of Youth Suite No. 1—FAIRIES AND GIANTS, *GR. 3, Vol. 1*
    Wand of Youth Suite No. 2—FOUNTAIN DANCE, *GR. 2*

Falla: La Vida Breve—SPANISH DANCE NO. *1, GR. 6, Vol. 1*

Faure: Dolly—BERCEUSE, *GR. 2*

Ginastera: Estancia—WHEAT DANCE, *GR. 4, Vol. 1*

Gliere: The Red Poppy—RUSSIAN SAILORS' DANCE, *GR. 6, Vol. 2*

Gluck: Iphigenie in Aulis—AIR GAI, *GR. 1*

Gottschalk-Kay: Cakewalk Ballet Suite—GRAND WALK-AROUND, *GR. 5, Vol. 1*

Gould: AMERICAN SALUTE, *GR. 5, Vol. 1*

Gounod: Faust Ballet Suite—WALTZ NO. 1, *GR. 3, Vol. 1*

Grainger: LONDONDERRY AIR, *GR. 4, Vol. 2*

Gretry:
    Cephale et Procris—GIGUE (Arr. by Mottl), *GR. 1*
    Cephale et Procris—TAMBOURIN (Arr. by Mottl), *GR. 2*

Grieg:
    Lyric Suite—NORWEGIAN RUSTIC MARCH, *GR. 4, Vol. 1*
    Peer Gynt Suite No. 1—IN THE HALL OF THE MOUNTAIN KING, *GR. 3, Vol. 2*

Griffes: THE WHITE PEACOCK, *GR. 5, Vol. 1*

Grofé: Death Valley Suite—DESERT WATER HOLE, *GR. 4, Vol. 1*

Guarnieri: BRAZILIAN DANCE, *GR. 6, Vol. 2*

Handel:
    Royal Fireworks Music—BOURREE MENUETTO NO. 2, *GR. 3, Vol. 2*
    Water Music—HORNPIPE, *GR. 2*

Hanson: Merry Mount Suite—CHILDREN'S DANCE, *GR. 3, Vol. 1*

Herbert:
    Babes in Toyland—MARCH OF THE TOYS, *GR. 2*
    Natoma—DAGGER DANCE, *GR. 3, Vol. 1*

Humperdinck: Hansel and Gretel—PRELUDE, *GR. 5, Vol. 2*

Holst: The Perfect Fool—SPIRITS OF THE EARTH, *GR. 6, Vol. 2*

Ibert:
    Divertissement—PARADE, *GR. 1*
    Histories No. 2—THE LITTLE WHITE DONKEY, *GR. 2*

Kabalevsky:
    The Comedians—MARCH, COMEDIANS GALOP, *GR. 3, Vol. 1*
    The Comedians—PANTOMIME, *GR. 1*

Khachaturian: Masquerade Suite—WALTZ, *GR. 4, Vol. 2*

Kodály:

    Hary Janos Suite—ENTRANCE OF THE EMPEROR AND HIS COURT, *GR. 4, Vol. 2*
    Hary Janos Suite—VIENNESE MUSICAL CLOCK, *GR. 2*

Lecuona: Suite Andalucia—ANDALUCIA, *GR. 4, Vol. 1*

Lully: Ballet Suite—MARCH, *GR. 3, Vol. 2*

MacDowell: Second (Indian) Suite—IN WARTIME, *GR. 5, Vol. 1*

Massenet: Le Cid—ARAGONAISE, *GR. 1*

McDonald:
    Children's Symphony (1st Movement)—LONDON BRIDGE; BAA, BAA, BLACK SHEEP, *GR. 3, Vol. 2*
    Children's Symphony (3rd Movement)—FARMER IN THE DELL; JINGLE BELLS, *GR. 2*

Menotti: Amahl and the Night Visitors—SHEPHERDS' DANCE, *GR. 4, Vol. 2*

Meyerbeer: Les Patineurs—WALTZ, *GR. 2*

Milhaud:
    Saudades do Brazil—COPACABANA, *GR. 4, Vol. 2*
    Saudades do Brazil—LARANJEIRAS, *GR. 2*

Moussorgsky:
    Pictures at an Exhibition—BALLET OF THE UNHATCHED CHICKS (Orchestrated by Ravel) *GR. 1*
    Pictures at an Exhibition—BYDLO (Orchestrated by Ravel) *GR. 2*

Mozart:
    Divertimento No. 17—MENUETTO NO. 1, *GR. 5, Vol. 2*
    Eine kleine Nachtmusik—ROMANZE, *GR. 4, Vol. 1*

Offenbach: The Tales of Hoffmann—BARCAROLLE, *GR. 3, Vol. 1*

Prokofiev:
    Children's Suite—WALTZ ON THE ICE, *GR. 3, Vol. 2*
    Summer Day Suite—MARCH, *GR. 1*
    Winter Holiday—DEPARTURE, *GR. 2*

Ravel:
    Mother Goose Suite—THE CONVERSATIONS OF BEAUTY AND THE BEAST, *GR. 5, Vol. 1*
    Mother Goose Suite—LAIDERONNETTE, EMPRESS OF THE PAGODAS, *GR. 4, Vol. 2*

Respighi:
    Brazilian Impressions—DANZA, *GR. 5, Vol. 2*
    Pines of Rome—PINES OF THE VILLA BORGHESE, *GR. 4, Vol. 1*

Rimsky-Korsakov: Le Coq d'Or Suite—BRIDAL PROCESSION, *GR. 4, Vol. 1*

Rossini: William Tell Overture—FINALE, *GR. 3, Vol. 1*

Rossini-Britten: Soirées Musicales—MARCH, *GR. 1*

Rossini-Respighi:
    The Fantastic Toyshop—CAN-CAN, *GR. 2*
    The Fantastic Toyshop—TARANTELLA, *GR. 3, Vol. 2*

Saint-Saens: Carnival of the Animals—THE SWAN, *GR. 3, Vol. 2*

Scarlatti-Tommasini: The Good-Humored Ladies—NON PRESTO MA A TEMPO DI BALLO, *GR. 4, Vol. 2*

Schubert: Symphony No. 5—FIRST MOVEMENT, *GR. 5, Vol. 1*

Schumann: Scenes from Childhood—TRAUMEREI, *GR. 4, Vol. 2*

Shostakovich:
    Ballet Suite No. 1—PETITE BALLERINA, *GR. 2*
    Ballet Suite No. 1—PIZZICATO POLKA, *GR. 1*

Sibelius: Karelia Suite—ALLA MARCIA, *GR. 5, Vol. 1*

Smetana: The Bartered Bride—DANCE OF THE COMEDIANS, *GR. 6, Vol. 2*

Sousa:
    SEMPER FIDELIS, *GR. 3, Vol. 2*
    STARS AND STRIPES FOREVER, *GR. 4, Vol. 2*

Strauss, R.: Der Rosenkavalier—SUITE, *GR. 6, Vol. 1*

Stravinsky:
    The Firebird Suite—BERCEUSE, *GR. 1*
    The Firebird Suite—INFERNAL DANCE OF KING KASTCHEI, *GR. 5, Vol. 2*

Taylor: Through the Looking Glass—GARDEN OF LIVE FLOWERS, *GR. 3, Vol. 2*

Tchaikovsky:
    The Sleeping Beauty—PUSS-IN-BOOTS AND THE WHITE CAT, *GR. 3, Vol. 1*
    The Sleeping Beauty—WALTZ, *GR. 4, Vol. 1*
    Swan Lake—DANCE OF THE LITTLE SWANS, *GR. 1*
    Symphony No. 4—FOURTH MOVEMENT, *GR. 6, Vol. 2*

Thomson:
    Acadian Songs and Dances—THE ALLIGATOR AND THE COON, *GR. 3, Vol. 2*
    Acadian Songs and Dances—WALKING SONG, *GR. 1*

Vaughan Williams:
    FANTASIA ON "GREENSLEEVES," *GR. 6, Vol. 2*
    The Wasps—MARCH PAST OF THE KITCHEN UTENSILS, *GR. 3, Vol. 1*

Villa-Lobos: Bachianas Brasileiras No. 2—THE LITTLE TRAIN OF THE CAIPIRA, *GR. 3, Vol. 1*

Wagner: Lohengrin—PRELUDE TO ACT III, *GR. 6, Vol. 1*

Walton: Facade Suite—VALSE, *GR. 6, Vol. 2*

appendix c

Series 1

ANIMALS AND CIRCUS (BOL #51)

CARNIVAL OF THE ANIMALS, Saint-Saens. (Introduction, Royal March of the Lion, Hens and Cocks, Fleet Footed Animals, Turtles, the Elephant, Kangaroos, Aquarium, Long Eared Personages, Cuckoo in the Deep Woods, Aviary, Pianists, Fossils, The Swan, Finale)
CIRCUS POLKA, Stravinsky
UNDER THE BIG TOP, Donaldson. (Marching Band, Acrobats, Juggler, Merry-Go-Round, Elephants, Clowns, Camels, Tightrope Walker, Pony Trot, Marching Band.)

NATURE AND MAKE-BELIEVE (BOL #52)

MARCH OF THE DWARFS, Grieg
ONCE UPON A TIME SUITE, Donaldson. (Chicken Little, Three Billy Goats Gruff, Little Train, Hare and the Tortoise.)
THE LARK SONG (Scenes of Youth), Tchaikovsky
LITTLE BIRD, Grieg
DANCE OF THE MOSQUITO, Liadov

635

FLIGHT OF THE BUMBLE BEE, Rimsky-Korsakov

SEASON FANTASIES, Donaldson. (Magic Piper, The Poet and his Lyre, The Anxious Leaf, The Snowmaiden)

TO THE RISING SUN (Fjord and Mountain, Norwegian Suite 2), Torjussen

CLAIR DE LUNE, Debussy

PICTURES AND PATTERNS (BOL #53)

PIZZICATO (Fantastic Toyshop), Rossini-Respighi

MARCH-TRUMPET AND DRUM (Jeux d'Enfants), IMPROMPTU-THE TOP (Jeux d'Enfants), Bizet

POLKA (Mlle. Angot Suite), GAVOTTE (Mlle. Angot Suite), Lecocq

INTERMEZZO (The Comedians), Kabalevsky

GERMAN WALTZ-PAGANINI (Carnaval), Schumann-Glazounov

BALLET PETIT, Donaldson

MINUET, Mozart

A GROUND, Handel

CHOPIN (Carnaval), Schumann-Glazounov

VILLAGE DANCE, Liadov

EN BATEAU (In a Boat), Debussy

HARBOR VIGNETTES, Donaldson (Fog and Storm, Song of the Bell Buoy, Sailing)

MARCHES (BOL #54)

ENTRANCE OF THE LITTLE FAUNS, Pierne

MARCH, Prokofieff

POMP AND CIRCUMSTANCE #1, Elgar

HUNGARIAN MARCH (Rakoczy), Berlioz

COL. BOGEY MARCH, Alford

MARCH OF THE LITTLE LEAD SOLDIERS, Pierne

MARCH (Love for Three Oranges), Prokofiev

CORTEGE OF THE SARDAR (Caucasian Sketches), Ippolitov-Ivanov

MARCHE MILITAIRE, Schubert

STARS AND STRIPES FOREVER, Sousa

THE MARCH OF THE SIAMESE CHILDREN (The King and I), Rodgers

DANCES, PART I (BOL #55)

DANCE OF THE CAMORRISTI, Wolf-Ferrari

DANCA BRASILEIRA, Guarnieri

GAVOTTE, Kabalevsky

SLAVONIC DANCE #1, Dvořák

HOE-DOWN (Rodeo), Copland

FACADE SUITE, Walton (Polka, Country Dance, Popular Song)

HUNGARIAN DANCE #5, Brahms

SKATER'S WALTZES, Waldteufel

MAZURKA (Masquerade Suite), Khatchaturian

GALOP (Masquerade Suite), Khatchaturian

DANCES, PART II (BOL #56)

FOLK DANCES FROM SOMERSET (English Folk Song Suite), Vaughan-Williams
JAMAICAN RUMBA, Benjamin
BADINERIE, Corelli
DANCE OF THE COMEDIANS, Smetana
CAN CAN (Mlle. Angot Suite), Lecocq
GRAND WALTZ (Mlle. Angot Suite), Lecocq
TRITSCH-TRASCH POLKA, Strauss
TARANTELLA (Fantastic Toyshop), WALTZ (Fantastic Toyshop), Rossini-Respighi
ESPAÑA WALTZES, Waldteufel
ARKANSAS TRAVELER, Guion
RUSSIAN DANCE (Gayne Suite #2), Khatchaturian

FAIRY TALES IN MUSIC (BOL #57)

CINDERELLA, Coates
SCHERZO (Midsummer Night's Dream), Mendelssohn
MOTHER GOOSE SUITE, Ravel (Pavane of the Sleeping Beauty, Hop o' My
    Thumb, Laideronette, Empress of the Pagodas, Beauty and the Beast, The
    Fairy Garden)

STORIES IN BALLET AND OPERA (BOL #58)

SUITE FROM AMAHL AND THE NIGHT VISITORS, Menotti (Introduction, March
    of the Three Kings, Dance of the Shepherds)
HANSEL AND GRETEL OVERTURE, Humperdinck
NUTCRACKER SUITE, Tchaikovsky (Overture Miniature, March, Dance of the
    Sugar-Plum Fairy, Trepak, Arabian Dance, Chinese Dance, Dance of the
    Toy Flutes, Waltz of the Flowers)

LEGENDS IN MUSIC (BOL #59)

DANSE MACABRE, Saint-Saëns
PEER GYNT SUITE #1, Grieg (Morning, Asa's Death, Anitra's Dance, In the Hall
    of the Mountain King)
SORCERER'S APPRENTICE, Dukas
PHAETON, Saint-Saëns

UNDER MANY FLAGS (BOL #60)

THE MOLDAU, Smetana
LAPLAND IDYLL (Fjord and Mountain, Norwegian Suite #2), Torjussen
FOLK SONG (Fjord and Mountain, Norwegian Suite #2), Torjussen
LONDONDERRY AIR, Grainger
FINLANDIA, Sibelius
LONDON SUITE, Coates (Covent Garden, Westminster, Knightsbridge March)

AMERICAN SCENES (BOL #61)

GRAND CANYON SUITE, Grofé (Sunrise, Painted Desert, On the Trail, Sunset, Cloudburst)

MISSISSIPPI SUITE, Grofé (Father of Waters, Huckleberry Finn, Old Creole Days, Mardi Gras)

Series 2

MASTERS IN MUSIC (BOL #62)

JESU, JOY OF MAN'S DESIRING, Bach
BOURREE FROM FIREWORKS MUSIC, Handel
VARIATIONS (from "Sunrise" Symphony), Haydn
MINUET (from Symphony #40), Mozart
SCHERZO (from Seventh Symphony), Beethoven
WEDDING DAY AT TROLDHAUGEN, Grieg
RIDE OF THE VALKYRIES, Wagner
TRIUMPHAL MARCH (Aida), Verdi
HUNGARIAN DANCE #6, Brahms
THIRD MOVEMENT, SYMPHONY #1, Mahler

CONCERT MATINEE (BOL #63)

CHILDREN'S CORNER SUITE, Debussy, (Doctor Gradus ad Parnassum, Jumbo's Lullaby, Serenade of the Doll, The Snow is Dancing, The Little Shepherd, Golliwog's Cakewalk)
SUITE FOR STRING ORCHESTA, Corelli-Pinelli (Sarabande, Gigue, Badinerie)
MINUET (from "Surprise" Symphony), Haydn
ANVIL CHORUS, Verdi ("Il Trovatore")
NORWEGIAN DANCE IN A (#2), Grieg
TRAUMEREI, Schumann

MINIATURES IN MUSIC (BOL #64)

CHILDREN'S SYMPHONY, Zador
THE BEE, Schubert
GYPSY RONDO, Haydn
WILD HORSEMEN, Schumann
HAPPY FARMER, Schumann
LITTLE WINDMILLS, Couperin
ARIETTA, Leo
MUSIC BOX, Liadov
FUNERAL MARCH OF THE MARIONETTES, Gounod
DANCE OF THE MERRY DWARFS (Happy Hypocrite), Elwell
LITTLE TRAIN OF CAIPIRA, Villa-Lobos

MUSIC, USA (BOL #65)

SHAKER TUNE (Appalachian Spring), Copland
CATTLE & BLUES (Plow that Broke the Plains), Thomson
FUGUE AND CHORALE ON YANKEE DOODLE (Tuesday in November), Thomson
PUMPKINEATERS LITTLE FUGUE, McBride
AMERICAN SALUTE, Gould
POP GOES THE WEASEL, Cailliet
LAST MOVEMENT, SYMPHONY #2, Ives

ORIENTAL SCENES (BOL #66)

WOODCUTTER'S SONG, Koyama
THE EMPEROR'S NIGHTINGALE, Donaldson
SAKURA (Folk tune), played by koto and bamboo flute

FANTASY IN MUSIC (BOL #67)

THREE BEARS, Coates
CINDERELLA, Prokofiev (Sewing Scene, Cinderella's Gavotte, Midnight Waltz,
    Fairy Godmother)
MOON LEGEND, Donaldson
SLEEPING BEAUTY WALTZ, Tchaikovsky

CLASSROOM CONCERT (BOL #68)

ALBUM FOR THE YOUNG, Tchaikovsky. (Morning Prayer, Winter Morning,
    Hobby Horse, Mamma, March of the Tin Soldiers, Sick Doll, Doll's Burial,
    New Doll, Waltz, Mazurka, Russian Song, Peasant Plays the Accordion,
    Folk Song, Polka, Italian Song, Old French Song, German Song, Nea-
    politan Dance Song, Song of the Lark, Hand-organ Man, Nurse's Tale,
    The Witch, Sweet Dreams, In Church)
OVER THE HILLS, Grainger
MEMORIES OF CHILDHOOD, Pinto. (Run, Run; Ring Around the Rosie; March;
    Sleeping Time; Hobby Horse)
LET US RUN ACROSS THE HILL, Villa-Lobos
MY DAUGHTER LIDI, TEASING, GRASSHOPPER'S WEDDING, Bartok
DEVIL'S DANCE, Stravinsky
LITTLE GIRL IMPLORING HER MOTHER, Rebikov

Series 3

MUSIC OF THE DANCE: STRAVINSKY (BOL # 69)

FIREBIRD SUITE (L'Oiseau de Feu) (Koschai's Enchanted Garden, Dance of the
    Firebird, Dance of the Princesses, Infernal Dance of Koschai, Magic Sleep
    of the Princess Tzarevna, Finale: Escape of Koschai's Captives.)

SACRIFICIAL DANCE from "The Rite of Spring" (Le Sacre du Printemps)
VILLAGE FESTIVAL from "The Fairy's Kiss" (Le Baiser de la Fée)
PALACE OF THE CHINESE EMPEROR from "The Nightingale" (Le Rossignol)
TANGO, WALTZ AND RAGTIME from "The Soldier's Tale" (L'Histoire du Soldat)

MUSIC OF THE SEA AND SKY (BOL #70)

CLOUDS (Nuages), Debussy
FESTIVALS (Fêtes), Debussy
MERCURY from The Planets, Holst
SEA PIECE WITH BIRDS, Thomson
OVERTURE TO "THE FLYING DUTCHMAN" (Der Fliegende Hollander), Wagner
DIALOGUE OF THE WIND AND SEA from The Sea (La Mer), Debussy

SYMPHONIC MOVEMENTS, NO. 1 (BOL #71)

FIRST MOVEMENT, SYMPHONY No. 40, Mozart
SECOND MOVEMENT, SYMPHONY No. 8, Beethoven
THIRD MOVEMENT, SYMPHONY No. 4, Tchaikovsky
SECOND MOVEMENT, SYMPHONY No. 4, Schumann
THIRD MOVEMENT, SYMPHONY No. 3, Brahms
FOURTH MOVEMENT, SYMPHONY No. 3, Saint-Saens

SYMPHONIC MOVEMENTS, No. 2 (BOL #72)

FIRST MOVEMENT, SYMPHONY No. 9, ("From the New World"), Dvorak
FIRST MOVEMENT, SYMPHONY No. 5, Beethoven
FIRST MOVEMENT, (Boisterous Bourrée), A SIMPLE SYMPHONY, Britten
SECOND MOVEMENT, SYMPHONY No. 2, Hanson
FIRST MOVEMENT, SYMPHONY No. 2, Sibelius

SYMPHONIC STYLES (BOL #73)

SYMPHONY No. 99 ("Imperial"), Haydn (Adagio: Vivace Assai, Adagio, Minuetto, Vivace)
CLASSICAL SYMPHONY, Prokofiev (Allegro, Larghetto, Gavotte: Non troppo allegro, Molto vivace)

TWENTIETH CENTURY AMERICA (BOL #74)

EL SALON MEXICO, Copland
DANZON from "Fancy Free," Bernstein
EXCERPTS, SYMPHONIC DANCES from "West Side Story," Bernstein
AN AMERICAN IN PARIS, Gershwin

U.S. HISTORY IN MUSIC (BOL #75)

A LINCOLN PORTRAIT, Copland
CHESTER from NEW ENGLAND TRIPTYCH, Schumann

PUTNAM'S CAMP from "Three Places in New England," Ives
INTERLUDE from FOLK SONG SYMPHONY, Harris
MIDNIGHT RIDE OF PAUL REVERE from Selections from McGuffey's Readers,
    Phillips

OVERTURES (BOL #76)

OVERTURE TO "THE BAT" (Die Fledermaus), Strauss
ACADEMIC FESTIVAL OVERTURE, Brahms
OVERTURE TO "THE MARRIAGE OF FIGARO," Mozart
ROMAN CARNIVAL OVERTURE, Berlioz
OVERTURE TO "WILLIAM TELL," Rossini (Dawn, Storm, Calm, Finale)

SCHEHERAZADE BY RIMSKY-KORSAKOV (BOL #77)

The Sea and Sinbad's Ship, Tale of the Prince Kalendar, The Young
Prince and the Princess, The Festival at Bagdad

MUSICAL KALEIDOSCOPE (BOL #78)

ON THE STEPPES OF CENTRAL ASIA, Borodin
IN THE VILLAGE FROM CAUCASIAN SKETCHES, Ippolitoff-Ivanoff
EXCERPTS, POLOVTSIAN DANCES FROM "PRINCE IGOR," Borodin
RUSSIAN SAILORS' DANCE FROM "THE RED POPPY," Gliere
L'ARLESIENNE SUITE No. 1, Bizet (Carillon, Minuet)
L'ARLESIENNE SUITE No. 2, Bizet (Farandole)
PRELUDE TO ACT *1*, "CARMEN," Bizet
MARCH TO THE SCAFFOLD, from Symphonie Fantastique, Berlioz

MUSIC OF THE DRAMA: WAGNER (BOL #79)

"LOHENGRIN" (Overture to Act 1, Prelude to Act 3)
"THE TWILIGHT OF THE GODS" (Die Götterdämmerung) (Siegfried's Rhine Jour-
    ney)
"THE MASTERSINGERS OF NUREMBERG" (Die Meistersinger von Nürnberg)
    (Prelude, Dance of the Apprentices and Entrance of the Mastersingers)
"TRISTAN AND ISOLDE" (Love Death)

PETROUCHKA BY STRAVINSKY (BOL #80)

COMPLETE BALLET SCORE WITH NARRATION

ROGUES IN MUSIC (BOL #81)

TILL EULENSPIEGEL, Strauss
LIEUTENANT KIJE, Prokofiev Birth of Kije, Troika
HARY JANOS, Kodály (Viennese Musical Clock, Battle and Defeat of Napoleon,
    Intermezzo, Entrance of the Emperor)

MUSICAL PICTURES: MOUSSORGSKY (BOL #82)

PICTURES AT AN EXHIBITION (Promenade Theme, The Gnome, The Old Castle, Tuileries, Ox-Cart, Ballet of Chicks in Their Shells, Goldenberg and Schmuyle, The Market Place at Limoges, Catacombs, The Hut of Baga Yaga, The Great Gate of Kiev)

NIGHT ON BALD MOUNTAIN

ENSEMBLES, LARGE AND SMALL (BOL #83)

YOUNG PERSON'S GUIDE TO THE ORCHESTRA, Britten
CANZONA IN C MAJOR FOR BRASS ENSEMBLE AND ORGAN, Gabrieli
CHORALE: AWAKE, THOU WINTRY EARTH, Bach
FOURTH MOVEMENT, "TROUT" QUINTET, Schubert
THEME AND VARIATIONS FOR PERCUSSION QUARTET, Kraft
THEME AND VARIATIONS from SERENADE FOR WIND INSTRUMENTS, Mozart
   (K361)

CONCERTOS (BOL #84)

FIRST MOVEMENT, PIANO CONCERTO, Grieg
FOURTH MOVEMENT, PIANO CONCERTO No. 2, Brahms
THIRD MOVEMENT, VIOLIN CONCERTO, Mendelssohn
SECOND MOVEMENT, GUITAR CONCERTO, Castelnuovo-Tedesco
THIRD MOVEMENT, CONCERTO IN C FOR TWO TRUMPETS, Vivaldi

MUSICAL IMPRESSIONS: RESPIGHI (BOL #85)

PINES OF ROME (Pines of the Villa Borghese, Pines Near a Catacomb, Pines of the Appian Way)
FOUNTAINS OF ROME (The Fountain of Valle Giulia at Dawn, The Triton Fountain at Morning, The Trevi Fountain at Midday, The Villa Medici Fountain at Sunset)
THE BIRDS (Prelude)

FASHIONS IN MUSIC (BOL #86)

ROMEO AND JULIET (Fantasy-Overture), Tchaikovsky
LITTLE FUGUE IN G MINOR, Bach
SUITE No. 2 FROM "DAPHNIS AND CHLOË," Ravel
ROMANZE FROM A LITTLE NIGHT MUSIC (Eine kleine Nachtmusik), Mozart
PERIPETIA FROM FIVE PIECES FOR ORCHESTRA, Schoenberg

appendix d

Allyn and Bacon, Inc., Boston 02210. THIS IS MUSIC.
American Book Company, New York 10003. MUSIC FOR YOUNG AMERICANS.
Follett Publishing Company, Chicago 60607. DISCOVERING MUSIC TOGETHER.
Ginn and Company, Boston 02117. THE MAGIC OF MUSIC.
Holt, Rinehart and Winston, Inc., New York 10017. EXPLORING MUSIC.
Prentice-Hall, Inc., Englewood Cliffs, N.J. 07632. GROWING WITH MUSIC.
Silver Burdett Company, Morristown, N.J. 07960. MAKING MUSIC YOUR OWN.
Summy-Birchard, Evanston, Illinois 60204. BIRCHARD MUSIC SERIES.

index of sources of songs mentioned in this book

Reveille, F-5, SB-3
Riddle Song, SWC
Rig-a-Jig-Jig, AB-1,4, ABC-k, G-3, H-2, PH-2,5, SB-k,1, EM
Ring the Banjo, AB-5, ABC-6
Rock Island Line, PH-5, EM
Roll Over, EM
Row, Row, Row Your Boat, ABC-3, F-3, G-3, H-2, Sil-1, SB-1, SWC
Rune, Sil's *Music Near and Far*

Sakura (Cherry Blossom), G-4, H-4, Sil-4, SB-3
Sally Go Round, AB-k, F-3, SB-1, EM
Sandy Land, H-3, Sil-2,3,4
Santa Lucia, ABC-6, F-5, H-5
Shanty Boys in the Pine, AB-5
Shoo Fly, ABC-1, H-2, Sil-2
Shortnin' Bread, ABC-4
Simple Gifts, G-5, H-5, SB-5
Sing Your Way Home, AB-5, ABC-3,6, G-4, H-5, PH-4, SWC
Skip to My Lou, ABC-1, F-2,3, G-4, H-2,5, Sil-1,4, SB-2,3, SWC
Sleep, Baby, Sleep, G-2, H-1,2, PH-4, SB-1, EM
So Long, AB-5, F-5, H-5, PH-6, SWC
Song of Peace (Finlandia), F-6
Song of the Gingerbread Children, F-4
Sourwood Mountain, AB-6, ABC-5, H-5, Sil-6
Sparrow's Song, F-4, SWC
Springfield, Mountain, Sil-3, EM
St. Paul's Steeple (Bells in the Steeple), AB-2, SWC
Standin' in the Need of Prayer, EM
Stodola Pumpa, AB-6, H-4
Streets of Laredo, SWC
Summer Has Come, F-6
Susy, Little Susy, F-4, G-3, H-3, SB-3, EM
Swing Low, Sweet Chariot, AB-5, ABC-5, F-4, G-5, H-5, Sil-6, SWC

Taps, AB-4, ABC-4, F-5, PH-6, SB-3
Ten Little Indians, AB-1, EM
There's a Long, Long Trail, PH-5
There Was a Little Woman, SWC
This Old Man, AB-1,4, F-2, H-1, SB-1, SWC
Three Blind Mice, AB-4, ABC-1, F-1,3, H-3
Tideo, EM
Tinga Layo, AB-2, F-4, H-3, SWC
Tisket, a Tasket, EM
Today Is Monday, EM
Toodola, AB-1,2, H-1, SB-k,2
Turkey in the Straw, F-6
Twelve Days of Christmas, AB-4, ABC-4, F-4, G-4, Sil-5,6 SB-5
Twinkle, Twinkle, Little Star, AB-1,2,4, F-1,2, G-1,2, H-2, SB-k, EM

Up on the Housetop, AB-1, G-1, H-1, PH-2, SB-1, SWC
United Nations Hymn (World Anthem), AB-6

Wait for the Wagon, AB-k, ABC-2
Wayfaring Stranger, ABC-6, F-6, G-5, Sil-6
We Wish You a Merry Christmas, AB-3, ABC-1, F-3, G-1,2, H-4, PH-2, Sil-k,1,2,4, SWC
Weggis Song, H-4, Sil-4
We Three Kings of Orient Are, F-4, G-3, SWC

index of songs

index